**PEARSON**

# COMPUTER CONCEPTS
# IST 101

## Custom Edition for Mercer County Community College

Taken from:
*Technology In Action Complete,* Ninth Edition
by Alan Evans, Kendall Martin, Mary Anne Poatsy

*Computer Literacy for IC3 Unit 3: Living Online,* First Edition
by John Preston, Sally Preston, Robert L. Ferrett

Cover Art: PhotoDisc/Getty Images

Taken from:

*Technology In Action Complete*, Ninth Edition
by Alan Evans, Kendall Martin, and Mary Anne Poatsy
Copyright © 2012, 2011, 2010, 2009, 2008 by Pearson Education
Published by Prentice Hall
Upper Saddle River, New Jersey 07458

*Computer Literacy for IC3 Unit 3: Living Online*, First Edition
by John Preston, Sally Preston, and Robert L. Ferrett
Copyright © 2010 by Pearson Education
Published by Prentice Hall
Upper Saddle River, New Jersey 07458

Pearson Learning Solutions, 501 Boylston Street, Suite 900, Boston, MA 02116
A Pearson Education Company
www.pearsoned.com

Printed in the United States of America

3 4 5 6 7 8 9 10 V092 17 16 15 14 13 12

000200010271682254

CM/CK

ISBN 10: 1-256-80867-9
ISBN 13: 978-1-256-80867-1

**Grateful acknowledgment is made to the following sources for permission to reprint material copyrighted or controlled by them:**

"Information Literacy Progression Standards: For use in New Jersey Colleges and Universities," by The Shared Information Literacy Committee of VALE, the User Education Committee of ACRL/NJLA, and the Academic Reference Librarians of CJRLC, October 2009, by permission of the authors.

"Evaluation Criteria," by Susan E. Beck, reprinted from The Good, The Bad & The Ugly: or, Why It's a Good Idea to Evaluate Web Sources, April 27, 2009.

"In Text Citations: The Basics," by Joshua Paiz et al., reprinted from *http://owl.english.purdue.edu,* March 14, 2012, Purdue OWL.

"APA Style Workshop," by Kristen Seas and Allen Brizee, reprinted from *http://owl.english.purdue.edu,* April 21, 2010, Purdue OWL.

"Reference List: Basic Rules," by Joshua Paiz et al., reprinted from *http://owl.english.purdue.edu,* May 23, 2012, Purdue OWL.

"Reference List: Electronic Sources (Web Publications)," by Joshua Paiz et al., reprinted from *http://owl. english.purdue.edu,* June 6, 2012, Purdue OWL.

Text arrangement by Andrea Lynch, Associate Professor at Mercer County Community College

# Contents at a Glance

# Contents

## Chapter 1

## Chapter 2

# Chapter 3

## Understanding and Assessing Hardware: Evaluating Your System

# Chapter 4

## Technology in Focus: Under the Hood

# Chapter 5

## Digital Lifestyle: Managing Digital Data and Devices

# Chapter 6

## Technology in Focus: Information Technology Ethics

# Chapter 7

## Application Software: Programs That Let You Work and Play ....................................................................................202

# Chapter 8

## Using System Software: The Operating System, Utility Programs, and File Management

# Chapter 9

## Behind the Scenes: Databases and Information Systems

# Chapter 10

## Using the Internet: Making the Most of the Web's Resources

# Chapter 11

## Information Literacy

# Chapter 12

# Chapter 13

# Dedication

For my wife Patricia, whose patience, understanding, and support continue to make this work possible . . . especially when I stay up past midnight writing! And to my parents, Jackie and Dean, who taught me the best way to achieve your goals is to constantly strive to improve yourself through education.

**Alan Evans**

For all the teachers, mentors, and gurus who have popped in and out of my life.

**Kendall Martin**

For my husband Ted, who unselfishly continues to take on more than his fair share to support me throughout this process; and for my children, Laura, Carolyn, and Teddy, whose encouragement and love have been inspiring.

**Mary Anne Poatsy**

# About the Authors

## Alan Evans, MS, CPA

aevans@mc3.edu

Alan is currently a faculty member at Moore College of Art and Design and Montgomery County Community College teaching a variety of computer science and business courses. He holds a B.S. in accounting from Rider University and an M.S. in information systems from Drexel University, and he is a certified public accountant. After a successful career in business, Alan finally realized his true calling was education. He has been teaching at the college level since 2000. Alan enjoys giving presentations at technical conferences and meets regularly with computer science faculty and administrators from other colleges to discuss curriculum development and new methods of engaging students.

## Kendall Martin, PhD

kmartin@mc3.edu

Kendall has been teaching since 1988 at a number of institutions, including Villanova University, DeSales University, Arcadia University, Ursinus College, County College of Morris, and Montgomery County Community College, at both the undergraduate and graduate level.

Kendall's education includes a B.S. in electrical engineering from the University of Rochester and an M.S. and a Ph.D. in engineering from the University of Pennsylvania. She has industrial experience in research and development environments (AT&T Bell Laboratories) as well as experience with several start-up technology firms.

As an Associate Professor at Montgomery County Community College, Kendall works with area entrepreneurs to connect them with the College community.

## Mary Anne Poatsy, MBA

mpoatsy@mc3.edu

Mary Anne is a senior faculty member at Montgomery County Community College, teaching various computer application and concepts courses in face-to-face and online environments. She enjoys speaking at various professional conferences about innovative classroom strategies. She holds a B.A. in psychology and education from Mount Holyoke College and an MBA in finance from Northwestern University's Kellogg Graduate School of Management.

Mary Anne has been in teaching since 1997, ranging from elementary and secondary education to Montgomery County Community College, Gwynedd-Mercy College, Muhlenberg College, and Bucks County Community College, as well as training in the professional environment. Before teaching, she was a vice president at Shearson Lehman Hutton in the Municipal Bond Investment Banking Department.

# Acknowledgments

*First, we would like to thank our students. We constantly learn from them while teaching, and they are a continual source of inspiration and new ideas.*

We could not have written this book without the loving support of our families. Our spouses and children made sacrifices (mostly in time not spent with us) to permit us to make this dream into a reality.

Although working with the entire team at Pearson has been a truly enjoyable experience, a few individuals deserve special mention. The constant support and encouragement we receive from Jenifer Niles, Associate Vice President/Executive Acquisitions Editor, and Michael Payne, Editor in Chief, continually makes this book grow and change. Our heartfelt thanks go to Toni Ackley, our developmental editor. Toni, new to the Technology in Action project this edition, had a positive impact on the book, and we have benefited greatly from her creative ideas and efficient time management skills. In addition, Keri Rand, our editorial project manager, has done a fantastic job of coordinating all details of the project, and was especially helpful guiding us through the murky permissions process. As Media Project Manager, Alana Coles works tirelessly to ensure that the media accompanying the text is produced professionally and is delivered in a timely fashion. Despite the inevitable problems that crop up when producing multimedia, she handles all challenges with a smile. We also would like to extend our appreciation to Rhonda Aversa, our Production Project Manager, who works tirelessly to ensure that our book is published on time and looks fabulous. The timelines are always short, the art is complex, and there are many people with whom she has to coordinate tasks.

There are many people whom we do not meet in person at Pearson and elsewhere who make significant contributions by designing the book, illustrating, composing the pages, producing multimedia, and securing permissions. We thank them all. We would also like to thank the supplement authors for this edition: Lisa Hawkins, Julie Boyles, Linda Arnold, Hilda Federico, Tonya Pierce, Abigail Miller, Stefanie Emrich, Susan Fry, Terry Holly, Kevin Cleary, Stacy Everly, Sharon Behrens, Amy Rutledge, Wanda Gibson, Barbara Edington, and Lori Damanti.

And finally, we would like to thank the reviewers and the many others who contribute their time, ideas, and talents to this project. We appreciate their time and energy, as their comments help us turn out a better product each edition.

# Reviewers

Prentice Hall and the authors would like to thank the following people for their help and time in making this book what it is. We couldn't publish this book without their contributions.

| | |
|---|---|
| Nazih Abdallah | University of Central Florida |
| Allen Alexander | Delaware Technical & Community College |
| Joan Alexander | Valencia Community College—West |
| Beverly Amer | Northern Arizona University |
| Wilma Andrews | Virginia Commonwealth University |
| Gregg W. Asher, Ph.D. | Minnesota State University—Mankato |
| LaDonna Bachand | Santa Rosa Junior College |
| Carolyn Barren | Macomb Community College |
| Wendy Barron | Lehigh Carbon Community College |
| LeeAnn Bates | |
| Elise J. Bell, MA, Educ. | City College of San Francisco |
| Linda Belton | Springfield Technical Community College |
| Bob Benavides | Collin College |
| David Billings | Guilford Technical Community College |
| Kim Binstead, Ph.D | University of Hawaii at Manoa |
| Susan Birtwell | Kwantlen University College |
| Henry Bojack | Farmingdale State University of New York |
| Gina Bowers-Miller | HACC Harrisburg |
| Julie Boyles | |
| Brenda K. Britt | Fayetteville Technical Community College |
| Cathy J. Brotherton | Riverside Community College |
| Gerald U. Brown Jr. | Tarrant County College |
| Jeff Burton | Daytona Beach Community College |
| Kristen Callahan | Mercer County Community College |
| Judy Cameron | Spokane Community College |
| Jill Canine | Ivy Tech Community College of Indiana |
| Heather Cannon | Blinn College |
| Judy Cestaro | California State University—San Bernardino |
| Deborah Chapman | University of Southern Alabama |
| Gerianne Chapman | Johnson & Wales University |
| John P. Cicero, Ph.D | Shasta College—Redding, CA |
| Dan Combellick | Scottsdale Community College |
| Joann Cook | College of DuPage |
| Mark Connell | SUNY Cortland |
| Gail Cope | Sinclair Community College |
| Françoise Corey | California State University, Long Beach |
| John Coverdale | Riverside Community College |
| Thad Crews | Western Kentucky University |
| Doug Cross | Clackamas Community College |
| Geoffrey Crosslin | Kalamazoo Valley Community College |
| Becky Cunningham | Arkansas Tech University |
| Becky Curtin | Harper College |
| John Cusaac | Fullerton College |
| Paul Dadosky | Ivy Tech Community College |
| James Bac Dang | Tarrant County College |
| Marvin Daugherty | Ivy Tech |
| Ronald G. Deardorff | Shasta Community College |
| Joseph DeLibero | Arizona State University |

| | |
|---|---|
| K. Kay Delk | Seminole Community College |
| Charles DeSassure | Tarrant County College |
| Gretchen V. Douglas | State University of New York at Cortland |
| Susan N. Dozier | Tidewater Community College |
| Annette Duvall | Albuquerque Technical Vocational Institute |
| Laurie Eakins | East Carolina University |
| Roland Eichelberger | Baylor University |
| Bernice Eng | Brookdale Community College |
| James Fabrey | West Chester University |
| Deb Fells | Mesa Community College |
| Catherine L. Ferguson | University of Oklahoma |
| Marj Feroe | Delaware County Community College |
| Judy Firmin | Tarrant County College |
| Beverly Fite | Amarillo College |
| Mary Fleming | Ivy Tech Community College |
| Howard Flomberg | The Metropolitan State College of Denver |
| Richard A. Flores | Citrus College |
| Alicen Flosi | Lamar University |
| Linda Foster-Turpen | Central New Mexico Community College |
| Susan Fry | Boise State University |
| Yvonne Galusha | University of Iowa |
| Barbara A. Garrell | Delaware County Community College |
| Ernest Gines | Tarrant County College |
| Tim Gottleber | North Lake College |
| Kate Le Grand | Broward College |
| Bob Grazinski | Central Texas College |
| Sherry Green | Purdue University—Calumet Campus |
| Debra Gross | The Ohio State University |
| Vivian Haddad | Nova Southeastern University |
| Don A. Halcomb | Bluegrass Community and Technical College |
| Lewis Hall | Riverside City College |
| Rachelle Hall | Glendale Community College |
| Eric Hamilton | Community College of Denver |
| Bill Hammerschlag | Brookhaven College |
| Terry Hanks | San Jacinto College—South Campus |
| Susan Hanson | Albuquerque Technical Vocational Institute |
| Marie Hartlein | Montgomery County Community College |
| Ronda D. Hayes | North Lake College |
| Susan E. Hoggard | Tulsa Community College |
| Jim Hendricks | Pierce College |
| Catherine Hines | Albuquerque Technical Vocational Institute |
| Norm Hollingsworth | Georgia Perimeter College |
| Bill Holmes | Chandler-Gilbert Community College |
| Mary Carole Hollingsworth | Georgia Perimeter College |
| Sherry Hopkins | Anne Arundel Community College |
| Christie Jahn Hovey | Lincoln Land Community College |
| Jeffrey Howard | Finger Lakes Community College |
| John L. Howard | East Carolina University |
| Judy Irvine | Seneca College |
| Glen Johansson | Spokane Community College |
| Kay Johnson | Community College of Rhode Island |
| Stephanie Jones | South Plains College |
| Steve St. John | Tulsa Community College |

| Kathy Johnson | DeVry Chicago |
| Richard B. Kalman | Atlantic Cape Community College |
| Dr. K. Kamel | TSU |
| Darrel Karbginsky | Chemkeketa Community College |
| Linda Kavanaugh | Robert Morris University |
| Robert R. Kendi | Lehigh University |
| Annette Kerwin | College of DuPage |
| David Kight | Brewton-Parker College |
| Kai S. Koong | University of Texas Pan American |
| Frank Kuehn | Pikes Peak Community College |
| Jackie Lamoureux | Albuquerque Technical Vocational Institute |
| David K. Lange | Grand Valley State University |
| Joanne Lazirko | University of Wisconsin—Milwaukee |
| Michael R. Lehrfeld | Brevard Community College |
| Yvonne Leonard | Coastal Carolina University |
| Judith Limkilde | Seneca College—King Campus |
| Richard Linge | Arizona Western College |
| Christy Lopez | East Carolina University |
| Mike LoSacco | College of DuPage |
| Joelene Mack | Golden West College |
| Lisa Macon | Valencia Community College |
| Donna Madsen | Kirkwood Community College |
| Daniela Marghitu | Auburn University |
| Norma Marler | Catawba Valley Community College |
| Carol Prewitt Martin | Louisiana State University at Alexandria |
| Toni Marucco | Lincoln Land Community College |
| Evelynn McCain | Boise State University |
| Dana McCann | Central Michigan University |
| Lee McClain | West Washington University |
| Krista McClimans | Everett Community College |
| Sandra M. McCormack | Monroe Community College |
| Sue McCrory | Missouri State University |
| Phil McCue | Lone Star College—Montgomery |
| Helen McFadyen | Mass Bay Community College—Framingham |
| Charles J. McNerney Ph.D. | Bergen Community College |
| Dr. Dori McPherson | Schoolcraft College |
| Laura Melella | Fullerton College |
| Josephine Mendoza | California State University, San Bernardino |
| Mike Michaelson | Palomar College |
| Gina Bowers Miller | Harrisburg Area Community College |
| Johnette Moody | Arkansas Tech University |
| Dona Mularkey | Southern Methodist University |
| Rebecca A. Mundy | University of Southern California |
| Linda Mushet | Golden West College |
| Lisa Nademlynsky | Johnson & Wales University |
| Maguerite Nedreberg | Youngstown State University |
| Brad Nicolajsen | Carteret Community College |
| Omar Nooraldeen | Cape Fear Community College |
| Judy Ogden | Johnson County Community College |
| Connie O'Neill | Sinclair Community College |
| Claudia Orr | Northern Michigan University |
| James R. Orr | East Carolina University |
| Sung Park | Pasadena City College |

| | |
|---|---|
| **Brenda Parker** | Middle Tennessee State University |
| **Lucy Parker** | California State University, Northridge |
| **Patricia Partyka** | Schoolcraft College |
| **Woody Pekoske** | North Carolina State University |
| **Judy Perhamus Perry** | Riverside Community College—Norco Campus |
| **Carolyn Poe** | Lone Star College—Montgomery |
| **Mike Puopolo** | Bunker Hill Community College |
| **Paul Quan** | Albuquerque Technical Vocational Institute |
| **Ram Raghuraman** | Joliet Junior College |
| **Patricia Rahmlow** | Montgomery County Community College |
| **Shirley Reid** | Indian Hills Community College |
| **Ruth Robbins** | University of Houston—Downtown |
| **Teresa Roberts** | Wilson Community College |
| **Catherine J. Rogers** | Laramie County Community College |
| **Mary Rousseau** | Broward College, South Campus |
| **Russell Sabadosa** | Manchester Community College |
| **Peg Saragina** | Santa Rosa Junior College |
| **Judith Scheeren** | Westmoreland County Community College |
| **Samuel Scott** | Pierce College |
| **Vicky Seehusen** | The Metropolitan State College of Denver |
| **Ralph Shafer** | Truckee Meadows Community College—Reno |
| **Mirella Shannon** | Columbia College |
| **Laurie Evin Shteir** | Temple University |
| **Sheila Smart Sicilia** | Onondaga Community College |
| **Greg A. Simpson** | Phoenix College—Phoenix, AZ |
| **Robert G. Sindt** | Johnson County Community College |
| **Gary R. Smith** | Paradise Valley Community College |
| **Steven Singer** | Kapi'olani Community College |
| **Robert Smolenski** | Delaware County Community College |
| **Diane Stark** | Phoenix College |
| **James Stark** | Milwaukee Area Technical College |
| **Suzanne Mello Stark** | Community College of Rhode Island |
| **Kriss Stauber** | El Camino College |
| **Neal Stenlund** | Northern Virginia Community College |
| **Linda Stoudemayer** | Lamar Institute of Technology |
| **Catherine Stoughton** | Laramie County Community College |
| **Lynne Stuhr** | Trident Technical College |
| **Song Su** | East Los Angeles College |
| **Jim Taggart** | Atlantic City Community College |
| **John Taylor** | Hillsborough Community College—Brandon Campus |
| **Margaret Taylor** | College of Southern Nevada |
| **Dennie Templeton** | Radford University |
| **Joyce Thompson** | Lehigh Carbon Community College |
| **Lou Thompson** | University of Texas at Dallas |
| **Janine Tiffany** | Reading Area Community College |
| **Janet Towle** | New Hampshire Community Technical College—Nashua |
| **Goran Trajkovski** | Towson University |
| **Deborah Tyler** | Tarrant County College |
| **Pamella M. Uhlenkamp** | Iowa Central Community College—Fort Dodge, Iowa |
| **Erhan Uskup** | Houston Community College—Northwest |
| **Emily Vandalovsky** | Bergen Community College |
| **Bill VanderClock** | Bentley Business University |
| **Glenna Vanderhoof** | Missouri State University |

| | |
|---|---|
| **Michelle Vlaich-Lee** | Greenville Technical College |
| **Craig Watson** | Bristol Community College |
| **Karen Weil-Yates** | Hagerstown Community College |
| **Catherine Werst** | Cuesta College |
| **Janice L. Williams** | Seward County Community College |
| **Melanie Williamson** | Bluegrass Community and Technical College |
| **Steven H. White** | Anne Arundel Community College |
| **Barbara Yancy** | Community College of Baltimore County—Essex Camp |
| **Thomas Yip** | Passaic County Community College |
| **Mary Zajac** | Montgomery County Community College |
| **Mary T. Zegarski** | Northampton Community College |
| **Mary Ann Zlotow** | College of DuPage |

# Letter from the Authors

## Why We Wrote This Book

Our combined 46 years of teaching computer concepts have coincided with sweeping innovations in computing technology that have affected every facet of society. From iPads to Web 2.0, computers are more than ever a fixture of our daily lives—and the lives of our students. But although today's students have a greater comfort level with their digital environment than previous generations, their knowledge of the machines they use every day is still limited.

We wrote *Technology in Action* to focus on what matters most to today's student. Instead of a history lesson on the microchip, we focus on what tasks students can accomplish with their computing devices and what skills they can apply immediately in the workplace, the classroom, and at home. We strive to have the text as current as the publishing timelines will allow us, constantly looking for the next technology trend or gadget. We have augmented the text with weekly technology updates to help you keep your classroom on top of the latest breaking developments. The result is a learning system that sparks student interest by focusing on the material they want to learn (such as how to integrate computing devices into a home network) while teaching the material they need to learn (such as how networks work). The sequence of topics is carefully set up to mirror the typical student learning experience.

As they read through this text, your students will progress through stages of increasing difficulty:

1. Thinking about how technology offers them the power to change their society and their world
2. Examining why it's important to be computer fluent
3. Examining the basic components of the computer
4. Connecting to and exploring the Internet
5. Exploring software
6. Learning the operating system and personalizing the computer
7. Evaluating and upgrading computing devices
8. Exploring home networking and keeping the computer safe from hackers
9. Going mobile with smartphones, netbooks, iPads, and laptops
10. Going behind the scenes, looking at technology in more detail

We have written the book in a "spiraling" manner, intentionally introducing on a basic level in the earlier chapters those concepts that students have trouble with and then later expanding on those concepts in more detail when students have become more comfortable with them. Thus, the focus of the early chapters is on practical uses for the computer, with real-world examples to help the students place computing in a familiar context. For example, we introduce basic hardware components in Chapter 2, and then we go into increasingly greater detail on some hardware components in Chapter 6 and in the "Under the Hood" Technology in Focus feature.

The Behind the Scenes chapters venture deeper into the realm of computing through in-depth explanations of how programming, networks, the Internet, and databases work. They are specifically designed to keep more experienced students engaged and to challenge them with interesting research assignments.

We have also developed a comprehensive multimedia program to reinforce the material taught in the text and to support both classroom lectures and distance learning. The Helpdesk training content, created specifically for *Technology in Action*, enables students to take on the role of a helpdesk operator and work through common questions asked by computer users. Exciting Sound Byte multimedia—fully integrated with the text—expands student mastery of complex topics. Tech in Action Weekly delivers the latest news stories in technology to you for use in your classroom. Each is accompanied by specific discussion topics and activities to expand on what is within the textbook materials.

Now that the computer has become a ubiquitous tool in our lives, a new approach to computer concepts is warranted. This book is designed to reach the students of the twenty-first century and prepare them for the the role they can take in their country and their world.

# Visual Walk-Through

## TOPIC SEQUENCE
Concepts are covered in a spiraling manner between chapters to mirror the typical student learning experience.

**CHAPTER 2**

**CHAPTER 6**

**CHAPTER 6**

### Hardware First Introduced
Chapter 2 is the first time students read about introductory hardware. It is covered at the beginning level because this is their experience level at this point of the book.

### Hardware Taught in More Depth in Additional Chapters
In later chapters, students are taught hardware in greater depth because they are more experienced and comfortable working with their computer.

### How Cool is This?
Highlights the latest and greatest web sites, gadgets, and multimedia.

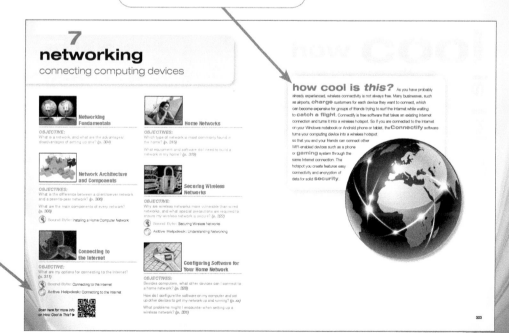

**7**

# networking
connecting computing devices

### Multimedia Cues
Visual integration of multimedia.

**Figure 3.30**

**Figure 10.14**

The **Ethics in IT** boxes examine the ethical dilemmas caused by technology.

The **Trends in IT** boxes explore newer topics involved in computing.

**Dig Deeper** boxes cover technical topics in depth to challenge advanced students.

**Bits and Bytes** teach good habits for safe computing.

**Multiple Choice and True/False**

**Technology in Focus**
Five special features that teach key uses of technology today.

# The Multimedia

**Companion Website**
Includes an interactive study guide, online end-of-chapter material, additional Internet exercises, and much more.

www.prenhall.com/techinaction

**Active Helpdesk**
Interactive training that puts the student in the role of a helpdesk staffer fielding questions from callers.

**Completely Revised**
Features textbook page references within each call and assessment at the end of each call.

Supervisor available to assist students.

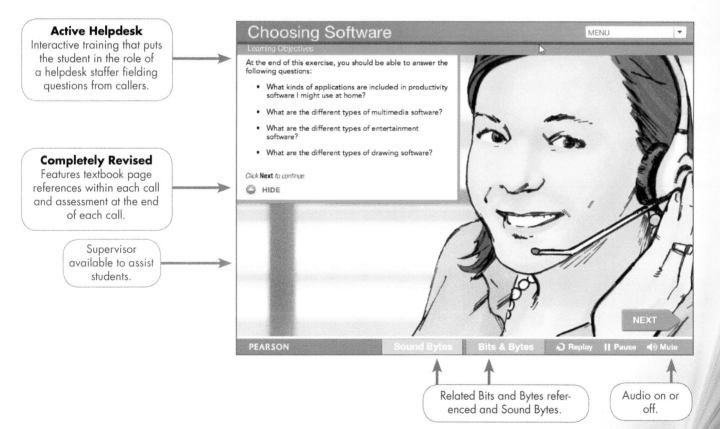

Related Bits and Bytes referenced and Sound Bytes.

Audio on or off.

**ninth**

# 9

**Transcript button** used
to turn transcript on or off.

**Sound Bytes**
Multimedia lessons
with video, audio,
or animation and
corresponding labs
featuring multiple-
choice quizzing.

Also available as
podcasts.

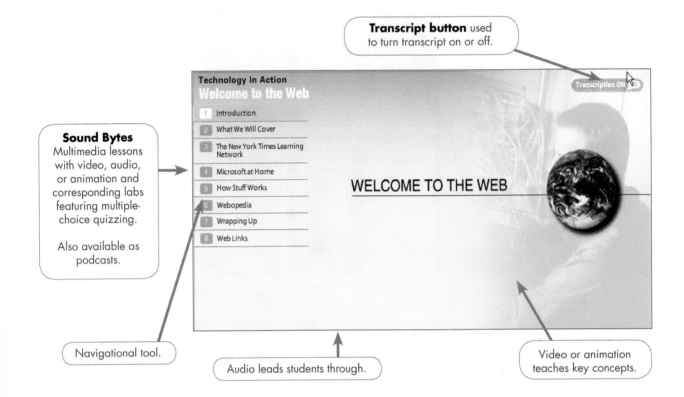

**Technology In Action**
**Welcome to the Web**

1 Introduction
2 What We Will Cover
3 The New York Times Learning Network
4 Microsoft at Home
5 How Stuff Works
6 Webopedia
7 Wrapping Up
8 Web Links

Transcription ON

WELCOME TO THE WEB

Navigational tool.

Audio leads students through.

Video or animation
teaches key concepts.

# Annotated Instructor Edition

Provided with each chapter are two divider pages like the ones outlined below.

## FRONT OF CHAPTER TAB

On the front side of each chapter tab, you will find the following categories:

**IN THE CLASSROOM:** Activities you can use in a classroom or in online classes, including:

- PowerPoint Presentations
- Discussion Exercises
- Active Helpdesk Calls
- Sound Bytes

**HOMEWORK:** Activities used out of class for assessment or preparation for the next chapter, including:

- Web Resource Projects
- Active Helpdesk Calls
- Sound Byte Labs
- Online Study Guides

**ASSESSMENT:**

- Blackboard
- WebCT
- TestGen
- myitlab

The back side of each chapter tab includes the relevant Sound Bytes for that chapter.

## FRONT OF ETHICS TAB

On the front of the Ethics tab, you will find the following:

**OPPOSING VIEWPOINTS TABLE:** Outlines debatable ethics topics that you can use in the classroom.

**KEYWORDS:** Provides you with additional words to search the Internet for more information related to the ethics topic.

For a list of the resources available for every chapter and where they are located, see the back of this tab.

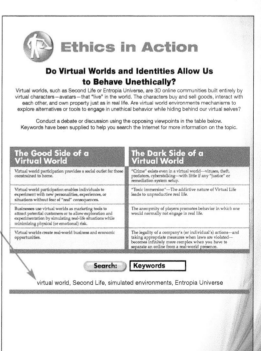

# Instructor Resource CD

**Instructor Resource CD**
- **NEW! Interactive Course Builder** to help you integrate all the instructor resources.
- **NEW! Recommended chapter lectures** written by the authors that you can customize.
- All resources included with the *Technology in Action* Instructional System.

Contact your local Pearson sales rep to learn more about the
***Technology in Action*** instructional system.

# using technology to change the world

David Grigg / iStockphoto.com

### More Than Just a Job

*OBJECTIVE:*
Beyond personal goals, what impact can you have on the world? *(p. 4)*

© Emrah Turudu / iStockphoto.com

### Technology and Our Society

*OBJECTIVE:*
How can knowledge of technology help you impact the direction of our society? *(p. 9)*

Brandon Alms / iStockphoto.com

### Technology on the World Stage

*OBJECTIVE:*
How can becoming proficient with technology help you understand and participate in important issues in the world at large? *(p. 4)*

Ximagination / Shutterstock.com

### Technology and Your Life

*OBJECTIVES:*
What does it mean to be "computer literate"? *(p. 13)*

How does being computer literate make you a savvy computer user and consumer? *(p. 14)*

How can becoming computer literate help you in a career? *(p. 16)*

 Sound Byte: The History of the Personal Computer

 Sound Byte: Questions to Ask Before You Buy a Computer

*Scan here for more info on How Cool Is This?*

# how cool is *this*?
At the Wake Forest Institute for Regenerative Medicine, researcher Dr. Anthony Atala heads a group working on replacement tissue and **organ** development. One project there uses ordinary desktop **printers** to create human organs! Instead of using ink, they "bioprint" with human **cells** layer after layer. In about 40 minutes they can "print" a two-chamber heart, which starts beating on its own about five hours later. Currently these are still experimental organs, but there is great hope that complex organs with lots of blood vessels like hearts, livers, and kidneys can be reproduced this way. The gap between the need for **transplant** organs and the supply is skyrocketing as the number of patients requesting organs has doubled in the last decade, while the number of transplants has remained about the same.

Science Photo Library / Alamy

## More Than Just a Job

Ask yourself: Why are you in this class? It may be that this class is required for your degree. Or it may be that you thought it would be useful for you to have better computer skills when you apply for a job. Both of these are great reasons to study computers and technology, but let's step back for a moment and try to see a bigger picture.

Technology today is not just a means for career advancement or just a necessary skill set for survival in society. It has become something more—a tool that allows an individual to make an impact far beyond his or her own life. So many movies dangle the same dream in front of us—being the girl or guy who saves the world, and gets to drive a nice car while doing it! Whether it's *Transformers* or *Spider-Man*, we are drawn to heroes because we want our work and our lives to mean something and benefit others.

The material in this book can be your ticket to doing just that, to influence and to participate in projects that are changing the world. In this opening chapter, we'd like to ask you to think about what your talents and skills in technology could let you contribute on a larger scale, beyond the benefits they will bring to you.

**Figure 1.1**

How big of a role did social media play in the transfer of power in Egypt in 2011?

## Technology on the World Stage

Political and global issues of recent times are showing that modern technology is galvanizing groups of people in new ways. As you work this semester to develop your understanding of technology, realize that you could become the next Wael Ghonim or Ory Okolloh. You will use technology to change the world.

### Political Issues

**Egypt** The end of 2010 saw a series of revolutions across the Arab and North African region. Protests or full-scale revolutions took place in Tunisia, Libya, Algeria, and Jordan. **Social networking** is the gathering together of groups of people using online tools to connect and exchange ideas. Social networking tools like Facebook and Twitter fueled social unrest in the face of repression and censorship in many countries. Egypt is one example that shows the impact of an individual armed with an understanding of modern technology.

The reigning government in Egypt had been in power for more than 30 years—the entire life of many young people in the country. Wael Ghonim, a Google marketing manager in Egypt, anonymously launched the Facebook page "We Are All Khaled Said" in June 2010. Khaled Said was an Egyptian businessman tortured and killed by authorities. The Facebook page became a tool that made people aware there were others who were dissatisfied with the direction of the country, even though they were not yet able to imagine other options. By January 2011, the government responded to the increasing unrest online by "turning off" the Internet for the entire country. The government told the four largest Internet providers to shut down and closed access to 93 percent of Egyptian networks. Protests against this shutdown turned violent, and Egyptian Internet providers began to restore service a few days later.

Back in the virtual world of Facebook and Twitter, thousands offered ideas on how they could protest meaningfully. Finally, a silent gathering near the sea in Alexandria was chosen. This movement from "virtual community" to physical community (see Figure 1.1) was a turning point, and by February 11, 2011, President Mubarak

**Figure** 1.2

The Ushahidi site used crisis mapping during the Kenyan election to quickly combine a torrent of reports into a useful mapping tool.

of Egypt had resigned. President Obama stated, "We had the privilege to witness history taking place. . . . Egypt will never be the same."

Social networking tools are providing a level of instant connection and instant distribution of information that is reshaping the world. For Wael Ghonim, it led to an opportunity to recast the future of his country. What can you do with social networking tools that will change the future of your community?

**Kenya** A single voice in Kenya combined with technology to create a tool that continues to change the world. In December 2007, angry Kenyans wielding machetes were battling the police in the streets. The closest election in Kenya's history had ended with the current president declaring victory despite suspicion and allegations of electoral fraud. Nairobi lawyer Ory Okolloh began to get messages describing acts of violence occurring all over the country. She tried to post them all on her blog site KenyanPundit, but she was quickly overwhelmed. She put out a request for help through the blog.

Within 72 hours, two programmers, Erik Hersman and Juliana Rotich, had created Ushahidi (Swahili for "testimony"). It is a **crisis mapping tool** that collects information from e-mails, text messages, blog posts, and Twitter tweets and maps them, making the information instantly publicly available (see Figure 1.2). The developers then made Ushahidi a free platform that anyone in the world could use. To date, it has been used during the earthquakes and tsunami in Japan, to battle election violence in the Congo, to observe events in the Gaza Strip, and to monitor the 2010 snow emergency in Washington, D.C. ("Snowmageddon").

From there, the development team created a second generation product called SwiftRiver. SwiftRiver addresses a key issue in collecting eyewitness accounts in real time during a crisis: What do you read first? As thousands of tweets and posts come in, how can we pull relevant information from all this data from the crowd? SwiftRiver uses filters to rate the submitters and the quality of the information to generate a measurement of the probability the information is accurate.

In what other ways could technology prove useful in helping us face times of crisis?

### Human Rights

Writer and futurist Jamais Cascio has presented ideas of how our current technological landscape might bring all citizens into a more engaged role in changing the world. In his TED talk "The Future We Will Create" (**www.ted.org**), Cascio discusses how a smartphone-carrying population can work to create a better world—more sustainable, more secure, and more desirable.

Having an international population armed with cameras and a means to quickly distribute their video allows the invisible to become visible in many ways (see Figure 1.3). This transparency can be used to let us see the consequences of our behavior directly, and make changes. The Witness Project, founded by Peter Gabriel, uses this strategy to stop human rights abuses throughout the world (**www.witness.org**). Their slogan is, "See it. Film it. Change it." ("See It. Film It. Change It." Copyright © 2011 by WITNESS. Reprinted by permission of WITNESS www.witness.org.) And video from the Witness Project has changed many lives; for example, it contributed to the arrest of warlords in the Democratic Republic of Congo for the recruitment of child soldiers. Using technology such as the Witness Project, what problems in your community could you shed light on and bring to the community's attention?

### The Environment

Efforts similar to those just described are working to document the environmental state of the world. Environmental successes can be collected together, along with evidence to document ecological crimes. What if each of the cell phones distributed around the world was equipped with integrated atmospheric sensors? Then millions of points around the world would be constantly reporting in on air and water quality. And what if these sensors could monitor for flu viruses? Tagged with geographical information, the data could be combined with maps for easy viewing and analysis. Ideas like these are being explored by UCLA researcher Dr. Deborah Estrin, the director of the Center for Embedded Network Sensing. Can you think of other ways that your cell phone could help you improve your society?

Thanks to technology, each of us is empowered with tools and opportunities to impact the world. Your reach can go far beyond what you see around you. Learn as much as you can about using your technology to its fullest potential, to enrich the world community.

### The Digital Divide

**Accessible Technology** If technology can provide every person with the power to change their country, even their world, what

**Figure 1.3**

The Witness Project uses the power of video and a grassroots movement to advocate for human rights around the world.

does it mean to be without access to technology? There is still a great gap between the levels of Internet access and the availability of technical tools in different regions of the world. The term coined for that gap, for the difference in ease of access to technology, is the **digital divide**. The danger of a digital divide is that it prevents us from using all of the minds on the planet to solve the problems of the planet. But that challenge also is being answered by the application of technology.

The Next Einstein Initiative (NEI) is a strategic plan to focus resources on the young talented mathematical minds of Africa (see Figure 1.4). By expanding the African Institute for Mathematical Sciences (AIMS) across the continent, the future of Africa can be profoundly changed. Cambridge professor Neil Turok founded AIMS to bring together the brightest young minds across Africa with the best lecturers in the world. He has described the power of the youthful intellect in Africa by saying, "If Africa is going to get fixed, it's by them, not by us." NEI has won funding from Google's Project $10^{100}$, a push to award $10 million to a set of five projects, selected by open public voting. By capturing the enthusiasm of the world with presentations distributed through ted.com and Project $10^{100}$, there is now an active push to create 15 additional AIMS centers across Africa.

There are smaller ways to address the digital divide as well. Traditional chalkboards gave way to whiteboards, which have given way to smartboards. Smartboards can display content on a computer screen, are touch interactive, and can easily record and store lecture content. But there is a price tag for all that functionality. Smartboard units can cost as much as $5,000, so they are much more common in affluent settings. A quick hack to the popular Nintendo Wii remote, however, makes it possible to create a smartboard for about $50. Researcher Johnny Lee of Google has developed, and freely distributes, software that uses the infrared camera in the tip of a Wii remote, as well as an infrared pen (which you can make for about $5) to create an inexpensive smartboard. In its first three months on Lee's Web site, the software for this was downloaded over half a million times. The final

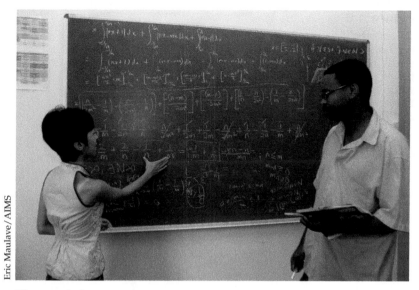

**Figure 1.4**

The Next Einstein Initiative is rallying the support of the world to identify mathematical genius.

product is not as full featured as competing products, but as Lee says, "you get about 80 percent of the way there, for about 1 percent of the cost."

**High Low Tech** The MIT Media Lab has a research group dedicated to integrating high- and low-tech materials and processes into other cultures. Projects like Fab FM have created radio kits that can be produced and assembled at home. The Open Source Consumer Electronics project studies ways that traditional electronic circuit boards and components can be more easily shared, modified, and produced. The Junkyard Jumbotron from the MIT Center for Future Civic Media is another example of a software solution that allows low-tech parts to imitate the utility of expensive high-tech tools. The Jumbotron lets you combine a range of displays into a single virtual screen. Any kind of screen can become part of the jumbo image as long as it runs a Web browser, so laptops, smartphones, and smart televisions all can be converted on the spot to become an instant Jumbotron screen (see Figure 1.5).

There is no exaggerating the range and severity of problems facing our world, from environmental threats to dangers brought on by how we treat each other. Your understanding of technology could provide the means to change the course of our future. How will you use these powers to improve your own world?

**Figure** 1.5

The Junkyard Jumbotron lets users create a single screen from laptops, tablets, smartphones—anything with a Web browser.

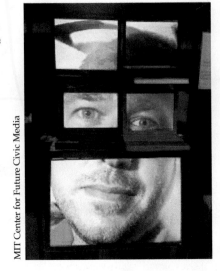

MIT Center for Future Civic Media

MIT Center for Future Civic Media

## Ethics in IT: The Digital Divide and the Mobile Bridge

The digital divide, the gap between those with easy access to technology and those with little to no access (see Figure 1.6), is a social problem that leads to more complex social issues down the road. Lack of access to the Internet and computers means that people don't develop computer skills, leading to less chance of success in career and business. Less familiarity with the Internet can lead to less civic engagement and a lower level of active, engaged citizenship. So how should we attack the problem of the digital divide?

Perhaps the answer is to promote mobile devices as a means for low-income families to access the Internet. Recent studies from the University of Michigan show that without Internet access at home, teens from low-income households (family income under $30,000 a year) are more likely than their wealthier counterparts to use their cell phones to go online. So the widening penetration of cell phones might be the answer to ending the digital divide. Or is it? It depends on how you define the digital divide. If merely having access to the Internet means you have crossed the divide, the increase of mobile plan usage by lower income families is a great step.

But could it be that this "solution" just continues the problem in a new disguise? Going online using a cell phone plan is the most expensive of all options, and data transfer speeds are among the slowest. So the teens with the least money are likely paying the most to get the slowest online experience. And they are more likely to be paying for it themselves, as opposed to teens from wealthier households in which, according to the same University of Michigan study, the teens are more likely to be on family plans paid for by someone else. So by not having available free Internet access, is our society placing an unfair burden on just those groups least likely to be able to afford access?

"The willingness of poor people to pay for Internet access underscores the idea that net access is not just 'nice to have' but that it is increasingly seen as a necessity," the researchers wrote. But if your main access to the Internet is through mobile usage, does that help develop a wider range of computer skills? Often teen cell usage is limited to managing online social networks, playing games, or listening to music. Computer tasks and skills that could lead to economic advancement, like filling out job applications or running a business, are not yet handled easily on mobile devices.

Will the increasing penetration of smartphones and faster cellular Internet access eliminate the digital divide in the United States? Should our government intervene and make sure there is sufficient free access for all? Is it ethical to deprive the poorer segment of our society of a needed commodity? Answering challenging questions about technology is part of being an informed citizen.

Grant Alexander Waters

**Figure** 1.6

Can we bridge the digital divide through mobile devices? Should we?

# Technology and Our Society

Technology is allowing us to redefine very fundamental parts of our social makeup. How we think, how we connect with each other, how we purchase and consume products—all of these areas of our society are shifting rapidly because of technology.

## Technology Impacts How We Think

**What We Think About** What do you think about when you get home after school or work—when you are officially on your own time? In the late twentieth century, the most common trend was thinking about what to buy next. Or perhaps what to watch next, what to listen to next, what to read next—information and products were being served at an amazing rate, and a pattern of consumption became habit. As more and more Web applications began to appear that allowed each individual to become the "creator" of the Web, a new kind of Internet came into being. It was nicknamed Web 2.0, and now everyone could collaborate internationally at the click of a mouse. The twenty-first century has seen a dramatic shift—the generation of a **creative surplus**. Clay Shirky, author of *Cognitive Surplus: Creativity and Generosity in a Connected Age*, coined this term to describe the ability of the world's populace to volunteer and collaborate on large projects. The world's population has an estimated 1 trillion hours a year of free time. When that is coupled with the available media tools, and with a generosity and need to share, projects like Ushahidi and the Witness Project emerge.

Not only heart-stopping civic-minded projects appear online—there are many sites like LOLCats and video channels of backyard accidents as well. But modern theories of motivation show that what pushes people to apply their free time to projects, for no money, is the excitement of autonomy, mastery, and purpose (see Figure 1.7). **Autonomy** is the freedom to work without constant direction and control. **Mastery** is the feeling of confidence and excitement from seeing your own skills progress. So many people complete a full week of work and then play a musical instrument for hours at home, not to make money, but to feel their mastery of the instrument grow. **Purpose** is simply the understanding that you are working for something larger than yourself. Together, these three play into how we are fundamentally wired and produce incredibly motivated behavior. As we learn more about the "technology" of motivation, electronic technology offers motivated people the means to connect and to work easily with video and media. Their creative surplus becomes a powerful resource to change the world.

**Figure 1.7**

Our understanding of human motivation can play a role in our use of technology to impact society.

**How We Think of Each Other** We are trained by our society to adopt certain ideas about gender. From pink or blue booties all the way to major marketing media campaigns, specific messages and stereotypes about gender are broadcast to us constantly. Marketing often relies on identifying and exploiting specific stereotypes to sell products. If you fall into a certain demographic, say "men between the ages of 25 and 34," then your buying behavior is predicted along certain lines. Although marketing is very tuned to demographics, many groups find themselves underrepresented. For example, the highly influential Nielsen ratings of television do not even measure viewers over the age of 54. Another effect of this age bias is that certain standard storylines appear repeatedly in entertainment—movies for young men featuring fast cars, or "chick flicks" to appeal to young women.

How has the startling rise of social media networks impacted this? Online it is difficult to ascertain someone's true age—marketers only have access to your path through a particular Web site to try to determine your income or gender. But it is very easy to determine what interests you as you move around the Web. People form into groups based not on their age or income, but on their common interests. When

Joanna Blakely of the Norman Lear Center at the University of Southern California began to study the relationship between gender and online usage, she found that women outnumber men in their use of social networking. They also spend much more time on social sites. As marketers move toward relying on information from social networks, they will be increasingly driven by a female perspective and by a more complex model of what certain groups are attracted to than the classic clichés of the past.

### How We Connect

**Connecting Through Music** In most societies, people connect intimately in gatherings, local celebrations, and festivals through shared experiences. Technology has added breadth to that aspect of our lives as well. Eric Whitacre's Virtual Choir, shown in Figure 1.8, is one example. As a wannabe rock star, Whitacre was introduced to classical choir music in college, and the experience transformed his life. He is now a professional classical composer and conductor. He began the idea of a virtual choir by posting a video of himself conducting one of his works, "Lux Aurumque," to YouTube. The idea was that listeners would follow his lead and, as they heard the piano track, each would

**Figure 1.8**

The Virtual Choir 2.0 performance of "Sleep" included over 2,000 singers from 58 countries.

s70/ZUMA Press/Newscom

record their part of the piece as either a soprano, alto, tenor, or bass. The submitted videos were then edited together, the audio aligned, and the first piece from the Virtual Choir was released with 50 recorded voices.

> ## Tools like DYTHR represent a huge shift in how we are informed and who controls the information that governs our lives.

His next project, Virtual Choir 2.0 performing "Sleep," was released in April 2011 and was even larger in scale. It included 2,052 videos from 58 different countries. A blog connected the members of the choir and built a real sense of community and connection between members. Take a glance at the Virtual Choir Earth View (**www.ericwhiteacre.com/the-virtual-choir/earth-view**), which displays the physical location of each voice. As Whitacre remarked, ". . . human beings will go to any lengths necessary to find and connect with each other."

**Connecting in New Ways** Ze Frank is an artist working to explore the ways we connect now that our virtual lives are so expanded. Frank has organized numerous projects that illustrate the new ways we can connect virtually. He initiated one project named *A Childhood Walk* that invites people to go into Google Street View and record a walk that they used to take over and over as a child. People often have strong memories reappear, and Frank gathered together those memories along with photos from Google Street View to create a gallery (**www.zefrank.com/the_walk**). For the people who created these experiences, and for the audience that viewed the gallery, the results were powerful and emotional.

Another example of shifts in how we connect is demonstrated by the DYTHR project from MIT graduate students Grace Woo and Szymon Jakubczak. As people using DYTHR walk around with their mobile devices, they can broadcast a short message (see Figure 1.9). Other phones, while scanning for wireless networks, pick up and display the messages. If a message seems important, you can tap it and re-broadcast it. The more popular messages, as determined by the crowd, then begin to trickle up to the top of the list. So the crowd itself is writing the headlines, broadcasting them, and filtering them by popular demand. Tools like DYTHR represent a huge shift in how we are informed and who controls the information that governs our lives. No Internet connection or cell phone tower is required, so it is very difficult to censor. What other changes will technology bring to how we gather news and distribute it?

### How We Consume

Technology is changing all aspects of how we purchase and consume goods—from strategies for convincing you to purchase a

**Figure** 1.9
DYTHR lets information be created, distributed, and filtered by users themselves in real time.

Brian van der Brug/Los Angeles Times/MCT/Newscom

**Figure** 1.10

Best Buy uses QR tags on each product tag to direct shoppers to the Best Buy site for reviews.

certain product to the mechanics of how you buy and own things.

**Marketing** New strategies in marketing and communications are counting on the fact that so many people have a cell phone with a camera and Internet access. A technology named **QR (quick response) codes** lets any piece of print in the real world host a live link to online information and video content. From your smartphone, simply run your QR app and hold the phone near the QR image anywhere you see it—on a product, in an advertisement, on a sign or a storefront—and your phone takes you directly to a display of information. It might be a Web site, a video, a schedule, or a social network. QR tags are being used widely in retail (see Figure 1.10), because studies show 82 percent of shoppers go to the Internet on their phone before a purchase anyway. You'll even see them on the opening page of each chapter of this book!

Marketers also have to be aware of the phenomenon of **crowdsourcing**—checking in with the voice of the crowd. Consumers are using apps like MobileVoice to check people's verdict (the "crowd") on the quality of an item. Forward-thinking companies are using this input to improve their products and services. TaxiHack, for example,

allows phone users to comment on New York City cab drivers, and AT&T has an app to let customers report locations of coverage gaps.

Recent studies show that 93 percent of adults in the United States ages 18–29 now have a cell phone. Combined with the explosion in popularity of social networking sites, consumers' experiences are changing. Shopping now begins with price comparison tools like ShopSavvy and RedLaser. These "location aware" tools begin by scanning the barcode of the item and then comparing prices with nearby stores and also with the best prices available online. Once you've selected a store, many different mobile apps let you take advantage of mobile coupons, called mobicoupons. A smartphone can simply read the barcode on the item, and then will display a barcode for a coupon. The cashier scans the mobicoupon right at the register. More and more sites are appearing that offer some type of mobile coupon, including Zavers, Yowza, MobiQpons, and Cellfire. Future trends in this area include a tighter integration with the information customer loyalty programs already store about you. Based on location and your past buying preferences, specialized coupons could be designed and delivered through the mobicoupon system.

**Access Versus Ownership** Even the idea of ownership is evolving under technological pressures. The shift of information to a digital form is allowing us to change our relationship to objects. Items like bicycles and cars can become "subscriptions" instead of large one-time purchases. Call a Bike is a program run in Germany. At most major street corners, there is a rack of Call a Bikes (see Figure 1.11). Place a call to the phone number printed on the bike, and it texts you a code you can use to unlock the bike lock. Ride the bike to where you're going. When you arrive, relock it. The amount of time you rode it automatically is billed (by the minute) to your phone.

Zipcar is another system using the digital communication of information to change our lifestyle habits. Many cities and most major universities now offer a Zipcar program. Residents sign up for the program and receive a key that has an RFID microchip inside. All cars are connected to a central network. You can open a Zipcar car and start the engine only when your specific key is scheduled to open and start it. GPS technology is used to track where the car is, whether it has been dropped off at the right location, and how far it has been driven. The entire process is transparent to Zipcar members. Members have 24/7 access to a vehicle—a truck, a hybrid, a convertible—when they need it, with very little advance notice, for a cost of about $7 an hour (gas and insurance included!).

These models are spreading now to smaller goods. **Swap.com** supports people so they can trade books, video games, and DVDs with one another, using the power of peer-to-peer connections to find the best set of matches for their used DVD set of *Seinfeld* in exchange for a season of *Curb Your Enthusiasm*. Rachel Botsman and Roo Rogers make the case in their book *What's Mine Is Yours: The Rise of Collaborative Consumption* that the real fuel beneath these services is a shift in our acceptance of sharing. **Collaborative consumption** implies that we are joining together as a group to use a specific product more efficiently. We are so constantly connected with each other, we have again found the power of community. Adding in the pressure of mounting environmental concerns and a global financial crisis, we are migrating toward collaborative consumption. There are more and more opportunities to redistribute the things we have purchased, share our lives, and share the services a product provides, instead of owning it outright. On average a car is used 1 hour a day—the other 23 hours a day it is not helping you or any of your neighbors. As Kevin Kelly, editor of *Wired* magazine, framed it, we are moving toward a time where we design around a new idea " . . . where access is better than ownership."

# Technology and Your Life

Technology is creating huge changes in the world scene as well as how we behave socially, but it is also important to you on a more personal level. The more you understand technology, the greater your productivity can be and the better prepared you'll be for any career.

### Boost Your Productivity

Technology now allows you to be very active in critical social and global issues. In order to take advantage of such power you need to move beyond being just a casual computer user and achieve computer literacy. Being **computer literate** means being familiar enough with computers that you

**Figure 1.11**

Call a Bike uses digital technology to change our lifestyle from one of ownership to one of "subscription."

**Figure** 1.12

Do you know what all the words in a computer ad mean? Can you tell whether the ad includes all the information necessary to make a purchasing decision?

| | |
|---|---|
| **Processor:** | Intel i7-965 Extreme, Factory O'Cd to 3.73 GHz |
| **RAM:** | 12 GB Tri Channel Corsair DDR3 (1066 MHz) |
| **Video:** | ATI Radeon HD 5870 X2 with 1 GB DDR5 |
| **Audio:** | Creative Labs X-Fi Elite Pro; HDA 7.1 surround channel sound |
| **Network:** | Native Gigabit Ethernet |
| **Optical Drive:** | Blu-ray burner |
| **Storage Drive:** | 1 TB Serial ATA hard drive with support for up to 5 additional drives with RAID options |
| **Ports:** | 8 USB and 2 USB 3.0<br>2 DVI and 1 S-Video<br>2 IEEE 1394<br>1 S/PDIF out |
| **Physics Accelerator:** | Ageia PhysX Card |
| **Cooling:** | Two-stage liquid cooling system |
| **Portable Storage:** | Bluetooth wireless 19-in-1 media hub with VoIP stereo headset |
| **Operating System:** | Windows 7 Ultimate 64-bit |

NEW!

Norman Chan/
Shutterstock.com

Norman Chan/
Shutterstock.com

rozbyshaka/
Shutterstock.com

understand their capabilities and limitations (see Figure 1.12), and you know how to use them efficiently.

Once you can use computers in an efficient manner, you'll see changes in your own relationship with technology. You'll be a better consumer when it comes time to purchase computers, peripherals, and technology services. You'll be more sought after as a new hire and more productive as an employee. Your understanding of key concepts in technology can "future-proof" you, letting you easily and quickly react to the next round of new technologies.

### Be a Savvy Computer User

Let's look at how to become a savvy computer user and consumer. What does this mean? Here are a few examples. If you are not a savvy user now, don't worry—all these topics and more are covered in the remaining chapters.

- **Avoiding hackers and viruses.** Do you know what hackers and viruses are? Both can threaten a computer's security. Being aware of how hackers and viruses operate and knowing the damage they can do to your computer can help you avoid falling prey to them.

- **Protecting your privacy.** You've probably heard of identity theft—you see and hear news stories all the time about people whose "identities" are stolen and whose credit ratings are ruined by "identity thieves." But do you know

how to protect yourself from identity theft when you're online?

- **Understanding the real risks.** Part of being computer literate means being able to separate the real privacy and security risks from things you don't have to worry about. For example, do you know what a *cookie* is? Do you know whether it poses a privacy risk for you when you're on the Internet? What about a *firewall?* Do you know what one is? Do you really need one to protect your computer?

- **Using the Internet and the Web wisely.** Anyone who has ever searched the Web can attest that finding information and finding good information are two different things. People who are computer literate make the Internet a powerful tool and know how to find the information they want effectively. How familiar with the Web are you, and how effective are your searches?

- **Avoiding online annoyances.** If you have an e-mail account, are you sure you know all the tricks you need to use e-mail appropriately (see Figure 1.13)? Chances are you've received electronic junk mail, or **spam.** How can you avoid being overwhelmed by spam? What about adware and spyware— do you know what they are? Do you know the difference between those and viruses, worms, and Trojan horses? Do you know which **software** programs, the instructions that tell the computer

## Questions to Ask Before You Buy a Computer

This Sound Byte will help you consider important questions to ask before you buy a computer, such as whether you should get a laptop or a desktop, or whether you should purchase a new computer or a used or refurbished one.

**Figure** 1.13

Understanding how to use e-mail effectively is just one example of what it means to be computer literate.

what to do, you should install on your computer to avoid online annoyances?

• **Being able to maintain, upgrade, and troubleshoot your computer.** Learning how to care for and maintain your computer and knowing how to diagnose and fix certain problems can save you a lot of time and hassle. Do you know how to upgrade your computer if you want more memory, for example? Do you know which software and computer settings can help you keep your computer in top shape?

Everywhere you go, you see ads like the one in Figure 1.12 for computers and other devices: laptops, printers, monitors, cell phones, digital cameras, and GPS (global positioning system) devices. Do you know what all the words in the ad mean? What is *RAM?* What is a *CPU?* What are *MB, GB, GHz,* and *cache?* How fast do you need your computer to be, and how much memory should it have? Understanding computer

terminology and keeping current with technology will help you better determine which computers and devices match your needs.

Finally, becoming computer literate means knowing which technologies are on the horizon and how to integrate them into your home setup when possible (see Figure 1.14). Can you connect your laptop to a wireless network? What is Bluetooth, and does your computer have it? Can a USB 3.0 flash drive be plugged into an old USB 1.0 port? For that matter, what is a USB port? How much memory should your cell phone have? Knowing the answers to these and

**Figure** 1.14

Can you identify all of these devices? Do you know how to get them all to work well together?

other questions will help you make better purchasing decisions.

The benefits of being computer literate will help you in your career and in running your personal life. This book and course will make you computer literate. Chapter 3 shows you how to know if your hardware is beginning to limit your computer's performance, and how to upgrade or shop for a new system. In Chapter 10 you'll find out how to get the most from the Web, while staying free from the spam and clutter Internet surfing can leave behind.

You'll be able to save money, time, and endless frustration by having a strong background in the basics of how computers and computer systems operate.

### Prepare for Your Career

Computer careers are on the rise. Regardless of which profession you pursue, if computers are not already in use in that career, they most likely will be soon. **Information technology (IT)** is a field of study focused on managing and processing information and the automatic retrieval of information. Information technology includes computers, telecommunications, and software deployment. IT careers are on the rise, and several of the fastest-growing occupations are computer related. New technology in the workplace is creating a demand for new skill levels from employees. A study from the National Research Council concludes that by the year 2030, computers will displace humans in 60 percent of the current occupations. It will be more critical than ever for employees to have advanced skills. For more information about computers and the workplace, see the Technology in Focus section, "Careers in IT." So, let's begin with a look at how computer systems are used in a wide range of careers.

We all are used to seeing computers at the checkout counter in stores, at the check-in area at an airport, and so on, but computers are being used in many ways that you probably aren't aware of. Before we begin looking at a computer's parts and how it operates, let's take a look at a whole range of industries and examine how computers are a part of getting work done. Becoming truly computer literate will undoubtedly help you perform your job more effectively. It also will make you more desirable as an employee and more likely to earn more and advance your career. Whether you plan on a career in one of these fields or will just be a user of their products and services, your life will be affected by the use of computers in areas including retail, the arts, law enforcement, the military, agriculture, and more.

### Retail: Working in a Data Mine

Businesses accumulate a lot of data, but how do they manage to make sense of all of it? How do they separate the anomalies from the trends? They use a technique known as **data mining**, the process of searching huge amounts of data with the hope of finding a pattern (see Figure 1.15). For example, large retailers often study the data gathered from register terminals to determine which products are selling on a given day and in a specific location. In addition to inventory control systems, which help managers figure out how much merchandise they need to order to replace stock that is sold, the process of data mining opens the door to more detail. Managers can use mined data to determine that if a certain product is to sell

Mclek/Shutterstock.com    Richard Peterson/Shutterstock.com    Dmitriy Shironosov/Shutterstock.com

Simon Krzic/Shutterstock.com

Saleee/Shutterstock.com

yuyangc/Shutterstock.com

Dmitrije Paunovic/Shutterstock.com

**Figure 1.15**

Data mining is the art of combining huge volumes of raw data into views that provide insight.

well, they must lower its price—especially if they cut the price at one store and see sales increase, for example. Data mining thus allows retailers to respond to consumer buying patterns.

Did you ever wonder how Amazon or Netflix can suggest items that fit your taste? Or how such Web sites automatically display lists of items people bought after they ordered the camera you just picked out? Data mining can keep track of the purchases customers are making, along with their geographic data, past buying history, and lists of items they examined but did not purchase. This can be translated into extremely specific marketing that is immediate and customized to your shopping experience. This is the motivation behind all of the discount cards that grocery stores and drugstores offer. In exchange for tracking your personal buying habits, they offer you some kind of special pricing. How much is your private information worth?

**Arts: Ink, Paints, and a Laptop?**
Some design students think that because they're studying art, there is no reason for them to study computers. However, unless you plan to be a "starving artist," you'll probably want to sell your work. To do so, you'll need to showcase your designs and artistic creations so that prospective employers/customers can view them. Wouldn't it be helpful if you knew how to manage a Web site like the one shown in Figure 1.16?

Using computers in the arts and entertainment fields goes far beyond using the Internet. Dance and music programs like the ones at the Atlanta Ballet and the Juilliard School of Music use computers to create new performances for audiences. A live dancer can be wired with sensors that are connected to a computer that captures

> # Using computers in the arts and entertainment fields goes far beyond using the Internet.

the dancer's movements. Based on the data it collects, the computer generates a virtual dancer on a screen. The computer

# MADELEINEHIGHLAND

*"ONLINE PORTFOLIO"*

### NEW  FASHION ILLUSTRATION: LOOKING TO THE PAST

Often when I'm feeling creative block take hold, I'll look at fashion from the early couture masters, such as Paul Poiret, Mariano Fortuny, and Chanel. This particular garment was inspired by a 1930's Chanel evening wear ensemble.

**Figure 1.16**
Artists/designers such as Madeleine Highland use Web sites to showcase their creations (**http://madeleinehighland.wordpress.com**).

operator can easily manipulate this virtual dancer, as well as change the dancer's costume, with the click of a mouse. This allows artists to create new experiences for the audience.

Of course, not all artwork is created using traditional materials such as paint and canvas. Many artists today work exclusively with computers. Mastery of software programs such as Adobe Illustrator, Adobe

Photoshop, and Corel Painter is essential to creating digital art.

Other artists are pushing the envelope of creating art with computers even further. For example, MacArthur Fellow and artist Camille Utterback uses a computer to create works of art that react to the presence—and the absence—of movement of the viewers in the gallery. When no one is near the art piece, the image paints a small

---

## Today's teachers need to be at least as computer savvy as their students.

---

series of dots. However, as onlookers in the gallery move closer to the work, a camera mounted on the ceiling of the art gallery captures the onlookers' movements and dimensions. A computer with specialized software then uses this captured data to create smears of color and patterns of lines that reflect their movements. Because the image itself is created from the current and past movements and sizes of the gallery patrons, the work looks different each time it is viewed. You can learn more about Utterback's digital art at **www.macfound.org**.

**Video Game Design: A Long Way from Pac-Man** Revenues from video game sales in the United States are now larger than the movie industry's box office. Computer games sold more than 273 million units in 2009, and rapid growth is projected to continue over the next decade. The field is competitive, and games must be creative to grab their audience. Large-scale games are

impossible to create on your own—you must be part of a team. The good news is that because computer games are best developed for a local market by people native to that market, game development will most likely stay in the United States instead of being **offshored** (sent to other countries), as many other types of programming jobs have been.

You'll need an in-depth knowledge of computers to pursue a career in game programming or as a gaming artist. Mastering software animation tools, such as Autodesk 3ds Max, will enable you to create compelling new worlds and new characters like those in the story-driven role-playing game Final Fantasy XIII (see Figure 1.17).

**Education: Teaching and Learning**
Today's teachers need to be at least as computer savvy as their students. Computers are part of most schools, even preschools. In fact, at many colleges, students are required to have their own computers. Courses are designed around course management software such as Blackboard or Moodle, so that students can communicate outside of class, take quizzes online, and find their class materials easily. Teachers must, therefore, have a working knowledge of computers to integrate computer technology into the classroom effectively.

The Internet has obvious advantages in the classroom as a research tool for students, and effective use of the Internet allows teachers to expose students to places students otherwise could not access. There are simulations and instructional software programs on the Web that are incredible learning tools. Teachers can employ these products to give students a taste of running a global business (see Figure 1.18) or provide the experience of the Interactive Body (**bbc.co.uk/science/humanbody**).

Many museums have virtual tours on their Web sites that allow students to examine objects in the museum collections. The Art Project is one collaboration of several museums that allows online visitors to explore over a thousand pieces of art using the same technology employed in Google Street View. A custom viewer lets visitors zoom into the artwork itself at high resolution (see Figure 1.19). The information panel takes you to related videos and other related Web sites. So, even if you teach in Topeka, Kansas, you can take your students on a virtual tour of the Tate Britain in London.

**Figure 1.17**

Using powerful software, game developers can create complex worlds and characters to satisfy even the most demanding gamer.

Serah, come with me. Your family's waiting.

Courtesy of Square Enix

**Figure 1.18**

Internet applications have become sophisticated learning resources. For example, IndustryMasters (**www .industrymasters.com**) allows students to compete online for domination of a global market while giving instructors the chance to introduce many business concepts.

But what about when you want to take your students to visit museums in person? Today, technology is often used to enhance visitors' experiences at museums. New York's Museum of Modern Art (MoMA), for example, offers a full range of options for tech-savvy visitors: old-fashioned museum audio guides, podcasts you can listen to with your smartphone, and multimedia tours that you can download through MoMA WiFi (**www.moma.org**) to your own MP3 device such as a Zune or an iTouch. These multimedia guides let you listen to music that the artist listened to when he or she was creating a particular work or look at other works that reflect

**Figure 1.19**

The Art Project presents you with an interactive walk through several museums. Thousands of pieces of work are displayed in high resolution with a pullout information panel (**www.googleart-project.com**).

**Figure** 1.20

Multimedia tours using mobile devices and wireless technology are commonplace in museums and galleries.

similar techniques or themes to those of the one you're viewing (see Figure 1.20). While looking at works by more modern artists, you can watch interviews with the artist explaining his or her motivation for the work. You can even connect quickly to other members of your group and direct them to specific works you want them to see. Being literate with technology may help make your museum tour even more memorable.

Computerized education in the classroom may prove to be the tool that helps teachers reach greater success, despite increasing class sizes and tightening financial constraints. The Khan Academy (**www.khanacademy.org**) is a terrific example. Salman Khan was an investment

analyst in Boston five years ago when he began to post videos to YouTube to teach algebra to his young cousins in New Orleans. Today his nonprofit Khan Academy contains over 2,200 videos, and over a million students a month use the site.

Part of the design of the Khan Academy is to use automated testing following each video series. Because the problems are automatically generated and graded, students can easily be fed similar problems until they show mastery by getting 10 in a row correct. This lets each student get repetitive drilling on just the areas they need to improve. The classroom teacher can follow what is happening in the classroom by using a dashboard (shown in Figure 1.21), a screen that shows which topics each student has mastered, which they are making progress with, and which have them spinning their wheels. Now a teacher can approach a student already knowing exactly what is frustrating them, avoiding the dreaded question, "Oh, what don't you understand?"

As an educator, being computer literate will help you integrate computer technologies like these constructively into lesson plans and interactions for your students.

**Figure** 1.21

The Dashboard of the Khan Academy shows exactly which topics a student has mastered and where he or she is failing to progress.

**Figure** 1.22

Tissue-rendering programs then add layers of muscles, fat, and skin to create faces that can be used to identify victims.

**Law Enforcement: Put Down That Mouse—You're Under Arrest!** Today, wearing out shoe leather to solve crimes is far from the only method available to investigators trying to catch criminals. Computers are being used in police cars and crime labs to solve an increasing number of crimes. For example, facial reconstruction systems like the one shown in Figure 1.22 can turn a skull into a finished digital image of a face, allowing investigators to proceed far more quickly with identification.

One technique used by modern detectives to solve crimes uses computers to search the vast number of databases on the Internet. Proprietary law enforcement databases such as the National Center for the Analysis of Violent Crime database enable detectives to analyze a wealth of information about similarities between crimes in an attempt to detect patterns that may reveal serial crimes. Where the law permits, detectives can also use their knowledge of wireless networking to intercept and read a criminal suspect's e-mail messages and chat sessions when he or she is online, all from the comfort of a car parked outside the suspect's home.

As detective work goes more high tech, so, too, does crime. To fight modern crime, a law enforcement specialty called computer forensics is growing. **Computer forensics** analyzes computer systems with specific techniques to gather potential legal evidence. For example, in 2009 Steven Zirko was convicted for two Chicago-area murders based on computer forensics work. FBI-trained computer forensics examiners scoured Zirko's computer and located searches for terms like "hire a hitman" and "GHB," the date rape drug. Zirko

also had used his computer to find the daily schedule for his victim's two school-aged children and to get directions to her home. This case is one of many solved by the use of computer forensics techniques. In many cases, files, videos, and conversations conducted using a computer can be recovered by forensics specialists and used as evidence of criminal activity.

## Computer forensics analyzes computer systems with specific techniques to gather potential legal evidence.

Computers are also used in training law enforcement officers to be more effective. For example, the Federal Bureau of Investigation (FBI) and the Transportation Security Administration (TSA) use computer-based training to teach officers to recognize lies and evasive behavior. Dr. Paul Ekman has spent a career studying *microexpressions*, brief (1/25th of a second) flashes of emotion. When a person is being deceptive, microexpressions, which cannot be controlled, reveal true emotions in his or her body language. The Microexpression Training Tool software system (**www .paulekman.com**), a program developed by Ekman's company, trains users to recognize emotions such as fear, disgust,

We are familiar with digital data—comfortable with carrying around music, some files, contact lists, and calendars. But where is your data when you need it? Today, your information is locked in your cell phone, your tablet computer, or your notebook computer. This mobility is revolutionary compared to the access of any prior generations, but it still requires you to take out your notebook, open it up, boot it up, and initiate a request for information. What lies ahead?

The Media Lab of MIT provides some great clues. The Fluid Interfaces group works to develop new tools to bring our data more directly into the physical world. One of the most promising of these new tools is called SixthSense (see Figure 1.23). It is a wearable device hanging around your neck consisting of a camera, a projector, and a mirror that can communicate with the Internet over wireless Bluetooth via the cell phone in your pocket. What SixthSense can do is augment your experience of reality by adding the information you need as you need it.

Say you are on your way to the airport and pull out your boarding pass. SixthSense uses pattern recognition to realize you are holding an airline ticket. It then goes out to the Internet to check if the flight is on time or if a gate change has been issued. If the flight is going to be late, the words "Delayed: 20 Minutes" would suddenly appear on the top of the boarding pass. The information is no longer trapped in your mobile device—it is part of your environment. Or say you are in a bookstore and select the title *Ambient Findability*. As you hold the book, its Amazon rating appears on the cover. You open to the inside sleeve, and the comments from readers at Amazon begin to scroll over the page. Then you can tap any one of those comments for more detail.

SixthSense is the product of work by Pranav Mistry and his advisor Patti Maes. The product can also respond to gestures, so when you make a rectangle with your fingers, it takes a photograph. When you reach your destination, any flat surface such as a wall or table can be used to "dump" your photos into a "pile." Using your hands, you can shuffle the images, or resize or rotate an image. Or draw a watch-sized circle on your wrist, and SixthSense displays an analog watch face on your arm.

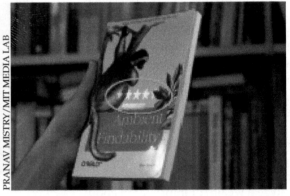

PRANAV MISTRY/MIT MEDIA LAB

PRANAV MISTRY/MIT MEDIA LAB

**Figure 1.23**

SixthSense recognizes what information you need added to your environment and displays it automatically.

contempt, and anger in these flashes of microexpressions. You can try the online demo to see if you are a "natural," one of the rare people who can recognize and read emotion without training.

**Medicine: The Chip Within** When you mention implanting technology into the human body, some people conjure up images of the Terminator, a futuristic cybernetic life form from the movie *The Terminator*. But the more realistic goals of modern biomedical chip research are to provide technological solutions to physical problems and to provide a means for positively identifying individuals.

We are at a stage when biology and technology are fusing. Figure 1.26 shows a nerve cell grown on a silicon chip. The cell was cultured on the chip until it formed a network with nearby cells. The chip contains a transistor that stimulates the cell above it, which in turn passes the signal to neighboring neurons.

In fact, your hand is as good a flat surface as any to SixthSense (see Figure 1.24). Need to make a phone call? SixthSense will display a keypad on your palm. Tap out the number on the virtual keypad, and one touch of the red CALL button that appears on your palm places your call.

The shirt of the person walking toward you will also work as a projection surface. When a person walks up to us, we don't often pull out our cell phone and Google them before speaking, but as a person approaches a SixthSense wearer, it recognizes their face, heads off to their Facebook page or blog, and scans the most recent entries. It then projects the keywords that describe the person and their interests on their clothing as you watch them approach.

Currently SixthSense is small but not very stylish. The product is constructed from off-the-shelf components costing about $350. Within a few years its inventors believe it can be produced as a button-sized device, costing less than a cell phone costs now. You can monitor the progress of this device at **www.pranavmistry.com/projects/sixthsense**.

There are a number of smartphone apps available right now that use the integrated compass and camera of the phone to add information to your environment. New York Nearest Subway is a $2 app that "augments" reality. **Augmented reality** is a combination of our normal sense of the objects around us with an overlay of information displayed. The image seen through the camera's lens provides a baseline, and additional information can be displayed over the image (see Figure 1.25).

This kind of direct integration of digital information with the physical world around us is a hallmark of our digital future. Augmented reality combines the digital information we have accumulated in an immediate and spontaneous manner. So where will your new reality take you?

Kyodo via AP Images

**Figure** 1.25

Augmented reality apps let you look through your phone's camera and see the world with extra information superimposed.

PRANAV MISTRY / MIT MEDIA LAB

**Figure** 1.24

Any surface can become an input device using SixthSense.

One potential application of biomedical chip implants is to provide sight to the blind. Macular degeneration and retinitis pigmentosa are two diseases that account for the majority of blindness in developing nations. Both diseases result in damage to photoreceptors in the retina. (Photoreceptors convert light energy into electrical energy that is transmitted to the brain, allowing us to see.) Researchers at MIT and the Boston Retinal Implant Project are experimenting

Sebastian Kaulitzki / Fotolia

**Figure** 1.26

Researchers are working on creating implantable chips to repair damaged nerves and restore movement and sensation to parts of the body.

## NASA Wants You . . . to Learn

As you read this chapter, hundreds of satellites are orbiting the globe and taking wonderfully detailed pictures of Earth. Until recently, these photos weren't available to the general public. However, thanks to NASA (and U.S. taxpayer dollars) and some savvy software developers, an application called World Wind is now making some 10 trillion bytes of imagery available to you. Do you need a picture of Mount Fuji for your science project or an aerial picture of your house for your PowerPoint presentation? Just download the software from learn.arc.nasa.gov, and you're ready to go. You'll find several terrific learning applications here as well. Virtual Lab lets you pretend you have your own scanning electron microscope, and Moonbase Alpha is a game built off of the Unreal engine, complete with 3D graphics, team play, and the ability to do in-play chatting. With a few clicks, you can have interactive learning resources that open the world to you.

with a microchip that would attach to the outside of the eye. The chip would take over processing from damaged photoreceptors and transmit electrical images to the brain. Biomedical chips such as these exemplify the types of medical devices you may "see" in the future.

One type of chip is already being implanted in humans as a means of verifying a person's identity. Produced by Positive ID and called *VeriMed*, this "personal ID chip" is about the size of a grain of rice and is implanted under the skin. When exposed to radio waves from a scanning device, the chip emits a signal that transmits its unique serial number to the scanner. The scanner then connects to a database that contains the name, address, and medical conditions of the person in whom the chip has been implanted.

The creators of VeriMed envision it helping keep Alzheimer's patients safe and being used with other devices (such as electronic ID cards) to provide tamperproof security measures. If someone stole your credit card, that person couldn't use it if a salesclerk had to verify your identity by scanning a chip in your arm before authorizing a transaction.

Currently, nonimplant versions of identity chips are used in hospitals. When chips are attached with bands to newborn infants, the hospital staff can monitor the location of any baby instantly. Elevators and doors are designed to allow only certain people to enter with a specific baby, even if the hospital power is interrupted. Although the use of these tags is becoming more common-

**Figure 1.27**

No bigger than the period at the end of this sentence, the Hitachi µ-chip can hold digital information, which can then be read when it passes a detector.

REUTERS/Eriko Sugita/Landov

> ...it remains to be seen whether people generally will decide that the advantages of having personal identity and medical data quickly available justifies having chips implanted into their bodies.

place, it remains to be seen whether people generally will decide that the advantages of having personal identity and medical data quickly available justifies having chips implanted into their bodies.

Hitachi has a similar device, called the μ-chip ("mu chip"), which is smaller than the period at the end of this sentence (see Figure 1.27). Those concerned with privacy issues worry because the μ-chip could be easily attached to, or ingested by, a person without his or her knowledge. On the other hand, researchers are excited by the possibility of using the μ-chip to monitor the safety of the food supply chain and how it might be mixed into paints to monitor heat and moisture conditions and be embedded in paper and plastics.

**Science: Simulating Reality** Thanks to a partnership between the National Severe Storms Lab and the National Center for Supercomputing Applications, tornado forecasting may be getting more accurate (see Figure 1.28). Scientists have been able to create a model so detailed that it takes

nine days for a supercomputer to generate it, even though the computer is executing 4 trillion operations each second. Simulations also can model the structure of solar magnetic flares, which can interfere with broadcasts on Earth. By studying the data produced by these simulations, forecasters hope to improve their predictions about weather phenomena.

Other technological applications in the sciences are being used on some of the oldest sites on Earth. The ancient site of Pompeii has been under the intense scrutiny of tourists and archaeologists for decades. Sadly, decades of foot traffic and hundreds of years of exposure to the elements have eroded portions of the ruins. Today, scientists are using three-dimensional scanners and imaging software to capture a detailed record of the current condition of the ruins. The virtual re-creation of the ruins is so lifelike that archaeologists can study the ruins on screen instead of at the actual site. Using the scans as well as satellite imagery, aerial photography, and other

Steve Bloom Images/Alamy

National Oceanic and Atmospheric Administration (NOAA)

**Figure 1.28**

Software that combines radar information in new ways increases the accuracy of tornado predictions and allows for earlier warning of threatened towns.

URN:5940874 (Press Association via AP Images)

**Figure** 1.29

Robots with articulated joints that mimic human limbs can balance, stand, walk, and even hug.

us to explore the nature of being human and the nature of machines.

Psychologists and computer scientists are jointly conducting research to develop computer systems that respond to human affect and emotional expression, as well as enable computer systems to develop social and emotional skills. **Affective computing** is computing that relates to emotion or deliberately tries to influence emotion. Most computers you are familiar with can perform calculations and do the tasks they are programmed for much faster than humans can, but they fail miserably in telling a good joke or modifying their behavior based on your frustration. This wide gap in the computing abilities of computers versus their emotional abilities is the target of research in affective computing.

One project to emerge is the emotional-social prosthesis (ESP) device developed by a group at the MIT Media Lab. The ESP system is targeted at helping people who have autism. Autistic individuals can have extremely high intelligence, but do not easily sense nonverbal cues such as facial expressions and tone of voice. ESP is a wearable system that isolates the movements and facial expressions of people, interprets what their mood and intention probably are, and communicates this information back to the user.

Another project at the Media Lab will help people who have difficulty maintaining focus on a specific task. This project centers on the creation of computer systems

data, scientists will eventually be able to re-create missing portions of the ruins in a virtual model. And scientists won't stop at Pompeii. This method will soon be used to make records of other decaying sites.

**Psychology: You Should Smile . . . Now** Science fiction shows and movies such as *Transformers* have always been populated with robots that emulate humans, seemingly effortlessly. So, when will we have Bumblebee, C-3PO, or the Terminator laughing at our jokes or bringing us our favorite snack when they recognize we're sad? It is a question that pushes that can analyze a person's movements, watch how the person uses the mouse, and interpret the pressure patterns on the chair in which the person is seated. That data is used to determine the individual's level of attention. The computer could then interrupt an individual who is beginning to lose concentration and refocus him or her on a certain task.

While engineers work to create computers that can understand us emotionally, psychologists and computer scientists are also working to evolve systems toward a more human appearance (see Figure 1.29). A human-like robot named Robonaut 2 (R2) is a permanent resident of the Interna-

tional Space Station (see Figure 1.30). The R2 has a torso, two arms, and two hands. Developed jointly by General Motors and NASA, it can use the same tools as station astronauts.

**Figure 1.30**

R2 works side by side with astronauts in space.

Image courtesy of NASA

**summary**

**1. Beyond just personal goals, what impact can you have on the world?**

Your own goals of increasing your personal knowledge and improving your career options will be met by mastering the material here. But skill and knowledge of technology can do more—it can allow you to impact the world at large.

**2. How can becoming proficient with technology help you understand and participate in important issues in the world at large?**

Whether it is political issues, environmental issues, or questions addressing the global digital divide, it is important that you become proficient with technology to be able to participate in the discussion. Technology can be the means by which you find your voice in the world and impact others in meaningful ways, as we see happening in many examples from around the world.

**3. How can knowledge of technology help you impact the direction of our society?**

Technology is changing how we think, how we connect with each other, and how we purchase and consume products and services. You can become a creator of new pieces of music, connect with people from around the world, and collaborate to create or consume by using current technology.

**4. What does it mean to be "computer literate"?**

Computer literacy goes beyond knowing how to use a mouse and send e-mail. If you are computer literate, you understand the capabilities and limitations of computers and know how to use them wisely. Being computer literate also enables you to make informed purchasing decisions, use computers in your career, and understand the many ethical, legal, and societal implications of technology today. Anyone can become computer literate.

**5. How does being computer literate make you a savvy computer user and consumer?**

By understanding how a computer is constructed and how its various parts function, you'll be able to get the most out of your computer. Among other things, you'll be able to avoid hackers, viruses, and Internet headaches; protect your privacy; and separate the real risks of privacy and security from those you don't have to worry about. You'll also be better able to maintain, upgrade, and troubleshoot your computer; make good purchasing decisions; and incorporate the latest technologies into your existing equipment.

**6. How can becoming computer literate help you in a career?**

As computers become more a part of our daily lives, it is difficult to imagine any career that does not use computers in some fashion. Understanding how to use computers effectively will help you be a more productive and valuable employee, no matter which profession you choose.

 **Companion Website**

The Companion Website includes a variety of additional materials to help you review and learn more about the topics in this chapter. Go to: *www.pearsonhighered.com/techinaction*

**key terms**

buzzwords

## Word Bank

- affective computing
- augmented reality
- autonomy
- collaborative consumption
- computer literate

- creative surplus
- crisis mapping tools
- crowdsourcing
- data mining
- digital divide

- information technology (IT)
- mastery
- purpose
- social networking

**Instructions:** Fill in the blanks using the words from the Word Bank above.

Technology allows each of us to become a powerful force in changing the world. It might be that we use (1) _____ to help during a time of unexpected disaster. Perhaps we can help address the gap between those with easy access to technology and those with limited access, the (2) _____, using modern tools. We are all much more connected through the development of (3) _____ systems. Because we can share our skills and knowledge so easily, the (4) _____ available is producing even more tools and free software. There is an increasing incentive to use (5) _____ to reduce pressures on the environment and share the use of objects. Technology is also helping those with social disabilities as new tools from the area of (6) _____ help people integrate better into society. (7) _____ is growing as we are blending the information available to us directly into our environment with tools like SixthSense. Our understanding of human motivation is becoming more refined so we can capitalize on the things that engage people, to use and create solutions. (8) _____, a sense of independence; (9) _____, the ability to improve your skill level; and (10) _____, the drive to help beyond just your own immediate needs, are forces that will direct us toward solving the challenges we face locally, socially, and globally.

becoming computer literate

Using the key terms and ideas you learned in this chapter, write a one- or two-paragraph summary for your younger brother to motivate him to learn more than just how to log in to Xbox Live. Discuss the importance of being computer literate to address global and social concerns. Discuss how your brother's career will need him to become computer literate. Using the Internet, find additional examples to support your position.

**Instructions:** Answer the multiple-choice and true–false questions below for more practice with key terms and concepts from this chapter.

## Multiple Choice

1. Which is NOT a technology that has been used to deliver assistance during times of crisis?
   a. Ushahidi
   b. QR codes
   c. SwiftRiver
   d. e-mail

2. Artists interface with technology often, but cannot yet
   a. use computers to generate images that respond to the environment.
   b. use computers to create a virtual storefront.
   c. use software to suggest plot endings.
   d. use software to create and enhance virtual performances.

3. People who do not read emotion easily in others hope for new progress in the field of
   a. affective computing.
   b. data mining.
   c. bioprinting.
   d. forensic science.

4. Studies reveal that human motivation is fostered by
   a. increasing levels of mastery.
   b. the ability to self-direct.
   c. directing your work toward a higher goal than just your own needs.
   d. all of the above.

5. Collaborative consumption is when people get together to
   a. find the best prices on products.
   b. exchange reviews on services and goods they have purchased.
   c. fight diseases of the respiratory tract.
   d. increase the use of a single product by sharing access to it.

6. Social networking tools
   a. played a part in revolutions in 2011.
   b. are limited to social dating.
   c. have encouraged increased censorship in the United States.
   d. include software like Microsoft Office and Adobe Illustrator.

7. Computer forensics uses computer systems and technology to
   a. simulate a person's anatomical system.
   b. train law enforcement officers to be more effective.
   c. create a crisis map.
   d. gather potential legal evidence.

8. IT is the abbreviation for
   a. information training.
   b. Internet training.
   c. Internet technology.
   d. information technology.

9. Which of the following allows retailers to respond to consumer buying patterns?
   a. RFID tags
   b. data mining
   c. smart labels
   d. Bluetooth technology

10. The crisis of a growing digital divide is being addressed by
    a. Ushahidi.
    b. the Next Einstein project.
    c. the Freecycle program.
    d. building faster computers.

## True-False

_____ 1. Researchers believe that microchips may one day restore sight to the blind.

_____ 2. QR codes let companies track your past purchases and customize offers for you.

_____ 3. Supercomputers can accurately forecast tornadoes within minutes.

_____ 4. Criminal investigators may find evidence on a computer, but that evidence cannot be used in court.

_____ 5. Many modern museums offer WiFi networks and multimedia downloads to their patrons to enrich their experience.

### 1. Computer Literacy

In your college career, you'll be spending time understanding the requirements of the degree program you choose. At many schools, computer literacy requirements exist either as incoming requirements (skills students must have before they are admitted) or as outgoing requirements (skills students must prove they have before graduating). Does your program require specific computer skills? Which skills are these? Should they be required? How can students efficiently prove that they have these skills? How often does the set of skills need to be reviewed and updated?

### 2. The Mind of the Mob

Crowdsourcing is the gathering of data in real time, as it happens, from a growing crowd of people. Because of the large number of students who now own phones with Internet access, crowdsourcing on campus could start to be useful. In what settings would making decisions based on information from a gathering crowd on campus be valuable? How would you react to your professor using a form of crowdsourcing to determine your grade on an essay?

### 3. Mobile Push

A mobile application called Keyring allows you to download and store all the rewards program cards you use for the supermarket, Best Buy, the pharmacy, and so on. You can quickly scan from your phone "card" to the register at checkout and also let the companies push coupons and information to you. Would a system like this be useful on your campus? What kind of information could the college push to your mobile device that would be helpful?

### 4. Recycle, Repair, Redistribute

The Microsoft authorized refurbisher program and TechSoup both help provide resources to people in need to reduce the barrier of the digital divide. These organizations recycle hardware and supply software inexpensively to needy families. How could a program be set up at your school to make people aware of these options? Could students donate materials or retrofit systems as part of their coursework? As part of a club activity? How could you make these programs work for your community?

### 5. Military Computing

Review the computer science programs at the U.S. Air Force Academy (**www.usafa .af.mil**), the U.S. Military Academy at West Point (**www.usma.edu**), and the U.S. Naval Academy (**www.usna.edu**). What specific courses or paths of study do these institutions have that are specific to military settings? What information do the departments' Web sites provide on why an understanding of computers matters to the military? How would this training support a transition from a military career to the civilian workplace?

# A Culture of Sharing

## Problem

As more and more peer-to-peer music sharing services appeared, like BitTorrent and LimeWire, many felt a culture of theft was developing. Some argued there was a mindset among young people that property rights for intellectual works need not be respected and that people should be able to download, for free, any music, movies, or other digital content they wanted.

But there is another view of the phenomenon. Some are suggesting that the amount of constant access to each other—through texting, e-mail, blogging, and the easy exchange of digital content—has created a culture of trust and sharing. This Team Time will explore both sides of this debate in three different parts of our lives—finance, travel, and consumerism.

## Task

Each of the three groups will select a different area to examine—finance, travel, or consumerism. The groups will find evidence to support or refute the idea that a culture of sharing is developing. The finance group will want to explore projects like the Grameen Bank (**www.grameenbank.com**) and Kiva (**www.kiva.org**). The travel group should examine what is happening with **www.couchsurfing.org** to start their research. The team investigating consumerism will want to take a look at goods exchange programs like Freecycle (**www.freecycle.org**).

## Process

1. Divide the class into three teams.

2. Discuss the different views of a "culture of sharing." With the other members of your team, use the Internet to research up-and-coming technologies and projects that would support your position. Because people use social media tools to connect into groups to exchange ideas, does it promote trust? Does easy access to digital content promote theft, or has the value of content changed? Are there other forces like the economy and environmental state of the world that play a role in promoting a culture of sharing? What evidence can you find to support your ideas?

3. Present your group's findings to the class for debate and discussion.

4. Write a strategy paper that summarizes your position and outlines your predictions for the future. Will the pace of technology promote a change in the future from the position you are describing?

## Conclusion

The future of technology is unknown, but we do know that it will impact the way our society progresses. To be part of the developments that technology will bring, no matter what area of the culture you are examining, will take good planning and attention. Begin now—learn how to stay on top of technology.

**ethics project**

# Should Information Be Free?

In this exercise, you will research and then role-play a complicated ethical situation. The role you play might or might not match your own personal beliefs; regardless, your research and use of logic will enable you to represent the view assigned. An arbitrator will watch and comment on both sides of the arguments, and together team members will agree on an ethical solution.

In this chapter you saw how the crisis mapping tool Ushahidi was able to collect and present information in times of political and environmental crisis. This allowed everyone to be involved in gathering the actual facts about what was happening and in helping to address very specifically the needs of people who were lost and hurt. The free exchange of information from the crowd is being used to mobilize a large number of people and provide positive action.

## Problem

WikiLeaks is another example of a tool that gathers information and "frees" it by presenting it to the entire world. Whistleblowers and secret and classified media have been exposed to the world community through publication via WikiLeaks. WikiLeaks founder Julian Assange, however, is facing a range of international criminal charges.

What is the nature of information? Should it be "free"—available without censure or government controls? Is there a limit—should only certain information be free while other bits need to be kept away from the public for the greater good?

## Research Areas to Consider

- WikiLeaks
- Ushahidi
- Electronic Frontier Foundation
- Government 2.0

## Process

1. Divide the class into teams.

2. Research the areas cited above and devise a scenario in which information needs to be restricted.

3. Team members should write a summary that provides background information for their character—for example, a government official, an accused criminal, or an injured victim of a natural disaster—and details their character's behaviors to set the stage for the role-playing event. Then team members should create an outline to use during the role-playing event.

4. Team members should arrange a mutually convenient time to meet for the exchange, using either the chat room feature of MyITLab or the discussion board feature of Blackboard or by meeting in person.

5. Team members should present their case to the class or submit a PowerPoint presentation for review by the rest of the class, along with the summary and resolution they developed.

## Conclusion

As technology becomes ever more prevalent and integrated into our lives, more and more ethical dilemmas will present themselves. Being able to understand and evaluate both sides of the argument, while responding in a personally or socially ethical manner, will be an important skill.

# looking at computers
## understanding the parts

Login/ Shutterstock.com

### Understanding Your Computer

**OBJECTIVES:**

What exactly is a computer, and what are its four main functions? *(p.40)*

What is the difference between data and information? *(p. 40)*

What are bits and bytes, and how are they measured? *(p. 40)*

 **Sound Byte:** Binary Numbers Interactive

 **Active Helpdesk:** Understanding Bits and Bytes

### Input Devices and Output Devices

**OBJECTIVES:**

What devices do I use to get data into the computer? *(p. 43)*

What devices do I use to get information out of the computer? *(p. 51)*

 **Sound Byte:** Tablet and Notebook Tour

 **Active Helpdesk:** Using Input Devices

 **Active Helpdesk:** Using Output Devices

© Wildcat123 | Dreamstime.com

### Processing, Memory, and Storage

**OBJECTIVES:**

What's on the motherboard? *(p. 59)*

Where are information and programs stored? *(p. 61)*

 **Sound Byte:** Virtual Computer Tour

© Iofoto | Dreamstime.com

### Ports and Power Controls

**OBJECTIVE:**

How are devices connected to the computer? *(p. 63)*

 **Active Helpdesk:** Exploring Storage Devices and Ports

 **Sound Byte:** Port Tour: How Do I Hook It Up?

ImageZoo/Alamy

### Setting It All Up

**OBJECTIVE:**

How do I set up my computer to avoid strain and injury? *(p. 67)*

 **Sound Byte:** Healthy Computing

*Scan here for more info
on How Cool Is This?*

# how cool is *this?*

The **3D experience** is pretty common at the movies, and even on some TVs, but how about on your laptop? Computer manufacturers, such as Sony, Asus, and Acer, are producing **high-end laptops** that have 3D viewing capabilities. That means that **games, photos, movies, and Web sites** can be experienced in 3D. These machines are targeted toward **gamers and 3D movie enthusiasts,** and require high-end graphics components, such as the 3D kit by NVIDIA that includes a combination of a sophisticated graphics processor unit and monitor, software, and **specialized 3D glasses** to achieve the 3D effects. If you're not thrilled with wearing those stylish glasses to enjoy the 3D special effects, then you might want to hold out for a No-Glasses 3D laptop by Toshiba, currently in the prototype stage, which uses the laptop's Web camera and eye-tracking technology to create the 3D effects.

Stockbyte/Getty Images

# Understanding Your Computer

After reading Chapter 1, you can see why becoming computer literate is so important. But where do you start? You've no doubt gleaned some knowledge about computers just from being a member of society. However, although you have undoubtedly used a computer before, do you really understand how it works, what all its parts are, and what these parts do? In this section, we discuss what a computer does and how its functions make it such a useful machine.

### Computers Are Data Processing Devices

Strictly defined, a **computer** is a data processing device that performs four major functions:

1. **Input:** It gathers data, or allows users to enter data.

2. **Process:** It manipulates, calculates, or organizes that data into information.

3. **Output:** It displays data and information in a form suitable for the user.

4. **Storage:** It saves data and information for later use.

**What is the difference between data and information?** People often use the terms *data* and *information* interchangeably. Although they may mean the same thing in a simple conversation, the actual distinction between data and information is an important one.

In computer terms, **data** is a representation of a fact, a figure, or an idea. Data can be a number, a word, a picture, or even a recording of sound. For example, the number 7135553297 and the names Zoe and Richardson are pieces of data. Alone, these pieces of data probably mean little to you.

**Information** is data that has been organized or presented in a meaningful fashion. When your computer provides you with a contact listing that indicates Zoe Richardson can be reached by phone at (713) 555-3297, then the previous data suddenly becomes useful—that is, it becomes information.

**How do computers interact with data and information?** Computers are excellent at **processing** (manipulating, calculating, or organizing) data into information. When you first arrived on campus, you probably were directed to a place where you could get an ID card. You most likely provided a clerk with personal data (such as your name and address) that was entered into a computer. The clerk then took your picture with a digital camera (collecting more data). This information was then processed appropriately so that it could be printed on your ID card (see Figure 2.1). This organized output of data on your ID card is useful information. Finally, the information was probably stored as digital data on the computer for later use.

### Bits and Bytes: The Language of Computers

**How do computers process data into information?** Unlike humans, computers work exclusively with numbers (not words). To process data into information, computers need to work in a language they understand. This language, called **binary language**, consists of just two digits: 0 and 1. Everything a computer does, such as processing data, printing a report, or editing a photo, is broken down into a series of 0s and 1s. Each 0 and 1 is a **binary digit**, or **bit** for short. Eight binary digits (or bits) combine to create one **byte**. In computers, each letter of the alphabet, each number, and each special character (such as the @ sign) consists of a unique

**Figure 2.1**

Computers process data into information.

Input data → Processing data into information → Output information

combination of eight bits, or a string of eight 0s and 1s. So, for example, in binary language, the letter K is represented as 01001011. This equals eight bits, or one byte. (We discuss binary language in more detail in the Technology in Focus section "Under the Hood.")

**What else can bits and bytes be used for?** You've probably heard the terms *kilobyte (KB)*, *megabyte (MB)*, and *gigabyte (GB)*. Bits and bytes not only are used as the language that tells the computer what to do, but also are what the computer uses to represent the quantity of data and information that it inputs and outputs. Word processing files, digital pictures, and even software are represented inside a computer as a series of bits and bytes. These files and applications can be quite large, containing thousands or millions of bytes.

To make it easier to measure the size of these files, we need units of measure larger than a byte. Kilobytes, megabytes, and gigabytes are therefore simply amounts of bytes. As shown in Figure 2.2, a **kilobyte (KB)** is approximately 1,000 bytes, a **megabyte (MB)** is about 1 million bytes, a

**gigabyte (GB)** is around 1 billion bytes, and a **terabyte (TB)** is around 1 trillion bytes. As our information-processing needs have grown, so too have our storage needs. Today, personal computers are capable of storing terabytes of data, and many business computers can store up to a petabyte (one thousand terabytes) of data. The Google search engine processes more than 1 petabyte of user-generated data per *hour*—that's a lot of bytes!

**How does your computer process bits and bytes?** Your computer uses a combination of hardware and software to process data into information and enables you to complete tasks such as writing a letter or playing a game. An anonymous person once said that hardware is any part of a computer that you can kick when it doesn't work properly. A more formal definition of **hardware** is any part of the computer you can physically touch. However, a computer needs more than just hardware to work: It also needs some form of software (computer programs). Think of a book without words or a CD without music. Without words or music, these two common items are just shells that hold nothing.

**Figure 2.2** | HOW MUCH IS A BYTE?

| Name | Abbreviation | Number of Bytes | Relative Size |
|------|--------------|-----------------|---------------|
| Byte | B | 1 byte | Can hold one character of data. |
| Kilobyte | KB | 1,024 bytes ($2^{10}$ bytes) | Can hold 1,024 characters, or about half of a double-spaced typewritten page. |
| Megabyte | MB | 1,048,576 bytes ($2^{20}$ bytes) | Can hold approximately 768 pages of typed text. |
| Gigabyte | GB | 1,073,741,824 bytes ($2^{30}$ bytes) | This is approximately 786,432 pages of text. 500 sheets of paper is approximately 2 inches, so this represents a stack of paper 262 feet high. |
| Terabyte | TB | 1,099,511,627,776 bytes ($2^{40}$ bytes) | This represents a stack of typewritten pages almost 51 miles high. |
| Petabyte | PB | 1,125,899,906,842,624 bytes ($2^{50}$ bytes) | The stack of pages is now 52,000 miles high, or approximately one-fourth the distance from the Earth to the moon. |
| Exabyte | EB | 1,152,921,504,606,846,976 bytes ($2^{60}$ bytes) | The stack of pages is now 52 million miles high, or just about twice the distance between the Earth and Venus. |
| Zettabyte | ZB | 1,180,591,620,717,411,303,424 bytes ($2^{70}$ bytes) | The stack of pages is now 52 billion miles high. That's some 20 times the distance between the Earth and Pluto. |

Similarly, a computer without software is a shell full of hardware components that can't do anything. Software is the set of computer programs that enables the hardware to perform different tasks. There are two broad categories of software: application software and system software.

When you think of software, you are most likely thinking of application software. **Application software** is the set of programs you use on a computer to help you carry out tasks such as writing a research paper. If you've ever typed a document, created a spreadsheet, or edited a digital photo, for example, then you've used a form of application software.

**System software** is the set of programs that enables your computer's hardware devices and application software to work together. The most common type of system software is the operating system (OS)—the program that controls the way in which your computer system functions. It manages the hardware of the computer system, such as the monitor and the printer. The operating system also provides a means by which users can interact with the computer. We'll cover software in greater depth in Chapters 7 and 8. For the rest of this chapter, we'll explore the basic components of computer hardware.

## Types of Computers

### Are all computers the same?

Considering the amount of amazing things computers can do, they are really quite simple machines. You learned in the previous section that a basic computer system is made up of software and hardware. There are two basic designs of computers: portable and stationary. A **notebook computer** (or laptop computer) is a portable computer that has a keyboard, a monitor, and other devices integrated into a single compact case. Notebooks are powered by a battery unit or an

### Figure 2.3

(a) A tablet PC has a monitor that swivels to become a touch-sensitive input device; (b) an all-in-one computer does not need a separate tower.

AC adapter. A **netbook** is a small, lightweight notebook computer that is generally 7 to 10 inches wide and has a longer battery life than a notebook computer. A **tablet PC** is similar to a notebook computer, but the monitor swivels and folds flat (see Figure 2.3a). Users then input data and commands primarily by using a special pen called a stylus across the touch screen, and input text by pressing keys on the virtual keyboard. In 2010, Apple introduced the iPad, which began a new class of mobile computers. A **tablet computer,** such as the Apple iPad or Motorola XOOM, is a mobile computer integrated into a flat multitouch-sensitive screen. It uses an onscreen virtual keyboard, but separate keyboards can be connected via Bluetooth or wires (see Figure 2.14 later in this chapter). A **desktop computer** is intended for use at a single location, and therefore is stationary. Most desktop computers consist of a separate case that houses the main components of the computer plus peripheral devices. A **peripheral device** is a component, such as a monitor or keyboard, that is connected to the computer. An **all-in-one computer,** such as the Apple iMac (Figure 2.3b) or HP TouchSmart, eliminates the need for a separate tower because these computers house the computer's processor and memory in the monitor unit. Many all-in-one models, such as the TouchSmart, also incorporate touch-screen technology.

### Are there other types of computers?

Although you may never come into direct contact with the following types of computers, they are still important to our society:

- A **mainframe** is a large, expensive computer that supports hundreds of users simultaneously. Mainframes are often used in insurance companies, for example, where many people are working on similar operations, such as claims processing, all at once. Your college also may use mainframe computers to handle the multitude of processing needs throughout the campus. Mainframes excel at executing many different computer programs at the same time.

- A **supercomputer** is a specially designed computer that can perform complex calculations extremely rapidly. Supercomputers are used in situations in which complex models requiring intensive mathematical calculations are needed (such as weather forecasting or atomic energy research). The main difference between a supercomputer and a mainframe is that supercomputers are designed to execute a few programs as quickly as possible, whereas mainframes are designed to handle many programs running at the same time but at a slower pace.

- An **embedded computer** is a specially designed computer chip that resides in another device, such as your car or the electronic thermostat in your home. Embedded computers are self-contained computer devices that have their own programming and typically do not receive input from you or interact with other systems.

In the following sections, we look more closely at your computer's hardware. Each part has a specific purpose that coordinates with one of the functions of the computer—input, processing, output, or storage (see Figure 2.4). Additional devices, such as modems and routers, help a computer communicate with the Internet and other computers to facilitate the sharing of documents and other resources. We begin our exploration of hardware by looking at your computer's input devices.

## Input Devices

An **input device** enables you to enter data (text, images, and sounds) and instructions (user responses and commands) into the computer. The most common input devices are the keyboard and the mouse. A **keyboard** is used to enter typed data and commands, and a **mouse** is used to enter user responses and commands.

There are other input devices as well. Microphones input sounds, and scanners and digital cameras input nondigital text and digital images, respectively. A **stylus** is an input device that looks like a skinny pen but has no ink. You use it like a mouse or pen to tap commands or draw on a screen.

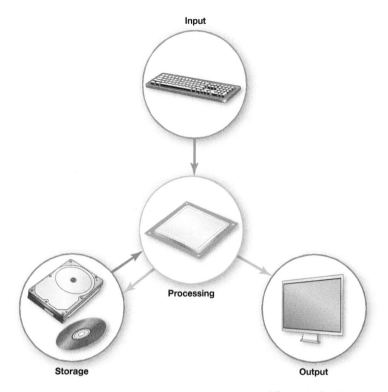

**Figure 2.4**

Each part of the computer serves a special function.

### Keyboards

**Aren't all keyboards the same?** Most desktop and notebook computers come with a standard **QWERTY keyboard**. This keyboard layout gets its name from the first six letters in the top-left row of alphabetic keys on the keyboard and is the standard English-language keyboard layout. Over the years, there has been some debate over what is the best keyboard layout. The QWERTY layout was originally designed for typewriters and was meant to slow typists down and prevent typewriter keys from jamming. Although the QWERTY layout is considered inefficient because it slows typing speeds, efforts to change to more efficient layouts, such as that of the Dvorak keyboard, have not been met with much public interest. The Dvorak keyboard (see Figure 2.5) is an alternative

© Editorial Image, LLC./Alamy

**Figure 2.5**

DVORAK keyboard layout.

Did you know that you can change your keyboard layout from the QWERTY format to the Dvorak format without buying a new keyboard? You can use the Windows operating system to customize the keyboard by changing the keyboard layout. The keyboard layout controls which characters appear on the screen when you press the keys on your keyboard. Computer users who suffer from a repetitive strain injury such as carpal tunnel syndrome and who would like to use the Dvorak keyboard layout may find it useful to switch layouts. You can also switch layouts to conform to different foreign languages.

To change the keyboard layout to the Dvorak layout, for example, you first must install a new language format. To do so, from the Control Panel, select Change keyboards or other input methods. Click the Keyboards and Languages tab, and then select the change keyboards button in the Region and Language dialog box. Click the Add button in the Text Services and Input Languages dialog box, scroll down to English (United States), and click the box next to United States-Dvorak. (There are also choices for left-hand and right-hand Dvorak keyboards. See Figure 2.6). Click OK. The Dvorak language has been installed. To switch to the new layout, click the keyboard icon that now appears in the taskbar and click United States-Dvorak.

You might also find it useful to cover the keys on the keyboard with stickers of the corresponding characters of the newly configured layout, so the characters on your keyboard match up to the new layout.

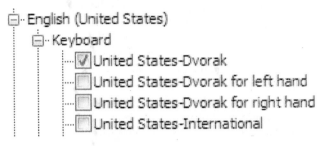

**Figure 2.6**

You can customize the layout of your keyboard using the Windows operating system.

>To change the keyboard layout, open Control Panel, click **Change keyboards or other input methods** in the Clock, Language and Region section. Click the **Change keyboards** . . . button. Click the **Add** button, scroll to find and then check the appropriate keyboard, then click **OK**.

keyboard layout that puts the most commonly used letters in the English language on "home keys," which are the keys in the middle row of the keyboard. The Dvorak keyboard's design reduces the distance your fingers travel for most keystrokes, increasing typing speed.

**What's special about notebook keyboards?** To save space and weight, some of the smaller notebook keyboards (14" and under) are more compact than standard desktop keyboards and, therefore, have fewer keys. To retain the same functionality as a standard keyboard, many of the notebook keys have alternate functions. For example, many notebook keyboards do not have a separate numeric keypad. Instead, some letter keys function as number keys when they are pressed in combination with another key such as the function (Fn) key. The keys you use as numeric keys on notebooks have number notations on them so you can tell which keys to use (see Figure 2.7).

**Figure 2.7**

On many notebooks, certain letter keys can function as number keys.

Alan Ford/Alamy

**What are some alternative keyboards?** The size of notebook keyboards and other portable computer devices have become quite compact. Flexible keyboards are a terrific alternative if you want a full-sized keyboard for your notebook. You can roll one up, fit it in your backpack, and plug it into the USB port when you need to use it. The virtual laser keyboard (see Figure 2.8) is about the size of a cellular phone, and is another compact keyboard alternative. It projects the image of a keyboard, and sensors detect the motion of your fingers as you "type" on a desk or other flat surface. Data is transmitted via **Bluetooth** technology, which is a wireless transmission standard that facilitates the connection of electronic computing devices such as cell phones, smartphones, and computers to peripheral devices such as keyboards and headsets. We'll discuss Bluetooth in further detail in Chapter 5.

Gamers love keyboards such as the DX1 from Ergodex. These keyboards allow placement of the keys in any position on the keyboard pad. The keys can be programmed to execute individual keystrokes or macros (a series of tasks) to perform specific tasks. This makes it easy for gamers to configure a keyboard in the most desirable way for each game they play.

**How can I use my keyboard most efficiently?** All keyboards have the standard set of alphabetic and numeric keys that

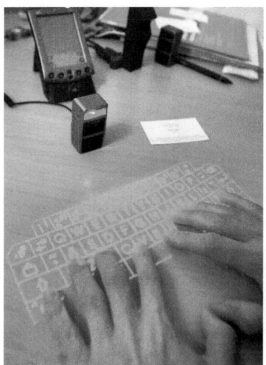

**Figure** 2.8

The virtual laser keyboard projects the image of a QWERTY keyboard on any surface. Sensors detect typing motions, and data is transmitted to a computing device via Bluetooth technology.

AP Photo/Martin Meissner

you regularly use when typing. As shown in Figure 2.9, many keyboards for notebook and desktop computers have additional keys that perform special functions.

Knowing how to use these special keys will help you improve your efficiency:

- The numeric keypad allows you to enter numbers quickly.

**Figure** 2.9

Keyboards have a variety of keys that help you work more efficiently.

Toggle and other keys

Internet controls

Multimedia controls

Numeric keypad

Function keys

Cursor control keys

Alt key

Windows key

Control (Ctrl) key

Artur Synenko/Shutterstock.com

- Function keys act as shortcut keys you press to perform special tasks. They are sometimes referred to as the "F" keys because they start with the letter F followed by a number. Each software application has its own set of tasks assigned to various function keys. For example, the F2 key moves text or graphics in Microsoft Word but allows editing of the active cell in Microsoft Excel. Many keys are universal: the F1 key is the Help key in most applications.
- The Control (Ctrl) key is used in combination with other keys to perform shortcuts and special tasks. For example, holding down the Ctrl key while pressing the B key adds bold formatting to selected text. The Alt key works with other keys to execute additional shortcuts and special tasks. (On Macs, the Control function is the Apple key or Command key, and the Alt function is the Option key.)

- The Insert key is a *toggle key* because its function changes between one of two options each time you press it: When toggled on, the Insert key inserts new text within a line of existing text. When toggled off, the Insert key replaces (or overwrites) existing characters with new characters as you type. Other toggle keys that switch between an on state and an off state include the Num Lock key and the Caps Lock key.
- The Windows key is specific to the Windows operating system. Used alone, it opens the Start menu, although you can use it in combination with other keys to perform shortcuts. For example, in Windows 7 and Vista, pressing the Windows key plus the M key minimizes all windows, and the Windows key plus the L key locks a computer (a good habit to get into when you leave a computer you use in a group setting such as a business office unattended).

**Are all conventional keyboards connected to the computer via wires?** Wireless keyboards provide additional flexibility because you are not tethered to the computer by wires. Instead, wireless keyboards are powered by batteries. They send data to the computer using a form of wireless technology that uses radio frequency (RF). A radio transmitter in the keyboard sends out radio wave signals that are received either through a small receiving device that is plugged into a USB port or a Bluetooth receiving device that is contained in the system unit. RF keyboards used on home computers can be placed as far as 6 feet to 30 feet from the computer, depending on their quality. RF keyboards that are used in business conference rooms or auditoriums can be placed as far as 100 feet away from the computer.

### Mice and Other Pointing Devices

**What kinds of mice are there?** The mouse type you're probably most familiar with is the **optical mouse**. An optical mouse uses an internal sensor or laser to detect the mouse's movement. The sensor sends signals to the computer, telling it where to move the pointer on the screen. Optical mice do not require a mouse pad, though you can use one to enhance the movement of the mouse on an uneven surface, or to protect your work surface from being scratched.

## Keystroke Shortcuts

Did you know that you can combine certain keystrokes to take shortcuts within an application, such as Microsoft Word, or within the operating system itself? The following are a few of the most helpful Windows shortcuts. Use them to make more efficient use of your time. For more shortcuts for Windows-based PCs, visit **www.support.microsoft.com**. For a list of shortcuts for Macs, see **www.apple.com/support**.

| Text Formatting | File Management | Cut/Copy/Paste | Windows Controls |
|---|---|---|---|
| **Ctrl+B** Applies (or removes) **bold** formatting to/from selected text | **Ctrl+O** Opens the Open dialog box | **Ctrl+X** Cuts (removes) selected text from document and stores in Clipboard | **Alt+F4** Closes the current window |
| **Ctrl+I** Applies (or removes) *italic* formatting to/from selected text | **Ctrl+N** Opens a new document | **Ctrl+C** Copies selected text to Clipboard | **Windows Key+Tab** Cycles through open programs using Flip 3D |
| **Ctrl+U** Applies (or removes) underlining to/from selected text | **Ctrl+S** Saves a document | **Ctrl+V** Pastes selected text (previously cut or copied) from Clipboard | **Windows Key+L** Locks the computer |
| | **Ctrl+P** Opens the Print dialog box | | **Windows Key+F** Opens the Search (Find Files) dialog box |

**Figure 2.10**

Customizable mice offer programmable buttons and adjustable fittings to meet most any need.

If you have special ergonomic needs, or want to be able to customize the functionality of your mouse beyond that of a standard optical mouse, there are plenty of options from which to choose. Most mice have two or three buttons that enable you to execute commands and open shortcut menus. (Mice for Macs sometimes have only one button.) As shown in (Figure 2.10), many mice, such as the Naga Epic by Razer, have additional programmable buttons and wheels that let you quickly maneuver through Web pages or games. The Cyborg R.A.T. 9 is customizable to fit any size hand and grip style, and comes with adjustable weights for optimal fit and control.

**Are there wireless mice?** Just as there are wireless keyboards, there are wireless mice. Wireless mice are similar to wireless keyboards in that they use batteries and send data to the computer by radio frequency or Bluetooth technologies. If you have an RF wireless keyboard, then your RF wireless mouse and keyboard usually can share the same RF receiver. Wireless mice for notebooks have their own receivers that often clip into the bottom of the mouse for easy storage when not in use.

Apple has developed Magic Mouse, the first multi-touch wireless mouse (see Figure 2.11a). The top surface of the mouse, which is virtually the mouse itself, is the button. Use your finger to scroll in any direction, swipe your finger across the mouse to move through Web pages and photos, and tap on the mouse to click and double-click.

Small, compact devices like the MoGo Mouse (see Figure 2.11b) are designed for portability. The MoGo Mouse fits into a peripheral slot on the side of a notebook; this slot serves to store the mouse, protect it, and charge its battery all at the same time. The MoGo Mouse is wireless and uses Bluetooth technology to transmit data to the notebook.

**What other tasks can be done with a mouse?** Manufacturers of mice are constantly releasing new models that allow you to perform useful tasks with a few clicks of the mouse. On some mouse models, Microsoft and Logitech provide features such as the following:

- **Magnifier:** Pulls up a magnification box that you can drag around the screen to enhance viewing of hard-to-read images. This feature is often used by people with visual disabilities.
- **Web search:** Allows you to quickly highlight a word or phrase and then press the search button on the mouse to start a Web search.
- **File storage:** Includes a wireless USB receiver that contains flash memory to store or back up your files.

**Figure 2.11**

(a) The Magic Mouse by Apple has multi-touch technology. (b) The MoGo Mouse is a portable mouse that stores and charges in a PC Card slot.

## A touch screen is a display screen that responds to commands initiated by a touch with a finger or a stylus.

**Do notebook computers include a mouse?** Most notebooks have an integrated pointing device such as a **touch pad (or trackpad)**, a small, touch-sensitive area at the base of the keyboard (see Figure 2.12). To use the touch pad, you simply move your finger across the pad. Mac notebooks include multi-touch trackpads, which do not have buttons, but are controlled by various one-, two-, three-, and four-finger actions. For example, scrolling is controlled by brushing two fingers along the trackpad in any direction; swiping four fingers either left or right views all open applications as icons. Most touch pads are sensitive to taps, interpreting them as mouse clicks. Many notebooks also have buttons beneath the pads to record mouse clicks. Some notebooks incorporate a **trackpoint device**, a small, joystick-like nub that allows you to move the cursor with the tip of your finger.

**What input devices are used with games?** Game controllers such as joysticks, game pads, and steering wheels are also considered input devices because they send data to the computer. Game controllers, which are similar to the devices used on gaming consoles such as the Xbox 360 and the PlayStation, are also available for use with computers. They have buttons and miniature pointing devices that provide input to

the computer. Force-feedback joysticks and steering wheels deliver data in both directions. They translate your movements to the computer and translate its responses into forces on your hands, creating a richer simulated experience. Most game controllers, such as those for Rock Band and the Wii system, are wireless to provide extra mobility.

### Touch Screens

**How else can I input data and commands?** You've seen and used touch-sensitive screens in fast-food restaurants, airport check-in kiosks, and ATM machines for quite some time. A **touch screen** is a display screen that responds to commands initiated by a touch with a finger or a stylus. Touch screens are becoming increasingly popular on many computing devices, especially smartphones such as the Droid and iPhone,

Nathan Alliard/Photononstop/Glowimages.com

**Figure** 2.13

Virtual keyboards are found on tablets and other touch-screen devices.

and tablet computers such as the iPad and XOOM. Tablet PCs were one of the first devices with touch-screen capabilities. Although all tablet PCs have built-in keyboards that allow you to type text just as you would with a normal keyboard, the touch-screen functionality often makes it a better choice when inputting with a keyboard is impractical or unwieldy. Tablets, such as the iPad, and other touch-screen devices, use a virtual keyboard (see Figure 2.13) that displays on screen when input of text is required. These keyboards show basic keyboard configurations, and use special keys to switch to numeric, punctuation, and other special keys.

**Figure** 2.12

Touch pads and trackpoint devices take the place of a mouse on notebook computers.

© Yongkai | Dreamstime.com

Trackpoint device

Touch pad

**Tablet and Notebook Tour**

In this Sound Byte, you'll take a tour of a tablet PC and a notebook computer, learning about the unique features and ports available on each.

All-in-one desktop PCs, as well as some other desktop and notebook computers, have touch screens, and portable media players (PMPs) such as the Apple iPod Touch have touch capability, as do some portable gaming devices such as the Nintendo DS.

email

PDF

Facebook

**Figure 2.14**

The Livescribe Echo Smartpen captures writing and stores it in a flash drive for later transfer to a computer. No typing is required!

If you want to create digital notes, but cannot afford a computer, or don't want to always be lugging around a notebook, you can use a digital pen like the one shown in Figure 2.14. This pen works in conjunction with a **flash drive** (a portable electronic storage device that connects to a USB port on a computer). You can write with the pen on any conventional paper. The pen captures your writing and then wirelessly transmits and stores it in the flash drive. When the flash drive is connected to a computer, you can use software to translate your writing into digital text.

## Image Input

**How can I input digital images into my computer?** Digital cameras, camcorders, and cell phones are common devices for capturing pictures and video, and all of them are considered input devices. Digital cameras and camcorders are usually used in remote settings (away from a computer) to capture images and video for later downloading to the computer. These devices either connect to a computer with a data cable or transmit data wirelessly. The computer automatically recognizes these devices when they are connected and makes the input of the digital data to the computer simple and easy. Scanners can also input images. They work similar to a photocopy machine, but instead of generating the image on paper, they create a digital image, which can then be printed, saved in storage, or e-mailed.

**How do I capture live video from my computer or device?** A **webcam** is a small camera that sits on top of a computer monitor (connected to the computer by a cable) or is built into a notebook or tablet computer. Although webcams are able to capture still images, they are used mostly for capturing and transmitting live video, and some have incorporated HD quality. Videoconferencing technology allows a person using a computer equipped with a webcam and a microphone to transmit video and audio across the Internet. Video call sites such as ooVoo (see Figure 2.15) make it easy to video conference with as many as twelve people. You can also exchange files, swap control of computers, and text

**Figure 2.15**

Video conferencing is simplified with software from **www.ooVoo.com**.

AP Photo / Livescribe

If you were asked to cite an example of unethical behavior while using a computer, you could easily provide an answer. You've probably heard news stories about people using computers to commit such crimes as unleashing viruses or committing identity theft. You may also have read about students who were prosecuted for illegally sharing copyrighted material such as videos. Or perhaps you heard about the case where the school district was monitoring students through notebook computer webcams without the students' knowledge. All of these are examples of unethical behavior while using a computer. However, if you were asked what constitutes ethical behavior while using a computer, could you provide an answer just as quickly?

Loosely defined, ethics is a system of moral principles, rules, and accepted standards of conduct. So what are the accepted standards of conduct when using computers (see Figure 2.16)? The Computer Ethics Institute developed the Ten Commandments of Computer Ethics, which is widely cited as a benchmark for companies that are developing computer usage and compliance policies for employees. These guidelines are applicable for schools and students as well. The ethical computing guidelines listed below are based on the Computer Ethics Institute's work.

### Ethical Computing Guidelines

1. Avoid causing harm to others when using computers.
2. Do not interfere with other people's efforts at accomplishing work with computers.
3. Resist the temptation to snoop in other people's computer files.
4. Do not use computers to commit theft.
5. Agree not to use computers to promote lies.
6. Do not use software (or make illegal copies for others) without paying the creator for it.
7. Avoid using other people's computer resources without appropriate authorization or proper compensation.
8. Do not claim other people's intellectual output as your own.
9. Consider the social consequences of the products of your computer labor.
10. Only use computers in ways that show consideration and respect for others.

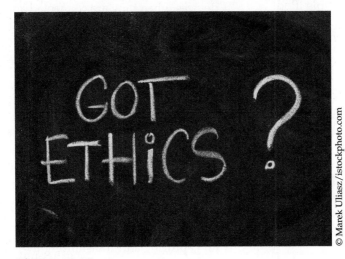

**Figure 2.16**

Make sure the work you claim as your intellectual output is the product of your intellect alone.

The United States has enacted laws that support some of these guidelines, such as Guideline 6, the breaking of which would violate copyright laws, and Guideline 4, which is enforceable under numerous federal and state larceny laws. Other guidelines, however, require more subtle interpretation as to what behavior is unethical because there are no laws designed to enforce them.

Consider Guideline 7, which covers unauthorized use of resources. The college you attend probably provides computer resources for you to use for coursework. But if the college gives you access to computers and the Internet, is it ethical for you to use those resources to run a business on eBay in between classes or on the weekends? Although it might not be technically illegal, you are tying up computer resources that could be used by other students for their intended purpose: learning and completing coursework. (This behavior also violates Guidelines 2 and 10.)

Throughout the chapters in this book, we touch on many topics related to these guidelines. So keep them in mind as you study, and think about how they relate to the actions you take as you use computers in your life.

---

message during the call. There is also a mobile application to make it easy to conference on the go.

### Sound Input

**Why would I want to input sound to my computer?** In addition to letting others hear you in a video conference, equipping your computer to accept sound input opens up a variety of other possibilities. You can conduct audio conferences with work colleagues, chat with friends or family over the Internet instead of using a phone, record podcasts, and more. Inputting sound to your computer requires using a **microphone** or **mic**, a device that allows you to capture sound waves (such as your voice) and transfer them to digital format on your computer. Most notebook computers come with built-in microphones, and some desktop computers come with inexpensive microphones.

**What types of microphones are available?** Unidirectional microphones pick up sound from only one direction. These are best used for recording podcasts with a single voice or making phone calls over the Internet with only one person on the sender's end of the call. Omnidirectional microphones pick up sounds from all directions at once (see Figure 2.17). These mics are best for recording more than one voice, such as during a conference call when you need to pick up the voices of multiple speakers. Bidirectional microphones receive sound equally from the front and back of the mic, and are especially good for interviews.

Clip-on microphones (also called *lavalier microphones*) are useful in environments such as presentations, where you need to keep your hands free for other activities (such as writing on a whiteboard) or move around the room. Many of these microphones are wireless.

Close-talk microphones, which are usually attached to a headset, facilitate using speech-recognition software, videoconferencing, or making telephone calls. With a microphone attached to a headset, your hands are free to perform other tasks while you speak, such as making notes or referring to paper documents, and the headset allows you to listen as well.

**What input devices are available for people with disabilities?** Many people who have physical challenges use computers often, but they sometimes need special input devices to access them. For visually impaired users, voice recognition is an obvious option. For those users whose visual limitations are less severe, keyboards with larger keys are available. Keyboards that display on a touch screen can make input easier for some individuals. These keyboards are displayed as graphics on the computer monitor. The user presses the keys with a pointing device or simply presses on the touch-screen monitor. There are also keyboards designed for individuals who can only use one hand, such as the Maltron keyboard.

People with motor control issues may have difficulty with pointing devices. To aid such users, special trackballs are available that can easily be manipulated with one finger and can be attached to almost any surface, including a wheelchair. When arm motion is severely restrained, head-mounted pointing devices can be used. Generally, these involve a camera mounted on the computer monitor and a device attached to the head (often installed in a hat). When the user moves his or her head, the camera detects the movement, which controls the cursor on the screen. In this case, mouse clicks are controlled by a switch that can be manipulated by the user's hands or feet or even by using an instrument that fits into the mouth and senses the user blowing into it.

> **Many people who have physical challenges use computers often, but they sometimes need special input devices to access them.**

*Blue Microphones*

**Figure 2.17**

Professional-quality microphones are essential for producing quality podcasts. The Blue Yeti can easily switch among four settings to provide the best sound recording in any situation.

## Output Devices

An **output device** enables you to send processed data out of your computer in the form of text, pictures (graphics), sounds (audio), or video. One common output device is a **monitor** (sometimes referred to as a **display screen**), which displays text, graphics, and video as soft copies (copies you can see only on screen). Another common output device is the **printer**, which creates hard copies (copies you can touch) of text and graphics. Speakers and earphones (or earbuds) are the output devices for sound.

## Monitors

**What are the different types of monitors?** The most common type of monitor is a **liquid crystal display (LCD)**. An LCD monitor, also called a flat-panel monitor, is light and energy efficient. Some newer monitors use **light-emitting diode (LED)** technology, which is more energy efficient, and may have better color accuracy and thinner panels than traditional LCD monitors. These flat panel monitors have replaced the cathode ray tube (CRT) monitor. CRT monitors are difficult to find or buy because they have become **legacy technology**, or computing devices or peripherals that use techniques, parts, and methods from an earlier time that are no longer popular. Although legacy technology may still be functional, it is

quickly being replaced by newer technological advances. This doesn't mean that if you have a CRT monitor that is functioning well you should replace it with an LCD monitor. However, when your CRT monitor fails, you will most likely only be able to replace it with an LCD monitor. **Organic light-emitting diode (OLED) displays** use organic compounds that produce light when exposed to an electric current. Unlike LCDs and LEDs, OLEDs do not require a backlight to function and therefore draw less power and have a much thinner display, sometimes as thin as 3 mm (see Figure 2.18). They are also brighter and more environmentally friendly than LCDs. Because of their lower power needs, OLED displays run longer on a single battery charge than do LEDs, which is why OLED technology is currently being used in small screens of mobile devices such as cell phones, portable media players, and digital cameras.

**How do LCD monitors work?** Monitor screens are grids made up of millions of tiny dots, each of which is called a **pixel**. Illuminated pixels create the images you see on your monitor. Each pixel is actually composed of three subpixels of red, blue, and green; some newer TVs on the market have added a fourth color: yellow. LCD monitors are made of two or more sheets of material filled with a liquid crystal solution (see Figure 2.19). A fluorescent panel at the back of the LCD monitor generates light waves. When electric current passes through the liquid crystal solution, the crystals move around and either block the fluorescent light or let the light shine through. This blocking or passing of light by the crystals causes images to form on the screen. The various combinations of red, blue, and green make up the components of color we see on our monitors.

AP Photo/Jae C. Hong, file

### Figure 2.18

Because they do not need a backlight, OLED displays are much thinner, making LCD screens seem bulky.

### Figure 2.19

A magnification of a single pixel in an LCD monitor.

Rear glass

Colored light

Polarizer

Front glass

Unpolarized white light from backlight

Polarizer

Liquid crystals

Color filters

**What factors affect the quality of an LCD monitor?** When choosing an LCD monitor, there are several factors to consider, such as aspect ratio and resolution. The **aspect ratio** is the width-to-height proportion of a monitor. Traditionally, aspect ratios have been 4:3, but newer monitors are available with an aspect ratio of 16:9 or 16:10. The screen **resolution**, or the clearness or sharpness of the image, reflects the number of pixels on the screen. An LCD monitor may have a native (or maximum) resolution of 1600 × 1200 meaning it contains 1,600 vertical columns with 1,200 pixels in each column. The higher the resolution, the sharper and clearer the image will be, but generally the resolution of an LCD monitor is dictated by the screen size and aspect ratio. Although you can change the resolution of an LCD monitor beyond its native resolution, the images will become distorted. Generally, you should select a monitor with the highest resolution available for the screen size (measured in inches).

Other factors to consider when judging the quality of an LCD monitor include the following:

- **Contrast ratio:** This is a measure of the difference in light intensity between the brightest white and the darkest black that the monitor can produce. If the contrast ratio is too low, colors tend to fade when you adjust the brightness to a high or low setting. A contrast ratio between 400:1 and 1,000:1 is preferable. Some monitors may sport a dynamic contrast ratio that may be 10,000:1 or 50,000:1. This measurement is taken when the backlight is turned off completely; normal contrast ratio measurements have the backlight dimmed to its lowest setting but not completely off. Unfortunately, in normal use, the backlight is not turned off, so the dynamic contrast ratio is not a relevant measure, unless you are using an LED monitor.
- **Viewing angle:** An LCD's viewing angle, which is measured in degrees, tells how far you can move to the side of (or above or below) the monitor before the image quality degrades to unacceptable levels. For monitors that measure 17 inches or more, a viewing angle of at least 150 degrees is usually recommended.
- **Brightness:** Measured as candelas per square meter (cd/m$^2$) or *nits*, brightness is a measure of the greatest amount of light showing when the monitor is displaying pure white. A brightness level of 300 cd/m$^2$ or greater is recommended.
- **Response time:** This is the measurement (in milliseconds) of the time it takes for a pixel to change color. A lower response time value means faster transitions; therefore, moving images will appear less jerky on the monitor.

**Is a bigger screen size always better?** The bigger the monitor, the more you can display, and depending on what you want to display, size may matter. In general, the larger the panel, the larger number of pixels it can display. For example, a 27-inch monitor can display 2560 × 1440 pixels, while a 21.5-inch monitor may only be able to display 1680 × 1050 pixels. However, most new monitors have at least a 1920 × 1080 resolution that is required to display Blu-ray movies. Larger screens can also allow you to view multiple documents or Web pages at the same time, creating the

 **Testing and Calibrating Your PC Monitor**

BITS AND BYTES

Most new PC monitors do not need color or tint adjustments, but some can benefit from a few tweaks that will ultimately enhance your video experience. This might be especially important if you are a Web designer, digital photographer, or graphic professional. In those professions, especially, you want to make sure the colors are displayed on the monitor as accurately as possible. Before you start the calibration process, check that your monitor is set to the "native" resolution (usually the recommended setting). Some monitors have their own calibration program; otherwise, you can work through the adjustments manually or use the display utility in your operating system. If you are running Windows 7, you can use the Display Color Calibration utility found by clicking the Start button, clicking the Control Panel, and then clicking Appearance and Personalization. Click Display, and then in the Navigation Pane, click Calibrate color. The Display Color Calibration utility will check the gamma, brightness, contrast, and color balance settings. Gamma describes the relationship between the varying levels of brightness that a monitor can display. Brightness determines how dark colors appear on your display. When brightness is set too high, dark colors appear washed out. Contrast determines how white and light colors display. (Note that most notebook computers do not have controls to adjust contrast.) Color balance makes adjustments to the red, blue, and green controls.

effect of using two separate monitors side by side. Again, be mindful of cost. Buying two smaller monitors might be cheaper than buying one large monitor. For either option—a big screen or two screens—you should check that your computer has a special adapter card to support these video display devices.

**What other features should I look for in an LCD monitor?** Some monitors, especially those on notebook computers, come with convenient built-in features such as speakers, webcams, and microphones. A built-in multiformat card reader is convenient to display images directly on the monitor or to download pictures quickly from a camera memory card to the PC. Another nice feature to look for in a desktop LCD monitor is a built-in USB port. This will enable you to connect extra peripherals easily without reaching around the back of the PC. In addition, if you want to connect a gaming console or DVD/Blu-ray player, you should look for monitors with video ports for easy access.

**How do I show output to a large group of people?** Crowding large groups of people around your computer isn't practical. However, it is possible to use a **projector**, a device that can project images from your computer onto a wall or viewing screen. Projectors are commonly used in business and education settings such as conference rooms and classrooms. These projectors are small and light-weight, and some, like the 3M MPro 150 (see Figure 2.20), are small enough to fit into the palm of your hand! These portable projectors are ideal for businesspeople that have to make presentations at client locations. *Entertainment projectors*, such as the Wonderwall, include stereo speakers and an array of multimedia connectors, making them a good option for use in the home to display TV programs, DVDs, digital images, or video games in a large format. If your laptop is equipped with an HDMI port, you can connect your laptop

directly to an HDTV. Although you could connect your laptop with a DVI port, by using HDMI, you only need the one cable, eliminating the need for additional audio cables.

### Printers

**What are the different types of printers?** There are two primary categories of printers: inkjet and laser, both of which are considered nonimpact printers. A **nonimpact printer** sprays ink or uses laser beams to transfer marks onto the paper. Today, nonimpact printers have replaced impact printers almost entirely. An **impact printer** has tiny hammerlike keys that strike the paper through an inked ribbon, making marks on the paper. The most common impact printer is the dot-matrix printer. The only place you may see a dot-matrix printer is at a company that still uses them to print multipart forms. For most users, dot-matrix printers are truly legacy technology.

**What are the advantages of inkjet printers?** An **inkjet printer** (see Figure 2.21) is the standard type of printer found in most homes. Inkjet printers are popular because they are affordable and produce high-quality color printouts quickly and quietly. Inkjet printers work by spraying tiny drops of ink onto paper and are great for printing black-and-white text as well as color images. In fact, when loaded with the right paper, higher-end inkjet printers can print images that look like professional-quality photos. One thing to consider when buying an inkjet

**Figure 2.21**

Inkjet printers are popular among home users, especially with the rise of digital photography. Many inkjet printers are optimized for printing photos from digital cameras.

TheVectorminator/Shutterstock.com

**Figure 2.20**

Inexpensive projectors are showing up more frequently in business and the home to provide large images for movie viewing and gaming.

Courtesy of 3M

## How Touch Screens Work

Touch-screen technology was developed in 1971, and used primarily with ATMs and fast-food order displays. The technology for monitors and other displays was made popular by the iPod Touch, and is now in many smartphones, tablet computers, and notebook and desktop monitors. But how do touch-screen monitors know where you're touching? How do they know what you want them to do?

The basic idea behind touch screens is pretty straightforward—when you place your finger or stylus on a screen, it changes the state that the device is monitoring. The location of the touch is then translated into a command. Three basic systems are used to recognize a person's touch: resistive, capacitive, and surface acoustic wave. All of these systems require the basic components of a touch-responsive glass panel, controller, and software driver, combined with a display and computer processor.

The *resistive system* maps the exact location of the pressure point created when a user touches the screen. The *capacitive system* (see Figure 2.22) uses the change in the electrical charge on the glass panel of the monitor that is created by the user's touch, to generate a location. The third technology, *surface acoustic wave system*, uses two transducers (electrical devices that convert energy from one form to another) that are placed along the *x* and *y* axes of the monitor's glass plate. Reflectors, which are also placed on the glass, are used to reflect an electric signal sent from the sending transducer to the receiving transducer. The receiving transducer determines whether the signal has been disturbed by a touch event, and locates the touch instantly. Then, with all three systems, the display's software driver translates the touch into something the operating system can understand, similar to how a mouse driver translates a mouse's movements into a click or drag.

Because the resistive system uses pressure to register a touch, it doesn't matter if the touch is created by a finger or another device. A capacitive system must have conductive input, so generally a finger is required. The surface acoustic wave system allows touches by any object.

The iPhone introduced another complexity to the touch-screen system—a multi-touch user interface. In addition to just pressing the screen in one location, multi-touch technology can process multiple simultaneous touches on the screen. For example, pinching or spreading out the thumb and finger together enables the display to zoom out and in, respectively. The features of each touch, such as size, shape, and location, are also determined. A touch-sensitive screen, like the one used with the iPhone and iPad and with many other smartphones and tablet computers, arranges the capacitors in a coordinate system so the circuitry can sense changes at each point along the grid (see Figure 2.23). Consequently, every point when touched on the grid generates its own signal, and can do so even simultaneously as another signal is also being generated. The signals are then relayed to the device's processor. This allows the device to determine the location and movement of simultaneous touches in multiple locations.

**Figure** 2.22

Some basic touch screens use a capacitive system to detect touches and translate them into meaningful commands that are understood by the computer's operating system.

After detecting the position and type of touch occurring on the display, the device's processor combines this information with the information it has about the application that is in use, and what was being done in the application when the touch occurred. The processor relays that information to the program in use and the command is executed. All of this happens seemingly instantaneously.

**Figure** 2.23

Multi-touch screens use a coordinate-based grid to arrange the capacitors so the circuitry can detect and respond to multiple touches occurring at the same time.

printer is the type and cost of the ink cartridges the printer needs. Some printers use two cartridges: black and color. Other printers use four or more cartridges, typically black, magenta, cyan, and yellow.

**Why would I want a laser printer?** Laser printers (see Figure 2.24) are most often used in office or classroom settings because they have a faster printing speed than inkjet printers and produce higher-quality printouts. A **laser printer** uses laser beams and static electricity to deliver toner (similar to ink) onto the correct areas of the page. Heat is used to fuse the toner to the page, making the image permanent. In the past, laser printers generally were not found in the home because of their high purchase price and because they did not produce great color images. Recently, however, the quality and speed have improved and the price of color laser printers has fallen dramatically, making them highly price competitive with high-end inkjet printers. If you print a high volume of pages, consider a laser printer. When you include the price of ink or toner in the overall cost, laser printers can be more economical than inkjets.

**Are there wireless printers?** One reason you may have bought a notebook was to be able to use a computer without the restriction of wires. Wireless printing offers you the same freedom. In addition, wireless printers allow several people to print to the same printer from different places. There are two different types of wireless printers: WiFi and Bluetooth. Both WiFi and Bluetooth printers have a range of up to approximately 300 feet. WiFi, however, sends data more quickly than Bluetooth. If your printer is not Bluetooth enabled, you can add Bluetooth by plugging a Bluetooth adapter into a USB port. This lets you take advantage of a great printing solution for photos stored on your cell phone or any other Bluetooth-enabled portable device.

**Can I carry my printer with me?** Although some inkjet printers are small enough to carry with you, you may want to consider a printer designed for portability for added mobility and flexibility. These compact printers can connect to your computer, camera, or smartphone via Bluetooth technology, or with a USB port. Portable printers are often compact enough to fit in a briefcase, are lightweight, and can run on battery power as well as AC power.

**Are there any other types of specialty printers?** An **all-in-one printer** is a device that combines the functions of a printer, scanner, copier, and fax into one machine. Popular for their space-saving convenience, all-in-one printers can use either inkjet or laser technology. A **plotter** is another type of printer. Plotters produce oversize pictures that require the drawing of precise and continuous lines, such as maps, detailed images (see Figure 2.25), and architectural plans. Plotters use a computer-controlled pen that provides a greater level of precision than the series of dots that laser or inkjet printers are capable of making.

**Figure 2.24**

Laser printers print quickly and offer high-quality printouts.

**Figure 2.25**

Plotters are large printers used to print oversize images, maps, and architectural plans.

Courtesy of Xerox Corporation

A **thermal printer**, such as the one shown in Figure 2.26, is another kind of specialty printer. These printers work either by melting wax-based ink onto ordinary paper (a process called *thermal wax transfer printing*) or by burning dots onto specially coated paper (a process called *direct thermal printing*). They are used in stores to print receipts and in airports for electronic ticketing. Many models, such as the printers that car rental agencies use to give you an instant receipt when you drop off your rental car, feature wireless infrared technology for complete portability. Thermal printers are also emerging as a popular technology for mobile and portable printing in conjunction with smartphones and similar devices.

**How do I select the best printer?** There is a printer for every printing need. First, you need to decide what your primary printing need is. If you will use your printer mostly to print digital images, then you will want to select a photo printer. If not, then a general-purpose printer will be a better choice. General-purpose printers have a finer, faster text output, whereas photo printers have a more distinctive color output. It's also important to determine whether you want just a printer or a device that prints and scans, copies, or faxes (an all-in-one). In addition, you should decide whether you want an inkjet or laser printer, and whether or not you want to print wirelessly. Once you have narrowed down the type of printer you want, the following criteria will help you determine the best model to meet your needs.

- **Speed:** A printer's speed determines how many pages it can print per minute. Print speed is expressed as *pages per minute* or *ppm*. The speed of inkjet printers has improved over the years, and many inkjet printers now print as fast as laser printers. Printing speeds vary by model and range from 8 ppm to 38 ppm for both laser and inkjet printers. Text documents printed in black and white print faster than documents printed in color.
- **Resolution:** A printer's resolution (printed image clarity) is measured

**ACTIVE HELP-DESK** Using Output Devices

In this Active Helpdesk call, you'll play the role of a helpdesk staffer, fielding calls about different output devices, including the differences between LCD and CRT monitor technologies and between inkjet and laser printers and the advantages and disadvantages of each.

Zebra Technologies

**Figure 2.26**

Thermal printers are often used to print receipts.

in dots per inch (dpi), which is the number of dots of ink in a one-inch line. The higher the dpi, the greater the level of detail and quality of the image. You'll sometimes see dpi represented as a horizontal number multiplied by a vertical number, such as 600 × 600, but you may also see the same resolution simply stated as 600 dpi. The dpi will differ for color output than for black and white output. For general-purpose printing, 1,200 dpi is sufficient. For printing photos, 4,800 dpi is better. The dpi for professional photo-quality printers is twice that.

- **Color output:** If you're using an inkjet printer to print color images, four-color printers (cyan, magenta, yellow, and black) or six-color printers (four-color plus light cyan and light magenta) offer the highest-quality output. Although some printers come with a single ink cartridge for all colors and others have two ink cartridges (one for black and one for color), the best setup is to have an individual ink cartridge for each color so you can replace only the specific color cartridge that is empty. Color laser printers have four separate toner cartridges (black, cyan, magenta, and yellow), and the toner is blended in various quantities to produce the entire color spectrum.
- **Use and cost of the printer:** If you will be printing mostly black-and-white, text-based documents or will be sharing your printer with others, then a black-and-white laser printer is best because of its printing speed and

overall economy for volume printing. If you're planning to print color photos and graphics, then an inkjet printer or color laser printer is a must, even though the cost per page will be higher. Keep in mind a printer's reported duty cycle. A duty cycle is a manufacturer's figure that refers to how long a machine can keep operating before it needs a rest, or what percentage of the time it's designed to be in use. For a printer, the duty cycle generally refers to the number of printed pages the printer can reliably produce on a monthly basis. If you buy a printer with a duty cycle of 1,000 copies per month, and you generally only print 100 copies a month, then you will have overpurchased. Alternatively, exceeding the duty cycle estimates might lead to printer malfunctions.

- **Cost of consumables:** You should carefully investigate the cost of consumables (such as printer cartridges and paper) for any printer you are considering purchasing because the cost of inkjet cartridges often can exceed the cost of the actual printer when purchased on sale. Reviews in consumer magazines such as *PC World* and *Consumer Reports* can

help you evaluate the overall cost of producing documents with a particular printer.

### Sound Output

**What are the output devices for sound?** Most computers include inexpensive speakers. A **speaker** is an output device for sound. These speakers are sufficient to play the standard audio clips you find on the Web and usually enable you to participate in videoconferencing or phone calls made over the Internet. However, if you plan to digitally edit audio files or are particular about how your music sounds, then you may want to upgrade to a more sophisticated speaker system, such as one that includes subwoofers (special speakers that produce only low bass sounds) and surround-sound speakers. A **surround-sound speaker** is a system of speakers and audio processing that envelops the listener in a full 360-degree field of sound. Wireless speaker systems are available now to help you avoid cluttering up your rooms with speaker wire. We discuss surround sound in more detail in Chapter 3.

If you work in close proximity to other employees or travel with a notebook, then you may need to use headphones or earbuds for your sound output to avoid

---

 **BITS AND BYTES**

## Does It Matter What Paper I Print On?

The quality of your printer is only part of what controls the quality of a printed image. The paper you use and the printer settings that control the amount of ink used are equally important. If you're printing text-only documents for personal use, then using low-cost paper is fine. You also may want to consider selecting draft mode in your printer settings to conserve ink. However, if you're printing more formal documents such as résumés, you may want to choose a higher-quality paper (determined by the paper's weight, whiteness, and brightness) and adjust your print setting to "normal" or "best."

The weight of paper is measured in pounds, with 20 pounds being standard. A heavier paper may be best for projects such as brochures, but be sure to check that your printer can handle the added thickness. The degree of paper whiteness is a matter of personal preference. Generally, the whiter the paper, the brighter the printed

color. However, for more formal documents, such as résumés, you may want to use a creamier color. The brightness of paper usually varies from 85 to 94. The higher the number, the brighter the paper, and the easier it is to read printed text. Opacity, or the "show through" of print from one side to the other, or to the next sheet, is especially important if you're printing on both sides of the paper because it determines the amount of ink that shows through from the opposite side of the paper.

If you're printing photos, then paper quality can have a big impact on the results. Photo paper is more expensive than regular paper and comes in a variety of textures ranging from matte to high gloss. For a photo-lab look, high-gloss paper is the best choice. Semigloss (often referred to as satin) is good for portraits, while a matte surface is often used for black-and-white photo printing.

---

distracting other people. Both devices will plug into the same jack on the computer that speakers connect to, so using them with a computer is easy. Studies of users of portable media players have shown that hearing might be damaged by excessive volume, especially when using earbuds, because they fit into the ear canals. Exercise caution when using these devices.

## Processing and Memory on the Motherboard

We just looked at the components of your computer that you use to input and output data. But where does the processing take place, and where is the data stored? The **motherboard** is the main circuit board that contains the central electronic components of the computer, including the computer's processor (its brain), its memory, and the many circuit boards that help the computer function (see Figure 2.27). On a desktop, the motherboard is located inside the **system unit**, the metal or plastic case that also houses the power source and all the storage devices (CD/DVD drive and hard drive). With a notebook computer, the system unit is combined with the monitor and the keyboard into a single package.

**What's on the motherboard?** Recall that the motherboard is the main circuit board that contains the set of chips that powers the system, including the central processing unit (CPU). The motherboard also houses ROM, RAM, and cache, the chips that provide the short-term memory for the computer. The motherboard also includes slots for **expansion cards** (or **adapter cards**), which are circuit boards that provide additional functionality. Typical expansion cards found in the system unit are the sound and video cards. A **sound card** provides a connection for the speakers and microphone, whereas a **video card** provides a connection for the monitor. Many low-end

computer models have video and sound capabilities integrated into their motherboards. High-end models use expansion cards to provide video and sound capabilities. Other expansion cards provide a means for network and Internet connections. These include the **modem card**, which provides the computer with a connection to the Internet via a traditional phone line, and a **network interface card (NIC)**, which enables your computer to connect with other computers or to a cable modem to facilitate a high-speed Internet connection. Lastly, some expansion cards provide additional USB and FireWire ports.

### Figure 2.27

A motherboard contains the CPU, the memory (RAM) modules, and slots for expansion cards.

Expansion slots

Memory (RAM) slots

CPU

Ports

S.Dashkevych/Shutterstock.com

## Memory

**What exactly is RAM?** **Random access memory (RAM)** is the place in a computer where the programs and data the computer is currently using are stored. RAM is much faster to read from and write to than the hard drive and other forms of storage. The processor can request the RAM's contents, which can be located, opened, and delivered to the CPU for processing in a few nanoseconds (billionths of a second). If you look at a motherboard, you'll see RAM as a series of small cards (called *memory cards* or *memory modules*) plugged into slots on the motherboard.

Because the entire contents of RAM are erased when you turn off the computer, RAM is a temporary or **volatile storage** location. To save data permanently, you need to save it to the hard drive or to another permanent storage device such as a CD or flash drive. You can think of RAM as the computer's temporary memory and the hard drive as permanent memory.

**Does the motherboard contain any other kinds of memory besides RAM?** In addition to RAM, the motherboard also contains a form of memory called **read-only memory (ROM)**. ROM holds all the instructions the computer needs to start up when it is powered on. Unlike data stored in RAM, which is volatile storage, the instructions stored in ROM are permanent, making ROM a nonvolatile storage location, which means the data is not erased when the power is turned off.

### Processing

**What is the CPU?** The **central processing unit** (**CPU**, or **processor**) is sometimes referred to as the "brains" of the computer because it controls all the functions performed by the computer's other components and processes all the commands issued to it by software instructions. Modern CPUs can perform as many as tens of billions of tasks per second without error, making them extremely powerful components.

**How is processor speed measured?** Processor speed is measured in units of hertz (Hz). Hertz means "machine cycles per second." A machine cycle is the process of the CPU getting the data or instructions from RAM and decoding the instructions into something the computer can understand. Once the CPU has decoded the instructions, it executes them and stores the result back into system memory. Current systems run at speeds measured in **gigahertz (GHz)**, or billions of machine cycles per second. Therefore, a 3.8 GHz processor performs work at a rate of 3.8 billion machine cycles per second. It's important to realize, however, that CPU clock speed alone doesn't determine the performance of the CPU.

**What else determines processor performance?** Although speed is an important consideration when determining processor performance, CPU performance also is affected by other factors. One factor is the number of *cores*, or processing paths, a processor has. Initially processors could handle only one instruction at a time. Now, processors have been designed so that they can have two, four, and even eight different paths, allowing them to process more than one instruction at a time (see Figure 2.28). Applications such as virus protection software and the operating system, which are always running behind the scenes, can have their own processors, freeing up the other processor to run other applications such as a Web browser, Word, or iTunes more efficiently.

**Besides the number of cores, are there other factors that determine processing power?** In addition to the number of cores in a processor, you should consider other factors such as cache memory and front side bus (FSB). Front side bus determines how fast data is exchanged between the CPU and RAM. These factors will be discussed in greater detail in Chapter 3. The "best" processor will depend on your particular needs and is not always the processor with the highest GHz and the greatest number of cores. Intel, one of the leading manufacturers of computer processor chips, has created a pictorial rating system for CPU chips. Intel uses one to five stars to illustrate the relative computing power of each type of CPU within the Intel line of processors.

**Figure 2.28**

Two or more are faster than one! With their multi-core processors, Intel CPUs can work in parallel, processing two or more separate programs at the same time instead of switching back and forth between them.

Single path vs. dual path processors for data

Single core processor          Dual core processor

# Storing Data and Information

Earlier we characterized RAM as temporary or volatile memory because the entire contents of RAM are erased when you turn off the computer. Thus, if you want to permanently save the files you're working on, as well as your music, digital images, and any software applications you use, you need to store them in a location other than RAM. To save your data and information permanently, you need to save it to the hard drive or to another permanent storage device such as an external hard drive, DVD, or flash drive.

## Hard Drives

**Are there different kinds of hard drives?** The **hard disk drive (HDD or hard drive)** is your computer's primary device for permanent storage of software and documents. The hard drive is a **nonvolatile storage** device, meaning it holds data and the instructions your computer needs permanently, even after the computer is turned off. Today's internal hard drives (see Figure 2.29a), with capacities of as much as 3 terabytes (TB), can hold more data than would fit in the books in a school's library. External hard drives (see Figure 2.29b) offer similar storage capacities, but reside outside the system unit, and connect to the computer via a USB or FireWire port. The most common type of hard drive has moveable parts—spinning platters, a moving arm with a read/write head—that can fail and lead to devastating disk failure. However, recently, the **solid-state drive (SSD)** has become a more feasible option for desktop and laptop storage. SSDs have no moving parts, so they are more efficient, run with no noise, emit very little heat, and require very little power. In addition, they are less likely to fail after being bumped or dropped. The small portable flash drives that you may carry around in your pocket use solid state technology.

Some permanent storage devices are located in your desktop or notebook computer in a space called a **drive bay**.

There are two kinds of drive bays—internal and external—as described below:

- Internal drive bays cannot be seen or accessed from outside the system unit. Generally, internal drive bays are reserved for internal hard drives. An **internal hard drive** usually holds all permanently stored programs and data.

- External drive bays can be seen and accessed from outside the system unit. External drive bays house CD and DVD drives, for example. On desktop computers, sometimes there are empty external drive bays that can be used to install additional drives. These extra spaces are covered by a faceplate on the front panel. Notebook computers generally do not give you the ability to add additional drives. Such expansion is done by attaching an external drive to the computer through a USB port.

## Flash Storage

**How can I take my files with me?** There are many options available to take data with you. For large portable storage needs, there are portable **external hard drives**, which are small enough to fit into your pocket and have storage capacities of 1 or 2 TB (or larger). These devices are small and lightweight and are enclosed in a protective case. They attach to your computer via the USB port (see Figure 2.30). Most of these portable external hard drives, such as My Passport, do not use solid state technology, so care should be taken when transporting them.

A flash drive, sometimes referred to as a jump drive, USB drive, or thumb drive, uses

a

b

Ragnarock/Shutterstock.com

utflytter/Shutterstock.com

**Figure** 2.29

(a) Internal hard drives hold the data and instructions that the computer needs and are inaccessible from outside the system unit. (b) High-capacity external hard drives are often used to back up data on internal hard drives.

## Taking Care of Flash Drives

Flash drives have become a convenient means of portable storage, primarily because of their diminutive physical size, but also because of their expansive storage capacities. Although they are fairly rugged and withstand much abuse, flash drive failures can occur. Therefore, it is important to know how to care for your flash drive to extend its useful life, and to keep your data safe.

1. Like any other mechanical device, do not submerge a flash drive in water or expose it to extreme temperatures. Take care to not leave it where it's at risk of being spilled on.

2. Keep the end covered or closed when not plugged into the computer. This prevents dust and other particles from interfering with the connections.

3. Never defrag a flash drive. It is not necessary, and can reduce the life expectancy of the drive.

4. A flash drive has a limited amount of writes in its lifetime. Depending on the device, it can be 10,000 or 100,000, which seems like a lot, but over years of extensive use, could add up. It's best to make edits to documents on the computer, and then transfer the finished document to your flash drive.

5. Remember to remove the flash drive correctly. All files and folders must be closed, with no active documents running, before the device is removed. To properly stop the device, use the "Safely remove hardware" feature in the taskbar, or select Eject from Windows Explorer. Mac users should select Eject from the Finder menu. If you find that you cannot stop the flash drive by these methods, you will need to power down the computer first before removing the drive.

**Figure 2.30**

Smaller external hard drives enable you to take a significant amount of data and programs on the road with you.

solid-state flash memory, storing information on an internal memory chip. Because a flash drive contains no moving parts, it is quite durable. It is also tiny enough to fit into your pocket, making it a very convenient means of portable storage. Often flash drives are combined with other devices such as pens or pocketknives (see Figure 2.31) for added convenience. Despite their diminutive size, flash drives have significant storage capacity—currently

as much as 256 GB. Flash drives plug into USB ports. When you plug a flash drive into your computer's USB port, it appears in the Windows or Macintosh operating system as another disk drive. You can write data to it or read data from it in the same manner as reading and writing data to and from hard drives.

Another convenient means of portable storage is a **flash memory card** such as a Memory Stick or CompactFlash card. Like the flash drive, memory cards use solid-state flash memory. Most desktops and notebooks include slots for flash memory cards, but if your computer is not equipped, there are memory card readers that can be plugged into a USB port. Flash memory cards let you transfer digital data between your computer and devices such as digital cameras, smartphones, video cameras, and printers. Although incredibly small—some are even smaller than the size of a postage stamp—these memory cards have capacities that exceed the capacity of a DVD. We discuss flash memory in more detail in Chapter 5.

### Optical Storage

**What other kinds of storage devices are available?** Internal hard drives are used to store your data, files, and installed software programs. Hard drives store their data on magnetized platters. Also included on most desktop and notebook computers is at least one **optical drive** that can read from and maybe even write to CDs, DVDs, or

**Figure 2.31**

Flash drives are a convenient means of portable storage, and come in many different shapes and sizes.

Blu-ray Discs. Data is saved to a **compact disc (CD)**, **digital video** (or **versatile**) **disc (DVD)**, or **Blu-ray Disc (BD)** as tiny pits that are burned into the disc by a high-speed laser. CDs were initially created to store audio files. DVDs are the same size and shape as CDs but can hold more data. DVDs that store data on just one side and in one layer can store about seven times more data. If you're looking for more storage capacity, a double-sided/single-layer DVD is the next step. These discs have up to 8.5 GB of storage, and a double-sided/double-layer DVD can store nearly 16 GB of data. What if you want even more storage capacity? Blu-ray is the latest incarnation of optical storage to hit the market. Blu-ray Discs, which are similar in size and shape to CDs and DVDs, can hold as much as 50 GB of data—enough to hold approximately 4.5 hours of movies in the high-definition (HD) digital format that has become so popular. Many systems are now available with BD-ROM drives and even Blu-ray burners. External BD drives are another inexpensive way to add HD storage capacity to your system.

Figure 2.32 shows the storage capacities of the various portable storage media used in your computer system.

# Connecting Peripherals to the Computer

Throughout this chapter, we have discussed peripheral devices that input, store, and output data and information. A **port** is a place through which a peripheral device attaches to the computer so that data can be exchanged between it and the operating system. Many ports are located on the back of a notebook computer and the system unit of a desktop computer. However, some commonly used ports are placed on the front and sides of many desktop and notebook computers (see Figure 2.33) for easier access when connecting devices such as flash drives or digital and video cameras.

### High-Speed and Data Transfer Ports

**What is the most common way to connect devices to a computer?**
A **universal serial bus (USB) port** is now the most common port type used to connect input and output devices to the computer. This is mainly because of a USB port's ability

**Figure 2.32** | STORAGE MEDIA CAPACITIES

| Medium | Image | Typical Capacity |
|---|---|---|
| Solid-state drive (SSD) | Oleksiy Mark/ iStockphoto.com | 5 TB or more |
| External portable hard drive | joel-t/ iStockphoto .com | 4 TB or more |
| Mechanical hard drive | © D. Hurst / Alamy | As much as 6 TB or more |
| Flash drive | Christopher Testi/ Shutterstock .com | 900 GB or more |
| Flash memory card | © Richard Naude/Alamy | 128 GB |
| Blu-ray (dual layer) | AP/Photo/ PRNewsFoto/Sony Electronics Inc. | 50 GB |
| Blu-ray (BD) | © Coyote-Photography .co.uk/Alamy | 25 GB |
| DVD DL (dual layer) | © Studio 101/ Alamy | 8.5 GB |
| DVD | © Niels Poulsen/ Alamy | 4.7 GB |
| CD | © Studio 101/ Alamy | 700 MB |

**a**

**b**

USB ports

Audio/video ports

FireWire ports

S-video

Memory card slots

Ethernet port

alexkar08/Shutterstock

Suwan_bjp/Shutterstock.com

**Figure 2.33**

Many of the same ports appear on both (a) desktop and (b) notebook computers.

Courtesy of Seagate Technology, Inc.

**b**

**Figure 2.34**

(a) USB 3.0 and
(b) USB 2.0 connectors.

to transfer data quickly. USB 2.0 ports (see Figure 2.34b) are the current standard and transfer data at 480 megabits per second (Mbps), approximately 40 times faster than the original USB ports. USB ports can connect a wide variety of peripherals to the computer, including keyboards, printers, mice, smartphones, external hard drives, flash drives, and digital cameras. The new USB 3.0 standard provides transfer speeds of 4.8 Gbps, which is 10 times the speed of USB 2.0. In addition, USB 3.0 charges devices faster than its predecessor. USB 3.0 (shown in Figure 2.34a) (per new note with image) should quickly become the port of choice.

A traditional serial port sends data one bit (piece of data) at a time. Serial ports were often used to connect modems (devices used to transmit data over telecommunications lines) to the computer. Sending data one bit at a time was a slow way to communicate. A parallel port could send data between devices in groups of bits at speeds of 500 Kbps and was much faster than traditional serial ports.

Parallel ports were often used to connect printers to computers. The speed advantage offered by USB ports has made serial and parallel ports legacy technology.

**What are other types of ports?** You may also see other ports, such as **FireWire 400** and **FireWire 800**. The FireWire 400 interface moves data at 400 Mbps, while the FireWire 800 doubles the rate to 800 Mbps. Devices such as external hard drives, digital video cameras, portable music players, and digital media players all benefit from the speedy data transfer capabilities of FireWire. The FireWire 3200 standard, with data transfer rates of 3.2 Gbps, has been ratified but has yet to reach the market. FireWire 400 ports and connectors have two different configurations, as shown in Figure 2.35. FireWire 400 ports on computers generally have six pins, while FireWire ports on digital cameras have four pins.

To transfer data between the two devices, a special cable that has an appropriate connector at each end is needed. The faster FireWire 800 requires a nine-pin connection

6-pin

4-pin

© Editorial Image, LLC./Alamy

Ronald Hudson/Fotolia

**Figure 2.35**

FireWire ports come in different configurations, two of which are illustrated here.

and is found on storage devices such as external and portable hard drives.

## Connectivity and Multimedia Ports

### Which ports help me connect with other computers and the Internet?

Another set of ports on your computer helps you communicate with other computers. A **connectivity port** can give you access to networks and the Internet or enable your computer to function as a fax machine. To find a connectivity port, look for a port that resembles a standard phone jack but is slightly larger. This port is called an **Ethernet port** (see Figure 2.36). Ethernet ports transfer data at speeds up to 10,000 Mbps. You can use an Ethernet port to connect your computer to a digital subscriber line (DSL) or cable modem, or a network. Many computers still feature a second connectivity port that will accept a standard phone line connector. This jack is the **modem port**. It uses a traditional telephone signal to connect to the Internet over a phone line.

**Figure 2.36**

An Ethernet port and an Ethernet connector.

### How do I connect monitors and multimedia devices?

Other ports on the back and sides of the computer include the audio and video ports (see Figure 2.37). Video ports are necessary to hook up monitors. Whether you are attaching a monitor to a desktop computer, or adding a second, larger display to a notebook computer, you will use video ports. The **video graphics array (VGA)** port is the port to which CRT monitors connect. Many older LCD monitors also connect with a VGA port. The newer LCD monitors, as well as other multimedia devices such as televisions, DVD players, and projectors, connect to **digital video interface (DVI)** and **S-video (super video)** ports. Audio ports are where you connect headphones, microphones, and speakers to the computer.

### How can I connect my computer to TVs and gaming consoles?

The latest digital connector designed for use in high-definition home theater environments is a **high-definition multimedia interface (HDMI)**, a compact audio–video interface that carries both high-definition video and

VGA port

Speaker

Headphones

Microphone

**Figure 2.37**

Video ports connect your monitors and multimedia devices to the computer; audio ports are used to connect speakers, headphones, and microphones.

uncompressed digital audio on one cable. (DVI can only carry video signals.) Because HDMI can transmit uncompressed audio and video, there is no need to convert the signal, which could ultimately reduce the quality of the sound or picture. Most DVD players, TVs, and game consoles have at least one HDMI port (see Figure 2.38).

## Adding Ports: Expansion Cards and Hubs

### What if I don't have all the ports I need?

Because almost everything connects to your computer using USB ports, your desktop computer should have at least six USB ports, and a notebook computer should have at least three USB ports. Therefore, if you are looking to add the newest ports to an older computer or to expand the number of ports on your computer, you can use special expansion cards. You can install expansion cards into an open expansion slot on the motherboard in your desktop system unit to provide additional ports. If your notebook computer requires additional ports,

**Figure 2.38**

HDMI is the latest digital connector type for HD home theater equipment.

USB 3.0    USB 2.0  FireWire

a

© Andrew Kitching /Alamy

Express Card

Express card USB 3.0 (2 ports)

ExpressCard

b

© Editorial Image, LLC /Alamy

**Figure** 2.39

Expansion cards can (a) fit on the motherboard or (b) in a card slot to provide your computer with additional ports.

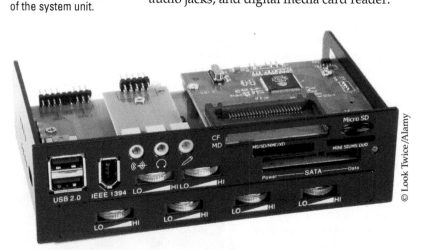

USB 2.0    IEEE 1394    LO    HI LO    HI

CF
MD    MS/SD/MMC/XD    MINI SD/MS DUO

Micro SD

Power    SATA    Data

LO    HI    LO    HI    LO    HI    LO    HI

© Look Twice/Alamy

**Figure** 2.41

You can use an empty drive bay to add additional ports and even a flash card reader to the front panel of the system unit.

you can add them with an express card adapter. Figure 2.39 shows an example of such expansion cards.

Another alternative is adding an expansion hub (shown in Figure 2.40). An expansion hub is a device that connects to one port, such as a USB port, to provide additional new ports. It works like the multiplug extension cords used with electrical appliances.

You also can add ports to an empty drive bay, giving you easy-to-reach new ports. one The shown in Figure 2.41, fits into a regular drive bay and adds front-panel access to two USB 2.0 ports, a FireWire port audio jacks, and digital media card reader.

Coolstuffexpress.com

**Figure** 2.40

If you don't have enough USB ports to support your USB devices, consider getting an expansion hub, which can add four or more USB ports to your system.

## Power Controls

**What's the best way to turn my computer on and off?** The **power supply,** which is housed inside the system unit, transforms the wall voltage to the voltages required by computer chips. A desktop system typically has a power-on button on the front panel of the system unit, though you may also find power-on buttons on some keyboards. On notebooks, the power-on button is generally located near the top of the keyboard. Powering on your computer from a completely turned off state, such as when you start your computer in the morning, is called a **cold boot**. Powering off your computer properly helps to save energy, keeps your computer more secure, and ensures that your data is saved. You can turn your computer off by pressing the computer's power button or using the Shut Down button on the Start menu.

**Should I turn off my computer every time I'm done using it?** Some people say you should leave your computer on at all times. They argue that turning your computer on and off throughout the day subjects its components to stress because the heating and cooling process forces the components to expand and contract repeatedly. Other people say you should shut down your computer when you're not using it. They claim that it's not as environmentally friendly, and you'll end up wasting money on electricity to keep the computer running all the time. Modern operating systems include power-management settings that allow the most power-hungry components of the system (the hard drive and monitor) to shut down after a short idle period. With the power-management options of Windows 7, for example, you really need to shut down your computer completely only when you need to repair or install hardware in the system unit or move the system unit to another location. However, if you use your computer only for a little while each day, it would be best to power it off completely after each daily use.

**Can I "rest" my computer without turning it off completely?** As mentioned earlier, your computer has power-management settings that help it conserve energy. In Windows 7, the two main methods of power management are Sleep and Hibernate. When your computer enters **Sleep mode**, all of the documents, applications, and data you were using remain in RAM (memory), where they are quickly accessible when you restart your computer.

**Hibernate** is another power-saving mode (available in systems with less than 4GB of RAM) that stores your data in memory and saves it to your computer's hard drive. In either Sleep or Hibernate mode, the computer enters a state of greatly reduced power consumption, which saves energy. The big advantage to using Hibernate is that if there is a power failure while your computer is conserving power, your information is protected from loss, because it is saved on the hard drive. To put your computer into Sleep or Hibernate, open the Start menu and select the appropriate Sleep or Hibernate option. To wake up your computer, tap a key on the keyboard or move the mouse. In a few seconds, the computer will resume with exactly the same programs running and documents displayed as when you put it to sleep.

In Windows 7, you can change what happens when you click the arrow next to the Shut Down button in the Start menu. By accessing the Power Options dialog box (see Figure 2.42), you can decide if you want your computer to Sleep, Hibernate, or Shut Down when you click the power button.

**What's the restart option in Windows for?** If you're using Windows 7, you have the option to restart the computer when you click the right arrow button next to the Shut Down button on the Start menu (see Figure 2.43). Restarting the system while it's powered on is called a **warm boot**. You might need to perform a warm boot if the operating system or other software application stops responding or if you have installed new programs. It takes less time to perform a warm boot than to power down completely and then restart all of your hardware.

**Figure 2.42**

You can determine what happens when you click the power button on your computer through Power Options.

>To access Power Options, click the **Start** button, click **Control Panel**, click **Hardware and Sound**, and then select **Power Options**.

## Setting It All Up

It's important that you understand not only your computer's components and how they work together but also how to set up these components safely. *Merriam-Webster's Dictionary* defines **ergonomics** as "an applied science concerned with designing and arranging things people use so that the people and things interact most efficiently and safely." ("Definition of ergonomics" from MERRIAM-WEBSTER'S COLLEGIATE® DICTIONARY, 11TH EDITION. Copyright © 2011 by Merriam-Webster,

**Figure 2.43**

The Start menu in Windows 7 presents several power options. For a warm boot, choose Restart. To power down the computer completely, choose Shut Down. To put your computer into a lower power mode, select Sleep or Hibernate.

>To select a particular power option, click the **Start** menu button in the taskbar and then click the right arrow button.

Incorporated (www.merriam-webster.com).
Reprinted by permission.) In terms of computing, ergonomics refers to how you set
up your computer and other equipment to
minimize your risk of injury or discomfort.

### Why is ergonomics important?

You don't have to have a desk job to run the
risk of becoming injured by working improperly on a computer. Studies suggest that
teenagers, on average, spend 31 hours online
each week. When you factor in other computer uses such as typing school reports and
playing video games, there is great potential
for injury. The repetitive nature of long-term
computer activities can place too much stress
on joints and pull at the tendons and muscles,
causing repetitive stress injuries such as carpal tunnel syndrome and tendonitis. These
injuries can take months or years to develop
to a point where they become painful, and
by the time you notice the symptoms, the
damage has already taken place. If you take
precautionary care now, you may prevent
years of unnecessary pain later on.

**How can I avoid injuries when
I'm working at my computer?** As
Figure 2.44 illustrates, it is important to
arrange your monitor, chair, body, and
keyboard in ways that will help you avoid
injury, discomfort, and eyestrain as you
work on your computer. The following
additional guidelines can help keep you
comfortable and productive:

- **Position your monitor correctly**. Studies
  suggest it's best to place your monitor at
  least 25 inches from your eyes. You may
  need to decrease the screen resolution to
  make text and images more readable at
  that distance. Experts recommend that
  the monitor be positioned either at eye
  level or so that it is at an angle 15 to 20
  degrees below your line of sight.

- **Purchase an adjustable chair.** Adjust
  the height of your chair so that your feet
  touch the floor. (You may need to use
  a footrest to get the right position.) The
  back support needs to be adjustable so
  that you can position it to support your
  lumbar (lower back) region. You should
  also be able to move the seat or adjust the
  back so that you can sit without exert-
  ing pressure on your knees. If your chair
  doesn't adjust, placing a pillow behind
  your back can provide the same support.

- **Assume a proper position
  while typing.** A repetitive
  strain injury (RSI) is a painful
  condition caused by repetitive
  or awkward movements of a
  part of the body. Improperly
  positioned keyboards are one
  of the leading causes of RSIs
  in computer users. Your wrists
  should be flat (not bent) with
  respect to the keyboard, and
  your forearms should be parallel to the floor. Additionally,
  your wrists should not be resting on the keyboard while typing. You can either adjust the
  height of your chair or install
  a height-adjustable keyboard
  tray to ensure a proper position. Specially designed ergonomic keyboards such as the
  one shown in Figure 2.45 can
  help you achieve the proper
  wrist position.

**Figure 2.44**

Using proper equipment
that is adjusted correctly
helps prevent repetitive
strain injuries while
working at a computer.

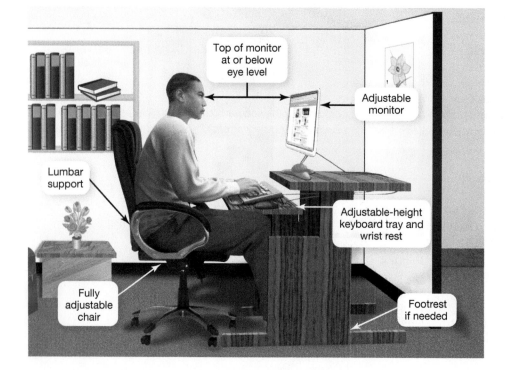

- **Take breaks from computer tasks.** Remaining in the same position for long periods of time increases stress on your body. Shift your position in your chair and stretch your hands and fingers periodically.

  Likewise, staring at the screen for long periods of time can lead to eyestrain, so rest your eyes by periodically taking them off the screen and focusing them on an object at least 20 feet away.

- **Ensure the lighting is adequate.** Ensuring that you have proper lighting in your work area is a good way to minimize eyestrain. To do so, eliminate any sources of direct glare (light shining directly into your eyes) or reflected glare (light shining off the computer screen) and ensure there is enough light to read comfortably. If you still can't eliminate glare from your computer screen, you can purchase an antiglare screen to place over your monitor. Look for ones that are polarized or have a purplish optical coating. These will provide the greatest relief.

**Figure 2.45**
Ergonomic keyboards that curve and contain built-in wrist rests help maintain proper hand position and minimize wrist strain.

Dmitry Melnikov/Shutterstock

**Is ergonomics important when using mobile devices?** Working with mobile computing devices presents interesting challenges when it comes to injury prevention. For example, many users work with notebooks resting on their laps, placing the monitor outside of the optimal line of sight and thereby increasing neck strain. The table in Figure 2.46 provides guidelines on preventing injuries when computing on the go.

So whether you're computing at your desk or on the road, consider the ergonomics of your work environment. Doing so will help you avoid injury and discomfort.

**Figure 2.46** | PREVENTING INJURIES WHILE ON THE GO

|  | PDA/Smartphone RSIs | PMP Hearing Damage | Small-Screen Vision Issues | Lap Injuries | Back, Neck, and Shoulder Injuries |
|---|---|---|---|---|---|
| Malady | Repetitive strain injuries (such as DeQuervain's tendonitis) from constant typing of instant messages. | Hearing loss from high decibel sound levels in earbuds or headphones. | Blurriness and dryness caused by squinting to view tiny screens on mobile devices. | Burns on legs from heat generated by notebook. | Pain caused from carrying notebook (messenger) bag hung over your shoulder. |
| Preventative measures | Restrict length and frequency of messages, take breaks often, and perform other motions with your thumbs and fingers during breaks to relieve tension. | Turn down volume (you should be able to hear external noises such as people talking), use software programs that limit sound levels (not over 60 decibels), and use external, over-ear style headphones instead of earbuds. | Blink frequently or use eye drops to maintain moisture level in eyes, after 10 minutes take a break and focus your eyes on something at least 8 feet away for 5 minutes, use an adequate amount of light, increase the size of fonts. | Place a book, magazine, or notebook cooling pad between your legs and your notebook. | Use a conventional backpack with two shoulder straps, lighten the load by only carrying essential equipment, and consider buying a lightweight notebook. |

## Innovations in Printing

With the advent of the computer, many speculated that we would become a paperless society. Instead of saving printed documents and other output as was done prior to the PC, information would be saved in a digital state: hard drives replacing filing cabinets, online photo buckets replacing photo albums and scrapbooks, and e-books replacing our favorite novels and textbooks. Hard drive capacities do enable us to save more digital content and online storage systems enable us to save pictures and other files to "the cloud." Additionally, e-book readers have increased in popularity. But, has all of this push toward digital content begun to make the printer obsolete? Surprisingly, no. In this digital age, more than ever, people still have a deep-rooted need to see, feel, mark, share, or use their digital images or information in a physical form. New technologies that push the boundaries of printing, such as inkless printing, printing from the cloud, and 3D printing, are being developed and refined.

### Inkless Printing

We've all experienced it: needing to print out an important document only to find that our print cartridge is so low that either nothing prints, or the resulting document appears in varying shades of pink and green. Inkless printing avoids this dilemma by eliminating the need for print cartridges altogether. Inkless printing systems, such as that developed by Zink, store ink in the paper itself, rather than in toner or ink cartridges. The Zink printer heats the color crystals in the paper with precise heat pulses of specific duration and temperature to produce a full color print. This technology is currently being used in small portable camera and printer devices such as Dell's Wasabi printer and PoGo by Polaroid (see Figure 2.47). The PoGo instant digital camera has an integrated printer, and the PoGo instant digital printer connects to your cellphone or digital camera via Bluetooth to print pictures on the go.

The PrePeat is an innovative office printer that uses no ink or toner because it uses rewritable plastic sheets made from PET plastic that can be erased and reprinted about 1,000 times per sheet. The heat-sensitive plastic sheets are fed into the printer and a line thermal head either prints a new document in black and white or erases an existing document and reprints another, allowing you to re-use paper again and again. This technology is ideal for documents that are only read once, such as office memos or emails. Although the technology is very expensive (the printer is about $5,500 and each sheet of special paper is $3.30), it provides another lead into helping reduce the incredible toll paper and ink printing has on our environment.

### Cloud Printing

What happens if you want to print something from your smartphone or tablet? With the growing proliferation of mobile devices, the need to send a print document to a printer is increasing, but as yet unavailable. Currently, to print a document you must have a printer associated with your

AP Photo/Jae C. Hong

**Figure 2.47**

Using an inkless printing system, the PoGo instant digital camera and printer make printing on the go possible.

computer. Usually this is not a problem because at home, school, or in the office, there is generally one printer, and all the PCs connected to it have the right software and cables or wireless capabilities. But, to print something from your mobile device, the solution has been to transfer the document via e-mail to a Web-based storage service such as Dropbox so a printer-connected computer could access it. Not surprisingly, Google has released Google Cloud Print in beta form, a service that enables "any application (web, desktop, or mobile) on any device to print to any printer."

In Google's vision, there would be "cloud-aware" printers (see Figure 2.48). Such printers would need neither a PC connection of any kind nor a print driver. The printer is simply registered with one or more cloud print services and awaits print jobs. Cloud-aware printers don't exist yet, but Google is hoping that manufacturers will see the universal need and interest in this concept and begin to develop the appropriate software and hardware. In the meantime, Google has provided a work-around for traditional printers—those that are in our homes, schools, and offices. Installing a small piece of software gives the legacy printer a proxy that registers the printer with Google Cloud Print, and printing requests can then be sent via the cloud, directed to the traditional printer.

### 3D Printing

Printing a 3D model of a proposed building or new prototype is common for architects and engineers. The process builds a model one layer at a time from the bottom up. The procedure begins by spreading a layer of powder on a platform. Then, depending on technology, uses nozzles similar to those in an inkjet printer to spray tiny drops of glue at specific places to solidify the powder, or it is solidified through a melting process. The printer repeats solidifying layers of powder until the model is built to specifications. This technology has spurred the manufacturing of a variety of consumer goods, from toys to clothing. Shapeways (**www.shapeways.com**) uses 3D printing to enable anyone to turn their 3D designs into real physical models. Then, those models can be personalized, bought, or sold through Shapeways' online community.

3D printing is being used in the medical community as well. Bespoke Innovations (**www.bespokeinnovations.com**) is using 3D printing to create prosthetic limbs with more life-like form and textures, as well as giving the recipient the ability to further personalize the prosthetic to include tattoos! As mentioned in Chapter 1, researchers at Wake Forest Institute for Regenerative Medicine have developed a way to use similar inkjet technologies to build heart, bone, and blood vessel tissues in the lab, as well as to "print" restorative cells directly into a soldier's wound at the site where the injury occurred, thus significantly improving the soldier's chances of survival.

Taking traditional technologies, such as inkjet printing, and applying them to solve current human struggles is a long and tedious process, but without these pioneers experimenting with different applications, society would advance a lot more slowly.

**Figure** 2.48
"Cloud aware" printers will only need an Internet connection and then could be accessed from any mobile device.

## 1. What exactly is a computer, and what are its four main functions?

Computers are devices that process data. They help organize, sort, and categorize data to turn it into information. The computer's four major functions are: (1) input: gather data, or allow users to enter data; (2) process: manipulate, calculate, or organize that data; (3) output: display data and information in a form suitable for the user; and (4) storage: save data and information for later use.

## 2. What is the difference between data and information?

Data is a representation of a fact or idea. The number 3 and the words *televisions* and *Sony* are pieces of data. Information is data that has been organized or presented in a meaningful fashion. An inventory list that indicates that "three Sony televisions" are in stock is processed information. It allows a retail clerk to answer a customer query about the availability of merchandise. Information is more powerful than raw data.

## 3. What are bits and bytes, and how are they measured?

To process data into information, computers need to work in a language they understand. This language, called *binary language*, consists of two numbers: 0 and 1. Each 0 and each 1 is a binary digit, or bit. Eight bits create one byte. In computers, each letter of the alphabet, each number, and each special character consists of a unique combination of eight bits (one byte)—a string of eight 0s and 1s. For describing large amounts of storage capacity, the terms *megabyte* (approximately 1 million bytes), *gigabyte* (approximately 1 billion bytes), and *terabyte* (approximately 1 trillion bytes) are used.

## 4. What devices do I use to get data into the computer?

An input device enables you to enter data (text, images, and sounds) and instructions (user responses and commands) into a computer. You use keyboards to enter typed data and commands, whereas you use the mouse to enter user responses and commands. Keyboards and mice come in both wired and wireless versions, as well as other special layouts and designs to fit almost every need.

Touch screens are display screens that respond to commands initiated by a touch with a finger or a stylus. Images are input into the computer with scanners, digital cameras, camcorders, and cell phones. Live video is captured with webcams and digital video recorders. Microphones capture sounds. There are many different types of microphones, including desktop, headset, and clip-on models.

## 5. What devices do I use to get information out of the computer?

Output devices enable you to send processed data out of your computer. It can take the form of text, pictures, sounds, or video. Monitors display soft copies of text, graphics, and video, while printers create hard copies of text and graphics. LCDs are the most popular type of monitor.

There are two primary categories of printers used today: inkjet and laser. Specialty printers are also available. These include all-in-one printers, plotters, and thermal printers. When choosing a printer, you should be aware of factors such as speed, resolution, color output, and cost.

Speakers are the output devices for sound. Most computers include speakers, with more sophisticated systems including subwoofers and surround sound.

## 6. What's on the motherboard?

The motherboard, the main circuit board of the system, contains a computer's central processing unit (CPU), which coordinates the functions of all other devices on the computer. The performance of a CPU is affected by the speed of the processor (measured in gigahertz), the amount of cache memory, the speed of the front side bus (FSB), and the number of processing cores. RAM, the computer's volatile memory, is also located on the motherboard. RAM is where all the data and instructions are held while the computer is running. ROM, a permanent type of memory, is responsible for housing instructions to help start up a computer. The motherboard also houses a set of slots for expansion cards, which have specific functions that augment the computer's basic functions. Typical expansion cards found in the system unit are the sound and video cards.

## two

**7. Where are information and programs stored?**

To save programs and information permanently, you need to save them to the hard drive or to another permanent storage device such as a CD, DVD, or flash drive. The hard drive is your computer's primary device for permanent storage of software and files. The hard drive is a nonvolatile storage device, meaning it holds the data and instructions your computer needs permanently, even after the computer is turned off. Mechanical hard drives have spinning platters on which data is saved, whereas newer solid-state hard drives (SSD) use solid-state memory, similar to that used with flash drives. External hard drives are essentially internal hard drives that have been made portable by enclosing them in a protective case and making them small and lightweight. Optical drives that can read from and write to CD, DVD, or Blu-ray Discs are another means of permanent, portable storage. Data is saved to compact discs (CDs), digital video discs (DVDs), and Blu-ray Discs (BDs) as tiny pits that are burned into the disc by a high-speed laser. Flash drives are another portable means of storing data. Flash drives plug into USB ports. Flash memory cards let you transfer digital data between your computer and devices such as digital cameras, smartphones, video cameras, and printers.

**8. How are devices connected to the computer?**

There are a wide variety of ports that allow you to hook up peripheral devices (such as your monitor and keyboard) to your system.

The most common type of port used to connect devices to a computer is the USB port. USB technology has replaced serial ports and parallel ports, which are now considered legacy technology. USB 2.0 is the current standard but will be quickly replaced by the newer, faster USB 3.0 standard. FireWire ports provide additional options for data transfer.

Connectivity ports, including Ethernet ports and modem ports, give you access to networks and the Internet and enable your computer to function as a fax machine. Multimedia ports include VGA, DVI, and S-video ports. They connect the computer to monitors and other multimedia devices. Audio ports are where you connect headphones, microphones, and speakers to the computer. HDMI ports are used as a connection between monitors, TVs, and gaming consoles and work with both audio and video content.

**9. How do I set up my computer to avoid strain and injury?**

*Ergonomics* refers to how you arrange your computer and equipment to minimize your risk of injury or discomfort. This includes positioning your monitor correctly, buying an adjustable chair that ensures you have good posture while using the computer, assuming a proper position while typing, making sure the lighting is adequate, and not looking at the screen for long periods of time. Other good practices include taking frequent breaks and using other specially designed equipment such as ergonomic keyboards. Ergonomics is also important to consider when using mobile devices.

 **Companion Website**

The Companion Website includes a variety of additional materials to help you review and learn more about the topics in this chapter. Go to: *www.pearsonhighered.com/techinaction*

## Word Bank

- CPU
- DVI
- ergonomics
- external hard drive
- FireWire
- inkjet printer
- laser printer

- LED
- microphone
- monitor
- mouse
- notebook
- optical mouse
- QWERTY

- RAM
- ROM
- speakers
- SSD
- system unit
- USB
- webcam

**Instructions:** Fill in the blanks using the words from the Word Bank above.

Jackie had been getting a sore back and stiff arms when she sat at her desk, so she redesigned the (1) _____ of her notebook setup. She placed the notebook in a stand so the (2) _____ was elevated to eye level and was 25 inches from her eyes. She decided to improve her equipment in other ways. Her (3) _____ was old, so she replaced it with a wireless (4) _____ that didn't need a mouse pad. To plug in the wireless receiver, she used a(n) (5) _____ port on the front of her (6) _____. She considered buying a larger (7) _____ keyboard with a number pad so she could more easily input numeric data. Because she often printed papers for her classes, Jackie decided to buy a printer that could print text-based pages quickly. Although she decided to keep her (8) _____ to print photos, she decided to buy a new (9) _____ to print her papers faster. While looking at printers, Jackie also noticed widescreen (10) _____ monitors that would provide a larger display than that on her notebook, so she bought one on sale. She hooked up the monitor to the (11) _____ port on the back of the notebook. Jackie also bought a(n) (12) _____ that was attached to a headset and a(n) (13) _____ so she could talk to her friends over the Internet. Jackie also knew she had to buy a(n) (14) _____ to back up all her files. Finally, knowing her system could use more memory, Jackie checked out prices for additional (15) _____.

There is such a variety of computers on the market today. Each type of device satisfies a different need—for example, a notebook computer is good for those who do not want to be tied down to working in one spot, while netbook computers are also great mobile devices, but their diminutive size may be a limiting factor for some users.

**Instructions:** Create a presentation that details the differences between all-in-one, desktop, notebook, tablet PC, tablet, and netbook computers. Include the pros and cons of each device, and list what kind of users may benefit from using each device. You should also incorporate images for each device. You may use the Internet for information, device pictures, and illustrations, but remember to credit all sources.

**Instructions:** Answer the multiple-choice and true–false questions below for more practice with key terms and concepts from this chapter.

## Multiple Choice

**1.** What is a gigabyte?
   a. one million bytes
   b. one billion bytes
   c. one billion bits
   d. one trillion bits

**2.** The type of computer that might help run your refrigerator or car is
   a. a mainframe computer.
   b. a supercomputer.
   c. an embedded computer.
   d. none of the above.

**3.** What enables your computer to connect with other computers?
   a. expansion card
   b. adapter card
   c. video card
   d. network interface card

**4.** Which is NOT a built-in input device for a notebook?
   a. trackpoint
   b. touch pad
   c. optical mouse
   d. none of the above

**5.** To add ports to your computer, what do you need?
   a. a digital media card reader
   b. an external hard drive
   c. an expansion card
   d. a flash memory card

**6.** Which holds the instructions the computer needs to start up?
   a. CPU     c. USB
   b. RAM     d. ROM

**7.** Which is TRUE about mainframe computers?
   a. They perform complex calculations rapidly.
   b. They support hundreds of users simultaneously.
   c. They execute many programs at a fast pace.
   d. They excel at running a few programs quickly.

**8.** Which is NOT important to consider when buying a printer?
   a. paper
   b. duty cycle
   c. cost of consumables
   d. resolution

**9.** Which type of microphone is best for recording a single voice?
   a. omnidirectional
   b. bidirectional
   c. unidirectional
   d. all of the above

**10.** What type of storage device can you use to transfer digital data between your computer and devices such as digital cameras?
   a. flash memory card
   b. optical drive
   c. connectivity port
   d. HDMI port

## True-False

_____ 1. Data and information are interchangeable terms.

_____ 2. The hard drive is an example of a nonvolatile storage device.

_____ 3. Ergonomics is important only with desktop computers, not mobile devices.

_____ 4. LED and LCD monitors are considered legacy technology.

_____ 5. The clock speed of the CPU is the only measure of a processor's expected performance.

1. **Study Abroad**

   You are preparing for your semester abroad in an immersion program in France. All the work you turn in will be written in French. Investigate the differences between a keyboard that you'd use in France and a traditional American English keyboard. What options do you have to incorporate an international keyboard into your notebook computer?

2. **Watching Device Demos**

   YouTube is a great resource for product demonstrations. Open your browser, navigate to the YouTube Web site (**www.youtube.com**), and search on any type of computer peripheral discussed in this chapter to see if you can find a demonstration of a cool product.

   How helpful are these demonstrations? Make a video demonstration of a computing device you have and post it to your course management system, or present it to your classmates (as specified by your instructor).

3. **Communicating with the Computer**

   You are involved in many group projects at school. Between your work, your classes, and other outside responsibilities, you are finding it difficult to always meet in person. Investigate the devices you would need to be able to have virtual group meetings.

4. **Turn Your Monitor into a TV**

   You've heard how easy it is to convert an LCD monitor into a TV. Your parents just bought a new computer and are giving you their old PC monitor. You need a new TV for your dorm room, so you decide to give it a try.

   a. What does your monitor need to retrofit it into a TV? What other devices do you need?
   b. How much will it cost? How much do new LCD TVs cost?
   c. Is this something you would consider doing? Why or why not?
   d. What would you do if your parents gave you their old LCD TV? Could you turn it into a monitor? If so, what would you need to do that?

5. **Green Computing**

   Reducing energy consumption and promoting the recycling of computer components are key aspects of many businesses' "green" (environmentally friendly) initiatives. Using the Web, research the following:

   a. What are the key attributes of the Energy Star and EPEAT Gold green PC certifications? Does your PC have these certifications?
   b. What toxic components are contained in computers and monitors? Where can you recycle computers and monitors in your area?
   c. Check out **www.goodcleantech.com** and find out which companies are currently working toward better green technology. If your school had to replace computers in a lab, which environmentally friendly company would you recommend? Why?

### 1. Backing up Your Work

You have embarked on a position as a freelance editor. You will be using your own computer. Until now you have not worried too much about backing up your data. Now, however, it's extremely important that you back up all your work frequently.

Research the various backup options that are available including online backup, external hard drives, and portable flash storage. What are the size limitations of each? What are the initial and ongoing costs of each? How frequently do the various options allow you to perform backups? Which option would you would choose, and why?

### 2. What Hardware Will You Use?

When you arrive at a new position for a company, your employer will most likely provide you with a computer. Based on the career you are in now or are planning to pursue, answer the following questions:

a. What kind of computer system would the company mostly likely provide to you—desktop, notebook, tablet PC, or something else? How does that compare with the type of system you would prefer to work with?
b. If you were required to use a type of computer you had never used before (such as a Mac instead of a PC), how would you go about learning to use the new computer?
c. What other devices might your employer provide? Consider such items as smartphones or printers. How important is it for these devices to conform to the latest trends?
d. Should you be able to use employer-provided equipment, such as a smartphone, for personal benefit? Does your answer differ if you have to pay for part or all of the device?

### 3. Exploring Monitors

You have been asked to help edit video for a friend. You have a great notebook computer, which is powerful enough to handle this type of task, but you need to buy a separate LCD monitor to hook up to your computer and are not exactly sure what to buy. You know it should be larger than 15 inches, capable of displaying HD, and can't cost more than $200.

a. Research five different monitors that would fit your needs. Create a table that lists each monitor and its specifications, including display type, screen size, aspect ratio, native resolution, and response time. Also list the types of ports and connectors the monitor has.
b. Note whether each monitor has HDMI. Why would HDMI capability be important or not important?
c. Research two LED monitors. Would an LED monitor be a viable option? Explain.
d. Explain which of the five monitors would best suit your needs and why.

### 4. Communications Devices

You have been assigned to create podcasts for the department in which you work. The podcasts will involve interviews and personal reflections, as well as capturing sound from groups of people. Investigate the best microphones for these jobs. Which type of microphone would work best for each type of function? Is there a microphone that could be used for all needs? If so, which one? Would buying one microphone be more economical than buying three different mics? Why or why not?

### 5. Choosing the Best Laser Printer

You are looking to replace your inkjet printer with a laser printer. You haven't decided whether a color laser printer is necessary.

a. What are the cost considerations between getting a laser printer and a color laser printer (i.e., initial costs, costs of cartridges, and so on)?
b. Investigate wireless and Bluetooth options. What are the considerations involved with regard to these features?
c. Investigate all-in-one laser printers that have printer, scanner, and fax capabilities. How much more expensive are they than laser printers? Are there any drawbacks to these multi-purpose machines? Do they perform each function as well as their stand-alone counterparts do? Can you print in color on these machines?

Based on your research, which printer would be your choice, and why?

**Instructions:** Some ideas are best understood by experimenting with them in our own minds. The following critical thinking questions are designed to demand your full attention but require only a comfortable chair—no technology.

### 1. Computer of the Future

Think about how mobile our computing devices have become and the convergence of different devices such as cameras, phones, and computers. What do you think the computer of the future will be like? What capabilities will it have that computers currently don't have? Do you see desktop computers becoming obsolete in the near future?

### 2. Table Monitors and Surface Monitors

Table monitors and surface monitors are tabletop devices that are designed to "grab" and manipulate objects on the display. Like an iPod Touch or iPhone, the display is multi-touch and can accept simultaneous input from multiple users, so the table monitor can be helpful with games or other products that require interactivity. Microsoft launched a product called Surface in 2007, and although it never really took off, you see similar devices featured on some TV crime-fighting shows as detectives manipulate crime evidence and photos. Why do you think this device never really captured the interest of the public? Would this be a useful object to have in your home, classroom, or office? Why or why not?

### 3. External Storage

Hard drives are great for storing data and information on your computer, but there are many reasons why you might want to have alternate storage devices. List various external and mobile storage devices that are discussed in this chapter, and describe the purposes and uses of each one. Note which of these device types you currently use, and for what purpose. Note also the device(s) you might have a need to use in the next year or so.

### 4. Ethics Violations

Review the Ethics piece in this chapter. Which of the Ten Commandments of Ethical Computing do you think your classmates have violated? Why do you think these violations occur, and what do you think could be done to reduce or eliminate such unethical behaviors?

### 5. "Smart" Cars

Cars are becoming more technically advanced every day. They are now able to parallel park by themselves, avoid collisions, alert you if you are falling asleep at the wheel, provide emergency response, and sense if you are going to back up over something inadvertently. What other technical advances do you see cars incorporating? Do you think that any of these current or potential advancements could result in unexpected negative consequences? If so, what?

### 6. iPad

The Apple iPad has been enthusiastically accepted because of its multi-touch screen, useful applications, and small, light frame. The iPad 2 includes two cameras, but it is without certain features that might make it even better. If Steven Jobs, the CEO of Apple, were to ask you for your advice as to what to include in the next version of the iPad, what would you suggest?

team time

# Which Mobile Device Is the Best?

## Problem

You have joined a small business that is beginning to evaluate its technology setup. Because of the addition of several new sales representatives and other administrative employees, many new computers need to be purchased. You are trying to decide which mobile devices would be better to purchase: notebook computers, tablet PCs, tablet computers (iPads), or a combination of these devices.

## Task

Split your class into small groups, divide each group into three teams, and assign the following tasks:

> Member A explores the benefits and downfalls of notebook computers.
> Member B explores the benefits and downfalls of tablet PCs.
> Member C explores the benefits and downfalls of tablet computers.

## Process

1. Form the teams. Think about what the technology goals are for the company and what information and resources you need to tackle this project.
2. Research and then discuss the components of each system you are recommending. Are any components better suited for the particular needs of certain types of employees (sales representatives versus administrative staff)? Consider all the input, output, processing, and storage devices. Are any special devices or peripherals required?
3. Consider the different types of employees in the company. Would a combination of devices be better than a single solution? If so, what kinds of employees would get which type of computer?
4. As a team, write a summary position paper. Support your system recommendation for the company. Each team member should include why his or her type of computer will be part of the solution or not.

## Conclusion

Notebooks, tablet PCs, and tablet computers have their own merits as computing systems. Being aware of the options in the marketplace, knowing how to analyze the trade-offs of different designs, and recognizing the different needs each type fulfills allows you to become a better consumer as well as a better computer user.

# Green Computing

Ethical conduct is a stream of decisions you make all day long. In this exercise, you will research and then role-play a complicated ethical situation. The role you play may or may not match your own personal beliefs but your research and use of logic will enable you to represent whichever view is assigned. An arbitrator will watch and comment on both sides of the arguments, and together the team will agree on an ethical solution.

Green computing—conducting computing needs with the least possible amount of power—is on everyone's minds. Although it's hard to argue with an environmentally conscious agenda, the pinch to our pocketbooks and the loss of some comforts sometimes makes green computing difficult. Businesses, including colleges, need to consider a variety of issues and concerns before jumping into a complete green overhaul.

## Research Areas to Consider

- End-of-life management: E-waste and recycling
- Energy-efficient devices
- Costs of green computing
- Government funding and incentives

## Process

Divide the class into teams.

1. Research the areas cited above and devise a scenario in which your college is considering modifying its current technology setup to a more green IT strategy.
2. Team members should write a summary that provides background information for their character—for example, environmentalist, college IT administrator, or arbitrator—and details their character's behaviors to set the stage for the role-playing event. Then, team members should create an outline to use during the role-playing event.
3. Team members should arrange a mutually convenient time to meet for the exchange, using the chat room feature of MyITLab, the discussion board feature of Blackboard, or meeting in person.
4. Team members should present their case to the class or submit a PowerPoint presentation for review by the rest of the class, along with the summary and resolution they developed.

## Conclusion

As technology becomes ever more prevalent and integrated into our lives, more and more ethical dilemmas will present themselves. Being able to understand and evaluate both sides of the argument, while responding in a personally or socially ethical manner, will be an important skill.

# chapter 3

# understanding and assessing hardware:
## evaluating your system

### Your Ideal Computer

**OBJECTIVE:**
How can I determine whether I should upgrade my existing computer or buy a new one? *(p. 84)*

### Evaluating the CPU Subsystem

**OBJECTIVE:**
What does the CPU do, and how can I evaluate its performance? *(p. 88)*

### Evaluating the Memory Subsystem: RAM

**OBJECTIVE:**
How does memory work in my computer, and how can I evaluate how much memory I need? *(p. 92)*

 Sound Byte: Using Windows 7 to Evaluate CPU Performance

 Active Helpdesk: Evaluating Your CPU and RAM

 Sound Byte: Memory Hierarchy Interactive

 Sound Byte: Installing RAM

### Evaluating the Storage Subsystem

**OBJECTIVE:**
What are the computer's storage devices, and how can I evaluate whether they match my needs? *(p. 95)*

 Sound Byte: Optical Media Reading and Writing Interactive
Sound Byte: Installing a Blu-ray Drive

### Evaluating the Video and Audio Subsystems

**OBJECTIVES:**
What components affect the quality of video on my computer, and how do I know if I need better video performance? *(p. 101)*

What components affect my computer's sound quality? *(p. 105)*

 Active Helpdesk: Evaluating Computer System Components

### Evaluating System Reliability and Making the Final Decision

**OBJECTIVE:**
How can I improve the reliability of my system? *(p. 107)*

# how cool is *this?*

It used to be that the case for a desktop computer was just a boring rectangular box—but no longer! Consider some of the new designs on the market. On the **Phobos** computer system by BFG Technologies, the front of the case features a **touch-panel LCD** that reports system performance parameters, controls music content, and presents a summary of storage and memory usage. There is also an integrated iPod/iPhone **docking station** on the top of the case. Or consider Falcon Northwest, which delivers **custom paint** jobs on its system cases—images from its library, your own image, or even a screen from your favorite game.

The Thermaltake Level 10 wins for pure **artistry**. It isolates all the major subsections—motherboard, power supply, hard drives, optical drives—in a separate physical space. Each section is hinged and can swing open for easy access. Made of aluminum, the entire case helps disperse heat . . . and looks cool doing it!

© Hugh Threlfall / Alamy

*Scan here for more info on How Cool Is This?*

# Your Ideal Computer

It can be hard to know if your computer is the best match for your needs. New technologies emerge so quickly, and it might be hard to decide if these are expensive extras or tools you would use. Do you need to be able to burn a Blu-ray Disc? Is a webcam really going to improve how you use your computer? Doesn't it always seem like your friend's computer is faster than yours anyway?

Maybe you could get more out of newer technologies, but should you upgrade the system you have or buy a new machine? In this chapter we'll begin by helping you design the optimal system for your needs. Then we'll examine all the subsystems of a computer and learn how to evaluate their performance and what upgrades are easily available to help you end up with a system you just love.

**What if I always struggle to get things done on my computer?** Do you ever wonder whether your computer is fine and you just need more training to get it to work smoothly? Or do you need a more sophisticated computer system? In this chapter we'll start by determining whether your current computer is meeting your needs. We'll begin by figuring out what you want your ideal computer to be able to do. You'll then learn more about important components of your computer—its CPU, memory, storage devices, and audio and video devices—and how these components affect system performance. Along the way, you'll find worksheets to help you conduct a system evaluation, and multimedia Sound Bytes that will show you how to upgrade various components in your system. You'll also learn about the many utilities available to help speed up and clean up your system. If it's time for you to buy a new computer, this chapter will provide you with important information you will need about computer hardware to make an informed purchasing decision.

**When is the best time to buy a new computer?** There never seems to be a perfect time to buy. It seems that if you can just wait a year, computers will inevitably be faster and cost less. Is this actually true?

As it turns out, it is true. In fact, a rule of thumb often cited in the computer industry, called **Moore's Law**, describes the pace at which CPUs (central processing units)—the small chips that can be thought of as the "brains" of the computer—improve. Named for Gordon Moore, the cofounder of the CPU chip manufacturer Intel, this rule predicts that the number of transistors inside a CPU will increase so fast that CPU capacity will double every 18 months. (The number of transistors on a CPU chip helps determine how fast it can process data.)

As you can see in Figure 3.1, this rule of thumb has held true for over 45 years. Imagine finding a bank that would agree to treat your money in this way. If you put 10 cents in that kind of savings account in 1965, you would have a balance of more than $800 million today! Moore himself, however, has predicted that around the year 2020 CPU chips will be manufactured in a different way, thus changing or eliminating the effects of Moore's Law altogether.

In addition to the CPU becoming faster, other system components also continue to improve dramatically. For example, the capacity of memory chips such as dynamic random access memory (DRAM)—the most common form of memory found in personal computers—increases about 60 percent every year. Meanwhile, hard drives have been growing in storage capacity by some 50 percent each year.

**So should I be buying a new computer every year?** No one wants to spend money every year just to keep up with technology. Even if money weren't a consideration, the time it would take to

**Figure 3.1**

Moore's Law predicts that CPUs will continue to get faster.

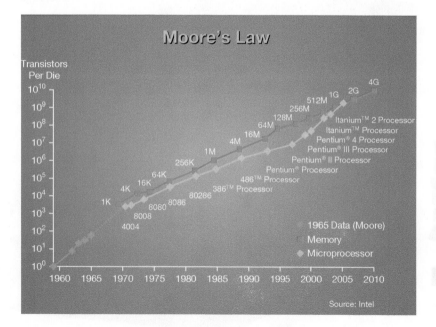

transfer all of your files and reinstall and reconfigure your software would make buying a new computer every year terribly inefficient. Landfills would be overflowing with tossed aside older equipment. Extending the life of a computer reduces the environmental and security concerns involved in the disposal of computers.

No one wants to keep doing costly upgrades that won't significantly extend the life of a system, either. How can you determine if your system is suitable or if it needs to be upgraded? Moreover, how can you know which is the better option—upgrading or buying a new computer? The first step is figuring out what you want your computer to do for you.

**But what if I'm just buying my first computer?** Even if you're a new computer user, you will still need to evaluate what you want your system to do for you before you buy. Being able to understand and evaluate computer systems will make you a more informed buyer. You will be comfortable answering questions like "What kinds of CPUs are there?" "How does the CPU affect system performance?" and "How much RAM do I need?"

**OK, how do I know what my ideal system is?** Consider what you want to be able to do with your computer. For example, do you need to bring your computer to school or work with you? Do you want to be able to edit digital photos and video? Do you want to watch and record Blu-ray Discs? Or do you mainly use your computer for word processing and Internet access? The worksheet in Figure 3.2 lists a number of ways in which you may want to use your computer. In the second column, place a check next to those computer uses that apply to you. Also, set a priority of high (1), medium (2), or low (3) in the rightmost column so that you can determine which features are most important to you.

Next, look at the list of desired uses for your computer and determine whether your current system can perform these activities. If there are things it can't do, you may need to purchase additional hardware or a new computer. For example, if you plan to edit digital video files or play games that require high video frame rates for smooth in-game motion, you may need to add more memory and upgrade your video card. Depending on the costs of the individual upgrade components, you may be better off buying a new system.

**Should that system come as a notebook or a desktop?** In this discussion, we'll only be considering full-size desktops and notebooks. If your main need is light weight and great portability, a netbook or a tablet may be a workable option. Netbooks and tablets are discussed in detail in Chapter 5.

To make the best decision, it's important to evaluate where you will use the computer. The main distinction between desktops and notebooks is portability. If you indicated in Figure 3.2 that you need to take your computer with you to work or school, or even want the flexibility to move from room to room in your house, a notebook is the best choice. If portability is not an absolute requirement, you should consider a desktop.

**How does a notebook compare to a desktop for value?** Desktop systems are invariably a better value than notebooks in terms of computing power gained for your dollar. Because of the notebook's small footprint (the amount of space it takes up), you pay more for each component. Each piece has had extra engineering time invested to make sure it fits in the smallest space. In addition, a desktop system offers more expandability options. It's easier to add new ports and devices because of the amount of room available in the desktop computer's design.

If a large monitor is important, desktops have an edge. Although 18-inch screens are now available on some notebooks, the weight of these systems (often more than 10 pounds) makes them really more of a "desktop replacement" than a portable computing solution. Light notebooks typically have 17-inch screens or smaller, while inexpensive 24-inch monitors are readily available for desktop solutions. If you need a large screen and portability, you may end up buying a notebook and a fixed desk monitor to connect to when you are at home, an extra cost.

Desktop systems also are more reliable. Because of the amount of vibration that a notebook experiences and the added exposure to dust, water, and temperature fluctuations that portability brings, notebooks often have a shorter lifespan than desktop computers. Manufacturers offer extended warranty plans that cover accidental damage and unexpected drops; however, such plans may be costly.

## Figure 3.2 | WHAT SHOULD YOUR IDEAL COMPUTER SYSTEM BE ABLE TO DO?

| Computer Uses | Have It | Want It! | Priority (High, Medium, Low) |
|---|---|---|---|
| **Portability Uses** | | | |
| Be light enough to carry easily | | | |
| Access the Internet wirelessly | | | |
| Print wirelessly | | | |
| Long battery life | | | |
| **Entertainment Uses** | | | |
| Play and record CDs and DVDs | | | |
| Play and record Blu-ray Discs | | | |
| Record and edit digital videos | | | |
| Record and edit digital music | | | |
| Capture and edit digital photos | | | |
| Play graphics-intensive games | | | |
| Show video across multiple monitors | | | |
| Transfer files wirelessly to mobile devices and other computers | | | |
| Transfer files using flash memory cards | | | |
| Upload media to social networking sites | | | |
| Have your peripheral devices work easily and speedily with your computer | | | |
| Purchase/rent music and videos from the Internet | | | |
| Talk with friends and family with live video and audio | | | |
| Stream television and movies | | | |
| Other | | | |
| **Educational Uses** | | | |
| Perform word processing tasks | | | |
| Use educational software | | | |
| Access library archives and subscribe to e-zines | | | |
| Create multimedia presentations | | | |
| Create backups of all your files | | | |
| Record notes with synchronized audio recordings | | | |
| Other | | | |
| **Business Uses** | | | |
| Create spreadsheets and databases | | | |
| Work on multiple software applications quickly and simultaneously | | | |
| Conduct online banking, pay bills online, or prepare your taxes | | | |
| Conduct online job searches or post résumés | | | |
| Synchronize your mobile device (phone/media player) with your computer | | | |
| Conduct online meetings with video and audio | | | |
| Organize business contacts and manage scheduling | | | |
| Other | | | |

**How long will a notebook be useful to me?** The answer to that question depends on how easy it is to upgrade your system. Take note of the maximum amount of memory you can install in your notebook because that cannot be changed a few years down the road. Internal hard drives are not easy for novices to install in a notebook, but by using a fast transfer port on your notebook, you can easily add an external hard drive for more storage space.

Notebooks are often equipped with an **ExpressCard** slot. ExpressCards (shown in Figure 3.3) can add a solid-state drive (SSD), eSATA and FireWire ports, and other capabilities to your system. You can add an ExpressCard that allows you to read flash memory cards such as Compact-Flash, Memory Sticks, and Secure Digital cards. As new types of ports and devices are introduced, like those for the USB 3.0 standard, they are manufactured in ExpressCard formats so you can make sure your notebook does not become obsolete before its time. Figure 3.4 summarizes the advantages and disadvantages of each style of computer.

**How am I going to learn to use my new system?** Of course, college courses like this one are a great idea! Colleges offer a number of other training options including online modules and weekend workshops. In addition, many online tutorials are available for software products. For specific questions or skills, be sure to check YouTube, iTunes U, and other podcast directories. Valuable series exist that answer your questions in step-by-step video demonstrations, such as MrExcel or Photoshop Quicktips. Some manufacturers, like Apple, offer classes at their stores for a yearly fee. Training shouldn't be an

afterthought. Consider the time and effort involved in learning about what you want your computer to do before you buy hardware or software.

**How can I turn my list into the exact system specifications?** Now that you have a better idea of your ideal computer system, you can make a more informed assessment of your current computer. To determine whether your computer system has the right hardware components to do what you ultimately want it to do, you need to conduct a **system evaluation**. To do this, you look at your computer's subsystems, see what they do, and check how they perform.

The following sections will examine each subsystem. At the end of each section, you'll find a small worksheet you can use

**Figure 3.3**
ExpressCards add functionality to your notebook.

**BITS AND BYTES**

## Moving to a New Computer Doesn't Have to Be Painful

Are you ready to buy a new computer but dread the prospect of transferring all your files and redoing all of your Windows settings? You could transfer all those files and settings manually, but Windows stores much information in the registry files, which can be tricky to update. So what do you do? Windows 7 incorporates Windows Easy Transfer, which lets you migrate files and settings from a Windows Vista system to a Windows 7 system via a network connection by using a flash drive or external hard drive or using optical media.

Alternatively, other PC migration software is available, such as Laplink's PC-mover, which is designed to make the transition to a new computer easier. For the latest information on such utilities, search for migration software online. You'll be ready to upgrade painlessly in no time. If you prefer to avoid the do-it-yourself option, support technicians at retail stores (such as the Geek Squad at Best Buy) will often perform the migration for a small charge.

**Figure 3.4** | DESKTOP VERSUS NOTEBOOK COMPUTERS—WHICH FITS YOU?

| Notebooks | Desktops |
|---|---|
| Portable: lightweight, thin | Best value: more processing power, memory, and storage capacity for lower price |
| Take up less physical space | More difficult to steal, less susceptible to damage from dropping or mishandling |
| Easier to ship or transport if the system needs repair | Easier to expand and upgrade |
| Smaller video display (18 inches or smaller) | Large monitors available (24 inches or larger) |

## Taking Your System Out of the Box

You just brought your brand-new machine home, and it's loaded up with all kinds of bloat! Here are two steps you can take right away to replace that bloat with truly useful software so you have the fresh beginning you were hoping for.

1. Remove the preinstalled trial programs and advertisements installed by most vendors. A quick way to do this is with the free program PC Decrapifier. Its wizard walks you through uninstalling the most common annoyances that came preloaded on your new system.

2. Grab the really valuable free software you will want to use. Consider loading OpenOffice.org, Firefox, Chrome, iTunes, Picasa, and Gimp. (These packages are discussed in more detail in the Technology in Focus section titled "Computing Alternatives.")

Now go enjoy your new machine!

to evaluate each subsystem on your computer. *Note:* This chapter discusses tools you can use to assess a Windows-based PC.

# Evaluating the CPU Subsystem

Let's start by considering the type of processor in your system. As mentioned in Chapter 2, your computer's central processing unit (CPU or processor) is critically important because it processes instructions, performs calculations, and manages the flow of

© 4kodiak/istockphoto.com

Sony Electronics Inc.

**Figure 3.5**

(a) The Intel i7 is the most advanced desktop CPU ever made by Intel. (b) The PlayStation 3 gaming console uses the Cell Broadband Engine to compute 230 billion floating point calculations per second (gigaflops).

information through a computer system. The CPU is responsible for turning raw data into valuable information through processing operations. The CPU is located on the motherboard, the primary circuit board of the computer system. There are several types of processors on the market including Intel processors (such as the Core family with the i7, i5,

i3, and the Centrino line) and AMD processors (such as the Athlon II and Phenom X4). The Intel Core i7 is the most advanced desktop CPU made by Intel. Figure 3.5 shows the i7 as well as the Cell Broadband Engine used in the PlayStation 3.

**How does the CPU work?** The CPU is composed of two units: the control unit and the arithmetic logic unit (ALU). The control unit coordinates the activities of all the other computer components. The ALU is responsible for performing all the arithmetic calculations (addition, subtraction, multiplication, and division). It also makes logic and comparison decisions such as comparing items to determine if one is greater than, less than, equal to, or not equal to another.

Every time the CPU performs a program instruction, it goes through the same series of steps. First, it *fetches* the required piece of data or instruction from RAM, the temporary storage location for all the data and instructions the computer needs while it is running. Next, it *decodes* the instruction into something the computer can understand. Once the CPU has decoded the instruction, it *executes* the instruction and *stores* the result to RAM before fetching the next instruction. This process is called a machine cycle. (We discuss the machine cycle in more detail in the Technology in Focus feature "Under the Hood" on page 122.) **What makes one CPU different from another?** The primary distinction between CPUs is processing power, which is determined by a number of factors:

- Number of cores
- Clock speed
- Amount of cache memory
- Front side bus performance

A **core** is a complete processing section from a CPU embedded into one physical chip. The **clock speed** of the CPU dictates how many instructions the CPU can finish in one second. The CPU's **cache memory** is a form of random access memory that can be reached much more quickly than regular RAM. The **front side bus (FSB)** is the main path for data movement within the system, carrying data from the CPU to memory, the video card, and other components on the motherboard.

**How does a multi-core CPU help me?** If you had a clone of yourself sitting next to you working, you could get twice as much done, and that is the idea of multi-core processing. CPUs began to execute more than one instruction at a time quite a while ago, when hyperthreading was introduced. **Hyperthreading** provides quicker processing of information by enabling a new set of instructions to start executing before the previous set has finished. The most recent design innovation for PC processors, an improvement upon hyperthreading, is the use of *multiple cores* on one CPU chip. With multiple core technology, two or more processors reside on the same chip, enabling the execution of two sets of instructions at the same time. Applications that are always running behind the scenes, such as virus protection software and your operating system, can have their own processor, freeing the other processor to run other applications such as a Web browser, Word, or iTunes more efficiently.

In Figure 3.6c, hyperthreading allows two different programs to be processed at one time, but they are sharing the computing resources of the chip. With multiple cores, each program has the full attention of its own processing core (see Figures 3.6a and 6.6b). This results in faster processing and smoother multitasking. It is possible to design a CPU to have multiple cores *and* hyperthreading. The Intel i7-990X has six cores, each one using hyperthreading, so it simulates having twelve processors!

**How does a CPU with a faster processor speed help me?** Each CPU is designed to run at a specific processing speed. The faster the clock speed, the more quickly the next instruction is processed. CPUs currently have clock speeds running between 2.1 GHz and 4 GHz (billions of steps per second). Some users even push their hardware to perform faster, overclocking their processor. Overclocking means that you run the CPU at a faster speed than

the manufacturer recommends. It produces more heat, meaning a shorter lifetime for the CPU, and usually voids any warranty.

**How does more cache memory help me?** Although clock speed is an important consideration when determining processor performance, CPU performance also is affected by the amount of cache memory. Because of its ready access to the CPU, cache memory gets data to the CPU for processing much faster than bringing the data in from RAM.

There are several levels of cache memory. These levels are defined by a chip's proximity to the CPU. Level 1 cache is a block of memory that is built onto the CPU chip itself for the storage of data or commands that have just been used. Level 2 cache is located on the CPU chip but is slightly farther away from the CPU, or it's on a separate chip next to the CPU and therefore takes somewhat longer to access. Level 2 cache contains more storage area than does level 1 cache. In the same way, some chips continue on to have a third cache, Level 3. Again, this level of cache is slower for the CPU to reach but larger in size.

**How does the front side bus impact performance?** The front side bus connects the processor (CPU) in your

**Four cores**
Intel® CORE i7
a

**Two cores**
Intel® CORE i5
b

**Hyperthreading**
Intel® Pentium®
c

**Figure 3.6**

(a) Some Intel processors have four cores able to run four programs simultaneously. (b) Some Intel processors have two cores. (c) The Intel Pentium 4 Hyperthreading operates with only one core, but it hyperthreads (working on two processes at once).

**Figure** 3.7 | PROCESSOR SPECIFICATIONS

| | Model | Number of Cores | Max Clock Speed | Max FSB | Max L3 Cache |
|---|---|---|---|---|---|
| Desktop Processors | i3-2100T | 2 | 2.50 GHz | 1333 MHz | 3 MB |
| | i5-2500 | 4 | 3.30 GHz | 1333 MHz | 6 MB |
| | i7-990X | 6 | 3.46 GHz | 1600 MHz | 12 MB |
| Notebook Processors | i3-380UM | 2 | 1.33 GHz | 800 MHz | 3 MB |
| | i5 Mobile 2410M | 2 | 2.30 GHz | 1333 MHz | 3 MB |
| | i7 Mobile 2920XM | 4 | 2.50 GHz | 1600 MHz | 8 MB |

**Figure** 3.8

The System Properties window identifies which CPU you have, as well as its speed.

>Click the **Start** button and then click **Computer** on the right panel of the **Start** menu. On the top toolbar, click **System Properties**.

computer to the system memory. Think of the front side bus as the highway on which data travels between the CPU and RAM. The total number of cars that whiz by in one minute would depend on the number of lanes of highway and the speed of the cars. Similarly, the throughput of the FSB depends on how much data it transfers per cycle (bytes) and its clock frequency (Hz). The faster the FSB is, the faster you can get data to your processor. The faster you get data to the processor, the faster your processor can work on it.

**How do I shop for a CPU?** Modern processors are defined by the combination of the number of cores, the processor speed, the front side bus performance, and the amount of cache memory. For example, Intel has several processor families, in a range of clock speeds, cache memory sizes, and FSB speeds, as shown in Figure 3.7. Even within the same processor family, though, there is a variety of choices. For example, the i7-990X

processor has six cores and a 12 MB cache, whereas the i7-860S processor has four cores and an 8 MB L3 cache.

Because so many factors influence CPU design, picking the fastest CPU for the kind of work you do involves researching performance benchmarks. **CPU benchmarks** are measurements used to compare performance between processors. Benchmarks are generated by running software programs specifically designed to push the limits of CPU performance. Articles are often published comparing a number of chips, or complete systems, based on their benchmark performance. Investigate a few, using sites like **www.cpubenchmark.net**, before you select the chip that is best for you.

**Why are there different CPU choices for notebooks and desktops?** Both Intel and AMD make processors that are specifically designed for notebook computers. Notebook processors not only need to perform quickly and efficiently, like their desktop counterparts, but also need better power savings to improve battery life. Processors used in notebooks work to combine low power consumption, to support long battery life, and more flexible wireless connectivity options. AMD features notebook processors like the Turion X2 Mobile and the AMD Mobile Sempron, while Intel has mobile versions of the i5 and i7 series.

**What CPU does my current computer have?** You can easily identify the type of CPU in your current system by accessing the System Properties. As shown in Figure 3.8, you can view basic information about your computer, including which CPU is installed in your system and its speed. More detailed information,

CPU model          CPU clock speed

like the FSB speed and the amount of cache memory, is not shown in this screen. You can find those values by checking the manufacturer's Web site for the specific model number of CPU shown. For example, the CPU illustrated here is the Intel i7, version 960.

**How can I tell whether my CPU is meeting my needs?** You can tell if your CPU speed is limiting your system performance by watching how busy the CPU is as you work. Even if your CPU meets the minimum requirements specified for a particular software application, if you're running other software at the same time, you need to check how well the CPU is handling the entire load. Keep in mind that the workload your CPU experiences will vary considerably during your work day. Even though it might run Word just fine, it may not be able to handle running Word, Photoshop, iTunes, and Movie Maker at the same time. The percentage of time that your CPU is working is referred to as **CPU usage**.

Figure 3.9 helps you evaluate the factors that determine whether your CPU is meeting your needs.

A utility that measures information such as CPU usage and RAM usage is incredibly useful, both for considering whether you should upgrade and for investigating if your computer's performance suddenly seems to drop off for no apparent reason. On Windows systems, the program Task Manager gives you easy access to all this data. Mac OS X has a similar utility named Activity Monitor, which is located in your Applications folder in the Utilities folder.

**SOUND BYTE**

**Using Windows 7 to Evaluate CPU Performance**

In this Sound Byte, you'll learn how to use the utilities provided by Windows 7 to evaluate your CPU's performance. You'll also learn about shareware utilities (software that you can install and try before you purchase it) that expand on the capabilities the Task Manager utility provides.

To use Task Manager to view information on CPU usage, right-click an empty area of the taskbar, select Start Task Manager, and click the Performance tab, as shown in Figure 3.10a. The **CPU usage graph** records your CPU usage for the past several seconds. (Note: If you have multiple cores and hyperthreading, you will see several CPU usage curves listed.) Of course, there will be periodic peaks of high CPU usage, but if you see that your CPU usage levels are greater than 90 percent during most of your work session, a faster CPU will contribute a great deal to your system's performance. If you use the Windows gadgets, you can add a CPU Meter gadget to track both CPU and RAM usage (see Figure 3.10b). To see exactly how to use the Task Manager and the CPU Meter gadgets, watch the Sound Byte "Using Windows 7 to Evaluate CPU Performance."

**Will improving the performance of the CPU be enough to improve my computer's performance?** You may think that if you have the best processor,

**Figure 3.9** | HOW IS YOUR CPU PERFORMING?

| | Current System | Dream System |
|---|---|---|
| What is my computer's CPU speed? | | |
| How much cache memory is on the CPU*? | | |
| What is the FSB speed*? | | |
| What is the benchmark score for your CPU? (try **www.cpubenchmark.net**) | | |
| What kind of multilevel processing does the CPU have—multiple cores, hyperthreaded, etc.? | | |
| Is the CPU usage value below 90% during most of my daily tasks? | | |

*You can find these numbers by checking the manufacturer's specifications for your model of CPU.

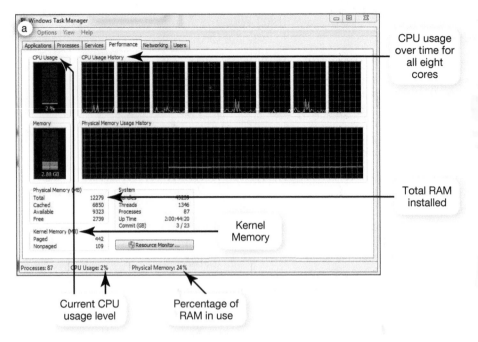

CPU usage over time for all eight cores

Total RAM installed

Kernel Memory

Current CPU usage level

Percentage of RAM in use

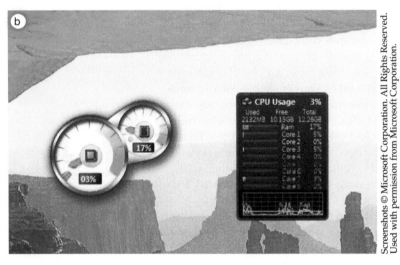

**Figure 3.10**

(a) The Performance tab of the Windows Task Manager utility shows you how busy your CPU actually is. (b) Windows gadgets let you follow CPU performance easily.

>In an empty area of the taskbar, right-click, select **Start Task Manager**, and click the **Performance** tab.

you will have the best system. However, upgrading your CPU will affect only the processing portion of the system performance, not how quickly data can move to or from the CPU. Your system's overall performance depends on many factors, including the amount of RAM installed as well as hard drive speed. Your selection of CPU may not offer significant improvements to your system's performance if there is a bottleneck in processing because of insufficient RAM or hard drive performance.

# Evaluating the Memory Subsystem: RAM

**Random access memory (RAM)** is your computer's temporary storage space. Although we refer to RAM as a form of storage, it really is the computer's short-term memory. It remembers everything that the computer needs to process the data into information, such as data that has been entered and software instructions, but only when the computer is on. RAM is an example of **volatile storage**. When the power is off, the data stored in RAM is cleared out. This is why, in addition to RAM, systems always include **nonvolatile storage** devices for permanent storage of instructions and data when the computer is powered off. ROM memory, for example, holds the critical startup instructions. Hard drives provide the largest nonvolatile storage capacity in the computer system.

**Why not use a hard drive to store the data and instructions?** It's about one million times faster for the CPU to retrieve a piece of data from RAM than from a mechanical hard drive. The time it takes the CPU to grab data from RAM is measured in nanoseconds (billionths of seconds), whereas pulling data from a fast mechanical hard drive takes an average of 10 milliseconds (ms), or thousandths of seconds. Figure 3.11 shows the various types of memory and storage that are distributed throughout your system: CPU registers, cache, RAM, and hard drives. Each of these has its own tradeoff of speed versus price. Because the fastest memory is so much more expensive, systems are designed with much less of it. This principle is influential in the design of a balanced computer system and can have a tremendous impact on system performance.

**Are there different types of RAM?** Like most computer components, RAM has gone through a series of evolutions. In current systems, the RAM used most often comes in the form of double data rate 3 (DDR3) memory modules, available in several different speeds (1066 MHz, 1333 MHz, 1600 MHz). The higher the speed the better the performance. Double data rate 5 memory (DDR5), which has an even faster data transfer rate, is seen in high-performance video graphics cards. In older systems, other types of RAM may have been used, including dynamic RAM (DRAM), static RAM (SRAM), and synchronous DRAM (SDRAM).

RAM appears in the system on **memory modules** (or **memory cards**), small circuit boards that hold a series of RAM chips and fit into special slots on the motherboard (see Figure 3.12). Most memory modules in today's systems are packaged as *dual inline memory modules* (DIMMs).

On high-end systems, manufacturers may offer an option to purchase Corsair Dominator DDR3 modules. These are tested to high levels to guarantee optimum performance. A special heat exchanger is designed into the RAM module to help it operate at a lower temperature, making it more stable and more reliable. All of these factors boost the performance of the memory and make it popular with demanding video gamers.

If you're adding RAM to any system, you must determine what type your system needs. Consult your user's manual or the system manufacturer's Web site. In addition, many online RAM resellers, such as Crucial (**www.crucial.com**), can help you determine the type of RAM that is compatible with your system by running an automated system scan program on your computer.

**How can I tell how much RAM is installed in my computer and how it's being used?** The amount of RAM that is actually sitting on memory modules in your computer is your computer's **physical memory**. The easiest way to see how much RAM you have is to look in the System Properties window. (On the Mac, choose the Apple menu and then About This Mac.) This is the same tab you looked in to determine your system's CPU type and speed, and is shown in Figure 3.8. RAM capacity is measured in gigabytes (GB), and most machines sold today, especially those running Windows, have at least 4 GB of RAM. The computer in Figure 3.13 has 12 GB of RAM installed.

Windows 7 uses a memory-management technique known as **SuperFetch**. SuperFetch monitors which applications you use the most and preloads them into your system memory so that they'll be ready to go. For example, if you have Word running, Windows 7 stores as much of the information related to Word in RAM as it can, which speeds up how fast your application

**Figure 3.11**

A computer system's memory has many different levels, ranging from the small amounts in the CPU to the much slower but more plentiful storage of a mechanical hard drive.

**Figure 3.12**

A single memory module holds a series of RAM chips.

Hugh Threlfall/Alamy

**Figure 3.13**

The Resource Monitor's Memory tab shows a detailed breakdown of how the computer is using memory.

>In the Task Manager, click the **Performance** tab, click **Resource Monitor;** and then click the **Memory** tab.

**Figure** 3.14 | SAMPLE RAM ALLOCATION

| Application | RAM Recommended |
|---|---|
| Windows 7 (64 bit) | 2 GB |
| Microsoft Office Professional 2010 | 512 MB |
| Internet Explorer 9 | 512 MB |
| iTunes 10 | 1 GB |
| Adobe Photoshop Elements 9 | 2 GB |
| Total RAM required to run all programs simultaneously | 6 GB |

responds, because pulling information from RAM is so much faster than pulling it from the hard drive. This idea of caching the data you need in RAM, having it ready to use quickly when it is asked for, is different from how memory was used in earlier operating systems. You can watch this process work using the Resource Monitor, which shows in Figure 3.13 how the 12 GB of installed RAM is being used: 3 GB is running programs, 6 GB is holding cached data and files ready for quick access, and 3 GB is currently unused.

**How much RAM do I need?** Because RAM is the temporary holding space for all the data and instructions that the computer uses while it's on, most computer users need quite a bit of RAM. As you will learn in Chapter 8, the operating system is the main software application that runs the computer. Without it, the computer does not work. At a minimum, the system needs enough RAM to run the operating system.

The memory that your operating system uses is referred to as **kernel memory**. This memory is listed in a separate Kernel Memory table in the Performance tab. In Figure 3.10, the Kernel Memory table tells you that approximately 0.55 GB (total kernel memory) of the total 12 GB of RAM is being used to run the operating system. In fact, systems running all the new features

of Windows 7 should have a minimum of 1 GB of RAM, but for peak performance, at least 2 GB of RAM is recommended. However, because you run more applications than just the operating system, you will want to have more RAM than the just enough for the OS. New systems ship with at least 4 GB and high-end systems can come with 24 GB.

To determine how much RAM you need, list all the software applications you might be running at one time. Figure 3.14 shows an example of RAM requirements. In this example, if you are running your operating system, word processing and spreadsheet programs, a Web browser, a music player, and photo editing software simultaneously, then you will need a minimum of 6 GB of RAM. It's always best to check the system requirements of any software program before you buy it to make sure your system can handle it. System requirements can be found on the software packaging or on the manufacturer's Web site.

It's a good idea to have more than the minimum amount of RAM you need now, so you can use more programs in the future. Remember, too, that "required" means these are the minimum values recommended by the manufacturers, and having more RAM often helps programs run more efficiently. When upgrading RAM, the rule of thumb is to buy as much as you can afford but certainly no more than your system will handle.

**Adding RAM**

**Is there a limit to how much RAM I can add to my computer?** Every computer has a maximum limit on the amount of RAM it can support. A motherboard is

**SOUND BYTE**

**Memory Hierarchy Interactive**

In this Sound Byte, you'll learn about the different types of memory used in a computer system.

designed with a specific number of slots into which the memory cards fit, and each slot has a limit on the amount of RAM it can hold. To determine your specific system limits, check the system manufacturer's Web site.

In addition, the operating system running on your machine imposes its own RAM limit. For example, the maximum amount of RAM for the 32-bit version of Windows 7 is 4 GB, while the maximum memory you can install using the 64-bit version of Windows 7 Ultimate is 192 GB.

Review the considerations presented in Figure 3.15 to see if your system could benefit from an upgrade of additional RAM.

**Is it difficult or expensive to add RAM?** Adding RAM to a computer is fairly easy (see Figure 3.16). Be sure that you purchase a memory module that's compatible with your computer. Typically you simply line up the notches and then gently push the memory module in place. The new RAM you buy will come with installation instructions for your particular system, so be sure to read and follow those.

RAM is a relatively inexpensive system upgrade. The cost of RAM does fluctuate in the marketplace as much as 400 percent over

**Figure 3.15** | DO YOU NEED TO UPGRADE YOUR RAM?

| | Current System | Dream System |
|---|---|---|
| What is the maximum amount of RAM my system can hold?* | | |
| How much RAM does my system have? | | |
| What is the maximum amount of RAM I need for the applications I currently run? | | |
| Would I be willing to upgrade to an operating system that supports the amount of RAM I want? | | |

*Check the manufacturer's specifications for your system.

time, though, so if you're considering adding RAM, you should watch the prices of memory in online and print advertisements.

## Evaluating the Storage Subsystem

Remember, there are two ways data is stored on your computer: temporary storage and permanent storage. RAM is a form of temporary (or volatile) storage. The information residing in RAM is not stored permanently. It's critical to have the means to store data and software applications permanently.

Fortunately, several storage options exist. Storage devices include hard drives, USB flash drives, optical drives, SSD drives, and external hard drives. When you turn off your computer, the data that has been written to these devices will be available the next time the machine is powered on. These devices provide *nonvolatile* storage.

**Figure 3.16**

Adding RAM to a computer is quite simple and relatively inexpensive. On a notebook machine you often gain access through a panel on the bottom.

Editorial Image, LLC / Alamy

Editorial Image, LLC / Alamy

# When the operating system is installed on an SSD drive, the wakeup time of the system drops to just a few seconds because of the fast access.

### Hard Drive

**What makes the hard drive the most popular storage device?** With storage capacities exceeding 4 terabytes (TB), a **hard drive** has the largest capacity of any storage device. The hard drive is also a much more economical device than other options, because it offers the most gigabytes of storage per dollar. Most system units are designed to support more than one internal hard drive. The Apple Mac Pro has room for four hard drives, and the Thermaltake Level 10 (shown in the opening How Cool Is This?) can support six hard drives. Each one simply slides into place when you want to upgrade.

**How is data stored on a hard drive?** A hard drive is composed of several coated round, thin plates of metal stacked on a spindle. Each plate is called a **platter**. When data is saved to a hard drive platter, a pattern of magnetized spots is created on the iron oxide coating of each platter. When the spots are aligned in one direction, they represent a 1; when aligned in the other direction, the represent a 0.

These 0s and 1s are bits (or binary digits) and are the smallest pieces of data that computers can understand. When data stored on the hard drive platter is retrieved (or read), your computer translates these patterns of magnetized spots into the data you have saved.

**How quickly does a hard drive find information?** The hard drive's **access time**, the time it takes a storage device to locate its stored data and make it available for processing, is faster than that of other permanent storage devices, like optical drives. Mechanical hard drive access times are measured in milliseconds (ms), meaning thousandths of seconds. For large capacity drives, access times of approximately 12–13 milliseconds are typical. That's less than one-hundredth of a second. A DVD drive can take over 150 milliseconds to access data.

**Do mechanical hard drives have the fastest access times?** Not all hard drives have mechanical motors and moving parts. A **solid-state drive (SSD)** uses the same kind of memory that flash drives use. Because no spinning platters or motors are needed, SSDs run with no noise and very little heat, and require very little power. SSDs are very popular in laptops because of their lower power consumption and quiet, cool operation. Having no mechanical motors also allows solid state drives to offer incredibly fast access times, reaching data in only a tenth of a millisecond (0.1 ms). That is about 1,000 times faster than mechanical drives!

Storage capacities for SSD drives now range up to 2 TB, but that size SSD drive is very expensive. Smaller SSDs, around 256 GB, are increasingly being used as the boot (or startup) drive. When the operating system is installed on an SSD drive, the wakeup time of the system drops to just a few seconds because of its fast access. Systems designed like this often have a mechanical hard drive, or two, to provide large amounts of inexpensive storage space.

Figure 3.17 provides a listing of the various storage options and compares their access times.

**Figure 3.17**

Access times for nonvolatile storage options.

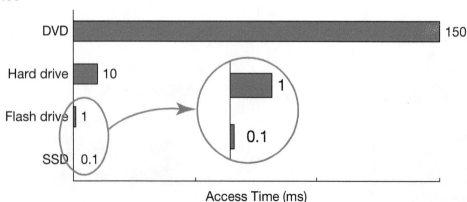

**Device**

Access Time (ms)

**How do I know how much storage capacity I have?** Typically, hard drive capacity is measured in gigabytes (GB), although hard drives with capacity in the terabytes (1 TB = 1,000 GB) are now available. Windows displays the hard drives, their capacity, and usage information, as seen in Figure 3.18. To get a slightly more detailed view, select a drive, and then right-click and choose Properties.

**How much storage do I need?** You need enough space to store the software applications you use, such as Microsoft Office, music players, and games. Then add space for all of the data files you own. If you have a large digital music library, that alone could require 30 to 50 GB. Do you keep all of your photographs on your hard drive? You may need another 40 GB or more for them. If you store digital video of television shows and movies, that could easily be 100 to 200 GB more, even higher if the videos are all high definition. Of course, the operating system also requires storage space. The demands on system requirements have grown with new versions of operating systems. Windows 7, the latest Microsoft operating system, can require up to 20 GB of available hard drive capacity, depending on the configuration. Figure 3.19 shows an example of storage calculation. If you plan to have a system backup on the same drive, be sure to budget for that room as well.

**How do hard drives connect to my system?** Internal hard drives connect using **Serial Advanced Technology Attachment (SATA)**. SATA hard drives use thin cables, and can transfer data quickly. (An older technology, Integrated Drive Electronics [IDE] was much slower.) Over 90 percent of new systems are using SATA drives now. There are currently two flavors of SATA—the original, which tranfers data at a rate of 3 gigabits per second (Gb/s) and the newer revision, which updates to a 6 Gb/s standard. If your motherboard supports the 6 Gb/s SATA, look for a hard drive that matches that data transfer rate to have the best performance. You can compare the actual data transfer rates of hard drives at sites that do performance benchmarking, like Tom's Hardware (**www.tomshardware.com**).

If you are adding an external hard drive to your system, there are two popular ports

**Figure 3.18**

In Windows, the free and used capacity of each device in the computer system are shown in the Computer window. The General tab of the Properties dialog box gives you more detailed information.

>To view the Computer window, click **Start**, and then click **Computer**. To view the pie chart, right-click the **C drive**, and select **Properties**.

to use. Many hard drives use a USB port to connect. The USB 3.0 standard is about 10 times faster than USB 2.0, so if your system supports USB 3.0 that is the better choice. Some computer systems offer an eSATA

| Figure 3.19 | SAMPLE HARD DRIVE SPACE REQUIREMENTS |
|---|---|
| **Application/Data** | **Hard Drive Space Required** |
| Windows 7 (64 bit) | 20 GB |
| Microsoft Office 2010 Professional | 3.5 GB |
| Adobe Photoshop Elements 9 | 2 GB |
| Roxio Creator 2011 | 3 GB installation space + 30 GB for working space = 33 GB |
| Video library of movies | 40 GB (about 20 HD movies) |
| Music library | 50 GB (about 7,000 songs) |
| Total storage in use | 148.5 GB |
| Full backup | 150 GB |
| Total required | 298.5 GB |

## HDTV on Your Notebook

If you are moving through your day with a notebook in tow, why not use it to pull up your favorite television shows? There are now several USB devices that allow your notebook or desktop to receive the high-definition television (HDTV) signals whizzing by in the airwaves.

Devices like the Pinnacle HDTV stick (see Figure 6.20) are USB digital TV tuners. One end plugs into any available USB port. The other end connects to the provided digital antenna. Software is included that allows you to schedule shows to record onto your hard drive, so your notebook essentially becomes a time-shifting digital video recorder. If you are at home, you can remove the antenna and connect to your home cable television signal. It's enough to make you think about buying a larger hard drive on your next computer!

AP Photo/Paul Sakuma

**Figure 3.20**

The Pinnacle HDTV stick allows you to watch and record high-definition television shows on your computer.

port, shown in Figure 3.21. This is an **external SATA** port that will connect to some external hard drive models. It allows a data transfer rate of up to 3 Gb/s. The theoretical limit of USB 3.0 is 5 Gb/s, so as that technology matures expect USB 3.0 to become the fastest way to connect an external drive.

**Do I want one huge drive or several smaller drives?** It depends on what is important to you: speed or security. If you purchase two smaller

**Figure 3.21**

An eSATA port allows you to connect an external hard drive that can transfer data at speeds faster than USB 2.0.

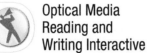

## Optical Media Reading and Writing Interactive

In this Sound Byte, you'll learn about the process of storing and retrieving data from CD-RW, DVD, and Blu-ray Discs. You'll be amazed to see how much precision engineering is required to burn MP3 files onto a disc.

drives, you can combine them using RAID technology. **RAID (redundant array of independent disks)** is a set of strategies for using more than one drive in a system. RAID 0 and RAID 1 are the most popular for consumer machines.

In a RAID 0 configuration, every time data is written to a hard drive, it is actually spread across two physical drives (see Figure 3.22a). The write begins on the first drive, and while the system is waiting for that write to be completed, the system jumps ahead and begins to write the next block of data to the second drive. This makes writing information to disk almost twice as fast as using just one hard drive. The downside is that if either of these disks fail, you lose all your data, because part of each file is on each drive. So RAID 0 is for those most concerned with performance.

In a RAID 1 configuration, all the data written to one drive is perfectly mirrored and written to a second drive (see Figure 3.22b). This provides you a perfect, instant by instant backup of all your work. It also means that if you buy two 1 TB drives, you only have room to store 1TB of data because the second 1 TB drive is being used as the "mirror." RAID 0 and RAID 1 configurations are available on many consumer systems and are even beginning to appear on notebook computers.

### Optical Storage

Optical drives are disc drives that use a laser to store and read data. Data is saved to a compact disc (CD), digital video disc (DVD), or Blu-ray Disc (BD) within established tracks and sectors, just like on a hard drive. However, unlike hard drives, which store their data on magnetized platters, optical discs store data as tiny pits that are burned into the disc by a high-speed laser. These pits are extremely small. For CDs and DVDs, they are less than 1 micron in diameter, so nearly 1,500 pits fit across the top of a pinhead. The pits on a Blu-ray Disc are only 0.15 microns in diameter, more than twice as small as the

**Figure** 3.22

(a) RAID 0 speeds up file read/write time. (b) RAID 1 gives you an instant backup.

pits on a DVD. As you can see in Figure 3.23, data is read from a disc by a laser beam, with the pits and nonpits (called *lands*) translating into the 1s and 0s of the binary code computers understand. CDs and DVDs use a red laser to read and write data. Blu-ray Discs get their name because they are read with a blue laser light. All of them collectively are referred to as **optical media**.

**Why can I store data on some discs but not others?** All forms of optical media come in prerecorded, recordable, and rewritable formats. The prerecorded discs—known as CD-ROM, DVD-ROM, and BD-ROM discs—are read-only

**Figure** 3.23

Blu-ray lasers have a shorter wavelength, so they can focus more tightly than earlier optical media.

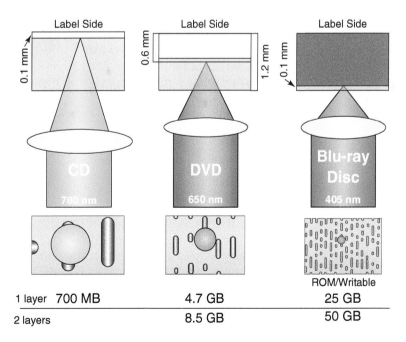

| | CD | DVD | Blu-ray Disc |
|---|---|---|---|
| 1 layer | 700 MB | 4.7 GB | 25 GB |
| 2 layers | | 8.5 GB | 50 GB |

The thin metal platters that make up a hard drive are covered with a special magnetic coating that enables the data to be recorded onto one or both sides of the platter. Hard drive manufacturers prepare the disks to hold data through a process called low-level formatting. In this process, concentric circles, each called a **track**, and pie-shaped wedges, each called a **sector**, are created in the magnetized surface of each platter, setting up a gridlike pattern that identifies file locations on the hard drive. A separate process called high-level formatting establishes the catalog that the computer uses to keep track of where each file is located on the hard drive. More detail on this is presented in the Dig Deeper feature "How Disk Defragmenter Utilities Work" in Chapter 8.

Hard drive platters spin at a high rate of speed, some as fast as 15,000 revolutions per minute (rpm). Sitting between the platters are special "arms" that contain read/write heads (see Figure 3.24). A **read/write head** moves from the outer edge of the spinning platter to the center, as frequently as 50 times per second, to retrieve (read) and record (write) the magnetic data to and from the hard drive platter. As noted earlier, the average total time it takes for the read/write head to locate the data on the platter and return it to the CPU for processing is called its access time. A new hard drive should have an average access time of approximately 12 ms.

Access time is mostly the sum of two factors: seek time and latency. The time it takes for the read/write heads to move over the surface of the disk, moving to the correct track, is called the **seek time**. (Sometimes people incorrectly refer to this as access time.) Once the read/write head locates the correct track, it may need to wait for the correct sector to spin to the read/write head. This waiting time is called **latency** (or **rotational delay**). The faster the platters spin (or the faster the rpm), the less time you'll have to wait for your data to be accessed. Currently, most hard drives for home systems spin at 7,200 rpm. Some people design their systems to have a faster hard drive run the operating system, such as the Western Digital Velociraptor, which spins at 10,000 rpm. They then add a slower drive with greater capacity for storage.

The read/write heads do not touch the platters of the hard drive; rather, they float above them on a thin cushion of air at a height of 0.5 microinches. As a matter of comparison, a human hair is 2,000 microinches thick and a particle of dust is larger than a human hair. Therefore, it's critical to keep your hard drive free from all dust and dirt, because even the smallest particle could find its way between the read/write head and the disk platter, causing a **head crash**—a stoppage of the hard drive that often results in data loss.

SSDs (solid-state drives) free you from worry about head crashes at all. The flash memory of SSDs means there are no platters, no motors, and no read/write arms in this style of hard drive. Instead, a series of cells are constructed in the silicon wafers. If high voltage is applied, electrons move in and you have one state. Reverse the voltage and the electrons flow in another direction, marking the cell as storing a different value. The limiting factor for SSDs' lifespan is how many times data can be written to a cell. But the current generation of SSDs are proving to have very strong performance over time. Intel, one manufacturer of SSDs, says its drives will last five years when being written to heavily (20 GB per day).

Capacities for hard drives in personal computers can exceed 4,000 GB (4 TB). Increasing the amount of data stored in a hard drive is achieved either by adding more platters or by increasing the amount of data stored on each platter. How tightly the tracks are placed next to each other, how tightly spaced the sectors are, and how closely the bits of data are placed affect the measurement of the amount of data that can be stored in a specific area of a hard drive platter. Modern technology continues to increase the standards on all three levels, enabling massive quantities of data to be stored in small places.

**Figure 3.24**

The hard drive is a stack of platters enclosed in a sealed case. Special arms fit in between each platter. The read/write heads at the end of each arm read from and save data to the platters.

optical discs, meaning you can't save any data onto them. Prerecorded CDs usually contain audio content, software programs, or games, whereas DVD-ROMs and BD-ROMs typically contain movies or prerecorded TV shows in regular or high definition, respectively. Recordable formats such as CD-R, DVD-R, and BD-R allow data to be written (saved or burned) to them. If you want to be able to use a form of optical media repetitively, writing and rewriting data to it many times, read/writeable formats such as CD-RW, DVD-RW, and BD-RE are available.

**Figure** 3.25 | DO YOU WANT TO UPGRADE YOUR STORAGE?

| | Have It | Want It! |
|---|---|---|
| What is my current hard drive capacity? | | |
| Do I want to have a very fast startup time (i.e., use an SSD drive for my operating system)? | | |
| Do I want to implement multiple drives in RAID 0 for performance? | | |
| Do I want to implement multiple drives in RAID 1 for instant backup? | | |
| Do I have a DVD-ROM drive? | | |
| Can I burn DVDs (i.e., do I have a DVD-RW drive)? | | |
| Can I play Blu-ray Discs (i.e., do I have a Blu-ray drive)? | | |
| Can I burn my own Blu-ray Discs (i.e., do I have a Blu-ray burner installed)? | | |
| Do I have a working data backup solution such as external backup drives or remote data storage? | | |
| Do I use any portable storage devices such as external hard drives? | | |

**Do I need separate players and burners for CD, DVD, and BD formats?** Although CDs and DVDs are based on the same optical technology, CD drives cannot read DVDs. Although Blu-ray discs are read with a different type of laser than CDs and DVDs, most Blu-ray players are backward compatible and can play DVDs and CDs. If you want to both play and record optical discs, you need to make sure your drive is a "burner" not just a player. Because recording drives are also backward compatible, you do not need separate burners for each form of media. A DVD burner will also record CDs, and a Blu-ray burner will most likely record both CDs and DVDs (although there may be some compatibility issues).

**Are some optical drives faster than others?** When you buy an optical drive, knowing the drive speed is important. Speeds are listed on the device's packaging. Record (write) speed is always listed first, rewrite speed is listed second, and playback speed is listed last. For example, a DVD-RW drive may have speeds of 24X8X12X, meaning that the device can record data at 24X speed, rewrite data at 8X speed, and play back data at 12X speed. For DVDs, the X after each number represents the transfer of 1.3 MB of data per second. So a DVD-RW drive with a 24X8X12X rating records data at 24 times 1.3 MB per second, or 31.2 MB per second. If you're

SOUND BYTE

Installing a Blu-ray Drive

In this Sound Byte, you'll learn how to install a Blu-ray drive in your computer.

in the market for a new DVD burner, then you'll want to investigate the drive speeds on the market and make sure you get the fastest one you can afford.

Blu-ray drives are the fastest optical devices on the market. Blu-ray technology defines 1X speed as 36 MB per second. Because BD movies require data transfer rates of at least 54 MB per second, most Blu-ray disc players have a minimum of 2X speeds (72 MB per second). Many units are available with 12X speeds.

**So how do my storage devices measure up?** The table in Figure 3.25 will help you determine if your computer's storage subsystem needs upgrading.

## Evaluating the Video Subsystem

How video is displayed depends on two components: your video card and your monitor. It's important that your system have the correct monitor and video card

**Figure** 3.26

Video cards have grown
to be highly specialized
subsystems.

Processor covered
by heat sink and fan

Video memory chips

Video memory chip

Connects to
VGA monitor

HDMI port to
digital monitor

Video memory chip

Clips into motherboard

S-video port to TV,
stereo, or VCR

Digital Video Interface (DVI)
port to digital monitor

to meet your needs. If you are considering loading Windows 7 on your system, or using your computer system to display files that have complex graphics, such as videos on Blu-ray or from your HD video camera, or even playing graphics-rich games with a lot of fast action, you may want to consider upgrading your video subsystem.

### Video Cards

**What is a video card?** A **video card** (or **video adapter**) is an expansion card that is installed inside your system unit to translate binary data into the images you view on your monitor. Modern video cards like the ones shown in Figures 3.26 and 3.27 are extremely sophisticated. They include ports that allow you to connect to different

video equipment such as the DVI ports for digital LCDs, HDMI ports to connect to high-definition TVs or gaming consoles, and the newer DisplayPort adapters. In addition, video cards include their own RAM, called **video memory**. Several standards of video memory are available, including graphics double data rate 3 (GDDR3) memory and the newer **graphics double data rate 5 (GDDR5)** memory. Because displaying graphics demands a lot of the CPU, video cards also come with their own graphics processing units (GPUs). When the CPU is asked to process graphics, those tasks are redirected to the GPU, significantly speeding up graphics processing.

**Is a GPU different from a CPU?** Just like a CPU, the **graphics processing unit (GPU)** performs computational work. However, a GPU is specialized to handle 3D graphics and image and video processing with incredible efficiency and speed. Figure 3.28 shows that the CPU can run much more efficiently when a GPU does all of the graphics computation.

Special lighting effects can be achieved with a modern GPU. Designers can change

**Figure** 3.27

Modern graphics cards, like this ASUS ARES, need massive fans for heat removal.

ASUSTek Computer, Inc.

**ACTIVE HELP-DESK**  Evaluating Computer System Components

In this Active Helpdesk call, you'll play the role of a helpdesk staffer, fielding calls about the computer's storage, video, and audio devices and how to evaluate whether they match your needs, as well as how to improve the reliability of your system.

Without a GPU

With a GPU

the type of light, the texture, and the color of objects based on complex interactions. Some GPU designs incorporate dedicated hardware to allow high-definition movies to be decoded or special physics engines to model water, gravity, and rigid body movements.

**Where is the GPU—on the motherboard or on the video card?** Basic video processing is sometimes integrated into the motherboard. However, high-end video cards that have their own GPUs are separate from the motherboard. These sophisticated video cards connect through the ultrafast PCI Express bus. The ASUS ARES actually uses two Radeon HD 5870 GPUs that work together to add even more processing punch. Cards like this one carry their own processing RAM space, which can range between 512 MB and 4 GB, depending on the model. Together they provide an unprecedented level of realism and detail in gaming environments.

**How can I tell how much memory my video card has?** Information about your system's video card can be found in the Advanced Settings of the Screen Resolution dialog box. To get to the Screen Resolution dialog box, right-click on your desktop and select Screen resolution. In the Screen Resolution dialog box, click the Advanced settings link. A window will appear that shows you the type of graphics card installed in your system, as well as memory information including total available graphics memory, dedicated video memory, system video memory, and shared system memory. The documentation that came with your computer should also contain specifications for the video card, including the amount of video memory it has installed.

**How much memory does my video card need?** The amount of memory your video card needs depends on what you want to display on your monitor. If you work primarily in Microsoft Word and conduct general Web searches, 256 MB is a realistic minimum. For the serious gamer, a 512 MB or greater video card is essential, although cards with as much as 2 or 3 GB are available in the market and are preferred. These high-end video cards, which have greater amounts of memory, allow games to generate smoother animations and more sophisticated shading and texture. Before purchasing new software, check the specifications to ensure your video card has enough video memory to handle the load.

**How many video cards can I add to a system?** For users who are primarily doing text processing or spreadsheet work, one video card is certainly enough. However, computer gamers and users of high-end visualization software often take advantage of the ability to install more than one video card at a time. Two or even three video cards can be used in one system. The two major video chipset manufacturers, Nvidia and ATI, have each developed their own standards supporting the combining of multiple video cards. For Nvidia this standard is named SLI and for ATI it is called CrossFire. When the system is running at very high video resolutions, such as 1920 × 1200 or higher, multiple video cards working together provide the ultimate in performance. If you are buying a new system and might be interested in employing multiple video cards, be sure to check whether the motherboard supports SLI or CrossFire.

**Figure 3.28**

The graphics processing unit (GPU) is specialized to handle processing of photos, videos, and video game images. It frees the CPU to work on other system demands.

## Figure 3.29 | BIT DEPTH AND COLOR QUALITY

| Bit Depth | Color Quality Description | Number of Colors Displayed |
|---|---|---|
| 4-bit | Standard VGA | 16 |
| 8-bit | 256-color mode | 256 |
| 16-bit | High color | 65,536 |
| 24-bit | True color | 16,777,216 |
| 32-bit | True color | 16,777,216 plus 8 bits to help with transparency |

### What else does the video card do?

The video card also controls the number of colors your monitor can display. The number of bits the video card uses to represent each pixel (or dot) on the monitor, referred to as **bit depth**, defines the color quality of the image displayed. The more bits, the better an image's color detail. A 4-bit video card

displays 16 colors, the minimum number of colors your system works with (referred to as Standard VGA). Most video cards today are 24-bit cards, displaying more than 16 million colors. This mode is called *true color mode* (see Figure 3.29).

### When is it time to get a new video card?

If your monitor takes a while to refresh when you are editing photos, surfing the Web, or playing a graphics-rich game, then the video card could be short on memory or the GPU is being taxed beyond its capacity. You can evaluate this precisely using the software that came with your card. For example, AMD Overdrive software monitors the GPU usage level, the current temperature, and the fan speed.

You also may want to upgrade if added features such as importing analog video are important to you. If you want to use multiple monitors at the same time, you also may need to upgrade your video card. Working with multiple monitors is a great advantage if you often have more than one application running at a time (see Figure 3.30). There are video cards that can support up to six monitors from a single card. "Surround Sight" allows you to merge all six monitors to work as one screen or to combine them into any subset—for example, displaying a movie on two combined screens, Excel on one monitor, Word on another, and a browser spread across the final two.

Review the considerations listed in Figure 3.31 to see if it might be time for you to upgrade your video card. On a desktop computer, replacing a video card is fairly simple: just insert the new video card in the correct expansion slot on the motherboard.

### BITS AND BYTES — Auto Tech

The automotive industry is pushing its own hardware technology advances. The OnStar system combines software running in the OnStar mirror with a full set of sensors distributed around the car to enable your car to call for help if it detects a crash and you are not responsive. OnStar reports the direction and number of impacts, rollover status, and the maximum velocity on impact so medical workers can come better prepared. If the vehicle is stolen, OnStar can find the location and report it to authorities, can send a signal to the vehicle forcing it to gradually slow down, and can lock out the ignition so it is impossible to restart the car. And once a month your car e-mails you with a report telling you how soon you need an oil change, what the air pressure is in all four tires, and if you need to make an appointment with the garage.

a

Courtesy of AMD

b

Courtesy of AMD

### Figure 3.30

Solutions like (a) AMD Eyefinity technology support (b) six monitors, which can be combined in any way.

**Figure** 3.31 | DO YOU NEED TO UPGRADE YOUR VIDEO CARD?

| | Have It | Want It! |
|---|---|---|
| What is the total amount of video memory on my video card? | | |
| How many monitors can my video card support? | | |
| Does my video card support the kind of ports I need: DVI? HDMI? DisplayPort? | | |
| Is my video card able to refresh the screen fast enough for the videos and games I play? | | |
| Can I import video through my video card? | | |
| Is my video card running at a high temperature? | | |

# Evaluating the Audio Subsystem

Computers output sound by means of speakers (or headphones) and a sound card. For many users, a computer's preinstalled speakers and sound card are adequate for the sounds produced by the computer itself—the beeps and so on that the computer makes. However, if you're listening to music, viewing HD movies, hooking into a household stereo system, or playing games with sophisticated soundtracks, you may want to upgrade your speakers or your sound card.

## Sound Card

**What does the sound card do?** Like a video card, a **sound card** is an expansion card that attaches to the motherboard inside your system unit. A sound card enables the computer to drive the speaker system. Most systems have a separate sound card, although low-end computers often have integrated the job of managing sound onto the motherboard itself.

**What does a basic sound card do for me?** Many computers ship with a **3D sound card**. The 3D sound technology advances sound reproduction beyond traditional stereo sound (where the human ear perceives sounds as coming from the left or the right of the performance area) and 3D sound is better at convincing the human ear that sound is omnidirectional, meaning that you can't tell from which direction the sound is coming. This tends to produce a fuller, richer sound than stereo sound. However, 3D sound is not surround sound.

**What is surround sound then?** **Surround sound** is a type of audio processing that makes the listener experience sound as if it were coming from all directions by using multiple speakers. The current surround sound standard is from Dolby. There are many formats available, including Dolby Digital EX and Dolby Digital Plus for high-definition audio. Dolby TrueHD is the newest standard. It features high-definition and lossless technology, which means no information is lost in the compression process. To create surround sound, Dolby takes digital sound from a medium (such as a Blu-ray Disc) and reproduces it in eight channels. Seven channels cover the listening field with placement to the left front, right front, and center of the audio stage, as well as the left rear and right rear, and then two extra side speakers are added, as shown in Figure 3.32. The eighth channel holds extremely low-frequency sound data and is sent to a subwoofer, which can be placed anywhere in the room. The name 7.1 surround indicates that there are seven speakers reproducing the full audio spectrum and one speaker handling just lower frequency bass sounds. There is also a 5.1 surround sound standard, which has a total of six speakers—one subwoofer, a center speaker, and four speakers for right/left in the front and the back. If you have a larger space or want precise location of sounds, use the newer 7.1 system.

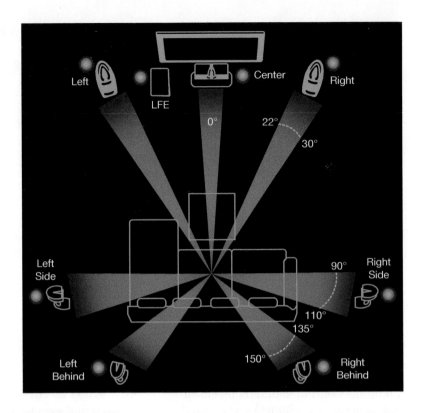

**Figure** 3.32

Dolby Digital 7.1 surround sound gives you better quality audio output.

To set up surround sound on your computer, you need two things: a set of surround-sound speakers and, for the greatest surround-sound experience, a sound card that is Dolby Digital–compatible.

**I don't need surround sound. Why else might I need to upgrade my sound card?** Most basic sound cards contain the following input and output jacks (or ports): microphone in, speaker out, and line in. This allows you to hook up a set of stereo speakers and a microphone. But what if you want to hook up a right and left speaker individually, or attach other audio devices to your computer?

To do so, you need more ports, which are provided on upgraded sound cards like the one shown in Figure 3.33.

With an upgraded sound card, you can connect portable media players, MIDI instruments, and recording equipment to your computer. Musicians often record music

Analog/Digital Output

Line Input Signal

Microphone Input

Line Output

Rear Speaker Output

FireWire (IEEE 1394)

**Figure** 3.33

In addition to improving sound quality, upgraded sound cards can provide additional ports for your audio equipment.

## ETHICS IN IT — Free (as in Speech, not Beer)

The open source software movement has flourished over the past decade. In response to increasing prices and the limitations placed on commercially available software, programmers began to donate time to design, develop, and support software systems. These products, like Gimp (a photo editing tool), were then made freely available.

In the world of hardware, a similar but a different approach called the open source hardware movement has flourished. Because hardware projects require materials and tools to assemble, products distributed as open source are not free in terms of cost, but they are free from any restrictions on how you modify them. Sample open source hardware projects include video game systems, audio equipment, and 3D printers.

Is open hardware good for the world? Does it undermine the intellectual property of others who want to create hardware resources and sell them for a profit? Does it foster a spirit of cooperation instead of competition that ultimately benefits all parties? What is the impact on developing countries if they have immediate access to hardware designs instead of being required to purchase these items from a for-profit company in a developed country? The future of open hardware is important to watch. Follow the future of open source hardware by keeping an eye on conferences like the Open Hardware Summit (**www.openhardwaresummit.org**), developer and supplier sites like littleBits (**littlebits.cc**), and homebrew blogs like Procrastineering (**procrastineering.blogspot.com**).

---

onto their computers by connecting guitars, keyboards, digital drums, or microphones directly to sound card ports. There are also external devices that will add RCA jacks for connecting guitars and the microphone ports you need for USB or XLR cables that come from recording mikes. For example, the E-MU Audio/MIDI Interface connects to your computer using USB and is a way to add connectivity for microphones and other instruments. To determine whether your audio subsystem is meeting your needs, review the table in Figure 3.34.

| Figure 3.34 | DO YOU NEED TO UPGRADE YOUR AUDIO SUBSYSTEM? | | |
|---|---|---|---|
| | | Have It | Want It! |
| Is the speaker quality high enough for the way I am using my computer? | | | |
| Is my sound card capable of 3D sound? | | | |
| Does my sound card support Dolby Digital surround sound? | | | |
| Do I have 5.1-channel surround sound or 7.1-channel surround sound? | | | |
| Do I have an HDMI port on the audio card? | | | |

## Evaluating System Reliability

Many computer users decide to buy a new system not necessarily because they need a faster CPU, more RAM, or a bigger hard drive, but because they are experiencing problems such as slow performance, freezes, and crashes. Over time, even normal use can cause your computer to build up excess files and to become internally disorganized. This excess, clutter, and disorganization can lead to deteriorating performance or, far worse, system failure. If you think your system is unreliable, see if the problem is one you can fix before you buy a new machine.

Proper upkeep and maintenance also may postpone an expensive system upgrade or replacement.

**What can I do to ensure my system performs reliably?** Here are several procedures you can follow to ensure your system performs reliably:

1. Clean out your Startup folder. Some programs install themselves into your Startup folder and run automatically each time the computer starts up, whether you are using them or not.

---

**Over time, even normal use can cause your computer to build up excess files and to become internally disorganized.**

---

This unnecessary load uses up RAM, leaving less for other programs. To minimize this problem, check your Startup folder by clicking Start > All Programs. Then click on the Startup folder and make sure all the programs listed are important to you. Right-click on any unnecessary program and select Delete to remove it from the Startup folder. Make sure you delete *only* programs you are absolutely sure are unnecessary. Another way programs sneak their way in is to load themselves into your system tray. Keep an eye on how many icons are in the system tray and uninstall any that you do not use frequently.

2. Clear out unnecessary files. Temporary Internet files can accumulate quickly on your hard drive, taking up unnecessary space. Running the Disk Cleanup utility is a quick and easy way to ensure your temporary Internet files don't take up precious hard drive space. Likewise, you should delete any unnecessary files from your hard drive regularly, because they can make your hard drive run more slowly.

3. Run spyware and adware removal programs. These often detect and remove different pests and should be used in addition to your regular antivirus package.

4. Run the Disk Defragmenter utility on your hard drive. When your hard drive becomes fragmented, its storage capacity is negatively affected. When you defragment (defrag) your hard drive, files are reorganized, making the hard drive work more efficiently. But remember that this only makes sense for mechanical drives. With no motors, there is no need to defrag an SSD drive. For a more complete discussion of the Disk Defragmenter, refer to Chapter 8.

The utilities that need to be run more than once, like Disk Cleanup, Disk Defragmenter, and the antivirus, adware, and spyware programs, can be configured to run automatically at any time interval you want. You can use Windows Task Scheduler or third-party programs like Norton Security Suite to set up a sequence of programs to run one after the other every evening while you sleep, and wake up each day to a reliable, secure system.

**My system crashes often during the day. What can I do?** Computer systems are complex. It's not unusual to have your system stop responding occasionally. If rebooting the computer doesn't help, you'll need to begin troubleshooting:

1. Check that you have enough RAM, which you learned how to do in the section "Evaluating the Memory Subsystem: RAM" earlier in this chapter. Systems with insufficient amounts of RAM often crash.

2. Make sure you have properly installed any new software or hardware. If you're using a Windows system, use the System Restore utility to "roll back" the system to a time when it worked more reliably. (To find System Restore, just type "restore" into the Start menu search box.) For Mac systems, Mac OS X Time Machine, shown in Figure 3.35, provides automatic backup and enables you to look through and restore (if necessary) files, folders, libraries, or the entire system.

3. If you see an error code in Windows, visit the Microsoft Knowledge Base (**support.microsoft.com**), an online resource for resolving problems with Microsoft products. This may help you determine what the error code indicates and how you may be able to solve the problem. If you don't find a satisfactory answer in the Knowledge Base, try copying the entire error message into Google and searching the larger community for solutions.

**Figure 3.35**

Mac's Time Machine restores files, folders, libraries, and, if necessary, the entire system.

**Can my software affect system reliability?** Having the latest version of software products makes your system much more reliable. You should upgrade or update your operating system, browser software, and application software as often as new patches (or updates) are reported for resolving errors. Sometimes these errors are performance-related; sometimes they are potential system security breaches.

If you are having a problem that can be replicated, use the Problem Steps Recorder to capture the exact steps that lead to it. In Windows 7, go to the Start menu and search for "psr." Run the Problem Steps Recorder and go through the exact actions that create the problem you are having. At any particular step, you can click the Annotate button and add a comment about any part of the screen. PSR then produces a documented report, complete with images of your screen and descriptions of each mouse movement you made. You can then e-mail this report, which is compressed in the WinZip format, to customer support to help technicians resolve the problem.

**How do I know whether updates are available for my software?** You can configure Windows so that it automatically checks for, downloads, and installs any available updates for itself, Internet Explorer, and other Microsoft applications such as Microsoft Office. From the Windows Control Panel, open System and Security and then Windows Update. Click Change Settings.

Many other applications now also include the ability to check for updates. Check under the Help menu of the product, and often you will find a Check for Updates command.

**What if none of this helps? Is buying a new system my only option?** If your system is still unreliable after these changes, then you have two options:

1. Upgrade your operating system to the latest version. There are substantial increases in reliability with each major release of a new operating system. However, upgrading the operating system may require hardware upgrades such as additional RAM, an updated graphics processor, and an even larger hard drive. The Microsoft Windows 7 Upgrade Advisor (a free download from **www.microsoft.com**) will scan your system to determine what upgrades might be required before you convert to Windows 7. Be sure to examine the *recommended* (not required) specifications of the new operating system.

2. Reinstall the operating system. As a last resort, you might need to reinstall the operating system. To do so, you'll want to back up all of your data files before the installation and be prepared to reinstall all your software after the installation. Make sure you have all of the original discs for the software installed on your system, along with the product keys, serial numbers, and any other activation codes so that you can reinstall them.

## Making the Final Decision

Now that you have evaluated your computer system, you need to shift to questions of *value*. How closely does your system come to meeting your needs? How much would it cost to upgrade the system you have to match what you'd ideally like your computer to do, not only today but also a few years from now? How much would it cost to purchase a new system that meets these specifications?

To decide whether upgrading or buying a new system has better value for you, you need to price both scenarios. Figure 3.36 provides an upgrade worksheet you can use to evaluate both the upgrade path and the new purchase path. Purchasing a new system is an important investment of your resources, and you want to make a well-reasoned, well-supported decision.

**What happens to my old computer?** Be sure to consider what benefit you might obtain by having two systems. Would you have a use for the older system? Would you be able to give it to a family member? If you decide to throw it away, consider the environmental impact. Mercury in LCD screens, cadmium in batteries and circuit boards, and flame retardant in plastic housings all are toxic. An alarming, emerging trend is that discarded machines are beginning to create an e-waste crisis.

**How could I recycle my old computer?** Instead of throwing your computer away, you may be able to donate

## Figure 3.36 | UPGRADE/NEW PURCHASE COMPARISON WORKSHEET

| Needs | Hardware Upgrade Cost | Included on New System? | Additional Expense If Not Included on New System |
|---|---|---|---|
| **CPU and RAM** | | | |
| CPU upgrade | | | |
| RAM upgrade | | | |
| **Storage** | | | |
| Hard drive upgrade | | | |
| SSD drive | | | |
| DVD-RW burner | | | |
| Blu-ray burner | | | |
| **Video and Audio** | | | |
| Video card upgrade | | | |
| Sound card upgrade | | | |

it to a nonprofit organization. Many manufacturers, such as Dell, offer recycling programs and have formed alliances with nonprofit organizations to help distribute your old technology to those who need it. Sites like Computers with Causes (**www.computerswithcauses.org**) organize donations of both working and nonworking

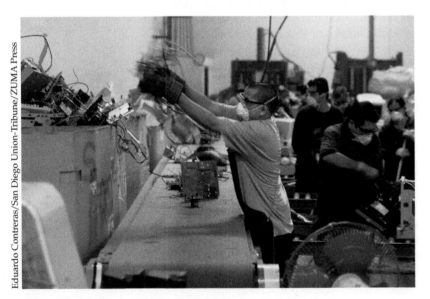

**Figure 3.37**

An electronics scrap recycler "demanufactures" printers, computers, and other electronics and then resells the usable parts.

computers, printers, and mice. You can also take your computer to an authorized computer recycling center in your area. The Telecommunications Industry Association provides an e-cycling information site you can use to find a local e-cycling center (**www.eiae.org**).

For companies that need to retire large quantities of computers, the risk of creating an environmental hazard is serious. Firms like GigaBiter (**www.gigabiter.com**) offer a solution. GigaBiter eliminates security and environmental risks associated with electronic destruction by first delaminating the hard drive and then breaking down the computer e-waste into recyclable products (Figure 3.37). The result of the final step is a sandlike substance that is 100 percent recyclable.

**Can I donate a computer safely, without worrying about my personal data?** Before donating or recycling a computer, make sure you carefully remove all data from your hard drive, or you could become the victim of identity theft. Credit card numbers, bank information, Social Security numbers, tax records, passwords, and personal identification numbers (PINs) are just some of the types of sensitive information that we casually record to our computers' hard drives. Just deleting files that contain proprietary personal information is not protection enough. Likewise, reformatting or erasing your hard drive does not totally remove data, as was proved by two MIT graduate students. They bought more than 150 used hard drives from various sources. Although some of the hard drives had been reformatted or damaged so the data was supposedly irrecoverable, the two students were able to retrieve medical records, financial information, pornography, personal e-mails, and more than 5,000 credit card numbers!

The U.S. Department of Defense suggests a seven-layer overwrite for a "secure erase." This means that you fill your hard drive seven times over with a random series of 1s and 0s. Fortunately, several programs exist for doing this. For PCs running Windows, look for Active@ Kill Disk, Eraser, or Cyber-Scrub. Wipe is available for Linux, and ShredIt X can be used for OS X. These programs provide secure hard drive erasures, either of specific files on your hard drive or of the entire hard drive.

# Thunderbolt: The New Standard for Data Transfer

Look at the back of your system and you no doubt see a messy collection of cables of every color, thickness, and design. USB cables to your printer, networking cables to the router, video cables to monitors, along with the requisite power cables, speaker cables, and maybe even a keyboard cable. Don't we all dream of a better day?

Well, that day may be near at hand. Intel has used fiber optics, the transmission of digital data through pure glass cable as thin as human hair, to develop a new input/output technology named Thunderbolt (developed under the codename Light Peak). Thunderbolt supports blazing fast transfer rates of 10 Gb/s, zooming past even the theoretical limit of the new USB 3.0 which is 4.8 Gb/s. How fast is that? Intel says that Thunderbolt could transfer a full length HD movie in under 30 seconds or copy over a library of music that would take a solid year to play through in just 10 minutes. And Thunderbolt can supply much more power to devices than the USB standard allows. It also has a very slim connector design, allowing laptop designers to make their systems even thinner (see Figure 3.38).

But one of the greatest hopes that comes with Thunderbolt is that the technology will be able to replace a number of different ports, cleaning up the cluttered design we see now on the sides of laptops and the backs of desktop units. The first devices using this technology appeared in May 2011 when Apple announced Thunderbolt ports on the MacBook Pro series. It looks like a single thin port that supports both the video standard DisplayPort and the bus standard PCI Express (see Figure 3.39). So Thunderbolt can connect monitors to computers using VGA, DisplayPort, DVI, or HDMI and can connect systems to external hard drives that use USB, FireWire, or eSATA. One Thunderbolt port can support several devices because the cables can be daisy-chained (connected one after another in a serial fashion), so having just one Thunderbolt port on a laptop allows you to connect up to six different peripherals to your system.

Thunderbolt technology also gives you two for one, because each connector can support two separate channels to send and receive data, each one still operating at the full 10 Gb/s bandwidth.

Thunderbolt port

**Figure** 3.38

Thunderbolt ports are very thin, allowing new design options.

What will this mean to laptop designers? Some speculate we'll see the heavy, heat-producing video cards that are integrated into gaming laptops become external graphics boxes. An incredibly thin, light laptop design would let you be wonderfully mobile all day, then when you come home you'd attach one cable. It would run from your Thunderbolt port to your 60" HDTV, then continue on to a separate graphics processor box. That same laptop is now running a huge HD monitor with a high-resolution graphics and physics engine.

Apple is not the only company that will be using the Intel technology. Hard drive companies like LaCie and Western Digital as well as audio/video processing companies like Avid and Apogee have announced Thunderbolt products. And the USB community may need to put up a bit of a fight to keep their standard around. But the allure of incredible speed, great versatility, and small, thin packaging is going to make the Thunderbolt technology a trend to watch.

Could Thunderbolt make USB a thing of the past?

**Figure** 3.39

Thunderbolt can carry two channels of information on the same connector.

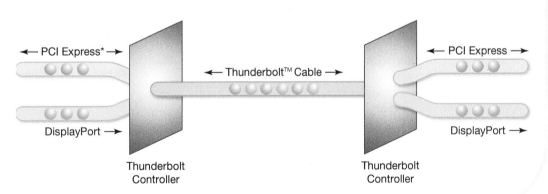

← PCI Express* →

← Thunderbolt™ Cable →

← PCI Express →

DisplayPort →

DisplayPort →

Thunderbolt Controller

Thunderbolt Controller

**1. How can I determine whether I should upgrade my existing computer or buy a new one?**

To determine whether you need to upgrade your system or purchase a new one, you need to define your ideal system and what you want it to do. Then you need to perform a system evaluation to assess the subsystems in your computer, including the CPU, memory, storage, video, and audio. Finally, you need to determine if it's economical to upgrade, or whether buying a new computer would be better.

**2. What does the CPU do, and how can I evaluate its performance?**

Your computer's CPU processes instructions, performs calculations, manages the flow of information through the computer system, and is responsible for processing the data you input into information. CPU speed is measured in gigahertz (billions of machine cycles per second). You can tell whether your CPU is limiting your system performance by watching how busy it is as you work on your computer. The percentage of time that your CPU is working is referred to as CPU usage, which you can determine by checking the Task Manager. Benchmarking software offers direct performance comparisons of different CPUs.

**3. How does memory work in my computer, and how can I evaluate how much memory I need?**

RAM is your computer's temporary memory. It remembers everything that the computer needs to process data into information. However, it is an example of volatile storage. When the power is off, the data stored in RAM is cleared out. The amount of RAM sitting on memory modules in your computer is your computer's physical memory. The memory your OS uses is kernel memory. At a minimum, you need enough RAM to run the OS plus the software applications you're using, plus a bit more to hold the data you will input.

**4. What are the computer's storage devices, and how can I evaluate whether they match my needs?**

Storage devices for a typical computer system may include a hard drive, an SSD drive, a flash drive, and CD and DVD drives. Blu-ray drives are gaining in popularity for viewing and burning high-density media. When you turn off your computer, the data stored in these devices remains. These devices are referred to as *nonvolatile* storage devices. Hard drives have the largest storage capacity of any storage device and are the most economical. Newer SSD drives have the fastest access time and data transfer rate of all nonvolatile storage options. CDs and DVDs have capacities from 700 MB to 17 GB, while Blu-ray discs can hold up to 50 GB. Portable flash drives allow easy transfer of 64 GB or more of data from machine to machine. To determine the storage capacity your system needs, calculate the amount of storage your software needs to reside on your computer. To add more storage or to provide more functionality for your system, you can install additional drives, either internally or externally.

**5. What components affect the quality of video on my computer, and how do I know if I need better video performance?**

How video is displayed depends on two components: your video card and your monitor. A video card translates binary data into the images you see. These cards include their own RAM (video memory) as well as ports that allow you to connect to video equipment. The amount of video memory you need depends on what you want to display on the monitor. A more powerful card will allow you to play graphics-intense games and multimedia.

6. **What components affect my computer's sound quality?**

Your computer's sound depends on your speakers and sound card. A sound card enables the computer to produce sounds. Users upgrade their sound cards to provide surround sound, and additional ports for audio equipment.

7. **How can I improve the reliability of my system?**

Many computer users decide to buy a new system because they are experiencing problems with their computer. However, before you buy a new system because you think yours may be unreliable, make sure the problem is not one you can fix. Run a full scan with antispyware and -adware software. Make sure you have installed any new software or hardware properly, check that you have enough RAM, run system utilities such as Disk Defragmenter and Disk Cleanup, clean out your Startup folder, remove unnecessary files from your system, and keep your software updated with patches. If you continue to have troubles with your system, reinstall or upgrade your OS, and, of course, seek technical assistance.

## Companion Website

The Companion Website includes a variety of additional materials to help you review and learn more about the topics in this chapter. Go to: ***www.pearsonhighered.com/techinaction***

**key terms**

## Word Bank

- access time
- cache memory
- cores
- CPU usage graph
- data transfer rate
- eSATA
- ExpressCards

- front side bus
- GDDR5
- GPU
- hard drive
- HDMI
- memory modules
- Moore's Law

- RAID 1
- RAM
- sound card
- SSD
- surround sound

**Instructions:** Fill in the blanks using the words from the Word Bank above.

Luis already has a desktop PC but just heard about a great deal on a new one. He decides to perform a system evaluation on his computer to see whether he should keep it or buy the new one. First, he watches the load on the processor using the (1)_____ in Windows. Because he has a multiple (2) _____ in his processor, there are multiple graphs to follow. Because he is often having system crashes, he begins to suspect his system is suffering from too little (3) _____. He has room for an additional two (4) _____ on his motherboard. Adding memory is something he learned how to do this semester, but would that be enough to make this machine fit his needs?

He visits the Intel Web site to check two other important factors on his model of CPU: the amount of (5) _____ and the speed of the (6) _____. It looks like the newer i7 processor would be much faster overall. It seems each generation of processors is so much faster than the last. That rule, (7) _____, is still holding true!

Luis continues to evaluate his system by checking out which components he has and which ones he'll need. He notes the storage capacity of his mechanical (8) _____ and decides he needs more room. Recently, he has been wishing his system had a(n) (9) _____ port. As it is, he is running out of space to store files. But the (10) _____, or the amount of time it takes to retrieve data from the disk drive, on any mechanical drive is slow compared to the (11) _____ in the new computer he's eyeing, which has no moving parts at all. Luis is really concerned about having a backup of his work so he's going to use two cheaper mechanical drives, connected in (12) _____ to guarantee immediate backup of every change. The new video card includes a specialized (13) _____ that can process 3D data with great speed. It would be great if he could take advantage of the 7.1 (14) _____ that is on the gaming software he runs.

It's tough to play the games he wants though since his current system doesn't meet the minimum video requirements for the newer games. The current video cards have blindingly fast (15) _____ memory, and some people even use multiple cards. Overall, with prices dropping, it seems like time to go buy that new system!

Rebecca has already built five or six PCs and tells you she can make a killer desktop system for you for under $1,300. But you do love the idea of having a light, compact notebook computer that could travel with you around campus and back and forth to work.

**Instructions:** Using the preceding scenario, write an e-mail to Rebecca describing to her what you need in your new system. Examine the specifications for both notebook and desktop systems in this price range and decide which one is best suited to you. Use key terms from the chapter and be sure your sentences are grammatically correct and technically meaningful.

**Instructions:** Answer the multiple-choice and true–false questions below for more practice with key terms and concepts from this chapter.

## Multiple Choice

1. Which statement about notebook computers is FALSE?
   - *a.* Notebooks typically have a longer lifespan than desktop computers.
   - b. Notebooks are typically less reliable than desktop computers.
   - c. Notebooks can be docked to larger monitors.
   - d. Notebooks are more difficult to expand or upgrade.

2. SSD is classified as what type of storage?
   - a. volatile
   - *b.* nonvolatile
   - c. video
   - d. cache

3. To document a problem you are having, you can use
   - a. Disk Cleanup.
   - *b.* Problem Steps Recorder.
   - c. PC Decrapifier.
   - d. Resource Monitor.

4. If you want your system to run reliably, you should
   - a. add all programs to the Startup folder.
   - b. save all of your temporary Internet files.
   - c. install programs in the system tray.
   - *d.* defragment the hard drive.

5. Which best describes RAID 0 technology?
   - a. Saved data is spread across two hard drives.
   - b. Data is written to one drive and mirrored to a second drive.
   - c. RAID 0 allows you to store twice the data.
   - *d.* RAID 0 provides an instant backup of your work.

6. CPUs have several internal components, including
   - *a.* L2 cache.
   - b. ALU.
   - c. level 1 cache memory.
   - d. all of the above.

7. Which is *not* a type of video port?
   - a. HDMI
   - b. DVI
   - *c.* USB 3.0
   - d. DisplayPort

8. A sound card that supports 7.1 surround sound will drive
   - a. seven speakers.
   - b. one speaker.
   - *c.* eight speakers.
   - d. Dolby headphones.

9. SuperFetch is a memory-management technique that
   - a. determines the type of RAM your system requires.
   - *b.* makes the boot-up time for the system very quick.
   - *c.* preloads the applications you use most into system memory.
   - d. defragments the hard drive to increase performance.

10. What is the name for the time it takes a storage device to locate its stored data and make it available for processing?
    - a. rotational latency
    - b. access time
    - *c.* data transfer rate
    - d. seek time

## True-False

_T_ 1. A quad core CPU with hyperthreading has eight virtual CPUs.

_T_ 2. The memory that your operating system uses is referred to as kernel memory.

_F_ 3. SSD hard drives need to be defragged but mechanical hard drives do not.

_F_ 4. Cache memory is a form of read-only memory that can be accessed more quickly by the CPU.

_F_ 5. GDDR5 memory is often used in eSATA drives.

making the
transition to...
next semester

## 1. Personalize Your System

Likely, you spend many hours each day working on your computer using it for school, work, communication, research, and entertainment. Your computer should be a device that fits you, fits your needs, and expresses who you are.

a. Begin with the computer's form. Would you select a notebook or a desktop? What features determine that decision?

b. Next consider performance. Which type of CPU do you need? How much RAM should be installed? What kind of hard drive storage would you select? Give specific price-to-value arguments for each decision.

c. Now consider expandability. If you need this system to last for four years, what kind of ports and expansion capabilities are necessary?

## 2. Convertibles

The line between the capabilities of a laptop and a portable tablet have become more and more blurred with the arrival of "convertible tablets." These systems can be detached from a base unit with a full size keyboard and then function as a lightweight touch screen tablet. What kind of user would find this an ideal solution? Do you anticipate this category of computer becoming more popular?

## 3. Go Small or Stay Home

Manufacturers are releasing a number of systems that are trying to capitalize on size—or the lack of size! Explore some of the small form factor (SFF) computers appearing on the market.

a. Research the Falcon Northwest FragBox (**www.falcon-nw.com**).

b. Examine the Apple Mac mini (**www.apple.com**).

c. Compare those systems with the Dell Zino HD (**www.dell.com**).

Why are these SFF computers appearing? What role do you see these systems fulfilling? What kind of performance and hardware would you recommend for such a system?

## 4. Do-It-Yourself Computer Design

Visit Newegg (**www.newegg.com**) and do a search on "do it yourself." You will find that Newegg has created a number of bundles, which are a set of components that cover the categories outlined in this chapter: the computer case, processor, RAM, storage, video, and audio.

a. Which system looks like the best match for your needs for school next semester? Why?

b. What is the price difference between building the system and purchasing a similar unit from a major manufacturer?

c. What skills would you need before you could assemble the computer yourself?

d. What additional components (hardware and software) would you need to complete the system?

## 5. How Does Your System Measure Up?

A number of tools are available to measure your system's performance. Explore the following tools and use one to gather data on your current system's performance.

a. Windows 7 Gadgets: Visit the Windows 7 Personalization Gallery (**windows.microsoft .com/en-US/windows/downloads/personalize**) and find gadgets to help you monitor system performance.

b. Windows 7 Resource Monitor: Use the Resource Monitor to collect data on CPU utilization and memory usage over a typical school day.

c. Benchmarking suites: Examine a sample of consumer benchmarking programs like PassMark's PerformanceTest, Primate Lab's Geekbench, and Maxon's Cinebench. Which subsystems do each of these products evaluate?

1. **Judging System Performance**

   As you learned in this chapter, the Resource Monitor provides a detailed breakdown of how the computer is using memory at any given time.

   a. Open the Resource Monitor, display the CPU tab, and open the Processes frame. What is your total CPU Usage? How many "virtual" CPUs does your machine have? Clicking on any of the column titles sorts that column, so clicking the Average CPU column shows you the applications currently using most of the CPU resources. What are the top two most intensive applications?

   b. Display the Memory tab. How much memory is in use? How much is available? Of the memory available, how much has been preloaded with data and files that Windows "thinks" you will need soon?

   c. Display the Disk tab. Click on the Processes with Disk Activity panel. Which programs are making the greatest total demand to read and write to the disk?

2. **More and More Monitors**

   Video cards that support three or even more monitors are very affordable and could be of great use in a number of businesses. Investigate a set of video cards that support three, six, or eight monitors. Research multi-monitor mounting systems. How would the following jobs best arrange multiple monitors to make their workday more efficient?

   a. Stockbroker          b. Software developer
   c. Airport traffic control    d. Author

3. **Room to Move**

   You are responsible for specifying the storage solution for an accounting customer's computer system. Your customer needs to always have redundancy—that is, multiple copies of the work they are doing—because of the secure nature of the records they keep and the length of time they are required to keep records. Prepare a report that describes the type of hard drive and optical storage you would recommend. Be sure to include performance specifications and price. Devise a list of questions you would need to ask your customer to be sure they have a system that meets their expectations.

4. **Video Connections**

   You have a position in a pharmaceutical research firm. Your group does simulations of protein folding to predict if a new drug will be effective. You collaborate daily with a team in India using video conferencing. Now you have found out you also have the responsibility of creating a series of training videos to teach the Indian team how to use the newest release of software. What video and processing hardware would your workstation need to tackle this? Specify the video card performance and the CPU and memory requirements you would have for this project.

5. **Let Me Tell You My Problem**

   You may be responsible for helping others solve various computer problems. Test out the Problem Steps Recorder in Windows 7 to see how the program can help you help them. Click the Start button and search for "psr." Run the program and click Start Record. Then just click between different applications, visit the Control Panel, and add an annotation. Save the file to your desktop and close the Problem Steps Recorder. View the annotated report. How could you use the Problem Steps Recorder to describe a problem or to gather information?

**Instructions:** Some ideas are best understood by experimenting with them in our own minds. The following critical thinking questions are designed to demand your full attention but require only a comfortable chair—no technology.

1. **More and More**

   The amount of storage we have available on hard disk drives has increased again and again. What has changed that we suddenly need such huge amounts of storage? How have our storage habits changed? What is the limit—what is the largest amount of storage you can imagine using? How will cloud networking impact our future need for storage?

2. **Emerging Technologies**

   Touch screens are now available in a range of sizes, from smartphones to iPads to larger products like the Microsoft Surface. Windows 7 has integrated support for touch screens. "Surround Sight" and 3D monitors are available in increasing numbers. What new technologies will last and become part of our collective experience? How will these technologies and devices change entertainment and how people interact with information? What future technologies would be on your wish list?

3. **The Early Adopter**

   We are all aware of the technology price curve: when first introduced, products have the highest prices and the most instability. As these products settle into the market, they become more reliable and the prices fall, sometimes very quickly. People who make those first release purchases are called *early adopters*. What are the advantages to being an early adopter? What are the disadvantages? How do you decide at what point you should step into the technology price curve for any given product?

4. **A Green Machine**

   Review the impacts of your computer during its entire lifecycle. How do the production, transportation, and use of the computer impact the increase of greenhouse gas emissions? How does the selection of materials and packaging impact the environment? What restricted substances (like lead, mercury, cadmium, and PVC) are found in your machine? Could substitute materials be used? How would the ultimate "green machine" be designed?

5. **System Longevity**

   If you purchase a computer system for business purposes, the Internal Revenue Service (IRS) allows you to depreciate its cost over five years. The IRS considers this a reasonable estimate of the useful lifetime of a computer system. What do you think most home users expect in terms of how long their computer systems should last? How does the purchase of a computer system compare with other major household appliances in terms of cost, value, benefit, life span, and upgrade potential?

# Many Different Computers for Many Different Needs

### Problem

Even within one discipline, there are needs for a variety of types of computing solutions. Consider the Communications department in a large university. Because it is such an interdisciplinary area, there are some groups involved in video production, some groups producing digital music, and some groups responsible for creating scripts and screenplays. The department as a whole needs to decide on a complete computing strategy.

### Process

Split your class into teams.

1. Select one segment of the Communications department that your team will represent: video production, digital music, or scripting. The video production team requires their labs to be able to support the recording, editing, and final production and distribution of digital video. The digital music group wants to establish a collegiate recording studio (in the model of the Drexel University recording label, Mad Dragon Records). The scripting group needs to support a collaborative community of writers and voice-over actors.

2. Analyze the computing needs of that division, with particular focus on how they need to outfit their computer labs.

3. Price the systems you would recommend and explain how they will be used. What decisions have you made to guarantee they will still be useful in three years?

4. Write a report that summarizes your findings. Document the resources you used and generate as much enthusiasm as you can for your recommendations.

### Conclusion

The range of available computing solutions has never been so broad. It can be a cause of confusion for those not educated in technology. But with a firm understanding of the basic subsystems of computers, it is precisely the pace of change that is exciting. Being able to evaluate a computer system and match it to the current needs of its users is an important skill.

# ethics project

## Benchmarking

In this exercise, you will research and then role-play a complicated ethical situation. The role you play might or might not match your own personal beliefs; in either case, your research and use of logic will enable you to represent the view assigned. An arbitrator will watch and comment on both sides of the arguments, and together the team will agree on an ethical solution.

### Problem

We have seen that for complex systems like computers, performance often is determined not by comparing the specifications of individual parts but by using benchmarks, software suites that test a full area of performance. There are benchmarks for battery life, for CPU performance, and for video performance. The results of these tests become a major force in marketing and selling the product.

There have been a number of claims of unethical conduct in the area of benchmarking. Companies have been accused of using out-of-date testing software to skew their results. Some companies have manipulated the settings on the machine to artificially raise their score (for example, turning off the display and wireless network before testing for battery life). Some companies have even accused their competition of colluding with the creator of the benchmark so that it is written to favor one product over another.

Where is the line between having a competitive edge and lying when it comes to hardware assessment?

### Research Areas to Consider

- SysMark 2002
- BAPCo
- MobileMark
- 2009 Nobel Prize for Physics

### Process

Divide the class into teams.

1. Research the areas cited above from the perspective of either an Intel engineer working on a new CPU, an AMD engineer working on a competing CPU, or a benchmark designer.
2. Team members should write a summary that provides factual documentation for the positions and views their character takes around the issue of equitable testing of hardware. Then, team members should create an outline to use during the role-playing event.
3. Team members should arrange a mutually convenient time to meet for the exchange, either using the chat room feature of MyITLab, the discussion board feature of Blackboard, or meeting in person.
4. Team members should present their case to the class, or submit a PowerPoint presentation for review by the rest of the class, along with the summary and resolution they developed.

### Conclusion

As technology becomes ever more prevalent and integrated into our lives, more and more ethical dilemmas will present themselves. Being able to understand and evaluate both sides of the argument, while responding in a personally or socially ethical manner, will be an important skill.

# Under the Hood

# IN FOCUS

SOME PEOPLE ARE DRAWN TO UNDERSTANDING things in detail, but many folks are happy just to have things work. If you use a computer, you may not have ever been tempted to "look under the hood." However, without understanding the hardware inside, you'll be faced with some real limitations. You'll have to pay a technician to fix or upgrade your computer. This won't be as efficient as fine-tuning it yourself, and you may find yourself buying a new computer sooner than necessary. If you're preparing for a career in information technology, understanding computer hardware will affect the speed and efficiency of the programs you design. And what about all those exciting advances you hear about? How do you evaluate the impact of a new type of memory or a new processor? A basic appreciation of how a computer system is built and designed is a good start.

We'll build on what you've learned about computer hardware in other chapters and go under the hood, looking at the components of your system unit in more detail. Let's begin by looking at the building blocks of computers: switches.

## Switches

The **system unit** is the box that contains the central electronic components of the computer. But how, exactly, does the computer perform all of its tasks? How does it process the data you input? The CPU performs functions like adding, subtracting, moving data around the system, and so on using nothing but a large number of on/off switches. In fact, a computer system can be viewed as an enormous collection of on/off switches.

### Electrical Switches

Computers work exclusively with numbers, not words. To process data into information, computers need to work in a language they understand. This language, called **binary language**, consists of just two numbers: 0 and 1. Everything a computer does, such as processing data or printing a report, is broken down into a series of 0s and 1s. **Electrical switches** are devices inside the computer that can be flipped between these two states: 1 and 0, signifying "on" and "off." Computers use 0s and 1s to process data because they are electronic, digital machines. They only understand two states of existence: on and off. Inside a computer these two possibilities, or states, are represented using the binary switches (or digits) 1 and 0.

You use various forms of switches every day. The on/off button on your DVD player is a mechanical switch: pushed in, it represents the value 1 (on), whereas

**Figure 4.1**

Water faucets can be used to represent binary switches.

popped out, it represents the value 0 (off). Another switch you use each day is a water faucet. As shown in Figure 4.1, shutting off the faucet so that no water flows could represent the value 0, whereas turning it on could represent the value 1.

Computers are built from a huge collection of electrical switches. The history of computers is really a story about creating smaller and faster sets of electrical switches so that more data can be stored and manipulated quickly.

**Vacuum Tubes** The earliest generation of electronic computers used devices called **vacuum tubes** as switches. Vacuum tubes act as computer switches by allowing or blocking the flow of electrical current. The problem with vacuum tubes is that they take up a lot of space, as you see in Figure 4.2. The first high-speed digital computer, the Electronic Numerical Integrator and Computer (ENIAC), was deployed in 1945. It used nearly 18,000 vacuum tubes as switches and filled approximately 1,500 square feet of floor space. That's about one-half the size of a standard high school basketball court! In addition to being large, the vacuum tubes produced a lot of heat and burned out frequently. Thus, vacuum tubes are impractical to use as switching devices in personal computers because of their size and reliability.

Since the introduction of ENIAC's vacuum tubes, two major revolutions have occurred in the design of switches, and consequently computers, to make them smaller and faster: the invention of the transistor and the fabrication of integrated circuits.

**Figure** 4.2

Computers can be constructed using vacuum tubes (see inset). The difference in size achieved by moving from tubes to transistors allowed computers to become desktop devices.

## Transistors

**Transistors** are electrical switches that are built out of layers of a special type of material called a **semiconductor**, which is any material that can be controlled to either conduct electricity or act as an insulator (to prohibit electricity from passing through). Silicon, which is found in common sand, is the semiconductor material used to make transistors.

By itself, silicon does not conduct electricity particularly well, but if specific chemicals are added in a controlled way to the silicon, it begins to behave like a switch (see Figure 4.3). The silicon allows electrical current to flow eas-

**Figure** 4.3

In "doping," a phosphorous atom is put in the place of a silicon atom. Because phosphorous has five electrons instead of four, the extra electron is free to move around.

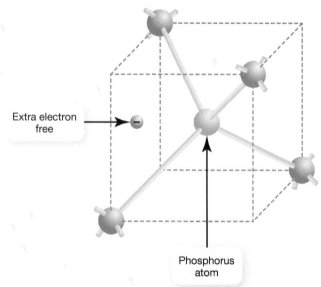

Extra electron free

Phosphorus atom

ily when a certain voltage is applied; otherwise, it prevents electrical current from flowing, thus behaving as an on/off switch. This kind of behavior is exactly what is needed to store digital information, the 0s (off) and 1s (on) in binary language.

Early transistors were built in separate units as small metal rods, with each rod acting as a single on/off switch. These first transistors were much smaller than vacuum tubes, produced little heat, and could quickly be switched from on to off, thereby allowing or blocking electrical current. They also were less expensive than vacuum tubes.

It wasn't long, however, before transistors reached their limits. Continuing advances in technology began to require more transistors than circuit boards could reasonably handle at the time. Something was needed to pack more transistor capacity into a smaller space. Thus, integrated circuits, the next technical revolution in switches, were developed.

**Integrated Circuits** **Integrated circuits** (or **chips**) are tiny regions of semiconductor material such as silicon that support a huge number of transistors (see Figure 4.4). Along with all the many transistors, other components critical to a circuit board (such as resistors, capacitors, and diodes) are also located on the integrated circuit. Most integrated circuits are no more than a quarter inch in size.

Because so many transistors can fit into such a small area, integrated circuits have enabled computer designers to create small yet powerful **microprocessors**, which are the chips that contain a CPU. The Intel 4004, the first complete microprocessor to be located on a single integrated circuit, was released in 1971, marking the beginning of the true miniaturization of computers. The Intel 4004 contained slightly more than 2,300 transistors. Today, more than 2 billion transistors can be manufactured in a space as tiny as the nail of your little finger!

This incredible feat has fueled an industry like no other. In 1951, the Univac I computer was the size of a large room. The processor memory unit itself, which cost more than $1 million to produce, was 14 feet long by 8 feet wide by 8.5 feet high and could perform about 1,905 operations per second. Thanks to advances in integrated circuits, the IBM PC released 30 years later took up just 1 cubic foot of space, cost $3,000, and performed 155,000 times more quickly.

**Figure** 4.4

Integrated circuits use advanced fabrication techniques to fit millions of transistors into a quarter inch of silicon. This is an integrated circuit with areas marked out in black to show memory units, logic sections, and input/output blocks.

Computers use on/off switches to perform their functions. But how can these simple switches be organized so that they let you use a computer to pay your bills online or write an essay? How can a set of switches describe a number or a word, or give a computer the command to perform addition? Recall that to manipulate the on/off switches, the computer works in binary language, which uses only two digits, 0 and 1. To understand how a computer works, let's first look at the special numbering system called the *binary number system*.

## The Binary Number System

A **number system** is an organized plan for representing a number. Although you may not realize it, you are already familiar with one number system. The **base 10 number system**, also known as **decimal notation**, is the system you use to represent all of the numeric values you use each day. It's called base 10 because it uses 10 digits, 0 through 9, to represent any value.

To represent a number in base 10, you break the number down into groups of ones, tens, hundreds, thousands, and so on. Each digit has a place value depending on where it appears in the number. For example, using base 10, in the whole number 6,954, there are 6 sets of thousands, 9 sets of hundreds, 5 sets of tens, and 4 sets of ones. Working from right to left, each place in a number represents an increasing power of 10, as shown here:

$$6{,}954 = 6 * (1{,}000) + 9 * (100) + 5 * (10) + 4 * (1)$$
$$= 6 * 10^3 + 9 * 10^2 + 5 * 10^1 + 4 * 10^0$$

Note that in this equation, the final number 1 is represented as $10^0$ because any number raised to the zero power is equal to 1.

Anthropologists theorize that humans developed a base 10 number system because we have 10 fingers. However, computer systems, with their huge collections of on/off switches, are not well suited to thinking about numbers in groups of 10. Instead, computers describe a number in powers of 2 because each switch can be in one of two positions: on or off. This numbering system is referred to as the **binary number system**.

The binary number system is also referred to as the **base 2 number system**. Even with just two digits, the

**SOUND BYTE**

## Where Does Binary Show Up?

In this Sound Byte, you'll learn how to use tools to work with binary, decimal, and hexadecimal numbers. (These tools come with the Windows operating system.) You'll also learn where you might see binary and hexadecimal values when you use a computer.

binary number system can still represent all the values that a base 10 number system can (see Figure 4.5). Instead of breaking the number down into sets of ones, tens, hundreds, and thousands, as is done in base 10 notation, the binary number system describes a number as the sum of powers of 2. Binary numbers are used to represent every piece of data stored in a computer: all of the numbers, all of the letters, and all of the instructions that the computer uses to execute work.

**Figure 4.5**

Computer humor—the value 2 is written as 10 in binary!

**Representing Integers** In the base 10 number system, a whole number is represented as the sum of ones, tens, hundreds, and thousands—that is, sums of powers of 10. The binary system works in the same way, but describes a value as the sum of groups of 1s, 2s, 4s, 8s, 16s, 32s, 64s, etc.—that is, powers of 2: 1, 2, 4, 8, 16, 32, 64, and so on.

Let's look at the number 67. In base 10, the number 67 would be six sets of 10s and seven sets of 1s, as follows:

$$\text{Base 10: } 67 = 6 * 10^1 + 7 * 10^0$$

One way to figure out how 67 is represented in base 2 is to find the largest possible power of 2 that could be in the number 67. Two to the eighth power is 256, and there are no groups of 256 in the number 67. Two to the seventh power is 128, but that is bigger than 67. Two to the sixth power is 64, and there is a group of 64 inside a group of 67.

| 67 has | 1 | group of | 64 | That leaves 3 and |
|---|---|---|---|---|
| 3 has | 0 | groups of | 32 | |
| | 0 | groups of | 16 | |
| | 0 | groups of | 8 | |
| | 0 | groups of | 4 | |
| | 1 | group of | 2 | That leaves 1 and |
| 1 has | 1 | group of | 1 | Now nothing is left |

So, the binary number for 67 is written as 1000011 in base 2:

$$\text{Base 2: } 67 = 64 + 0 + 0 + 0 + 0 + 2 + 1$$
$$= (1 * 2^6) + (0 * 2^5) + (0 * 2^4) + (0 * 2^3) +$$
$$(0 * 2^2) + (1 * 2^1) + (1 * 2^0)$$
$$= (1000011) \text{ base 2}$$

It is easier to have a calculator do this for you! Some calculators have a button labeled DEC (for decimal) and another labeled BIN (for binary). Using Windows, you can access the Scientific Calculator that supports conversion between decimal (base 10) and binary (base 2) by choosing Start, All Programs, Accessories, and then clicking Calculator. From the View menu, select Programmer. You can enter your calculation in decimal and instantly see the binary representation in 64 bits, as shown in Figure 4.6.

A large integer value becomes a very long string of 1s and 0s in binary! For convenience, programmers often use **hexadecimal notation** to make these expressions easier to use. Hexadecimal is a base 16 number system, meaning it uses 16 digits to represent numbers instead of the 10 digits used in base 10 or the 2 digits used in base 2. The 16 digits it uses are the 10 numeric digits, 0 to 9, plus six extra symbols: A, B, C, D, E, and F. Each of the letters A through F corresponds to a numeric value, so that A equals 10, B equals 11, and so on (see Figure 4.7). Therefore, the value 67 in decimal is 1000011 in binary or 43 in hexadecimal notation. It is much easier for computer scientists to use the two-digit 43 than the seven-digit string 1000011. The Windows Calculator in Programmer view also can perform conversions to hexadecimal notation. (You can watch a video showing you how to perform

**Figure 4.6**

The Windows Calculator in Programmer mode instantly converts from decimal values to binary.

conversions between bases using the Windows Calculator in the Sound Byte titled "Where Does Binary Show Up?")

**Representing Characters: ASCII** We have just been converting integers from base 10, which *we* understand, to base 2 (binary state), which the computer understands. Similarly, we need a system that converts letters and other symbols that *we* understand to a binary state that the computer understands. To provide a consistent means for representing letters and other characters, certain codes dictate how to represent characters in binary format. Older mainframe computers use Extended Binary-Coded Decimal Interchange Code (EBCDIC, pronounced "Eb-sih-dik"). However, most of today's personal computers use the American National Standards Institute (ANSI, pronounced "An-see") standard code, called the **American Standard Code for Information Interchange** (**ASCII**, pronounced "As-key"), to represent each letter or character as an 8-bit (or 1-byte) binary code.

Each binary digit is called a **bit** for short. Eight binary digits (or bits) combine to create one **byte**. We have been converting base 10 numbers to a binary format. In such cases, the binary format has no standard length. For example, the binary format for the number 2 is two digits (10), whereas the binary format for the number 10 is four digits (1010). Although binary numbers can have more or fewer than 8 bits, each single alphabetic or special character is 1 byte (or 8 bits) of data and consists of a unique combination of a total of eight 0s and 1s.

The ASCII code represents the 26 uppercase letters and 26 lowercase letters used in the English language, along with many punctuation symbols and other special characters, using 8 bits. Figure 4.8 shows several examples of ASCII code representation of printable letters and characters.

**Figure 4.7** | SAMPLE HEXADECIMAL VALUES

| Decimal Number | Hexadecimal Value | Decimal Number | Hexadecimal Value |
|---|---|---|---|
| 00 | 00 | 08 | 08 |
| 01 | 01 | 09 | 09 |
| 02 | 02 | 10 | A |
| 03 | 03 | 11 | B |
| 04 | 04 | 12 | C |
| 05 | 05 | 13 | D |
| 06 | 06 | 14 | E |
| 07 | 07 | 15 | F |

**Figure 4.8** | ASCII STANDARD CODE FOR A SAMPLE OF LETTERS AND CHARACTERS

| ASCII Code | Represents This Symbol | ASCII Code | Represents This Symbol |
|---|---|---|---|
| 01000001 | A | 01100001 | a |
| 01000010 | B | 01100010 | b |
| 01000011 | C | 01100011 | c |
| 01011010 | Z | 00100011 | # |
| 00100001 | ! | 00100100 | $ |
| 00100010 | " | 00100101 | % |

*Note:* For the full ASCII table, see **www.asciitable.com**.

**Representing Characters: Unicode** Because it represents letters and characters using only 8 bits, the ASCII code can assign only 256 (or $2^8$) different codes for unique characters and letters. Although this is enough to represent English and many other characters found in the world's languages, ASCII code cannot represent all languages and symbols, because some languages require more than 256 characters and letters. Thus, a new encoding scheme, called **Unicode**, was created. By using 16 bits instead of the 8 bits used in ASCII, Unicode can represent nearly 1,115,000 code points and currently assigns more than 96,000 unique character symbols (see Figure 4.9). The first 128 characters of Unicode are identical to ASCII, but because of its depth, Unicode is also able to represent the alphabets of all modern and historic languages and notational systems, including such languages and writing systems as Tibetan, Tagalog, Japanese, and Canadian Aboriginal syllabics. As we continue to become a more global society, it is anticipated that Unicode will replace ASCII as the standard character formatting code.

**Representing Decimal Numbers** The binary number system also can represent a decimal number. How can a string of 1s and 0s capture the information in a value such as 99.368? Because every computer must store such numbers in the same way, the Institute of Electrical and Electronics Engineers (IEEE) has established a standard called the *floating-point standard* that describes how numbers with fractional parts should be represented in the binary number system. Using a 32-bit system, we can represent an incredibly wide range of numbers. The method dictated by the IEEE standard works the same for any number with a decimal point, such as the number –0.75. The first digit, or bit (the sign bit), is used to indicate whether the number is positive or negative. The next eight bits store the magnitude of the number, indicating whether the number is in the hundreds or millions, for example. The standard says to use the next 23 bits to store the value of the number.

**Interpretation** *All* data inside the computer is stored as bits. Positive and negative numbers can be stored using signed integer notation, with the first bit (the sign bit) indicating the sign and the rest of the bits indicating the value of the number. Decimal numbers are stored according to the IEEE floating-point standard, and letters and symbols are stored according to the ASCII code or Unicode. All of these different number systems and codes exist so that computers can store different types of information in their on/off switches. No matter what kind of data you input in a computer—a color, a musical note, or a street address—that data will be stored as a string of 1s and 0s. The important lesson is that the interpretation of 0s and 1s is what matters. The same binary pattern could represent a positive number, a negative number, a fraction, or a letter.

How does the computer know which interpretation to use for the 1s and 0s? When your brain processes language, it takes the sounds you hear and uses the rules of English, along with other clues, to build an interpretation of the sound as a word. If you are in New York City and hear someone shout, "Hey, Lori!" you expect someone is saying hello to a friend. If you are in London and hear the same sound—"Hey! Lorry!"—you jump out of the way because a truck is coming at you! You knew which interpretation to apply to the sound because you had some other information—that you were in England.

Likewise, the CPU is designed to understand a specific language or set of instructions. Certain instructions tell the CPU to expect a negative number next or to interpret the following bit pattern as a character. Because of this extra information, the CPU always knows which interpretation to use for a series of bits.

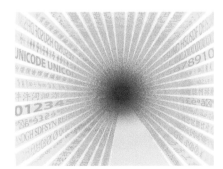

**Figure 4.9**

The written languages of the world require thousands of different characters, shown here. Unicode provides a system allowing digital representation of over 1,100,000 unique characters.

# The CPU Machine Cycle

Any program you run on your computer is actually a long series of binary code describing a specific set of commands the CPU must perform. These commands may be coming from a user's actions or may be instructions fed from a program while it executes. Each CPU is somewhat different in the exact steps it follows to perform its tasks, but all CPUs must perform a series of similar general steps. These steps, illustrated in Figure 4.10, are referred to as a CPU **machine cycle** (or **processing cycle**).

1. **Fetch:** When any program begins to run, the 1s and 0s that make up the program's binary code must be "fetched" from their temporary storage location in random access memory (RAM) and moved to the CPU before they can be executed.

2. **Decode:** Once the program's binary code is in the CPU, it is decoded into the commands the CPU understands.

3. **Execute:** Next, the CPU actually performs the work described in the commands.

   Specialized hardware on the CPU performs addition, subtraction, multiplication, division, and other mathematical and logical operations at incredible speeds.

4. **Store:** The result is stored in one of the **registers**, special memory storage areas built into the CPU, which are the most expensive, fastest memory in your computer. The CPU is then ready to fetch the next set of bits encoding the next instruction.

No matter what program you are running, be it a Web browser or a word processing program, and no matter how many programs you are using at one time, the CPU performs these four steps over and over at incredibly high speeds. Shortly, we'll look at each stage in more detail so that you can understand the complexity of the CPU's design, how to compare different CPUs on the market, and what enhancements you can expect in CPU designs of the future. But first, let's examine a few of the CPU's other components that help it perform its tasks.

## The System Clock

To move from one stage of the machine cycle to the next, the motherboard uses a built-in **system clock**. This internal clock is actually a special crystal that acts like a metronome, keeping a steady beat and thereby controlling when the CPU will move to the next stage of processing.

These steady beats or "ticks" of the system clock, known as the **clock cycle,** set the pace by which the computer moves from process to process. The pace, known as **clock speed,** is measured in hertz (Hz), a unit of measure that describes how many times something happens per second. Today's system clocks are measured in gigahertz (GHz), each of which represents 1 billion clock ticks per second. Therefore, in a 3 GHz system, there are 3 billion

**Figure** 4.10

The CPU machine cycle.

clock ticks each second. Computers with older processors would sometimes need one or more cycles to process one instruction. Today, however, CPUs are designed to handle more instructions more efficiently, and are, therefore, capable of executing more than one instruction per cycle.

## The Control Unit

The CPU, like any part of the computer system, is designed from a collection of switches. How can simple on/off switches "remember" the fetch-decode-execute-store sequence of the CPU machine cycle? How can they perform the work required in each of these stages?

The **control unit** of the CPU manages the switches inside the CPU. It is programmed by CPU designers to remember the sequence of processing stages for that CPU and how each switch in the CPU should be set (i.e., on or off) for each stage. With each beat of the system clock, the control unit moves each switch to the correct on or off setting and then performs the work of that stage.

Let's now look at each of the stages in the machine cycle in a bit more depth.

## Stage 1: The Fetch Stage

The data and program instructions the CPU needs are stored in different areas in the computer system. Data and program instructions move between these areas as they are needed by the CPU for processing. Programs (such as Microsoft Word) are permanently stored on the hard drive because it offers nonvolatile storage, meaning the programs remain stored there even when you turn the power off. However, when you launch a program (that is, when you double-click an icon to execute the program), the program, or sometimes only the essential parts of a program, is transferred from the hard drive into RAM.

The program moves to RAM because the CPU can access the data and program instructions stored in RAM more than 1 million times faster than if they are left on the hard drive. In part, this is because RAM is much closer to the CPU than the hard drive is. Another reason for the delay in transmission of data and program instructions from the hard drive to the CPU is the relatively slow speed of mechanical hard drives. The read/write heads have to sweep over the spinning platters, which takes time. Even non-mechanical SSD hard drives have slower access speeds than RAM. RAM is a type of memory that gives very fast, direct access to data. As specific instructions from the program are needed, they are moved from RAM into registers (the special storage areas located on the CPU itself), where they wait to be executed.

The CPU's storage area is not big enough to hold everything it needs to process at the same time. If enough memory were located on the CPU chip itself, an entire program could be copied to the CPU from RAM before it was executed. This certainly would add to the computer's speed and efficiency, because there would be no delay while the CPU stopped processing operations to fetch instructions from RAM to the CPU. However, including so much memory on a CPU chip would make these chips extremely expensive. In addition, CPU design is so complex that only a limited amount of storage space is available on the CPU itself.

**Cache Memory** The CPU doesn't actually need to fetch every instruction from RAM each time it goes through a cycle. There is another layer of storage, called **cache memory**, that has even faster access than RAM. The word *cache* is derived from the French word *cacher*, which means "to hide." Cache memory consists of small blocks of memory located directly on and next to the CPU chip. These memory blocks are holding places for recently or frequently used instructions or data that the CPU needs the most. When these instructions or data are stored in cache memory, the CPU can retrieve them more quickly than would be the case if it had to access the instructions or data in RAM.

Taking data you think you'll be using soon and storing it nearby is a simple idea but a powerful one. This is a strategy that shows up in other places in your computer system. For example, when you are browsing Web pages, it takes longer to download images than text. Your browser software automatically stores images on your hard drive so that you don't have to wait to

download them again if you want to go back and view a page you've already visited. Although this cache of files is not related to the cache storage space designed into the CPU chip, the idea is the same.

Modern CPU designs include several types of cache memory. If the next instruction to be fetched is not already located in a CPU register, instead of looking directly to RAM to find it, the CPU first searches Level 1 cache. **Level 1 cache** is a block of memory that is built onto the CPU chip to store data or commands that have just been used.

If the command is not located in Level 1 cache, the CPU searches Level 2 cache. Depending on the design of the CPU, **Level 2 cache** is either located on the CPU chip but slightly farther away from the CPU than Level 1, or is on a separate chip next to the CPU and therefore takes somewhat longer to access. Level 2 cache contains more storage area than does Level 1 cache. For the Intel Core i7, for example, the Level 1 cache is 64 kilobytes (KB) and the Level 2 cache is 1 megabyte (MB).

Only if the CPU doesn't find the next instruction to be fetched in either Level 1 or Level 2 cache will it make the long journey to RAM to access it.

The current direction of processor design is toward increasingly large multilevel CPU cache structures. Therefore, some newer CPUs, such as Intel's Core i7 processors, have an additional third level of cache memory storage called **Level 3 cache**. On computers with Level 3 cache, the CPU checks this area for instructions and data after it looks in Level 1 and Level 2 cache, but before it makes the longer trip to RAM (see Figure 4.11). The Level 3 cache holds between 2 and 12 MB of data. With 12 MB of Level 3 cache, there is storage for some entire programs to be transferred to the CPU for execution.

As an end user of computer programs, you do nothing special to use cache memory. In fact, you are not even able to see that caching is being used—nothing special lights up on your system unit or keyboard. The advantage of having more cache memory is that you'll experience better performance because the CPU won't have to make the longer trip to RAM to get data and instructions as often. Unfortunately, because it is built into the CPU chip or motherboard, you can't upgrade cache; it is part of the original design of the CPU. Therefore, as with RAM, when buying a computer it's important, everything else being equal, to consider buying the one with the most cache memory.

### Stage 2: The Decode Stage

The main goal of the decode stage is for the CPU's control unit to translate (or **decode**) the program's instructions into commands the CPU can understand. A CPU can understand only a tiny set of commands. The collection of commands a specific CPU can execute is called the **instruction set** for that system. Each CPU has its own unique instruction set. For example, the AMD Phenom II X6 six-core processor in a Gamer Mage system from iBuy-Power has a different instruction set than does the Intel Core i5 used in a Dell Inspiron notebook. The control unit

**Figure** 4.11

The CPU has multiple stages of internal memory, just a part of the overall hierarchy of memory storage.

interprets the code's bits according to the instruction set the CPU designers laid out for that particular CPU. Based on this process of translation, the control unit then knows how to set up all the switches on the CPU so that the proper operation will occur.

Because humans are the ones who write the initial instructions, all of the commands in an instruction set are written in a language called **assembly language**, which is easier for humans to work with than binary. Many CPUs have similar assembly commands in their instruction sets, including the commands listed here:

| ADD | Add |
|-----|-----|
| SUB | Subtract |
| MUL | Multiply |
| DIV | Divide |
| MOVE | Move data to RAM |
| STORE | Move data to a CPU register |
| EQU | Check if equal |

CPUs differ in the choice of additional assembly language commands selected for the instruction set. Each CPU design team works to develop an instruction set that is both powerful and speedy.

However, because the CPU knows and recognizes only patterns of 0s and 1s, it cannot understand assembly language directly, so these human-readable instructions are translated into long strings of binary code. The control unit uses these long strings of binary code called **machine**

**language** to set up the hardware in the CPU for the rest of the operations it needs to perform. Machine language is a binary code for computer instructions, much like the ASCII code is a binary code for letters and characters. Similar to each letter or character having its own unique combination of 0s and 1s assigned to it, a CPU has a table of codes consisting of combinations of 0s and 1s for each of its commands. If the CPU sees a particular pattern of bits arrive, it knows the work it must do. Figure 4.12 shows a few commands in both assembly language and machine language.

### Stage 3: The Execute Stage

The **arithmetic logic unit (ALU)** is the part of the CPU designed to perform mathematical operations such as addition, subtraction, multiplication, and division and to test the comparison of values such as *greater than, less than,* and *equal to.* For example, in calculating an average, the ALU is where the addition and division operations would take place. The ALU also performs logical OR, AND, and NOT operations. For example, in determining whether a student can graduate, the ALU would need to ascertain whether the student had taken all required courses AND obtained a passing grade in each of them. The ALU is specially designed to execute such calculations flawlessly and with incredible speed.

The ALU is fed data from the CPU's registers. The amount of data a CPU can process at a time is based in part on the amount of data each register can hold. The number of bits a computer can work with at a time is referred to as its **word size**. Therefore, a 64-bit processor can process more information faster than a 32-bit processor.

### Stage 4: The Store Stage

In the final stage, the result produced by the ALU is stored back in the registers. The instruction itself will explain which register should be used to store the answer. Once the entire instruction has been completed, the next instruction will be fetched, and the fetch-decode-execute-store sequence will begin again.

## Making CPUs Even Faster

Knowing how to build a CPU that can run faster than the competition can make a company rich. However, building a faster CPU is not easy. A new product launch must take into consideration the time it will take to design, manufacture, and test that processor. When the processor finally

## Figure 4.12 | REPRESENTATIONS OF SAMPLE CPU COMMANDS

| Human Language for Command | CPU Command in Assembly Language (Language Used by Programmers) | CPU Command in Machine Language (Language Used in the CPU's Instruction Set) |
|---|---|---|
| Add | ADD | 1110 1010 |
| Subtract | SUB | 0001 0101 |
| Multiply | MUL | 1111 0000 |
| Divide | DIV | 0000 1111 |

hits the market, it must be faster than the competition if the manufacturer hopes to make a profit. To create a CPU that will be released 36 months from now, it must be built to perform at least twice as fast as anything currently available.

Gordon Moore, the cofounder of processor manufacturer Intel, predicted more than 40 years ago that the number of transistors on a processor would double every 18 months. Known as **Moore's Law**, this prediction has been remarkably accurate—but only with tremendous engineering ingenuity. The first 8086 chip had only 29,000 transistors and ran at 5 MHz. Advances in the number of transistors on processors through the 1970s, 1980s, and 1990s continued to align with Moore's prediction.

However, there was a time near the turn of the 21st century when skeptics questioned how much longer Moore's Law would hold true. These skeptics were proved wrong with the microprocessor's continued growth in power. Today's Intel i7 chip has 774 million transistors—more than 18 times the transistor count of the Pentium 4 from the year 2000. Moreover, Intel's Itanium 9300 flaunts a whopping 2.3 billion transistors! How much longer can Moore's prediction hold true? Only time will tell.

Processor manufacturers can increase CPU performance in many different ways. One approach is to use a technique called *pipelining* to boost performance. Another approach is to design the CPU's instruction set so that it contains specialized, faster instructions for handling multimedia and graphics. In addition, some CPUs, such as Intel's i7 980X or the AMD Phenom II X6 processors, now have six independent processing paths inside, with one CPU chip doing the work of six separate CPU units. Some heavy computational problems are attacked by large numbers of computers actually clustered together to work at the same time.

### Pipelining

As an instruction is processed, the CPU runs sequentially through the four stages of processing: fetch, decode, execute, and store. **Pipelining** is a technique that allows the CPU to work on more than one instruction (or stage of processing) at a time, thereby boosting CPU performance.

For example, without pipelining, it may take four clock cycles to complete one instruction (one clock cycle for each of the four processing stages). However, with a four-stage pipeline, the computer can process four instructions at the same time. Like an automobile assembly line, instead of waiting for one car to go completely through each process of assembly, painting, and so on, you can have four cars going through the assembly line at the same time. When every component of the assembly line is done with its process, the cars all move on to the next stage.

Pipelined architectures allow several instructions to be processed at the same time. The ticks of the system clock (the clock cycle) indicate when all instructions move to the next process. The secret of pipelining is that the CPU is allowed to be fetching one instruction while it is simultaneously decoding another, executing a third, storing a fourth, and so on. Using pipelining, a four-stage processor can potentially run up to four times faster because some instruction is finishing every clock cycle rather than waiting four cycles for each instruction to finish. In Figure 4.13a, a non-pipelined instruction takes four clock cycles to be completed, whereas in Figure 13b, the four instructions have been completed in the same time using pipelining.

The number of stages in a pipeline depends entirely on design decisions. Earlier we analyzed a CPU that went through four stages in the execution of an instruction. The Intel Pentium 4 with hyper-threading featured a 31-stage pipeline, and the PowerPC G5 processor used a 10-stage pipeline. Thus, similar to an assembly line, in a 31-stage pipeline, as many as 31 different instructions can be processed at any given time, making the processing of information much faster. However, because so many aspects of the CPU design interact, you cannot predict performance based solely on the number of stages in a pipeline.

### Does Your Computer Need More Power? Team It Up!

The history of computing shows us that processing power increases tremendously each year. One strategy in use now for continuing that trend is cluster computing. If one computer is powerful, then two are twice as powerful—if you can get them to work together. A *computing cluster* is a group of computers, connected by specialized clustering software, that works together to solve complex equations. Most clusters work on something called the *balancing principle*, whereby computational work is transferred from overloaded (busy) computers in the cluster to computers that have more computing resources available. Computing clusters, although not as fast as supercomputers (single computers with extremely high processing capabilities), can perform computations faster than one computer working alone and are used for complex calculations such as weather forecasting and graphics rendering. You can now rent time on computing clusters through services like PurePowua (**www.purepowua .com**), where you can upload and remotely control your job from your desktop as it runs on a cluster of computers.

**a** Instruction Cycle, Non-Pipelined

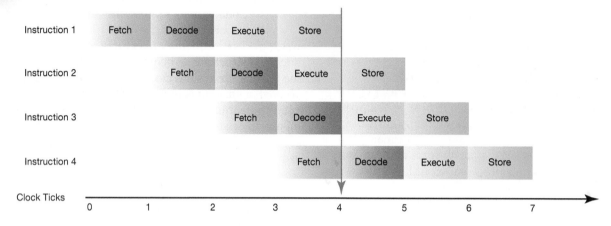

**b** Instruction Cycle, Pipelined

## Figure 4.13

Instead of (a) waiting for each instruction to complete, (b) pipelining allows the system to work on more than one set of instructions at one time.

There is a cost to pipelining a CPU as well. The CPU must be designed so that each stage (fetch, decode, execute, and store) is independent. This means that each stage must be able to run at the same time that the other three stages are running. This requires more transistors and a more complicated hardware design.

### Specialized Multimedia Instructions

Each design team that develops a new CPU tries to imagine what users' greatest needs will be in four or five years. Currently, several processors on the market reflect this consideration by incorporating specialized multimedia instructions into the basic instruction set.

Hardware engineers have redesigned the chip so that the instruction set contains new commands that are customized to speed up the work needed for video and audio processing. For example, Intel has integrated into its processor designs Streaming Single Instruction Multiple Data (SIMD) Extensions, adding a special group of 157 commands to the basic instruction set. These multimedia-specific instructions work to accelerate video, speech, and image processing in the CPU.

### Multiple Processing Efforts

Many high-end server systems employ a **quad processor design** that has four completely separate CPU chips on one motherboard. Often, these server systems can later be scaled so that they can accommodate four, six, or even twelve processors. The Cray Jaguar supercomputer has a total of 37,376 independent processors!

Meanwhile, Intel is promoting a technology called *multi-core processing* in its Core processor line of chips. Chips with dual-core processing capabilities have two separate parallel processing paths inside them, so they are almost as fast as two separate CPUs. It is not quite twice as fast because the system must do some extra work to decide which processor will work on which part of the problem and to recombine the results each CPU produces.

Dual-core processing is especially helpful because antivirus software and other security programs often run in the background as you use your system. A dual-core processor enables these multiple applications to execute much more quickly than with traditional CPUs. Six-core processors, like the Intel i7 Extreme Edition, are appearing in high-performance home-based systems now as well,

### Today's Supercomputers: The Fastest of the Fast

Supercomputers are the biggest and most powerful type of computer. Scientists and engineers use these computers to solve complex problems or to perform massive computations. Some supercomputers are single computers with multiple processors, whereas others consist of multiple computers that work together.

The top spot on the June 2011 TOP500 List was won by the Japanese K computer. It operates at a peak of more than 8 petaflops (or 8 quadrillion operations per second). That's almost 90,000 times faster than the fastest personal computer. In fact, the K computer is faster than the next five supercomputer systems on the TOP500 List combined!

Check out the current crop of the world's fastest supercomputers at the TOP500 site (**www.top500.org**).

executing six separate processing paths. Multiprocessor systems are often used when intensive computational problems need to be solved in such areas as computer simulations, video production, and graphics processing.

Certain types of problems are well suited to a parallel-processing environment. In **parallel processing**, there is a large network of computers, with each computer working on a portion of the same problem simultaneously. To be a good candidate for parallel processing, a problem must be one that can be divided into a set of tasks that can be run simultaneously. So, for example, a problem where millions of faces are being compared with a target image for recognition is easily adapted to a parallel setting. The target face can be compared at the same time to many hundreds of faces. But if the next step of an algorithm can be started only after the results of the previous step have been computed, parallel processing will present no advantages.

A simple analogy of parallel processing is a laundromat. Instead of taking all day to do five loads of laundry with one machine, you can bring all your laundry to a laundromat, load it into five separate machines, and finish it all in approximately the same time it would have taken you to do just one load on a single machine. In real life, parallel processing is used in complex weather forecasting to run calculations over many different regions around the globe; in the airline industry to analyze customer information in an effort to forecast demand; and by the government in census data compilation.

Thus, what you can continue to expect from CPUs in the future is that they will continue to get smaller and faster and consume less power. This fits with the current demands of consumers for more powerful portable computing devices.

At the most basic level of binary 1s and 0s, computers are systems of switches that can accomplish impressive tasks. By understanding the hardware components that make up your computer system, you can use your system more effectively and make better buying decisions.

## Multiple Choice

**Instructions:** Answer the multiple-choice questions below for more practice with key terms and concepts from this Technology in Focus feature.

1. Which is *not* a typical use of parallel processing systems?
   a. computer simulations
   b. word processing
   c. weather modeling
   d. graphics processing

2. What is another name for the base 10 number system?
   a. decimal notation
   b. binary number system
   c. hexadecimal notation
   d. integer system

3. Which encoding scheme can represent the alphabets of all modern and historic languages?
   a. base 2 number system
   b. Unicode
   c. ASCII
   d. scientific

4. Moore's Law is best described as
   a. an observation of the rate of increasing transistor density.
   b. a physical principle.
   c. a legal construct limiting performance.
   d. an advertising campaign by Intel.

5. To regulate the internal timing of a computer system, the motherboard uses
   a. a system clock.
   b. software simulation.
   c. RAM.
   d. a register.

6. Special areas of memory storage built into the CPU are known as
   a. switches.
   b. semiconductors.
   c. registers.
   d. integrated circuits.

7. Which is the correct set of steps in the machine cycle?
   a. execute, store, fetch, decode
   b. store, fetch, execute, decode
   c. decode, execute, fetch, store
   d. fetch, decode, execute, store

8. All data inside the computer is stored as
   a. bytes.
   b. bits.
   c. switches.
   d. cache memory.

9. Which statement about pipelining is *false?*
   a. Pipelining boosts CPU performance.
   b. Pipeline design is used in many modern CPUs.
   c. Pipelining requires a less complicated hardware design.
   d. Pipelining allows the computer to process multiple instructions simultaneously.

10. From fastest to slowest, which is the fastest sequence of accessing memory?
    a. RAM, Level 1 cache, Level 2 cache, Level 3 cache
    b. registers, Level 1 cache, Level 2 cache, RAM
    c. Level 1 cache, Level 2 cache, RAM, registers
    d. Level 2 cache, Level 1 cache, registers, RAM

# chapter 5

# digital lifestyle:

## managing digital data and devices

Marilyn Nieves/
Vetta/Getty Images

### A Digital Lifestyle

**OBJECTIVE:**

What are the changes that have brought us a digital lifestyle? *(p. 136)*

LockieCurrie/
iStockphoto.com

### Digital Telephony

**OBJECTIVES:**

How do cell phone and smartphone components resemble a traditional computer? *(p. 138)*

Why would I use VoIP? *(p. 147)*

 Sound Byte: Smartphones Are Really Smart

 Sound Byte: Connecting with Bluetooth

 Active Helpdesk: Keeping Your Data on Hand

Palsur/
iStockphoto.com

### Digital Media and Information

**OBJECTIVES:**

How is digital media different from analog? *(p. 149)*

How is digital media created and what changes has it brought? *(p. 151)*

How do I create and watch digital video? *(p. 159)*

 **Active Helpdesk:** Using Portable Media Players

© ryccio/
iStockphoto.com

### Digital Convergence

**OBJECTIVE:**

What new kinds of mobile devices are available? *(p. 166)*

*Scan here for more info on How Cool Is This?*

# how cool is *this?*

TiVo is not the only game in town. **PVR** (personal video recorder) software is now available, free of charge, for every style of operating system. Using a PVR, you can **record** standard or HD television broadcasts on your hard drive and then watch them when you have the time. **Free** programs like XBMC Media Center and MeediOS let you pause and rewind live TV shows and include features that allow you to automatically detect and **skip** commercials. You even have access to a TV **listings** guide and can schedule your PVR from any location using the Web.

# A Digital Lifestyle

Computers today are central to everyday life. Which part of your life isn't touched by some sort of computer or digital technology? Computer-like devices, such as smartphones and iPads, are everywhere. Much of your entertainment—playing games, watching movies and television, and downloading songs—is probably delivered digitally via the Internet.

Do you really understand how all this digital technology works? Do you know all of your options so you can enjoy the digital devices and digital media you purchase to the fullest extent? In this chapter, we explore the key aspects of your digital life—digital telephony, digital media, and digital convergence—and help you understand how the related technologies work so you can use them to your best advantage.

**When did everything go "digital"?** It used to be that everything was analog. Today, no matter what you're interested in—music, movies, television, radio, stock prices—digital information is the key. All forms of entertainment have migrated to the digital domain (see Figure 5.1). Phone systems and television signals are now digital streams of data. MP3 files encode digital forms of music, and digital cameras and video cameras are now commonplace. In Hollywood, feature films are being shot entirely with digital equipment, and many movie theaters use digital projection equipment. Satellite radio systems such as SiriusXM satellite radio and HD Radio are broadcast in digital formats.

**What is special about digital?** Any kind of information can be digitized (measured and converted to a stream of numeric values). Consider sound. It is carried to your ears by sound waves, which are actually patterns of pressure changes in the air. Images are our interpretation of the changing intensity of light waves around us. These sound and light waves are called **analog** waves or continuous waves. They illustrate the loudness of a sound or the brightness of the colors in an image at a given moment in time. They are continuous signals because you would never have to lift your pencil off the page to draw them; they are just long, continuous lines.

First-generation recording devices such as vinyl records and analog television broadcasts were designed to reproduce these sound and light waves. A needle in the groove of a vinyl record vibrates in the same pattern as the original sound wave. Analog television signals are actually waves that tell an analog TV how to display the same color and brightness as is seen in the production studio. However, it's difficult to describe a wave, even mathematically. The simplest sounds, such as that of middle C on a piano, have the simplest shapes, like the one shown in Figure 5.2a. However, something like the word *hello* generates a highly complex pattern, like the one shown in Figure 5.2b.

**What advantages do digital formats have over analog ones?** Digital formats describe signals as long strings of numbers. This digital representation gives us a simple way to describe sound and light waves exactly so that sounds and images can be reproduced perfectly each time. In addition, we already have easy ways to distribute digital information, such as streaming movies or attaching files to a Facebook message. Thus, digital information can be reproduced exactly and distributed easily. Both give it huge advantages over an analog format.

**How can a sequence of numbers express complicated analog shapes?** The answer is provided by something called *analog-to-digital conversion*. In analog-to-digital conversion, the incoming analog signal is measured many times each second. The strength of the signal at each

| **Figure 5.1** | ANALOG VERSUS DIGITAL ENTERTAINMENT | |
|---|---|---|
| | **Analog** | **Digital** |
| Publishing | Magazines, books | Ebooks, ezines |
| Music | Vinyl record albums and cassette tapes | CDs and MP3 files |
| Photography | 35-mm single-lens reflex (SLR) cameras / Photos stored on film | Digital cameras, including digital SLRs / Photos stored as digital files |
| Video | 8-mm, VHS, and Hi8 camcorders / Film stored on tapes | High-definition digital video (DV) cameras / Film stored as digital files; distributed on DVD and Blu-ray Discs and streamed |
| Radio | AM/FM radio | HD Radio / Sirius/XM satellite radio |
| Television | Conventional broadcast analog TV | High-definition digital television (HDTV) |

**Figure** 5.2

(a) This is an analog wave showing the simple, pure sound of a piano playing middle C. (b) This is the complex wave produced when a person says "Hello."

measurement is recorded as a simple number. The series of numbers produced by the analog-to-digital conversion process gives us the digital form of the wave. Figure 5.3 shows analog and digital versions of the same wave. In Figure 5.3a, you see the original, continuous analog wave. You could draw that wave without lifting your pencil from the page. In Figure 5.3b, the wave has been digitized and is no longer a single line; instead, it is represented as a series of points or numbers.

**How has the change from analog to digital technologies affected our lifestyle?** When the market for communication devices for entertainment media—like photographs, music, and video—switched over to a digital standard, we began to have products with new and useful capabilities. Small devices can now hold huge collections of a variety of types of information. We can interact with our information any time we like, in ways that, prior to the conversion to digital media, had been

**Figure** 5.3

(a) A simple analog wave. (b) A digitized version of the same wave.

too expensive or too difficult to learn. The implications of the shift to digital media are continually evolving.

## Digital Telephony

Communication has changed radically in the digital age. Chapter 10 will discuss the use of wikis, blogs, RSS feeds, and other Web-based tools for connecting people and their ideas. All of these software applications are dependent on digital information.

Hardware devices that support communication also have evolved because of digital technologies. **Telephony**, the use of equipment to provide voice communications over a distance, has shifted from an analog science to a digital one. In this section, we examine cell phones, smartphones, and Voice over Internet Protocol (VoIP) devices to see how they are changing to meet modern communication needs.

### Cell Phones and Smartphones

**What's the difference between a cell phone and a smartphone?** The **cellular phone** (or **cell phone**) has evolved from a clunky, boxlike device to a compact, fully featured communication and information storage device. Cell phones offer all of the features available on a traditional telephone system, including automatic redial, call timers, and voice mail capabilities. Most cell phones also feature voice-activated dialing, which is important for hands-free operation. In addition, many cell phones offer Internet access, text messaging, personal information management (PIM) features, voice recording, GPS services, and digital image and video capture. In fact, the category of inexpensive phones equipped with many of these abilities is now referred to as *feature phones*.

**Smartphones** extend the power of a cell phone. A smartphone requires a data plan from the cell phone provider. This is logical because a smartphone user is likely to spend a lot of time accessing the Internet to upload and download data. Most smartphones have larger screen areas, WiFi accessibility, and enough computing power to run versions of programs like Microsoft Excel or even video editing software.

**Are cell phones and smartphones computers?** Cell phones and smartphones have the same components as any computer: a processor (central processing unit, or CPU), memory, and input and output devices, as shown in Figure 5.4. Cell/smartphones also require their own operating system (OS) software and have their own application software. So modern cell phones and smartphones are computers.

### How Cellular Works

**How do cell phones use digital signals?** When you speak into a cell phone, the sound enters the microphone as a sound wave. Because analog sound waves need to be digitized (that is, converted into a sequence of 1s and 0s that the cell phone's processor can understand), an **analog-to-digital converter chip** converts your voice's sound waves into digital signals. Next, the digital data must be compressed, or squeezed, into the smallest possible space so that it will transmit more quickly to another phone. The processor cannot perform the mathematical operations required at this stage quickly enough, so a specialized chip called the **digital signal processor** is included in the cell phone to handle the compression work. Finally, the digital data is transmitted as a radio wave through the cellular network to the destination phone.

When you receive an incoming call, the digital signal processor decompresses the incoming message. An amplifier boosts the signal to make it loud enough, and it is then passed on to the speaker.

**What's "cellular" about a cell phone?** A set of connected "cells" makes up a cellular network. Each cell is a geographic area centered on a **base transceiver station**, which is a large communications tower with antennas, amplifiers, receivers, and transmitters. When you place a call

---

**BITS AND BYTES**

### Phoning Home—Accessing Your Home Computer from Your Cell Phone

An estimated 1 billion cellular phones that aren't considered smartphones are currently deployed. But you can still do some very advanced things with a non-smartphone. For example, you can use it to access your home computer remotely and retrieve that big presentation you need for this afternoon. Remote access services such as GoToMyPC (**www.gotomypc.com**) and LogMeIn (**www.logmein .com**) can help and are free of charge. As long as you have a browser on your cell phone and a data plan with your provider, you can access the files on your computer from your phone without installing any software on the cell phone. (Versions are also available for tablets like the iPad.) You may not have to trade in that low-end cell phone yet. Just try getting it to work a little harder!

on a cell phone, a base station picks up the request for service. The station then passes the request to a central location called a **mobile switching center**. The reverse process occurs when you receive an incoming call. A telecommunications company builds its network by constructing a series of cells that overlap in an attempt to guarantee that its cell phone customers have coverage no matter where they are.

As you move during your phone call, the mobile switching center monitors the strength of the signal between your cell phone and the closest base station. When the signal is no longer strong enough between your cell phone and the base station, the mobile switching center orders the next base station to take charge of your call. When your cell phone "drops out," it may be because the distance between base stations was too great to provide an adequate signal.

### Cell Phone Components

**What does the processor inside a cell/smartphone do?** Although the processor inside a cell/smartphone is obviously not as fast or as high-powered as a processor in a desktop computer, it is still responsible for a great number of tasks. The processor coordinates sending all of the data among the other electronic components inside the phone. It also runs the cell/smartphone's operating system, which provides a user interface so that you can change phone settings, store information, play games, and so on. Popular processors for cell/smartphones include the Qualcomm Snapdragon, the Apple A4, and the Marvell XScale processor. Some processors use dual-core processing technology, which is also used in some desktop processors.

When shopping for a new phone, be well prepared. Use published benchmarking results to compare performance. These benchmarks are often published on the *PC Magazine* Web site (**www.pcmag.com**) or at *Wired* (**www.wired.com**).

**Is there a standard operating system for cell/smartphones?** Each cell/smartphone manufacturer makes its own small changes to the operating system and designs its own user interface. So when moving between different cell/smartphones, you will likely see a different set of commands and icons.

There are a number of operating systems in the cell/smartphone market now. Many

smartphones use the Windows Phone 7 operating system. Apple's iPhone uses iOS, a version of the OS X operating system that is used in Apple's personal computers. The HP Pre uses its own in-house-developed webOS. These operating systems are required to translate the user's commands into instructions for the processor.

There are several free operating systems that a manufacturer can use as a base for its cell/smartphone operating system. The most successful open source OS is the Android collection developed by Google. Other open source mobile operating systems include Meego, Symbian, and Openmoko. The advantage of an open source mobile OS is that you can leverage the creativity of many developers in creating great applications and new phone designs.

Figure 5.5 illustrates some of the different and creative user interfaces featured among cell/smartphone operating systems.

**What does the memory chip inside a cell/smartphone do?** The operating system and the information you save in your cell/smartphone, such as phone numbers and addresses, need to be stored in memory. The operating system is stored in read-only memory (ROM) because the phone would be useless without that key piece of software. As you learned earlier, two kinds of memory are used in computers: volatile memory, which requires power to

Speaker

Liquid crystal display

Keypad

Microphone

Memory chip

CPU

**Figure** 5.4

Inside your cell phone, you'll find a CPU, a memory chip, input devices such as a microphone and a keypad, and output devices such as a display screen and a speaker.

a

b

c

**Figure** 5.5

(a) iOS 5, (b) Windows Phone 7, and (c) Android are all cellular operating systems.

store data, and nonvolatile memory, which stores data even when the power is turned off. ROM is nonvolatile, or permanent, memory. This means that when you turn off your phone, the data that is stored in ROM, which includes the operating system, remains in memory.

Other phone data, such as ring tones, is stored in separate internal memory chips. Full-featured cell phones have as many as 200 MB of internal memory and support additional memory through micro SD flash cards that can store up to 64 GB, as shown in Figure 5.6. Micro SD cards are easy to install in a phone, while some models simply have external slots for an SD card. You can use that storage for contact data, ring tones, images, songs, videos, and even software applications such as language translators or video games. Not every smartphone allows memory upgrades in this way, however. For example, the iPhone series does not allow you to add any memory.

**Figure** 5.6

You can insert additional memory by installing a micro SD flash card in a smartphone.

**What input and output devices do cell/smartphones use?** The primary input devices for a cell/smartphone are a microphone and a keypad. Some phones, such as the Samsung Impression (see Figure 5.7a), offer both a hidden keyboard and a touch-sensitive screen. The Apple iPhone provides a software-based keyboard (see Figure 5.7b) that supports more than 40 languages.

Cell phones often include a digital camera for capturing photos and video. These cameras are catching up to the quality level of standalone point-and-shoot cameras. For example, the Droid X2 offers a high-quality 8-megapixel (MP) camera with flash and video capture, and the Nokia N8 sports a 12 MP camera with Carl Zeiss lenses. Most cameras on cell/smartphones can record video as well as take still shots. Picture and video messaging is popular with many cell/smartphone users. They can transmit photos and video files via e-mail, post the files to Web sites such as Facebook, or send them directly to other phones.

Cell phone output devices include a speaker and a liquid crystal display (LCD). Higher-end models include full-color, high-resolution LCD screens. Newer on the market are OLED (organic light-emitting diode) displays, which allow very bright, sharp imaging and draw less power.

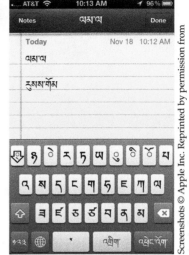

**Figure 5.7**

(a) The Samsung Impression includes a touch screen and a built-in QWERTY keyboard. (b) The Apple iPhone has a touch keyboard that supports more than 40 languages and a range of character sets.

High-resolution displays are becoming increasingly popular because more people are using their cell/smartphones to send and receive the digital images included in multimedia text messages and e-mail, and even to watch TV (see Figure 5.8).

Cell/smartphone and cable providers are teaming up to deliver broadcast TV programs directly to cell/smartphones through services such as Verizon V CAST and Sprint TV. A developing standard named Mobile DTV allows cell/smartphones or other mobile devices like tablets to receive free broadcasts from television stations. Cable providers and vendors like Netflix also provide streaming video content to mobile devices. With all this video content, having a high-quality screen is becoming more and more important.

**SOUND BYTE** — Smartphones Are Really Smart

In this Sound Byte, you'll learn how to use a smartphone as a powerful tool to communicate, calculate, and organize your workload.

**Figure 5.8**

The Mobile DTV system allows local TV stations to broadcast live, digital content to mobile devices.

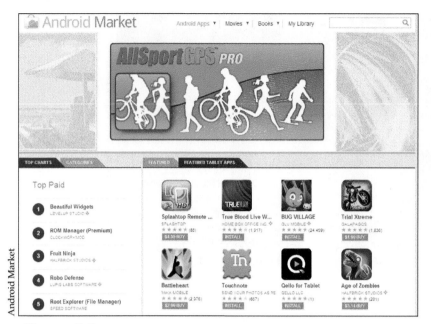

**Figure 5.9**

The Android Market is one of many online stores delivering software for mobile devices.

**Figure 5.10**

The Windows Sync Center makes it easy to arrange for synchronization of all your mobile devices.

>To launch Sync Center, click the **Start** button, select **Control Panel**, and double-click the **Sync Center** icon.

**What cell/smartphone software is available?** The operating system of most mobile devices comes with a standard collection of software such as a to-do list, contact manager, and calendar. Modified versions of application software such as Microsoft Word, Excel, Outlook, and PowerPoint are available for some high-end smartphones. A variety of games, tools, and reference applications are available from numerous software companies. A good source to locate software applications for your phone is GetJar (**www.getjar.com**). Many manufacturers have Web-based software stores, like iTunes for the Apple iPhone and the BlackBerry App World for RIM's BlackBerry devices. The Android developer community has held competitions to spur

the creation of new software applications for Android-based phones. Many software applications are available for Android through the Web and the Android Market (see Figure 5.9).

### Synchronizing

**How do I move information from my computer to my smartphone?** There are two main ways to transfer information between your phone and computer—wired and wireless. Let's start by looking at wired solutions. The high-density micro SD cards available for phones have room for thousands of songs, videos, or data files. Some phones are designed with a flash card that can be easily removed and slipped directly into a flash card reader on the computer. Almost all phones are designed with a USB port. Some have a mini-USB connector, while other models require a special cable to connect the phone to standard USB port. Once connected using a USB data cable, your phone will appear on your computer like an additional flash drive, and you can drag and drop files to it. You can also charge your phone through the USB cable.

You can coordinate the changes you make to your to-do lists, schedules, and other files on your phone with the files on your home or office computer. This process of updating your data so that the files on your cell/smartphone and computer are the same is called **synchronizing** or **syncing**. To synchronize your computer and the device, simply connect your phone via the appropriate USB cable.

Microsoft has recognized the vast increase in portable computing devices by integrating synchronization into the

Windows operating system. The Sync Center (see Figure 5.10), which is accessed from the Control Panel, allows you to set up automatic or manual synchronization. Make sure the device you are trying to set up synchronization parameters for is connected to your computer and then launch the Sync Center. Select the Set up new sync partnerships option to view available devices and configure their synchronization options.

**How do I transfer information to and from my phone wirelessly?** There are multiple technologies for handling wireless file transfer. **Bluetooth** technology uses radio waves to transmit data signals over short distances (approximately 30 feet for Bluetooth 1 and 60 feet for Bluetooth 2 and 3). Bluetooth 3 devices are the newest on the market and have a throughput about eight times faster than Bluetooth 2. Most cell/smartphones on the market today are Bluetooth-enabled, meaning they include a small Bluetooth chip that allows them to transfer data wirelessly to any other Bluetooth-enabled device. One benefit Bluetooth has over infrared, a wireless connection used in the past, is that a direct line of sight does not have to be present between two devices for them to communicate. You also can use Bluetooth

to synchronize your device with your computer. Bluetooth accessories such as earpieces, mice, keyboards, and even stereo headsets are available.

Another way to wirelessly transfer data to your phone is to use a WiFi 3G/4G connection through a cloud service. A number of Web services are now available to synchronize your e-mail, files, contacts, and calendars instantly and wirelessly. SugarSync, for example, will automatically wirelessly sync folders of data and the photos on your Android phone to your home computers (see Figure 5.11). These Web services

**Figure** 5.11

A cloud service allows you to keep the information on your phone instantly in sync with your other computing devices.

follow the model of "cloud computing," where Internet-based services and resources are distributed to users instead of being installed as an application on the user's computer. Apple's iOS 5 has integrated cloud support into several of the applications like Calendar, iTunes, PhotoStream, Contacts, and Mail.

There are other providers of wireless synchronization for mobile devices. Google Sync works with iPhones, Blackberry phones, Symbian, and Windows Mobile devices. All of your Google e-mail, calendar events, and contacts are automatically backed up online instantly on the Google servers. Even the Amazon Kindle uses wireless synchronization so that if you read a bit further in your e-book on your phone, when you get to your office, the Kindle software on your PC will have automatically updated to bookmark the new page you're on.

### Text Messaging

**What is SMS?** Short message service **(SMS)**—often just called *text messaging*—is a technology that allows you to send short text messages (comprising up to 160 characters) over mobile networks. To send SMS messages from your cell/smartphone, you use the keypad or a pre-saved template and type your message. You can send SMS messages to other mobile devices or to any e-mail address. You also can use SMS to send short text messages from your home computer to mobile devices such as your friend's cell/smartphone.

**How does SMS work?** SMS uses the cell phone network to transmit messages. When you send an SMS message, an SMS calling center receives the message and delivers it to the appropriate mobile device using

something called *store-and-forward* technology. This technology allows users to send SMS messages to any other SMS device in the world.

Many SMS fans like text messaging because it allows the receivers to read messages when it is convenient for them and is quicker than e-mail. Companies now support texting in many ways, so for example, your bank may allow you to text commands to request account balances or details about your last transaction, and the bank will text the requested information back to you. As shown in the table in Figure 5.12, several companies provide useful services based on text messaging.

If you plan to do a lot of texting, check the phone's feature list in advance and look for a phone with a good text prediction algorithm. With such an algorithm, typing a single letter pulls up a list of popular words beginning with that letter, saving you typing time. For example, the T9 (Text on 9 keys) algorithm also "learns" from your usage patterns and displays the most-used word first.

**Can I send and receive photos and videos using a cell/smartphone?** SMS technology allows you to send only text messages. However, an extension of SMS called **multimedia message service (MMS)** allows you to send messages that include text, sound, images, and video clips to other phones or e-mail addresses. MMS messages actually arrive as a series of messages; you view the text, then the image, and then the sound, and so on. You can then choose to save just one part of the message (such as the image), all of it, or none of it. MMS users can subscribe to financial, sports, and weather services that will "push" information

**Figure 5.12** | TEXT MESSAGING INFORMATION SERVICES

| SMS Code | Service Name | Web site | Description |
|---|---|---|---|
| 466453 (google) | Google SMS Search | **www.google.com/mobile/sms** | Obtains information such as addresses, phone numbers, driving directions, sports scores, and movie listings from the Google search engine. |
| 44636 (4Info) | 4INFO | **alerts.4info.com** | Similar to Google SMS, but also handles flight information and mobile coupons. |
| 242 242 (cha cha) | ChaCha | **www.chacha.com** | Human "guides" provide answers to any question in conversational English. |
| 3109043113 | 411 sms | **www.411sms.com** | Offers address and phone listings, turn-by-turn directions, movie showtimes, stock quotes, hot spot locations, dictionary definitions, horoscopes, and foreign language translations. |

to them, sending it automatically to their phones in MMS format.

### Mobile Internet

**How do I get Internet service for my smartphone?** Just as you have an Internet service provider (ISP) for Internet access for your desktop or notebook computer, you must have a **wireless Internet service provider** (or **wireless ISP**) to connect your smartphone to the Internet. Phone companies that provide phone calling plans (such as T-Mobile, Verizon, and AT&T) usually double as wireless ISPs. An Internet connectivity plan or text messaging plan is usually known as a **data plan**. Data charges are separate from phone calling charges and are provided at rates different from voice calls. Most carriers provide separate plans for different levels of texting usage and for various levels of data transfer to and from Internet sites. Before subscribing to a data plan, you should assess your needs: How often do you download new wallpaper, ring tones, or games? Do you use your smartphone's Internet access to download files from e-mails or from your company Web site? Begin by estimating how many kilobytes of data you transfer up and down from the Internet each month. Then select a plan that provides adequate service at a good price.

**At what speed is digital information transferred to my smartphone?** A smartphone connection is much slower than the Internet connection you have at your home. Although broadband speeds of 50 megabits per second (Mbps) are achievable at home using a cable or fiber-optic connection, your smartphone will connect at a much lower speed, depending on which technology you are using (see Figure 5.13).

Providers have introduced many smartphones based on two standards that support fast data transfer technologies:

**Figure 5.13** | CELLULAR CONNECTION SPEEDS

| Network | Availability | Speed (Mbps) |
| --- | --- | --- |
| 3G | 300 major markets | 0.6–2.3 |
| WiFi | WiFi hot spots | 4–5 |
| 4G | Major cities | 5–12 |

*Note:* Speeds will vary depending on provider and location.

3G and 4G. 3G brought mobile device data transfer rates as high as 1.4 Mbps (or more, under ideal conditions). Uploading the video clip you just recorded at the park or downloading a large PDF file from your company intranet is quicker if you are in range of a WiFi signal. But 3G does have some advantages over WiFi. It is more reliable and less susceptible to interference. Moreover, you won't have to hunt for a WiFi hot spot, because 3G blankets most major urban areas with connectivity.

4G networks are now rolling out across the United States. The promise of 4G is incredible: mobile connection speeds of up to 100 Mbps! Currently, most providers

**Figure 5.14**

A MiFi device turns your 3G phone signal into a WiFi connection for you and four of your friends.

AP Images/PRNewsFoto/ Verizon Wireless

## Make Your Cell/Smartphone Deliver

Carriers offer many additional services for your cell/smartphone. MusicID, for example, allows you to identify a song easily. Just hold your phone close to the radio's speaker for 15 seconds. You will then receive a text message with the name of the artist and the song. MusicID has a database of more than 3 million songs, so you can be the first to grab those new titles.

Other services can be added to your cell/smartphone plan. For example, you can subscribe to high-definition radio stations over your cell/smartphone. The extra fee allows you to stream more than 50 channels of commercial-free digital radio through your phone. Many phones are equipped for navigation services such as AT&T Navigator. Navigator delivers turn-by-turn instructions to you over your phone and displays real-time traffic information.

cannot deliver true 4G speeds, but deliver speeds of 3 Mbps to 6 Mbps. These options are faster than 3G but do not meet the rate required to be true 4G, so they are referred to as "near 4G" networks. The expansion of 4G will usher in a new generation of mobile devices and applications that will continue to expand how we think of mobile computing.

### Can I use my 3G signal to create a WiFi hotspot for my other devices?

There are devices available that will instantly create a mobile hot spot for you. MiFi (pronounced "my fi") devices, like the Verizon model shown in Figure 5.14, are often available free with a new account from major Internet providers like Verizon and Sprint. The MiFi can fit in a shirt pocket and run for up to four hours on a single charge. It connects to the Internet through the 3G wireless phone network and then distributes the WiFi signal over an area of 30 feet. These personal hot spots can then support up to five WiFi-enabled devices.

Another approach is **tethering**, which makes sure that as long as you have a 3G signal, your computer can access the Internet even when it tells you there are no available wireless networks. Several phones offer this capability. For example, an iPhone 4 can connect your notebook computer through wireless Bluetooth, and

Opera Mini

### Figure 5.15

Microbrowser software like Opera lets you quickly switch between open browser windows.

then provide Internet access through the 3G network signal.

### How do smartphones display content from the Internet?

On smartphones that have a limited amount of screen space, it is difficult to view Web pages without a great deal of horizontal scrolling. This is because most Web sites are designed for viewing on desktop monitors, which have much wider pixel widths than mobile screens. To enhance your Internet browsing experience on mobile devices, special microbrowser software runs on your phone. **Microbrowser** software provides a Web browser that is optimized to display Web content effectively on the smaller screen (see Figure 5.15). Popular versions of microbrowser software include Internet Explorer Mobile (included with the Windows Mobile OS), Safari on the iPhone, and Opera Mobile. Opera Mobile uses special small-screen rendering technology to reformat the Web images to fit on your smartphone screen, then zooms in with a simple tap. For the best Web experience, consider a phone that has a large screen, such as the HTC HD2, which boasts a 4.3-inch HD touch screen.

More and more Web sites are being created with content specifically designed for wireless devices. This specially designed content, which is text-based and contains no graphics, is written in a format called **Wireless Markup Language (WML)**. Content is designed so that it fits the smaller display screens of handheld mobile devices.

### How convenient is e-mail on a cell/smartphone?

A popular feature of cell/smartphones with Internet access lets users check e-mail. BlackBerry handhelds were the first devices that were optimized to check e-mail. BlackBerry pioneered the "push" technology that delivers your e-mail automatically to your phone, so you do not have to deliberately ask for current mail to be delivered. Now many other systems also offer "push" technology. With Internet access, users can always send or receive e-mail through Web-based e-mail accounts like Gmail or Yahoo!

If receiving and sending e-mail while on the go is mission critical for you, check out smartphones with larger displays and integrated keyboards that make it easier to read and respond to messages.

### Cell Phone/Smartphone Security

**Can I get a virus on my cell/smartphone?** Although viruses can already infect cell/smartphones, manufacturers and software engineers are bracing themselves for a tidal wave of viruses targeted to cell/smartphones. With half of users reporting that they send confidential e-mails using their phones and one third of users indicating that they access bank account or credit card information, cell/smartphones are the next most likely realm of attack by cybercriminals. The potential of cell/smartphone viruses ranges from the mildly annoying (certain features of your phone stop working) to the costly (your phone is used without your knowledge to make expensive calls).

Symantec, McAfee, and F-Secure are the leading companies currently providing antivirus software for mobile devices. Products are designed for specific cell/smartphone operating systems; for example, Symantec Mobile Security has versions for the Android, Windows Mobile, Blackberry, and Symbian OS. Often businesses will have their information technology department install and configure an antivirus solution like this for all the phones used in the organization.

Although viruses plaguing cell/smartphones have not yet reached the volume of viruses attacking PC operating systems, with the proliferation of mobile devices it is expected that such virus attacks will increase. If no antivirus program is available for your phone's operating system, the best precautions are common sense ones. Check the phone manufacturer's Web site frequently to see whether your cell/smartphone needs any software upgrades that could patch security holes. In addition, remember that you should not download ring tones, games, or other software from unfamiliar Web sites.

**How do I keep my cell/smartphone number private?** It seems that every time you fill out a Web form someone is asking for your phone number. If you are concerned about widely distributing your cell/smartphone number and potentially inviting lots of unwanted solicitation calls, you should consider using a virtual phone number. A virtual phone number is a phone number you create that can be assigned to ring on existing phone numbers. Companies such as Telusion (**www.tossabledigits.com**) will sell you a virtual number. Then, when you are filling out a registration form for some Web service, you can input your virtual phone number in the Web form instead of giving out your number. When you set up the virtual account, you can restrict the hours that you will receive calls from that number, and if you are receiving many unwanted calls, you can disable the virtual number without affecting your cell/smartphone service.

### Voice over Internet Protocol

Digital telephone services cover more than just mobile phones. Cell phone service is still not 100 percent reliable, and dropped calls and poor reception are a problem in many areas. In addition, the call quality of landline phone service is often superior to cell/smartphone call quality. Landline phones can also be digital using a technology named VoIP (Voice over Internet Protocol). Often people who run home businesses maintain a landline to ensure high voice quality of calls. In many instances, landline phone plans can be cheaper than cell/smartphone plans, especially for international calls.

**How is VoIP different from regular telephone service?** Voice over Internet Protocol (VoIP) is a form of voice-based Internet communication that turns a standard Internet connection into a means to place phone calls, including long-distance calls. Traditional telephone communications use analog voice data and telephone connections. In contrast, VoIP uses technology similar to that used in e-mail to send your voice data digitally over the Internet.

**Computer**

**VoIP phone**

**WiFi Device**

**INTERNET**

**DSL/Cable modem**

**Phone adapter**

**Computer**

**Phone**

**Figure 5.16**

Depending on your VoIP service, you can hold conversations through a computer, a special VoIP telephone, or a regular telephone with an adapter.

**What do I need to use VoIP?** For the simplest and least costly VoIP service, you need speakers, a microphone, an Internet connection, and a VoIP provider (see Figure 5.16). Depending on the provider you choose, you also may need to install software or a special adapter.

**Who are some VoIP providers?** Skype is one very well-known provider. Creating a VoIP account with Skype (**www .skype.com**) is similar to creating an instant messaging (IM) account. Skype requires that both callers and receivers have the company's free software installed on their computers. With Skype you can change your online status, look at your contact list, and even integrate the service into your Facebook news feed. Other VoIP services, such as Vonage (**www.vonage.com**), are a bit more complicated to set up and are not free. Major ISPs, like Comcast or Verizon, also provide VoIP phone services as an option you can package with your Internet or cable television plan.

One limitation of VoIP used to be that when you made a call, you had to be at your computer. As VoIP moves out to mobile devices, however, it is possible to place VoIP calls from any WiFi hot spot. For example, there are Skype applications available for mobile devices, like the iPad and the Sony Vita. You can make free calls to other Skype users or make low-cost calls to non-Skype users.

**What are the advantages and disadvantages of VoIP?** For people who make many long-distance phone calls, the advantage of VoIP is it's free or low cost. Portability is another advantage because all you need is an Internet connection. With Internet accessibility so abundant, you can keep in touch with friends and family no matter where you are. As long as you are covered by a WiFi signal, you can plug in your headset or IP phone, sign on to your VoIP service, and make your call.

Although VoIP is affordable and convenient, it does have drawbacks. Some people regard sound quality and reliability issues as VoIP's primary disadvantages. Another drawback is the loss of service if power is interrupted. Although many traditional phones do not depend on electricity, your Internet connection and IP phone do. One serious drawback when VoIP service was first offered to the public was the inability for 911 calls to be traced back to the caller, unlike with a traditional phone. The FCC now requires all VoIP providers to provide traceable 911 services.

Another issue with VoIP is security. Security risks are similar to the risks associated with e-mail and include the problem of fraud. Spam or having a hacker break into a VoIP system to make unauthorized calls are serious but avoidable problems. In addition, encryption services that convert data into a form that is not easily understood by unauthorized people are being deployed to help protect the very nature of calls made over the Internet. Despite these concerns, VoIP continues to enjoy explosive growth, and the technology will continue to improve.

**What new features come with having an Internet-based digital phone at home?** Once you are using an Internet-based digital phone system, new features become possible. You can have your telephone messages automatically bundled up as e-mails and sent to your account. If you are watching television and a call comes in, it can be displayed on the screen with caller ID information. Some learning management systems also use VoIP. For example if you are using MyITLab with this course, you can call your professor through VoIP without having their personal phone number.

## Digital Media and Information

The entertainment industry has become an all-digital field. Today, books, movies, music, and photographs are created using digital recording devices, processed using digital software systems, and delivered over digital distribution channels. Let's explore what this means for you.

### Digital Publishing

**Are books dead?** The publishing industry is in the process of migrating to digital materials. **Electronic text (etext)** is textual information stored as digital information so it can be stored, manipulated, and transmitted by electronic devices. With the increasing usage of etext, the market for printed materials is changing dramatically. In 2011, Amazon released a corporate report showing over the past year, for every 100 print books sold, it had sold 105 Kindle ebooks. Several authors, such as Stieg Larsson and James Patterson, have each sold over a million ebooks.

**eReaders** are devices that can display etext and have supporting tools, like note taking, bookmarks, and integrated dictionaries. They are selling at a brisk pace with a dizzying range of offerings in the market, including the Amazon Kindle, Barnes and Noble NOOK, and Sony eReader. Tablets are also helping to popularize the digitized ebook and the electronic versions of major magazines and newspapers. There is evidence that this is increasing all kinds of book buying, not just digital books. In 2011 Amazon had its greatest growth rate in sales, for all products combined, of the past ten years.

There are two popular technologies in representing digital text. Electronic ink (E ink) is a very crisp, sharp grayscale representation of text. The "page" is composed of millions of microcapsules with white and black particles in a clear fluid. Electronic signals can make each spot appear either white or black. E Ink devices reflect the light that shines on the page, like ordinary paper,

## How Do You Find Your WiFi?

Detecting a nearby WiFi signal is important if you are looking for Internet connectivity while you are on the move. Some notebooks have a built-in WiFi scanner that displays a row of lights on the case whenever a WiFi signal is available. Keychain fobs that light up when they detect WiFi signals in the vicinity are also available.

If you are running Windows 7, the Connect to a Network dialog box (accessible from the Network and Sharing Center) shows the strength of all wireless networks within range of your computer.

At ThinkGeek (**www.thinkgeek.com**), you may find the most easy-to-use WiFi detector ever. The WiFi Detector t-shirt and the WiFi baseball cap have a logo that lights up to indicate the signal strength of a nearby WiFi network (see Figure 5.17). Find your WiFi and look . . . well, look geeky while doing so!

**Figure** 5.17

The WiFi Detector T-shirt and cap make a statement— a geeky statement.

and are not backlit. It is designed to mimic reading regular paper and is more comfortable for many people. E Ink gives great contrast and is much easier to read in direct sunlight. Examples of devices using E Ink include the Amazon Kindle and the Barnes and Noble NOOK.

Another option for presenting etext is high-resolution backlit monitors seen in readers like the iPad or the NOOK Color. These illuminate themselves instead of depending on room lighting conditions. The glass does reflect glare, though, which makes them hard to use in bright, direct sunlight. Some people experience more fatigue in reading from a backlit device than when using E Ink. Also note that electronic

**Figure** 5.18

The two main technologies for etext display are high-resolution backlit color screens, like on the iPad, and E Ink grayscale displays, like on the Amazon Kindle.

ink readers have a battery life of a month or two on a charge while high-resolution color readers hold a single charge for 8–10 hours. Be sure to try both, shown in Figure 5.18, under a variety of conditions before you make a purchase decision.

**Do I need a dedicated device just for reading etexts?** No. There are software versions of the Kindle and the NOOK that are free downloads and run on either PC or Apple computers. Other texts that have no copyrights can be downloaded and read directly on a computer either as a PDF file or using software like the Microsoft Reader or the MobiPocket reader.

**What features make eReaders popular?** One big allure of digital publishing is distribution. Ease of access to digital books is very attractive. Even a 1,000-page book can be delivered directly to your eReader in under a minute. An incredible array of titles is available—over 950,000 books are available in just the Amazon Kindle store. In addition, there are millions of texts without copyright that are available for free. Most texts are available at a lower price than they would be in paper.

The basic features of ereading offer many advantages over paper books. Integrated dictionaries pull up a definition just by highlighting a word. The Kindle, for example, can work with both English and German dictionaries, a help in reading foreign works. Note taking and marking highlights are supported so the text can be searched by your own notes or for specific terms. Notes you make on the book can be shared easily with others. URL links or links to a glossary can be live in the book. Bookmarks are immediately pushed through cloud technology so you can read on one device and pick up with the most current bookmark on another device.

**What kinds of file formats are used in electronic publishing?** Digital formats for publishing vary. Amazon uses a proprietary format (.azw extension), so books purchased for a Kindle are not transportable to a non-Kindle device. An open format also exists, ePub. Some eReaders support the ePub file format. There is an ePub reader plugin available for the browser Firefox and several standalone software ePub readers like Stanza or MobiPocket Reader.

There are a number of vendors associated with eReader devices. Amazon sells the Kindle device and it connects directly to the Amazon Kindle store. The Barnes and Noble NOOK device works with the

**Figure 5.19**

Ebooks and audio books can be borrowed freely at most public libraries.

Barnes and Noble ebookstore. There are also many publishers selling ebooks online that can be read on any kind of device. Textbooks can be purchased in ebook format directly from the publisher; for example, the technology publisher O'Reilly has an online ebookstore. Another option is companies like CourseSmart, which offers a yearlong subscription to a digital text that then times out and disappears from your device.

Libraries are now including ebook and audiobook lending as part of their mission (Figure 5.19). Most libraries allow you to borrow up to ten ebooks at a time. There is never a late fee; the book just times out and disappears from your device when the borrowing period expires. Products like the Overdrive Media Console (**search.over-drive.com**) let you search to find which area library has the book you want. Log in to the library Web site and you can download a text any time of day or night. Libraries have a specific number of copies of each ebook title so you may be added to a waitlist if all the copies are checked out, just like with paper books.

Or you might be able to borrow an ebook from a friend. Lending of ebooks is now becoming a popular feature of eReader systems. The Barnes & Noble NOOK, for example, has a Lend Me feature on certain books. An eligible book can be loaned once for a period of 14 days.

Another source of free reading is Project Gutenberg. This repository site is a collection of over 36,000 free books in ePub, Kindle, and PDF formats. It contains books that are free in the United States because their copyright has expired. The catalog includes many classic titles like *War and Peace* by Leo Tolstoy or mystery novels by Agatha Christie.

Self-publishing is much easier in the age of digital texts. You can self-publish into the Amazon Kindle Store in a matter of minutes and earn a 70% royalty of sales. Companies like Smashwords (**www.smashwords.com**) take a Microsoft Word document from you, formatted to their specifications, and then make your book available through a number of vendors like the Apple iBooks store,

Barnes and Noble, and the Sony eReader store. Your book can also be distributed as an app to mobile marketplaces like the Android Market or the Apple App Store. Sites like Lulu.com include social marketing for your book so that you can promote it. They offer services from editors, designers, and marketers as well.

### Digital Music

**How is digital music created?** All digital media, whether an image, a song, or a video, has the same basis—digitized information. Figure 5.20 shows the process of digitally recording a song:

1. Playing music creates analog waves.

2. A microphone feeds the sound waves into a chip called an *analog-to-digital converter (ADC)* inside the recording device.

3. The ADC digitizes the waves into a series of numbers.

4. This series of numbers can be recorded onto CDs and DVDs or sent electronically.

5. On the receiving end, a playback device such as a CD player or DVD player is fed that same series of numbers. Inside the playback device is a *digital-to-analog converter (DAC)*, a chip that converts the digital numbers to a continuous analog wave.

6. That analog wave tells the receiver how to move the speaker cones to reproduce

Singer playing music

Analog wave

ADC

Digital format
28,36,42,
84,120,126,
120,98,98...

Optical Disc

DAC

Speaker

28,36,42,
84,120,126,
120,98,98...

**Figure** 5.20

During the complete recording process, information changes from analog form to digital data and then back again to analog sound waves.

the original waves, resulting in the same sound as the original.

More precisely, the digital wave will be *close* to exact. How accurate it is, or how close the digitized wave is in shape to the original analog wave, depends on the sampling rate of the ADC. The **sampling rate** specifies the number of times the analog wave is measured each second. The higher the sampling rate, the more accurately the original wave can be re-created. However, higher sampling rates also produce much more data, and therefore result in bigger files. For example, sound waves on CDs are sampled at a rate of approximately 44,000 times a second. This produces a huge list of numbers for even a single minute of a song!

When sounds or image waves are digitized, it means that analog data is changed into digital data—from a wave into a series of numbers. The digital data is perfectly reproducible and can be distributed easily on CDs and DVDs or through the airwaves. The data also can be easily processed by a computer.

**Are all music files MP3 files?** The letters at the end of a file name (the file extension) indicate how the data in the file is organized. MP3 is the name of just one type of file format used to store digital music, but many others exist, such as AAC and WMA. If you buy a song from the iTunes Music Store, for example, you receive an .aac format file. There are also many video formats such as DivX, MPEG-4 (which usually has an .mp4 extension), WMV, and XviD. All file formats compete on sound and video quality and *compression*, which relates to how small the file can be and still provide high-quality playback. Be sure to check what kind of files your audio device understands before you store music on it.

**How can I carry music files easily?** **Portable media players (PMPs)** are small portable devices (such as iPods) that enable you to carry your digital audio files around with you. Many PMPs handle video and still images as well as music files.

Depending on the PMP, you can carry several hours of music or video—or

**Figure** 5.21 | SOME PORTABLE MEDIA PLAYERS AND THEIR CHARACTERISTICS

| | Media Capacity | Built-in Flash Memory | Hard Drive Capacity | Connection to Computer | Other Features |
|---|---|---|---|---|---|
| Sansa Fuze Player | 2,000 songs or 24 hours of video | 2 GB to 8 GB | None, but 16 GB micro SD card supported | USB 2.0 | FM radio, voice recorder, and available "radio" cards prefilled with 1,000 songs |
| Zune HD | As many as 16,000 songs or 20 hours of HD video | 16 GB to 64 GB | None | USB 2.0 or wireless | Has HD radio, OLED screen, and multitouch navigation |
| Apple iPod touch | As many as 14,000 songs or 80 hours of video | 8 GB to 64 GB | None | USB 2.0 | Weighs only 4.05 ounces; flash memory enables skip-free playback |
| Apple iPod classic | As many as 40,000 songs or 200 hours of video | None | 160 GB | USB 2.0 | Has calendar feature that syncs with Outlook; can serve as a small, portable hard drive |
| Archos 7 | As many as 2,000 songs or 24 hours of video | 2 GB to 8 GB | None, but 32 GB SDHC card supported | USB 2.0 | Includes 7" screen display, WiFi, and touch screen |

possibly your entire music collection—in an incredibly small device. For example, an Apple iPod classic with a 160 GB hard drive is 4.1 inches by 2.4 inches (and only 0.41 inch thick), yet it can hold as many as 40,000 songs or 200 hours of video. The most compact players are slightly larger than a flash drive (although they hold less than 160 GB). Figure 5.21 shows several models of PMPs, all of which connect to computers via USB 2.0 ports.

**Are PMP devices the only choice for portable media management?** No, a number of electronic devices now incorporate the capability to carry electronic files and play music and video files. For example, netbooks, cell/smartphones, tablets, and mobile gaming systems also have support for playing both music and videos.

**How do I know how much digital media a PMP can hold?** The number of songs or hours of video a portable media player can hold depends on how much storage space it has. Most PMPs use built-in **flash memory**, a type of nonvolatile memory, to store files. Most PMPs that support video use a hard drive instead of flash memory and can store a much greater amount of music and video. Less expensive PMPs use flash memory ranging from 1 GB to 32 GB, whereas models that are more expensive use built-in hard drives, which provide as much as 160 GB of storage. Some of the PMPs that use flash memory allow you to add storage capacity by purchasing removable flash memory cards.

Another factor that determines how much music a player can hold is the quality of the MP3 music files. The size of an MP3 file depends on the digital sampling of the song. The same song could be sampled at 320 kbps or 64 kbps. The size of the song file will be five times larger if it is sampled at 320 kbps rather than the lower sampling rate of 64 kbps. The higher the sampling rate, the better quality the sound—but the larger the file size.

**How do you control the size of an MP3 file?** If you are *ripping*, or converting, a song from a CD into a digital MP3 file, you can select the sampling rate yourself. You decide by considering what quality sound you want, as well as how many songs you want to fit onto your MP3 player. For example, if your player has 1 GB of storage and you have ripped songs at 192 kbps, you could fit about 694 minutes of music onto the player. The same 1 GB could store 2,083 minutes of music if it were sampled at 64 kbps. Whenever you are near your computer, you can connect your player and download a different set of songs, but you always are limited by the amount of storage your player has.

**What if I want to access more music or video than the memory on my PMP allows?** Some PMPs allow you to add memory by inserting removable flash memory cards. Flash memory cards are quiet and light, use tiny amounts of power, and slide into a special slot in the player. If you've ever played a video game on PlayStation or Xbox and saved your progress to a memory card, then you have used flash memory. Because flash memory is nonvolatile, when you store data on a flash memory card, you won't lose it when you turn off the player. In addition, flash memory can be erased and rewritten with new data. PMPs use a variety of different types of flash cards. Check your manual and then review the coverage of flash media in Chapter 2 for more details.

Another solution is to use a service that streams the music to you over WiFi or 3/4G networks. Companies like Rhapsody and Spotify charge a monthly subscription fee that entitles you to listen to any of the millions of tracks in their catalog. The music is not yours to own, however—if you stop your subscription you no longer have any access to the music. But because it is streamed to you, it also does not take up space on your device drive. Some streaming services offer options to allow some downloading; for example, your last 100 played songs may be actually stored on your device.

**How do I transfer media files to my portable media player?** All portable media players come with software that enables you to transfer audio and video files from your computer to the player. As noted earlier, players that hold thousands of songs and hours of video use internal hard drives to store the files. For example, devices such as Apple iPods can hold several gigabytes of data. To move large volumes of data

**ACTIVE HELP-DESK**  Using Portable Media Players

In this Active Helpdesk call, you'll play the role of a helpdesk staffer, fielding calls about portable media players, what they can carry, and how they store data.

between your computer and your PMP, you want a high-speed port. Most PMPs use a USB 2.0 port, which allows you to transfer two dozen MP3 files to the iPod in less than 10 seconds.

New services are appearing that will automatically push music to your mobile device. Apple's iOS 5 operating system supports iCloud technology. This means that as soon as you purchase a new song from iTunes, it is automatically pushed to all your registered iTunes devices—your Mac, your PC, your iPod touch, and your iPhone.

**What if I want a lot of people to listen to my digital music?** PMPs are great for individual listening, but to share music from a PMP, you have to connect it to an alternative device. Many audio receivers now come with a port or a dock so that you can connect a PMP device directly to them as another audio input source, like a Blu-ray player or a television. Most new cars are equipped with an auxiliary input to the speaker system to support connecting a PMP; others have a fully integrated software system that displays and runs the PMP playlists. Many Ford models use the Microsoft Sync system to allow you to navigate through your playlists with just voice commands. There are alarm clocks and home speaker docks that can mate, even wirelessly, with a PMP and broadcast brilliant sound.

**How did the shift to digital music impact the music industry?** The initial MP3 craze was fueled by sites such as MP3.com, which originally stored its song files on a public server with the permission of the original artists or recording companies. Therefore, you were not infringing on a copyright by downloading songs from sites such as MP3.com (which still exists and now provides free music in streaming format).

Napster was a file exchange site created to correct some of the annoyances found by users of MP3.com. One such annoyance was the limited availability of popular music in MP3 format. With the MP3 sites, if you found a song you wanted to download, the link to the site on which the file was found often no longer worked. Napster differed from MP3.com because songs or locations of songs were not stored in a central public server, but instead were "borrowed" directly from other users' computers. This process of users transferring files between computers is referred to as **peer-to-peer (P2P) sharing**. Napster also provided a search engine dedicated to finding specific MP3 files. This direct search and sharing eliminated the inconvenience of searching links only to find them unavailable.

The problem with Napster was that it was so good at what it did. Napster's convenient and reliable mechanism to find and download popular songs in MP3 format became a huge success. The rapid acceptance and use of Napster—at one point, it had nearly 60 million users—led the music industry to sue the site for copyright infringement, and Napster was closed in June 2002. Napster has since reopened as a music site that sells music downloads and is sanctioned by the recording industry.

The reaction of the recording industry was to continue to enforce its absolute ownership over digital forms of its music. The industry even filed legal actions against individuals who had downloaded large amounts of music from Internet sites. This heavy-handed reaction to the new era of digital music ultimately backfired and left the music industry scrambling. Overall music sales have dropped significantly each year for the last decade. The recording industry is still trying to counter losing CD sales to digital forms of music. The approach they took early on did not allow them to adapt quickly enough to the new business models required by the shift to digital technologies.

**So if I don't pay for a music download . . . is it illegal?** Although you need to pay for most music you download, some artists post songs for free. Business models are still evolving as artists and recording companies try to meet audience needs while also protecting their own intellectual property rights. Several different approaches exist. One is to deliver something called *tethered downloads*, in which you pay for the music and own it, but are subject to restrictions on its use.

Another approach is to offer *DRM-free* music, which is music without any **digital rights management (DRM)**. DRM is a system of access control that allows only limited use of material that has been legally purchased. It may be the song can only run on certain devices or a movie can only be viewed a certain number of times. A DRM-free song can be placed on as many computers or players as you wish. These song files can be moved freely from system to system.

**Why buy any music if peer-to-peer (P2P) sharing sites are still operating?** When Napster was going through its legal turmoil, other P2P Web sites were quick to take advantage of a huge opportunity. Napster was "easy" to shut down because it used a central index server that queried other Napster computers for requested songs. Current P2P protocols (such as BearShare) differ from Napster in that they do not limit themselves to sharing only MP3 files. Video files are obtainable easily on P2P sites. More importantly, these sites don't have a central index server. Instead, they operate in a true P2P sharing environment in which computers connect directly to other computers. This makes them a prime source of unwanted viruses and spyware.

The argument these P2P networks make to defend their legality is that they do not run a central server like the original Napster, but only facilitate connections between users. Therefore, they have no control over what the users choose to trade. These legal nuances were not enough to keep the LimeWire service active, and it was shut down by court order in 2010. Note that not all P2P file sharing is illegal. For example, it is legal to trade photos or movies you have created with other folks over a P2P site.

People who oppose such file-sharing sites contend that the sites know their users are distributing files illegally and breaking copyright laws. Be aware that having illegal content on your computer, deliberately or by accident, is a criminal offense in many jurisdictions.

**Will PMPs eliminate radio stations?** Radio stations have always had certain advantages: early access to new music, and personalities and conversations that add to the listening experience. However, the Internet allows artists to release new songs to their fans immediately (on sites such as Facebook) and without relying on radio airtime. This opens up new channels for artists to reach an audience and changes the amount of power radio stations have in the promotion of music. Many radio stations have increased listenership by making their stations available through Internet sites and by broadcasting in high-definition quality.

**Can I create my own radio station?** Another development that competes with radio (and television) is *podcasting*. In

## Trick Out Your iTouch/iPhone

With more than 10 billion iTouch/iPhone apps downloaded, the App Store is a proven success. Some apps are games, some are just gimmicks, but many are great tools for a student. iFlipr is an app that connects you to 2.7 million flash cards. You can study for the MCAT exam or build and share your own custom flash card deck. iHomework organizes your teacher contact info, due dates for assignments, and research materials, and learning management systems like Blackboard have their own mobile apps. AudioNote lets your iPhone record audio in sync with handwritten notes you write down. Can't find the app you are dreaming of? The iPhone Developer University program is free and supports students and faculty in designing and coding mobile apps.

Chapter 10 you will read that podcasting allows users to download audio and video content and then listen to those broadcasts on their PMPs whenever they want. Podcasting is paving the way for anyone to create a radio or television show at home and distribute it easily to an audience. Using free software such as Audacity (**audacity.sourceforge.net**) and a microphone, you can record voice-overs, sequence songs, and generate special effects for your recordings. Loyal fans can use podcasting software such as Juice (**juicereceiver.sourceforge.net**) or iTunes to find a podcast's latest episode and automatically transfer it to their portable media players. Plugging your iPod into a data port on your computer causes the iPod to search iTunes for new content from the podcasters you subscribe to and then automatically transfers the new files to your iPod. Podcasts are easy to subscribe to and download using iTunes (see Figure 5.22).

**What if I want to publicize my band's music?** Digital music has made

Screenshot © Apple Inc. Reprinted by permission from Apple Inc.

**Figure 5.22**

iTunes makes it easy to subscribe to and manage podcasts.

distributing your own recordings very simple. You can make your own creations available using apps like ReverbNation (**www.reverbnation.com**). You can quickly create a Web page for your band, post your songs, and start building a fan base through Facebook, for example. ReverbNation will send you reports detailing who is listening to your music and what they are saying about it. ReverbNation is also a way to connect with independent recording labels and to find places that want to book your band.

### Digital Photography

**What is "analog" photography?** Before digital cameras hit the market, most people used some form of 35-mm single-lens reflex (SLR) camera. When you take a picture using a traditional SLR camera, a shutter opens, creating an aperture (a small window in the camera) that allows light to hit the 35-mm film inside. Chemicals coating the film react when exposed to light. Later, additional chemicals develop the image on the film, and the image is printed on special light-sensitive paper. A variety of lenses and processing techniques, special equipment, and filters are needed to create printed photos from traditional SLR cameras.

**What is different about digital photography?** Digital cameras do not use film. Instead, they capture images on electronic sensors called *charge-coupled device (CCD) arrays* and then convert those images to digital data, long series of numbers that represent the color and brightness of millions of points in the image. Unlike traditional cameras, digital cameras allow you to see

your images the instant you shoot them. Most camera models can now record digital video as well as digital photos.

**How do I select a digital camera?** With hundreds of models to choose from, where do you begin? The first question to answer is whether you want a compact "point-and-shoot" model camera or a more serious digital SLR. The larger digital SLR cameras allow you to switch among different lenses and offer features important to serious amateur and professional photographers (such as depth-of-field previewing). Although having such flexibility in moving up to a larger zoom lens is a great advantage, most of these cameras are also larger, heavier, and use more battery power than the tiny point-and-shoot models. Think about how you will be using your camera and decide which model will serve you best in the long run.

Next, you'll want to evaluate the quality of the camera on a number of levels. One great resource to use is Digital Photography Review (**www.dpreview.com**). The site's camera reviews evaluate a camera's construction as well as its features, image quality, ease of use, and value for the cost. In addition, the site provides comparisons to similar camera models by other manufacturers and feedback from owners of those models. Links are provided to several resellers, making it easy to compare prices as well.

**Why not just use the camera on my cell/smartphone?** Many cell/smartphones include a digital camera. These cameras often provide lower resolutions than stand-alone models and inferior lenses. Many features that photographers rely on are not often available in the cameras included on phones, such as different types of autofocus, image stabilization algorithms, and smile shutter, which waits to take a shot until your subject is smiling.

**What determines the image quality of a digital camera?** The overall image quality is determined by many factors: the quality of the lenses used, the file format and compression used, and the color management software. Another part of what determines the image quality of a digital camera is its **resolution**, or the number of data points it records for each image captured. A digital camera's resolution is measured in megapixels (MP). The prefix *mega* is short for millions. The word *pixel* is short for picture element, which is a single dot in a digital image. Point-and-shoot models typically offer resolutions from 10 MP to 15 MP. Professional digital SLR cameras, such as the Canon EOS-5D Mark II, can take photos at resolutions as high as 21.1 MP, but they sell for thousands of dollars.

If you're interested in making only 5″ × 7″ or 8″ × 10″ prints, a lower-resolution camera is fine. However, low-resolution images become grainy and pixelated when pushed to make larger-size prints. For example, if

flash card. The most common file types supported by digital cameras are raw uncompressed data (RAW) and Joint Photographic Experts Group (JPEG). Raw files have different formats and extensions depending on the manufacturer of a particular camera. The raw file records all of the original image information, so it is larger than a compressed JPEG file. JPEG files can be compressed just a bit, keeping most of the details, or compressed a great deal, losing some detail. Most cameras allow you to select from a few different JPEG compression levels.

Often cameras also support a very low-resolution storage option, enabling you to create files that you can easily attach to e-mail messages. This low-resolution setting typically provides images that are not useful for printing but are so small that they are easily e-mailed. Even people who have slow Internet connections are able to quickly download and view such images on-screen.

**How do I move photos to my computer?** Transferring photos to your computer allows you to store them and frees your flash card for reuse. Digital cameras have a built-in USB 2.0 port. Using a USB 2.0 cable, you can connect the camera to your computer and copy the converted images as

---

## When you choose to compress your images, you will lose some of the detail, but in return, you'll be able to fit more images on your flash card.

---

you tried to print an 11″ × 14″ enlargement from a 2 MP image taken using your cell/smartphone's camera, the image would look grainy; you would see individual dots of color instead of a clear, sharp image. The 10 MP to 15 MP cameras on the market now have plenty of resolution to guarantee sharp, detailed images even with enlargements as big as 11″ × 14″.

**What file formats are used for digital images?** To fit more photos on the same size of flash memory card, digital cameras allow you to choose from several different file types in order to compress the image data into less memory space. When you choose to compress your images, you will lose some of the detail, but in return, you'll be able to fit more images on your

uncompressed files or in a compressed format as JPEG files. Another option is to transfer the flash card from your camera directly to the built-in memory card reader on your computer. Some camera models support wireless network connections so that you can transfer the images without the fuss of putting a cable in place. If your model doesn't, you can purchase a memory card with built-in WiFi: the Eye-Fi. Eye-Fi will wirelessly transfer your photos to Google Picasa, Facebook, or one of thirty other Web destinations. Eye-Fi Mobile X2 will upload images directly from your camera to your iPad or phone as well. It will also back up the photos and videos you take with your camera to your home computer. And when you are away from home, Eye-Fi comes with hot spot access so you can upload for free from any McDonald's, Starbucks, hotel, or airport.

**Can I make my old photos digital?** Obviously, not every document or image you have is in an electronic form. What about all the photographs you have already taken? What about an article from a magazine or a hand-drawn sketch? How can these be converted into digital format?

Digital scanners convert paper text and images into digital formats. Most scanners today are integrated into an all-in-one printer that supports printing, copying, and scanning with one unit. You can place any flat material on the glass surface of the scanner and convert it into a digital file. Most

.com) and Shutterfly (**www.shutterfly.com**), store your images and allow you to organize them into photo albums or to create hard-copy prints, mugs, T-shirts, or calendars.

Photo printers for home use are available in two technologies: inkjet and dye sublimation. The most popular and inexpensive ones are inkjet printers. As noted in Chapter 2, some inkjet printers are capable of printing high-quality color photos, although they vary in speed and quality. Some include a display window so that you can review the image as you stand at the printer, whereas others are portable, allowing you to print your photos wherever you are. Some printers even allow you to crop the image right

---

## Photo printers for home use are available in two technologies: inkjet and dye sublimation.

---

scanner software allows you to store the converted images as TIFF files or in compressed form as JPEG files. Some scanners include hardware that allows you to scan film negatives or slides as well or even insert a stack of photos to be scanned in sequence.

Scanner quality is measured by its resolution, which is given in dots per inch (dpi). Most modern scanners can digitize a document at resolutions as high as 4,800 × 9,600 dpi, in either color or grayscale mode. The scanner software will also typically support optical character recognition (OCR). OCR software converts pages of handwritten or typed text into electronic files. You can then open and edit these converted documents with traditional word processing programs such as Microsoft Word.

**How do I print a digital image?** You can print a digital image using a professional service or your own printer. Most photo printing labs, including the film processing departments at stores such as Walmart and Target, offer digital printing services, as do many high-end online processing labs. The paper and ink used at processing labs are higher quality than what is available for home use and produce heavier, glossier prints that won't fade. You can send your digital photos directly to local merchants such as CVS and Walgreens for printing using Windows Live Photo Gallery. Online services, such as Flickr (**www.flickr**

at the printer without having to use special image editing software.

Unlike inkjet printers, which use an inkjet nozzle, dye-sublimation printers produce images using a heating element. The heating element passes over a ribbon of translucent film that has been dyed with bands of colors. Depending on the temperature of the element, dyes are vaporized from a solid into a gas. The gas vapors penetrate the photo paper before they cool and return to solid form, producing glossy, high-quality images. If you're interested in a printer to use for printing only photographs, a dye-sublimation printer is a good choice. However, some models print only specific photo sizes, such as 4" × 6" prints, so be sure the printer you buy will fit your long-term needs.

**Do I need to print out my photos?** You may decide not to print your photos at all. As noted earlier, online albums let you share your photos without having to print them. There are a number of digital scrapbooking sites that let you electronically design scrapbooks. Portable devices, such as tablets and cell/smartphones, also enable you to carry and display your photos. The iPad, for example, can be connected wirelessly to a TV and deliver slide shows of your photographs, complete with musical soundtracks you have selected. As we will mention in Chapter 12, if you have networked your home, a television connected to your network (or to a network-enabled device like a PlayStation 3 or a networked Blu-ray player) can display all the photos and videos stored on your computer.

### Digital Video

**Where does digital video come from?** Digital video comes from several sources, but now people often create their own digital videos. As a video creator, you may purchase dedicated digital camcorders to record digital video. Most cell/smartphones can record video, and digital cameras take video as well as digital still shots. Webcams also work as inexpensive devices for creating digital video.

There are many other sources of digital video available to you now. Television is broadcasting in digitally formatted signals. The Internet delivers a huge amount of digital video through Google Video, YouTube, communities like Vimeo (**www.vimeo.com**), and webcasting sites like Ustream (**www.ustream.tv**). Sites like Hulu (**www.hulu.com**) rebroadcast many current television shows as well as films and movie trailers. Many pay services are available to deliver digital video to you. These include on-demand streaming from cable providers, iTunes, Netflix's Instant Watch films, and Amazon's Instant Video download service.

**How do I record my own digital video?** Video equipment for home use stores information in a digital video (DV) format. This allows the cameras to be incredibly small and light. Such cameras don't require any tapes at all; they store hours of video on built-in hard drives or flash cards. Some models even record directly to DVD discs.

You can easily transfer video files to your computer and, using video editing software, edit the video at home, cutting out sections, resequencing segments, and adding titles. To do the same with analog videotape would require expensive and complex audio/video equipment available only in video production studios. You can save (or write) your final product on a CD or DVD and play it in your home DVD system or on your computer.

For true videophiles, cameras and burners are now available for high-definition video format.

**What if I decide to add some special effects and a sound track?** Video editing software presents a storyboard or timeline with which you can manipulate your video file, as shown in Figure 5.23. You can review your clips frame by frame or trim them at any point. You can order each segment on the timeline in whichever sequence you like and correct segments for color balance, brightness, or contrast.

In addition, you can add transitions to your video such as those you're used to seeing on TV—fades to black, dissolves, and so on. Just select the type of transition you want from the drop-down list and drag that icon into the timeline where you want the transition to occur.

Video editing software also lets you add titles, animations, and audio tracks to your video, including background music, sound effects, and additional narration. You can adjust the volume of each audio track to switch from one to the other or have both playing together. Finally, you can preview all of these effects in real time.

There is a lot to learn about digital video editing, and with the number of choices available, it is easy to be overwhelmed. Examine online tutorial resources such as Izzy Video podcasts (**www.izzyvideo.com**) to learn how to make the most impact with the editing and effects you apply to your raw video footage.

**Figure 5.23**

Adobe Premiere Elements allows you to build a movie from video clips and add sound tracks and special effects.

Effects  Transitions  Titles  Themes

Clip Art

Video track

Audio track

Music track

**What kinds of files will I end up with?** Once you're done editing your video file, you can save or export it in a variety of formats. Figure 5.24 shows some of the popular video file formats in use today, along with the file extensions they use.

Your choice of file format for your finished video will depend on what you want to do with your video. For example, the QuickTime streaming file format is a great choice if your file is really large and you plan to post it on the Web. The Microsoft AVI format is a good choice if you're sending your file to a wide range of users, because it's extremely popular and is commonly accepted as the standard video format for the Windows Media Player.

You also can try different compression choices to see which one does a better job of compressing your particular file. A **codec** (*co*mpression/*dec*ompression) is a rule, implemented in either software or hardware, that squeezes the same audio and video information into less space. Some information will be lost using compression, and there are several different codecs to choose from, each claiming better performance than its competitors. Commonly used codecs include MPEG-4, H.264, and DivX. There is no one codec that is always superior—a codec that works well for a simple interview may not do a good job compressing a live-action scene.

**What if I want a DVD with a menuing system?** If you want a DVD or Blu-ray with a menuing system, you can use special authoring software such as Pinnacle Studio HD or Adobe Encore. These DVD/Blu-ray software packages often include preset selections for producing video for specific mobile devices. These programs can also create final discs that have animated menu systems and easy navigation controls, allowing the viewer to move quickly from one movie or scene to another. Home DVD and Blu-ray players as well as gaming systems such as PlayStation and Xbox can read these discs.

**What is the quickest way to get my video out to viewers?** Because of the popularity of videos on the Web, products and services are now available that let you quickly upload your videos. Many mobile devices, such as smartphones and tablets, record HD video, and applications like Ustream allow you to broadcast live over the Web as you record. If you want to distribute your video through YouTube, there is a special Mobile Upload Profile that you can set up for your account. Once your unique e-mail address has been assigned, you can submit a video that you have on your phone to YouTube by e-mailing the file to the account address.

Of course, it is illegal for you to upload videos you do not own. You also cannot take

**Figure 5.24** | TYPICAL FILE FORMATS FOR DIGITAL VIDEO

| Format | File Extension | Notes |
|---|---|---|
| QuickTime | .qt<br>.mov | You can download QuickTime player without charge from **www.apple.com/quicktime**. The pro version allows you to build your own QuickTime files. |
| Moving Picture Experts Group (MPEG) | .mpg<br>.mpeg<br>.mp4 | MPEG-4 video standard adopted internationally in 2000; recognized by most video player software. |
| Windows Media Video | .wmv | Microsoft file format recognized by Windows Media Player (included with the Windows OS). |
| Microsoft Video for Windows | .avi | Microsoft file format recognized by Windows Media Player (included with the Windows OS). |
| RealMedia | .rm | Format from RealNetworks; popular for streaming video. You can download the player for free at **www.real.com**. |
| Adobe Flash Video | .flv | Adobe Flash video format, sometimes embedded in Shockwave files (*.swf). |

**Figure** 5.25
Webcams are small enough to make them part of any activity.

a piece of a copyrighted video and post it publicly. The Ethics in IT section in this chapter presents several legal and ethical situations that are important for you to be aware of as a content creator in the digital age.

Webcasting, or broadcasting your video live to an audience, is another option that has become simpler. Inexpensive webcams (costing from $25 to $100) can be easily attached to your desktop or notebook computer. Many models of monitors have built-in webcams. Webcam models that are more expensive have motors that allow you to automatically rotate to track the sound, and some webcams are small enough that they can be mounted on your bike or helmet (see Figure 5.25). Services such as YouTube offer Quick Capture buttons, so with one click, your video can be recorded through your webcam and delivered to the Internet.

**How can I distribute my video to the greatest number of viewers?** Sites like **www.justin.tv** or **www.ustream.tv** let you quickly set up to webcast your video as it is captured to a live Internet audience. You can also display an interactive chat next to the video feed. Both the chat and the video are captured and archived for viewers who missed the live broadcast. iTunes offers free distribution of video podcasts, so you can build a following there for your video work.

There are also options for distributing your movie based on social media seeding. Distrify is an application that helps you to post your trailer on your Web site and allow viewers to immediately download the film, as well as add it to their Facebook page. This viral approach to marketing your own creation connects you directly with your audience and eliminates any cost of distribution.

**Is all video digital now?** The switch to digital video as a broadcasting medium has happened over the past few years. In June 2009, all television stations were required to make the move to digital signal broadcasting. You can go to **www.DTV.gov** to keep current on using conversion boxes to allow older television sets to operate with the new digital signal.

Movie production studios have also been moving toward digital video for many years. George Lucas, a great proponent of digital technology, filmed *Star Wars Episode II: Attack of the Clones* completely in digital format way back in 2002. It played in a special digital release at digital-ready theaters. The film *Slumdog Millionaire*, a 2009 film shot mainly in digital technologies, won the Academy Award for Cinematography. *Avatar*, currently the top-grossing film of all time, both was shot digitally and forced theaters to convert to digital projection

So you just returned from your trip to the Grand Canyon and all your friends are raving about the quality of the photographs you took. You decide to put the photographs out on Flickr so your friends can see them. You also think that maybe someone might see your photos and want to use them in a commercial publication such as a magazine. Because you own the copyright to your photos, you control how they can be used—and you want to protect your rights. You add a disclaimer to Flickr indicating that all rights are reserved on your photos. Anyone who wants to use them will need to contact you and request permission.

All of a sudden, you are bombarded by dozens of requests for permission to use your photographs for all sorts of purposes. A high school student in Illinois wants to feature one of your photos on her travel blog. A church in Georgia wants to use a photo for their newsletter to illustrate a story about a church member's trip to Arizona. An advertising agency in Seattle wants to modify your sunrise photo by inserting a family on a camping trip into the photo. You want to be ethical and protect your ownership rights as well (maybe the ad agency might even pay you!), but how are you going to manage all these photo permission requests?

**Copyleft**, a play on the word copyright, is designed for this situation. Copyleft is a term for various licensing plans that enable copyright holders to grant certain rights to the work while retaining other rights. The GNU General Public License is a popular copyleft license that is used for software. For other works, the Creative Commons, a nonprofit organization, has developed a range of licenses that can be used to control rights to works.

Creative Commons has various types of licenses available based on the rights you wish to grant. The company provides a simple form to assist you with selecting the proper license for your work. Creative Commons provides two licenses at **www.creativecommons.org/about/licenses** that could simplify your life. An *attribution license* permits others to copy, distribute, and display your copyrighted work, but only if they give you credit in the way you specify. Under this license, the high school student could use one of your photos as long as he or she gave you credit.

A *noncommercial license* allows anyone to copy, distribute, and display your work, but only for noncommercial purposes. The church in

Georgia could use one of your photos under this license because it is not profiting from its use.

Both of these licenses can also be used to cover **derivative works**. A derivative work is based on the original work (one of your photos) but is modified in some way. The ad agency that wants to modify one of your photos is seeking permission to create a derivative work. If you had used an attribution license, the ad agency could use your work for a derivative purpose, but only if it attributed the original work to you as the author. If you had used a noncommercial license, the ad agency could not use your work to make a profit for itself.

The obvious advantage to using these Creative Commons licenses is that people won't constantly annoy you with permission requests to use your work. These licenses explain exactly how you are willing to have your work be used. Also, many advocates of copyleft policies feel that creativity is encouraged when people are free to modify other people's work instead of worrying about infringing on copyright.

Opponents of Creative Commons licenses often complain that these licenses have affected their livelihoods. If millions of images are out on Flickr with Creative Commons licenses that permit free commercial use, professional photographers might have a tougher time selling their work. Furthermore, Creative Commons licenses are irrevocable. If you make a mistake and select the wrong license for your work, or you later find out a work is valuable and you've already selected a license that allows commercial use, you're out of luck.

Many people find listings of Creative Commons licenses confusing. If there is a Creative Commons disclaimer at the bottom of a group of photos, does that mean all the photos are available under that license, or just some of them? What actually constitutes commercial use? Is displaying Google Adsense ads on your blog commercial use?

Each of us needs to carefully consider the value of our intellectual property and decide how best to conduct our digital livelihood. Understanding the meaning of copyright, and copyleft, is important both so that you respect the rights of others and so that you can simplify your life in granting permission rights to the works you create.

---

equipment to show the film. Moving to digital projection also allows a theater to show live concerts and sports events.

**How is HD different from "plain" digital?** HD stands for **high definition**. It is a standard of digital television signal that guarantees a specific level of resolution and a specific *aspect ratio*, which is the rectangular shape of the image. A 1080 HD TV displays 1,920 vertical lines and 1,080 horizontal lines of video on the screen, which is over six times as many pixels as standard definition. The aspect ratio used is 16:9, which makes the screen wider, giving it the same proportions as the rectangular shape

of a movie theater screen (see Figure 5.26). This allows televisions to play movies in the widescreen format that they were created for, instead of "letterboxing" the film with black bars on the top and the bottom of the screen.

**What types of connectivity are provided on modern television sets?** As video sources have increased, so have the number and types of connectors on a television. A typical HD set has at least three HDMI connectors, allowing game consoles, Blu-ray players, and cable boxes to be connected and produce the highest-quality output. HDMI is a single cable, with just one plug, that carries all of the video and all of the audio information. That means there is one connector, not three for different parts of the video signal and another two for the stereo sound signals!

Many sets have a built-in SD card reader. This allows users to display slide shows of photographs captured by their digital cameras. A PC VGA port is also included on most sets. This allows you to feed your computer's output video signal directly to the television so you can display an Internet browser or work on your files on the big screen. Sets are now incorporating a wireless network adapter so the set can stream video from the Internet without having a separate computer connected. Several manufacturers are offering TV sets that stream Internet content.

Samsung offers "smart television" models that have access to a Samsung app store and can download a YouTube app, Google Maps, Vimeo, or hundreds of others. Sony's Internet TV is a collaboration with Google. It allows a single search utility to check for content on the Internet, on your stored recorded programs, and on the TV guide listing, and contains a full browser and upgradeable operating system.

**What advantages are there to watching digital video on my television?** Because the signal can be stored into computer memory as it is delivered, a digital video television show can be paused, or can be rewound in real time. Other information services can be integrated with the broadcast; so if a telephone call came through during the show, a pop-up could appear identifying the caller. In the future, there will be more interactivity integrated so you can participate in live polls or chats on-screen as the show is broadcast.

**Can I record the digital video that comes over my television?** There are a variety of digital video recorders (DVRs) available to record the digital video from your television. These can record in either standard or HD quality and store the information on a hard drive. Useful features include being able to record two shows at once, being able to download movie

**NTSC**

**HDTV**

Extra image area

Letterbox

Pichugin Dmitry/Shutterstock.com

purchases or rentals from the Internet directly to the DVR unit, and easily moving stored content to a mobile device like an iPad or a smartphone. Using a DVR, you can pause live TV or set up a schedule to capture every episode of a series, no matter when it airs. Models like TiVo even recommend new shows you might like based on what you have been watching. If you don't want to purchase a DVR or pay the monthly subscription fee for DVR service, you can install PVR (personal video recording) software on your computer, as we mentioned at the opening of the chapter. When connected to your cable signal, programs like BeyondTV (**www.snapstream.com**) turn your computer itself into a DVR.

**How else can I get digital video to my TV?** In addition to the broadcast content coming in to your TV, there are a number of streaming sources of digital video.

**Figure 5.26**

(a) Standard-definition television has a more "square" aspect ratio, while (b) high-definition television matches the 16:9 ratio used in the motion picture industry without resorting to (c) letterboxing.

**Figure** 5.27

Slingbox can send your digital television content to your tablet, notebook, or phone, wherever you may be.

Cable providers offer a wide range of on-demand video services. Many older films, television episodes, and shows such as exercise classes are offered free of charge. Other premium content, like new-release movies, is offered for a fee. Just one click and you can instantly watch any offered movie for 24 hours, with full control—stopping, starting, and rewinding. Other providers, like Netflix, also offer streaming video content. While Netflix's original business model was to ship members discs physically in the mail, they now also offer Watch Instantly. Thousands of movies and TV series are available with just a click. You can view these shows on a television through any gaming console, a PC, an iPad, or a specialized device like the Roku digital video player.

**Can I get digital video to watch on my portable device?** Yes. Many DVR units, like TiVo, support software that allows you to transfer recorded shows to files on your PC and format them for viewing on a mobile device. There are also devices like Slingbox that take the video from your television and broadcast it to you over the Internet. With Slingbox, you can be in another room, or another country, and control and watch

your home television on your notebook or your smartphone (see Figure 5.27).

### Digital Navigation

**How has digitized information impacted navigation?** Built and operated by the U.S. Department of Defense, the **global positioning system** (GPS) is a network of 21 satellites (plus 3 working spares) that constantly orbits the Earth. GPS devices use an antenna to pick up the signals from these satellites and use special software to transform those signals into latitude and longitude. Using the information obtained from the satellites, GPS devices determine the geographical location anywhere on the planet to within 3 feet (see Figure 5.28). The exact accuracy depends on such things as atmospheric conditions and interference from obstacles like mountains or buildings. Because they provide such detailed positioning information, GPS devices are now used as navigational aids for aircraft, recreational boats, and automobiles, and they even come in handheld models for hikers.

**How do I get GPS in my car?** Stand-alone GPS devices have dropped dramatically in price and size. Small, handheld units deliver turn-by-turn instructions and real-time traffic information. Several manufacturers, like Garmin and Magellan, make stand-alone GPS devices that can be mounted onto the windshield of your car.

GPS units are available with a wide range of features. Garmin, for example, offers numerous services on its line of GPS units. A Map mode displays your location and the current speed limit on a map that is updated in real time as you drive. When you enter a series of destinations into the unit, an optimal route is developed for you. A voice warns you of lane changes and approaching turns, giving you directions using the actual street name (such as "Turn right on Hancock Avenue"). Lane Assist flips into a 3D display mode and shows you how to navigate through lane changes in highway merges (see Figure 5.29). If you miss a turn, the unit automatically recalculates the required route and gives you directions to get back on course. Flip to another screen, and it shows you how far you have to drive to the next gas station, restaurant, or hospital. Some models automatically mark the location of your car when you remove them from the vehicle, and can give you step-by-step directions back to your car.

In addition, most automotive companies now offer GPS systems as an installed

**Figure 5.28**

GPS computes your location anywhere on Earth from a system of orbiting satellites.

**Figure 5.29**

In addition to the driving applications shown, the Garmin nüvi series GPS devices are also able to provide Internet services.

option in their vehicles. Of course, GPS navigation can be added to any vehicle by using GPS on a mobile device like a smartphone.

**Do GPS devices carry other information?** Full-featured GPS models such as the Garmin nüvi 1490 series include MP3 players, audio book players, and the capability to display photos and connect to the Internet. Using Internet services such as MSN Direct, your GPS can keep you informed about the weather, traffic backups, local movie times, and even local gas prices.

**How does GPS help me in an emergency?** By the end of 2005, every cell/smartphone had to include a GPS chip. The Federal Communications Commission (FCC) mandated this to enable the complete rollout of the Enhanced 911 (E911) program. E911 automatically gives dispatchers precise location information for any 911 call. It also means your phone records may include this precise tracking information, which indicates where you are when you make a call.

**Can I use the GPS chip on a family member's cell/smartphone?** Cellular phone providers offer plans (for a monthly fee) that allow you to track where a phone is at any given time via a Web site.

For example, AT&T's service Family Maps allows parents to track all of the phones on their family plan in real time. Locations of all phones are displayed over the Web on a map, or the service will send an automatic text message alert with the phone's location at a specific time each day. So a parent could have a text or e-mail sent with their daughter's phone location each day at 3 P.M. to be sure she made it home from school. The person being tracked cannot turn off the service.

## Digital Convergence

Once you are comfortable with digital communication and digital media, you'll want to be able to communicate and to access your music, books, and media all the time. Access to your digital assets is required in a modern business environment and is a great benefit in your personal life.

There is a wide range of devices that grant you mobile access to your digital resources. As more and more computing power is available in mobile processors, mobile devices have evolved to be able to do multiple tasks. **Digital convergence**, the

**Figure** 5.30

Tablets do not have hardware keyboards but can be paired wirelessly with a keyboard if desired.

© Pixellover RM 4 / Alamy

**Figure** 5.31

The Asus Padphone lets you share the processor of the Phone with a tablet shell.

use of a single unifying device to handle media, Internet, entertainment, and telephony needs, is expressed in the range of devices now on the market.

Let's decide if you need more than one mobile device and which device is the right one for you.

**What are the main categories of mobile devices?** There are several major categories of mobile devices available now. Feature phones and smartphones were discussed earlier in this chapter. They have a wide set of abilities but are limited in computing power, display size, and keyboard size. **Netbooks** run a fully featured operating system but weigh in at 2 pounds or less. An **Internet tablet** is another type of very light, very portable device. Internet tablets do not offer full-size hardware keyboards but can be easily paired with a keyboard using Bluetooth (see Figure 5.30). The top-selling Apple iPad has a 9.7" multitouch screen and weighs in at only 1.5 pounds. The iPad runs a mobile OS named iOS and runs mobile touch versions of popular Apple productivity software Pages, Numbers, and Keynote. The iPad also supports video viewing, music, Internet browsing, and thousands of apps.

Netbooks and Internet tablets both carry files, music, and videos as well as provide specialized services. Then there is the full range of notebooks and tablet computers, and new blends of various features

are appearing in new devices all the time. For example, the Asus Padphone (see Figure 5.31) is a hybrid of a phone and a tablet "shell" that can be powered by the phone when a larger display is needed. Figure 5.32 lists the main features of several different mobile device categories.

**What if I don't need a full notebook computer but do need Internet access?** Lightweight Internet tablets have exploded in popularity. Manufacturers offer two versions of models, one with WiFi connectivity only and one with both WiFi and cellular connectivity (3G). Tablets have high-resolution multi-touch sensitive screens, integrated webcams, and GPS capabilities. There are models in a wide variety of sizes, with a range of operating systems and specifications (see Figure 5.33).

If a tablet is too expensive a solution, there are also netbooks and mobile gaming systems. Netbooks pack major computing power into a tiny package, and manufacturers try to extend battery life as long as possible. Screen sizes are typically between 8" and 10", and keyboards are less than full sized. Netbooks often come with a Windows operating system. Some users opt to install a flavor of Linux, however, because Linux requires fewer resources than Windows. Solid-state hard drives are a good choice for netbooks because they use less power and produce less heat. Many models include integrated webcams as well as Bluetooth, so

**Figure 5.32** | MOBILE DEVICES: PRICE, SIZE, WEIGHT, AND CAPABILITIES

| Device | Relative Price | Approximate Size | Approximate Weight | Standard Capabilities |
|---|---|---|---|---|
| Cell phone | $$ (Includes cost for the phone, a monthly plan, and Internet access) | 5" × 2" × 0.5" | 0.25 lb. | Voice, e-mail, some application software, and Internet connectivity |
| PMP | $$–$$$ | 4" × 2" × 0.5" | 0.25 lb. | Storage of digital music, video, and other digital files; no Internet access |
| Smartphone | $$–$$$ | 4.5" × 2" × 0.75" | 0.25 lb. | Camera, PIM capabilities, GPS, compass, application software, and access to the Internet |
| Internet tablet | $$$–$$$$ | 10" × 7" × 0.3" | 0.5 lb. | Webcam, GPS, phone calls using VoIP, sharp resolution, and widescreen display |
| Netbook | $$$ | 10" × 7" | 1–2 lbs. | 8" and 10" screens and full-featured operating systems and applications; hardware keyboard. |
| Tablet PC | $$$$ | 10" × 8" × 1" | 1–3 lbs. | PIM capabilities, access to application software, access to the Internet, and special handwriting- and speech-recognition capabilities |
| Notebook | $$$$–$$$$$ | 10" × 13" × 2" | 5 to 8 lbs. | All the capabilities of a desktop computer plus portability |

while netbooks are small and light, they still can serve many functions.

Mobile game systems have interesting combinations of features as well. The Sony Vita can play video games but also includes a Web browser, Skype, and an RSS reader. It uses Sony Memory Sticks to store data.

The screen is a 5″ OLED widescreen design with great clarity and brightness. With two cameras, a touch-sensitive screen, a rear touch pad, a gyroscope, an accelerometer, and dual analog control sticks, the Vita is a unique mobile offering.

**Figure 5.33**

iPad2 . . . Xoom . . . Galaxy? There are over 75 tablets on the market now. Finding the right digital device can be a challenge.

© oliver leedham / Alamy

# Near Field Communication

Mobile devices have changed many aspects of our daily lives, and that trend will continue with the expansion of near field communication (NFC). NFC technology allows a device with an NFC chip to communicate with another NFC device with just a single touch. Data can be exchanged, or financial transactions can be processed just by bringing the devices within an inch of each other. This simple-sounding type of wireless communication has the potential to create a major shift in how we live.

Because NFC has such a short range (up to 1.5 inches) it is being used for secure credit card transactions. Both MasterCard and Visa are piloting programs that would allow cellular phones to "tap and go," meaning phone owners would no longer carry physical credit cards. Instead they could simply wave their phone near an NFC checkout device and have the transaction processed.

This seems similar to the Visa PayWave or MasterCard PayPass programs in place in some areas, where the credit card itself can simply be "waved" near a reader to process the transaction. But NFC acceptance would open the door to much, much more. Imagine waving your phone past an NFC reader at checkout and having it automatically transmit the proper loyalty card information, select and process any appropriate coupon offers, and pay all at once (see Figure 5.34). In countries like Japan, Spain, and Germany, NFC ticketing programs are already in place. The Deutsche Bahn rail system allows users to tap their phones to an NFC tag when they get on the train, and another on departing. The fare is automatically calculated and billed to their credit card monthly. The new "digital wallet" would be a single storage place for all of your financial needs.

But you also use your wallet to carry ID information. NFC can handle that as well. The swipe cards that verify your identity for entry into secure areas can be replaced using NFC to exchange stored virtual credentials. The same technology could replace doors protected with PIN numbers or anywhere a username/password verification is used. So opening a door or logging into a computer could all be managed with a tap of your NFC-enabled phone.

At the time of this writing, there are not many phones on the U.S. market with NFC chips, but all major carriers have announcements planned. Google has announced a mobile app known as Google Wallet that will collect your loyalty cards, gift cards, receipts, boarding passes, tickets, and keys within your phone.

So imagine a time, soon, when you are out to dinner with friends and need to split the bill. Your NFC phone is already linked to your PayPal account and you simply wave your phone next to your friend's phone to transfer him your share of the bill. Some are predicting the worldwide NFC market will grow to be worth $50 billion by 2014, making this a trend to watch.

YOSHIKAZU TSUNO / AFP / Getty Images / Newscom

**Figure 5.34**
NFC-equipped phones will shift how we handle financial transactions and identify ourselves.

**summary**

1. **What are the changes that have brought us a digital lifestyle?**

   The increased use of digital information has led to a period of greater creativity and control of our data. In a digital format, information is easy to carry, manipulate, and exchange. This has led to revolutionary changes in communication, entertainment media, and mobile computing.

2. **How do cell phone and smartphone components resemble a traditional computer?**

   Like a traditional computer, a cell/smartphone has a central processor, memory, and an operating system. These components work in the same way as in a computer to process information and support communications, software applications, and other services.

3. **Why would I use VoIP?**

   VoIP allows inexpensive communication using a computer or a WiFi-enabled phone. Because it is based on a digital format for information, it can support services like automatic delivery of phone messages to an e-mail account or texts to a mobile device.

4. **How is digital media different from analog?**

   Digital media is based on a series of numeric data comprising number values that were measured from the original analog waveform. As a string of numbers, a digital photo or video file can be easily processed by modern computers.

5. **How is digital media created and what changes has it brought?**

   Digital publishing is allowing a variety of new distribution methods into the industry. eReaders and online bookstores are bringing changes to the models of how to sell printed materials. Digital music is created by combining pure digital sounds with samples of analog sounds. It has meant changes for the recording industry, for performers, and for music listeners. It is now inexpensive to carry a music library, to create new songs, and to distribute them worldwide.

6. **How do I create and watch digital video?**

   You can create digital video using any digital camera, webcam, or digital camcorder. Digital editing software allows you to add transitions, effects, and sound tracks. There are a great many sources of digital video, including free sources like YouTube and JustIn, as well as pay-per-view services like Amazon Video On Demand or cable providers' streaming video options.

7. **What new kinds of mobile devices are available?**

   There is a wide array of mobile devices, and each has a unique set of tools and software collected together. Internet tablets, netbooks, and mobile gaming devices each have specific advantages. Digital convergence has brought us single devices that have the capabilities that used to require four or five separate tools. We now see products that allow us to interact with information in ways that had been too expensive or difficult before.

 **Companion Website**

The Companion Website includes a variety of additional materials to help you review and learn more about the topics in this chapter. Go to: *www.pearsonhighered.com/techinaction*

## Word Bank

- analog-to-digital converter
- Bluetooth
- cell phone
- digital convergence
- GPS
- Internet tablet
- microbrowser
- MMS
- netbook
- P2P
- PMP
- sampling rate
- smartphone
- SMS
- synchronize
- telephony
- VoIP
- webcam

**Instructions:** Fill in the blanks using the words from the Word Bank above.

Ananda knows that everything seems to be "digital" these days. In the past, she carried a traditional SLR camera but now she simply uses her (1) _____ to take photos. She can connect wirelessly to the computer to transfer the images because the phone supports (2) _____. Sometimes she doesn't bother to do that because she has already sent a(n) (3) _____ message to a friend with the image. Her old phone couldn't do that because it only supported (4) _____. If she upgraded to a(n) (5) _____, she could actually make many refinements and edits to the image without transferring it to the computer at all.

Nigel is a real fan of technology, and so he has selected a(n) (6) _____ instead of a cell/smartphone. He's always near a WiFi signal, so he doesn't need an actual phone. He doesn't even pay for traditional phone service at home, where he uses (7) _____ instead of a landline. He's fallen in love with his new device for many reasons. It can give him driving directions with its built-in (8) _____. The (9) _____ software displays full HTML Web pages right on the device. He used to have to sync his device each night, but now he uses wireless (10) _____ technology to synchronize instantly.

Niti can't quite decide what device will work best for his new life. He's moving to California and plans to be outside a lot, so he wants something very light. He thinks the two-pound (11) _____ might be ideal because he doesn't really need a full keyboard or a huge screen. When he's out biking, he has plans to wear his (12) _____ on his helmet and keep a video record of his excursion. He downloads free songs offered by bands that are just starting out from a(n) (13) _____ site. The songs have a much lower (14) _____ than he usually demands, but at least they don't take up much space on his hard drive. He's heard that electronics are merging with clothing more and more, so maybe soon (15) _____ will lead to a T-shirt that can take care of his mobile music needs!

**Instructions:** Write a report providing answers to the questions posed below, using as many of the key terms from the chapter as you can. Be sure the sentences are grammatically and technically correct.

You have a limited budget to spend on technology tools and toys in the years you will be a student. You are considering communication, entertainment media, and your need to be able to work and connect with your information when you are not at home. Which digital media services and products would you definitely invest in? How would you justify their value? What kinds of services and products would you use that are free or low cost? Has the migration to a digital lifestyle given you more freedom and creativity or just caused you more annoyance and expense?

**Instructions:** Answer the multiple-choice and true–false questions below for more practice with key terms and concepts from this chapter.

## Multiple Choice

**1.** Which is *not* a factor that determines the quality of images taken with a digital camera?
  a. lens quality
  b. resolution
  c. file format
  d. eye-Fi

**2.** Cloud technology is important to mobile device owners because it
  a. allows you to carry video files.
  b. transmits weather and radar information.
  c. means you no longer need Internet access.
  d. allows instant synchronization of multiple devices.

**3.** The operating system of your cell/smartphone is stored in
  a. read-only memory.
  b. the display.
  c. the digital signal processor.
  d. random-access memory.

**4.** The quickest way to distribute your band's new song to a lot of listeners is to
  a. use an application to post it on Facebook.
  b. you cannot legally distribute music freely.
  c. e-mail the song to local radio stations.
  d. hand out CDs that you burned.

**5.** P2P is an acronym for
  a. packet-to-packet networking.
  b. peer-to-peer sharing.
  c. person-to-person texting.
  d. power-to-power delivery.

**6.** An analog signal is different from a digital signal because
  a. it is continuous.
  b. it has only specific discrete values.
  c. it is easier to duplicate.
  d. it is easier to transmit.

**7.** Flash memory is a type of
  a. nonvolatile memory.
  b. hard drive memory.
  c. SSD memory.
  d. volatile memory.

**8.** VoIP is phone service that
  a. works even when the electricity goes out.
  b. works over an Internet connection.
  c. requires no special setup for a secure connection.
  d. has extremely high quality and is very reliable.

**9.** Which of the following is *not* true about modern televisions?
  a. They incorporate wireless connectivity.
  b. They allow other services, like caller ID, to be integrated.
  c. You can purchase apps for them.
  d. They run word processing and spreadsheet software.

**10.** Which service allows you to use your cell/smartphone to send messages that contain images?
  a. MMS     b. ISP
  c. SMS     d. MiFi

## True–False

_____ 1. Digital convergence means that all cellular networks will become 4G.

_____ 2. Digital music files must be converted to the MP3 format if they are transferred to a mobile device.

_____ 3. A codec is the algorithm that compresses and decompresses video files.

_____ 4. If your digital camera doesn't support wireless connectivity, you can use a memory card with built-in WiFi.

_____ 5. Some Internet-enabled devices use Skype instead of cell phone service for voice communications.

1. **Choosing Mobile Devices to Fit Your Needs**

   As a student, which devices discussed in this chapter would have the most immediate impact on the work you do each day? Which would provide the best value (that is, the greatest increase in productivity and organization per dollar spent)? Consider the full range of devices, from cell/smartphones to notebook systems.

2. **Ready . . . Set . . . Act!**

   As a student, you often give presentations or take on student teaching assignments. What would be the steps for creating a digital video recording of one of your presentations? What tools would you need to record? What kind of file would you end up producing? How would you distribute the video to a live Internet audience? How would you make a DVD of the performance?

3. **Author, Author**

   As a new author of fantasy stories, you have written a collection of fiction shorts. You decide to publish them yourself. What options are there for you to use? How do they compare/contrast?

4. **Choosing the Best Phone**

   Your friend wants to trim down the number of different devices that she carries. Visit the most popular cellular providers' Web sites and research options. Compare at least three different models of phones and list their price, music storage capacity, built-in memory, and expandability options.

   a. Which of the three models you compared is the best value for your friend? Why?
   b. What special features does the phone you chose have? What accessories would you recommend your friend buy to make the phone more useful?
   c. Would you suggest buying a refurbished phone? Why or why not?

5. **iTunes U**

   Download a free copy of iTunes software. In the iTunes Store, explore the iTunes U podcast directory, which contains free audio and video lectures published by major universities.

   a. Look for the MIT Open Courseware collection. How many lectures are available?
   b. If each lecture were 90 minutes on average and approximately 200 MB in size, how much storage would it take to save all of the video lectures in every course published by MIT?
   c. Is there a mobile device that can store and play that much content? What devices could store the lectures from all of the courses in mathematics offered by MIT Open Courseware?

1. **Corporate Mobile Communications Needs**

   Imagine your company is boosting its sales force and looking to the future of mobile technology. Your manager has asked you to research the following issues surrounding mobile communications for the company:

   a. Do mobile communication devices present increased security risks? What would happen if you left a cell/smartphone at a meeting and a competitor picked it up? Are there ways to protect your data on mobile devices?

   b. Can viruses attack cell/smartphones? Is there any special software on the market to protect mobile devices from viruses? How much would it cost to equip 20 devices with virus protection?

   c. Is there a role for mobile communication devices even if employees don't leave the building? Which devices would be important for a company to consider for use within corporate offices? Are there software solutions that would work as well?

   d. Should employees be allowed to use smartphones provided by the company for personal use even though files related to personal use might eat up potentially valuable memory and space? What restrictions should be put on personal use to protect the privacy of proprietary company information contained on the devices?

2. **5G and 4G Communications**

   The most recent generation of telecommunications (nicknamed "4G" for fourth generation) is currently allowing the speed of cellular network transmissions to hit 3–6 Mbps. In the near future, full 4G speeds of closer to 100Mbps will be available. But what is beyond that?

   What is in place for the development of a 5G system? How do 4G and 5G compare to current broadband access over wired networks? What implications does that have for information access and e-commerce? What download speed would be ideal? Upload speed? How would it change how you communicate?

3. **Subscription Versus Ownership**

   With the arrival of reliable, fast, networked digital information, businesses can track the location and status of all kinds of objects, such as cars and bicycles. This is introducing a new business model different from individual ownership—now using a car can become a "subscription" service.

   What options are there for "subscribing" to a car instead of owning one? How about for a bicycle? Are there other businesses you can identify that would be able to take advantage of digital information and become subscription services instead of vendors of a physical product? What are the advantages to the consumer of subscription over ownership? What are the drawbacks?

4. **Too Much Media?**

   Imagine you are a manager of 18 employees, all of whom work with constant Internet access. As a manager, what concerns might you have about their use of corporate bandwidth to download and view media files? Do you think it would benefit your business to block any MP3 file transfers? Should you put in place a block to prevent access to sites that store huge numbers of streaming videos? As a manager, are there concerns you might have if employees have digital cameras on their cell/smartphones? Would your answers be different in an academic setting?

### 5. Mobile Devices on the Highway

Mobile devices used in vehicles are becoming the norm in today's society. Consider the following:

a.  Several car manufacturers provide Bluetooth option packages for their vehicles. What advantages are there to having Bluetooth connectivity in your car? Are there any disadvantages?

b.  Examine the Microsoft Sync software package. List the features and services it provides. If you were a salesperson with a territory that you covered by car, how would Sync help you?

critical thinking questions

**Instructions:** Some ideas are best understood by experimenting with them in our own minds. The following critical thinking questions are designed to demand your full attention but require only a comfortable chair—no technology.

### 1. Digital Entertainment

Can you name a style of media that has not made the shift to digital? What advantages does digital photography offer? Digital video? What disadvantages come along with a digital format for entertainment media? Has the growth in digital media promoted an increased understanding between people or has it created more isolation?

### 2. The Ultimate Style

As mobile devices continue to evolve, they have become lighter and smaller, and we are beginning to see a convergence of computing and clothing.

a. What would the ultimate convergent mobile clothing be for you? Is there a limit in weight, size, or complexity?
b. Can you imagine uses for technology in fashion that would support better health? Better social relationships? A richer intellectual life?

### 3. Reinvent Yourself

The arrival of digital information has forced major shifts in several industries, such as publishing, music recording, and film. How has each industry reacted? Have they each found ways to reinvent the products and services they deliver to match the challenge of the Digital Age? What other industries have had to realign their business model because of digital information?

### 4. Too Much Information?

Consider the following questions:

a. Your rental car has a GPS installed. After you return it, the rental company uses the GPS data to determine whether you have driven the car at speeds above the speed limit. It then issues fines for violations of the rental contract. Does this lead to safer highways? Is it an infringement of your privacy?
b. Would you agree to insert a GPS-enabled tracking chip into your pet? Your child? What legislation do you think should be required regarding use of the tracking data from your phone records? Would you be willing to sell that information to marketing agencies? Should that data be available to the government if you were suspected of a crime?

### 5. Electronic Publishing

Explore the specifications of the Sony Portable Reader, the Barnes & Noble NOOK, the Amazon Kindle, and the Apple iPad. How would your study habits change if your textbooks were only delivered to you in electronic format on one of these devices? What unique advantages would there be? What disadvantages would there be? How would using such a device compare with just receiving the book as an electronic file, such as a PDF document, to your notebook computer?

**team time**

# "... and one will rule them all."

### Problem

Digital convergence posits the dream of one device that can do it all, for everyone. But there are so many different mobile devices saturating the market that many people are left in a state of confusion. Either they are buying too many devices and not using them, or they are paralyzed from buying anything because of the dilemma of too many choices.

### Task

For each client scenario described below, the group will select the minimum set of devices that would support and enhance the client's life.

### Process

1. Consider the following three clients:

   - A retired couple who now travel for pleasure a great deal. They want to be involved in their grandchildren's lives and will need support for their health , finances, and personal care as they age.
   - A young family with two children, two working parents, and a tight budget.
   - A couple in which each individual is a physician and they both adore technology.

2. Make two recommendations for your client in terms of digital technologies that will enhance their business or their lifestyle. Discuss the advantages and disadvantages of each technology. Consider value, reliability, computing needs, training needed, and communication needs, as well as expandability for the future.

3. As a group, prepare a final report that considers the costs, availability, and unique features of the recommendations you have made for each client.

4. Bring the research materials from the individual team meetings to class. Looking at the clients' needs, make final decisions as to which digital technologies are best suited for each client.

### Conclusion

Digital information has allowed the development of a new style of living, both at home and at work. With so many digital solutions on the market today, recommending digital communication, media management, and mobility options needs to focus on converging to the minimum set of tools that will enhance life without adding complication to it.

# When Everyone Has a Voice

In this exercise, you will research and then role-play a complicated ethical situation. The role you play might or might not match your own personal beliefs; in either case, your research and use of logic will enable you to represent the view assigned. An arbitrator will watch and comment on both sides of the arguments, and together the team will agree on an ethical solution.

## Background

Much of the world's population is now equipped with Internet-ready camera phones. Sensors on these phones could measure for viruses or compute pollution indexes, while the cameras could be used to document a range of human behavior. This could create changes in political movements, art, and culture as everyone's experience is documented and shared.

## Research Areas to Consider

- Evgeny Morozov RSA Animate
- Mobilebehavior.com
- Witness project
- Center for Embedded Network Sensing

## Process

Divide the class into teams.

1. Research the sources cited above and devise a scenario in which mobile access could make an impact politically or environmentally, positively or negatively.

2. Team members should write a summary that provides background information for their character—for example, business owner, politician, reporter, and arbitrator—and details their character's behaviors to set the stage for the role-playing event. Then, team members should create an outline to use during the role-playing event.

3. Team members should arrange a mutually convenient time to meet for the exchange, either using the collaboration feature of MyITLab, the discussion board feature of Blackboard, or meeting in person.

4. Team members should present their case to the class, or submit a PowerPoint presentation for review by the rest of the class, along with the summary and resolution they developed.

## Conclusion

As technology becomes ever more prevalent and integrated into our lives, more and more ethical dilemmas will present themselves. Being able to understand and evaluate both sides of the argument, while responding in a personally or socially ethical manner, will be an important skill.

# TECHNOLOGY

© Sean Locke/iStockphoto.com

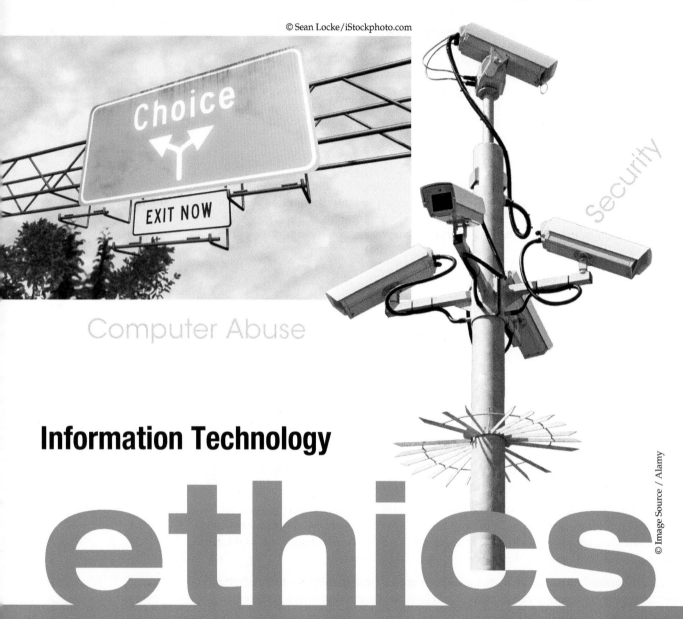

Security

Computer Abuse

© Image Source / Alamy

## Information Technology

# ethics

In this Technology in Focus section, we explore what ethics is, how your personal ethics develop, and how your personal ethics fit into the world around you. We'll also examine how technology and ethics affect each other and how technology can be used to support ethical conduct. Finally, we'll examine several key issues in technology ethics today, including the areas of social justice, intellectual property rights, privacy, e-commerce, free speech, and computer abuse.

# IN FOCUS

Intellectual Property

Robin Lund/Shutterstock.com

Censorship

John Wiese/iStockphoto.com

People speak of ethics—and the lack of ethics—casually all the time, but the ethical choices that individuals make are an extremely serious matter and can have a far-reaching impact. It is important to have a clear idea of what ethics are, what your personal ethics are, and how personal ethics fit into the world at large.

## Ethics in Computing

You just bought a new notebook computer. You know you can go to BitTorrent to download the latest summer blockbuster movie and its soundtrack. You also probably know this is unethical. Although pirating music and videos is a valid example of unethical behavior, it has been overused as an illustration of the ethical challenges of technology. There is a vast range of ethical issues surrounding technology (as shown in Figure 6.1), several of which we will discuss in this section. Many other issues are discussed in the Ethics in IT sections of each chapter throughout the book.

## What Is Ethics?

Ethics is the study of the general nature of morals and of the specific moral choices made by individuals. Morals involve conforming to established or accepted ideas of right and wrong (as generally dictated by society), and are usually viewed as black and white. Ethical issues often involve subtle distinctions, such as the difference between fairness and equity. Ethical values are the guidelines you use to make decisions each day. For example, the person in front of you at the coffee shop drops a dollar on the floor and doesn't notice it. Do you tell him or her about it, or do you pick up the dollar and use it to pay for your coffee?

**Doesn't everyone have the same basic ethics?** There are many systems of ethical conduct. Relativism is a theory that holds that there is no universal moral truth and that instead there are only beliefs,

perspectives, and values. Everyone has his or her own ideas of right and wrong, and so who are we to judge anyone else? Another ethical philosophy is situational ethics, which states that decision making should be based on the circumstances of a particular situation and not on fixed laws.

Many other ethical systems have been proposed over time, some of which are defined by religious traditions. For example, the expression "Judeo-Christian ethics" refers to the common set of basic values shared across the Jewish and Christian religious traditions. These include behaviors such as respecting property and relationships, honoring one's parents, and being kind to others.

**Are laws established to guide people's ethical actions?** Laws are formal, written standards designed to apply to everyone. Laws are enforced by government agencies (such as the police, the Federal Bureau of Investigation, the Food and Drug Administration, and so on) and interpreted by the courts. It is not possible to pass laws that cover every possible behavior that human beings can engage in. Therefore, societal ethics provides a general set of unwritten guidelines for people to follow.

**Rule utilitarianism** is an ethical theory that espouses establishing moral guidelines through specific rules. The idea behind this system is that if everyone adheres to the same moral code, society as a whole will improve and people will be happier. Many societies follow this system in general terms, including the United States. For instance, laws against nudity in public places (except for a few nude beaches) in the United States help define public nudity as immoral.

**Don't some people behave unethically?** Although many valid systems of ethical conduct exist, sometimes people act in a manner that violates the beliefs they hold or the beliefs of the ethical system they say they follow. **Unethical behavior** can be defined as not conforming to a set of approved standards of social or professional behavior. For instance, using your phone to text message a test answer to your friend during an exam is prohibited by many colleges' rules of student conduct. This behavior is different from amoral behavior, in which a person has no sense of right and wrong and no interest in the moral consequences of his or her actions.

**Figure 6.1**

Ethics in computing covers a wide range of areas, not just privacy and security.

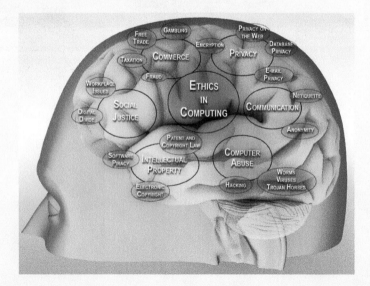

**Is unethical behavior a euphemism for illegal activity?** Unethical behavior does not have to be illegal. An example of an unethical but not illegal practice is supermarket slotting fees. These are fees that some supermarkets charge to produce companies and product manufacturers for the privilege of having their products placed on store shelves. This is considered unethical by many people because it puts smaller companies, which often don't have the financial resources to pay these fees, at a disadvantage.

Not all illegal behavior is unethical. Civil disobedience, which is manifested by intentionally refusing to obey certain laws, is used as a form of protest to effect change in extreme situations. Gandhi's nonviolent resistance to the British rule of India, which led to India's establishment as an independent country, is an example of civil disobedience. Although the British were ruling India, is it ever ethical for one country to control another country's people?

**Which system of ethics works best?** There is no universal agreement on which is the best system of ethics. Most societies use a blend of different systems. Regardless of the ethical system of the society in which you live, all ethical decisions are greatly influenced by personal ethics.

consequences of your decisions today might lead to an unhappy result for you in the short term. For instance, to get the job of your dreams, should you exaggerate a bit on your résumé and say you've already finished your college degree, even though you are still one credit short? Is this lying? Is such behavior justified in this setting? After all, you do intend to finish that last credit, and you would work really hard for this company if you were hired. If you tell the truth and state that you haven't finished college yet, then you might be passed over for the position. Making this choice is an ethical decision (see Figure 6.2).

**How do a person's ethics develop?** Many elements contribute to your ethical development (see Figure 6.3). Naturally, your family has a major role in establishing the values you cherish in your own life, and these might include a cultural bias toward certain moral positions. Your religious affiliation is another major influence in your ethical life, because most religions have established specific codes of ethical conduct. How these sets of ethics interact with the values of the larger culture is often challenging. Issues such as abortion, the

**Figure 6.2**

It would be nice if there were signposts to ethical conduct, but the issues are complex.

**Figure 6.3**

Many different forces shape your ethical worldview.

## Personal Ethics

**What are personal ethics?**
Every day you say certain things and take specific actions, and at each point you are making decisions based on some criterion. It may be that you are trying to care for the people around you, or are trying to eliminate a source of pain or anger in your life. Your words and actions may also be driven by a combination of criteria. As you choose your words and actions, you are following a set of personal ethics—a checklist of personal decisions you have compiled to organize your life. Some people have a clear, well-defined set of principles they follow. Others' ethics are inconsistent or are applied differently in similar situations.

It can be challenging to adhere to your own ethical system if the

Family
Don't litter.

Religion
Don't tell lies.

Experience
Don't speed or you'll get a ticket.

Your ethical behavior

Teachers
Don't cheat on tests or you'll fail.

death penalty, and war force confrontations between personal ethical systems and the larger society's established legal-ethical system.

As you mature, your life experiences also affect your personal ethics. Does the behavior you see around you make sense within the ethical principles that your family, your church, or your first-grade teacher taught you? Has your experience led you to abandon some ethical rules and adopt others? Have you modified how and when you apply these laws of conduct, depending on what is at stake?

**What if I'm not sure what my personal ethics are?** When you have a clear and firm idea of what values are most important to you, it may be easier to handle situations in your professional and your personal life that demand ethical action. Follow these steps to help define your personal ethics:

1. **Describe yourself.** Write down words that describe who you are, based on how others view you. Would a friend describe you as honest, or helpful, or kind?

2. **List your beliefs.** Make a list of all the beliefs that influence your decision making. For example, would you be comfortable working as a research assistant in a lab that infected animals with diseases and used them for medical research? How important is it to you that you never tell a lie? Consider whether your answers to each of these questions are "flexible." Are there situations in which your answers might change (say, if a friend were ill or in danger)?

3. **Identify external influences.** Consider the places where you work and live and how you relate to the people you see during the day. Are there things that you would like to change about these

relationships that would merit listing them in a code of ethics?

4. **Consider "why."** After writing down your beliefs, think about why you believe them. Have you accepted them without investigation? Do they stand up in the context of your real-world experiences? For which of these values would you make short-term sacrifices in order to uphold your beliefs?

5. **Prepare a statement of values.** It can be useful to distill what you have written into a short list. By having a well-defined statement of the values you hold most important in your own life, which you can refer to in times of challenge, it will be easier for you to make ethical decisions.

**Are there tangible benefits to ethical living?** Society has established its own set of rules of conduct in the form of laws. Ignoring or being inconsistent in following these principles can surely have an immediate impact. Whether it is complying with a law that affects the way your business is run, or with a law that affects your personal life (don't exceed the speed limit or you'll receive a fine), decision-making principles that work with society's legal boundaries can make your life much simpler.

More and more research is showing the health benefits of ethical living. When your day-to-day decisions are in conflict with the values you consider most important as a human being, you often develop stress and anger. Constant conflict between what you value and what actions you are forced to take can lead to a variety of types of mental and physical damage.

Perhaps even happiness itself is a result of living ethically (see Figure 6.4).

**Figure 6.4**

The field of positive psychology shows that living and working ethically affects your happiness.

Cheating
Stealing
Selfishness
Lying

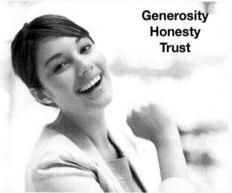
Generosity
Honesty
Trust

**Positive psychology** is a new focus in the field of psychology. Pioneered by Dr. Martin Seligman of the University of Pennsylvania, this field works to discover the causes of happiness instead of addressing the treatment of mental dysfunctions. Dr. Seligman's research has shown that, by identifying your personal strengths and values, and then aligning your life so that you can apply them every day, you can experience an increase in happiness (and a decrease in depression) equivalent to the effects of antidepressant medication and therapy. Thus, finding a way to identify and then apply your ethics and values to your daily life can have an impact on your health and happiness.

## Personal Ethics and Your Worldview

**How do my personal ethics fit into the world at large?** All of your actions, words, and even thoughts are controlled by your personal ideas of right and wrong. But do your ethics shift when you go to work? Your employer expects you to follow the ethics and rules of conduct that the owner has established for the business. Although each person at your workplace may be trying to follow corporate ethical guidelines, each person will follow them differently based on his or her personal ethics. Person A may feel it is acceptable to tell white lies to get more funding for his project, whereas Person B might believe that telling the truth at all times is the best and only way that she can foster the teamwork and cooperation necessary to complete a project.

This doesn't mean that individuals need to blindly follow practices they feel are unethical or detrimental to society at large. Most **whistle-blowers** are people that report businesses to regulatory agencies for committing illegal acts. Other whistle-blowers expose unethical (but still legal) acts by their employers by publicizing unethical behavior through various media outlets.

In summary, when you are working in a business environment, your ethics are guided by the ethical principles that are defined by the business owner or management, but you are still ultimately guided by your personal ethics.

**How do employers affect personal ethics?** Should your employer have control (or even input) about your conduct outside of the office? Do behavior, integrity, and honesty off the job relate to job performance? They might. But even if they don't, your actions could reflect poorly on your employer from your employer's perspective. Consider Ellen Simonetti, who was fired by Delta Airlines for blogging. Even though Ms. Simonetti never mentioned Delta Airlines by name on her blog ("Queen of the Sky: Diary of a Dysfunctional Flight Attendant"), Delta Airlines objected to photos that she posted of herself and fellow flight attendants in their Delta uniforms. Delta Airlines felt that the photos were inappropriate and portrayed negative images of Delta Airlines employees. Another example is Jillian Tomlinson, the Australian surgeon who was suspended by her employer for discussing medical procedures, her work environment, and fellow employees, and for posting CAT scans of patients on her blog (although patient names were not revealed). Therefore, although your ethics might dictate one mode of behavior, you need to consider how your employer might view your actions (see Figure 6.5).

**How does making ethical choices in a business setting differ from making personal ethical choices?** Most personal ethical decisions involve few people, unless the decision results in a significant impact on society. When making ethical choices in the business world, give careful consideration to the stakeholders of the business. **Stakeholders** are those people or entities who are affected by the

**Figure 6.5**

Is your boss watching you? Does that make you more or less inclined to behave ethically?

"The new hidden cameras will allow us to see if anyone is violating our privacy policy by reading someone else's email."

Mike Shapiro/CartoonStock

operations of a business. Before making an ethical choice for a business, you need to consider the effect that choice will have on all of the stakeholders. Typical stakeholders for most businesses are customers, suppliers, employees, investors (shareholders), financial lenders, and society.

For instance, suppose you decide to cut costs in your restaurant by hiring undocumented workers. While this might boost profits in the short term, the long-term impact on stakeholders can be severe. Potential employees who are eligible to work in the United States will be denied jobs. If you are caught using undocumented workers, fines will be levied against the business, which will cause investors to lose money and may affect the company's ability to repay lenders. The negative publicity from being caught may cause a downturn in business, which, in turn, might force layoffs of employees or even closure of the business. Your simple decision on cutting costs isn't as simple as it may seem!

## Technology and Ethics: How One Affects the Other

In both good and bad ways, technology affects our community life, family life, work environment, education, and medical research, to name only a few areas of our lives. Because technology moves faster than rules can be formulated to govern it, how technology is used is often left up to the individual and the guidance of his or her personal ethics.

Technology constantly challenges our ethics as individuals and as a society. In the rest of this Technology in Focus feature, we will explore some issues involving the relationship between technology and ethics. Specifically, we will examine situations in which ethics and technology touch each other: social justice (whistle-blowing), intellectual property (international piracy), privacy (personal privacy and technology), e-commerce (geolocation), electronic communication issues (free speech), and computer abuse (cyberbullying).

Ethical considerations are never black and white. They are complex, and reasonable people can have different yet equally valid views. We present alternative viewpoints in each setting for you to consider and discuss. Figure 6.6 summarizes these issues.

## Using Computers to Support Ethical Conduct

Although there are many opportunities to use computers and the Internet unethically, many more ways are available to use technology to support ethical conduct.

Many charitable organizations use the Internet and other technology tools for fundraising. When the earthquake and tsunami struck Japan in 2011, the Red Cross, the Salvation Army (see Figure 6.7), and other charities received many pledges via text

**Figure 6.6** | ETHICS IN COMPUTING

| TOPIC | ETHICAL DISCUSSION | DEBATE ISSUE |
|---|---|---|
| Social justice | Are there limits to whistle-blowing? | Does technology provide too easy an access for whistle-blowing? |
| Intellectual property | Do entire countries support software piracy? | Can we impose our values and intellectual property laws on the world? |
| Privacy | Is personal privacy a casualty of the modern age? | Should personal privacy be protected? |
| E-commerce | Do geolocation devices and applications threaten privacy? | Do the benefits of geolocation devices and applications outweigh the risks? |
| Electronic communication | When does big business limit free speech? | Should companies allow the Chinese government to dictate when to curtail free speech? |
| Computer abuse | Whose responsibility is it to monitor cyberbullying? | Should parents bear all the responsibility of monitoring cyberbullying, or should it be in the hands of public officials? |

message from donors' phones. Many people also made donations through charities' Web sites.

And as we discussed in Chapter 1, the Internet is also a tool for organizing aid to areas in crisis. When a major earthquake struck Haiti in 2010, Ushahidi allowed organizations and individuals conducting relief efforts to collect and disseminate the latest information on victims and aid efforts. More recently, after the devastating tornado hit Joplin, Missouri, in May 2011, folks used the Red Cross Web site and Facebook to locate friends and family members. The level of personal interaction the Web supports and the speed at which information can be exchanged is allowing computer technology to support ethical conduct in powerful new ways.

When you spot unethical behavior at your company, you need a fast, secure way to report it to the appropriate members of management. The Sarbanes–Oxley Act requires companies to provide mechanisms for employees and third parties to report complaints, including ethics violations. These mechanisms are required to provide the employees with anonymity. In addition, many businesses are using their Web sites to allow whistle-blowers to report wrongdoing anonymously, replacing previous e-mail and telephone hotline systems, which did not shield employees from being identified. With an electronic system, it is easier for a company to sort and classify complaints and designate them for appropriate action.

Electronic systems such as intranets and e-mail are also excellent mechanisms for informing employees about ethics policies. Storing ethics guidelines electronically on a company intranet ensures that employees have access to information whenever they need it. By using e-mail, a company can communicate new policies, or changes to existing policies, to employees quickly and efficiently.

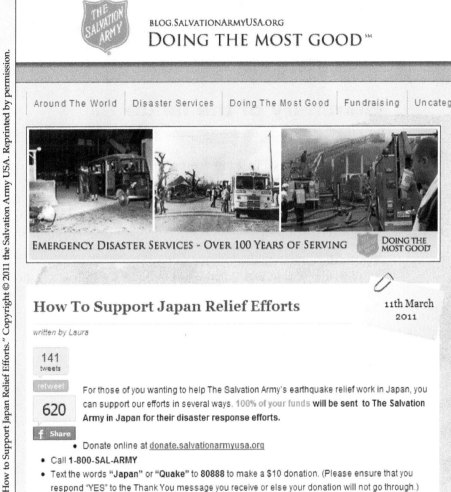

**Figure** 6.7

Using technology, including text messaging, helps charities facilitate donations.

Throughout your life, you will encounter many ethical challenges relating to information technology. Your personal ethics—combined with the ethical guidelines your company provides and the general ethical environment of society—will guide your decisions.

For further information on ethics, check out the following Web sites:

- ethics.csc.ncsu.edu
- www.ethicscenter.net
- www.business-ethics.com
- www.businessethics.org

# Social Justice

## Whistle-Blowing with Web 2.0

### Summary of the Issue

In a free democracy, are there still things the public does not have a right to see? What about military secrets? What about ongoing negotiations with foreign governments? Should corporate whistle-blowers be able to distribute the documents and materials they have that allege abuses? Historically, there have been tight controls over access to the media, and exceptions have been rare. One famous case is the Pentagon Papers, a 7,000-page U.S. government report on policy and planning for the Vietnam War. State department official Daniel Ellsberg leaked the document in 1971, and it was published by *The New York Times*. A complicated series of lawsuits was then filed against *The New York Times* for making the document public.

With the tools of Web 2.0, the entire model for the distribution of information has shifted, and now everyone has the ability to create content for the Web. WikiLeaks (www .wikileaks.org) is using that ability to make private and public documents available for viewing. WikiLeaks has described itself as "a public service designed to protect whistle-blowers, journalists, and activists who have sensitive materials to communicate to the public." *Time* magazine said of WikiLeaks, "[I]t could become as important a journalistic tool as the Freedom of Information Act."

Does society have a responsibility to use technology to help achieve social justice? Where are the boundaries of that responsibility? One controversial WikiLeaks case was the leak of a video showing a U.S. Army helicopter strike from 2007 in Baghdad that claimed the lives of several civilians including two children (see Figure 6.8). An Army intelligence analyst delivered the classified combat video to WikiLeaks in 2010. Another video leaked showed a May 2009 air strike near the Afghanistan village of Garani that killed nearly 100 civilians, mostly children. The Pentagon had released a report on that event but refused to show video of the attack to reporters.

### Questions to Think About and Research

1. Is the staff of WikiLeaks responsible for the accuracy and quality of the information it releases?

2. If information leaked through WikiLeaks leads to the death of an undercover officer, who is responsible for the consequences of the publication of information?

3. Does providing the public with official Pentagon updates of military missions mean that video of these events also must be released?

4. How does the meaning of "free speech" change as technology makes distribution of information universal and immediate? Do protections need to be modified?

# POINT

## Technology Provides Access to Information

The advocates of WikiLeaks argue that it allows an unprecedented means for those without power to hold those with power accountable for their actions.

1. If information can only be leaked if you happen to find an interested journalist, is society really protected?
2. Technology is not responsible for the actions or the consequences of the actions of people.
3. Technology has provided new tools that expose cover-ups, corruption, and abuses of power.

# COUNTERPOINT

## Technology Should Only Allow Controlled Access to Information

Critics maintain that the anonymity that WikiLeaks provides makes it difficult to check the accuracy of anything reported on the Web site.

1. The small staff of WikiLeaks cannot verify the accuracy of each document to the level of professional journalists.
2. If technology is used irresponsibly, it can cause panics because the information is available to so many people so quickly.
3. If each person in an organization can easily leak confidential information, the integrity of national security or of corporate security is at risk.

YouTube Screenshot Copyright © 2011 by Google, Inc. Reprinted by permission.

**Figure** 6.8

What boundaries should there be on the availability of sensitive information?

# Intellectual Property

## International Pirates

### Summary of the Issue

Intellectual property (such as music, writing, and software) is protected by copyright law. But there have been challenges in enforcing these standards in other countries. What happens to "fair trade" if some countries refuse to enforce copyright laws? How should the trade partners of these countries respond?

The Business Software Alliance (BSA) estimated that in 2010, 79 percent of China's computers ran on pirated software (see Figure 6.9). For comparison, the BSA estimated piracy in Denmark and Sweden at levels of 25 percent. This discrepancy means that businesses in China do not have to budget for software for operating systems or for productivity software, and that gives Chinese businesses an immediate advantage in the international marketplace. Although some companies, like Microsoft, continue to do business in China despite the piracy, smaller companies cannot survive. Tom Adams, the chief executive of Rosetta Stone, pulled his company and its language training software products out of China. He describes China as a "kleptocratic society" and worries about the amount of theft of his software in that environment.

The chief executives of twelve major software companies—Microsoft, Adobe, Autodesk, Symantec, and others—have pressured the U.S. administration and lawmakers to put more pressure on China to crack down on illegal copying. With a potential market of more than 1 billion people, and an increasing number of technologically hungry purchasers, companies dread the idea of missing out on the Chinese market. But if China continues to have such disinterest in following international copyright laws, there may be a migration of foreign business to other Asian countries. Corporations like Microsoft are considering moving Asian operations to India or Indonesia because their enforcement of intellectual property laws is more stringent than in China.

It is not just China that has weakly enforced copyright laws. U.S. lawmakers recently singled out five countries that are not doing enough to prevent piracy of music, movies, and software: Canada, China, Mexico, Russia, and Spain. "We are losing billions and billions of dollars because of the lack of intellectual property protections," said Senator Orrin Hatch of Utah. "These five countries have been robbing Americans." ("China and Canada among top on US piracy watch list" by Chris Lefkow, May 19, 2010. Copyright © 2010 by AFP. Reprinted by permission.) The BSA estimated the loss at more than $51 billion per year, although there is debate around the exact value.

Most people have had the opportunity to participate in the piracy of copyrighted materials through illegal peer-to-peer sharing and the use of torrents. Now that behavior is multiplied to the level of nations, and the consequences are still being explored.

### Questions to Think About and Research

1. Should a government be penalized for failing to actively enforce the laws it has within its own country? If so, what should the penalties be, and how should they be enforced?

2. Does each government have the right to make its own decision on a stand against piracy?

3. How can other countries respond to international piracy?

4. Does individual piracy have any connection to the enforcement of copyright laws on an international level?

# POINT

## International Copyright Protections Need to Be Vigorously Enforced

Artists and software developers depend on the integrity of the protection of intellectual property, both within the United States and internationally, to make a fair profit on their work.

1. If other countries do not fight piracy, artists and developers have a disadvantage in the marketplace.

2. By allowing massive piracy, these other countries are stealing from the United States.

3. Every country needs to have a common understanding and enforcement of intellectual property laws for trade to be fair and beneficial to everyone.

# COUNTERPOINT

## Global Business Demands Understanding Other Cultures

Most countries have laws on their books regarding intellectual property. It is not the job of the United States to tell a foreign government how to conduct internal affairs.

1. The existing laws on intellectual property have worked to serve the interests of these countries. If U.S. companies do not want to sell to the billion-person market of China, that is their choice.

2. Piracy exists within the United States, so it is hypocritical to be chastising foreign governments for software piracy.

3. Companies can pursue restitution for piracy through the foreign court systems.

© MARK/epa/Corbis

**Figure 6.9**

The issues of intellectual property play an important role in international trade.

# Privacy

## Does Social Media Erode Personal Privacy?

### Summary of the Issue

Like respect and dignity, privacy is a basic human right. What, exactly, is privacy? Simply stated, privacy is the right to be left alone to do as one pleases. The idea of privacy is often associated with hiding something (a behavior, a relationship, or a secret). However, privacy really means not being required to explain your behavior to others. But social media sites such as Facebook are inherently about sharing information with others. Does this mean there is no such thing as personal privacy (see Figure 6.10) on social media sites?

Facebook and other social media sites earn revenue by sharing information about their users with advertisers. This helps businesses target advertisements to individuals who might be more interested in their products and services. But social media sites have recently been criticized for making their privacy policies and controls too obscure. Champions of personal privacy argue that sites that make information sharing the default option or "opt-out" (that is, users have to make a specific request or change a specific setting to stop their information from being shared) expose users to misuse of their personal details. Also, social media sites often track and store user actions and preferences (such as "liking" something on Facebook). Personal privacy advocates are suspicious of how this information is used and to whom it is sold.

Web site owners argue that the entire premise of social media is built on sharing information, which makes it easy for others to find an individual. Social media administrators feel that information sharing improves the users' experience by tailoring advertisements and offers to their specific interests. And because most social media sites do not charge users for the service, the owners of the sites need ways to generate revenue, and their most valuable asset is the information that users provide about themselves.

The large social media sites (such as Facebook) have been responding to concerns by modifying their privacy settings and making it easier for users to select which information is shared and with whom. But critics still argue that users do not have enough control over opting out of sharing information. The control and privacy of information will continue to be a fine balancing act for the foreseeable future with companies trying to make money while appeasing the concerns of privacy advocates. Leaving a trail of electronic breadcrumbs is to a certain extent inevitable. But cleaning up or hiding your "trail" is still important to many users, not because they are trying to hide something but because they just value their basic right of privacy.

### Questions to Think About and Research

1. Should you be able to decide exactly what information on a social networking site you share with others? Would you be willing to pay for this privilege?

2. Do you know what your privacy settings are on the social media sites you use? Is there any information being shared publicly that you weren't aware was being shared?

3. Should social media sites be allowed to sell information collected on your surfing habits without your permission? Is this practice legal in the United States?

4. Is there any information on sites you use that you want to restrict people from seeing? Do these sites allow you to restrict the information you wish to protect?

## POINT

### Social Media Sites Should Protect Personal Privacy

The advocates of protecting privacy in the United States argue that the right to privacy is a basic human right that should be afforded to everyone. Personal privacy concerns should outweigh the business needs of a corporation.

1. Social media sites have an inherent duty to protect the data of their users.

2. If site owners are collecting information by recording users' surfing habits, they might misuse or lose control of the data.

3. Default privacy settings should all be opt-in, allowing users the ultimate control over who views their data.

## COUNTERPOINT

### Social Media Sites Are Entitled to Freely Share Information

Advocates for unrestricted sharing of information feel that business concerns outweigh privacy concerns. Social media sites offered free of charge must make money to survive, and therefore need to be able to provide information to third parties to generate revenue.

1. The "cost" of using the site is the agreement to share some of your personal information.

2. Users can make their own privacy decisions and choose not to post or share sensitive information (opt out).

3. In the digital age, loss of a certain amount of privacy is inevitable.

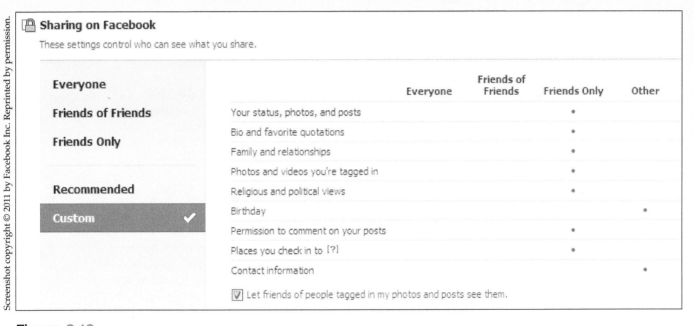

**Figure 6.10**

What information are you sharing on Facebook?

# E-Commerce

## Geolocation: Marketing Tool or Invasion of Privacy?

### Summary of the Issue

"Where are you?" is the burning social-networking question these days, and your smartphone probably has the answer. The technology is called geolocation (see Figure 6.11), and most smartphones have a GPS (global positioning system) chip that uses satellite data or cell towers to calculate your exact position. Services such as Foursquare, Gowalla, Brightkite, and Loopt are all hoping that you will use them in the process, so you can use geolocation to find your friends or let your friends find you. Through the apps, you can receive recommendations of places to visit or things to do nearby. Some apps, such as Loopt and Gowalla, have created partnerships with local establishments that generate freebies, special offers, and travel tips. Businesses are using geolocation apps to promote their products and offer rewards for "check-ins" to help drive customers to their location.

But the question remains, when you leave your home and announce your constant whereabouts through tweets and check-ins, do you lose some of your privacy in exchange for "fun" and "convenience"? Although you can set certain levels of privacy in the apps, there is still the potential for someone with bad intentions (stalkers, robbers) to follow your updates. For example, the Web site Please Rob Me (**www.PleaseRobMe.com**) was set up to illustrate how telling the world where you are at all times may not be such a great idea. After generating much discussion and awareness, the Web site exists, but no new content is being added. Regardless, the message from the authors of the PleaseRobMe site is clear:

> The danger is publicly telling people where you are. This is because it leaves one place you're definitely not . . . home. So . . . on one end we're leaving lights on when we're going on a holiday, and on the other we're telling everybody on the Internet we're not home. It gets even worse if you have 'friends' who . . . enter your address, to tell everyone where they are. Your address . . . on the Internet . . . Now you know what to do when people reach for their phone as soon as they enter your home. That's right, slap them across the face.
>
> –Excerpt from "PleaseRobMe" by Barry Borsboom, Boy van Amstel, Frank Groeneveld from www.pleaserobme. com. Copyright © 2010 Barry Borsboom, Boy van Amstel, Frank Groeneveld. Reprinted with permission.

In addition to opening yourself up to potential robbery, geolocation devices also can track the activities you might not want publicized, and that once documented can later be used against you.

It wasn't long ago that we were concerned about using our real names online, but now we are comfortable with sharing our exact location in a very public way. As Facebook CEO Mark Zuckerberg said, "People have really gotten comfortable not only sharing more information and different kinds, but more openly and with more people." But does such acceptance justify neglecting to maintain certain levels of privacy? Again, it seems that technology has moved more quickly than society can address the potential risks and dangers.

### Questions to Think About and Research

1. Do the benefits of geolocation outweigh the risks?
2. What other devices besides cell phones track and record our movements/locations as digital records?
3. How have social networks increased the risks of geolocation privacy?
4. What risks do geolocation pose for college students? How can users mitigate those risks?

# POINT

## Geolocation Devices Do Not Threaten Privacy

The advocates of using geolocation devices with minimal concern for threatened privacy are those who believe the social norm has shifted, and people have become comfortable with sharing more information.

1. Businesses are adopting geolocation apps as a part of their social media strategy in order to drive customers to their business. They would lose revenue if such activities ceased.

2. As the devices and apps become better and more precise, they may become useful as public safety and news-gathering devices.

3. Society may need to reevaluate its views about how much privacy is needed in people's digital lives, as well as assume greater responsibility for making sensible decisions about sharing information through the Internet.

# COUNTERPOINT

## Geolocation Devices Are a Threat to Privacy

The advocates for tighter privacy controls and awareness campaigns about the potential risks of using geolocation devices suggest that the threats are too big to ignore. Society has become too complacent with privacy issues.

1. Privacy settings on apps and GPS devices should be more restrictive to avoid broadcasting one's location and risking personal assault.

2. Laws and regulations will need to be created as to the use and distribution of digital location information.

3. Consumers need to be educated about geolocation and the ways it can impact them so that they are able to make informed choices.

Michael D. Brown/Shutterstock.com

**Figure 6.11**

Geolocation applications help you find cool places and businesses. But who do you want to find you with geolocation?

# Electronic Communication

## Does Free Speech Have a Price?

### Summary of the Issue

In early 2006 when Google launched its search engine services in China, it conceded to Beijing's demands that it self-censor its search engine, restricting search results for sensitive information such as the details of the Tiananmen Square protests and of human rights groups. This decision prompted much discussion, with some condemning Google's decision for putting business profits over basic human rights. Google justified its actions by stating that a company must operate within the rules of the market in which it operates and that the benefits of increased access to information for people in China "outweighed our discomfort in agreeing to censor some results." And, compared to search results from Baidu, the leading Chinese search engine, Google was not censoring all information. However, in 2010, Google announced that it was no longer willing to censor search results and moved the site to Hong Kong where it hopes there will be less censorship. The departure was a reaction to a sophisticated targeted cyberattack that Google believes was done to gather information on Chinese human rights activists. Google had about a 35 percent market share.

Microsoft, also in the Chinese market with its new search engine, Bing, announced in response to Google's departure that it had no plans to leave. Microsoft has only a 1 percent share of the market, so the decision to stay has huge upside potential. The question remains as to how Microsoft will manage search information. When Microsoft started in China, searches on controversial topics weren't just blocked in China, they were blocked from everyone around the world (see Figure 6.12). Microsoft corrected that, but some current searches show that although they are not censoring as much as Baidu, they are still censoring less than Google was. Microsoft says it is trying to do the right thing. Before honoring any censor requests, Microsoft insists that Chinese authorities make legally binding requests in writing. Microsoft, along with Google and Yahoo!, joined Global Network Initiative (**www.globalnetworkinitiative.org**), a group that has established a code of conduct for free expression and privacy. The goal of GNI is to help companies do the right thing under difficult circumstances. However, it's too early to tell whether Microsoft will indeed follow Google's path or remain and abide by China's censorship requirements.

### Questions to Think About and Research

1. Will Google's move from Mainland China to Hong Kong have a major impact on China's censorship laws?

2. Will Microsoft's compliance with censorship laws further Beijing's cooperation on combating software piracy in China? Are Microsoft's financial incentives even deeper than just Internet market share?

3. Can the U.S. government compel technology companies to take a firmer stance on free speech in China and elsewhere by instituting criminal charges if U.S. companies do not take reasonable steps to protect human rights?

# POINT

## U.S. Companies Should Comply with Local Laws

Those in favor of Microsoft's actions to remain in China feel that if a company chooses to operate in a foreign country, it knows the local laws and should be prepared to work within those laws as it does business. It is not the place of a company to try to change laws of foreign countries.

1. Microsoft conducts businesses in other countries that have censorship laws, so why not participate in China?

2. Working in China does not mean a company supports all of China's policies.

3. Microsoft's presence, as muted as it is, continues to advance the slow progress the Chinese government is making toward democracy. U.S. companies can ethically stay in China if they make an effort to improve human rights there. U.S. companies operating in China should agree on guidelines that respect human rights.

4. A U.S. company's presence has no impact on reform—reform must come from within.

# COUNTERPOINT

## U.S. Companies Should Put What Is Right Ahead of What Is Financially Expedient

Those who are in favor of Google's actions are believers that international corporations should begin to take a firm stance against governments that do not promote basic human rights.

1. China will never change unless there are financial and political incentives to do so. Google's departure helps pressure the Chinese government

2. Google's withdrawal from China threatens the viability of many advertising resellers in China. Will this added pressure help or hinder human rights efforts?

3. Google's decision to leave helps put pressure on China's government to play by global standards. It cannot expect to compete in the global marketplace while refusing to have a global exchange of ideas.

CENSORSHIP

kentoh/Shutterstock.com

**Figure** 6.12

Is free speech possible in countries (such as China) where information availability is restricted by law?

# Computer Abuse

## Cyberbullying—Who Should Protect Children from Each Other?

### Summary of the Issue

Cyberbullying is just like normal bullying, but it involves the use of digital technologies such as the Internet, cell phones, or video (see Figure 6.13). Instead of a bully chasing someone on the playground at recess, cyberbullying involves minors (children) harassing, threatening, humiliating, embarrassing, or tormenting other minors by means of technology. Cyberbullying is a child-on-child process that might result in criminal charges depending upon the type of incident.

There are many types of cyberbullying. The main types are as follows:

- Bombarding a victim with harassing instant messages or text messages
- Stealing a password and then using the victim's account to embarrass the victim by sending harassing, threatening, or lewd messages while pretending to be the victim
- Spreading rumors or lies on social networking sites
- Posting embarrassing photos or videos on the Web (such as candid nude shots taken in a locker room)
- Infecting the victim's computer with malware, usually to spy on the victim

The effects of cyberbullying can be devastating. For children, their standing in peer groups is a critical component of their self-worth. Adults have freedom in their lives to change bad situations, such as changing jobs, when they feel their esteem is under attack. Children often feel powerless because they have such limited options. Children don't usually have the option of changing schools without uprooting the entire family. Aside from developing severe feelings of depression, rage, frustration, and powerlessness, suicide can often be the unfortunate result, as in the case of student and soccer player Alexis Pilkington, who at 17 committed suicide in 2010 after being repeatedly taunted on social networking sites.

Unfortunately, cyberbullying is often difficult for adults to detect because the bullying often takes place online and anonymously. Signs that a child is a victim of cyberbullying are often the same signs related to various types of depression. A child may suddenly lose interest in normal activities, be reluctant to go to school, lose his or her appetite, have trouble sleeping, appear upset after using the Internet, or experience unusual mood swings (such as bursting into tears for no apparent reason). Signs that a child might be perpetrating cyberbullying include excessive Internet use, sending large volumes of text messages, clearing the computer screen when others enter a room, or conducting clandestine Internet activities (refusal to say what they are doing). Vigilance over children's online activities is obviously key to spotting both victims and perpetrators of cyberbullying.

But who is responsible for monitoring children? Parents obviously need to protect their children, but bullying usually doesn't happen until children are repeatedly exposed to other groups of children such as in daycare or school. So then, should teachers and caregivers shoulder the major responsibility for detecting, reporting, and mitigating cyberbullying? Children often spend more time in school during the day than they spend under the supervision of their parents. But cyberbullying activities don't just take place in school. Most children have access to the Internet at home and can carry on campaigns of terror from the privacy of their own bedroom (see Figure 6.14).

Children themselves could also be made part of the solution. Research shows that one of the best ways to prevent bullying is to make children aware of what behaviors constitute bullying and the consequences of their actions.

Although there is currently no federal law prohibiting cyberbullying, many state laws have been passed that address this issue. Anti-cyberbullying laws tend to place the burden of detection on the schools. For instance, the Massachusetts law requires school employees to report bullying when they become aware of it to the school administration. But unlike many other states, the law also requires training for school employees in the detection and prevention of bullying. Most legislatures are reluctant to pass laws that instruct parents on how to raise their children because this tends to raise issues about personal freedom. Therefore, the focus so far has been primarily on teachers and caregivers detecting cyberbullying. But a coordinated effort between parents and teachers may be a better approach.

## Questions to Think About and Research

1. What should parents do to protect their children from cyberbullying? How can parents protect their children when the children are not under their direct supervision?

2. What level of responsibility should school employees have for protecting children from cyberbullying?

3. Should there be federal laws that make cyberbullying a crime? If so, how would these laws be enforced?

4. What types of education for children would be beneficial in preventing cyberbullying? When should these programs begin, and how often should children be required to participate?

© Rawdon Wyatt / Alamy

**Figure 6.13**

Cyberbullying involves the use of digital technologies both to bully and to disseminate acts of bullying.

# Computer Abuse

## POINT

### Parents Must Protect Their Children from Cyberbullying

Proponents of parental responsibility for detecting and preventing cyberbullying feel that it is a personal behavior issue. Individuals are responsible for their own behavior as long as it doesn't harm others. Parents should be allowed to educate their children according to their own standards of behavior and preferences in terms of moral behavior (such as religion).

1. Parents are ultimately responsible for protecting their children.

2. Bullying is a personal behavior issue, and all decisions regarding personal freedom and behavior should be made by parents.

3. Because educating children about bullying is key to preventing it, decisions about the content of such training needs to be controlled by parents.

## COUNTERPOINT

### Schools Must Bear the Major Responsibility for Protecting Students from Cyberbullying

Cyberbullying affects society because it can severely damage an individual's self-esteem. Cyberbullying is similar to other hate crimes and should enlist public officials (such as educators) in enforcement of the laws.

1. Parents do not supervise their children 24/7 and therefore require help from other responsible adults to protect their children.

2. Parents need to be assured that publicly funded institutions such as schools and libraries are "safe havens" where their children will not be exposed to malicious activities.

3. Educators have better resources than most parents for teaching children about the serious effects of cyberbullying.

Chris Whitehead/Getty Images

**Figure 6.14**
Cyberbullying should be stopped, but by whom?

# Multiple Choice

**Instructions:** Answer the multiple-choice questions below for more practice with key terms and concepts from this Technology in Focus feature.

1. Which theory states that there is no universal moral truth?
   a. Relativism
   b. Ethical behavior
   c. Amoral behavior
   d. Personal ethics

2. The ethical theory that states that society as a whole will improve if everyone adheres to the same moral code is known as
   a. rule utilitarianism.
   b. societal ethics.
   c. moral prescription.
   d. personal ethics.

3. Which ethical philosophy states that decision making should be based on the circumstances surrounding a given situation, not fixed laws?
   a. Societal ethics
   b. Judeo-Christian ethics
   c. Relativism
   d. Situational ethics

4. Which of the following statements is *false*?
   a. Individuals who apply ethics inconsistently exhibit amoral behavior.
   b. All ethical decisions are greatly influenced by personal ethics.
   c. Unethical behavior is not always illegal.
   d. Life experience affects an individual's personal ethics.

5. Not conforming to a set of approved ethical standards is known as
   a. societal behavior.
   b. unethical behavior.
   c. amoral behavior.
   d. unprofessional behavior.

6. The field of psychology that theorizes that happiness results from ethical living is known as
   a. principled psychology.
   b. positive psychology.
   c. moral psychology.
   d. affirmative psychology.

7. Which system of ethics is most widely agreed upon to be the best system?
   a. Rule utilitarianism
   b. Relativism
   c. Situational ethics
   d. There is no universally agreed-upon best system.

8. Which is *not* a tangible benefit of ethical living?
   a. Improved health
   b. A simpler lifestyle
   c. Happiness
   d. Increased motivation

9. Which of the following actions would *not* help to identify your personal ethics?
   a. Describe yourself.
   b. Identify the influences of your work environment.
   c. Conduct a genealogic study of your extended family.
   d. Prepare a list of values that are most important to you.

10. Ethical decisions in business affect which of the following?
    a. The employees
    b. The business's clients and customers
    c. The suppliers and financial lenders
    d. The stakeholders

# application software:
## programs that let you work and play

### The Nuts and Bolts of Software

**OBJECTIVE:**
What's the difference between application software and system software? *(p. 204)*

### Web-Based Applications

**OBJECTIVE:**
What are Web-based applications, and how do they differ from traditional modes of software distribution? *(p. 204)*

### Productivity and Business Software

**OBJECTIVES:**
What kinds of applications are included in productivity software? *(p. 206)*

What kinds of software do small and large businesses use? *(p. 216)*

 **Sound Byte:** Creating Web Queries in Excel 2010

### Media and Entertainment Software

**OBJECTIVES:**
What are the different types of media and entertainment software? *(p. 220)*

What are the different types of drawing software? *(p. 227)*

 **Sound Byte:** Enhancing Photos with Image Editing Software

 **Active Helpdesk:** Choosing Software

### Buying, Installing, and Uninstalling Software

**OBJECTIVES:**
How can I purchase software or get it for free? *(p. 228)*

How do I install, uninstall, and start software? *(p. 235)*

 **Active Helpdesk:** Buying and Installing Software

### Getting Help with Software

**OBJECTIVE:**
Where can I go for help when I have a problem with my software? *(p. 237)*

*Scan here for more info on How Cool Is This?*

# how cool is *this?*

You've just returned from a great **vacation** and want to relive your wonderful experience. Looking at traditional digital images is nice, but wouldn't it be better if you could create a **3D walkthrough** of your favorite places? Upload your pictures to the 20 GB of free storage space of Microsoft's **Photosynth** and relive your experience in 3D. Photosynth takes a selection of photos, examines them for similarities to estimate the shape of the subject, and determines the vantage point from which each photo was taken. Using this information, Photosynth then **stitches** the images together to create a 3D effect. Check out some that others have done at **www.photosynth.net**, and then go make one from your own photos!

## The Nuts and Bolts of Software

A computer without software is like a sandwich without filling. Although a computer's hardware is critical, a computer system does nothing without software.

**What is software?** Technically speaking, the term **software** refers to a set of instructions that tells the computer what to do. An instruction set, also called a **program**, provides a means for us to interact with and use the computer, even if we lack specialized programming skills. Your computer has two basic types of software: system software and application software.

- **System software** includes software such as Windows and Mac OS X, which help run the computer and coordinate instructions between application software and the computer's hardware devices. System software includes the operating system and utility programs (programs in the operating system that help manage system resources). We discuss system software in detail in Chapter 8.
- **Application software** is the software you use to do tasks at home, school, and work. You can do a multitude of things with application software, such as writing letters, sending e-mail, paying taxes, creating presentations, editing photos, and taking an online course, to name a few.

Figure 7.1 shows the various types of application software that you can use to be productive—at home and at work. In addition, applications are available to produce and edit media as well as for entertainment. Lastly, there are applications that are more applicable to business uses, whether it's for a home office, big business, specialty business, or not-for-profit organization. In this chapter, we look at each of these types in detail, starting with productivity software. By no means does this exhaust all the types of software that are in use. Other types of software, such as Web browsers, virus protection, backup and recovery, and utility software are in use every day. These types of software are discussed elsewhere in this book.

## Web-Based Applications

**Does all application software require installation on my computer?** Most application software you acquire, whether by purchasing a CD or DVD at a retail store or by downloading the software from a Web site, must be installed on your computer before use.

There is a relatively new trend toward a distribution model of on-demand software deployment, referred to as **Software as a Service (SaaS)** that many software developers are taking advantage of. With the SaaS

**Figure 7.1**

Application software enables computer users to do a variety of tasks.

**Figure** 7.2

Microsoft Web Apps are similar to the full-featured versions of Word, Excel, PowerPoint, and OneNote, but the Web applications have fewer options available. The functionality and user interface are the same.

delivery model, the application is hosted online by the vendor and made available to the customer over the Internet. These applications are also referred to as **Web-based applications**. Web-based applications are run from software stored completely on a Web server instead of the traditional model that requires software to be purchased and installed on individual machines or network servers.

**What kinds of Web-based applications are available?** Along with its release of Office 2010, Microsoft made available Microsoft Office Web Apps. Office Web Apps are online versions of Word, Excel, PowerPoint, and OneNote, but with fewer tabs than the installed versions (see Figure 7.2).

Google Docs (**www.docs.google.com**) is a Web-based suite of productivity software with word processing, spreadsheet, and presentation capabilities. Sites such as Zoho (**www.zoho.com**) and ThinkFree (**www .thinkfree.com**) offer Web-based applications that cover not only word processing, presentation, and spreadsheet needs, but also a wealth of other business applications such as project management, three-

dimensional (3D) drawing, and customer relationship management software. Some other examples of Web-based applications include Intuit's QuickBooks online, Salesforce.com, and Citrix Online.

**What advantages do Web-based applications have?** As long as you have a Web browser, you can access your files, which are stored securely online. Although many of these free applications are not as fully featured as their installable counterparts, most can read and export to many different file formats and can be used with other software packages. Besides being able to access your documents from any computer or smartphone that has Internet access, Web-based applications are great for collaboration. You can invite people to share your files and work together in real time, watching as others make changes to the document.

**Is all Web-based software free?** Although most Web-based software programs are free, some Web sites charge a fee for their online products. Microsoft Office 365 is a subscription-based service that includes Microsoft Office Web Apps plus other Web-based services such as Exchange (for e-mail, calendar, and contacts) and Lync (for instant messaging, video calls, and online meetings). Google Apps for Business is similar to Office 365 and is free for businesses with up to 10 users, and then has a per user charge. TurboTax Online (**www.turbotax.com**) is a version of the popular tax preparation software that you can access online to prepare your tax returns. Although the standard version is free, you're charged for the more full-featured product. In addition to saving you the hassle of software installation, TurboTax Online stores your information in a secure location so you can retrieve it anytime.

# Productivity Software for Home and Office

One reason to have a computer is to make it easier to tackle the tasks you have in your daily life. Productivity software is all about helping you do that, making it easier to keep your budget, send letters, or keep track of the kids' school events. It's safe to say you regularly use some form of productivity software already. **Productivity software** includes programs that enable you to perform various tasks required at home, school, and business. This category includes word processing, spreadsheet, presentation, database, and personal information manager (PIM) programs.

### Word Processing Software

**What is the best software to use to create general documents?** Most students use **word processing software** to create and edit documents such as research papers, letters, and résumés. Because of its general usefulness, word processing software is the most widely used application. Word processing software has a key advantage over its ancestral counterpart, the typewriter: You can make revisions and corrections without having to retype an entire document. Instead, you can quickly and easily insert, delete, and move pieces of text, as well as move and insert text from one document into another seamlessly. Microsoft Word is the most popular word processing program.

**Are there free or more affordable software alternatives?** If you're looking for a more affordable alternative to software such as Microsoft Word or other Microsoft Office products, you may want to consider downloading free open source software. **Open source software** is program code that is publicly available and has few restrictions. Unlike **proprietary software**, which is neither free nor open source, the code can be copied, distributed, or changed without the stringent copyright protections of software products you purchase.

Writer, a word processing program from the OpenOffice.org suite (**www.openoffice.org**), and AbiWord (**www.abiword.com**) are gaining in popularity because they are available as free downloads from the Internet. Both AbiWord and Writer have many of the same features as the higher-priced Word, making either a great choice for cost-conscious consumers (see Figure 7.3). Keep one thing in mind when you choose an open source software product: support. Unlike Microsoft Office and other proprietary applications, these applications offer little or no formal support. Instead, open source applications are supported from their

**BITS AND BYTES**

## Finding the Right Software

There are millions of applications, and new ones are developed and released every day. How can you find the right application to meet your needs? What are the cool new applications, or the ones that just don't work? The editors and analysts at *PC Magazine* have put together AppScout (**www.appscout.com**), which provides reviews of the best software, Web sites, and Web applications. AppScout might be a good place to check first when you are in need of a new application.

community of users across Web sites and newsgroups.

**How do I control the way my documents look?** An advantage of word processing software is that you can easily create professional-looking documents. With the extensive formatting options available, you can change fonts, font styles, and sizes; add colors to text; adjust margins; add borders to portions of text or entire pages; insert bulleted and numbered lists; and organize your text into columns. You also can insert pictures from your own files or from a gallery of images and graphics, such as clip art and SmartArt, which are included with the software. You also can enhance the look of your document by creating an interesting background or by adding a "theme" of coordinated colors and styles throughout your document. Figure 7.4 shows what a document can look like when formatting options found in many word processing applications are incorporated. Although many of the open source and Web-based applications have great formatting capabilities, most are not as fully featured as Microsoft Word.

**What special tools do word processing programs have?** You're probably familiar with the basic tools of word processing software. Most applications come with some form of spelling and grammar checker and a thesaurus, for example.

Designs and other visual effects

Bibliography tool organizes sources

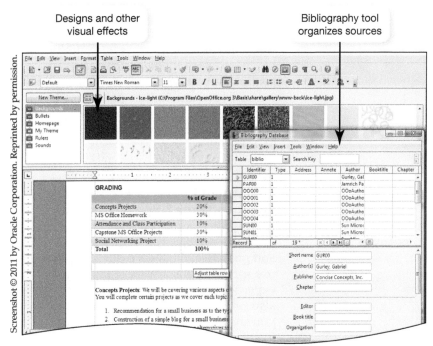

**Figure 7.3**

Writer, the word processing program in the OpenOffice .org suite, has many of the same features as Word.

Another popular tool is the find-and-replace tool that allows you to search for text in your document and automatically replace it with other text.

**Figure 7.4**

Nearly every word processing application has formatting features to give your document a professional look.

Drop cap

Section headings

Two-column text

Social Networking

Privacy vs. Security

Formatted headers

Bullets and numbering

Protect Yourself

WordArt

The average user is unaware of many interesting word processing software tools. For example, did you know that you could translate words or phrases into another language or automatically correct your spelling as you type? You also can automatically summarize key points in a text document, add bibliographical references, and include illustrations with different picture styles.

### Spreadsheet Software

**Why would I need to use spreadsheet software?** Spreadsheet software—such as Microsoft Excel and OpenOffice.org Calc—enables you to do calculations and numerical analyses easily. You can use spreadsheet software to track your expenses and create a simple budget. You also can use it to determine how much you should be paying on your student loans, car loan, or credit card bills each month. You know you should pay more than the minimum payment to spend less on interest, but how much more can you afford to pay, and for which loan? Spreadsheet software can help you evaluate different scenarios, such as planning the best payment strategy.

**How do I use spreadsheet software?** The basic element in a spreadsheet program is the worksheet, which is a grid consisting of columns and rows. As shown in Figure 7.5, the columns and rows form individual boxes called *cells*. Each cell can be identified according to its column and row position. For example, a cell in column A, row 1 is referred to as "cell A1." You can enter several types of data into a cell:

- **Text:** Any combination of letters, numbers, symbols, and spaces. Text is often used as labels to identify the contents of a worksheet or chart.
- **Values:** Numerical data that represent a quantity or an amount and are often the basis for calculations.
- **Formulas:** Equations that you build yourself using addition, subtraction, multiplication, and division, as well as values and cell references. For example, in Figure 7.5, you would type the formula "=B8-B22" (without quotation marks) to calculate net income for September.
- **Functions:** Formulas that are preprogrammed into the spreadsheet software. Functions help you with calculations

**Figure 7.5**

Spreadsheet software enables you to calculate and manipulate numerical data easily with the use of built-in formulas.

**Creating Web Queries in Excel 2010**

In this Sound Byte, you'll learn what Excel Web queries are, as well as how to use them effectively.

ranging from the simple (such as adding groups of numbers) to the complex (such as determining monthly loan payments), without you needing to know the exact formula. Therefore, in Figure 7.5, to calculate the total of all income sources for the month of September you could use the built-in SUM function, which would look like this: =SUM(B4:B7).

The primary benefit of spreadsheet software is its ability to recalculate all functions and formulas in the spreadsheet automatically when values for some of the inputs change. For example, as shown on the spreadsheet on the right side of Figure 7.5, you can insert an additional row (Memberships), change a value (September clothing expense), and then recalculate the results for Total Expenses and Net Income without having to redo the worksheet from scratch.

Because automatic recalculation enables you to see immediately the effects that different options have on your spreadsheet, you can quickly test different assumptions in the same analysis. This is called a *what-if analysis*. Look again at Figure 7.5 and ask, "What if I add $50 to my clothing expense? What impact will such an increase have on my total budget?"

**What kinds of graphs and charts can I create with spreadsheet software?** Sometimes it's easier to see the meaning of numerical information when it is shown in a graphical format such as a chart. As shown in Figure 7.6, most spreadsheet applications allow you to create a variety of charts, including basic column charts, pie charts, and line charts, with or without three-dimensional (3D) effects. In addition to these basic charts, you can use stock charts (for investment analysis) and scatter charts (for statistical analysis), or create custom charts. New in Excel 2010 are sparklines, which are small charts that fit into a single cell. Sparklines (see Figure 7.7) make it easy to show data trends.

**Are spreadsheets used for anything besides financial analysis?** There are so many powerful mathematical

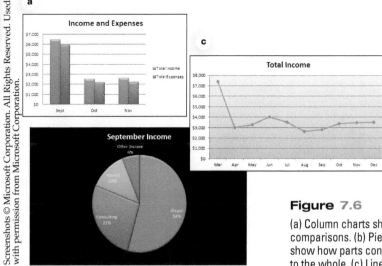

**Figure 7.6**

(a) Column charts show comparisons. (b) Pie charts show how parts contribute to the whole. (c) Line charts show trends over time.

functions built into spreadsheet programs that they can be used for serious numerical analyses or simulations. For example, an Excel spreadsheet can be designed to compute the output voltage at a point in an electrical circuit or to simulate customer arrival and wait times. In these settings, spreadsheet programs can often solve problems that formerly required custom programming. Many spreadsheet applications also have limited database capabilities and can sort, filter, and group data.

| | Current | 1 Year History | | |
| | | Trend | High | Low |
| --- | --- | --- | --- | --- |
| Microsoft | $ 25.79 | | 30.54 | 20.26 |
| Apple | $ 255.96 | | 261.09 | 125.83 |
| Intel | $ 20.95 | | 22.84 | 15.72 |
| Hewlett Packard | $ 46.05 | | 53.15 | 34.35 |
| Dell | $ 13.24 | | 16.2 | 11.57 |

Sparklines

**Figure 7.7**

Sparklines, a new feature for Excel 2010, are tiny graphs that fit into a single cell.

## Presentation Software

**What software do I use to create presentations?** You've probably sat through presentations during which the speaker's topic was displayed in slides projected on a screen. These presentations can be the most basic of outlines, containing only a few words and simple graphics, or elaborate multimedia presentations with animated text, graphic objects, and colorful backgrounds. You use **presentation software** such as Microsoft PowerPoint, OpenOffice.org

**Figure 7.8**

Several programs allow you to create presentation materials: (a) Microsoft Office PowerPoint 2010, (b) OpenOffice.org Impress, and (c) Zoho Show.

Impress, or Zoho Show (shown in Figure 7.8) to create these types of dynamic slide shows. Because these applications are simple to use, you can produce high-quality presentations without a lot of training. With some of the new capabilities in PowerPoint 2010, you can embed online videos, as well as change the color, add effects, and even trim video rate videos, as well. Prezi is free for basic services, or you can pay an annual fee for greater online storage space, and the ability to work offline and to make your presentations private.

> ## Because these applications are simple to use, you can produce high-quality presentations without a lot of training.

clips without the need for a separate video editing program. Prezi (**www.prezi.com**) is an online program that has an innovative way to produce presentations. Rather than being restricted to static slides, Prezi uses a larger canvas, which enables you to relate ideas better by zooming in to view the finer details and zooming out to see the bigger concept. You can also rotate the canvas for added visual interest. Prezi can incorpo-

**How do I create a presentation?**
Using the basic features included in presentation software, creating a slide show is simple. To arrange text and graphics on your slides, you can choose from a variety of slide layouts. These layouts give you the option of using a single or double column of bulleted text, various combinations of bulleted text, and other content such as clip art, graphs, photos, and even video clips.

You also can lend a theme to your presentation by choosing from different design templates. You can use animation effects to control how and when text and other objects enter and exit each slide. Slide transitions add different effects as you move from one slide to the next during the presentation.

## Database Software

### How can I use database software?

**Database software** such as Oracle, MySQL, and Microsoft Access are powerful applications that allow you to store and organize data. FileMaker Pro, Bento, and FileMaker Go are database alternatives for Windows, Mac OS X, and iOS. As mentioned earlier, spreadsheet applications include limited database features and are easy to use for simple database tasks such as sorting, filtering, and organizing data. However, you need to use a more robust, fully featured database application to manage larger and more complicated groups of data that contain more than one table; to group, sort, and retrieve data; and to generate reports.

Traditional databases are organized into fields, records, and tables, as shown in Figure 7.9. A field is a data category such as "First Name," "Last Name," or "Street Address." A record is a collection of related fields such as "Douglas, Seaver, Printing Solutions, 7700 First Avenue, Topeka, KS, 66603, (888) 968-2678." A table groups related records such as "Sales Contacts."

### Make a Winning Presentation

Undoubtedly, you have sat through bad presentations. Don't make your audience sit through another one! Here are some tips for designing good presentations:

- **Color:** Avoid using clashing text and background colors. Instead, choose dark text on a light background or light text on a dark background.
- **Bullets:** Use bullets for key points. Limit the number to four to six bulleted points per slide.
- **Text:** Limit the amount of text on a slide to about six words per bullet point. Avoid full sentences and paragraphs.
- **Images:** Images can convey a thought or illustrate a point. Make sure any text over an image can be read easily. In Microsoft PowerPoint, consider using SmartArt diagrams for interesting visual text arrangements.
- **Font size and style:** Keep the font size large enough to read from the back of the room. Avoid script or fancy font styles. Use only one or two font styles per presentation.
- **Animation and background audio:** Keep to a minimum. They can be distracting.

### How do you benefit when businesses use database software?

FedEx, UPS, and other shipping companies let customers search their online databases for tracking numbers, allowing customers to get instant information on the status of their packages. Other businesses use databases to keep track of clients, invoices, and personnel information. Often that information is available to a home computer user. For example, at Amazon.com you can use the company's Web site to access the entire history of all the

Table

Field

Record

## Figure 7.9

In databases, information is organized into tables, fields, and records.

**Figure** 7.10

OneNote is a great way to collect and organize notes and other information. The files are readily searchable, and easy to share.

purchases you have made. Amazon, iTunes, Craigslist, and Pandora all rely on databases to organize their information.

## Note Taking Software

**Is there software to help with note taking?** Programs are available to help students take notes during lectures and organize and maintain their lecture notes and the recordings they create from lectures. Microsoft OneNote first became popular with those who had tablet PCs, because it allows users to write their notes directly onto the tablet and later convert the handwritten text to digital text. OneNote works equally as well with a notebook or desktop computer, and has continued to develop into a powerful note taking and organizational tool. There is also a OneNote app for the iPad.

Notes can be organized into tabbed sections, similar to a multi-subject spiral-bound notebook, that provide further help in organizing and reorganizing pages (see Figure 7.10). By activating LinkedNotes from another Office application, your notes are tied directly to the specific point in the presentation or document you are reviewing, so you can jump to that exact point when you review your notes. With one click, Web links can be

quickly integrated and audio or video recordings of lectures can be added. Students can search for a term across the full set of digital notebooks they have created during the semester, helping them to find connecting ideas among their courses. You can also have a stripped-down version of OneNote running so you can jot down notes or refer to your notes as you work in other applications.

Because OneNote has co-authoring and version tracking capabilities, it's also perfect for organizing team and other collaborative projects. Omnioutliner is another great note and outlining tool for Mac computers and the iPad that allows you to easily do many tasks such as take notes, manage to-do lists, and plan events.

**Are there free or portable note taking applications?** There are several free and online note taking options available to help you take full-blown notes or just jot down a quick reminder. Some are even available for your smartphone. Evernote (**www.evernote.com**), for example, allows you to take notes via the Web, your phone, or your computer and then sync your notes between the Web, your phone, and any computer. You can save text, audio, and images, as well as screen captures, Web pages, and photos. The beauty of Evernote is that everything is searchable. SoundNote (**www.soundnote.com**), an iPad app, is similar to Evernote, but also has a drawing feature and the ability to handle longer audio recordings. Sticky Notes (**www.sticky-notes.net**) are digital equivalents to paper sticky notes. These notes can be customized, saved, and shared via e-mail, and they even have reminders.

## Personal Information Manager (PIM) Software

**Which applications should I use to manage my time, contact lists, and tasks?** Most productivity suites contain some form of **personal information manager (PIM) software** such as Microsoft Outlook or Lotus Organizer. Chandler (**www.chandlerproject.org**) is another PIM program that is open source and, therefore, free. These programs strive to replace the management tools found on a traditional desk—a calendar, address book, notepad, and to-do list, for example. Some PIMs contain e-mail management features so that you not only can receive and send e-mail messages, but also organize them into various folders, prioritize them, and coordinate them with other activities in your calendar (see Figure 7.11).

If you share a network at home or at work and are using the same PIM software as others on the network, you can use a PIM program to check people's availability before scheduling meeting times. Whether coordinating a team project or a family event, you can create and electronically assign tasks to group members by using a PIM. You can even track each person's progress to ensure that the tasks are finished on time.

Outlook also coordinates with OneNote, so you can create appointments, meeting

with any smartphone that runs on the Android operating system. Toodledo (**www .toodledo.com**) is an effective to-do manager that syncs with your smartphone and your desktop so you can always have all your tasks at hand wherever you are.

## Productivity Software Features

### What tools can help me work more efficiently with productivity software?

Whether you are working on a word processing document, spreadsheet, database, or slide presentation, you can make use of several tools to increase your efficiency:

- A **wizard** is a systematic guide that walks you through the steps necessary to complete a complicated task. At each

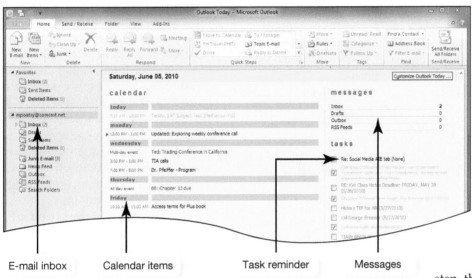

E-mail inbox    Calendar items    Task reminder    Messages

**Figure 7.11**

The Outlook Today feature in Microsoft Outlook includes common PIM features such as a summary of appointments, a list of tasks, and the number of new e-mail messages.

requests, and tasks directly in OneNote. If you're taking notes in a lecture or meeting, and the need to create a follow-up appointment comes up, you can do so without leaving the OneNote application.

### Are there Web-based PIM programs?

Many Web-based e-mail clients, such as Yahoo! and Google, have developed coordinating calendar and contacts programs similar to Microsoft Outlook. Yahoo! includes Notepad for jotting down notes and tasks. Google's calendar and contacts sync with Outlook so you can access your Outlook calendar information by logging into Google, giving you access to your schedule anywhere you have access to a computer and an Internet connection. It also syncs

step, the wizard asks you questions. Based on your responses, the wizard helps you complete that portion of the task. When you install software, you are often guided by a wizard.

- A **template** is a predesigned form. Templates are included in many productivity applications. They provide the basic structure for a particular kind of document, spreadsheet, or presentation. Templates can include specific page layout designs, formatting and styles relevant to that particular document, and automated tasks (macros). Typical templates allow you to lay out a professional-looking résumé, structure a home budget, or communicate the results of a project in a presentation.

- A **macro** is a small program that groups a series of commands so they will run as a single command. Macros are best used to automate a routine task or a complex series of commands that must be run frequently. For example, a teacher may write a macro to sort the grades in her grade book automatically in descending order and to highlight those grades that add up to less than a C average. Every time she adds the results of an assignment or test, she can set up the macro to run through that series of steps automatically.

### Software Suites

**What's a software suite?** A **software suite** is a group of software programs that have been bundled as a package. You can buy software suites for many different

**Figure 7.12**

Software suites provide users with a cheaper method of obtaining all of the software they want to buy in one bundle.

categories of software, including productivity, graphics, and virus protection (see Figure 7.12). Microsoft Office 2010 is the standard for proprietary software suites, and is available for both Windows-based and Apple computers. Apple offers productivity software for Macs in its iWork suite.

**Which applications do productivity software suites contain?** Most productivity software suites contain similar basic components, such as word processing, spreadsheet, presentation, and PIM software. However, depending on the version and manufacturer, they may also include other types of applications, such as database, note taking, or desktop publishing software. When you are shopping for software, it is important to figure out which bundle is the right one for your needs. For example, Microsoft Office 2010 is bundled in different ways; the three bundles that are available for individual purchase are described in Figure 7.13. Starter 2010, also from Microsoft, has stripped down versions of Word and Excel and includes advertising. Starter 2010 is installed by the computer manufacturer, and replaces Microsoft Works. Be sure to research carefully the bundling options for software you are buying.

**What are the advantages of software suites?** It is cheaper to buy a software suite than to buy each program individually. Another benefit of software suites is the compatibility between programs. Because the programs bundled in a software suite come from the same company, they work well together (that is, they provide for better integration) and share common features, toolbars, and menus. For example, when using applications in the Microsoft Office suite, you can seamlessly create a spreadsheet in Excel, import it into Access, and then link a query created in Access to a Word document. It would be much harder to do the same thing using different applications from a variety of software developers. Another example of a productivity suite is Apple iWork, which includes word processing (Pages), presentation (Keynote), and spreadsheet (Numbers) applications. Each program in the iWork suite can access and share certain common elements such as photographs.

Figure 7.13

Microsoft Office 2010 suites that are best for home, work, or school.

| Application | Function | Home and Student 2010 | Home and Business 2010 | Professional 2010 |
|---|---|---|---|---|
| Word | Word processing | X | X | X |
| Excel | Spreadsheet | X | X | X |
| PowerPoint | Presentation | X | X | X |
| Access | Database | | | X |
| Outlook | PIM | | X | X |
| Publisher | Desktop publishing | | | X |
| OneNote | Note taking | X | X | X |

## Personal Financial Software

**What software can I use to prepare my taxes?** Everyone has to deal with taxes, and having the right computer software can make this burden much simpler and keep it completely under your control. **Tax preparation software** such as Intuit TurboTax and H&R Block At Home enable you to prepare your state and federal taxes on your own instead of hiring a professional. Both programs offer a complete set of tax forms and instructions, as well as videos that contain expert advice on how to complete each form. Each company also offers free Web-based versions for federal forms and instructions. In addition, error-checking features are built into the programs to catch mistakes. TurboTax also can run a check for audit alerts, file your return electronically, and offer financial planning guidance to help you effectively plan and manage your financial resources in the following year (see Figure 7.14). Remember, however, that the tax code changes annually, so you must obtain an updated version of the software each year.

**Which software can I use to help keep track of my personal finances?** Financial planning software helps you manage your daily finances. Intuit Quicken, AceMoney, and YNAB are popular examples. Financial planning programs include electronic checkbook registers and automatic bill payment tools. With these features, you can print checks from your computer or pay recurring monthly

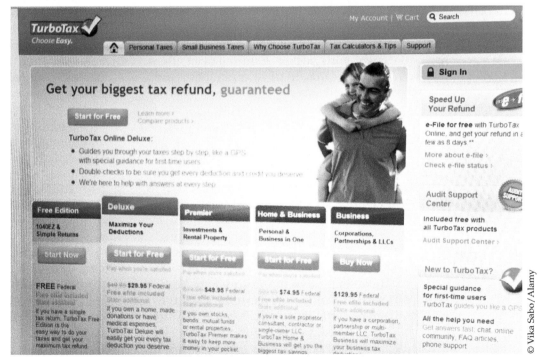

Figure 7.14

Tax preparation software such as Intuit TurboTax enables you to prepare and file your taxes using a guided, systematic process.

© Vika Sabo/Alamy

payments, such as rent or student loans, with automatically scheduled online payments. The software records all transactions, including online payments, in your checkbook register. In addition, you can assign categories to each transaction and then use these categories to create budgets and analyze your spending patterns.

Some financial planning applications also coordinate with tax preparation software. Quicken, for example, integrates seamlessly with TurboTax, so you never have to go through your checkbook and bills to find tax deductions, tax-related income, or expenses. Many banks and credit card companies also offer online services

**Figure 7.15**

Mint.com is an online financial management tool. An extensive online community provides helpful tips and discussions with other people in similar situations.

that download a detailed monthly statement into Quicken. Quicken even offers a credit card. All of your purchases are organized into categories and are downloaded automatically to your Quicken file to streamline your financial planning and record keeping.

**Are there Web-based financial planning programs?** Web-based programs such as Mint (**www.mint.com**) (see Figure 7.15) and Yodlee MoneyCenter (**www.yodlee.com**) are rapidly gaining in popularity. Both are great at analyzing your spending habits and offering advice on how to manage your spending better. Like some other full-featured applications such as Quicken, you can track your investment portfolio as well. Because they are Web-based, you can monitor and update your finances from any computer in a private and secure setting. Each product also has versions of its applications to load on smartphones, so your information is con-

veniently accessible. Users also have access to a network of other users with whom to exchange tips and advice.

## Business Software for Home and Office

With the amount of power available in a typical home computer, you have more opportunities than ever to run a business from your home. No matter what service or product you provide, there are common types of software that will be helpful in your business. Accounting software will help manage the flow of money, and desktop publishing and Web page creation tools will help you market and develop your new enterprise. A number of software packages are designed to organize and help with the daily operations of a typical business. If you ever plan to run a business from your own home, or even if you are just a user of large business products and services, it is helpful to know what functions business software can perform.

### Home Business Software

**Which programs are good for small-business owners?** If you have a small business or a hobby that produces income, then you know the importance of keeping good records and tracking your expenses and income. **Accounting software** helps small-business owners manage their finances more efficiently by providing tools for tracking accounts receivable and accounts payable. In addition, these applications offer inventory management, payroll, and billing tools. Examples of accounting applications are Intuit QuickBooks and Peachtree by Sage. Both programs include templates for invoices, statements, and financial reports so that small-business owners can create common forms and reports.

**What software can I use to lay out and design newsletters and other publications?** Desktop publishing (DTP) software allows you to incorporate and arrange graphics and text in your documents in creative ways. Although many word processing applications allow you to use some of the features that are hallmarks of desktop publishing, specialized desktop publishing software such as Microsoft

Publisher, QuarkXPress, and Adobe InDesign allows professionals to design books and other publications that require complex layouts (see Figure 7.16).

**What tools do desktop publishing programs include?** Desktop publishing programs offer a variety of tools with which you can format text and graphics. With text formatting tools, you easily can change the font, size, and style of your text and arrange text on the page in different columns, shapes, and patterns. You also can import files into your documents from other sources, including elements from other software programs (such as a chart from Excel or text from Word) and image files. You can readily manipulate graphics with tools that crop, flip, or rotate images or modify the image's color, shape, and size. Desktop publishing programs also include features that allow you to publish to the Web.

**What software do I use to create a Web page?** Web page authoring software allows even the novice to design interesting and interactive Web pages, without knowing any HyperText Markup Language (HTML) code. Web page authoring applications often include wizards, templates, and reference materials to help you easily complete most Web page authoring tasks. More experienced users can take advantage of these applications' advanced features, such as features that enable you to add headlines and weather information, stock tickers, and maps to make your Web content current, interactive, and interesting. Microsoft Expression Web and Adobe Dreamweaver are two of the programs to which both professionals and casual page designers turn.

**Are there other ways to create Web pages?** If you need to produce only the occasional Web page and do not need a separate Web page authoring program, you'll find that many applications include features that enable you to convert your document into a Web page. For example, in some Microsoft Office applications, if you choose to save a file as a Web page, the application will automatically convert the file to a Web-compatible format.

### Large Business Software

There is an application for almost every aspect of business. There are specialized programs for marketing and sales, finance, point of sale, general productivity, project management, security, networking, data management, e-commerce, and human resources, to name just a few. In the following sections, we discuss some of these specialized programs from this seemingly endless list.

Tool palette · Style Sheets palette · Colors palette · Measurements palette · Page Layout palette

**Figure 7.16**
Major publishing houses use professional publishing programs such as QuarkXPress to lay out the pages of textbooks.

**Figure 7.17**

A Gantt chart in Microsoft Project gives project managers a visual tool for assigning personnel and scheduling and managing tasks.

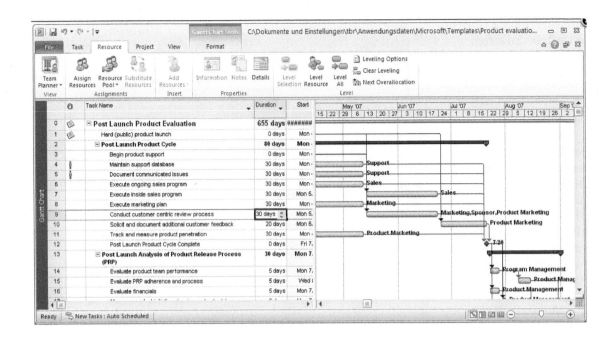

### What software do businesses use for planning and management?

Planning is a big part of running a successful business. Software programs such as Palo Alto Software's Business Plan Pro and Marketing Plan Pro help users write strategic and development plans for general business and marketing needs. Another category of business planning software is **project management software**, such as Microsoft Project. This type of software helps project managers create and modify scheduling charts like the one shown in Figure 7.17, which help them plan and track specific tasks and coordinate personnel resources.

**Customer relationship management (CRM) software** stores sales and client contact information in one central database. Sales professionals use CRM programs to get in touch with and follow up with their clients. These programs also include tools that enable businesses to assign quotas and create reports and charts that document and analyze actual and projected sales data. CRM programs coordinate well with PIM software such as Outlook and can be set up to work with smartphones. GoldMine from FrontRange Solutions is one example of a CRM program.

An **enterprise resource planning (ERP) system** lets a business consolidate multiple systems into one and improve coordination of these business areas across multiple departments. ERP systems are used to control many "back office" operations and processing functions such as billing, production, inventory management, and human resources management. These systems are implemented by third-party vendors and matched directly to the specific needs of a company. Oracle and SAP are well-known companies that sell ERP software.

### What software helps business travelers?

**Mapping programs** are useful for nonprofessionals traveling to unfamiliar locations. More users now turn to an **online mapping service** such as Google Maps, MapQuest, Yahoo! Maps, or Google Earth than to a more traditional mapping software program because the online services are easily accessible with any Internet connection and are updated more frequently than offline ones. Mapping programs, which can

## Need a Way to Share Files? Try PDF

Say you've created a file in Microsoft Excel, but the person to whom you want to send it doesn't have Excel, or any spreadsheet software, installed on his computer. Further, you do not want the contents of the original file to be changed. What do you do in these situations? One solution is to create a PDF file. Portable Document Format (PDF) is a file format you can create with Adobe Acrobat or CutePDF Writer, a free program available from **www.cutepdf.com.** These programs transform any file, regardless of its application or platform, into a document that can be shared, viewed, and printed by anyone who has Adobe Reader. If you are using Microsoft Office 2010 or OpenOffice.org, you can create PDF files easily with a built-in feature. Adobe Reader (available from **www.adobe.com**), the program you need to read all PDF files, is a free download.

work in conjunction with a global positioning system (GPS), are available in versions for smartphones and for cars.

**Is mapping software just used to assist with travel?** Travel is only one of several applications that use mapping technologies to assist businesses in making complex decisions and managing complex systems. Many companies use a geographic information system (GIS) to assist with managing, analyzing, and displaying data, most often in spatial or map form (see Figure 7.18). These maps are used by power companies to manage electric grids, by water distribution companies to manage water distribution, by shipping and transportation companies to determine the most efficient routes, and even by school districts to manage the flow of students to the appropriate schools. Many of these systems are complex, proprietary ones such as those produced by ESRI. Google Earth and interactive maps like Google Maps are simple and free examples of basic forms of a GIS.

**What software is used with e-commerce?** It seems that every business has an online presence to display company information or products, handle online sales, or offer customer service and support. Depending on the size of the company and its specific needs, it may use products such as IBM's WebSphere, Go-Emerchant, and ProStores Business from ProStores (an eBay company). These products offer bundled Web site creation and hosting services, shopping cart setup, and credit card processing services. For larger businesses, specialized software to handle each aspect of e-commerce is available; alternatively, a large business might develop proprietary software tailored to its specific needs.

### Specialized Business Software

Some applications are tailored to the needs of a particular company or industry. Software designed for a specific industry is called **vertical market software**. For example, the construction industry uses software such as Sage Master Builder, which features estimating tools to help construction companies bid on jobs. It also integrates project management functions and accounting systems that are unique to the construction industry.

Other examples of vertical market software include property management

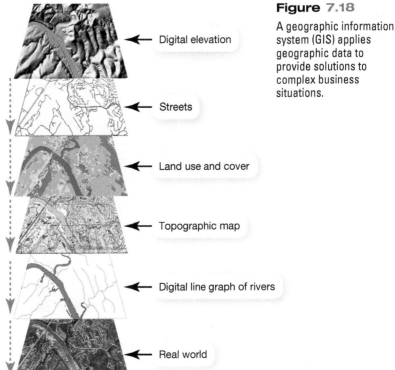

**Figure 7.18**

A geographic information system (GIS) applies geographic data to provide solutions to complex business situations.

- Digital elevation
- Streets
- Land use and cover
- Topographic map
- Digital line graph of rivers
- Real world

software for real estate professionals; ambulance scheduling and dispatching software for emergency assistance organizations; and library automation software that combines cataloging, circulation, inventory, online catalog searching, and custom report printing.

In addition to these specific business applications, which companies can buy off the shelf, programs often are custom developed to address a company's specific needs.

**What software is used to make 3D models?** Engineers use **computer-aided design (CAD)** programs to create automated designs, technical drawings, and 3D model visualizations. Specialized CAD software such as Autodesk's AutoCAD is used in areas such as architecture, the automotive industry, aerospace, and medical engineering.

With CAD software, architects can build virtual models of their plans and readily visualize all aspects of design before actual construction. Engineers use CAD software to design everything from factory components to bridges. The 3D nature of these programs allows engineers to rotate their models and make adjustments to their designs where necessary, thus eliminating costly building errors.

© Lloyd Sutton / Alamy

**Figure 7.19**

Google's SketchUp is a free 3D modeling application.

CAD software also is being used in conjunction with GPS devices for accurate placement of fiber-optic networks around the country. The medical engineering community uses CAD to create anatomically accurate solid models of the human anatomy, allowing them to develop medical implants quickly and accurately. The list of CAD applications keeps growing as more and more

```
Home Media          Digital image editing software
Software
                    Digital audio software

                    Digital video editing software

                    Media management software
```

**Figure 7.20**

There are many varieties of graphics and multimedia software.

industries realize the benefits CAD can bring to their product development and manufacturing processes.

Many graphics, animation, video, and gaming systems use applications from Autodesk called Autodesk 3ds Max and Autodesk Maya to create 3D models with complex textures and lighting models. Autodesk 3ds Max and Autodesk Maya

are complex and rich programs. A slightly simpler package is the open source program Blender (**www .blender.org**), which is available free of charge. A simple, Web-based, and fairly full-featured free 3D modeling application is Google's SketchUp (**sketchup.google.com**) (see Figure 7.19). SketchUp designs coordinate well with other Google applications so, for example, you could easily import a 3D image of a deck you created in SketchUp into a Google Earth image of your home.

## Media Software for Home

From movies and television to music and photography, the entertainment world is becoming digital. Your computer can help you create, organize, and modify digital images, songs, and movies, if you have the right software. **Multimedia software** includes image, video, and audio editing software; animation software; and other specialty software required to produce computer games, animations, and movies. In this section, we look at several popular types of multimedia software, as shown in Figure 7.20.

### Digital Image Editing Software

**What can I do with a digital image that I can't do with a photograph?** Once the image information is in a digital format (taken with a digital camera or scanned), you can use it easily with all your other software. For example, you can store a digital picture of each person in your Outlook contacts list or add a digital image you captured into a newsletter you are writing.

Products such as Microsoft Photo Story and Google Picasa, which are both free downloads, make it easy for you to use your collection of digital images in new ways. In Photo Story, you can add text, music, and camera movement to create a fully featured slide show with your images. Using Picasa, you can create a poster or several different styles of collages from your images.

**Figure 7.21**

You can create collages of your favorite images using Google's Picasa.

**What software can I use to edit my photos?** As its name implies, **image editing software** (sometimes called **photo editing software**) enables you to edit photographs and other images. Image editing software includes tools for basic modifications to digital images such as removing red-eye; modifying contrast, sharpness, and color casts; or removing scratches or rips from scanned images of old photos. Many of these software packages include painting tools such as brushes, pens, and artistic media (such as paints, pastels, and oils) that allow you to create realistic-looking images. Some include templates so you can insert your favorite pictures into preformatted pages for digital scrapbooks or greeting cards. Image editing programs such as Adobe Photoshop Elements and Roxio PhotoSuite are geared toward the casual home user. Google

Picasa (**picasa.google.com**) is another popular application in the online photo editing, storing, and sharing field (see Figure 7.21). Picasa, which is a free download, not only lets you organize and edit your photos, but also stores your photos on the Web. This makes it very easy to share photos by creating Web albums. Picasa helps you send images to your friends, your mobile devices, or your blog by automatically resizing a huge 12-megapixel image to a more manageable size for electronic transmission. With Picasa, you can then attach the image to an outgoing e-mail message, or transfer the image directly to your blog or to a mobile device such as an iPad or smartphone.

**What image editing programs might a professional use?** Often graphic designers use digital photos and images as a basis for their designs and then modify these images within image editing software to create their final products.

Adobe Photoshop and Corel PaintShop Photo Pro are fully featured image editing applications. GIMPshop (**www.gimpshop .com**) is a free download that has most of the features offered by the more expensive applications. They each offer sophisticated tools for tasks like layering images (placing pictures on top of each other) and masking images (hiding parts of layers to create effects such as collages). Designers use

 **SOUND BYTE**

Enhancing Photos with Image Editing Software

In this Sound Byte, you'll learn tips and tricks on how to best use image editing software. You'll learn how to remove the red-eye from photos and incorporate borders, frames, and other enhancements to produce professional effects.

Most likely you have a Facebook account as well as a Web-based e-mail account such as Gmail or Hotmail that you access every day. You put your pictures on Facebook and you can see them from anywhere you can access the Internet—from home, school, or work—and you can view them on your PC, your smartphone, or your friend's notebook. Similarly, you can always check your e-mail from any computing device. You might also use Dropbox to store your files instead of carrying around a flash drive, and you might have purchased your textbooks from Amazon rather than going to your local bookstore. For your last group project, you and your teammates might have used Google Docs because it was easiest for all of you to access and collaborate on at any time. By doing any of these activities, you have participated in cloud computing.

So what is cloud computing? From the term, you might think it is something magical—and that somehow your pictures and files are floating around in space. But, in reality, your pictures, e-mail, and any other files that are stored on the Web, as well as the software that you access from the Web, are housed in data centers or server farms. These data centers and server farms are basically warehouses full of computers and servers, and they are being created all over the world, providing us with "cloud storage." Being able to work from the cloud eliminates the need to have everything stored on your own computer's disk drives, which can be restricting if you are away from your computer. Instead, cloud computing gives you access to your favorite pictures, music, files, and programs anytime you like, anywhere you like, as long as you have access to the Internet. In addition, cloud computing facilitates collaboration and communication among multiple users, and can cut down on administrative tasks for organizations maintaining large amounts of computer hardware and software.

Technically, there are two sides to cloud computing: the front end and the back end. The front end is the side we see as users, and includes our computer and the application required to access the cloud computing system—generally a Web browser like Internet Explorer or Google Chrome. Some systems have unique applications that provide network access to clients. The back end consists of the various computers and servers that house the files and programs you access "on the cloud" (see Figure 7.22). A central server that uses a special kind of software called middleware (that allows networked computers to communicate with each other), monitors the demands on the system to ensure everything runs smoothly. The computers in the data centers or server farms are designed to work together, adjusting to the varying degrees of demand placed on them at any point in time. Companies like Facebook have had to increase the amount of servers dedicated to their users as the popularity and functionality of Facebook has increased, for example.

Google is one of the first true explorers in the cloud, building applications such as Google Docs, Gmail, and Chrome in an effort to eventually create a completely virtual operating environment. A fully functioning operating environment would enable users to sign in and have "their" computer setup (desktop configurations and images, programs, files, and other personalized settings) pop up on whatever computer they are using. Additionally, cloud computing would reduce the need for all of us to have the fastest computers with the most memory and storage capabilities. Instead, we could all have simple front-end terminals with basic input and output devices because the computers on the back end will be providing all the computing muscle. We are not quite there yet, but those days are inevitably coming.

these more sophisticated tools to create the enhanced digital images used commercially in logos, advertisements, and on book and CD covers.

**Are there Web-based programs available to edit, share, and store my photos?** One great advantage of taking digital images is that you can easily share the images via the Internet. Initially, we had to send images as e-mail attachments—and our exuberance in sending several images at the same time often clogged someone's inbox. Several online photo sharing and photo storing sites, such as Snapfish (**www.snapfish.com**), Kodak (**www.kodak.com**), and Shutterfly (**www.shutterfly.com**), enable you to upload your digital images from your computer, create photo albums, and share them with friends and family. These sites offer printing and card-making services as well.

Flickr (**www.flickr.com**) is probably one of the best of these online photo management and photo sharing applications. It lets you organize your images and then share them publicly with millions of users, or just with your closest friends and family. Discussion boards are available so that groups can exchange comments about the images, just as you would if you were passing them around the dinner table. In addition, taking advantage of online mapping technologies, Flickr enables you to link your images to a map so that you can show exactly where you took the images or see where others took theirs.

### Digital Audio Software

**Why would I have digital audio files on my computer?** Best-selling novels, newspapers, and radio shows all can be purchased as audio files from sellers such as Audible, Inc. (**www.audible.com**). Huge numbers of

"The Internet Cloud"

Google Docs

amazon

Gmail

**Figure 7.22**

There are two sides to cloud computing: the side we see as users, and the banks of computers and servers that house the files and programs we access.

Sure, there are some problems with cloud computing that users need to be aware of, such as what happens when the Internet goes down. Security and privacy are also very big concerns for cloud computing. Right now, the security of information stored on the Web is built on trusting that the passwords we set and the security systems that the data centers put in place are able to keep our information away from unauthorized users. Because even the devices in these large data centers and server farms inevitably will break down, the cloud computing systems have redundant systems to provide backup. However, for critical files that you must have, it might be a good idea to not completely rely on the cloud, and to have your own backup files. Like losing electricity, if the Internet goes down, you would have to go without, but having a backup system in place for the critical files and programs will help to reduce the inconvenience and loss of productivity while access to the Internet is being restored. But, you can't mitigate all the risks if you store all the files on your own personal computers, so you have to weigh these disadvantages against the strong advantages of the convenience of having your information when and where you want it, and the ability to have better collaboration.

free audio files are also available through the phenomenon of *podcasting*, the distribution of audio files such as radio shows and music videos over the Internet. Offered by subscription, these audio files are delivered to your computer free with the release of each episode. You may also choose to extract (*rip*) your CD collection to store on your computer. In addition, with programs such as MAGIX Music Maker or Apple GarageBand, you can compose your own songs or soundtracks with virtual instruments, voice recorders, synthesizers, and special audio effects. You may quickly have several gigabytes of audio files on your hard drive before you even know it!

**Why are MP3 files so popular?** MP3, short for MPEG-1 Audio Layer 3, is a type of audio compression format that reduces the file size of traditional digital audio files so that they will take up less storage capacity. It is also a standard of digital audio compres-

sion, which has made it possible to transfer and play back music on personal media players. For example, a typical CD stores between 10 and 15 songs in uncompressed format, but with files in MP3 format, the same CD can store between 100 and 180 songs. The smaller file size not only lets you store and play music in less space, but also allows quick and easy distribution over the Internet. Ogg Vorbis (or just Ogg) is a free, open source audio compression format alternative.

**What can digital audio software programs do?** You can find hundreds of digital audio applications that allow you to copy, play, and organize MP3 files. Most digital audio software programs, such as Apple iTunes, Windows Media Player, and Musicmatch Jukebox, enable you to do the following:

- *MP3 recording* allows you to record directly from streaming audio and other software or microphone sources to MP3 format.

- *CD ripping* allows you to copy or extract CDs and encode to the MP3 format.

- *CD burning* allows you to create your own CDs from your MP3 collection.

- *Encoding and decoding* is done by *encoders*, programs that convert files to MP3 format at varying levels of quality. Most ripping software has encoders built in to convert the files directly into MP3 format.

- *Format conversion* programs allow you to convert MP3 files to other digital audio formats such as WAV (Waveform Audio File Format), WMA (Windows Media Audio), and AIFF (Audio Interchange File Format).

**Can I edit audio files?** Audio **editing software** includes tools that make editing your audio files as easy as editing your text files. Software such as the open source Audacity (**http://audacity.sourceforge .net**) and Sony Sound Forge Pro 10 (**www .sonycreativesoftware.com**) enable you to perform such basic editing tasks as cutting dead air space from the beginning or end of the song or clipping a portion from the middle. Audio Acrobat (**http://marketersmojo.audioacrobat .com**), a Web-based program, makes it easy to record and stream audio and video, and hosts your audio files, as well. You also can add special sound effects, such as echo or bass boost, and remove static or hiss from your MP3 files. These applications support recording sound files from a microphone or any source you can connect through the input line of a sound card.

### Digital Video Editing Software

**What kind of software do I need to edit my digital videos?** With the boom of digital camcorders and the improved graphics capabilities on home computers, many people are experimenting with **digital video editing software**. Several video editing applications are available at a wide range of prices and capabilities. Although the most expensive products (such as Adobe Premiere Pro and Apple's Final Cut Pro) offer the widest range of special effects and tools, some moderately priced video editing programs have enough features to keep the casual user happy. Windows Live Movie Maker and Apple iMovie have intuitive drag-and-drop features that make it simple to create professional-quality movies with little or no training (see Figure 7.23). Windows Live Movie Maker (**http://download.live.com/moviemaker**) is a free download from Microsoft. Other software developers offer free trial versions so that you can decide whether their product meets your needs before purchasing it.

**Does video editing software support all kinds of video files?** Video files come in a number of formats such as flash video (FLV for YouTube), MPEG-1, MPEG-2, MPEG-4, VCD, SVCD, DVD, AVI, WMV, MOV, and even AVCHD, a format for high-definition video. Many of the affordable video editing software packages support most types of video files.

**Figure 7.23**

Video editing programs such as Apple iMovie make it easy to create and edit movies.

Video clips in clips pane

Window used to view or edit movie clips

Movie clips display in clip viewer

GTrans icon controls transition effects between clips

Anthony Devlin/PA Wire URN:10299603 (Press Association via AP Images)

Album covers flow in smooth display

iTunes social network

Genius recommendations based on song composition

Smart playlists select song lists based on your criteria

**Figure 7.24**

Software programs such as iTunes help you manage all the music files on your computer. You can sort, filter, and search your collection by artist, album, or category, and you can create playlists.

For more information on video editing software, see the section "Digital Video" on page 159 of Chapter 5.

**In what format are the videos I watch on my portable media player?** Videos that can be watched on portable media players, such as Apple's iPods, are in the MP4 (MPEG-4) video format. This format stores digital audio and digital video streams, as well as other items, such as text for subtitles and still images. Similar to the MP3 format, MP4 compresses the audio and video content into a more manageable file size. Most MP4 files have the file extension .mp4. However, Apple has created other MPEG-4 extensions to identify specific content such as .m4b, which is often used to identify audio book and podcast files, and .m4r, which is used to identify ringtone files for the iPhone.

### Media Management Software

**How do I manage the audio, video, and image files on my system?** Many people add hundreds or even thousands of files to their systems by purchasing music and downloading images and video. Your hard drive is a convenient place to store all your music and images, but only if you can find what you're looking for!

Software such as Windows Media Player, Winamp, and Apple iTunes allows you to organize audio and video files so that you

can sort, filter, and search your music collection by artist, album, or category (see Figure 7.24). Using these programs, you can manage individual tracks, generate playlists, and even export the files to a database or spreadsheet application for further manipulation. When you burn the songs to a CD, the programs can print liner notes that you can place inside the CD case.

## Entertainment Software for Home

As the term implies, **entertainment software** is designed to provide users with thrills, chills, and all-out fun! Computer games make up the vast majority of entertainment software. These digital games began with Pong, Pac-Man, and Donkey Kong, and have evolved to include many different categories, including action, driving, puzzles, role-playing, card-playing, sports, strategy, and simulation games. Entertainment software also includes other types of computer applications, such as drawing software.

### Gaming Software

**Do I need special equipment to run entertainment software?** As with any software, you need to make sure your system has enough processing power, memory (RAM), and hard drive capacity to run the

**Figure** 7.25

Computer controllers can be specialized. Rock Band controllers include a guitar, a drum set, and a microphone.

program. Because games often push the limit of sound and video quality, be sure your system has the appropriate sound cards, video cards, speakers, monitor, and DVD drives.

Some gaming software may require a special controller. Some games, such as Steel Battalion, Rock Band, and many games in the Nintendo Wii system, are sold with their own specialized controllers (see Figure 7.25). These controllers also can be adapted to your computer. Complex programs can benefit from configurable wireless controllers such as the Cyborg Evo.

**Can I make video games?** Now that video games represent an industry

with revenue of more than $20 billion each year, designing and creating video games is emerging as a desirable career opportunity. Professionally created video games involve artistic storytelling and design, as well as sophisticated programming. Major production houses such as Electronic Arts use applications that are not easily available to the casual home enthusiast. However, you can use the editors and game engines available for games such as EverQuest, Oblivion, and Unreal Tournament to create custom levels and characters to extend the game.

If you want to try your hand at creating your own video games, multimedia applications such as Unity, Adobe Flash, and RPG Maker VX provide the tools you need to explore game design and creation. The program GameMaker (**www.yoyogames.com**) is a free product that allows you to build a game without any programming; key elements of the new game creation are dragged and dropped into place. Alice (**www.alice.org**) is another free environment to check out. It lets you easily create 3D animations and simple games.

### Educational Software

**What kinds of educational applications are there?** Although a multitude of educational software products are geared toward the younger set, software developers have by no means ignored adult markets. In addition to all the products relating to the younger audience, there are software products that teach users new skills such as typing, languages, cooking, and playing the guitar. Preparation software for

**Figure** 7.26

Lumosity features games to exercise your brain to improve memory, processing speed, attention, and multitasking capabilities.

students who will be taking the SAT, GMAT, LSAT, and MCAT exams is also popular. In addition, there are many computer and online brain training games and programs designed to improve the health and function of our brains. Lumosity (**www.lumosity.com**) is one such site that has a specific "workout" program (see Figure 7.26), and can be played on the PC and on your smartphone. Brain Age[2] (**www.brainage.com**) has software for the Nintendo DS and is designed for players of all ages.

**What types of programs are available to train you to use software or special machines?** Many programs provide tutorials for popular computer applications. These programs use illustrated systematic instructions to guide users through unfamiliar skills. Some training programs, known as **simulation programs**, allow users to experience or control the software as if it were the actual software or an actual event. Such simulation programs include commercial and military flight training, surgical instrument training, and machine operation training. Often these simulators can be delivered on CD or DVD or over the Internet.

One benefit of these simulated training programs is that they safely allow users to experience potentially dangerous situations such as flying a helicopter during high winds. Consequently, users of these training programs are more likely to take risks and learn from their mistakes—something they could not afford to do in real life. Simulated training programs also help prevent costly errors. Should something go awry, the only cost of the error is restarting the simulation program.

 Choosing Software

In this Active Helpdesk call, you'll play the role of a helpdesk staffer, fielding calls about the different kinds of multimedia software, educational and reference software, and entertainment software.

**Do I need special software to take courses online?** As long as you have a compatible Web browser, online classes will be accessible to you. Depending on the content and course materials, however, you may need a password or special plug-ins to view certain videos or demos.

 **How to Open Unknown File Types**

Normally, when you double-click a file to open it, the program that is associated with the selected file runs automatically. For example, when you double-click a file with a .doc or.docx extension, the file will open in Microsoft Word. However, if the file has no extension or Windows has no application currently associated with that file type, an "Open with" dialog box appears and asks what program you want to use to open the file. In other cases, a document may open with a program other than the one you wanted to use. This is because many applications can open several file types, and the program you expected the file to open in is not currently the program associated with that file type. To assign a program to a file type or to change the program to open a particular file type, follow these instructions:

1. Click the Windows Explorer icon, which is pinned to the Windows 7 taskbar by default.
2. Use the search and navigation tools in Windows Explorer to locate the file you want to change. (For example, you can search for all Word files by searching for *.doc or *.docx.) Right-click on the file, and then point to Open With.
3. A list of programs installed on your computer will appear. Click the program that you want to use to open this type of file. If you are sure the selected file type is the one that should always be used, then also check "Always use the selected program to open this kind of file" check box, and then click OK.

When you double-click that file in the future, the file will open in the program you selected.

Taking classes over the Internet is rapidly becoming a popular method of learning because it offers greater schedule flexibility for busy students. Although some courses are run from an individually developed Web site, many online courses are run using **course management software** such as Blackboard, Moodle, and Angel. These programs provide traditional classroom tools such as calendars and grade books over the Internet. Special areas are available for students and professors to exchange ideas and information through the use of chat rooms, discussion forums, and e-mail. Other areas are available for posting assignments, lectures, and other pertinent class information.

### Drawing Software

**What kind of software should I use for simple illustrations?** Drawing software (or **illustration software**) lets you create or edit two-dimensional, line-based drawings. You can use drawing software to create technical diagrams or original nonphotographic drawings, animations, and illustrations using standard drawing and painting tools such as pens, pencils, and paintbrushes.

**Figure 7.27**

The drawing program Visio lets you create different types of diagrams easily with drag-and-drop options.

You also can drag geometric objects from a toolbar onto the canvas area to create images and use paint bucket, eyedropper, and spray can tools to add color and special effects to the drawings.

**Are there different types of drawing software?** Drawing software is used in both creative and technical drawings. Applications such as Adobe Illustrator include tools that let you create professional-quality creative and technical illustrations. Illustrator's tools help you create complex designs, such as muscle structures in the human body, and use special effects, such as charcoal sketches. Its warping tool allows you to bend, stretch, and twist portions of your image or text. Because of its many tools and features, Illustrator is one of the preferred drawing software programs of most graphic artists.

There are many software packages to help plan the layout of rooms, homes, and landscapes, such as those offered by Broderbund. Microsoft Visio is a program used to create technical drawings, maps, basic block diagrams, networking and engineering flowcharts, and project schedules, but it can also be used by the more casual designer. Visio uses project-related templates with special objects that you drag onto a canvas. For example, Visio allows you to quickly drag and drop objects to create diagrams like the one shown in Figure 7.27.

Visio also provides brainstorming templates to help you organize your thoughts and ideas.

# Buying Software

These days, you no longer need to go to a computer supply store to buy software. You can find software in almost any retail environment. In addition, you can purchase software online, through catalogs, and at auctions.

**Where can I buy software directly from the Internet?** As with many other retail products, you can buy and download software directly from many companies and retail Web sites such as Microsoft (**www.microsoft.com**) and Amazon (**www.amazon.com**). You also can use the Internet to buy software that is custom developed for your specific needs. Companies such as Ascentix Corporation (**www.ascentix.com**) act as intermediaries between you (the software user) and a software developer, who tweaks open source software code to meet your particular needs.

When buying software from the Internet, you should also request that the software be sent to you on CD or DVD, if this is available. Without a physical copy of the software, it is much more difficult to reinstall the software if you change computers or if your hard drive crashes. If a physical copy is not available, make sure you create a backup and keep it in a safe place.

The Microsoft .NET program (**www.microsoft.com/net**) offers software over the Internet for all devices—not just computers—that have a connection to the Internet. Therefore, you can download software specifically for your smartphone by using .NET. In addition, the Mac OS X operating system integrates online software purchases through the App Store feature.

## Software Licenses

**Don't I own the software I buy?** Most people don't understand that, unlike other items they purchase, the software they buy doesn't belong to them. The only thing they're actually purchasing is a license that gives them the right to use the software for their own purposes as the *only* user of that copy. The application is not theirs to lend.

## "There's an App for That!"

How many of us have said or heard that phrase, indicating that we are seemingly always within access of a program that can be easily downloaded onto our mobile device that will keep us ever connected, entertained, informed, organized, and productive, no matter where we are or what we are doing?

The Apple iPhone started the trend toward mobile applications when the App Store was launched in mid-2008 along with the release of the iPhone. The app craze has been strong from the beginning, and the growth is staggering: 1 billion apps were downloaded in nine months from the Apple App Store (compared to the three years it took to download 1 billion music tracks from iTunes), and 10 billion apps were downloaded by January 2011, only two and a half years after the App Store was opened. Now there are hundreds of thousands of mobile applications created for not just the Apple iPhone, but also for the Android, Blackberry, and other smartphones. In addition, the iPad and other similar tablet devices have their own sets of apps.

Nearly 82 percent of adults have cell phones, and about one-quarter of adults do not have a home landline phone. In addition, cell phones have become "smarter," with the capability of accessing the Internet and multitasking. Combine that with a society that is becoming increasingly dependent on access to instant information, and having access to mobile apps is the perfect solution to the perfect storm—an apps culture has emerged (see Figure 7.28).

According to a recent study conducted by the Pew Research Center's Internet and American Life Project, most of the apps downloaded are entertainment related (games, music, food, travel, and sports) and information based (maps, banking, weather, and news). And according to a separate study conducted by the Nielsen Company, most apps are used in our downtime while watching television, waiting for something, or shopping and running errands. They were least used in a classroom or a meeting.

Similar to the Mac versus PC battle where most software is developed for one or the other platform, not both, mobile apps are also platform specific. If you have a smartphone powered by the Android operating system, you can only use apps from the Android Market. If you

**Figure 7.28**

Apps that run on small mobile devices such as smartphones and tablets have created an apps culture.

© Arrow | Dreamstime.com

have an iPhone, you can only use apps from Apple's App Store. But, if you were to compare the two leading app marketplaces, is there a significant difference between the two? The answer is yes . . . and no.

Apple has the clear advantage by being the first in the market—and therefore has nearly twice as many apps as what is in Android Market. Of the apps that have been developed, Apple has tightly controlled the types of applications that can appear in the App Store; Google, on the other hand, has let developers basically put up anything they want in the Android Market without asking permission. Therefore, many apps on the Android Market can be considered "junk," but others are quite useful even though they would not pass Apple's strict requirements.

Both stores provide simple means to navigate through the hundreds of thousands of apps. Each store has arranged apps into categories, and differentiates between the free, most popular, and newly released. However, Apple has begun to group apps together in kits such as apps for "Students," "Movie Lovers," and "Working Out." And the Genius tab is very helpful by recommending apps based on your existing library.

All in all, the trend toward delivery and use of mobile apps has taken off at full speed and is quickly becoming a way of life for many smartphone users.

## What is a software license?

A **software license**, also known as an **End Users License Agreement (EULA)**, is an agreement between you, the user, and the software company (see Figure 7.29). You accept this agreement before installing the software on your machine. It is a legal contract that outlines the acceptable uses of the program and any actions that violate the agreement. Generally, the agreement will state who the ultimate owner of the

**Figure 7.29**

You must accept the terms of the software license before using the product.

Used with permission from Microsoft

Microsoft Software License Terms

MICROSOFT SOFTWARE LICENSE TERMS
MICROSOFT OFFICE 2010 DESKTOP APPLICATION SOFTWARE
Below are three separate sets of license terms. Only one set applies to you. To determine which license terms apply to you check the license designation printed either on your product key, near the product name on your Certificate of Authenticity, or on the download page if you obtained your product key online. If your designation is FPP, then the Retail License Terms below apply to you. If your designation is OEM, then the OEM License Terms below apply to you. If your designation is Product Key Card or PKC, then the Product Key Card License Terms below apply to you. If you need assistance finding your license type, please go to: www.microsoft.com/office/eula to determine which license you have.

1. RETAIL LICENSE TERMS.
These license terms are an agreement between Microsoft Corporation (or based on where you live, one of its affiliates) and you. Please read them. They apply to the software named above, which includes the media on which you received it, if any. Printed-paper license terms, which may come with the software, may replace or modify an on-screen license terms. These terms also apply to any Microsoft

Print                                                          OK

Can I Borrow Software That I Don't Own?

A computer user who copies an application onto more than one computer is participating in **software piracy**, unless his or her license specifically provides for multiple distributions. When software users purchase software, they are purchasing a license to use it, rather than purchasing the actual software. That license tells you how many times you can install the software, so it is important to read it. If you make more copies of the software than the license permits, you are pirating (see Figure 7.30). Historically, the most common way software has been pirated among computer users has been by supplementing each other's software library by borrowing installation CDs and installing the software on their own computers. Larger-scale illegal duplication and distribution by counterfeiters are quite common as well. In addition, the Internet provides various ways to copy and distribute pirated software illegally.

Is it really a big deal to copy a program or two? As reported by the Business Software Alliance, over 40 percent of all software is pirated. Not only is pirating software unethical and illegal, but the practice has financial impacts on all software consumers. The financial loss to the software industry is estimated to be valued at over $50 billion. This loss decreases the amount of money available for further software research and development, while increasing the up-front costs to legitimate consumers.

To determine whether you have a pirated copy of software installed on your computer at work or at home, you should conduct a software audit. The Business Software Alliance Web site (**www.bsa.org/usa**) has several free third-party software audit tools that help you identify and track licensed and unlicensed software installed on your computer and networks. These programs check the serial numbers of the software installed on your computer against software manufacturer databases of official licensed copies and known fraudulent copies. Any suspicious software installations are flagged for your attention.

As of yet, there's no such thing as an official software police force, but if you're caught with pirated software, severe penalties do exist. A company or individual can pay up to $150,000 for each software title copied. In addition, you can be criminally prosecuted for copyright infringement, which carries a fine of up to $250,000 or a five-year jail sentence or both.

Efforts to stop groups that reproduce, modify, and distribute counterfeit software over the Internet are in full force. Software manufacturers also are becoming more aggressive in programming mechanisms into software to prevent repeated installations. For instance, with many Microsoft products, installation requires you to activate the serial number of your software with a database maintained at Microsoft. This is different from the traditional "registration" that enrolled you voluntarily and allowed you to be notified of product updates. Activation is required, and failure to activate your serial number or attempting to activate a serial number that has been used previously results in the software going into a "reduced functionality mode" after the fiftieth time you use it. Therefore, without activation, you would not be able to save documents in Office.

**Figure 7.30**

Making more copies than the permitted number is pirating software, and is illegal.

© Lepro/iStockphoto.com

software is, under what circumstances copies of the software can be made, and whether the software can be installed on any other machine. Finally, the license agreement will state what, if any, warranty comes with the software.

**Do you always buy just one license?** Some software is purchased with a single license to cover one person's specific use. These licenses cannot be shared, and you cannot "extend" the license to install the software on more than one of your computers. However, Apple offers a Family Pack Software License Agreement that permits a user to install some of its software legally on as many as five computers that are in the same household, and some versions of Microsoft Office come with the ability to install the software on up to three computers in the same household. Businesses and educational institutions often buy multiuser licenses that allow more than one person to use the software. Some multiuser licenses are per-seat and limit the number of users overall, while others, called *concurrent licenses,* limit the number of users accessing the software at any given time.

**Does open source software require a license?** As you learned earlier, anyone using open source software has access to the program's code. Therefore, open source software programs can be tweaked by another user and redistributed. A free software license, the GNU General Public License, is required and grants the recipients the right to modify and redistribute the software. Without such license, the recipient would be in violation of copyright laws. This concept of redistributing modified open source software under the same terms as the original software is known as **copyleft**. Thus, all enhancements, additions, and other changes to copyleft software must also be distributed as free software.

### Pre-Installed Software

**What application software comes with my computer?** Virtually every new computer comes with an operating system as well as some form of application software, although the particular applications depend on the hardware manufacturer and computer model. You usually can count on your computer having some form of productivity software preinstalled, such as Windows Live Essentials, which includes Photo Gallery, Movie Maker, Mail, and Messenger, as well as Microsoft Office Starter. Multimedia-enriched computers also may offer graphics software or a productivity suite that includes Web page authoring software.

Some manufacturers can include applications on your new computer that they hope you will try, so as to build interest in their product. Some of these applications, especially virus protection software, are trial versions for which a user gets a short-term temporary software license. When the license expires, the software disables (but is still installed), and a permanent license must be purchased to reinstate the software.

**Are there any problems associated with pre-installed software?** There is such generous space on system hard drives these days that leaving pre-installed applications on a system isn't problematic from a storage perspective. However, having so many pre-installed programs on your system can degrade the system performance by allocating memory away from active applications. For notebook computers, such software can also reduce battery life. If you

## Getting Rid of the Bloat

You have a new computer and expect blazing fast speeds. Unfortunately, the manufacturer included lots of software that you don't want or need, and you know it degrades performance and slows down startup and shutdown times. To get rid of bloatware, you can install an application such as PC Decrapifier (**www.pcdecrapifier .com**), or if you prefer to do this yourself, consider some of these tips:

1. **Trial Antivirus Software:** Although it's absolutely necessary to have antivirus software on your new machine, often, you can transfer the unexpired portion of your license from your old machine to your new one. If that is the case, uninstall the trial version immediately, because you will be bombarded with registration prompts once the trial version expires.

2. **Toolbars:** Although toolbars can be useful, you want to select those that are most useful to you, and having too many can be repetitive. Many computers come with Google or Yahoo! toolbars installed, and possibly others. You can go through Programs and Features in the Control Panel to uninstall any unwanted toolbars.

3. **Manufacturer-Specific Software:** Some computer manufacturers also install their own software. Some of these programs can be useful, while others are help features and update reminders, which are also found in your operating system. You can remove any or all of these support applications, and instead just check the manufacturer's Web site periodically for any updates or new information.

don't use the software or don't renew the license, then the software just clogs up your system unnecessarily. For this reason, this pre-installed software is referred to as **bloatware**. The best thing to do is to delete the programs.

**Can I get the manufacturer to uninstall or install software before shipping?** Several years ago, Dell began to allow buyers of certain computers to decline unwanted bloatware. Dell also included an extra uninstall utility program on certain computers to make it easier to remove unwanted software. On the other hand, if you know you'll need a particular type of software not offered as standard on your new computer, you may want to see if the computer manufacturer has a special offer that will allow you to add that particular software at a reduced price. Sometimes, initially buying software through the hardware manufacturer is less expensive than buying software on the retail market. This is not always the case, so do some comparative pricing before you buy.

**If my computer crashes, can I get the pre-installed software back?** Although some pre-installed software, such as bloatware, is not necessary to replace if your computer crashes, other software such as the operating system is critical to reinstall. Most manufacturers use a separate partition on the hard drive that holds an image, or copy, of the pre-installed software. However, it's not always possible to reboot from the partitioned hard drive, especially when your computer crashes, so one of the first things you should do after you purchase a new computer is create a restore disc. Generally the manufacturer will have placed a utility on your system, or you can use the utility included in Windows 7, to create a restore disc. To create a restore disc with Windows 7, click the Start menu, select Control Panel, and then select System and Security. From there, select Backup and Restore, and then click Create a system repair disc from the Navigation Pane. Next, insert a blank DVD in your DVD drive and select the drive. Click Create disc. Once the copy has been made, label the disc and put it away in a safe place.

### Discounted Software

**Is there discounted software for students?** Software manufacturers understand that students and educators often need to use software for short periods of time because of specific classes or projects. In addition, they want to encourage you to learn with their product, hoping you'll become a long-term user of their software. Therefore, if you're a student or an educator, you can purchase software that is no different from regularly priced software at prices that are sometimes substantially less than general consumer prices.

Campus computer stores and college bookstores sometimes offer discounted prices to students and faculty who possess a valid ID. Online software suppliers such as Journey Education Marketing (**www.journeyed.com**), CampusTech, Inc. (**www.campustech.com**), and Academic Superstore (**www.academicsuperstore.com**) also offer popular software to students at reduced prices.

**Can I buy used software?** Often you can buy software through online auction sites such as eBay. If you do so, be sure that you are buying licensed (legal) copies. Computer shows that display state-of-the-art computer equipment are generally good sources for software. However, here, too, you must exert a bit of caution to make sure

you are buying licensed copies and not pirated versions.

### Freeware and Shareware

**Can I get software for free legally?** **Freeware** is any copyrighted software that you can use for free. Plenty of freeware exists on the Web, ranging from games and screen savers to business, educational, graphics, home and hobby, and system utility software

---

**Campus computer stores and college bookstores sometimes offer discounted prices to students and faculty who possess a valid ID.**

---

programs. To find free software, type "freeware" in your search engine. Good sources of a large variety of freeware programs are Butterscotch (**www.butterscotch.com**), and Freeware Home (**www.freewarehome.com**).

Although they do not charge a fee, some developers release free software and request that you send them an e-mail message to thank them for their time in developing the software and to give them your opinion of it. Such programs are called *e-mailware*.

Another option is to search for an open source program to fit your needs. Open source programs are free to use on the condition that any changes you make to improve the source code also must be distributed for free. SourceForge (**www.sourceforge.net**) is an excellent site to begin your hunt for a group that may already have built a solution that will work for you.

While much legitimate freeware exists, some unscrupulous people use freeware to distribute viruses and malware. Be cautious when installing such programs, especially if you are unsure of the provider's legitimacy.

**Can I try new software before it is really released?** Some software developers offer beta versions of their software free

Tucows, Inc.

**Figure 7.31**

Tucows downloads is a useful site for finding shareware and freeware applications. The site provides product reviews, hardware requirements, and details about the limitations of free versions of software.

of charge. A **beta version** is an application that is still under development. By distributing free beta versions, developers hope users will report errors, or bugs, they find in their programs. Many beta versions are available for a limited trial period, and are used to help the developers correct any errors before they launch the software on the market.

**Is it still freeware if I'm asked to pay for the program after using it for a while?** One model for distributing software is to run a version free of charge for only a limited time. These are fully functional packages, but they expire if not purchased within a certain timeframe. This is referred to as **shareware**. Shareware is not freeware. Shareware software is distributed free, but with certain conditions. Sometimes the software is released on a trial basis only and must be registered after a certain period of time. For example, Tech-Smith Corporation (**www.techsmith.com**) offers Snagit Screen Capture and Camtasia Studio for free for a 30-day period, after which time you must purchase the software to continue using it. If you use the software after the initial trial period is over,

then you are breaking the software license agreement.

Software developers put out shareware programs to get their products into users' hands without the added expense and hassle of marketing and advertising. Therefore, quite a few great programs are available as shareware, and they can compete handily with programs on retail shelves. For a listing of other shareware programs, visit the CNET site Tucows (**www.tucows.com/downloads**), shown in Figure 7.31.

**Can shareware programmers make me pay for their shareware once I have it?** The whole concept of shareware assumes that users will behave ethically and abide by the license agreement. However, to protect themselves, many developers have incorporated code into the program to stop it from working completely or to alter the output slightly after the trial period expires.

**Are there risks associated with installing beta versions, freeware, and shareware or downloading them from the Internet?** Not all files available as shareware and freeware will work on your computer. You easily can crash your system, and may even need to reinstall your operating system as a result of loading a freeware or shareware program that was not written for your computer's operating system.

Of course, by their very nature, beta products are unlikely to be bug free, so you always run the risk of something going awry with your system. Unless you're willing to deal with potential problems, it may be best to wait until the last beta version is released. By that time, most of the serious bugs will have been worked out.

As a precaution, you should be comfortable with the reliability of the source before downloading a freeware, shareware, or beta version of software. If it's a reliable developer whose software you are already familiar with, you can be more certain that a serious bug or virus is not hiding in the software. However, downloading software from an unknown source could potentially put your system at risk of contracting a virus.

A good practice to establish before installing any software on your system is to use the Windows 7 operating system's Restore feature and create a *restore point*. That way, if anything goes wrong during installation, you can restore your system to the way it was before you started. (We discuss the System Restore utility in Chapter 8.) Also, make sure that your virus protection software is up-to-date.

 **ACTIVE HELP-DESK** Buying and Installing Software

In this Active Helpdesk call, you'll play the role of a helpdesk staffer, fielding calls about how to best purchase software or get it for free, how to install and uninstall software, and where you can go for help when you have a problem with your software.

### Software Versions and System Requirements

**What do the numbers after software names indicate?** Software companies change their programs to repair problems (or bugs) or add new or upgraded features. Generally, they keep the software program's name but add a number to it to indicate that it is a different version. Originally, developers used numbers only to indicate different software versions (major upgrades) and releases (minor upgrades). Today, however, they also use years (such as Microsoft Office 2010) and letters (such as WordPerfect Office X5) to represent version upgrades.

**When is it worth buying a newer version?** Although software developers suggest otherwise, there is no need to rush out and buy the latest version of a software program every time one is available. Depending on the software, some upgrades may not be sufficiently different from the previous version to make it cost-effective for you to buy the newest version. Unless the upgrade adds features that are important to you, you may be better off waiting to upgrade every other release. You also should consider whether you use the software frequently enough to justify an upgrade and whether your current system can handle the new system requirements of the upgraded version.

**If I have an older version of software and someone sends me files from a newer version, can I still open them?** Software vendors recognize that people work on different versions of the same software. Vendors, therefore, make new versions backward compatible, meaning that they can recognize (open) files created with older versions. However, some software programs are not forward compatible, so older versions cannot recognize files created on newer versions of the same software.

**How do I know whether the software I buy will work on my computer?** Every software program has a set of **system requirements** that specify the minimum recommended standards for the operating system, processor, primary memory (RAM), and hard drive capacity. Sometimes there are other specifications for the video card, monitor, CD drive, and other peripherals. These requirements generally are printed on the software packaging or are available at the manufacturer's Web site. Before installing software on your computer, ensure that your system setup meets the minimum requirements by having sufficient storage, memory capacity, and processing capabilities.

## BITS AND BYTES

When you download software from the Web, you can run a download or you can save it (see Figure 7.32). What's the difference? When you select Run, the program is downloaded to your machine, and generally stored in Temporary Internet Files. Then the file is "run," meaning that it is loaded into memory and the operating system runs it. Use the Run option when you need to use the downloaded file on a limited basis, such as a song or video that you only plan to watch once or twice. Some installation programs actually install the software on your machine in a permanent location when Run is selected.

When you select Save (or sometimes Save As) on a download, the file will be copied to your hard disk. There may be an AutoRun program associated with the file that starts the installation automatically. Otherwise, you may need to navigate to the stored location and execute (or run) the file independently. The big difference is that the saved file is not downloaded into a temporary location. Use Save when you want to keep the file for a longer period of time, or when you want to control where the file or program is saved.

**Figure 7.32**

When downloading software you have the choice of Run or Save.

# Installing, Uninstalling, and Starting Software

Before you use most software, you must permanently place it, or install it, on your system. The installation process will differ slightly depending on whether you've purchased the software from a retail outlet and have an installation CD or have downloaded it from the Internet. Deleting or uninstalling software from your system requires that you take certain precautions to ensure you remove all associated programs as well.

**How do I install software?** When you purchase software, the program files may come on a CD or a DVD, or they may be available as a download from the Web. When installing programs from a CD or DVD, an installation wizard automatically opens when you insert the disc. By following the steps indicated by the wizard, you can install the application on your system. If the wizard doesn't open automatically for some reason, the best way to install the software is to go to the Start menu, select the Control Panel, click Programs, and then click on the Programs and

Features icon. This launches the installation wizard.

**How is the installation process different for software I download from the Web?** When you download software from the Web, you typically do not get an installation disc. Instead, everything you need to install and run the downloaded program is contained in one file that has been compressed (or zipped) to make the downloading process quicker. For the most part, these downloaded files unzip or decompress themselves and automatically start or launch the setup program. During the installation and setup process, these programs select or create the folder on your computer's hard drive in which most of the program files will be saved. Usually, you can select a different location if you desire. Either way, note the name and location of the files, because you may need to access them later.

**What do I do if the downloaded program doesn't install by itself?** Some programs you download do not automatically install and run on your computer. Although the compressed files may unzip automatically as part of the download process, the setup program may not run without some help from you. In this case, you need to locate the files on the hard drive (this is why you must remember the location of the files) and find the program that is controlling the installation (usually named *setup.exe* or sometimes *install.exe*). Files ending with the .exe extension are executable files or applications. All the other files in the folder are support, help, and data files. Once the setup program begins, you will be prompted to take the actions necessary to complete the installation.

**What's the difference between a custom installation and a full installation?** One of the first steps in the installation wizard asks you to decide between a full installation and a custom installation. A **full installation** will copy all the files and programs from the distribution disc to the computer's hard drive. By selecting **custom installation**, you can decide which features you want installed on the hard drive. Installing only the features you know you want allows you to save space on your hard drive.

**Can I just delete a program to uninstall it?** An application contains many different files—library files, help files, and other text files—in addition to the main file you use to run the program. By deleting only the main file, or only the icon on your desktop, you are not ridding your system of all the pieces of the program. In addition, some applications make changes to a variety of settings, and none of these will be restored if you just delete the desktop icon or remove the main file from your programs list.

Some programs place an Uninstall Program icon in the main program folder on the Start menu. Using this icon runs

the proper cleanup routine to clear out all of the files associated with the application, and also restores any settings that have been changed. If you can't locate the uninstall program for a particular application, click the Start menu, and then click Control Panel. Under Programs, click Uninstall a program. This will give you a list of applications installed on your system; from this list, you can choose which application you would like to uninstall.

**Is there a best way to start an application?** The simplest way to start an application is by clicking its icon in the All Programs list found on the Start menu. Every program that you install on your system is listed in All Programs on the Start menu. However, in Windows 7, if you find you use only a few programs often, you can place a shortcut to those programs on the taskbar or pin it to the Start menu. To place a program on the taskbar or pin it to the Start menu, right-click the program icon on your desktop or right-click the program name on the Start menu. From the shortcut menu that is displayed, select Pin to Taskbar or Pin to Start Menu. Windows then places an icon for this program on the taskbar or Start menu (see Figure 7.33). To uninstall a pinned icon from the Start Menu or a taskbar icon, right-click the icon and select "Remove from this list" or "Unpin this program from taskbar," respectively.

There is virtually an application for almost anything you want or need to do on your computer, whether it is school or work related or just for entertainment purposes. And there are a variety of types of almost every application, such as proprietary, open source, Web-based, freeware, and shareware. Have fun exploring all the various possibilities!

**Figure 7.33**

For quick access to an application you use often, you can create shortcuts on the Start Menu or taskbar.

**Figure** 7.34

Microsoft Office gives you tips on tasks you're working on and answers specific questions you have about using online and offline resources.

## Getting Help with Software

If you need help while you are working with software, you can access several different resources to find answers to your questions. For general help or information about a product, many manufacturers' Web sites offer answers to frequently asked questions (FAQs).

**Where can I find help while I'm working in an application?** Some programs offer online help and support. Online help may consist of documentation comparable to a user's manual. However, many applications' online help allows you to chat over the Internet with an online support team member. Some applications are context sensitive and offer task-specific help or screen tips to explain where your cursor is resting.

In Microsoft Office applications, you will see a question mark icon on the far top right of the program screen. This icon takes you to the main Help interface. **Integrated help** means that the documentation for the product is built directly into the software so you don't need to keep track of bulky manuals. You can type your question, search for a term, or browse the Help topics (see Figure 7.34). Like many software packages, Microsoft Office offers help documentation, which is installed locally on your machine, and online help resources, which are updated continually.

Finally, the Help menu, found in the File tab of most Microsoft applications, lets you choose to search an index or content outline to find out the nature of almost any Microsoft application feature.

**Where do I go for tutorials and training on an application?** If you need help learning how to use a product, the product's developer may offer online tutorials or program tours that show you how to use the software features. Often, you can find good tutorials by searching the Internet. MalekTips (**www.malektips.com**), for example, includes a vast array of multimedia help files; you can find podcasts for applications such as Excel and Photoshop in iTunes; and even YouTube has some helpful videos.

**summary**

### 1. What's the difference between application software and system software?

Application software is the software you use to do everyday tasks at home, school, and work. Application software includes productivity software, such as word processing and finance programs; media software, such as applications used for image and video editing; home and entertainment software, such as games or educational programs; and business software for small and large businesses. System software is the software that helps run the computer and coordinates instructions between application software and the computer's hardware devices. System software includes the operating system and utility programs.

### 2. What are Web-based applications, and how do they differ from traditional modes of software distribution?

Web-based applications are those that are hosted online by the vendor and made available to the customer over the Internet. This distribution model of on-demand software deployment is also referred to as Software as a Service (SaaS). Unlike traditional software that needs to be installed on individual machines or network servers, Web-based applications are accessed via an Internet connection to the host server. The appeal of Web-based applications is that they can be accessed from any machine that has an Internet connection and they can facilitate collaboration because many people can access the same file and work together in real time.

### 3. What kinds of applications are included in productivity software?

Productivity software programs include word processing, spreadsheet, presentation, note taking, personal information manager (PIM), and database programs. You use word processing software to create and edit written documents. Spreadsheet software enables you to do calculations and numerical and what-if analyses easily. Presentation software enables you to create slide presentations. Note taking software provides a convenient means to take extensive notes or to just jot down a few thoughts. You can easily organize and search your notes. PIM software helps keep you organized by putting a calendar, address book, notepad, and to-do lists within your computer. Database programs are powerful applications that allow you to store and organize data. Individuals can also use software to help with business-like tasks such as preparing taxes and managing personal finances.

### 4. What kinds of software do small and large businesses use?

Businesses, including home businesses, use software to help them with finance, accounting, strategic planning, marketing, and Web-based tasks common to most businesses. In addition, businesses may use specialized business software (or vertical market software) that is designed for their specific industry.

### 5. What are the different types of media and entertainment software?

Multimedia software includes digital image, video, and audio editing software; animation software; and other specialty software required to produce computer games. Many software programs are available for playing, copying, recording, editing, and organizing multimedia files. Because modern users have so many audio, video, and image files, many software solutions are available for organizing and distributing these types of files.

### 6. What are the different types of drawing software?

Drawing software includes a wide range of software programs that help you create and edit simple line-based drawings or create more complex designs for both imaginative and technical illustrations. Floor plans, animations, and mind maps are some of the types of images that can be created.

### 7. How can I purchase software or get it for free?

Almost every new computer system comes with some form of software to help you accomplish basic tasks. You must purchase all other software unless it is freeware or open source code, which you can download from the Web for free. You can also find special software called shareware you can run free of charge for a test period. Although you can find software in many stores, as a student you can purchase the same software at a reduced price with an academic discount. When you purchase software, you are actually purchasing the license to use it, and therefore must abide by the terms of the licensing agreement you accept when installing the program.

**8. How do I install, uninstall, and start software?**

When installing and uninstalling software, it's best to use the uninstall feature provided in the software, or if not included to use the uninstall feature that comes with the operating system. Most programs are installed using an installation wizard that walks you through the installation. Other software programs may require you to activate the setup program, which then will begin the installation wizard. Using the uninstall feature of the operating system when uninstalling a program will help you ensure that all additional program files are removed from your computer.

**9. Where can I go for help when I have a problem with my software?**

Most software programs have a Help feature built into the program with which you can search through an index or subject directory to find answers. Some programs group the most commonly asked questions into a single frequently asked questions (FAQ) document. In addition, many free and fee-based help and training resources are available on the Internet and through booksellers.

## Companion Website

The Companion Website includes a variety of additional materials to help you review and learn more about the topics in this chapter. Go to: **www.pearsonhighered.com/techinaction**

**key terms**

# seven

## Word Bank

- application software
- beta version
- financial planning software
- freeware
- illustration software
- image editing software
- integrated help
- presentation

- productivity software
- shareware
- software piracy
- software suite
- spreadsheet
- system requirements
- system software

- templates
- Web-based applications
- wizards
- word processing

**Instructions:** Fill in the blanks using the words from the Word Bank above.

Roxanne has just enrolled in college and is deciding which software she must have. She knows she's going to need some (1) _____ applications for all the different tasks she'll have to do at school and at home. She has been told it's better to buy these applications as a(n) (2) _____ instead of individually since it's usually less expensive. In picking out which bundle of software to purchase, she looks for the one that has a(n) (3) _____ software to help her create slide shows, and a(n) (4) _____ program to help her write papers, and a(n) (5) _____ program for her finance classes. Roxanne is also aware of many interesting (6) _____ such as Google Docs and Dropbox that are available on the Internet and that she can access anywhere she has an Internet connection. Lastly, to keep track of her finances, Roxanne knows she'll need some type of (7) _____.

As a graduation present, Roxanne received a new digital camera. She needs to install the (8) _____ that came with her camera to edit and manage her digital pictures. Although she's used the software a couple of times on her parents' computer, she is still glad for the (9) _____ feature to assist her with specific feature-related questions and the (10) _____ that provide systematic guides to help her do things.

Roxanne especially likes the decorative preformatted (11) _____she can use to insert pictures and make them seem professional. She also knows of some (12) _____ games she can download without cost from the Internet and other (13) _____ programs that she could try but eventually pay for. It's tempting for her to borrow software from her friends, but she knows that it's considered (14) _____. She also knows that before installing any of the programs she must check the (15) _____ to determine if the software is compatible with her system as well as whether the system has enough resources to support the software.

Using key terms from this chapter, write a letter to a new business owner advising them of the types of software they should get to help them run their company. Make sure you identify the type of business in the letter, and think of all possible software that would fit that specific type of business in addition to general business software that most businesses would require.

**Instructions:** Answer the multiple-choice and true–false questions below for more practice with key terms and concepts from this chapter.

## Multiple Choice

**1.** The minimum set of recommended standards for a program is known as the
a. operating system.
b. system requirements.
c. setup guide.
d. installation specs.

**2.** Software that is available on-demand via the Internet is called
a. proprietary software.
b. Web-based software.
c. productivity software.
d. Internet software.

**3.** What type of software enables you to create dynamic slide shows?
a. word processing
b. spreadsheet
c. presentation
d. database

**4.** Which is NOT an advantage of using a software suite?
a. The cost is cheaper than buying programs individually.
b. The programs provide for better integration.
c. The programs integrate easily with programs from other software suites.
d. The programs share common features such as toolbars.

**5.** Image, video, and audio editing software belong in the category of what kind of software?
a. gaming software
b. multimedia software
c. photo enhancing software
d. production software

**6.** What kind of software is responsible for back office operations such as billing and inventory?
a. enterprise resource planning
b. project management
c. business accounting
d. personal information

**7.** Which of the following is true about open source software?
a. The program code is confidential.
b. The program can be changed and freely distributed.
c. The program can be freely distributed as long as the program code is not changed.
d. The program code is subject to copyright protection.

**8.** A small program that groups a series of commands so they will run as a single command is called a
a. wizard.
b. macro.
c. template.
d. function.

**9.** Which program can you use when you are taking notes in class?
a. SoundNote
b. EverNote
c. OneNote
d. all of the above

**10.** What is another name for Software as a Service (SaaS)?
a. Web-based application
b. ERP software
c. apps
d. software suite

## True–False

_____ 1. A macro is a small program that groups a series of commands so that they run as a single command.
_____ 2. When you need help with software, you should use the program's help features or manufacturer FAQs, not online help like podcasts or YouTube videos.
_____ 3. System software includes the operating system and utility programs.
_____ 4. A software suite is a group of programs bundled as a package.
_____ 5. When you buy software, you then own it and can do anything you'd like with it, including giving it to a friend to install on their machine.

1. **Picture Perfect**

   You just spent the summer volunteering in a remote village in Africa, and you have tons of pictures you want to share with friends and family. For your friends, it's easy to upload them into Facebook, but you don't want to give your family access to your Facebook account. Research different Web sites that you would consider using to upload your pictures to show your family. Create a table that lists the different services along with the pros and cons of each site. Discuss which services you would use and explain your reasoning.

2. **Software Help**

   Because your friends know you like technology, they always are coming to you for advice and help with their software. While you don't mind helping out your friends, there are some great Web sites that they also can go to. Create a presentation that explains the various ways they can get free help about all their software questions. Begin the presentation with a list of FAQs and hyperlink each question to the slide that contains the answer.

3. **Collaborating with Software**

   You have been assigned the dreaded group project. For once you have a great group of students to work with, but none of your schedules line up so you can meet in person. You decide to use Web-based applications because you have heard they are great for collaborating online. Research the differences between Google Docs and Microsoft Web Apps. Are there differences between the two products, such as getting accounts, working simultaneously, or reviewing the history of changes made to documents? Which would you recommend to your group to use for this project, and why?

4. **Choices, Choices**

   There are many word processing software options. Describe the decision process you would use to choose among a free Web-based word processing application, an open source word processing application, and a standard packaged application if you are:

   a. Traveling abroad for a semester, visiting 15 different cities, and not carrying a notebook with you
   b. Staying at home for the term and compiling a capstone report using several hundred researched sources of information
   c. Working with three people from other colleges on a joint paper that will be presented at a conference at the end of the term

5. **Using OneNote**

   You have been assigned a research paper, which will be very extensive. You are required to collect information for the paper throughout the semester, so you need a good system to keep your notes, readings, and data organized. You've heard OneNote is a great tool for just this type of project, but since you have never used the software, you do not know where to start. Go to Microsoft Online and search on "Templates for OneNote." Find several good templates that will help you get started. What are the features of the templates you chose? Discuss which template you would most likely use, and why.

### 1. Required Software for the Job

Almost every profession requires some use of technology and software. Identify the field you would like to enter upon graduation, and then after doing some research, compile a list of applications you expect to use in your job. If possible, list a proprietary application, as well as open source and Web-based alternatives. Note those applications for which you will need training. If your chosen field currently does not require software, discuss why that may be the case. Do you foresee a time when software may be helpful? If so, what kind of software might that be?

### 2. Read and Understand the EULA

Before anyone installs or downloads software they have to accept the end user license agreement (EULA). Most of us rarely take the time to read a license agreement, but often there is important information stored in the EULA that a user should know about. Find an end user license agreement for a software product that you use frequently (such as Facebook or iTunes) and read it. Look particularly at the privacy policies and the sharing features. Write a brief summary about the types of information contained in the EULA.

### 3. Tracking Your Personal Finances

You are finally out on your own—graduated from college and working your first job. It's time to track how much you spend versus what you are earning. You really don't want to live from paycheck to paycheck, and want to begin a savings plan to build a rainy-day fund. Investigate online financial planning sites such as Mint (**www.mint .com**) and Yodlee (**www.yodlee.com**) and then choose the one that seems best to you. If you can, download a version of the software for your smartphone. Track your expenses for a few weeks, and identify areas in which you can cut back on your spending. What are the features of the software that you like? Discuss how this may or may not help you in your goal of achieving financial independence.

### 4. Going Beyond PowerPoint

Your boss is tired of looking at presentations with the same designs and features and has asked you to research different presentation software packages. In particular, she has suggested you look into Prezi (**www.prezi.com**) and SlideRocket (**www .sliderocket.com**). Using one of these software applications (both have free trials), create a presentation that compares these two products to Microsoft PowerPoint, Apple Keynote, and OpenOffice.org Impress.

critical thinking questions

**Instructions:** Some ideas are best understood by experimenting with them in our own minds. The following critical thinking questions are designed to demand your full attention but require only a comfortable chair—no technology.

1. **Can You Reuse Software?**

   Several years ago you purchased Adobe Acrobat so you could make PDFs and edit and mark up PDFs. You have since changed computers, and your version of Acrobat is not compatible with the operating system on your new computer. You are required to purchase an upgrade of Adobe Acrobat to run on the new machine. Your sister wants to install the old version of Adobe Acrobat on her computer since you're not using it anymore. Do you think this will be legal to do? Why or why not?

2. **What's Your App?**

   Small applications are being developed every day for smartphones. If you have a smartphone, what applications are the most useful to you? If you do not, what kind of app do you think would be the most useful? Describe an app that is currently not available that would be your "killer app."

3. **Media Management**

   Less than a decade ago, most home users had few media files on their computer systems. Today, many users have a library of music, a collection of digitized movies, personal photo collections, and even a large set of recorded television shows. Examine three different software packages on the market today for managing these materials. What features do they need to make the PC the primary entertainment device for a home? What would make users move their PC from the office into the living room?

4. **Living on the Cloud**

   Cloud computing is becoming more popular, and many users are working from the cloud and not even realizing it. What kinds of software applications are you using that are completely Web-based? Why do you use them instead of installed software applications? Envision a time when all software is Web-based and describe how being totally on the cloud would be an advantage. Also list some of the disadvantages a cloud-based environment might present.

5. **Software Myths and Misconceptions**

   There are several myths and misconceptions about software, such as the 24-hour rule, the 80/20 rule, and the Abandonment rule. The 24-hour rule claims a person can download software for 24-hours, and then have the choice of deleting it or buying it. The 80/20 rule implies that for single-use licenses, a person can install software on both a work and home computer as long as work use is not more than 80 percent, and home use is not greater than 20 percent. The Abandonment rule claims that one can use software if it is no longer supported or created by a company that is no longer in business. Explain how you think each of these is a violation of copyright law.

team time

## Software for Startups

### Problem

You and your friends have decided to start Recycle Technology, a not-for-profit organization that would recycle and donate used computer equipment. In the first planning session, the group recognizes the need for certain software to help them with various parts of the business such as tracking inventory, designing notices, mapping addresses for pickup and delivery, and soliciting residents by phone or e-mail about recycling events, to name a few.

### Task

Split your class into as many groups of four or five as possible. Make some groups responsible for just locating free or Web-based software solutions, and other groups responsible for finding proprietary solutions. Another group could be responsible for finding mobile app solutions. The groups will present and compare results with each other at the end of the project.

### Process

1. Identify a team leader who will coordinate the project and record and present results.
2. Each team is to identify the various kinds of software that Recycle Technology needs. Consider software that will be needed for all the various tasks needed to run the organization such as communication, marketing, tracking, inventory management, and finance.
3. Create a detailed and organized list of required software applications. Depending on your team, you will specify either proprietary software or open source software.

### Conclusion

Most organizations require a variety of software to accomplish different tasks. Compare your results with those of other team members. Were there applications that you didn't think about, but that other members did? How expensive is it to ensure that even the smallest company has all the software required to carry out daily activities, or can the needs be met with free, open source products?

# Open Source Software

Ethical conduct is a stream of decisions you make all day long. In this exercise, you will research and then role-play a complicated ethical situation. The role you play might or might not match your own personal beliefs; in either case, your research and use of logic will enable you to represent the view assigned. An arbitrator will watch and comment on both sides of the arguments, and together the team will agree on an ethical solution.

## Problem

Proprietary software has set restrictions on use and can be very expensive; while open source software is freely available for users to use as is, or change, improve, and redistribute. Open source software has become acceptable as a cost-effective alternative to proprietary software, so much so that it is reported that the increased adoption of open source software has caused a drop in revenue to the proprietary software industry. But determining which software to use involves more than just reducing the IT budget.

## Research Areas to Consider

- Open source software (Linux, OpenOffice.org suite, and Mozilla.org)
- Proprietary software (Microsoft Windows and Office, Apple Mac OS X and iWork)
- Copyright licensing
- Open source development

## Process

1. Divide the class into teams.
2. Research the areas cited above and devise a scenario in which someone is a proponent for open source software but is being rebuffed by someone who feels "you get what you pay for" and is a big proponent of using proprietary software.
3. Team members should write a summary that provides background information for their character—for example: open source proponent, proprietary developer, or arbitrator—and details their character's behaviors to set the stage for the role-playing event. Then, team members should create an outline to use during the role-playing event.
4. Team members should arrange a mutually convenient time to meet for the exchange, either using the collaboration features of MyITLab, the discussion board feature of Blackboard, or meeting in person.
5. Team members should present their case to the class, or submit a PowerPoint presentation for review by the rest of the class, along with the summary and resolution they developed.

## Conclusion

As technology becomes ever more prevalent and integrated into our lives, more and more ethical dilemmas will present themselves. Being able to understand and evaluate both sides of the argument, while responding in a personally or socially ethical manner, will be an important skill.

# chapter 8

# using system software

## the operating system, utility programs, and file management

### Operating System Fundamentals

**OBJECTIVES:**

What software is included in system software? *(p. 250)*

What are the different kinds of operating systems? *(p. 251)*

What are the most common operating systems? *(p. 251)*

 Ferenc Szelepcsenyi / Shutterstock.com

### What the Operating System Does

**OBJECTIVES:**

How does the operating system provide a means for users to interact with the computer? *(p. 256)*

How does the operating system help manage resources such as the processor, memory, storage, hardware, and peripheral devices? *(p. 258)*

How does the operating system interact with application software? *(p. 262)*

 **Active Helpdesk:** Managing Hardware and Peripheral Devices: The OS

Ivancovlad / Shutterstock.com

### The Boot Process: Starting Your Computer

**OBJECTIVE:**

How does the operating system help the computer start up? *(p. 263)*

 **Active Helpdesk:** Starting the Computer: The Boot Process

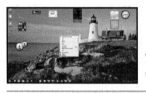

### The Desktop and Window Features

**OBJECTIVE:**

What are the main desktop and window features? *(p. 266)*

 Sound Byte: Customizing Windows

Stanislav Popov / Shutterstock.com

### Organizing Your Computer: File Management

**OBJECTIVES:**

How does the operating system help me keep my computer organized? *(p. 268)*

 **Active Helpdesk:** Organizing Your Computer: File Management

 Sound Byte: File Management

Infoimages / Shutterstock.com; Tuomas Kujansuu / iStockphoto.com

 Windows 7

### Utility Programs

**OBJECTIVE:**

What utility programs are included in system software, and what do they do? *(p. 275)*

 **Active Helpdesk:** Using Utility Programs

 Sound Byte: File Compression
Sound Byte: Hard Disk Anatomy Interactive
Sound Byte: Letting Your Computer Clean Up After Itself

*Scan here for more info on How Cool Is This?*

# how cool is *this?*

Have you ever wanted to capture what appears on your **monitor screen**? You can use the PrtScn (print screen) key on your keyboard, but that captures only the active window, and only onto the clipboard. You then need to crop and save the file for that **screen capture** to be useful. There are also screen capture software programs that you can purchase. However, Windows 7 includes the **Snipping Tool**, and Mac OS has **Grab**

to capture an entire screen image or to "grab" a free-form or rectangular "snip" of any window or object on the screen. Once captured, you can use the Snipping Tool or Grab to **annotate**, save, or **share** the object. In Windows 7, you can find the Snipping Tool by clicking the Start button, selecting All Programs, and then opening the Accessories folder. In Mac OS, Grab is found in Utilities. For more features, try **Jing** (**www .techsmith.com/jing**), a freeware tool from Tech-Smith. Jing not only captures still screen shots, but

siloto/Shutterstock.com

also records video of on-screen action. You can share Jing files over the Web, via instant messaging, or by e-mail.

# System Software Basics

As you learned in the previous chapter, there are two basic types of software on your computer: application software and system software. **Application software** is the software you use to do everyday tasks at home and at work. **System software** is the set of programs that helps run the computer and coordinates instructions between application software and the computer's hardware devices. From the moment you turn on your computer to the time you shut it down, you are interacting with system software. System software consists of two primary types of programs: the operating system and utility programs.

**What does system software do?** System software manages the computer's resources. The **operating system (OS)** component of system software is a group of programs that controls how your computer system functions. The OS manages the computer's hardware, including the processor (also called the *central processing unit*, or *CPU*), memory, and storage devices, as well as peripheral devices such as the monitor and printer. The OS also provides a consistent means for software applications to work with the CPU, and it is responsible for the management, scheduling, and coordination of tasks as well as system maintenance. Your first interaction with the OS is the **user interface**—the features of the program such as the desktop, icons, and menus that allow the user to communicate with the computer system.

System software also includes utility programs. A **utility program** is a small program that performs many of the general housekeeping tasks for the computer, such as system maintenance and file compression.

**Do all computers have operating systems?** Every computer, from the smallest notebook to the largest supercomputer, has an operating system. Even cell phones, game consoles, automobiles, and some appliances have operating systems. The role of the OS is critical; the computer cannot operate without it. As explained more fully in the section of this chapter titled "What the Operating System Does," the operating system coordinates the flow of data and information through the computer system by coordinating the hardware, software, user interface, processor, and system memory.

**Are all operating systems alike?** Although most computer users can name only a few operating systems, many types exist. Some operating systems, such as those found in household appliances and car engines, are embedded in the device and don't require any user intervention at all. Some are proprietary systems developed specifically for the devices they manage. Some operating systems are available for personal and business use to run on personal computers or mobile devices (see Figure 8.1), and other operating systems coordinate resources for many users on a network. These operating systems were traditionally classified into categories, depending on the number of users they served (single user or multiple users) and the tasks they performed (single task or multitasks). However, as devices begin to converge in their functionalities, and the operating systems continue to become more powerful, the distinction in the traditional categorization of operating systems begins to blur.

For example, personal computers were at one time run by single-task, single-user operating systems such as the **Microsoft Disk Operating System (MS-DOS)**. MS-DOS (or DOS) was

**Figure** 8.1

Different operating systems are found on personal computers and mobile devices.

the first widely installed operating system in personal computers. Compared to the operating systems we are familiar with today, DOS was a highly user-unfriendly OS. To use it, you needed to type specific commands, and didn't have the option to click on **icons** (pictures that represent an object such as a software application or a file or folder) or choose from a **menu** or list of commands.

Eventually, operating systems such as Apple's Mac OS and Microsoft's Windows replaced DOS because these systems allowed a single user to **multitask**, that is, to perform more than one process at a time. (The Mac and Windows operating systems are discussed in more detail later in this chapter.)

Then, networking capabilities were added to these personal computer operating systems to facilitate sharing peripheral devices and Internet access among multiple computers at home. These systems, although still traditionally used as single-user, multitask operating systems, technically became multiuser, multitask operating systems because of their networking capabilities. Similar transitions are happening with mobile devices, as cell phones and PDAs (personal digital assistants) converge to smartphones and incorporate the functionalities of cameras and personal media players. Although smartphones were initially single-task devices, with combined functionalities, the newer devices are beginning to add multitasking capabilities.

In the next section, we will look at different types of operating systems that work with a variety of computers.

## Types of Operating Systems

Operating systems can be categorized by the type of device in which they are installed, such as robots and specialized equipment with built-in computers, mainframes and network computers, mobile devices, and personal computers.

### Real-Time Operating Systems

**Why do machines with built-in computers need an operating system?** Machinery that is required to perform a repetitive series of specific tasks in an exact amount of time requires a **real-time operating system (RTOS)**. Real-time operating systems, also referred to as *embedded systems*, require minimal user interaction. This type of operating system is a program with a specific purpose, and it must guarantee certain response times for particular computing tasks; otherwise, the machine is useless. The programs are written specifically for the needs of the devices and their functions. Therefore, there are no commercially available standard RTOS software programs. Devices that must perform regimented tasks or record precise results—such as measurement instruments found in the scientific, defense, and aerospace industries—require real-time operating systems. Examples include digital storage oscilloscopes and the Mars Reconnaissance Orbiter.

**Where else are RTOSs in use today?** You also encounter real-time operating systems in everyday life. They are in devices such as fuel-injection systems in car engines, automobile "infotainment" systems, inkjet printers, VoIP phones, and some medical devices, as well as some common appliances. Real-time operating systems are also found in many types of robotic equipment. Television stations use robotic cameras with real-time operating systems that glide across a suspended cable system to record sports events from many angles (see Figure 8.2).

**What kind of operating system controls a simple cell phone?** Unlike smartphones, simple cell phones are single-function devices; they only require operating systems that perform one task at a time. These devices generally have **firmware**, instructions permanently installed onto computer chips. Some firmware can be updated by connecting the device to the computer and downloading an upgrade from the manufacturer's Web site. Other devices, such as portable audio players, digital cameras, and gaming consoles, also use firmware.

### Operating Systems for Networks, Servers, and Mainframes

**What kind of operating system do networks use?** A **multiuser operating system** (also known as a **network operating system**) enables more than one user to access the computer system at one time by efficiently handling and prioritizing requests from multiple users. Networks (groups of computers connected to each other for the purposes of communicating and sharing resources) require a multiuser operating

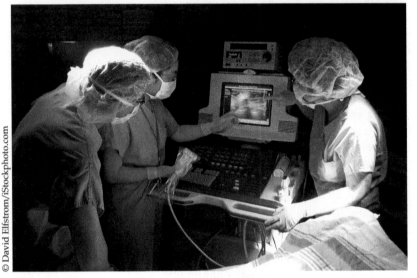

**Figure** 8.2

Devices such as TV sky cameras, cars, and medical equipment use real-time operating systems.

**What is UNIX?** UNIX is a multiuser, multitask operating system used as a network operating system, primarily with mainframes, although it is also often found on PCs. Developed in 1969 by Ken Thompson and Dennis Ritchie of AT&T's Bell Labs, the UNIX code was initially not proprietary—in other words, no company owned it. Rather, any programmer was allowed to use the code and modify it to meet his or her needs. Later, AT&T licensed the UNIX program code to the Santa Cruz Operation Group. UNIX is a brand that belongs to the company The Open Group, but any vendor that meets testing requirements and pays a fee can use the UNIX name. Individual vendors then modify the UNIX code to run specifically on their hardware. HP/UX from Hewlett-Packard, Oracle Solaris from Oracle Corporation, and AIX from IBM are some of the UNIX systems currently available in the marketplace.

**What other kinds of computers require a multiuser operating system?** Large corporations with hundreds or thousands of employees often use powerful computers known as *mainframes*. A **mainframe** is responsible for storing, managing, and simultaneously processing data from all users. Mainframe operating systems fall into the multiuser category. Examples include UNIX and IBM's IBM i and z/OS.

Supercomputers also use multiuser operating systems. Scientists and engineers use supercomputers to solve complex problems or to perform massive computations. Some supercomputers are single computers with multiple processors, whereas others consist of multiple computers that work together.

### Operating Systems for Mobile Devices

**What kind of operating system does a smartphone use?** A **smartphone** does more than let the user make and answer phone calls. It also has productivity, media player, and camera features, as well as Web connectivity. Examples of smartphones include BlackBerry devices, Apple iPhone, HTC Thunderbolt, and Palm Pre. The most common operating systems that can be found on smartphones include Symbian by Nokia, BlackBerry by RIM, Windows Mobile by Microsoft, iPhone iOS by Apple, Android by Google, and webOS by Palm.

system because many users simultaneously access the **server**, which is the computer on a network that manages network resources such as printers.

The latest versions of Microsoft Windows and Mac OS X can be considered network operating systems; they enable users to set up basic networks for use in homes and small businesses. (A more complete discussion of Microsoft Windows and Mac OS can be found in the "Operating Systems for Personal Computers" section.) In larger networks, a more robust network operating system is installed on the server and manages all user requests, ensuring they do not interfere with each other. For example, on a network where users share a printer, the network would ensure the printer produces only one document at a time in the order in which the requests are made. The OS is therefore responsible for managing all the printer requests and making sure they are processed one at a time. Examples of network operating systems include Windows Server, Linux, and UNIX.

Initially, although multifunctional, smartphones were only capable of doing one task at a time. Now most modern smartphones have modest multitasking capabilities such as checking e-mail while on a phone call. Some, such as the iPhones on the AT&T network, provide greater multitasking and allow a user to talk while surfing the Web or using apps at the same time.

**Do gaming consoles and personal media players require an operating system?** Gaming systems, like Microsoft's Xbox 360, the Nintendo Wii, and the Sony PlayStation (see Figure 8.3), as well as personal media players like Microsoft's Zune and Apple's iPod, all require some form of customized system software that is developed specifically for the particular device. The system software includes system programs that control the device, as well as other programs that come with the personal media player or the gaming device. For example, the programs included with most portable media players allow users to manage music files on the player and to rip audio CDs. The operating systems on gaming consoles support Web browsing and file storage of media and photos as well as playing DVDs and games.

Florea Marius Catalin/iStockphoto.com

Lee Pettet/iStockphoto.com

**Figure 8.3**

Gaming devices such as the Nintendo Wii and PlayStation 3 have their own system software.

## Operating Systems for Personal Computers

**What is the Microsoft Windows operating system?** Microsoft **Windows** began as an operating environment that worked with MS-DOS and incorporated a user-friendly interface like the one that was first introduced with Apple's operating system. In 1995, Microsoft released Windows 95, a comprehensive update that made changes to the user interface and incorporated multi-tasking capabilities. Windows XP was another major update; it provided networking capabilities in its consumer editions. The newest release of Microsoft's operating system, **Windows 7**, follows Windows Vista, and builds on the security and user interface upgrades that

the Windows Vista release provided. It also gives users with touch-screen monitors the ability to use touch commands to scroll, resize windows, pan, and zoom. What was once an operating system on which only one user could perform one task at a time is now a more robust operating system that can support home networking tasks. Over time, Windows improvements have concentrated on increasing user functionality and friendliness, improving Internet capabilities, and enhancing file privacy and security.

**What is the difference between the various editions of Windows 7 operating systems?** With each new version of its operating system, Microsoft continues to make improvements. However, it's still not a one-size-fits-all operating system. Windows 7 comes in several editions to accommodate different users. Those that are available for home users are Starter and Home Premium. Windows 7 Professional can be used by the home user, but is targeted toward small-business users. Windows 7 Ultimate is a full-featured operating system intended for businesses, but is available to home users as well. In addition, there are 32-bit and 64-bit versions of Windows. The 32-bit version is built for computers that have up to 4 GB of RAM. For those systems with more than 4 GB of RAM, a 64-bit version is required. Figure 8.4 outlines the features and benefits of each edition of Windows 7.

**What is the Mac Operating System?** In 1984, **Mac OS** became the first commercially available operating system to incorporate a graphical user interface (GUI) with user-friendly point-and-click technology.

**Does it matter what operating system is on my computer?** The type of processor in the computer determines which operating system a particular personal computer uses. The combination of operating system and processor is referred to as a computer's **platform**. For example, Microsoft Windows operating systems are designed to coordinate with a series of

**Figure 8.4** | WINDOWS 7 EDITIONS

| Edition | Description |
|---|---|
| Windows 7 Starter | This edition is designed to run on small netbooks and is for those users who have basic computing requirements. There is no Aero interface, and only 32-bit versions are available. |
| Windows 7 Home Premium | This edition incorporates multimedia functions as core components. No extra software is needed to run DVDs and other audio and video files. Networking as well as file and peripheral sharing across PCs are included. |
| Windows 7 Professional | As its name implies, this edition is aimed at the business market but is also appropriate for the advanced home user. This edition builds on Windows 7 Home Premium and features advanced networking capabilities. |
| Windows 7 Ultimate | This is the "ultimate" operating system for high-end PC users, gamers, multimedia professionals, and PC enthusiasts. |

processors from Intel Corporation and Advanced Micro Devices (AMD), which share the same or similar sets of instructions. Originally, the Macintosh operating systems worked primarily with PowerPC processors from the Motorola Corporation and IBM, which were designed specifically for Apple computers. However, in 2006, Apple discontinued the use of PowerPC processors, and now uses Intel processors.

Most application software is also operating system dependent. For example, there are special Mac versions of Microsoft Office, Adobe Photoshop Elements, Intuit Quicken, and other "traditional" PC software applications.

**Can I have more than one operating system on my computer?** Some Mac users may want to have both Mac OS X and Windows on their machines. Or, you might want to test drive the newest operating system on your computer without uninstalling the previous version before you commit to an upgrade. Or perhaps you would like to have a Linux distribution to work with, in addition to your Windows operating system. The generous size of today's hard drives, as well as some additional software capabilities, enables users to run multiple operating systems on a single machine. A standard utility included in Mac OS X called Boot Camp allows you to boot into either Windows or OS X. But, if you want to run both Mac OS X and Windows operating systems at the same time, you could create virtual drives using virtualization software such as Parallels or VMware Fusion.

**What are Web-based operating systems?** Now that broadband Internet access and providing computer resources via the Internet (cloud computing) are becoming more commonplace, prototypes for Web-based operating systems are being developed. Actually, the terms *Web-based operating environment* and *portable or Web desktop* might be more accurate, because one still needs a computer, operating system, and Web browser to access a Web-based OS. The concept behind this movement is to enable complete portability of a user's computer experience.

Currently, most applications and files we use have been installed and saved on a specific computer and can be used only on that computer. A Web-based operating environment would allow users to access applications and content via the Web, regardless of the machine they are using. This means you would not need to lug your notebook computer everywhere you go. Instead, you would only need to find a computer that had Internet access to be able to have all of your applications and documents ready for you to resume work. Currently you could cobble together a similar experience by accessing Google Docs, Yahoo! Mail, and Dropbox, but with far less efficiency because that requires managing several different accounts and logins. A Web-based OS would enable you to have access to all of your settings and preferences, even a customized desktop image, as well as working documents, stored in an individual Web-based account for you to access anywhere and on any machine at any time.

Google is taking steps toward developing a complete Web-based system. Its Google Docs application and Chrome browser are the initial components of a completely Web-based operating environment. Another innovator in the Web desktop field is the open source product eyeOS (**www.eyeos.org**).

**SOUND BYTE**

**Customizing Windows**

In this Sound Byte, you'll find out how to customize your desktop. You'll learn how to configure the desktop, set up a screen saver, change pointer options, customize the Start menu, and manage user accounts.

## Upgrading Your Operating System

If you have had your computer for a year or two, you may be faced with the decision of whether to upgrade to the newest release version of your operating system (such as going from Windows Vista to Windows 7). Here are a few key things to consider before taking the plunge:

- **Is your current operating system still supported?** When it deploys new versions of operating systems, the company may stop supporting older versions. If your current version will no longer be supported, it's best to upgrade to a newer version.

- **Are there significant features in the new version that you want?** Operating systems are often upgraded to provide extra security, better performance, and additional features that are intended to make your computer experience more efficient, and perhaps even more fun. But, if the only features the new version offers are ones you don't need or can live without, you should reconsider upgrading.

- **Will your hardware work with the new OS?** Check the minimum operating requirements (required RAM, processor speed, hard drive space, etc.) of the new version to ensure that your computer can handle the workload of the new software. You will also need to

make sure drivers for the new OS are available for all your hardware devices and peripherals to ensure they will work properly with the new OS. Microsoft has made this easy with Windows Upgrade Advisor, which you can download from Microsoft's Web site. The Upgrade Advisor scans your hardware, devices, and installed programs for compatibility, advises you on how to resolve any issues found, and recommends what you should do before upgrading.

- **Is your application software compatible with the new version of the OS?** Usually, application software works fine with a new version of an OS. Sometimes it doesn't. Check with the software vendors regarding compatibility, especially if you're upgrading to a 64-bit system. Although Windows 7 has a compatibility feature that allows you to run some software in an earlier version of the operating system if it is not compatible with Windows 7, it doesn't work with all older file formats.

Before starting the upgrade, you should back up all your data files so you won't lose anything accidentally during the upgrading process. Backup and Restore in Windows makes this job less of a hassle.

---

**What is Linux?** Linux is an open source operating system designed for use on personal computers and as a network operating system. Open source software is freely available for anyone to use or modify as they wish. The Linux operating system is based on the central programming code of an operating system, and the rest of the code is from the GNU (pronounced "g-noo") Project and other sources. Linux began in 1991 as a part-time project of Finnish university student Linus Torvalds, who wanted to create a free OS to run on his home computer. He posted his OS code to the Web for others to use and modify. It has since been tweaked by scores of programmers as part of the Free Software Foundation GNU Project (**www.gnu.org**).

Linux has a reputation as a stable OS that is not subject to crashes or failures. Because the code is open and available to anyone, Linux can be modified or updated quickly by hundreds of other programmers around the world to meet virtually any new operating system need. For example, only a few weeks were necessary

to get the Linux OS ready for the Intel Xeon processor, a feat unheard of in proprietary OS development. Some Linux-based operating systems have been modified to run on iPods and gaming systems. Linux is also gaining popularity among computer manufacturers, which have begun to ship it with some of their latest PCs.

**Where else is Linux used?** Android, the new operating system developed by Google, is Linux-based. Because the overall size of Android is much smaller than that of Windows, many netbook users choose to use it in place of the factory-installed Windows operating system (see Figure 8.5). It is also popular on smartphones. Another Linux-based newcomer to the OS market is MeeGo, a joint project between Nokia and Intel, which is designed for smartphones, netbooks, and entry-level personal computers.

**Where can I get Linux?** You can download open source versions of Linux for free from Linux distributors such as Mandriva, Ubuntu, Fedora, Suse, Debian GNU/Linux, and Gentoo Linux. However,

© Oleksiy Maksymenko Photography/Alamy

**Figure 8.5**

Developed by Google, the Android operating system is based on Linux and runs easily on netbooks.

Proprietary software such as Microsoft Windows and Mac OS is developed by corporations and sold for profit. This means that the **source code**, the actual lines of instructional code that make the program work, is not accessible to the general public. Without being able to access the source code, it's difficult for a user to modify the software or see exactly how the program author constructed various parts of the system.

Restricting access to the source code protects companies from having their programming ideas stolen, and it prevents customers from using modified versions of the software. However, in the late 1980s, computer specialists became concerned that large software companies (such as Microsoft) were controlling a large portion of market share and driving out competitors. They also felt that proprietary software was too expensive and contained too many bugs (errors).

These people felt that software should be developed without a profit motive and distributed with its source code free for all to see. The theory was that if many computer specialists examined, improved, and changed the source code, a more full-featured, bug-free product would result. Hence, the open source movement was born.

So, if an operating system such as Linux is free and relatively bug-free, why does Windows, which users must pay for, have such a huge market share, and why does Linux have less than 1 percent of the desktop market? One reason is that corporations and individuals have grown accustomed to one thing that proprietary software makers can provide: technical support. It is almost impossible to provide technical support for open source software because anyone can freely modify it; thus, there is no specific developer to take responsibility for technical support. Similarly, corporations have been reluctant to install open source software extensively because of the cost of the internal staff of programmers that must support it.

Companies such as Red Hat, Ubuntu, and Xandros have been combating this problem. Red Hat offers a free, open source operating system called Fedora (see Figure 8.6). In addition, Red Hat has modified the original Linux source code and markets a version, Red Hat Enterprise Linux, as a proprietary program. Fedora is the testing ground for what eventually goes into this proprietary program. Red Hat Enterprise Linux 6 is the current system on the market, and comes in versions for servers and desktops. Purchasers of Red Hat Enterprise Linux receive a warranty and technical support. Packaging open source software in this manner has made its use much more attractive to businesses. As a result, many Web servers are hosted on computers running Linux.

**Figure 8.6**

Companies like Red Hat provide free or low-cost Linux software, such as Fedora, but technical support is not often available.

several versions of Linux are more proprietary in nature and must be purchased. These versions come with support and other features that are not generally associated with the open source Linux. Red Hat has been packaging and selling versions of Linux since 1994 and is probably the best-known Linux distributor. For a full listing and explanation of all Linux distributors, visit DistroWatch (**www.distrowatch.com**).

## What the Operating System Does

As shown in Figure 8.7, the operating system is like an orchestra's conductor. It coordinates and directs the flow of data and information through the computer system.

In doing so, the OS performs several specific functions:

- It provides a way for the user to interact with the computer.
- It manages the processor, or CPU.
- It manages the memory and storage.
- It manages the computer system's hardware and peripheral devices.
- It provides a consistent means for software applications to work with the CPU.

In this section, we look at each of these functions in detail.

### The User Interface

**How does the operating system control how I interact with my computer?** The operating system provides a user interface that enables you to interact with the computer. As noted earlier, the first personal computers had a DOS operating system with a command-driven interface, as shown in Figure 8.8a. A **command-driven interface** is one in which you enter commands to communicate with the computer system. The DOS commands were not always easy to understand; as a result, the interface proved to be too complicated for the average user. Therefore, PCs were used primarily in business and by professional computer operators.

The command-driven interface was later improved by incorporating a menu-driven interface, as shown in Figure 8.8b. A **menu-driven interface** is one in which you choose commands from menus displayed on the screen. Menu-driven interfaces eliminated the need for users to know every command because they could select most of the commonly used commands from a menu. However, they were still not easy enough for most people to use.

**What kind of interface do operating systems use today?** Current personal computer operating systems such as Microsoft Windows and Mac OS use a **graphical user interface**, or **GUI** (pronounced "gooey"). Unlike command- and menu-driven interfaces, GUIs display graphics and use the point-and-click technology of the mouse and cursor, making them much more user-friendly.

Linux-based operating systems do not have a single default GUI interface. Instead, users are free to choose among many commercially available and free interfaces, such as GNOME and KDE, each of which provides a different look and feel. For example, GNOME (pronounced "gah-NOHM") actually allows you to select which interface (Windows or Mac) you'd like your system to have. This means that if you're using Linux for the first time, you don't have to learn a new interface; you just use the one you're most comfortable with.

**Figure 8.7**
The operating system is the orchestra conductor of your computer, coordinating its many activities and devices.

Manages computer hardware and peripherals

Provides a user interface

The Operating System

Provides a consistent interaction between applications and CPU

Manages memory and storage

Manages the processor

**Figure 8.8**

(a) A command-driven interface. (b) A menu-driven interface.

## Sugar: The Sweet OS for Every Child

The Internet is a fantastic tool, but only if you can access it. In an effort to give children in developing countries a better opportunity to "learn, share, and create," the One Laptop per Child (OLPC) initiative was founded by Nicholas Negroponte and other faculty from MIT Media Lab, in conjunction with partners such as Google, AMD, and News Corporation. The mission of OLPC (**www.laptop .org**) is to ensure that all school-aged children in lesser-developed communities receive their own personal computers so that they are no longer excluded from the educational, economic, and entertainment benefits that computers can provide. Laptops have been distributed to over 2 million children worldwide. Most of the users are in Latin America and Africa, in countries such as Uruguay, Peru, Mongolia, Nigeria, Ethiopia, and Rwanda. Uruguay, for example, is the first major country in the world that is using the OLPC program to provide laptops to every elementary school child.

This ambitious project to develop and distribute a low-cost notebook computer (currently, the cost is $199) would provide access to electronic textbooks and other learning aids—and eventually the Internet. The main thrust of the project is to overcome the so-called digital divide (the gap between people who have access to computers and those who don't) and provide computing resources to everyone regardless of their financial means.

Courtesy of One Laptop Per Child

### Figure 8.9

The XO can be easily converted from a traditional notebook to an e-book reader. A new tablet-like device, the XO-3, is currently being developed, and is scheduled for release in 2012.

The notebook itself is revolutionary in design (see Figure 8.9). Called the XO (the latest version is XO-1.5), the notebook is small and has a comfortable, child-sized, built-in handle. It also has a tablet-like monitor that can twist to turn the notebook into an electronic book (e-book) reader, which is critical in areas where books are hard to come by. The outside of the notebook is rugged and child-friendly. In addition, it is power efficient, running on less than one-tenth the power a standard notebook requires. Because access to electricity is minimal in many of the project's target areas, the notebook is self-powered by an easy-to-use pull string.

At the core of the XO laptop is Sugar, the operating system. It is based on open source code components from Red Hat's Fedora version of the Linux operating system, but has a user interface that is completely different from Windows, Mac OS, or Linux. The developers really thought about how the users of the notebook would interact with the device. The OLPC notebooks will most likely be the first computer that many of these children use, and so the user interface was designed to be as intuitive as possible.

The operating system focuses on activities rather than on applications. When the machine powers up, the first image is that of the XO man (an O on top of an X) in the middle of a circle. It is surrounded by icons that represent home, friends, and neighborhood. The computer

## Processor Management

**Why does the operating system need to manage the processor?** When you use your computer, you are usually asking the CPU to perform several tasks at once. For example, you might be printing a Word document, chatting with your friends on Facebook, watching a movie using the Blu-ray drive, and working on an Excel spreadsheet—all at the same time, or at least what appears to be at the same time. Although the processor is the powerful brain of the computer, processing all of its instructions and performing all of its calculations, it needs the OS to arrange for the execution of all these activities in a systematic way, creating the appearance that everything is happening simultaneously.

To do so, the operating system assigns a slice of its time to each activity that requires the processor's attention. The OS must then switch among different processes millions of times a second to make it appear that everything is happening seamlessly. Otherwise, you wouldn't be able to watch a movie and print at the same time without experiencing delays in the process.

**How exactly does the operating system coordinate all the activities?** When you create and print a document in Word while also watching a Blu-ray movie, for example, many different devices in the computer system are involved, including your keyboard, mouse, Blu-ray drive, and printer. Every keystroke, every mouse click, and each signal to the printer and from the includes a built-in microphone and webcam for children to create their own multimedia. For example, the multimedia tool allows children to add music to their drawings. Other activities include browsing the Internet, chatting, text editing, and playing games. At the core of each activity is the ability to collaborate, which facilitates the community learning experience. To enhance collaboration, the notebooks are all interconnected in a wireless mesh network, providing the potential for every activity to be a networked activity. Browsing, for example, would no longer be an isolated, individual activity; it could also be a collaborative group experience (see Figure 8.10a). Wireless capabilities also help extend the community beyond its physical borders. These computers make it possible for a child in Africa, for example, to connect with another child in Latin America.

In addition, the operating system uses a journaling technique for arranging and organizing files (see Figure 8.10b). The file system records what the child has done (rather than just what the student has saved), working as a scrapbook of the student's interactions with the computer as well as with peers. The journal can be tagged, searched, and sorted in a variety of ways.

Another general concept behind the operating system is that children learn through doing, so the software puts an emphasis on tools for exploration and expression, as well as encouraging students to learn by helping each other. Because Sugar is built on an open source platform, it also encourages students to explore how it works and to modify the code to meet their individual preferences.

The OLPC is not the only organization interested in increasing the reach of technology to those in less-developed nations. Intel has gone forward with its own program and produced the Classmate PC. Although the Classmate PC is more closely aligned with the traditional Windows-based PC model—it runs on either Windows or the open source OS Mandriva Discovery 2007 (a version of Linux)—it offers some of the

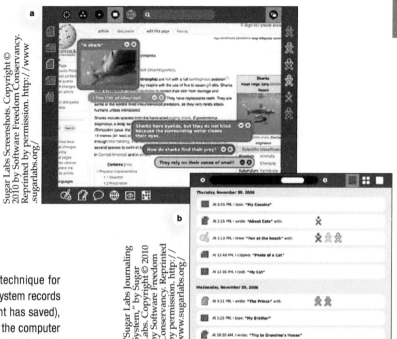

**Figure** 8.10

(a) One student shares a browsing experience with several others.
(b) The journaling system chronicles what the student saves as well as the student's interaction with the machine and with others.

same user-friendly hardware features as the XO machine does, such as the swivel monitor that converts to a tablet PC. Some reviewers and followers of both projects have offered the opinion that the Classmate PC is better suited for the older student user, whereas the XO laptop is geared toward a younger, less sophisticated user. With so many children waiting to be exposed to technology and to a more fun and intuitive learning process, there is most likely room in the market for both machines.

Blu-ray drive creates an action, or **event**, in the respective device (keyboard, mouse, Blu-ray drive, or printer) to which the operating system responds.

Sometimes these events occur sequentially (such as when you type characters one at a time), but other events involve two or more devices working concurrently (such as the printer printing while you continue to type and watch a movie). Although it looks as though all the devices are working at the same time, in fact, the OS switches back and forth among processes, controlling the timing of events the processor works on.

For example, assume you are typing and want to print a document. When you tell your computer to print your document, the printer generates a unique signal

called an **interrupt** that tells the operating system that it is in need of immediate attention. Every device has its own type of interrupt, which is associated with an **interrupt handler**, a special numerical code that prioritizes the requests. These requests are placed in the interrupt table in the computer's primary memory (random access memory, or RAM). The operating system processes the task assigned a higher priority before processing a task that has been assigned a lower priority. This is called **preemptive multitasking**.

In our example, when it receives the interrupt from the printer, the operating system suspends the CPU's typing activity and Blu-ray activity, and puts a "memo" in a special location in RAM called a *stack*.

The memo is a reminder of what the CPU was doing before it started to work on the printer request. The CPU then retrieves the printer request from the interrupt table and begins to process it. On completion of the printer request, the CPU goes back to the stack, retrieves the memo it placed about the keystroke or Blu-ray activity, and returns to that task until it is interrupted again, in a very quick and seamless fashion.

**What happens if there is more than one document waiting to be printed?** The operating system also coordinates multiple activities for peripheral devices such as printers. When the processor receives a request to send information to the printer, it first checks with the operating system to ensure that the printer is not already in use. If it is, the OS puts the request in another temporary storage area in RAM, called the *buffer*. The request then waits in the buffer until the **spooler**, a program that helps coordinate all print jobs currently being sent to the printer, indicates the printer is available. If more than one print job is waiting, a line (or *queue*) is formed so that the printer can process the requests in order.

### Memory and Storage Management

**Why does the operating system have to manage the computer's memory?** As the operating system coordinates the activities of the processor, it uses RAM as a temporary storage area for instructions and data the processor needs. The processor then accesses these instructions and data from RAM when it is ready to process them. The OS is therefore responsible for coordinating the space allocations in RAM to ensure that there is enough space for all of the pending instructions and data. It then clears the items from RAM when the processor no longer needs them.

**Does the amount of RAM on a system control the type of OS I get?** Until recently, the maximum amount of RAM found on most personal computers was 4 GB. That was considered a lot! Now, many personal computer systems that are reasonably priced provide for 8 GB or more of RAM. Systems that offer more than 4 GB of RAM require a 64-bit version of Windows. Although there are other factors involved in determining what operating system you get, determining the bit-version is important. At the moment, not all ap-

plications and devices are compatible with 64-bit systems. If you purchase a 64-bit system, you will need to make sure that all your hardware and software programs are updated to work well with the 64-bit version of your operating system. To assist you in this process, Micro-soft has created the Windows 7 Upgrade Advisor. This downloadable free program checks to determine whether your computer is compatible in all respects with Windows 7, including the 64-bit compatibility. If there is incompatibility, Windows 7 allows you the option of running in a compatibility mode to emulate a 32-bit system.

**Can my system ever run out of RAM?** RAM has limited capacity. Like most users, over time you will expand how you use your computer by adding new software and new peripherals. Most computers sold for home use have between 2 and 12 GB of RAM. If you have an older system with 1 or 2 GB of RAM, it might be sufficient if you're running a few programs at the same time. But, if you start installing and using software with greater RAM requirements, your system might not respond well. For example, if you want to upgrade to Windows 7, the minimum requirement for the operating system using minimal capabilities is 1 GB of RAM. Such limited RAM requirements are fine if you are using a netbook that is running Windows 7 Starter edition. However, most other systems that run more robust editions of Windows 7 may be challenged if they have only 1 GB of RAM, especially if you run graphic-intensive programs such as Adobe Photoshop, many gaming applications, or even the latest version of Microsoft Office. If you want to incorporate the translucent Aero user interface themes that are available in some versions of Windows 7, your system should have at least 2 GB of RAM and a video card with at least 256 MB of RAM. As you add and upgrade software and increase your usage of the computer system, you will likely find that the amount of RAM you once found to be sufficient is no longer enough.

**What happens if my computer runs out of RAM?** When there isn't enough RAM for the operating system to store the required data and instructions, the operating system borrows from the more spacious hard drive. This process of optimizing RAM storage by borrowing hard drive space is called **virtual memory**. As shown in Figure 8.11, when more RAM is needed, the operating system swaps out from RAM the data or instructions that have not been recently used and moves them to a temporary storage area on the hard drive called the **swap file** (or **page file**). If the data or instructions in the swap file are needed later, the operating system swaps them back into active RAM and replaces them in the hard drive's swap file with less active data or instructions. This process of swapping is known as **paging**.

**Can I ever run out of virtual memory?** Only a portion of the hard drive is allocated to virtual memory. You can manually change this setting to increase the amount of hard drive space allocated, but eventually your computer system will become sluggish as it is forced to page more and more often. This condition of excessive paging is called **thrashing**. The solution to this problem is to increase the amount of RAM in your system so that it will not be necessary for it to send data and instructions to virtual memory.

**How does the operating system manage storage?** If it weren't for the operating system, the files and applications you save to the hard drive and other storage locations would be an unorganized mess. Fortunately, the OS has a file-management system that keeps track of the name and location of each file you save and the programs you install. We will talk more about file management later in this chapter.

### Hardware and Peripheral Device Management

**How does the operating system manage the hardware and peripheral devices?** Each device attached to your computer comes with a special program called a **device driver** that facilitates communication between the hardware device and the operating system. Because the OS must be able to communicate with every device in the computer system, the device driver translates the device's specialized commands into commands that the operating system can understand, and vice versa. Devices would not function without the proper device drivers because the OS would not know how to communicate with them.

**Do I always need to install drivers?** Today, most devices, such as flash drives, mice, keyboards, and many digital cameras, come with the driver already installed in Windows. The devices whose drivers are included in Windows are called Plug and Play devices. **Plug and Play (PnP)** is a software and hardware standard designed to facilitate the installation of new hardware in PCs by including in the OS the drivers these devices need in order to run. Because the OS includes this software, incorporating a new device into your computer system seems automatic. Plug and Play enables users to plug a new device into a port on the system unit, turn on the computer, and immediately play (use) the device. The OS automatically recognizes the device and its driver without any further user manipulations of the system.

Data and instructions not recently used

OS

RAM

Data and instructions needed now

Hard drive's swap file

brontazavra/Shutterstock.com

Tim Dobbs/Shutterstock.com

**What happens if the device is not Plug and Play?** Some current devices, such as many types of printers and many older devices, are not Plug and Play. When you install a non–PnP device, you will be prompted to insert the driver that was provided with the device. If you obtain a non-PnP device secondhand and do not receive the device driver, or if you are required to update the device driver, you can often download the necessary driver from the manufacturer's Web site. You can also go to Web sites such as DriverZone.com (**www.driverzone.com**) or DriverGuide (**www.driverguide.com**) to locate drivers.

**Can I damage my system by installing a device driver?** Occasionally, when you install a driver, your system may become unstable (that is, programs may stop responding, certain

**Figure 8.11**

Virtual memory borrows excess storage capacity from the hard drive when there is not enough capacity in RAM.

Locate driver in device list and click for device properties

Click to revert to previous driver

**Figure 8.12**

The Roll Back Driver feature in Windows removes a newly installed driver and replaces it with the last one that worked.

>To access the Device Manager window, click the **Start** button, **Control Panel, Hardware and Sound group**; then in the **Devices and Printers** group, click the **Device Manager** link. To display the Properties dialog box, double click on a device, then select **Properties.** Click the **Driver** tab.

actions may cause a crash, or the device or the entire system may stop working). Although this is uncommon, it can happen. Fortunately, to remedy the problem, Windows has a Roll Back Driver feature that removes a newly installed driver, and replaces it with the last one that worked (see Figure 8.12).

### Software Application Coordination

**How does the operating system help application software run on the computer?** Application software feeds the CPU the instructions it needs to process data. These instructions take the form of computer code. Every computer program, no matter what its type or manufacturer, needs to interact with the CPU. For programs to work with the CPU, they must contain code that the CPU recognizes. Rather than having the same blocks of code for similar procedures in each program, the operating system includes the blocks of code—each called an **application programming interface (API)**—that application software needs in order to interact with the OS. Microsoft DirectX, for example, is a group of multimedia APIs built into the

Windows operating system that improves graphics and sounds when you're playing games or watching video on your PC.

**What are the advantages of using APIs?** To create applications that can communicate with the operating system, software programmers need only refer to the API code blocks when they write an application. They don't need to include the entire code sequence in the application. APIs not only prevent redundancies in software code, but also make it easier for software developers to respond to changes in the operating system.

Large software developers such as Microsoft have many applications under their corporate umbrella and use the same APIs in all or most of their applications. Because APIs coordinate with the operating system, all applications that have incorporated these APIs have similar interface features, such as toolbars and menus. Therefore, many features of the applications have the same look. An added benefit to this system is that applications sharing these formats can easily exchange data with each other. As such, it's easy to create a chart in Microsoft Excel from data in Microsoft Access and incorporate the finished chart into a Microsoft Word document.

## The Boot Process: Starting Your Computer

Many things happen quickly between the time you turn on the computer and the time when it is ready for you to start using it. As you learned earlier, all data and instructions (including the operating system) are stored in RAM while your computer is on. When you turn off your computer, RAM is wiped clean of all its data (including the OS). How does the computer know what to do when you turn it on if there is nothing in RAM? It runs through a special boot process (or start-up process) to load the operating system into RAM. The term *boot*, from *bootstrap loader* (a small program used to start a larger program), alludes to the straps of leather, called *bootstraps*, that men used to use to help them pull on their boots. This is the source of the expression "pull yourself up by your bootstraps."

**ACTIVE HELPDESK**

Managing Hardware and Peripheral Devices: The OS

In this Active Helpdesk call, you'll play the role of a helpdesk staffer, fielding calls about how the operating system manages memory, storage, hardware, and peripheral devices.

More so than ever, we are concerned about sustainability and using products that will have little to no long-term impact on the planet. Since the majority of users leave PCs on at night or for long periods of time for various reasons, a lot of energy is wasted.

Fortunately, the newest operating systems have better power management control features. In Windows 7, notebook users can adjust their power management settings with just one click by hovering over the battery in the task pane.

You can make some easy changes to help extend the life of your notebook battery and waste less power, including:

- Lowering the brightness and dimming the display while the system is idle. By default, Windows 7 dims the display if the system is idle for 2 minutes on battery power, or 5 minutes when plugged in.

- Set the timer to turn off the display or put the computer to sleep more quickly (see Figure 8.13).

**Figure 8.13**

Adjusting the power management setting in Windows can help to extend the life of your battery and waste less power.

**What are the steps involved in the boot process?** As illustrated in Figure 8.14, the **boot process** consists of four basic steps:

1. The basic input/output system (BIOS) is activated by powering on the CPU.

2. The BIOS checks that all attached devices are in place (called a **power-on self-test** or **POST**).

3. The operating system is loaded into RAM.

4. Configuration and customization settings are checked.

**How can I tell if my computer is entering the boot process?** When you boot up on a PC with Windows or on a Mac, you will see the Windows or Mac OS logo display on the monitor, indicating the progress of the start-up process. Once the boot process has completed, the computer is ready to accept commands and data. Let's look at each of these steps in more detail.

### Step 1: Activating BIOS

**What's the first thing that happens after I turn on my computer?** In the first step of the boot process, the CPU activates the **basic input/output system (BIOS)**. BIOS (pronounced "BAHY-ohs") is a program that manages the exchange of data

between the operating system and all the input and output devices attached to the system, hence its name. BIOS is also responsible for loading the OS into RAM from its permanent location on the hard drive.

BIOS itself is stored on a special read-only memory (ROM) chip on the motherboard. Unlike data stored in RAM, data stored in ROM is permanent and is not erased when the power is turned off.

### Step 2: Performing the Power-On Self-Test

**How does the computer determine whether the hardware is working properly?** The first job BIOS performs is to ensure that essential peripheral devices are attached and operational. As mentioned already, this process is called the power-on self-test, or POST. The POST consists of a test on the video card and video memory, a BIOS identification process, and a memory test to ensure that memory chips are working properly.

The BIOS compares the results of the POST with the various hardware configurations that are permanently stored in CMOS (pronounced "see-moss"). CMOS, which stands for *complementary metal-oxide semiconductor*, is a special kind of memory that uses almost no power. A little battery provides

**STEP 2:** BIOS conducts power-on self-test.

**STEP 1:** CPU activates BIOS.

ROM chip

CPU

**STEP 3:** BIOS loads OS to RAM.

**STEP 4:** Configuration and customization settings checked, and desktop displays.

**Figure** 8.14

The boot process.

Maxx-Studio/Shutterstock.com

Arno van Dulmen/Shutterstock.com

Ragnarock/Shutterstock.com

enough power so that the CMOS contents will not be lost after the computer is turned off. CMOS contains information about the system's memory, types of disk drives, and other essential input and output hardware components. If the results of the POST compare favorably to the hardware configurations stored in CMOS, the boot process continues. If new hardware has been installed, this will cause the POST to disagree with the hardware configurations in CMOS, and you will be alerted that new hardware has been detected.

### Step 3: Loading the Operating System

**How does the operating system get loaded into RAM?** When the first two steps are successfully completed, BIOS goes through a preconfigured list of devices in its search for the drive that contains the **system files**, which are the main files of the operating system. When it is located, the operating system loads into RAM from its permanent storage location on the hard drive.

Once the system files are loaded into RAM, the **kernel** (or **supervisor program**) is loaded. The kernel is the essential component of the operating system. It is responsible for managing the processor and all other components of the computer system. Because it stays in RAM the entire time your computer is powered on, the kernel is said to be *memory resident*. Other parts of the OS that are less critical stay on the hard drive and are copied over to RAM on an as-needed basis so that RAM is managed more efficiently. These programs are referred to as *nonresident*. Once the kernel is loaded, the operating system takes over control of the computer's functions.

### Step 4: Checking Further Configurations and Customizations

**When are the other components and configurations of the system checked?** CMOS checks the configuration of memory and essential peripherals in the beginning of the boot process. In this last phase of the boot process, the operating system checks the registry for the configuration of other system components. The **registry** contains all of the different configurations (settings) used by the OS and by other applications. It contains the customized settings you put into place, such as mouse speed and the display settings, as well as instructions as to which programs should be loaded first.

**Why do I sometimes need to enter a login name and password at the end of the boot process?** In a networked environment, such as that found at most colleges, the operating system serves many users. To determine whether a user is authorized to use the system (for example, whether a user is a valid student or college employee), authorized users are given a login name and password. The verification of your login name and password is called **authentication**. The authentication process blocks unauthorized users from entering the system.

On your home computer, you also may need to input a password to log in to your user account on your computer after your computer has completely booted up. Even in a home environment, all users with access to a Windows computer can have their own user accounts. Users can set up a password to protect their account from being accessed by another user without permission.

**How do I know if the boot process is successful?** The entire boot process takes only a few minutes to complete. If the entire system is checked out and loaded properly, the process completes by displaying a desktop screen image. The computer system is now ready to accept your first command.

### Handling Errors in the Boot Process

**What should I do if my computer doesn't boot properly?** Sometimes problems occur during the boot process. Fortunately, you have several options for correcting the situation. If you have recently installed new software or hardware, try uninstalling it. (Make sure you use the Uninstall a program feature in the Control Panel to remove the software.) If the problem no longer occurs when rebooting, you have determined the cause of the problem and can reinstall the device or software. If the problem does not go away, the first option is to restart your computer in Safe mode.

**What is Safe mode?** Sometimes Windows does not boot properly, and you end up with a screen that says "Safe Mode" in the corners, as shown in Figure 8.15. Alternatively, you can boot directly into Safe mode by pressing the F8 key during the boot process before the Windows logo ap-

**Starting the Computer: The Boot Process**

In this Active Helpdesk call, you'll play the role of a helpdesk staffer, fielding calls about how the operating system helps the computer start up.

pears. **Safe mode** is a special diagnostic mode designed for troubleshooting errors. When the system is in Safe mode, only essential devices—such as the mouse, keyboard, and monitor—function. Even the regular graphics device driver will not be activated in Safe mode. Instead, the system runs in the most basic graphics mode, eliminating any screen images and nonessential icons and resulting in a neutral screen. While in Safe mode, you can use the **Device Manager**, a feature in the operating system that lets you view and change the properties of all devices attached to your computer. Safe mode boots Windows with only the original Microsoft Windows drivers that are required to boot the computer.

If Windows detects a problem in the boot process, it will add **Last Known Good Configuration** to the Windows Advanced Options Menu (also accessible by pressing the F8 key during the boot process). Every

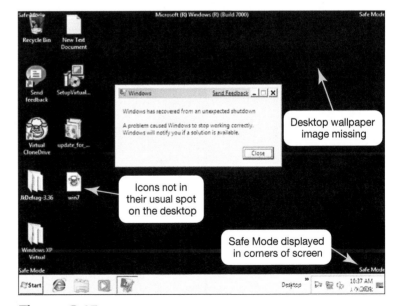

**Figure 8.15**

If there is an error in the boot process, your system might boot into Safe mode. Safe mode offers functionality that is limited but sufficient to allow you to perform diagnostic testing.

time your computer boots successfully, a configuration of the boot process is saved. When you choose to boot with the Last Known Good Configuration, the operating system starts your computer by using the registry information that was saved during the last shutdown. Safe mode and Last Known Good Configuration are the two most widely used methods of booting into Windows when a user cannot do so with the current configuration. Finally, if all other attempts to reboot fail, try a System Restore to roll back to a past configuration. System Restore is covered in more detail later in this chapter.

**What should I do if my keyboard or another device doesn't work after I boot my computer?** Sometimes during the boot process, BIOS skips a device (such as a keyboard) or improperly identifies it. Your only indication that this sort of problem has occurred is that the device won't respond after the system has been booted. When that happens, you can generally resolve the problem by rebooting. If the problem persists, you may want to check the operating system's Web site for any patches (or software fixes) that may resolve the issue. If there are no patches or the problem persists, then you may want to get technical assistance.

## The Desktop and Window Features

The **desktop** is the first interaction you have with the operating system and the first image you see on your monitor. As its name implies, your computer's desktop puts at your fingertips all of the elements necessary for a productive work session. They are items that are typically found on or near the top of a traditional desk, such as files and folders.

**What are the main features of the Windows desktop and Start menu?** The very nature of a desktop is that it lets you customize it to meet your individual needs. As such, the desktop on your computer may be different from the desktop on your friend's computer, or even from the desktop of another account user on the same computer. In recent versions of Windows, many features that were once only found on the desktop have moved to the Start menu and the taskbar, including access to documents, programs, and computer drives and devices (see Figure 8.16). You can always create shortcuts on your desktop to these features if you find that's more convenient.

On the desktop you'll find:

- **Recycle Bin:** Location for deleted files and folders from the C drive only. Deleted files in the Recycle Bin can be recovered easily before the Recycle Bin is emptied.

- **Gadgets:** An easy-to-use miniprogram that gives you information at a glance or quick access to frequently used tools including weather information, calendar items, calculators, games, photo albums, and system tools.

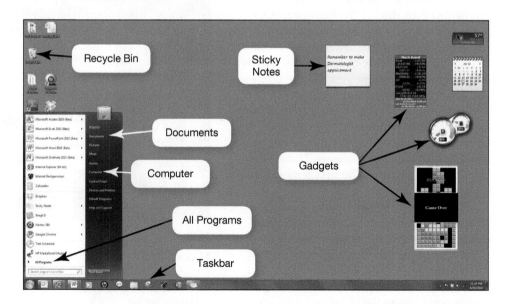

**Figure** 8.16

The Windows 7 desktop puts the most commonly used features of the operating system at your fingertips.

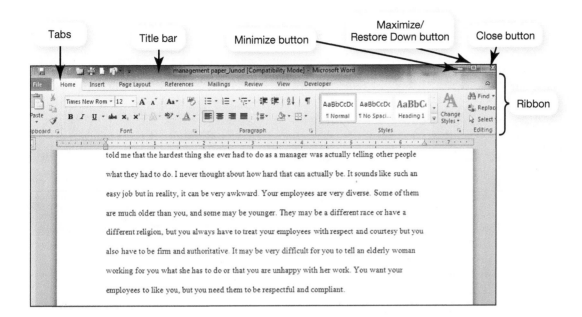

**Figure** 8.17

Most windows in a graphical user interface have the same common elements.

- **Taskbar:** Displays open and favorite applications for easy access. You can point to an icon to preview windows of open files or programs, or move your mouse over a thumbnail to preview a full-screen image. Or right-click an icon to view a Jump List—the most recently or commonly used files or commands for that application.

In the Windows 7 Start menu, you'll find:

- **Documents:** A convenient organizational tool that enables you to keep all your documents in one place. You can further organize your Documents folder with subfolders, similar to the way a traditional filing system is organized.

- **Computer:** Provides easy access to disk drives and system and network devices.

- **All Programs:** In the Start menu, this provides access to all programs available in the system. To prevent taking up valuable screen space, a limited number of programs displays. Use the scrollbar to gain access to programs not immediately visible. Instant Search can facilitate locating a program.

### What are common features of a window?

One feature introduced in the graphical user interface is **windows** (with a lowercase *w*), the rectangular panes on your computer screen that display applications running on your system. Most programs have windows that include **toolbars**, which have **icons** (shortcuts to frequently used

tasks) and **scrollbars** (bars that appear at the side or bottom of the screen that control which part of the information is displayed on the screen). As shown in Figure 8.17, the newer versions of Microsoft Office have begun to organize toolbars into a **ribbon** interface. The ribbon is further organized into task-specific tabs with relevant commands. Using the Minimize, Maximize/Restore Down, and Close buttons, you can open, close, and resize windows.

### How does the Mac desktop compare with Windows?

Although the Mac OS X and the Windows operating systems are not compatible, they are extremely similar in terms of functionality.

As illustrated in Figure 8.18, both Windows and Mac operating systems use windows, menus, and icons. They both also have streamlined mechanisms to access commonly used applications. Macs feature a Dock and a Dashboard with widgets. A **widget** is a mini-application that enables quick access to frequently used tools and activities (such as stock prices, to-do lists, and games). The latest version of Windows has a **taskbar** with Dock-like capabilities and **gadgets** that provide functionality similar to that of the Mac widgets.

### How can I see more than one window on my desktop at a time?

You can easily arrange the windows on a desktop so that they sit next to each other either horizontally or vertically. You also can arrange windows by cascading them so that they overlap one another, or you

Widgets (Mac)/
Gadgets (Windows)

Files

Icons

Windows

Access to
applications

**Figure** 8.18

Although not compatible
with each other, the
Windows OS and the
Mac OS have many
similar features.

can simply resize two open windows
so that they appear on the screen at the
same time.

Showing windows side by side or stacked
on top of each other makes accessing two
or more active windows more convenient.
To do so, right-click the taskbar and select
"Show Windows Stacked" or "Show Windows Side by Side." When you want to undo
the arrangement, right-click the taskbar again
and select "Undo Show Stacked" (or "Undo
Show Side by Side"). To bring a window
back to its full size, click the Restore button
in the top right corner of the window. Windows 7 introduces the "snap" feature, which
is another new way to view windows side by
side. Simply drag a window to either the left
or right so the pointer touches the side of the
desktop, and Windows will automatically
resize and snap that window in place.

**Figure** 8.19

The Windows Flip 3D feature gives you the ability to move through live images of
open windows.

>To access Windows Flip, hold down the Windows key and then press Tab.

Windows Vista and 7 offer two more
ways to navigate through open windows.
To see live thumbnail images of open windows, press Alt + Tab to access Windows
Flip. Pressing the Windows key + Tab initi-
ates the Windows Flip 3D feature. You can
then "flip" through open windows in a stack
by pressing Tab multiple times, or by using
the scroll wheel on your mouse or the arrow
keys on your keyboard. The open windows
appear in a three-dimensional configuration,
as shown in Figure 8.19.

**Can I move or resize the windows
once they are tiled?** Regardless of
whether the windows are tiled, you can
resize them and move them around the
desktop. You can reposition windows on
the desktop by using the mouse to point to
the title bar at the top of the window and,
while holding down the left mouse button,
drag the window to a different location. To
resize a window, place your mouse pointer
over any side or corner of a window until it
changes to a double-headed arrow [↕]. You
can then left-click and drag the window to
the new desired size. Aero Shake is a feature that allows you to grab a window by
its title bar and "shake" it (hold the cursor
on the title bar and quickly move the window back and forth) to minimize all other
windows.

## Organizing Your Computer: File Management

So far you have learned that the operating system is responsible for managing the
processor, memory, storage, and devices,

and that it provides a mechanism whereby applications and users can interact with the computer system. An additional function of an operating system is to enable **file management**, which provides an organizational structure to the computer's contents. The OS provides a hierarchical **directory** structure that includes folders, libraries, and drives. In this section, we discuss how you can use this hierarchical structure to make your computer more organized and efficient.

### Organizing Your Files

**What exactly are a file, folder, and library?** Technically, a **file** is a collection of related pieces of information stored together for easy reference. A file in an operating system is a collection of program instructions or data that is stored and treated as a single unit. Files can be generated from an application such as a Word document or an Excel workbook. In addition, files can represent an entire application, a Web page, a set of sounds, or an image. Files are stored on the hard drive, a flash drive, or another permanent storage medium. As the number of files you save increases, it becomes more important to keep them organized in folders and libraries. A **folder** is a collection of files. Windows 7 introduces the concept of libraries. A **library** gathers files from different locations and displays them as if they were all saved in a single folder, regardless of where they are actually physically stored. Libraries don't store files and folders; rather, they provide easy access to a category of files no matter where they are stored. For example, you might have pictures stored all over your computer, including your external hard drive. Rather than looking through each separate location to view your pictures, you can access all of them more easily by looking in the Pictures library.

**How does the operating system organize files?** Windows organizes the contents of your computer in a hierarchical structure composed of drives, libraries, folders, subfolders, and files. The hard drive, represented as the C drive, is where you permanently store most of your files. Other storage devices on your computer are also represented by letters. The A drive has traditionally been reserved for a floppy drive, which you may or may not have installed on your computer. Any additional drives (such as flash or DVD drives) found on your

**BITS AND BYTES**

### How to Get the Most from Windows Libraries

Windows 7 introduced libraries, a new organizing feature that aggregates multiple folders into a single accessible location. To get the most out of using libraries, consider the following tips.

- **Add a new library:** There are four default libraries: Documents, Music, Pictures, and Videos. You can add a new library to collect other content, such as games. To do so, open Windows Explorer. In the Navigation Pane, right-click on Libraries, and click New. Type in a name for the new library. To add new locations to the library, open the new library and click on Include a Folder.

- **Share or collaborate with libraries:** Perhaps you have pictures saved on your laptop, your dad's desktop, and your mom's laptop. As long as all three computers are on the same Homegroup network, you can share each other's libraries by right-clicking the library name, clicking Share With, and then clicking either Homegroup option, depending on whether you want to allow editing privileges to those with whom you are sharing the library.

- **Create a backup library:** Do you store important data in a variety of folders on your computer? Even though it's best to back up your entire system, you might only need to back up specific folders. In that case, create a new library, and call it Backup. Add the folders you want to ensure are backed up, then point your backup software to that library.

computer are represented by other letters (D, E, F, and so on).

**How is the hard drive organized?** The C drive, or hard drive, is like a large filing cabinet in which all files are stored. As such, the C drive is the top of the filing structure of the computer system and is referred to as the **root directory**. All other libraries, folders, and files are organized within the root directory. There are areas in the root directory that the operating system has filled with files and folders holding special OS files. The programs within these files help run the computer and generally shouldn't be accessed. The Windows operating system also creates libraries called Documents, Pictures, Music, and Videos that store and organize your text, image, audio, and video files, respectively. Or you can create your own libraries, folders, or subfolders to modify the default filing system to better meet your needs.

**How can I easily locate and see the contents of my computer?** If you use a Windows PC, **Windows Explorer** is the main tool for finding, viewing, and managing the contents of your computer. It shows the location and contents of every drive, folder, and file. As illustrated in Figure 8.20, Windows Explorer is divided into two panes, or sections.

**Figure** 8.20

Windows Explorer lets you see the contents of your computer.

>**Click the Start** button, and then select **Computer**.

The navigation pane on the left shows the contents of your computer. It displays commonly accessed areas organized by Favorites and libraries (Documents, Music, Pictures, and Videos) as well as all the drives of the system (under Computer) and available networks. When you select a Favorite, library, drive, or network, the files and folders of that particular area are displayed in the right pane.

### How should I organize my files?

Creating folders is the key to organizing your files because folders keep related documents together. Again, think of your computer as a big filing cabinet that is filled with many folders. Those folders have the capacity to hold individual files, or even other folders that contain individual files. For example, you might create one folder called Classes to hold all of your class work. Inside the Classes folder, you could create folders for each of your classes (such as CIS110, MGT111, and HIS112). Inside each of those folders, you could create subfolders for each class's assignments, completed homework, research, notes, and so on.

Grouping related files into folders makes it easier for you to identify and find files. Which would be easier—going to the CIS110 folder to find a file or searching through the hundreds of individual files in Documents hoping to find the right one? Grouping files in a folder also allows you to move them more efficiently, so you can quickly transfer critical files needing frequent backup, for instance.

Sometimes it's not possible to put all similar files into one folder. For example, you might have PowerPoint files stored in separate folders that correspond to each particular class. If you want to always have quick access to your PowerPoint files, you could create a PowerPoint Library and specify the folders where the PowerPoint files are located. The PowerPoint Library would then gather the PowerPoint files from the different locations and display them as if they were all saved in a single folder.

### Viewing and Sorting Files and Folders

### Are there different ways I can view and sort my files and folders?

When you open any folder in Windows, the toolbar at the top displays a Views button. Clicking on the Views button offers you different ways to view the folders and files, which are discussed in more detail below. In some views, the folders are displayed as Live Icons, which is a feature that began in Windows Vista. Live Icons allows you to preview the actual contents of a specific file or folder without actually opening the file. Live Icons can be displayed in a variety of views.

- **Tiles view:** This view displays files and folders as icons in list form. Each icon represents the application associated with the file, and also includes the name and the size of the file, though the display information is customizable to include other data. The Tiles view also displays picture dimensions, a handy feature for Web page developers.

- **Details view:** This is the most interactive view. Files and folders are displayed in list form, and the additional file information is displayed in columns alongside the name of the file. You can sort and display the contents of the folder by any of the column headings, so you can sort the contents alphabetically by name or type, or hierarchically by date last modified or file size (see Figure 8.21). Right-click the column heading area to modify the display of columns.

- **List view:** This is another display of icons and names that are even smaller than in Tiles view. This is a good view if you have a lot of content in the folder and need to see most or all of it at once.

- **Small and Medium Icons views:** These views also display files and folders as icons in list form, but the icons are either small- or medium-sized, respectively. Additional file information displays in a ScreenTip (the text that appears when you place your cursor over the file icon).

- **Large and Extra Large Icons views:** Large Icons view (see Figure 8.22) shows the contents of folders as small images. There is also Extra Large Icons view, which shows folder contents and other icons as even larger images. Large Icons and Extra Large Icons views are the best to use if your folder contains picture files,

Sort files and folders by clicking the headers

or for PowerPoint presentations, because the title slide of the presentation will display, making it easier for you to distinguish among presentations. You may use the scale feature to adjust the size of the icons further. Additionally, a preview pane is available in this view. It allows you to view the first page of the selected document without having to open it completely (see Figure 8.22). For those folders that contain collections of MP3 files, you can download the cover of the CD or an image of the artist to display on any folder to identify that collection further.

**Figure 8.21**

Details view enables you to sort and list your files in a variety of ways to enable quick access to the correct file.

>To access Details view, right click anywhere in the Windows Explorer window, select View, and then select Details.

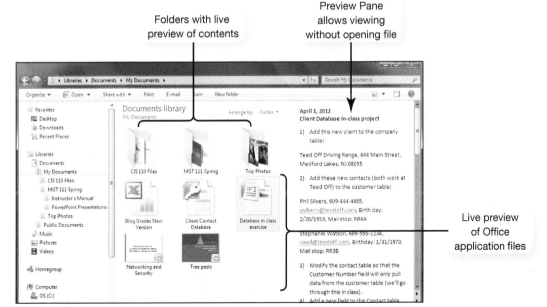

Folders with live preview of contents

Preview Pane allows viewing without opening file

Live preview of Office application files

**Figure 8.22**

The Large Icons view is an especially good way to display the contents of files and folders. The preview pane on the right enables you to see the first page of your document without first opening it.

>To access Large Icons view, from the command bar in any folder dialog box, click the **Views** arrow, and then select **Large Icons** view. To access the Preview Pane, click **Organize**, select **Layout**, and then select **Preview Pane**.

**What's the best way to search for a file?** You've no doubt saved a file and forgotten where you saved it, or have downloaded a file from the Internet and then were not sure where it was saved. What's the quickest way to find a file? Looking through every file stored on your computer could take hours, even with a well-organized file management system. Fortunately, the newer versions of Windows include Instant Search, a search feature found on the Start menu, which searches through your hard drive or other storage device (DVD or flash drive) to locate files that match criteria you provide. Your search can be based on a part of the name of the file or just a word or phrase in the file. You can also narrow your search by providing information about the type of file, which application was used to create the

file, or even how long ago the file was saved. Instant Search can also find e-mails based on your criteria. Instant Search is found in Windows Explorer, too, and is used to search the contents of current folders. Mac OS X has a similar feature called Spotlight.

### Naming Files

**Are there special rules I have to follow when I name files?** Files have names just like people. The first part of a file, or the **file name**, is similar to your first name, and is generally the name you assign to the file when you save it. For example, "bioreport" may be the name you assign a report you have completed for a biology class.

In a Windows application, an **extension**, or **file type**, follows the file name and a period or dot (.). Like a last name, this extension identifies what kind of family of files the file belongs to, or which application should be used to read the file. For example, if "bioreport" is a spreadsheet created in Microsoft Excel 2010, it has a .xlsx extension and its name is "bioreport.xlsx." If the bioreport file is a Word 2010 document, then it has a .docx extension and its name is "bioreport.docx." Figure 8.23 lists some common file extensions and the types of documents they indicate.

**Figure 8.23** | COMMON FILE NAME EXTENSIONS

| Extension | Type of Document | Application |
|---|---|---|
| .doc | Word processing document | Microsoft Word 2003 |
| .docx | Word processing document | Microsoft Word 2007 and 2010 |
| .sdw | Text | OpenOffice.org |
| .xlsx | Worksheet | Microsoft Excel 2007 and 2010 |
| .accdb | Database | Microsoft Access 2007 and 2010 |
| .pptx | Presentation | Microsoft PowerPoint 2007 and 2010 |
| .pdf | Portable Document Format | Adobe Acrobat or Adobe Reader |
| .rtf | Text (Rich Text Format) | Any program that can read text documents |
| .txt | Text | Any program that can read text documents |
| .htm or .html | HyperText Markup Language for a Web page | Any program that can read HTML |
| .jpg | Joint Photographic Experts Group (JPEG) image | Most programs capable of displaying images |
| .gif | Graphics Interchange Format (GIF) image | Most programs capable of displaying images |
| .bmp | Bitmap image | Windows |
| .zip | Compressed file | WinZip |

Imagine you are sending an e-mail to a diverse group of individuals. You are not sure what word processing software each of them uses, but you assume that there will be a mix of people who use Microsoft Word, iWorks, and Writer. How can you be sure that all users will be able to open the attachment regardless of the program installed on their computers? Save the file in Rich Text Format (.rtf), Portable Document Format (.pdf), or Plain Text (.txt) format. Rich Text Format and Plain Text files can be read by any modern word processing program, although some formatting may be lost when a document is saved in Plain Text format. Anyone can read a PDF file by downloading the free Adobe Reader from the Adobe Web site (**www.adobe.com**). To save files as RTF, PDF, or TXT files, simply change the file type when saving your file. In Microsoft Word, for example, you can select the file type in the Save as Type list shown in Figure 8.24.

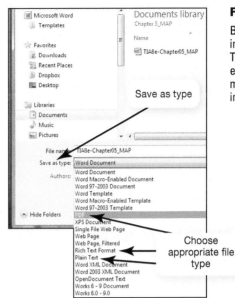

**Figure 8.24**

By changing a word processing file's type to PDF, RTF, or TXT, you can ensure that everyone can read your file, no matter which word processing program they use.

**Why is it important to know the file extension?** As shown in Figure 8.25, when you save a file created in most applications running under the Windows operating system, you do not need to add the extension to the file name; by default, it is added automatically for you. Mac and Linux operating systems do not require file extensions. This is because the information as to the type of application the computer should use to open the file is stored inside the file itself. However, if you're using the Mac or Linux operating system and will be sending files to Windows users, you should add an extension to your file name so that Windows can more easily open your files. You may also need to know the extension of files created in any of the Office 2007 or 2010 applications because they have a different file format than the earlier versions. The new versions of Office have an $x$ at the end of the extension to represent the XML file format. For example, files saved in Word 2010 have a .docx file extension, whereas files save in Word 2003 have a .doc file extension. A file created in Office 2007 or 2010 cannot be read with an earlier version of Office unless it is converted or saved in the earlier format. Finally, sometimes you are sent a file by e-mail, and cannot open it. Most likely, that's because your computer does not have the program needed to open the file. Sometimes, similar programs that you already have installed can be used to open the file, so it's helpful to know what the file extension is. Sites such as **www.filext.com** can help you identify the source program.

**Figure 8.25**

When you save a file in Microsoft Word 2010, you can select in what format you would like the file to be saved, such as a format compatible with Word 97–2003.

>The Save As features are displayed by selecting the File tab and then selecting Save As.

## Figure 8.26 | FILE NAMING CONVENTIONS

| | Mac OS X | Windows |
|---|---|---|
| **File and folder name length** | As many as 255 characters* | As many as 255 characters |
| **Case sensitive?** | Yes | No |
| **Forbidden characters** | Colon (:) | " / \ * ? <> \| : |
| **File extensions needed?** | No | Yes |
| **Path separator** | Colon (:) | \ |

*Note: Although Mac OS X supports file names with as many as 255 characters, many applications running on OS X still support only file names with a maximum of 31 characters.

**Are there things I shouldn't do when naming my files?** Each operating system has its own naming conventions, or rules, which are listed in Figure 8.26. Beyond those conventions, it's important that you name your files so that you can easily identify them. A file name such as "research.docx" may be descriptive to you if you're only working on one research paper. However, if you create other research reports later and need to identify the contents of these files quickly, you'll soon wish you had been more descriptive. Giving your files names that are more descriptive, such as bioresearch.docx or, better yet, bio101research.docx, is a good idea.

Keep in mind, however, that all files must be uniquely identified, unless they are saved are Documents for files, Music for audio files, Pictures for graphic files, and Videos for video files. Although you can create your own libraries, these default libraries are the beginning of a well-organized system.

You can determine the location of a file by its **file path**. The file path starts with the drive in which the file is located and includes all folders, subfolders (if any), the file name, and the extension. For example, if you were saving a picture of Andrew Carnegie for a term paper for a U.S. History course, the file path might be C:\Documents\HIS182\Term Paper\Illustrations\ACarnegie.jpg.

As shown in Figure 8.27, C is the drive on which the file is stored (in this case, the hard drive), and Documents is the file's primary folder. HIS182, Term Paper, and Illustrations are successive subfolders within the Documents main folder. Last is the file name, ACarnegie, separated from the file extension (in this case, jpg) by a period. Notice that there are backslash characters (\) in between

**Figure 8.27**

Understanding file paths.

C:\Documents\HIS182\Term Paper\Illustrations\ACarnegie.jpg

Drive   Primary Folder   Subfolders   File Name   Extension

in different folders or in different locations. Therefore, although files may share the same file name (such as "bioreport.docx" or "bioreport.xlsx") or share the same extension ("bioreport.xlsx" or "budget.xlsx"), no two files stored on the same device and folder can share *both* the same file name and the same extension.

**How can I tell where my files are saved?** When you save a file for the first time, you give the file a name and designate where you want to save it. For easy reference, the operating system includes libraries where files are saved unless you specify otherwise. In Windows, the default libraries the drive, primary folder, subfolders, and file name. This backslash character, used by Windows and DOS, is referred to as a **path separator**. Mac files use a colon (:), whereas UNIX and Linux files use the forward slash (/) as the path separator.

### Working with Files

**How can I move and copy files?** Once you've located your file with Windows Explorer, you can perform many other file-management actions such as opening, copying, moving, renaming, and deleting files. You open a file by double-clicking the file from its storage location. Based on the file extension, the operating system then determines which application needs to be started to open the requested file and opens the file within the correct application automatically. You can copy a file to another location using the Copy command. When you copy a file, a duplicate file is created and the original file remains in its initial location. To move a file from one location to another, use the Move command. When you move a file, the original file is deleted from its former location and saved in the new location.

**Where do deleted files go?** The **Recycle Bin** is a folder on the desktop where files deleted from the hard drive reside until you permanently purge them from your system. Unfortunately, files deleted from other drives (such as a DVD drive, flash drive, external hard drive, or network drive) do not go to the Recycle Bin but are deleted from the system immediately. (Mac systems have something similar to the Recycle Bin, called Trash, which is represented by a wastebasket icon. To delete files on a Mac, drag the files to the Trash on the Dock.)

**How do I permanently delete files from my system?** Files placed in the Recycle Bin or the Trash remain in the system until they are permanently deleted. To delete files from the Recycle Bin permanently, select Empty the Recycle Bin after right-clicking the desktop icon. On Macs, select Empty Trash from the Finder menu in OS X.

# Utility Programs

The main component of system software is the operating system. You have learned that the operating system is the single most essential piece of software in your computer system because it coordinates all the system's activities and provides a means by which other software applications and users can interact with the system. However, there is another set of programs included in system software, which are very important. Utility programs are small applications that perform special functions.

Some of these utility programs are incorporated into the operating system. For example, Windows has its own firewall and file-compression utilities. Other utility programs, such as antivirus and security programs, are sophisticated and require such frequent updating that they are offered as stand-alone programs or as Web-based services. Sometimes utility programs, such as Norton SystemWorks, are offered as

## Need to Recover a Deleted File?

Should you move a file to the Recycle Bin in error, you can restore the deleted file by clicking the Recycle Bin icon on the desktop, right-clicking the erroneously deleted file, and then selecting restore. Once you empty the Recycle Bin, getting the file back is difficult, but perhaps not impossible.

Because you don't see the file name anymore, it looks as if the file has been erased from the hard drive. However, only the reference to the deleted file is deleted permanently, so the operating system has no easy way to find the file. The file data actually remains on the hard drive until it is written over. For those files that have been deleted for a while, you can use a program such as FarStone's RestoreIT! or Norton Ghost. However, the longer you wait to recover a deleted file, the smaller your chances of a full recovery, because the probability increases that your file has been overwritten by other data.

software suites, bundled with other useful maintenance and performance-boosting utilities. Still other utilities, like Lavasoft's Ad-Aware, are offered as freeware or shareware programs and are available as downloads from the Web.

Figure 8.28 illustrates some of the various types of utility programs available within the Windows operating system as well as some alternatives available as stand-alone programs. In general, the basic utilities designed to manage and tune the computer hardware are incorporated into the operating system. The stand-alone utility programs typically offer more features or an easier user interface for backup, security, diagnostic, or recovery functions. For some Windows programs, like Task Manager and Task Scheduler, no good stand-alone alternative exists.

In this section, we explore many of the utility programs you'll find installed on a Windows 7 operating system. Unless otherwise noted, you can find Windows utilities in the Control Panel or on the Start menu by selecting All Programs, Accessories, and then System Tools.

### Display Utilities

**How can I change the appearance of my desktop?** Personalization, found in Appearance and Personalization on the Control Panel or by right-clicking any empty area on the desktop and selecting Personalize, has all the features you need to change the appearance of your desktop. It provides different options for the desktop background, screen savers, and window colors. Although Windows comes with many different background themes and screen saver options

**Figure 8.28** | UTILITY PROGRAMS AVAILABLE WITHIN WINDOWS AND AS STAND-ALONE PROGRAMS

| Windows Utility Program | Type of Document | Application |
|---|---|---|
| Windows Explorer File Compression | WinZip, StuffIt | Reduces file size |
| Backup and Disk Imaging | Acronis True Image, Norton Ghost, SkyDrive | Backs up important files, makes a complete mirror image of current computer setup |
| Disk Cleanup | McAfee Total Protection | Removes unnecessary files from hard drive |
| Disk Defragmenter | Norton Utilities, iDefrag | Arranges files on hard drive in sequential order |
| Error-checking (previously ScanDisk) | SeaTools (free download from www.seagate.com) | Checks hard drive for unnecessary or damaged files |
| System Restore | FarStone Snapshop, Acronis Backup and Security, Norton Ghost | Restores system to previous, stable state |
| Task Manager and Resource Monitor | | Displays performance measures for processes; provides information on programs and processes running on computer |
| Task Scheduler | | Schedules programs to run automatically at prescribed times. |

preinstalled, a vast array of downloadable options are available on the Web. Just search for "backgrounds" or "screen savers" on your favorite search engine to customize your desktop. Make sure you select one from a reputable source, though, because sometimes viruses and other unwanted or annoying files can also be downloaded with a desktop image or screensaver.

### The Programs and Features Utility

**What is the correct way to add new programs to the system?** When you install a new program, usually the program automatically runs a wizard (a step-by-step guide) that walks you through the installation process. If a wizard does not start automatically, you should open the Control Panel, click Programs, and then click Programs and Features. This prompts the operating system to look for the setup program of the new software and starts the installation wizard.

**What is the correct way to remove unwanted programs from my system?** Some people think that deleting a program from the Program Files folder on the C drive is the best way to remove a program from the system. However, most programs include support files such as a help file, dictionaries, and graphics files that are not located in the main program folder found in Program Files. Depending on the supporting file's function, support files can be scattered throughout various folders within the system. You would normally miss these files by deleting only the main program file or folder from the system. By selecting the individual program's own uninstall option, or the Windows uninstaller utility found in Programs in the Control Panel, you delete not only the main program file, but also all supporting files and most registry entries.

### File Compression Utilities

**What is file compression?** File compression makes a large file more compact, making it easier and faster to send over the Internet, upload to a Web page, or save onto a disc. As shown in Figure 8.29, Windows has a built-in **file compression utility** that takes out redundancies in a file (zips it) to reduce the file size. There are also several stand-alone freeware and shareware programs, such as WinZip (for Windows) and StuffIt (for Windows or Mac), that you can obtain to compress your files.

**How does file compression work?** Most compression programs look for repeated patterns of letters and replace these patterns with a shorter placeholder. The repeated patterns and the associated placeholder are cataloged and stored temporarily in a separate file called the *dictionary*. For example, in the following sentence, you can easily see the repeated patterns of letters.

**The rain in Spain falls mainly on the plain.**

**Figure 8.29**

(a) File compression is a built-in utility of the Windows operating system. (b) Compressing the PowerPoint document reduced the file size from 1935 KB to 1453 KB.

>To access the Windows file compression utility, right-click the file or folder that is to be compressed, select **Send to** from the shortcut menu, and then select **Compressed (zipped) folder**.

Although this example contains obvious repeated patterns (**ain** and **the**), in a large document the repeated patterns may be more complex. The compression program's algorithm (a set of instructions designed to complete a solution in a step-by-step manner) therefore runs through the file several times to determine the optimal repeated patterns to use to obtain the greatest compression.

**How effective are file compression programs?** The effectiveness of file compression—that is, how much a file's size is reduced—depends on several factors, including the type and size of the individual file and the compression method used. Current compression programs can reduce text files by 50 percent or more, depending on the file. However, some files, such as PDF files, already contain a form of compression, so they do not need to be compressed further. Other file types, especially some graphics and audio formats, have gone through a compression process that reduces file size by permanently discarding data.

  File Compression

In this Sound Byte, you'll learn about the advantages of file compression and how to use Windows to compress and decompress files. This Sound Byte also teaches you how to find and install file compression shareware programs.

For example, image files such as Joint Photographic Experts Group (JPEG), Graphics Interchange Format (GIF), and Portable Network Graphics (PNG) files discard small variations in color that the human eye may not pick up. Likewise, MP3 files permanently discard sounds that the human ear cannot hear. These graphic and audio files do not need further compression.

**How do I decompress a file I've compressed?** When you want to restore the file to its original state, you need to decompress the file so that the pieces of file that the compression process temporarily removed are restored to the document. Generally, the program you used to compress the file has the capability to decompress the file as well (see Figure 8.30).

### System Maintenance Utilities

**Are there any utilities that make my system work faster?** Disk Cleanup is a Windows utility that cleans, or removes, unnecessary files from your hard drive. These include files that have accumulated in the Recycle Bin as well as temporary files, which are files created by Windows to store data temporarily while a program is running. Windows usually deletes these temporary files when you exit the program, but sometimes it forgets to do this, or doesn't have time because your system freezes up or incurs a problem that prevents you from properly exiting a program. Disk Cleanup, found by clicking the

STEP 1: Right-click zipped folder.

STEP 2: Select Extract All...

STEP 3: Browse to storage location.

STEP 4: Extracted file displays in selected location.

**Figure 8.30**

The Extraction Wizard in Windows makes unzipping compressed folders and files easy.

Total space to be freed

Space freed with the selections

Description of folder contents

**Figure 8.31**

Using Disk Cleanup will help free space on your hard drive.

>Disk Cleanup is accessed by clicking **Start**, **All Programs**, **Accessories**, and then **System Tools**.

Start button, then selecting All Programs, Accessories folder, and then the System Tools folder, also removes temporary Internet files (Web pages stored on your hard drive for quick viewing) as well as offline Web pages (pages stored on your computer so you can view them without being connected to the Internet). If not deleted periodically, these unnecessary files can hinder efficient operating performance.

**How can I control which files Disk Cleanup deletes?** When you run Disk Cleanup, the program scans your hard drive to determine which folders have files that can be deleted and calculates the amount of hard drive space that would be freed by doing so. You check off which type of files you would like to delete, as shown in Figure 8.31.

**What else can I do if my system runs slowly?** Over time, as you add and delete information in a file or download updates to your software, the file pieces are saved in scattered locations on the hard drive. When the file is opened, locating all the pieces of the file takes extra time, making the operating system less efficient. Windows **Disk Defragmenter** regroups related pieces of files on the hard drive, thereby allowing the OS to work more efficiently. The process of collecting file fragments and putting them back together in a contiguous manner is known as optimization. You can find the Windows Disk Defragmenter utility by clicking the Start menu, then All Programs, Accessories, and then System Tools. Using the Windows Disk Defragmenter Analyzer feature, you should check several times a year to determine whether your drive needs to be defragmented. Macs do not have a defrag utility built into the system. Those users who feel the need to defrag their Mac can use iDefrag, an external program that can be purchased from Coriolis Systems.

**How do I diagnose potential errors or damage on my storage devices?** **Error-checking**, once known as ScanDisk, is a Windows utility that checks for lost files and fragments as well as physical errors on your hard drive. Lost files and fragments of files occur as you save, resave, move, delete, and copy files on your hard drive. Sometimes the system becomes confused, leaving references on the **file allocation table** or **FAT** (an index of all sector numbers in a table) to files that no longer exist or have been moved. Physical errors on the hard drive occur when the mechanism that reads the hard drive's data (which is stored as 1s or 0s) can no longer determine whether the area holds a 1 or a 0. These areas are called *bad sectors*. Sometimes Error-checking can recover the lost data, but more often, it deletes the files that are unnecessarily taking up space. Error-checking also makes a note of any bad sectors so that the system will not use them again to store data. To locate Error-checking, from the Start menu click Computer, right-click the disk you want to diagnose, select Properties, and select Tools. On Macs, you can use the Disk Utility to test and repair disks. You will find Disk Utility in the Utilities subfolder in the Applications folder on your hard drive.

**How can I check on a program that has stopped running?** If a program has stopped working, you can use the Windows **Task Manager** utility to check on the program or to exit the nonresponsive program. Although you can access Task Manager from the Control Panel, it is more easily accessible by pressing Ctrl + Alt and then the Delete key or by right-clicking an empty space on the taskbar at the bottom of your screen. The Applications tab of Task Manager lists all programs that you are using and indicates whether they are working properly (running) or have stopped improperly (not responding). You can terminate programs that are not responding by clicking the End Task button in the dialog box.

If you need further assistance because of a program error, it may be helpful to run an application debugger. Problem Steps Recorder (see Figure 8.32), a tool in Windows Vista and Windows 7, gathers information about the computer when there is a program error. When an error occurs, this tool automatically creates and saves a log. The log can then be viewed, printed, or delivered electronically to any technical support professional, who can then use this information to help diagnose the problem.

### System Restore and Backup Utilities

**Is there an undo command for the system?** Suppose you have just installed a new software program and your

## Problem Steps Recorder: Making Tech Support Easier

Have you ever been frustrated trying to clearly and accurately describe your problem or an error message you have received to a technical support person? Have you had trouble remembering the steps you took to encounter a problem? Or, are you on the other side, trying to help via the phone a friend or family member with their problems? If so, Windows 7 has a cool new feature called Problem Steps Recorder that you can use to capture all your mouse clicks and keystrokes (see Figure 8.32). In addition to capturing the clicks and keystrokes you make to reproduce the problem or error, the Problem Steps Recorder provides screen shots of your actions. The captured data is stored in a zipped file. You can then send the zipped file to your technical support person.

To start Problem Steps Recorder, click Start, type "psr.exe" in the search box, and press Enter. When Problem Steps Recorder displays, click the Start Record button and continue the steps to reproduce the problem or error. You can add comments as you go. The end result is a slideshow of all your actions, along with descriptions (in regular English—not code) of what you did.

**Figure 8.32**

The Problem Steps Recorder captures the clicks and keystrokes you make to reproduce a problem or error.

computer freezes. After rebooting the computer, when you try to start the application, the system freezes once again. You uninstall the new program, but your computer continues to freeze after rebooting. What can you do now?

The most recent versions of Windows have a utility called **System Restore** that lets you roll your system settings back to a specific date when everything was working properly. A **system restore point**, which is a snapshot of your entire system's settings, is made every week and prior to certain events, such as installing or updating software. You also can create a custom restore point manually. Should problems occur, if the computer was running just fine before you installed new software or a hardware

## Using Utility Programs

In this Active Helpdesk call, you'll play the role of a helpdesk staffer, fielding calls about the utility programs included in system software and what these programs do.

To understand how disk defragmenter utilities work, you must first understand the basics of how a hard disk drive stores files. A hard disk drive is composed of several platters, or round, thin plates of metal, that are covered with a special magnetic coating that records the data. The platters are about 3.5 inches in diameter and are stacked onto a spindle. There are usually two or three platters in any hard disk drive, with data stored on one or both sides. Data is recorded on hard disks in concentric circles called tracks. Each **track** is further broken down into pie-shaped wedges, each called a **sector** (see Figure 8.33). The data is further identified by clusters, which are the smallest segments within the sectors.

When you want to save (or write) a file, the bits that make up your file are recorded onto one or more clusters of the drive. To keep track of which clusters hold which files, the drive also stores an index of all sector numbers in a table. To save a file, the computer will look in the table for clusters that are not already being used. It will then record the file information on those clusters. When you open (or read) a file, the computer searches through the table for the clusters that hold the desired file and reads that file. Similarly, when you delete a file, you are actually not deleting the file itself, but rather the reference in the table to the file.

How does a disk become fragmented? When only part of an older file is deleted, the deleted section of the file creates a gap in the sector of the disk where the data was originally stored. In the same way, when new information is added to an older file, there may not be space to save the new information sequentially near where the file was originally saved. In that case, the system writes the added part of the file to the next available location on the disk, and a reference is made in the table as to the location of this file fragment. Over time, as files are saved, deleted, and modified, the bits of information for various files fall out of sequential order and the disk becomes fragmented.

Disk fragmentation is a problem because the operating system is not as efficient when a disk is fragmented. It takes longer to locate a whole file because more of the disk must be searched for the various pieces, greatly slowing down the performance of your computer.

How can you make the files line up more efficiently on the disk? At this stage, the disk defragmenter utility enters the picture. The defragmenter tool takes the hard drive through a defragmentation process in which pieces of files that are scattered over the disk are placed together and arranged sequentially on the hard disk. Also, any unused portions of clusters that were too small to save data in before are grouped, increasing the available storage space on the disk. Figure 8.34 shows before and after shots of a fragmented disk that has gone through the defragmentation process.

For more about hard disks and defragmenting, be sure to check out the Sound Byte "Hard Disk Anatomy Interactive."

Fragmented files on disk

Defragmented files on disk

**Figure 8.34**
Defragmenting the hard drive arranges file fragments so that they are located next to each other. This makes the hard drive run more efficiently.

Track

Sector

Cluster

**Figure 8.33**
On a hard disk platter, data is recorded onto tracks, which are further broken down into sectors and clusters.

device, you could restore your computer to the settings that were in effect before the software or hardware installation. System Restore does not affect your personal data files (such as Microsoft Word documents, browsing history, or e-mail), so you won't lose changes made to these files when you use System Restore.

**How does the computer remember its previous settings?** Every time you start your computer or install a new application or driver, Windows automatically

**Figure** 8.35

Setting a restore point is good practice before installing any hardware or software.

>The System Restore Wizard is found by clicking **Start**, **All Programs**, **Accessories**, **System Tools**. In the **System Tools** folder, click **System Restore**. The System Restore Wizard appears, with Restore Point shown on the second page of the Wizard.

creates a system restore point. You also can create and name your own restore points at any time. Creating a restore point is a good idea before making changes to your computer such as installing hardware or software. If something goes wrong with the installation process, Windows can reset your system to the restore point. As shown in Figure 8.35, Windows includes a System Restore Wizard that walks you through the process of setting restore points.

**How can I protect my data in the event something malfunctions in my system?** When you use the Windows **Backup and Restore** utility (found in the Control Panel), you can create a duplicate copy of all the data on your hard drive (or just the folders and files you specify) and copy it to another storage device, such as a Blu-ray Disc or external hard drive. A backup copy protects your data in the event your hard drive fails or files are accidentally erased. Although you may not need to back up every file on your computer, you should back up the files that are most important to you and keep the backup copy in a safe location. Mac OS X includes a backup utility called Time Machine that will automatically back up your files to a specified location. Apple also offers backup hardware called Time Capsules, which are wireless devices designed to work with Time Machine and record your backup data. Because Time Machine makes a complete image copy of your system, it can also be used to recover your system in the case of a fatal error.

If you encounter a non-recoverable error on a Windows machine that System Restore cannot repair, you can recover Windows from a system repair disc. A system repair disc is designed to fix problems with Windows 7. It will let you boot up Windows, and then give you options for repairing your system. It won't reinstall Windows 7 and it won't reformat your computer; it's

**SOUND BYTE**

**Hard Disk Anatomy Interactive**

In this Sound Byte, you'll watch a series of animations that show various aspects of a hard drive, including the anatomy of a hard drive, how a computer reads and writes data to a hard drive, and the fragmenting and defragmenting of a hard drive.

**Figure 8.36**

To keep your machine running in top shape, use Task Scheduler to schedule maintenance programs to run automatically at selected times and days.

>Task Scheduler is found by clicking **Start, All Programs, Accessories**, and then **System Tools**.

described previously on a routine basis. Depending on your usage, you may want to defrag your hard drive or clean out temporary Internet files periodically. However, many computer users forget to initiate these tasks. Luckily, the Windows **Task Scheduler** utility, shown in Figure 8.36, allows you to schedule tasks to run automatically at predetermined times, with no additional action necessary on your part.

### Accessibility Utilities

**Are there utilities designed for users with special needs?** Microsoft Windows includes an Ease of Access Center, which is a centralized location for assistive technology and tools to adjust accessibility settings. In the Ease of Access Center (see Figure 8.37), you can find tools to help you adjust the screen contrast, magnify the screen image, have screen contents read to you, and display an on-screen keyboard, as more fully explained in the following list. If you're not sure where to start or what settings might help, a questionnaire asks you about routine tasks and provides a personalized recommendation for settings that will help you use your computer. Some of these features are described below.

- **High Contrast:** Allows you to select a color scheme setting in which you can control the contrast between text and background. Because some visually impaired individuals find it easier to see white text on a dark background, there are color schemes that invert screen colors.

- **Magnifier:** A utility that creates a separate window that displays a magnified portion of the screen. This feature makes the screen more readable for users who have impaired vision.

just a means to get to the recovery tools that are incorporated into Windows. Sometimes your computer comes with these repair discs, but often they do not. If you do not have a system repair disc, you should create one before problems arise. With Windows 7, it is easy to create a system repair disc. Insert a blank disc into the DVD drive, click Start, and type "System Repair" in the Search box. Then, click Create a System Repair Disc, make sure the appropriate drive is showing, and click Create disc.

### The Task Scheduler Utility

**How can I remember to perform all these maintenance procedures?** To keep your computer system in top shape, it is important to run some of the utilities

Magnifier window

On-screen keyboard

**Figure 8.37**

Microsoft Windows includes an Ease of Access Center to help users with disabilities. It has handy accessibility features such as a magnifier and an on-screen keyboard.

>The Ease of Access Center is found by clicking **Start, All Programs, Accessories, Ease of Access**.

- **Narrator:** A very basic speech program that reads what is on screen, whether it's the contents of a window, menu options, or text you have typed. The Narrator coordinates with text utilities such as Notepad and WordPad as well as with Internet Explorer, but it may not work correctly with other programs. For this reason, Narrator is not meant for individuals who must rely solely on a text-to-speech utility to operate the computer.

- **On-Screen Keyboard:** Displays a keyboard on the screen. You type by clicking on or hovering over the keys with a pointing device (mouse or trackball) or joystick. This utility, which is similar to the Narrator, is not meant for every-day use for individuals with severe disabilities. A separate program with more functionality is better in those circumstances.

- **Windows Speech Recognition:** An effective tool that allows you to dictate text and control your computer by voice. The Speech Recognition utility is in the Ease of Access section of the Control Panel.

Whether you use Windows, OS X, Linux, or another operating system, a fully featured operating system is available to meet your needs. As long as you keep the operating system updated and regularly use the available utilities to fine-tune your system, you should experience little trouble from your OS.

### 1. What software is included in system software?

System software is the set of software programs that helps run the computer and coordinates instructions between application software and hardware devices. It consists of the operating system (OS) and utility programs. The OS controls how your computer system functions. Utility programs are programs that perform general housekeeping tasks for the computer, such as system maintenance and file compression.

### 2. What are the different kinds of operating systems?

There are many different kinds of operating systems. Real-time operating systems (RTOSs) require no user intervention. They are designed for systems with a specific purpose and response time (such as robotic machinery). Smartphones have their own specific operating systems, the latest of which allow the user to multitask. Current operating systems for desktops, notebooks, and netbooks have multitasking capabilities, as well as networking capabilities.

### 3. What are the most common operating systems?

Microsoft Windows is the most popular OS. It has evolved into a powerful multiuser operating system. The most recent release is Windows 7. Another popular OS is the Mac OS, which is designed to work on Apple computers. Apple's most recent release, Mac OS X, is based on the UNIX operating system. There are various versions of UNIX on the market, although UNIX is most often used on networks. Linux is an open source OS based on UNIX and designed primarily for use on personal computers, although it is often found as the operating system on servers.

### 4. How does the operating system provide a means for users to interact with the computer?

The operating system provides a user interface that enables users to interact with the computer. Most OSs today use a graphical user interface (GUI). Unlike the command- and menu-driven interfaces used earlier, GUIs display graphics and use the point-and-click technology of the mouse and cursor, making the OS more user-friendly. Common features of GUIs include windows, menus, and icons.

### 5. How does the operating system help manage resources such as the processor, memory, storage, hardware, and peripheral devices?

When the OS allows you to perform more than one task at a time, it is multitasking. To provide for seamless multitasking, the OS controls the timing of events the processor works on.

As the OS coordinates the activities of the processor, it uses RAM as a temporary storage area for instructions and data the processor needs. The OS is therefore responsible for coordinating the space allocations in RAM to ensure that there is enough space for the waiting instructions and data. If there isn't sufficient space in RAM for all the data and instructions, then the OS allocates the least necessary files to temporary storage on the hard drive, called *virtual memory*.

The OS manages storage by providing a file-management system that keeps track of the names and locations of files and programs. Programs called *device drivers* facilitate communication between devices attached to the computer and the OS. Device drivers translate the specialized commands of devices to commands that the OS can understand and vice versa, enabling the OS to communicate with every device in the computer system. Device drivers for common devices are included in the OS software, whereas other devices come with a device driver that you must install or download off the Web.

### 6. How does the operating system interact with application software?

All software applications need to interact with the CPU. For programs to work with the CPU, they must contain code that the CPU recognizes. Rather than having the same blocks of code appear in each application, the OS includes the blocks of code to which software applications refer. These blocks of code are called *application programming interfaces* (APIs).

**7. How does the operating system help the computer start up?**

When you start your computer, it runs through a special process called the *boot process*. The boot process consists of four basic steps: (1) The basic input/output system (BIOS) is activated when the user powers on the CPU. (2) In the POST check, the BIOS verifies that all attached devices are in place. (3) The operating system is loaded into RAM. (4) Configuration and customization settings are checked.

**8. What are the main desktop and window features?**

The desktop provides your first interaction with the OS and is the first image you see on your monitor once the system has booted up. It provides you with access to your computer's files, folders, and commonly used tools and applications. Windows are the rectangular panes on your screen that display applications running on your system. Common features of windows include toolbars, scrollbars, and Minimize, Maximize/Restore Down, and Close buttons.

**9. How does the operating system help me keep my computer organized?**

The OS allows you to organize the contents of your computer in a hierarchical structure of directories that includes files, folders, libraries, and drives. Windows Explorer helps you manage your files and folders by showing the location and contents of every drive, folder, and file on your computer. Creating folders is the key to organizing files because folders keep related documents together. Following naming conventions and using proper file extensions are also important aspects of file management.

**10. What utility programs are included in system software, and what do they do?**

Some utility programs are incorporated into the OS; others are sold as stand-alone off-the-shelf programs. Common Windows utilities include those that enable you to adjust your display, add or remove programs, compress files, defragment your hard drive, clean unnecessary files off your system, check for lost files and errors, restore your system to an earlier setting, back up your files, schedule automatic tasks, and check on programs that have stopped running.

## Companion Website

The Companion Website includes a variety of additional materials to help you review and learn more about the topics in this chapter. Go to: ***www.pearsonhighered.com/techinaction***

chapter

# eight

key terms

key terms

## Word Bank

- Backup and Restore
- Disk Cleanup
- Disk Defragmenter
- Error-checking
- file management
- files
- folders

- gadgets
- libraries
- Linux
- Mac OS
- operating system
- platform
- Safe mode

- Task Manager
- Task Scheduler
- utility programs
- virtual memory
- Windows Explorer

**Instructions:** Fill in the blanks using the words from the Word Bank above.

Vincent used (1) _____ to automatically schedule and run several (2) _____, those special-function programs that help with routine computer maintenance and repairs. Despite regularly running (3) _____ to help realign scattered file fragments on the hard drive, and (4) _____ to remove any unnecessary files, Vincent knew his computer was becoming progressively more sluggish. Vincent found he had to use the (5) _____ more frequently to check on programs that had stopped running, or to boot his system into (6) _____ so that he could perform further diagnostics while the computer was running in a limited state. Furthermore, Vincent knew with only 1 GB of RAM, his system was using (7) _____ and optimizing RAM storage by borrowing hard drive space. Vincent knew a hard drive error could happen at any time, so he had made a complete copy of his hard drive using the Windows (8) _____ utility. He relied on the (9) _____ tools to create an organized file system. He regularly created (10) _____ to better organize his files. He had been hearing lots of good reviews of Windows 7, Microsoft's new (11) _____ software, and in particular its additional file management feature, (12) _____, where he could access files, such as his pictures, from multiple locations in his computer system, without having to save them in a single folder. But many of his friends liked working with (13) _____, the Apple operating system. Both the PC and Mac operating systems included desktop features that Vincent found helpful, especially (14) _____ or widgets, the mini-programs that enable quick access to tools and activities such as calendars, stock prices, or weather indicators. Vincent wasn't sure which (15) _____ he would buy—a PC or a Mac—but he knew he needed to make a decision soon.

Using key terms from the chapter, write a letter to your 14-year-old cousin who just received her first computer, explaining the benefits of simple computer maintenance. First, explain any symptoms her computer may be experiencing, and then include a set of steps she can follow in setting up a regimen to remedy each problem. Make sure you explain some of the system maintenance utilities described in this chapter. Instruct your cousin on how to create a system repair disc and how to back up her files. Include any other utilities she might need, and explain why she should have them.

**Instructions:** Answer the multiple-choice and true–false questions below for more practice with key terms and concepts from this chapter.

## Multiple Choice

**1.** Which is an example of a smartphone operating system?
a. Symbian
b. Windows 7
c. Mac OS
d. webOS

**2.** Which OS does not have a user interface that incorporates point-and-click technology?
a. Windows 7
b. MS-DOS
c. Linux
d. Mac OS X

**3.** Which is the correct order of the boot process?
a. check settings, load BIOS into RAM, activate BIOS, conduct POST
b. load OS into RAM, check settings, conduct POST, activate BIOS
c. activate BIOS, conduct POST, load OS into RAM, check settings
d. conduct POST, load OS into RAM, activate BIOS, check settings

**4.** Which of the following is not a file management tool?
a. folders
b. Windows Explorer
c. libraries
d. groups

**5.** Which best describes Plug and Play (PnP)?
a. a means for the user to interact with the computer
b. enables the processor to handle multiple operations, seemingly at the same time
c. programming code in the OS that coordinates with software
d. a feature that facilitates the installation of peripheral devices with the inclusion of drivers in the OS

**6.** The term that defines excessive swapping of files between RAM and virtual memory is
a. thrashing.
b. multitasking.
c. caching.
d. paging.

**7.** Which term describes the pictures that represent an object such as a software application or a folder?
a. icons
b. gadgets
c. taskbars
d. widgets

**8.** Which statement about using APIs is *not* true?
a. APIs prevent redundancies in software code.
b. APIs make it easier for developers to respond to OS changes.
c. APIs allow application software to interact with the OS.
d. APIs make it possible to close non-responding software and restart the computer.

**9.** Which utility eliminates the inefficiencies of the computer hard drive?
a. System Restore
b. Disk Defragmenter
c. File Compression
d. Disk Cleanup

**10.** Which of the following would be considered an accessibility utility?
a. System Restore
b. Narrator
c. Screen Saver
d. Safe Mode

## True–False

_____ 1. All smartphones use the same operating system software.

_____ 2. The Android operating system is based on Microsoft Windows.

_____ 3. The amount of system RAM helps to determine which OS a computer uses.

_____ 4. Paging is the process of optimizing RAM storage by borrowing hard drive space.

_____ 5. Machines with built-in computers use real-time operating systems.

## 1. Organizing Your Files

Despite all the good advice, you may not have taken the time to organize your files on your computer. Click the Start button, and select Documents. Then, use the Snipping Tool to show your current file organization. If your system is well organized, explain how you set up your file management system. If you have not used file management features to organize your documents, develop a plan that outlines how you'll set up libraries, folders, and subfolders for your files.

## 2. Deciding On a New Computer

Your parents are getting you a new computer. Decide whether you want a desktop, notebook, or netbook and then describe how the choice may impact the operating system you get.

a. Discuss the advantages and disadvantages of Windows, Mac, and Linux operating systems.
b. Research whether you can use multiple operating systems on a single machine. Why might this be an important feature for you to consider?
c. Research how your smartphone and personal music player might sync with your computer's operating system.
d. Explain which system would be most useful to you.

## 3. Creating a Backup Plan

Your computer just shut down unexpectedly but, fortunately, you were able to get it back up and running without any loss of data. However, this was too close of a call, so you decide to back up your precious files once and for all. Research the specific steps you will need to take to initially create a backup and then maintain a current backup as your files change. Include in your research what stand-alone programs or operating system tools you will need to use, as well as any hardware devices or accessories you'll require. Then research the process of creating a disk image. What's the difference between creating a system backup and a disk image?

## 4. Portable Operating Systems

Traditionally, operating system files are stored permanently on your computer's hard drive. The operating system controls the user experience, so every computer you interact with (at home, at school, at your friend's house) may have different settings and features. Explore the concept of portable operating systems. What is a portable operating system? Why might it be useful to use one? Investigate a portable operating system, such as Slax or Ubuntu, and explain its features.

## 5. Smartphone OS

Your cell phone contract is up in a few weeks, and it's time to upgrade to a smartphone. Which smartphone would you buy, and why? What kind of OS does it have? What are the benefits and disadvantages of this OS compared to that of other smartphones? Is the smartphone OS compatible with the OS on your computer?

chapter

# eight

eight

making the
transition to...
the workplace

making the
transition to...
the workplace

1. **Using a Web-Based OS**

   Your new job requires you to collaborate and visit with sales and management teams within the United States as well as globally. Discuss the benefits and disadvantages of using a Web-based operating system as a means to help you perform your job better.

2. **Top Five Utility Programs**

   Create a list of the top five utilities you feel every computer should have. For each utility, discuss whether it is included in the operating system and/or if there are alternatives that can be downloaded for free or that can be purchased as stand-alone programs. Then, for each recommendation, include a review of the utility that has been written in the past year—make sure you document your sources.

3. **Accessibility Features**

   Windows offers a lot of great accessibility tools for those needing extra assistance. The vice president for human resources at the company you work for has asked you to research some stand-alone accessibility programs to determine what else, if anything, is available. List software that is available to help those who have special computing needs.

4. **Working with More Than One OS**

   The company you work for, which uses all Windows computers, has just acquired two other smaller companies, one that uses Macs and the other that uses Linux. Your boss, the CIO of the company, needs to decide what to do with all the various computer systems. You have been asked to provide information to your boss so that he can make an informed decision.

   a. What are the advantages and disadvantages of letting the acquired companies continue using their current systems?
   b. What are the advantages and disadvantages of converting all systems to one common system?

   As you research, consider factors such as technical support, training for a new system, compatibility of files and calendars among all employees in the company, cost of new hardware, stability of operating systems, needed frequency of upgrades, and software compatibility.

**Instructions:** Some ideas are best understood by experimenting with them in our own minds. The following critical thinking questions are designed to demand your full attention but require only a comfortable chair—no technology.

### 1. Market Dominance

Microsoft and Apple are large corporations and have control of most of the operating system markets. While there have been some innovative changes to each of their proprietary operating systems, does their size and market dominance prevent more innovation? Why or why not? Linux, as an open source environment, is poised for greater innovation. Why do you think the Linux operating system doesn't have a greater market share?

### 2. A Web-Based OS

Operating system interfaces have evolved from a text-based console format to the current graphical user interface. Many believe the OS of the future will be on the cloud (the Internet) and Web-based. Discuss the implications of this type of operating system. What are the potential security issues of a Web-based operating system?

### 3. To Hackintosh or Not: That Is the Question

Using Mac's Boot Camp, or virtualization software such as VMware, it's possible to install Windows on a Mac. It isn't quite as easy to install Mac OS X on a PC, but it can be done. Those PCs that have been modified so that Mac OS X can be run on them are given the name *Hackintosh*. What are the benefits of tweaking a PC to run Mac OS X? Is it okay to violate Apple's End User Licensing Agreement (EULA)? If Apple changed its EULA to allow the installation of its software onto PCs, would that ultimately hurt Apple-branded computers?

### 4. Your Own Gadget/Widget?

There are plenty of interesting Windows gadgets and Mac OS widgets available—some for fun, some to aid in productivity, some with specific utilitarian roles. Design or describe what the best gadget or widget for you would be. What features must it have? Why would you need it?

team time

## Choosing the Best OS

### Problem

You are the owner of a technology consulting firm. Your current assignments include advising several start-up clients on their technology requirements. The companies include a fashion design company, a small financial planning company, and an IT networking firm. The companies are holding off on buying anything until they hear from you as to the platform on which their computers should run. Obviously, one of the critical decisions for each company is the choice of operating system.

### Task

Recommend the appropriate operating system for each company.

### Process

1. Break up into teams that represent the three primary operating systems: Windows, Mac, or Linux. (Additional teams could be assigned to consider smartphone operating systems).

2. As a team, research the pros and cons of your operating system. What features does it have that would benefit each company? What features does it not have that each company would need? Why would your operating system be the appropriate (or inappropriate) choice for each company? Why is your OS better (or worse) than either of the other options?

3. Develop a presentation that states your position with regard to your operating system. Your presentation should have a recommendation and include facts to back it up.

4. As a class, decide which operating system would be the best choice for each company.

### Conclusion

Because the operating system is the most critical piece of software in the computer system, the selection should not be taken lightly. The OS that is best for a fashion design agency may not be best for a financial planning firm. An IT networking firm may have different needs altogether. It is important to make sure you consider all aspects of the work environment and the type of work that is being done to ensure a good fit.

# Software Piracy

In this exercise, you will research and then role-play a complicated ethical situation. The role you play may or may not match your own personal beliefs, but your research and use of logic will enable you to represent whichever view is assigned. An arbitrator will watch and comment on both sides of the arguments, and together the team will agree on an ethical solution.

## Problem

Software publishers spend millions of dollars developing new products. Illegal copies of software, including operating system software, rob the developers and their shareholders of their rightful profits. In addition, some say that pervasive software piracy, especially in China, could potentially threaten job loss for U.S. software companies. However, some people believe that when they buy the software, they have the right to distribute their copy as they like, thus violating the software license agreement they accepted when installing the software.

## Research Areas to Consider

- Software piracy

- Software licensing agreements

- CD piracy

- China antipiracy

## Process

1. Divide the class into teams.

2. Research the areas cited above and devise a scenario in which an individual has been accused of software piracy.

3. Team members should write a summary that provides background information for their character—for example, representative of a software developer, public consumer of the software, or arbitrator—and detail their character's behaviors to set the stage for the role-playing event. Then team members should create an outline to use during the role-playing event.

4. Team members should arrange a mutually convenient time to meet for the exchange, using the collaboration feature of MyITLab, the discussion board feature of Blackboard, or meeting in person.

5. Team members should present their case to the class or submit a PowerPoint presentation for review by the rest of the class, along with the summary and resolution they developed.

## Conclusion

As technology becomes ever more prevalent and integrated into our lives, more and more ethical dilemmas will present themselves. Being able to understand and evaluate both sides of the argument, while responding in a personally or socially ethical manner, will be an important skill.

# chapter 9

# behind the scenes:

## databases and information systems

DECKED BUILDER by Tan Thor Jen.
Copyright © Decked Studios.
Reprinted by permission.

### Database Basics

**OBJECTIVES:**

What is a database, and why is it beneficial to use databases? *(p. 296)*

What components make up a database? *(p. 298)*

What types of databases are there? *(p. 302)*

 **Active Helpdesk:** Understanding Database Management Systems

### How Databases Operate

Juri Samsonov / Fotolia

**OBJECTIVES:**

What do database management systems do? *(p. 304)*

How do relational databases organize and manipulate data? *(p. 312)*

 **Active Helpdesk:** Using Databases

 Sound Byte: Creating an Access 2010 Database

 Sound Byte: Improving an Access 2010 Database

© Mira / Alamy

### Database Warehousing and Storage

**OBJECTIVE:**

What are data warehouses and data marts, and how are they used? *(p. 317)*

patrimonio designs limited/Shutterstock

### Business Intelligence Systems and Data Mining

**OBJECTIVES:**

What is a business intelligence system, and what types of business intelligence systems are used by decision makers? *(p. 321)*

What is data mining, and how does it work? *(p. 327)*

 **Active Helpdesk:** Data Warehouses, Data Marts, and Information Systems

*Scan here for more info on How Cool Is This?*

# how cool is *this?*

Most useful sites on the Internet have databases integrated into them, or are actually databases themselves. One popular example is Twitter. But with the **millions** of Twitter users tweeting about all sorts of different things, how can you find Twitter users who generate tweets about subjects that fit your interests?

Justtweetit.com is a **database of Twitter** users that groups users by **logical topics of interest**. Are you an artist interested in following what other artists are tweeting about? Just click on the Artists link to find more than 550 active Twitter users who discuss art. What if you regularly tweet on a topic, such as fashion or video gaming, and want to have **more potential followers** find you? You can easily add yourself to the Justtweetit directory in the most appropriate of the hundreds of categories featured on the site. So start finding **more relevant tweets** today!

John Schwegel / Alamy

# Life Without Databases

A **database** is a collection of related data that can be easily stored, sorted, organized, and queried. By creating an organized structure for data, we hope to make data more meaningful and therefore more useful. In other words, we are attempting to turn data into information. But why should you learn about databases?

Although you may never be called upon to construct a database, you probably use databases every day. For example, you might search a database in an attempt to extract relevant information. A key attribute of databases is that information can be filtered so that you only see the information you really want. Understanding how databases work and what you can do with a database will help you use them more effectively. Let's look at two examples.

Have you checked Facebook today? If so, you used a database even though you probably didn't realize it. When you load your Facebook page, you see a News Feed of items your friends have posted on their Facebook pages. Facebook is using your list of friends to comb through their databases to provide you with what it thinks is relevant information—in other words, what your friends are saying today—to display on your News Feed. But you might have a different idea of what is relevant. You might only be interested in updates from your friends that include photos. Or perhaps you want to see only items with links to other pages. You can select these options on your News Feed, and Facebook changes your feed to only include the items you want to see and filters out any items that don't match the criteria you specified.

Or perhaps you want your News Feed to show all the latest updates, not just what Facebook thinks is most important. Selecting the option Most Recent on your News Feed sorts all the items posted by your friends with the newest posts on top. Sorting and filtering are key attributes of most databases.

Suppose you enjoy playing collectible card games such as Magic: The Gathering (MTG) or Yu-Gi-Oh!. Collectible card games like MTG present players with a wide variety of cards, that have been issued over the years, that can be used in building decks to compete with other players. Remembering all the available cards when trying to design a deck can be daunting. But database applications such as Decked Builder allow you to easily search for available cards based on key card attributes such as the type of card (creature or sorcery), color, and rarity (see Figure 9.1).

Although you may not have realized it, apps like Decked Builder are really searchable databases.

Filtering and sorting information to enhance its usefulness to you and searching for relevant information are just three useful aspects of databases. In the rest of this chapter, you'll learn about the inner workings of databases and other ways they can be used to provide relevant information quickly and easily.

### Should I use databases for managing all types of data?

Not every situation in which related data needs to be turned into organized information demands the complexity of a database. For simple tasks, lists are adequate. Often, word processing or spreadsheet software works for creating simple lists. A table you create in Microsoft Word can serve as a list, as can a spreadsheet you create in Microsoft Excel.

Figure 9.2 shows a simple "Books to Buy" list you might create in Excel before begin-

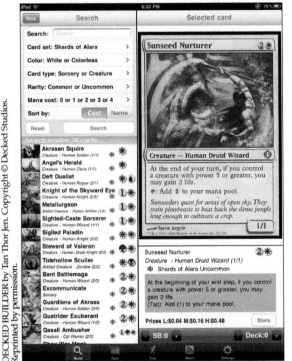

DECKED BUILDER by Tan Thor Jen. Copyright © Decked Studios. Reprinted by permission.

**Figure 9.1**

Decked Builder gives you the ability to search and filter information on Magic: The Gathering cards.

**Figure 9.2**

A simple list created as a spreadsheet in Microsoft Excel is often sufficient to organize simple tasks.

|   | A | B | C | D |
|---|---|---|---|---|
| 2 | **Books To Buy** | | | |
| 3 | | | | |
| 4 | **Class** | **Title** | **Author** | **Bought** |
| 5 | American Literature 1 | Anthology of American Literature, Volume 1 | McMichael et al. | |
| 6 | American Literature 1 | Moby Dick | Melville | Yes |
| 7 | American Literature 1 | The Last of the Mohicans | Cooper | Yes |
| 8 | English Composition 1 | The Academic Writer's Handbook | Rosen | |
| 9 | English Composition 1 | The Write Stuff: Thinking Through Essays | Sims | Yes |
| 10 | Intro to Business | Better Business | Solomon, Poatsy, Martin | Yes |

ning college. This list works well because it is simple and suited to just one purpose: to provide you with a list of the books you need to buy for a particular semester. If all the information that needed to be tracked were as simple as the information in Figure 9.2, there would be no need for databases.

**When is a list not appropriate?**
If complex information needs to be organized, or more than one person needs access to it, a list is not an efficient solution. For example, when you enrolled in college, you provided information about yourself to a number of people. This information included your name, your address, the classes you wished to take, and the meal plan you selected. Your school also tracks other information about you, such as your residence hall address. Consider the two lists shown in Figure 9.3. Figure 9.3a is a list the registrar's office might use to keep track of students, the classes they are taking, and the meal plan they selected. Figure 9.3b is a list the residence hall manager might use to track where students are housed.

**What's the problem with having two lists?** First, there is a great deal of duplicated data between the two lists in Figure 9.3. For example, each time Julio Garza registers for a class, his name and ad-

dress are entered. He needs to provide the same data to the residence hall manager when he receives his residence hall assignment. This **data redundancy**, though not a problem in the small lists in Figure 9.3, can be problematic when a college or university has 10,000 students. Imagine the time wasted by entering data multiple times, semester after semester. Imagine, too, the increased likelihood that someone will make a data entry mistake.

Second, each time the information in the list changes, multiple lists must be updated. If Mei Zhang moves, her data will need to be updated in all the lists that contain her address. It would be easy to overlook one or more lists or even one or more rows in the same list. This would lead to a state of **data inconsistency**. It would not be possible to tell easily which data was correct. In addition,

**Figure 9.3**

(a) A class registration list and (b) a list of residence hall assignments are two lists a college might create to keep track of student information.

**a**

**Class Registration List - Spring Semester**

| SID # | Last Name | First Name | Home Address | City | State | Zip Code | Class Code | Class Name | # Of Credits | Meal Plan # |
|---|---|---|---|---|---|---|---|---|---|---|
| 123456789 | Finkel | Susan | 645 Pine Street | Philadelphia | PA | 19102-5674 | CIS 110 | Computer Literacy | 3 | 1 |
| 123456789 | Finkel | Susan | 645 Pine Street | Philadelphia | PA | 19102-5674 | ENG 101 | English Comp 1 | 3 | 1 |
| 123456789 | Finkel | Susan | 645 Pine Street | Philadelphia | PA | 19102-5674 | HIS 103 | Western Civ 1 | 3 | 1 |
| 123456789 | Finkel | Susan | 645 Pine Street | Philadelphia | PA | 19102-5674 | CHE 140 | Chemistry | 4 | 1 |
| 123456789 | Finkel | Susan | 646 Pine Street | Philadelphia | PA | 19102-5674 | PSY 101 | Intro to Psychology | 3 | 1 |
| 789123456 | Garza | Julio | 421 West 3rd St | New Witten | SD | 57584-1234 | CIS 110 | Computer Literacy | 3 | 1 |
| 789123456 | Garza | Julio | 421 West 3rd St | New Witten | SD | 57584-1234 | SOC 101 | Intro to Sociology | 3 | 1 |
| 789123456 | Garza | Julio | 421 West 3rd St | New Witten | SD | 57584-1234 | PSY 101 | Intro to Psych | 3 | 1 |
| 678912345 | O'Connor | Leanne | 238 Grant Street | Beverly | MA | 01915-4333 | | | | |
| 567891234 | Stinson | Arthur | 345 Ryan Drive | Cedar Falls | IA | 50613-3232 | BIO 210 | Anatomy & Physiology 1 | 3 | 3 |
| 567891234 | Stinson | Arthur | 345 Ryan Drive | Cedar Falls | IA | 50613-3232 | ENG 101 | English Comp 1 | 3 | 3 |
| 567891234 | Stinson | Arthur | 345 Ryan Drive | Cedar Falls | IA | 50613-3232 | SOC 101 | Intro to Sociology | 3 | 3 |
| 456789123 | Zhang | Mei | 457 Blanchard St | Boston | MA | 01901-3424 | PSY 101 | Intro to Psychology | 3 | 2 |
| 456789123 | Zhang | Mei | 457 Blanchard St | Boston | MA | 01901-3424 | HIS 103 | Western Civ 1 | 3 | 2 |
| 456789123 | Zhang | Mei | 457 Blanchard St | Boston | MA | 01901-3424 | ENG 102 | English Comp 2 | 3 | 2 |

**b**

**Residence Hall Assignment List - Fall**

| SID # | Last Name | First Name | Home Address | City | State | Zip Code | Residence Hall Name | Room Number |
|---|---|---|---|---|---|---|---|---|
| 123456789 | Finkel | Susan | 645 Pine Street | Philadelphia | PA | 19102-5674 | Founder's Hall | 303 |
| 789123456 | Garza | Julio | 421 West 3rd St | New Witten | SD | 57584-1234 | Bauer Hall | 121 |
| 678912345 | O'Connor | Leanne | 238 Grant Street | Beverly | MA | 01915-4333 | Bauer Hall | 214 |
| 567891234 | Stinson | Arthur | 345 Ryan Drive | Cedar Falls | IA | 50613-3232 | Berger Quad | 317 |
| 456789123 | Zhang | Mei | 457 Blanchard St | Boston | MA | 98107-4356 | Mission | 223 |

notice that Susan Finkel's last record in Figure 9.3a contains a different street address than that shown in her other records. It's impossible to tell which address is correct, again resulting in data inconsistency.

In addition, correct data can be entered into a list but in an inconsistent format. Look at students Julio Garza and Mei Zhang in Figure 9.3a. Both are registered for PSY 101, but two different course names appear: Intro to Psychology and Intro to Psych. Are these the same course? Which name is the correct one? Confusion arises when data is inconsistently entered. Establishing data consistency is difficult to do with a list.

**Aside from data redundancy and inconsistency, are there any other problems with using lists instead of databases?** What if someone accidentally entered Arthur Stinson's enrollment data twice in the list in Figure 9.3a? Any reports (such as student bills) that are generated based on this list will be inaccurate because of the duplicate data. For example, Arthur would be sent two separate bills for his classes, resulting in confusion and headaches.

In Figure 9.3a, each student has selected one of the college's meal plans, and this data must be entered into each row. What if someone enters a nonexistent meal plan in one of the rows pertaining to Susan Finkel? This is not only wrong, but also can be confusing to anyone viewing the list. With a list, anything can be entered in a row or column, even if that information is incorrect.

In addition, information can be organized in many ways. Consider the list of residence hall assignments in Figure 9.3b, which is organized alphabetically by last name. This works well for the accounting clerk, who needs to generate bills for student housing. However, for the residence manager who wants to see which residence hall rooms are still vacant, it would be more useful to have the data organized by residence hall and room number. Reorganizing multiple lists in this way can be labor intensive.

A final problem with lists is how to handle incomplete data. In Figure 9.3a, Leanne O'Connor has enrolled in the college but has not yet selected a meal plan or registered for courses. Her known information has been entered, but it's impossible to tell by looking at her record whether data relating to her course registrations and meal plans is available and just was not entered, or is truly missing.

**Can't I just exercise caution and set rules for updating lists?** Carefully following the rules when you update a list like the ones shown in Figure 9.3 can address many of the problems mentioned, but there is still room for error. Being careful does not avoid the most pressing problems of lists: (1) the inability of the data to be shared and (2) data redundancy. Even if you could surmount all of these problems, you cannot easily change a list to accommodate the disparate needs of many users.

**How can I solve the problems associated with lists?** For single topics, a list is sufficient. However, for any complex data that needs to be organized or shared, using a database is the most practical and efficient way to avoid the pitfalls associated with using lists.

# Database Building Blocks

Almost any kind of data that needs organization and analysis can be put into a database. For example, eBay keeps track of the millions of items that users have for sale in a searchable database enabling you to find that used iPad you want to purchase. Media providers such as Netflix, which rents DVDs and streams video content to consumers, store subscribers' mailing addresses and payment information in a database. In this section, we explore the advantages of using databases as well as the terminology databases use to categorize data.

## Advantages of Using Databases

**How do databases make our lives easier?** Without databases, you could not store and retrieve large quantities of information easily. Consider airline reservation systems. Thousands of people fly across the United States on any given day. Without a database, it would be extremely difficult to keep track of such a large number of airline reservations. In addition, although you can look up information fairly quickly in a list, even extremely large electronic databases can provide the information you request in seconds. Databases provide three main advantages: They enable information sharing, they promote data integrity, and they allow the flexible use of data.

**How do databases make information sharing possible?** Consider student records at a college. As noted earlier, without databases, financial aid, admissions, and student housing would all need their own student lists (files). The information in these lists might not match because each department would maintain its own records. If a change had to be made in a student's address, all three lists (the financial aid file, the admissions file, and the student housing file) would have to be changed.

As shown in Figure 9.4, with a database only one file is maintained, which reduces the possibility of errors when data is entered or updated. It also increases efficiency, because there are no files to reconcile with each other. A database therefore provides for data centralization. There is no need for multiple lists. Each department that needs to use student information accesses it from the same set of data.

**How do databases promote data integrity?** Data integrity means that the data contained in the database is accurate and reliable. **Data centralization** goes a long way toward ensuring data integrity. Instead of being in multiple lists that have to be maintained, your name and address information is maintained in only one place. If you move, your address must be changed only once.

**How do databases provide flexibility?** Another significant advantage of databases is that they are flexibly organized, enabling you to reorganize the information they contain in a variety of ways to suit the needs of the moment. Think back to the earlier example regarding lists. The registrar and housing manager need to see different information. With a list, you can

organize information in only one way. If information is in a database, the registrar can easily view just the information she needs (such as the courses the student is taking). Likewise, the housing manager can easily view just the information he needs (such as the residence hall to which the student is assigned).

Data flexibility also makes information dissemination tasks easier. Suppose your school wants to send out a mailing about a new course to all business majors. Having the contact information of students available in a database makes it easy to merge the data, using an application such as Microsoft Word, and create personalized letters and address labels. Obviously, this would be much faster than generating these items manually, and the results should contain fewer errors. Thus, databases can manage larger amounts of data and process that data more efficiently.

**Financial Aid Office**

Student financial aid records are updated

*Sean Prior/Shutterstock.com*

A teacher enters student grades

*AVAVA/Shutterstock.com*

**Student Registration**

A student registers for classes and checks her grades

*Monkey Business Images/Shutterstock.com*

**Student Housing Office**

A student is assigned to a residence hall

*Tan Klan Khoon/Shutterstock.com*

**Student Information Database**

**Figure** 9.4

Using a database lets data be centralized, so that only one copy of relevant data must be maintained. All database users therefore access the same up-to-date information.

**Are there any disadvantages associated with databases?** Databases are more complex to construct and administer than lists. They also can be time-consuming and expensive to set up. Great care must be exercised in the design of databases to ensure they will function as intended. Although average individuals can design small databases, it is helpful to have an experienced **database administrator** (or **database designer**), an individual trained in the design and building of databases, to assist with the construction of large databases.

Data privacy concerns also arise when using databases. Think about how much information you've provided to your school. The school probably has records of your Social Security number, birth date, address, and credit card information. These are things an identity thief would love to get their hands on. For this reason, many colleges and universities no longer use Social Security numbers as student identification (ID) numbers. Instead, they create a unique student ID number when you register, which helps protect your Social Security number from falling into the wrong hands. Despite the increased complexity of databases and the issues surrounding privacy, however, the advantages of databases far outweigh the administrative disadvantages.

## Database Terminology

**How is data stored in a database?** Understanding how databases store information requires knowing the unique terminology developed to describe databases. As shown in Figure 9.5, databases have three main components: fields, records, and tables (or files).

## Fields

**What is a field?** A database stores each category of information in a **field**. Fields are displayed in columns. The city where a student lives can be found in the City field in the student information table shown in Figure 9.5. Each field is identified by a **field name**, which is a way of describing the field. Zip Code is a field name in the database in Figure 9.5. In a database, fields have other characteristics to describe them, including field data types and field size.

**What are data types?** When fields are created in the database, the user assigns those fields a **data type** (or **field type**). The data type indicates what type of data can be stored in the field.

Common data types are listed with examples in Figure 9.6 and are described in the remainder of this section.

- A **text field** can hold any combination of alphanumeric data (letters or numbers), but is most often used to hold words. Although text fields can contain numbers (such as telephone numbers), they are stored as text and therefore cannot be used in calculations.

- A **numeric field** stores numbers. Unlike values in text fields, values in numeric fields can be used to perform calculations. For instance, the numbers stored in numeric fields can be used to calculate tuition owed.

- A **computational field** (or **calculated field**) is a numeric field that stores the contents of a calculation, which is generated with a formula in the numeric field. This is similar to a formula computation in a spreadsheet cell.

- A **date/time field** holds data such as birthdays and due dates.

**Figure 9.5**

In a database, a category of information is stored in a field. A group of related fields is called a record, and a group of related records is called a table (or file).

## Figure 9.6 | COMMON DATA TYPES AND SAMPLE DATA

| Data Type | Used to Store | Examples |
|---|---|---|
| Text | Alphabetic or alphanumeric data | Cecilia<br>PSY 101 |
| Numeric | Numbers | 512<br>1.789<br>$1,230 |
| Calculated | Computational formulas | Credit hours × per-credit tuition charges |
| Date/Time | Dates and times in standard notation | 2/21/2016; 10:48 |
| Memo | Long blocks of text | Four score and seven years ago our fathers brought forth on this continent, a new nation, conceived in Liberty, and dedicated to the proposition that all men are created equal. |
| Object | Multimedia files or documents | MP3 file<br>AVI file |
| Hyperlink | A hyperlink to a Web page | www.pearsonhighered.com/techinaction |

- A **memo field** is like a text field but can hold long pieces of text. For example, a paragraph describing your high school achievements could be stored in a memo field.
- An **object field** holds items such as pictures, video clips, or documents.
- A **hyperlink field** stores hyperlinks to Web pages.

**What is meant by field size?** Field size defines the maximum number of characters or numbers that a field can hold. If a numeric field has a size of 5, it can hold a number as high as 99999. As a rule, you should tailor the field size to the length of the data it contains. If you define a field size of 50, space is reserved for 50 characters in that field, whether or not all 50 characters are used. Therefore, if you know that a character field will have a maximum of two characters, defining the field size as 50 wastes space and makes the files unnecessarily large. This can cause decreased database performance, especially in large databases.

### Records and Tables

**What are records and tables in databases?** A group of related fields is called a **record**. For example, a student's name, address, and telephone number comprise a record. A group of related records is called a **table** (or **file**). A database file can contain multiple tables. Tables usually are organized by a common subject. Figure 9.5 shows a table that contains records representing contact information for students.

### Primary Keys

**Can fields have the same values in the same table?** Yes, they can. It is possible that two students may live in the same town or have the same last name. However, to keep records distinct, each record must have one field that has a value unique to that record. This unique field is called a **primary key** or a **key field**. For example, as shown in Figure 9.7, in student records, the primary key is the student ID number (field name SID#). Establishing a primary

**Figure 9.7**

Unique student ID numbers make ideal primary keys, because even students with the same name won't have the same ID number.

| SID# | Last Name | First Name | Address | City | State | Zip Code |
|---|---|---|---|---|---|---|
| 123456789 | Finkel | Susan | 645 Pine Street | Philadelphia | PA | 19102-5674 |
| 345678912 | Garza | Julio | 32 Owen Ave | Lansdowne | PA | 19050-3423 |
| 789123456 | Garza | Julio | 421 West 3rd St | New Witten | SD | 57584-1234 |
| 678912345 | O'Connor | Leanne | 238 Grant Street | Beverly | MA | 01915-4333 |
| 567891234 | Stinson | Arthur | 345 Ryan Drive | | | 50613-3232 |
| 456789123 | Zhang | Mei | 457 Blanchard St | | | 01901-3424 |

Same name, different primary keys

## Music Database Helps You Find New Music

You probably have hundreds of songs that you listen to regularly. Wouldn't it be great if you could receive music recommendations based on the common attributes of music you already enjoy, instead of random comments from your friends or less reliable data such as buying patterns? Many Internet radio offerings, such as Last.fm (accessible through Xbox Live, smartphones, and the Web) and Pandora are designed to work this way.

The Music Genome Project provides such recommendations by analyzing songs and categorizing them in a database according to almost 400 different attributes, such as "breathy female lead vocalist" or "club rap roots." Pandora Internet Radio (**pandora.com**) currently uses the Music Genome Project to provide music to listeners based on their music preferences.

With Pandora, you can create radio stations that play music based on facts you provide, called seeds. Seeds can be either song titles or the names of musical artists (see Figure 9.8). So, if you enjoy music from The Black Eyed Peas or like the song "Rolling in the Deep" (by Adele), you would enter these as seeds for a Pandora station. Pandora then would play music with attributes similar to the seeds you provided. You can't control which songs will play, because they are served up randomly, but they will likely be songs you will enjoy, even if you have never heard them before.

**Figure 9.8**

Bloomberg via Getty Images

A Pandora radio "station" can be set up based on a seed for your favorite musical group.

---

key and ensuring that it is unique makes it impossible to duplicate records.

**What makes a good primary key?** We already have many numbers that follow us through our lives that make excellent primary keys. In the past, Social Security numbers were often selected as primary keys in databases containing data about individuals. As mentioned previously, concerns about identity theft have led many businesses to abandon Social Security numbers as the primary means of identifying individuals. Driver's license numbers are unique within a particular state, as are the license plate numbers on cars. State government agencies often use these numbers to track individuals and their transactions.

Primary keys don't have to be numbers that already represent something. For example, when you place an order with Amazon.com, your transaction gets a unique order number. This number is the Amazon database's primary key. You refer to this number when checking your order status, returning merchandise, and so on. It is essential to have a unique number for each order because it would be difficult to keep track of it without one.

## Database Types

Many different types of electronic databases have been used since the invention of the computer. The three major types of databases currently in use are relational, object-oriented, and multidimensional. Of these three, relational databases have the largest market share, but the market share of multidimensional databases is growing at a fast pace.

### Relational Databases

**What is a relational database?** A **relational database** organizes data in table format by logically grouping similar data into a **relation** (a table that contains related data). As discussed earlier, each record in a database table is assigned a primary key to ensure that the record is unique. In relational databases, tables are logically linked to each other by including their primary keys in other tables with related information.

For example, at your college, a database about students would have a table with student contact information (name, address, and phone number) and another table with class registration information (class number and class name). These two tables would be linked by a common field such as a student ID number.

**Who invented the relational database?** E. F. Codd first significantly defined the relational model in 1970. Since then, much research and development has been done on the relational database model, and the model has proven to be extremely reliable for storing and manipulating data.

### Object-Oriented Databases

**What is an object-oriented database?** An **object-oriented database** stores data in objects, rather than in tables. The models on which these databases are constructed evolved from the object-oriented programming paradigm, which caught on in the programming community in the late 1980s. Objects contain not only data, but also methods for processing or manipulating that data. This allows object-oriented databases to store more types of data than relational databases and to access that data faster.

For example, a "student" object that contains data about the courses a student is taking might also store the instructions for generating a bill for the student based on his or her course load. Because object-oriented databases store the instructions for doing computations in the same place as they store the data, they can usually process requests for information faster than can relational databases (which would only store the student information).

**Why would I use an object-oriented database?** Whereas relational databases excel in the storage of **structured (analytical) data** (such as "Bill" or "345"), object-oriented databases are more adept at handling unstructured data. **Unstructured data** includes nontraditional data such as audio clips (including MP3 files), video clips, pictures, and extremely large documents. Data of this type is known as a **binary large object (BLOB)** because it is actually encoded in binary form.

Object-oriented databases are based on complex models for manipulating data. These models are much more complex than relational database models. Because businesses today need to store a greater variety of data, object-oriented databases are becoming more popular. Many relational database systems have been expanded to include object-oriented components. For a business to use its data in an object-oriented database, it needs to undergo a costly conversion process. However, once this initial cost is overcome, the faster access and reusability of the database objects can provide advantages for large businesses.

Object-oriented databases also need to use a query language to access and manage data. A **query language** is a specially designed computer language that is used to manipulate data in or extract data from a database. Many object-oriented databases use **Object Query Language (OQL)**, which is similar in many respects to **SQL (Structured Query Language)**, a standard language used to construct queries to extract data from databases.

---

**ACTIVE HELP-DESK**

### Understanding Database Management Systems

In this Active Helpdesk call, you'll play the role of a helpdesk staffer, fielding calls about database management systems, what they do, and how people can use them.

---

### Multidimensional Databases

**What is a multidimensional database?** A **multidimensional database** stores data in more than two dimensions. This distinguishes it from a relational database, which stores data in two-dimensional tables. Multidimensional databases organize data in a cube format. Each data cube has a *measure attribute*, which is the main type of data that the cube is tracking. Other elements of the cube are known as *feature attributes*, which all describe the measure attribute in some meaningful way. For example, sales of automobiles (measure attribute) could be categorized by various dimensions such as region, automobile color, automobile model, time period (such as current month), or salesperson—all feature attributes (see Figure 9.9). In addition, the database could be constructed to define different levels within a particular feature attribute (such as state and town within a region).

**What are the advantages of multidimensional databases?** The two main advantages of multidimensional databases are that they can easily be

**Figure** 9.9

Multidimensional databases describe data in at least three dimensions.

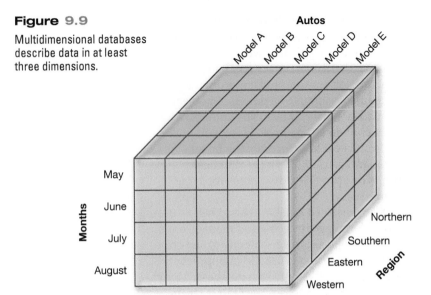

Autos

Model A   Model B   Model C   Model D   Model E

Months

May
June
July
August

Northern
Southern
Eastern
Western

Region

customized to provide information to a variety of users (based on their need), and they can process data much faster than pure relational databases can. The need for processing speed is especially critical when deploying a large database that will be accessed via the Internet. Therefore, large databases such as eBay that are accessed by many users needing to view data in different ways are usually designed as multi-dimensional databases. Oracle Corporation has slowly morphed its tried-and-true relational database into a multidimensional database in response to customer demand. This was primarily in response to customers who were using an Oracle database for applications deployed on the Web and needed better ways of storing and accessing image, audio, and video files. With multidimensional databases such as the current Oracle Database 11g, businesses do not have to abandon the proven relational database model, because multidimensional databases are based on proven relational database theory.

# Database Management Systems: Basic Operations

Databases are created and managed using a **database management system (DBMS)**. A DBMS is specially designed application software (such as Oracle Database or Microsoft Access) that interacts with the

user, other applications, and the database to capture and analyze data. The four main operations of a DBMS are

1. Creating databases and entering data
2. Viewing (or browsing) and sorting data
3. Querying (extracting) data
4. Outputting data

In the next sections, we look at each of these operations in detail.

## Creating Databases and Entering Data

**How do I create a database with a DBMS?** To create a database with a DBMS, you must first define the data to be captured. Therefore, you must create a description of the data. This description is contained in the database's files and is referred to as the **data dictionary** or the **database schema**. The data dictionary defines the name, data type, and length of each field in the database. Describing the data helps to categorize and analyze it and sets parameters for entering valid data into the database (such as a 10-digit number in a phone number field).

**How do I know what fields are needed in my database?** Careful planning is required to identify each distinct piece of data you need to capture. Each field should describe a unique piece of data and should never combine two separate pieces of data.

For example, for student registration at a college, capturing the student's name, street address, city, state, and zip code is important. But should a student's name be placed in one field or two? Because first and last names are separate pieces of data, you would want to create a separate field for each. For instance, suppose you wish to send an e-mail message to students addressing all of them by their first names (such as "Dear Geri"). If Geri's first and last names are in the same field in the database, it will be difficult to extract just her first name for the salutation.

**What does a data dictionary look like, and how do I create one?** In Microsoft Access, the data dictionary is called the Field Properties box. Figure 9.10a shows the Field Properties box for a database table in Access. The first step in creating an entry in the data dictionary is to create a field name. Field names must be unique within a table. In the table in

Figure 9.10a, the field name StateAbbreviation is used to store the abbreviation for the state where the student lives.

Second, you must define a data type for each field. For the StateAbbreviation field, you use a text data type because state abbreviations are expressed using characters. Third, you should set a maximum field size (in this case, two characters) for the field. Data in the field can be shorter than the maximum but can never exceed it. Sometimes the field name may not be meaningful to the user of the database even though it makes sense to the designer. The Caption value in Microsoft Access allows you to display a name of your choice on forms and reports.

Finally, you can set a **default value** for a field. A default value is the value the database uses for the field unless the user enters another value. Though not appropriate for first names, because they vary widely, default values are useful for field data that is frequently the same. For example, setting a default value for a state field saves users from having to enter it for each student if most students live in one state.

You need to repeat these steps for each field in the table. When completed, the resulting Student Information table, shown in Figure 9.10b, is ready for data entry.

The attributes, such as data type and field size, shown in Figure 9.10a are **metadata**: data that describes other data. Metadata is an integral part of the data dictionary. You need to build the data dictionary for each table you will use in a database before you enter data into the database. This also has the benefit of forcing you to consider up front the data you need to capture and the metadata that describes it.

**What happens if I forget to define a field in the data dictionary or if I want to add another one later?** Databases are extremely flexible. You can add fields as needed, but this does not negate the need for proper planning and design of a database. You will need to populate (enter data into) any new fields that are added to your database. This could be difficult if you suddenly need to add a field for birth dates to a database that already

contains records for 10,000 individuals. If you plan to use this field to analyze the data, you need to have a plan for accumulating birth dates to ensure the completeness of the data.

## Inputting Data

### How do I get data into the database?

After you create a data dictionary for each table (or file) in the database and establish the fields you want the database to contain, you can begin creating individual records in the database. There's an old-fashioned way to get data into these records: you can key it directly into the database. However, today, a great deal of data already exists in some type of electronic format, such as word processing documents and spreadsheets. Fortunately, most databases can import data electronically from other application files, which can save an enormous amount of keying.

When importing data, most databases usually apply filters to the data to determine that it is in the correct format as defined by the data dictionary. Nonconforming data is flagged (either on-screen or in a report) so that you can modify the data to fit the database's format.

**Figure 9.10**

(a) The Field Properties box, shown for the Student Information table in an Access database, represents the database's data dictionary. (b) The Student Information table, ready for data input, results from setting up the data dictionary in Figure 9.10a.

a

| Field Name | Data Type |
|------------|-----------|
| SID# | Number |
| Last Name | Text |
| First Name | Text |
| Address | Text |
| City | Text |
| StateAbbreviation | Text |
| Zip Code | Text |

Properties of highlighted field display below

General | Lookup

| | |
|---|---|
| Field Size | 2 |
| Format | |
| Input Mask | |
| Caption | State |
| Default Value | "OR" |
| Validation Rule | |
| Validation Text | |
| Required | No |

Field size set to 2

Displays instead of field name

Default value for State-Abbreviation field

b

| SID# ▾ | Last Name ▾ | First Name ▾ | Address ▾ | City ▾ | State ▾ | Zip Code ▾ |
|--------|-------------|--------------|-----------|--------|---------|------------|
| ✱ | | | | | OR | |

Figure 9.11

The input form used for entering data into the Student Information table.

In this Active Helpdesk call, you'll play the role of a helpdesk staffer, fielding calls about databases, their benefits, their components, and how relational databases organize and manipulate data.

in Figure 9.12. Each field has a label that indicates the data to be placed in the field. The data is represented by blank boxes. Notes have been added to the form to guide the users.

## Data Validation

**How can I ensure that only valid data is entered into the database?** One feature of most DBMSs is the capability to perform data validation. **Validation** is the process of ensuring that data entered into the database is correct (or at least reasonable) and complete. When you registered for college, for example, the admissions clerk most likely asked you for your phone number. A phone number in the United States usually comprises 10 digits formatted in the following fashion: (610) 555-1234. A **validation rule** is set up in the student database to alert the user if a clearly wrong entry, such as "#^#-&*%-#@#&," "(Har) ryJ-ones," or "4567," is entered in the phone number field instead of a valid 10-digit phone number.

Validation rules are generally defined as part of the data dictionary. Violations of validation rules usually result in an error message being displayed on the screen so that the error can be addressed. Common types of validation checks include range, completeness, consistency, and alphabetic and numeric checks.

**How does a range check work?** A **range check** ensures that the data entered into the database falls within a certain range of numbers. For instance, rates of pay for student jobs usually fall within a certain range. Therefore, for a student pay rate field, you could set a **field constraint** (a property that must be satisfied for an entry to be accepted into the field) to restrict pay rates to a range you define.

Figure 9.12 shows how you set up a range check in a data dictionary (in the Field Properties box) for an Access database. A validation rule restricts the entries for the Rate of Pay field to amounts between $7.25 (minimum rate of pay) and $20.00 (the maximum

### How can I make manual entry into a database more convenient?

For small databases, or databases in which no electronic information is to be imported, you can create an input form to speed data entry. An **input form** provides a view of the data fields to be filled, with appropriate labels to assist database users in populating the database. Figure 9.11 shows an example of an input form for the Student Information table shown

Figure 9.12

A validation rule set to restrict rates of pay to a certain range.

rate of pay for students at the college). If users tried to enter a rate of pay less than $7.25 or greater than $20.00, they would be notified of an invalid range error, and the input would not be accepted.

**What does a completeness check accomplish?** If you have ever bought anything online, you have probably encountered error messages generated by completeness checks. In database systems, fields can be defined as "required," meaning data must be entered into them. A **completeness check**, such as the one shown in Figure 9.13, ensures that all fields defined as required have data entered into them. When a user submits this form, the database performs a completeness check and, in this case, notices that the required "First Name" field was left blank. An error message then displays to alert the user of the omission.

**What is the function of a consistency check?** A **consistency check** compares the values of data in two or more fields to see if these values are reasonable. For example, your birth date and the date you enrolled in school are often in a college's database. It is not possible for you to have enrolled in college before you were born. Further, most college students are at least 16 years old. Therefore, a consistency check on these fields might ensure that your birth date is at least 16 or more years before the date when you enrolled in college.

**How are alphabetic and numeric checks used?** You may want to restrict fields to only alphabetic or numerical data (such as for names and student ID numbers). An **alphabetic check** confirms that only textual characters (such as "Robin") are entered in a field. A **numeric check** confirms that only numbers are entered in the field. With these checks in place, "$J2.5n" would not be accepted as the price of a product or a first name. Figure 9.14 shows how you can set such checks and custom error messages in Access.

Error message

Required field left blank

**Figure 9.13**

A database completeness check, like this one shown for myPearsonStore, ensures that all fields defined as required have data in them.

The field properties for the State field in Access is shown in Figure 9.14. The expression Like "??" tells Access to restrict entries for the State field to two alphabetic characters. Selecting "Yes" for the required attribute means that Access will not allow the field to be left blank. Error messages that display when validation checks fail can be customized by the user.

### Viewing and Sorting Data

**How can I view the data in a database?** Displaying the tables on-screen and **browsing** through the data (viewing

| Field Name | Data Type |
|---|---|
| SID# | Number |
| Last Name | Text |
| First Name | Text |
| Address | Text |
| City    Validation rule requires | Text |
| State    alpha characters | Text |
| Zip Code | Text |
| Cell Phone | Text |
| Rate of Pay | Currency |

General | Lookup

| Field Size | 2 |
|---|---|
| Format | |
| Input Mask | |
| Caption | |
| Default Value | "OR" |
| Validation Rule | Like "??" |
| Validation Text | Please enter a valid two letter state abbreviation |
| Required | Yes |
| Allow Zero Length | Yes |
| Indexed | No |

Error message for invalid entry

Field must contain data

**Figure 9.14**

An alphabetic check and a completeness check for the State field in an Access database.

# Structured Query Language (SQL)

To extract records from a database, you use a query language. Almost all relational and object-oriented databases today use Structured Query Language, or SQL. Oracle, Microsoft SQL Server, Microsoft Access, IBM DB2, and MySQL are examples of popular databases that use SQL.

When relational databases were first developed in the early 1970s, each DBMS software product contained its own query language. This meant that database administrators had to learn a new language whenever they worked with a different DBMS. The early query languages were mathematically based and often difficult to master. E. F. Codd, who has been called the father of relational databases, proposed a standardized query language when he worked at IBM in the mid-1970s.

The original language was called SEQUEL, short for *structured English query language*. The idea was to make queries easy by using English language–like sentence structure. Database software designers enthusiastically accepted the concept, developing a modified version of the original SEQUEL language, named SQL (pronounced "sequel"). Oracle first introduced SQL in a commercial database product in 1979. It has been the unofficial standard language for relational databases since then.

SQL uses relational algebra to extract data from databases. **Relational algebra** is the use of English-like expressions that have variables and operations, much like algebraic equations. Variables include table names, field names, or selection criteria for the data you wish to display.

Operations include directions such as *select* (which enables you to pick variable names), *from* (which tells the database which table to use), and *where* (which enables you to specify selection criteria). The two most common queries used to extract data using relational algebra are select queries and join queries.

A **select query** displays a subset of data from a table (or tables) based on the criteria you specify. A typical select query has the following format:

SELECT (Field Name 1, Field Name 2, ...)
FROM (Table Name)
WHERE (Selection Criteria)

The first line of the query contains variables for the field names you want to display. The FROM statement enables you to specify the table name from which the data will be retrieved. The last line (the WHERE statement) is used only when you wish to specify which records need to be displayed (such as all students with GPAs greater than 3.3). If you wish to display all the rows (records) in the table, then you do not use the WHERE statement. (See Figure 9.15.)

Suppose you want to create a cell phone list that includes all students from the Student Information table in Figure 9.15a. The SQL query you would send to the database would look like this:

**a**

| | SID# | Last Name | First Name | Address | City | State | Zip Code | Cell Phone |
|---|---|---|---|---|---|---|---|---|
| ⊞ | 123456789 | Finkel | Susan | 645 Pine Street | Philadelphia | PA | 19102-5674 | (610) 555-2367 |
| ⊞ | 789123456 | Garza | Julio | 421 West 3rd St | New Witten | SD | 57584-1234 | (454) 555-6512 |
| ⊞ | 678912345 | O'Connor | Leanne | 238 Grant Street | Beverly | MA | 01915-4333 | (303) 555-8723 |
| ⊞ | 567891234 | Stinson | Arthur | 345 Ryan Drive | Cedar Falls | IA | 50613-3232 | (427) 555-2398 |
| ⊞ | 456789123 | Zhang | Mei | 457 Blanchard St | Boston | MA | 01901-3424 | (302) 555-4976 |

*Query applied to this table*

SELECT (First Name, Last Name, Cell Phone)
FROM (Student Information Table)

*Query applied to this table*

SELECT (First Name, Last Name, Cell Phone)
FROM (Student Information Table)
WHERE (State = MA)

*Produces this output*

**b**

| First Name | Last Name | Cell Phone |
|---|---|---|
| Susan | Finkel | (610) 555-2367 |
| Mei | Zhang | (302) 555-4976 |
| Arthur | Stinson | (427) 555-2398 |
| Leanne | O'Connor | (303) 555-8723 |
| Julio | Garza | (454) 555-6512 |

*Produces this output*

**c**

| First Name | Last Name | Cell Phone |
|---|---|---|
| Leanne | O'Connor | (303) 555-8723 |
| Mei | Zhang | (302) 555-4976 |

**Figure 9.15**

When the query on the left is applied to the (a) Student Information table, it restricts the output to (b) only a phone list. The query on the right, which uses a WHERE statement, further restricts the phone list to (c) only students from Massachusetts.

SELECT (First Name, Last Name, Cell Phone)
FROM (Student Information Table)

Figure 9.15b shows the output from this query.

What if you want a phone list that only shows students from Massachusetts? In that case, you would add a WHERE statement to the query as follows:

SELECT (First Name, Last Name, Cell Phone)
FROM (Student Information Table)
WHERE (State = MA)

This query restricts the output to students who live in Massachusetts, as shown in Figure 9.15c. Notice that the State field in the Student Information table can be used by the query (in this case, as a limiting criterion), but the contents of the State field are not required to be displayed in the query results. This explains why the output shown in Figure 9.15c doesn't show the State field.

When you want to extract data that is in two or more tables, you use a **join query**. The query actually links (or joins) the two tables using the common field in both tables and extracts the relevant data from each. The format for a simple join query for two tables is as follows:

SELECT (Field Name 1, Field Name 2)
FROM (Table 1 Name, Table 2 Name)
WHERE (Table 1 Name.Common Field Name = Table 2 Name.Common Field Name)
AND (Selection Criteria)

Notice how similar this is to a select query, although the FROM statement must now contain two table names. In a join query, the WHERE statement is split into two parts. In the first part (right after WHERE), the relation between the two tables is defined by identifying the common fields between the tables. The second part of the statement (after AND) is where the selection criteria are defined.

The AND means that both parts of the statement must be true for the query to produce results (i.e., the two related fields must exist and the selection criteria must be valid). Figure 9.16 illustrates using a join query for the Student Information and Roster Master tables to produce a class roster for students.

**Figure 9.16**

This join query will display a student roster for each student in the Student Information table. Notice that the WHERE statement creates the join by defining the common fields (in this case SID#) in each table.

records) is an option with most databases. In many instances you'll only want to view the data, not display the entire table. For example, if you want to register for an additional course for the current semester, the admissions clerk would browse the roster database to determine which courses you are already taking. However, browsing through a large database is time consuming unless the records are in an order that makes your task easy.

**How can I reorder records in a database?** You can easily **sort** a database into the order that you need. Sorting a database involves organizing it in a new fashion. Figure 9.17a shows an Access data table in which the records were input in no particular order. By highlighting a column (in this case Last Name) and then clicking the Sort Ascending button, the database displays the

records in alphabetical order by last name, as shown in Figure 9.17b.

**What if I want to find a particular piece of data in a database?** Browsing records works for small databases, but if the amount of data you are managing is small, then you probably will just maintain it in a list anyway. To find data in a large database quickly and efficiently, you need to be able to request only the data you are seeking. Therefore, database management systems let you query the data to enable you to find what you're looking for.

### Extracting or Querying Data

**What is a query?** A **query** is a question or inquiry. A **database query** is a question you ask the database so that it provides you with the records you wish to view. When you query a database, you instruct it to search for a particular piece of data, such as a student's grade point average (GPA). Queries also enable you to have the database select and display records that match certain criteria, such as all of the students who have GPAs of 3.3 or higher.

**Is querying a database as simple as just asking the proper question?** All modern DBMSs contain a query language that the software uses to retrieve

**Figure 9.17**

(a) Shown is an unsorted table. Notice that the Last Name column is selected (highlighted) for sorting. Selecting the sorting option "Ascending" produces the sorted output (b) with the records sorted in ascending alphabetical order by last name.

and display records. A query language consists of its own vocabulary and sentence structure, which you use to frame the requests. Query languages are similar to full-blown programming languages but are usually much easier to learn. The most popular query language today is Structured Query Language, or SQL.

**Do I have to learn a query language to develop queries for my database?** Modern database systems provide wizards (or other tools) to guide you through the process of creating queries. Figure 9.18 shows an example of an Access wizard being used to create a query. Highlighting an available field and then clicking the arrow button adds the field to the selected fields list. Selected fields display in the query. Highlighting a field on the selected fields list and clicking the back arrow removes the field from the list. The wizard speeds up the process of creating queries, and also removes the need to learn a query language.

The Query Wizard can be found on the Create tab, in the Queries group. Click Query Wizard and select Simple Query Wizard. When you use the Simple Query Wizard, you're actually using SQL commands without realizing it. The Simple Query Wizard takes the criteria you specify and creates the appropriate SQL commands behind the scenes.

However, you may want to create your own SQL queries in Access, modify existing queries at the SQL language level, or view the SQL code that the wizard created. To do so, open a query and select SQL View from the View drop-down box on the Home tab of the Ribbon. This displays the SQL code that makes up the query. Figure 9.19 shows the SQL code that the query in Figure 9.18 created.

## Outputting Data

**How do I get data out of a database?** The most common form of

output for any database is a viewable (or printable) electronic report. Businesses routinely summarize the data within their databases and compile summary data reports. For instance, at the end of each semester your school generates a grade report for you that shows the classes you took and the grades you received.

**Can I transfer data from a database to another software application?** Database systems also can be used to **export** data to other applications. Exporting data involves putting it into an electronic file in a format that another application can understand. For example, the query shown in the wizard in Figure 9.18 may be used to generate a list of recipients for a form letter. In that case, the query output would be directed to a file that could be easily imported into Microsoft Word so that the data could be used in a mail merge process to generate letters.

**Figure 9.18**

(a) The Simple Query Wizard in Access displays all fields available in your table so that you can select the ones you need. (b) This information is displayed when you run the query defined in (a).

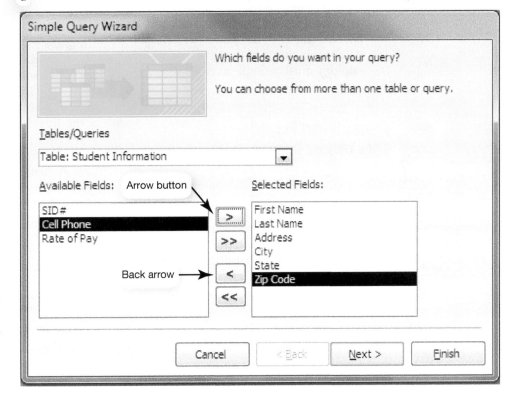

```
SELECT [Student Information].[First Name], [Student Information].[Last Name], [Student
Information].[Address], [Student Information].[City], [Student Information].[State], [Student
Information].[Zip Code]
FROM [Student Information];
```

**Figure 9.19**

The SQL View window shows the SQL code that the wizard created for the query in Figure 9.18. Although it is a relatively simple SELECT statement, it is much easier to create with the wizard.

In the next section, we look at the operation of relational databases and explore how relationships are established among tables in these databases.

# Relational Database Operations

As explained earlier, relational databases operate by organizing data into various tables based on logical groupings. For example, all student address and contact information (phone numbers, e-mail addresses, and so on) would be grouped into one table. Because not all of the data in a relational database is stored in the same table, a methodology must be implemented to link data between tables.

In relational databases, a link between tables that defines how the data is related is referred to as a **relationship**. To establish a relationship between two tables, both tables must have a common field (or column). Common fields contain the same data (such as student ID numbers), as shown in Figure 9.21. The fields do not have to have the same field name as long as they contain the same data.

Relationships in databases can take three forms: one-to-one, one-to-many, or many-to-many. A **one-to-one relationship** indicates that for each record in a table there is only one corresponding record in a related table. For example, a parking space can be occupied by only one car at a time, so a table that links assigned parking spaces to a table of faculty members (who are assigned parking spaces) would have a one-to-one relationship.

One-to-many relationships occur most frequently in relational databases. A **one-to-many relationship** is characterized by a record appearing only once in a table (such as the Student Information table in Figure 9.21) while appearing many times in the related Roster Master table. There is only one instance of a student ID in the Student Information table, but there can be many instances of the same student ID in the Roster Master table. Students can register for many classes, but each registration record can relate to only one student.

A **many-to-many relationship** is characterized by records in one table being related to multiple records in a second table and vice versa. For instance, a table of students could be related to a table of student employers. The employers could employ many students, and students could work for more than one employer.

## Normalization of Data

**How do I decide which tables I need and what data to put in them?** You create database tables (or files) for two reasons: to hold unique data about a person or thing and to describe unique events or transactions. In databases, the goal is to reduce data redundancy by recording data only once. This process is called **normalization** of the data. Yet the tables must still work well enough together to enable you to retrieve the data when you need it. Tables should be grouped using logical data that can be identified uniquely.

---

**BITS AND BYTES**

## iTunes Smart Playlists— They're Just Queries!

Ever built a smart playlist in iTunes? If so, you've created a database query. iTunes is just a relational database that manages your media. A smart playlist (see Figure 9.20) allows you to define multiple criteria to create a playlist. Say you want all songs in the genre Rock, except for the artist P!nk and the album *Monkey Business*. When you define these criteria as "match all" in the smart playlist creation window, you will get a smart playlist that contains the music you want. You have built a query that tells iTunes exactly what music to extract from the database and include in your playlist.

**Figure 9.20**

The iTunes Smart Playlist dialog box.

Screenshots © Apple Inc. Reprinted by permission from Apple Inc.

Let's look at an example. In Figure 9.22, the Class Registration List—Spring Semester contains a great deal of data about individual students and their course registration. However, each table in a relational database should contain a related group of data on a single topic. There are two distinct topics in this list: student contact information and student registration information. Therefore, this list needs to be divided into two tables so that the distinct data (contact data and registration data) can be categorized appropriately. Data about each student is duplicated in this table. Normalizing the data eliminates this duplication.

The Student Information table in Figure 9.23 organizes all of the student contact information found in Figure 9.22 into a separate table. Notice that the information for each student needs to be shown only once, instead of multiple times (as in the list in Figure 9.22). The unique primary key for this table is the student's ID number. Student information might be needed in a variety of instances and by a variety of departments, but it needs to reside only in this one database table, which many departments of the school can share.

**Student Information**

| | SID# | Last Name | First Name | Address | City |
|---|---|---|---|---|---|
| ⊞ | 123456789 | Finkel | Susan | 645 Pine Street | Philadelphia |
| ⊞ | 789123456 | Garza | Julio | 421 West 3rd St | New Witten |
| ⊞ | 678912345 | O'Connor | Leanne | 238 Grant Street | Beverly |
| ⊞ | 567891234 | Stinson | Arthur | 345 Ryan Drive | Cedar Falls |
| ⊞ | 456789123 | Zhang | Mei | 457 Blanchard St | Boston |

Common field in each table

**Roster Master Table**

| Registration | Class Code | SID# |
|---|---|---|
| 1 | CIS 110 | 123456789 |
| 2 | ENG 101 | 123456789 |
| 3 | HIS 103 | 123456789 |
| 4 | CHE 140 | 123456789 |
| 5 | PSY 101 | 123456789 |
| 12 | PSY 101 | 456789123 |
| 13 | HIS 103 | 456789123 |
| 14 | ENG 102 | 456789123 |

**Figure 9.21**

(a) The Student Information table and (b) the Roster Master table share the common field of student ID number. This allows a relationship to be established between the two tables.

**Class Registration List - Spring Semester**

| SID # | Last Name | First Name | Home Address | City | State | Zip Code | Class Code | Class Name | # Of Credits |
|---|---|---|---|---|---|---|---|---|---|
| 123456789 | Finkel | Susan | 645 Pine Street | Philadelphia | PA | 19102-5674 | CIS 110 | Computer Literacy | 3 |
| 123456789 | Finkel | Susan | 645 Pine Street | Philadelphia | PA | 19102-5674 | ENG 101 | English Comp 1 | 3 |
| 123456789 | Finkel | Susan | 645 Pine Street | Philadelphia | PA | 19102-5674 | HIS 103 | Western Civ 1 | 3 |
| 123456789 | Finkel | Susan | 645 Pine Street | Philadelphia | PA | 19102-5674 | CHE 140 | Chemistry | 4 |
| 123456789 | Finkel | Susan | 646 Pine Street | Philadelphia | PA | 19102-5674 | PSY 101 | Intro to Psychology | 3 |
| 789123456 | Garza | Julio | 421 West 3rd St | New Witten | SD | 57584-1234 | CIS 110 | Computer Literacy | 3 |
| 789123456 | Garza | Julio | 421 West 3rd St | New Witten | SD | 57584-1234 | SOC 101 | Intro to Sociology | 3 |
| 789123456 | Garza | Julio | 421 West 3rd St | New Witten | SD | 57584-1234 | PSY 101 | Intro to Psych | 3 |
| 678912345 | O'Connor | Leanne | 238 Grant Street | Beverly | MA | 01915-4333 | | | |
| 567891234 | Stinson | Arthur | 345 Ryan Drive | Cedar Falls | IA | 50613-3232 | BIO 210 | Anatomy & Physiology 1 | 3 |
| 567891234 | Stinson | Arthur | 345 Ryan Drive | Cedar Falls | IA | 50613-3232 | ENG 101 | English Comp 1 | 3 |
| 567891234 | Stinson | Arthur | 345 Ryan Drive | Cedar Falls | IA | 50613-3232 | SOC 101 | Intro to Sociology | 3 |
| 456789123 | Zhang | Mei | 457 Blanchard St | Boston | MA | 01901-3424 | PSY 101 | Intro to Psychology | 3 |
| 456789123 | Zhang | Mei | 457 Blanchard St | Boston | MA | 01901-3424 | HIS 103 | Western Civ 1 | 3 |
| 456789123 | Zhang | Mei | 457 Blanchard St | Boston | MA | 01901-3424 | ENG 102 | English Comp 2 | 3 |

**Figure 9.22**

The column headings in yellow are related to student contact data, whereas the column headings in red relate to enrollment information. To construct an efficient database, these topics should be contained in separate tables.

**Figure 9.23**

Student contact data is grouped in the Student Information table and needs to be entered only once for each student. The primary key for each record is a unique student ID number.

**Student Information**

| SID# | Last Name | First Name | Address | City | State | Zip Code |
|---|---|---|---|---|---|---|
| 123456789 | Finkel | Susan | 645 Pine Street | Philadelphia | PA | 19102-5674 |
| 789123 | | Julio | 421 West 3rd St | New Witten | SD | 57584-1234 |
| 678912 | | Leanne | 238 Grant Street | Beverly | MA | 01915-4333 |
| 567891234 | Stinson | Arthur | 345 Ryan Drive | Cedar Falls | IA | 50613-3232 |
| 456789123 | Zhang | Mei | 457 Blanchard St | Boston | MA | 01901-3424 |

*Primary Key*

Next, we could put the registration data found in Figure 9.22 for each student in a separate table, as shown in Figure 9.24. There is no need to repeat student name and address data in this table. Instead, each student can be identified by his or her student ID number. However, there are problems with this table. Each class name and class code has to be repeated for every student taking the course. Also,

| SID# | Class Code | Class Name | Credits |
|---|---|---|---|
| 123456789 | CHE 140 | Chemistry | 4 |
| 123456789 | CIS 110 | Computer Literacy | 3 |
| 123456789 | ENG | English Comp 1 | 3 |
| 123456789 | HIS | Western Civ 1 | 3 |
| 123456789 | PSY 101 | Intro to Psychology | 3 |
| 456789123 | ENG 102 | English Comp 2 | 3 |
| 456789123 | HIS 103 | Western Civ 1 | 3 |
| 456789123 | PSY 101 | Intro to Psychology | 3 |
| 567891234 | BIO 210 | Anatomy & Physiology 1 | 4 |
| 567891234 | ENG 101 | English Comp 1 | 3 |
| 567891234 | SOC 101 | Intro to Sociology | 3 |
| 789123456 | CIS 110 | Computer Literacy | 3 |

*SID# not unique*

*Duplicate data*

**Figure 9.24**

Although it contains related data (registration information), this table still contains a great deal of duplicate data and no usable primary key.

**Course Master Table**

| Class Code | Class Name | Credits |
|---|---|---|
| BIO 210 | Anatomy & Physiology 1 | 4 |
| CHE 140 | Chemistry | 4 |
| CIS 110 | Computer Literacy | 3 |
| ENG 101 | English Comp 1 | 3 |
| ENG 102 | English Comp 2 | 3 |
| HIS 103 | Western Civ 1 | 3 |
| PSY 101 | Intro to Psychology | 3 |
| SOC 101 | Intro to Sociology | 3 |

**Figure 9.25**

Related information about courses (class code, class name, and the credits for the class) is grouped logically in one table. The unique class code is the primary key.

there is no unique field that can be used as a primary key for this table. SID# cannot be used because it will be entered on multiple records when a student enrolls in more than one course. This presents another opportunity to normalize the data further.

**What can be done to fix the table in Figure 9.24?** In Figure 9.24, we have identified more data that should be grouped logically into another separate table: class code and class name. Therefore, we should create another table for just this information. This enables us to avoid repeating class names and codes. Figure 9.25 shows the Course Master table. Note that the Class Code is unique for every course and acts as a primary key in this table.

To solve the other problems with the table in Figure 9.24, we need a way to identify uniquely each student registered for a specific course. This can be solved by creating a course registration code (number) that will be unique and assigned by the database as records are entered. Figure 9.26 shows the resulting Roster Master table. Only three fields are needed: the registration code number (the unique primary key), the class code, and the student's ID number. This approach greatly minimizes duplicate data.

**How do I get the data in the tables to work together now that it is split up?** The entire premise behind relational databases is that relationships

**SOUND BYTE**

**Improving an Access 2010 Database**

In this Sound Byte, you'll learn how to create input forms, queries, and reports to simplify maintenance of your CD and DVD database. You'll follow along step by step, using Microsoft Access wizards to create and modify queries to suit your needs.

are established among the tables to allow the data to be shared. As noted earlier, to establish a relationship between two tables, the tables must have a common field (column). This usually involves the primary keys of a table.

For instance, to track registrations by student in the Roster Master table in Figure 9.26, the student ID number is the logical piece of data to use. The student ID number is the primary key in the Student Information table in Figure 9.23; however, in the Roster Master table, the student ID number is called a **foreign key**—the primary key of another table that is included for purposes of establishing relationships with that other table. Figure 9.27 shows the relationships that exist among the Course Master, Roster Master, and Student Information tables. Join lines indicate established relationships between tables. Tables must contain fields with common data; this establishes relationships between them. Relationships among tables can be established whenever you need them if common data fields exist in the tables.

Because relationships are vital to the operation of the database, it is important to ensure that there are no inconsistencies in the data entered in the common fields of two tables. Each foreign key (SID# in the Roster Master table in Figure 9.26) entered into the table must be a valid primary key from the related table (SID# from the Student Information table in Figure 9.23).

For instance, if 392135684 is not a valid student ID number for any student listed in the Student Information table, then it should not be entered into the Roster Master table. Each entry in the Roster Master table must correspond to a student (linked by his or her SID#) in the Student Information table.

| Roster Master Table | | |
|---|---|---|
| Registration | Class Code | SID# |
| 1 | CIS 110 | 123456789 |
| 2 | ENG 101 | 123456789 |
| 3 | HIS 103 | 123456789 |
| 4 | CHE 140 | 123456789 |
| 5 | PSY 101 | 123456789 |
| 6 | CIS 110 | 789123456 |
| 7 | SOC 101 | 789123456 |
| 8 | PSY 101 | 789123456 |
| 9 | BIO 210 | 567891234 |
| 10 | ENG 101 | 567891234 |
| 11 | SOC 101 | 567891234 |
| 12 | PSY 101 | 456789123 |
| 13 | HIS 103 | 456789123 |
| 14 | ENG 102 | 456789123 |

**Figure 9.26**

The Roster Master table shows only pertinent data related to a student's registration.

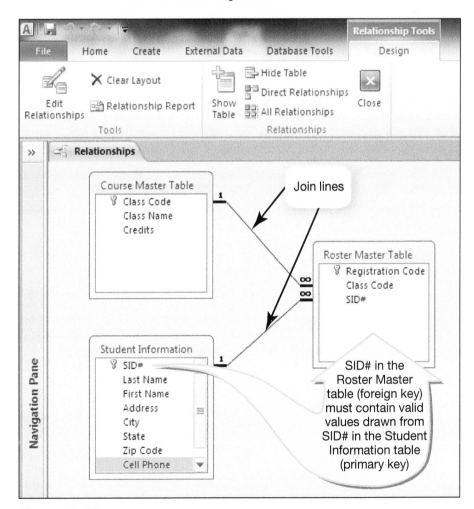

**Figure 9.27**

The Relationships screen in Microsoft Access visually represents the relationships established between tables.

Web 2.0 applications are mostly about enhancing communications and making it easy for users to create and disseminate their own content. So if you have a database that needs populating, why not seek help from the Web community to populate it, especially if it is designed as a resource for the masses.

The economy in the United States is largely a service-based economy. Businesses based in the United States tend to provide services to individuals or other businesses as the business climate has shifted away from manufacturing. Everyone needs haircuts and health care services, and many Americans love to eat out. But how do you find reliable service providers and good restaurants? Recommendations from friends and family are reliable, but what if no one in your circle of acquaintances knows of a good personal trainer or a great dentist? Why shouldn't the Internet be used to harness the power of millions of people's experiences to recommend reliable service providers? Two companies that have successfully plunged into this arena are Yelp and Angie's List.

Yelp (yelp.com) was conceived as the "yellow pages" for the 21st century. Yelp is free to use, and anyone can write a review of a business and post it to the site. The site has more than 15 million reviews of all types of businesses. Users can easily search the site, find service providers in their geographic area, and see what ratings (both good and bad) consumers gave them. Thinking about going to a Mexican restaurant in the San Jose area that you have never visited (see Figure 9.28)? A quick search on Yelp found more than 1500 restaurants that fit this broad criteria. Surely you'll be able to find one that fits your budget and that other people enjoyed visiting.

However, **Yelp.com** is not without its critics. Because Yelp allows anonymous posting, some people are afraid that businesses may try to up their ratings by posting their own positive reviews. And Yelp actively markets to businesses to pay for placement of ads on its site that some users may mistake for unsponsored reviews. (To avoid this kind of consumer misinterpretation, the Federal Communications Commission [FCC] now requires commercial Web sites to clearly identify reviews that are sponsored . . . but some consumers remain oblivious.) An alternative to Yelp that addresses these concerns is Angie's List.

Angie's List (**angieslist.com**) has the same basic premise as Yelp: to have individuals recommend businesses based on their experiences. However, whereas Yelp derives its revenue from advertising, Angie's List is a subscription service. Members pay a monthly fee to access the reviews on Angie's List. So what do you get for your fees that you don't get on Yelp? Angie's List does not permit anonymous reviews. This is a big benefit for business owners, because it makes it easier to contact dissatisfied customers and try to resolve issues. Angie's List also has a verification process with reviewers to ensure that businesses do not report on themselves. And businesses do not pay to advertise on Angie's List; they make the list only when they are reviewed by a consumer.

Both Yelp and Angie's List are searchable databases just like the other examples in this chapter. But whereas most companies usually populate databases with data that they generate or collect themselves, these Web sites rely on users to create their content. The databases still need to be well designed to capture this content, and there need to be processes in place to review the data entered for appropriateness. For instance, both Yelp and Angie's List would want to delete reviews that contained racist comments or hate speech. By harnessing the power of large groups of users to populate a database, the database owners can reap the rewards of saving time, effort, and money.

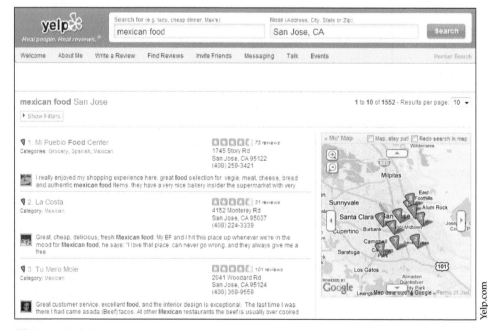

**Figure 9.28**
Yelp's database is populated with reviews created by users.

If this requirement is not applied to foreign keys, then a relationship cannot be enforced between tables.

**How do I ensure that a foreign key field contains a valid primary key from the related table?** To apply this restraint, when defining a relationship in a database, you have the option of enforcing referential integrity for that relationship. **Referential integrity** means that for each value in the foreign key of one table, there is a corresponding value in the primary key of the related table.

For instance, if you attempt to enter a record in the Roster Master table with an SID# of 156784522 and referential integrity is being enforced, the database checks to ensure that a record with SID# 156784522 exists in the Student Information table. If the corresponding record does not exist, then an error message displays. Establishing referential integrity between two tables helps prevent inconsistent data from being entered.

**Who manages the data in a database?** All of the data that is collected in databases needs to be stored and managed. Database administrators (DBAs) are the IT professionals responsible for designing, constructing, and maintaining databases. They review and manage data on an ongoing basis to ensure data is flowing smoothly into and out of the database. Figure 9.29 shows a view of the MySQL Enterprise Dashboard screen, a tool that is used primarily by DBAs when reviewing the performance of a database. Database administrators can monitor table usage and CPU utilization to help determine if database performance is acceptable.

In the next section, we explore how data is typically stored in large-scale business databases.

## Data Storage

At the simplest level, data is stored in a single database on a database server, and you retrieve the data as needed. This works fine for small databases and simple enterprises where all of the data you are interested in is in a single database. Problems can arise, however, when the data you need is in multiple places. Large storage repositories called *data warehouses* and *data marts* help solve this problem.

## Data Warehouses

**What is a data warehouse?** A data **warehouse** is a large-scale electronic repository of data that contains and organizes all the data related to an organization in one place. Individual databases contain a wealth of information, but each database's information usually pertains to one topic.

For instance, the order database at Amazon.com contains such information about book orders as the buyer's name, address, and payment information, and the book's name. However, the order database does not contain information on inventory levels of books, nor does it list suppliers from which out-of-stock books can be obtained. Data warehouses, therefore, consolidate information from disparate sources to present an enterprise-wide view of business operations.

**Is data in a data warehouse organized the same way as in a normal database?** Data in the data warehouse is organized by subject. Most databases focus on one specific operational aspect of business operations. For example, a large electronics retailer sells many types of electronics, such as televisions, computers, and mobile phones. Different departments in the retailer are responsible for each type of product and track the products they sell in different databases (one for television

**Figure 9.29**

The Enterprise Dashboard in MySQL helps DBAs review database performance.

## Emerging Technologies: Can Your Business Partner Deliver the Goods? Enhanced Databases Can Help You Decide!

You watch a weather forecast on television to gain information about the weather. The weather forecaster tells you that it will be sunny. When you get out of your car to go to class, rain is pouring down. Yes, you gathered relevant information. Too bad that it was inaccurate information!

Data and information stored in databases can be just as unhelpful as an inaccurate weather forecast if the information is incorrect or distorted. Although a poor weather report is probably nothing more to you than an inconvenience, accurate data in business is mission critical. Businesses rely on information in databases every day just to accomplish even routine tasks.

Developed to respond to business needs, **Alibaba.com** is one of the world's largest online business-to-business databases. Alibaba.com specializes in matching suppliers with buyers for all types of manufactured goods and raw materials. With the global nature of business, databases such as those maintained by Alibaba.com are essential tools that assist businesspeople in managing their global business. Figure 9.30 shows a search for short-sleeved women's cotton t-shirts in Vietnam. You could also use the terms "Vietnamese t-shirt manufacturers" in a search engine and you would probably find many leads. The information in the leads available online may be factually correct, but how do you determine how reliable these suppliers are?

There is a wealth of information online, provided by various sources, that you can use to evaluate potential suppliers before you contact them. However, it can be difficult for an individual to tell if the data has been altered or falsified. **Panjiva.com** is a Web site that also has a searchable database of over 1.5 million suppliers. However, the founders of Panjiva decided to make their database different. They gather data that indicates reliability of suppliers from sources such as government agencies, independent certification companies, nonprofit organizations, and customers.

Using the reliability information, Panjiva then creates ratings for companies (on a scale of 1 to 100) based on specific business performance criteria such as number of shipments to the U.S. market, their environmental record, and their capability to deliver shipments within promised time frames. Subscribers to Panjiva's database (companies such as The Home Depot) can then feel more comfortable about doing business with suppliers that Panjiva has rated for reliability.

Databases with enhanced information are the wave of the future in the business world. So, before you make that next crucial business decision, ask yourself how much you really know about your prospective business partner. If you don't know enough, then find a database that can make you feel more at ease.

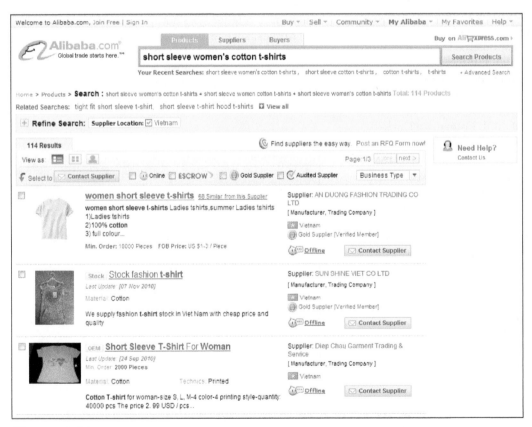

**Figure 9.30**

Using the database on **Alibaba.com**, a search for short-sleeved women's cotton t-shirts in Vietnam results in 114 links to vendors selling some type of women's t-shirt.

sales and one for mobile phone sales, for example), as shown in Figure 9.31.

These databases capture specific information about each type of electronics. The Television Sales database captures information about television features, installation costs, extended warranty details (and costs), and the cost of the television because this information is pertinent to determining the ultimate value of the television sale. The Mobile Phone Sales database captures information about the number of family members, calling and data plan features, and costs. But this database does not capture installation costs because they are not pertinent to mobile phones.

However, data on total electronic devices sold (and the resulting revenue generated) is critical to the management of the electronics retailer no matter what type of products are involved. Therefore, an electronics retailer's data warehouse would have a subject called Electronics Sales Subject (see Figure 9.31) that would contain information about *all* electronic devices sold throughout the company. The Electronics Sales Subject is a database that contains information from the other databases the company maintains. However, all data in the Electronics Sales Subject database is specifically related to electronics sales (as opposed to say appliances, which the retailer also carries).

From the Electronics Sales Subject database, it is easy for managers to produce comprehensive reports such as the Total Electronics Sales Report, as shown in Figure 9.31, which can contain information pertaining to all types of electronics sales.

**Are data warehouses much larger than conventional databases?** Data warehouses, unlike conventional databases, are vast repositories of information. The data contained within them is not operational in nature, but rather archival. Data warehouse data is **time-variant data**, meaning it doesn't all pertain to one period in time.

The warehouse contains current values, such as amounts due from customers, as well as historical data. If you want to examine the buying habits of a certain type of customer, then you need data about both current and prior purchases. Having time-variant data in the warehouse enables you to analyze the past, examine the present in

light of historical data, and make projections about the future.

**Populating Data Warehouses**

**How are data warehouses populated with data?** Source data for data warehouses can come from three places:

- Internal sources (such as company databases)
- External sources (suppliers, vendors, and so on)
- Customers or visitors to a company's Web site

Internal data sources are obvious. Sales, billing, inventory, and customer databases all provide a wealth of information.

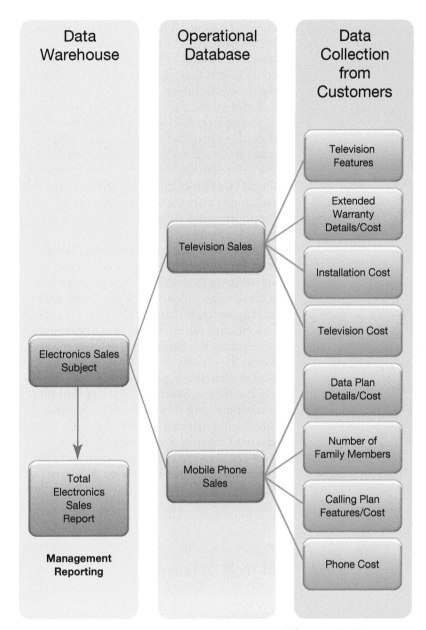

**Figure 9.31**

Data from individual databases is drawn together under appropriate subject headings in a data warehouse. Managers can then produce comprehensive reports that would be impossible to create from the individual databases.

However, internal information is not contained exclusively in databases. Spreadsheets and other ad hoc analysis tools may contain data that needs to be loaded into the data warehouse.

External data sources include vendors and suppliers that often provide data regarding product specifications, shipment methods and dates, electronic billing information, and so on. In addition, a virtual wealth of customer (or potential customer) information is available by monitoring the clickstream of the company Web site.

**What is a clickstream, and why is it important?** Companies can use software on their Web sites to capture information about each click that users make as they navigate through the site. This information is referred to as **clickstream data**. Monitoring the clickstream helps managers assess the effectiveness of a Web site. Using clickstream data capture tools, a company can determine which pages users visit most often, how long users stay on each page, which sites directed users to the company site, and the user demographics. Such data can provide valuable clues to what a company needs to improve on its site to stimulate sales.

## Data Staging

**Does all source data fit into the warehouse?** No two source databases are the same. Although two databases might contain similar information (such as customer names and addresses), the format of the data is most likely different in each database. Therefore, source data must be "staged" before entering the data warehouse. **Data staging** consists of three steps:

1. Extraction of the data from source databases
2. Transformation (reformatting) of the data
3. Storage of the data in the data warehouse

Many different software programs and procedures may have to be created to extract the data from varied sources and reformat it for storage in the data warehouse. The nature and complexity of the source data determine the complexity of the data staging process.

**Once the data is stored in the data warehouse, how can it be extracted and used?** Managers can query the data warehouse in much the same way you would query an Access database. However, because there is more data in the data warehouse, much more flexible tools are needed to perform such queries. Online analytical processing (OLAP) software provides standardized tools for viewing and manipulating data in a data warehouse. The key feature of OLAP tools is that they enable flexible views of the data, which the software user can easily change.

## Data Marts

**Is finding the right data in a huge data warehouse difficult?** Looking for the data you need in a data warehouse can be daunting when there are terabytes of data. Therefore, small slices of the data warehouse, each called a **data mart**, are often created. Whereas data warehouses have an enterprise-wide depth, the information in data marts pertains to a single department.

For instance, if you work in the sales department, you need accurate sales-related information at your fingertips—and you do not want to wade through customer service data, accounts payable data, and product shipping data to get it. Therefore, a data mart that contains information relevant only to the sales department can be created to

## BITS AND BYTES — CRM Tools Go Online

Even small businesses harness the power of databases to manage their customers. Customer relationship management (CRM) software contains sophisticated databases that are designed to manage and track all interactions with customers. Among other things, CRM software can 1) help salespeople manage their customer interactions, 2) provide communication paths for customers to solicit service and support, and 3) use analytical tools to identify the best prospects for marketing efforts based on customer interests and interactions with the company. Previously, CRM software was installed on salespeople's notebook computers or on servers at a company's home office. But with the widespread availability of wireless connections, many CRM products are now offered only online.

Zoho CRM is part of the online suite of free (and low-priced) tools offered by **www.zoho.com**. For a small business just getting started, Zoho CRM offers a free account for up to three users. Even though it is free, the software offers powerful features such as sales force automation (tracking customer leads and contacts), marketing automation (e-mail advertising campaigns), and customer support tracking and personal organization tools (calendars, to-do lists, call logging). And as the business grows, additional users can be added for a reasonable monthly fee. The database is stored totally online by Zoho, so it frees up a small business owner from the worries of database maintenance and backup.

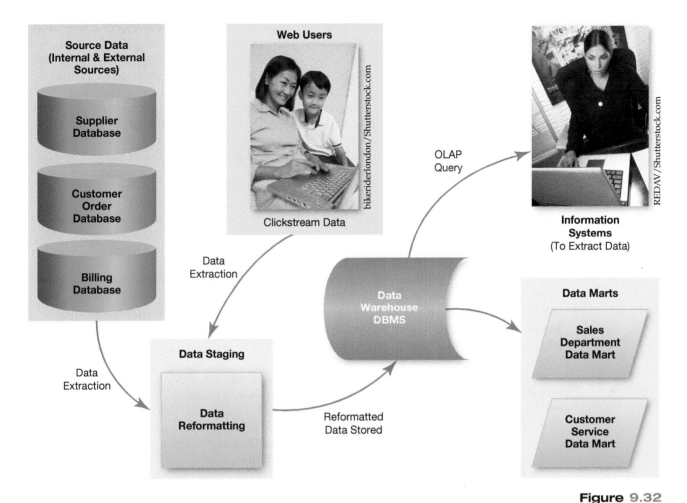

**Figure 9.32**

An overview of the data warehouse process.

make the task of finding this data easier. An overview of the data-warehousing process is illustrated in Figure 9.32. Data staging is vital because different data must be extracted and then reformatted to fit the data structure defined in the data warehouse's DBMS. Data can be extracted using powerful OLAP query tools, or it can be stored in specialized data marts for use by specific employee groups.

Now that you understand how databases are created and how data is stored in large-scale repositories, in the next section we'll explore the types of information systems that utilize databases to provide business intelligence to managers.

## Managing Data: Information and Business Intelligence Systems

Making intelligent decisions about developing new products, creating marketing strategies, and buying raw materials requires timely, accurate information. An **information system** is a software-based solution used to gather and analyze information. A system that delivers up-to-the-minute sales data on shoes to the computer of Zappos' president is one example of an information system. Databases, data warehouses, and data marts are integral parts of information systems because they store the information that makes information systems functional.

All information systems perform similar functions, including acquiring data, processing that data into information, storing the data, and providing the user with a number of output options with which to make the information meaningful and useful (see Figure 9.33). Most information systems fall into one of five categories: (1) office support systems, (2) transaction-processing systems, (3) management information systems, (4) decision support systems, and (5) enterprise resource planning (ERP) systems. Each type of system almost always involves the use of one or more databases.

The latter three types of systems are often classified as business intelligence systems. **Business intelligence systems** are used to analyze and interpret data to enable managers to make informed decisions about how best to run a business. Data warehouses and data marts are key components of business intelligence systems because they enable access to wide ranges of information gathered from multiple sources. Increased access to information usually enables business intelligence systems to provide better information to managers in a timely fashion, which can lead to enhanced decision making.

In the following sections, we'll examine each of the five types of systems in greater detail.

### Office Support Systems

**What does an office support system accomplish?** An office support system (OSS) is designed to improve communications and assist employees in accomplishing their daily tasks. Microsoft Office is an example of an OSS because it assists employees with routine tasks such as maintaining an employee phone list in Excel, designing a

**Figure 9.33**

All information systems perform similar functions, including acquiring data, processing that data into information, storing the data, and providing the user with a number of output options with which to make the information meaningful and useful.

sales presentation in PowerPoint, and writing customer letters using Word.

Modern OSSs include software tools with which you are probably familiar, including e-mail, word processing, spreadsheet, database, and presentation programs. Office support systems have their roots in manual, paper-based systems that were developed before computers. After all, maintaining a company phone listing was necessary long before computers were invented. A paper listing of employee phone extensions typed by an administrative assistant is an example of an early OSS. A modern OSS might publish this directory on the company's intranet (its internal network).

### Transaction-Processing Systems

**What is a transaction-processing system?** A transaction-processing system (TPS) keeps track of everyday business activities. For example, at your college, transactions that occur frequently include registering students for classes, accepting tuition payments, mailing advertisements, and printing course catalogs. Your college has TPSs in place to track these types of activities.

When computers were introduced to the business world, they often were first put to work hosting TPSs. Computers were much faster at processing large chunks of data than previous manual systems had been. Imagine having clerks type up tuition invoices for each student at a 10,000-student university. Obviously, a computer can print invoices much quicker from a database.

**How do transactions enter a TPS?** Transactions can be entered manually or electronically. When you order a sweater online, for example, you are providing data (such as your shipping address) that will reside in a TPS. When you purchase gasoline at a pay-at-the-pump terminal, the pump captures your credit card data and transmits it to a TPS, which automatically records a sale (gallons of gasoline and dollar value). Transactions are processed either in batches or in real time. Various departments in an organization then access the TPSs to extract the information they need to process additional transactions, as shown in Figure 9.34.

**What is batch processing?** Batch processing means that transaction data is accumulated until a certain point is reached, and then several transactions are processed all at once. Batch processing is appropriate for activities that are not time sensitive, such as developing a mailing list to mail out the new course catalogs that students have requested. The college could print a mailing label each time someone requests a catalog, but it is more efficient to batch the requests and process them all at once when the catalogs are ready to be addressed.

**How does real-time processing work?** For most activities, processing and recording transactions in a TPS occur in real time. **Real-time processing** means that the database is queried and updated while the transaction is taking place. For instance, when you register for classes online, if seats are still available for the classes you want, the database immediately records your registration in the class to ensure you have a seat. This **online transaction processing (OLTP)** ensures that the data in the TPS is as current as possible.

## Management Information Systems

**What is a management information system?** A **management information system (MIS)** provides timely and accurate information that enables managers to make critical business decisions (i.e., they provide business intelligence). MISs were a direct outgrowth of TPSs. Managers quickly realized that the data contained in TPSs could be an extremely powerful tool only if the information could be organized and output in a useful form. Today's MISs are often built in as a feature of TPSs.

**What does an MIS provide that a TPS does not?** The original TPSs were usually designed to output detail reports. A **detail report** provides a list of the transactions that occurred during a certain time period. For example, during registration periods at your school, the registrar might receive a detail report that lists the students who registered for classes each day. Figure 9.35a shows an example of a detail report on daily enrollment.

Going beyond the detail reports provided by TPSs, MISs provide summary reports and exception reports. A **summary report** provides a consolidated picture of detailed data. These reports usually include some calculation (totals) or visual displays of information (such as charts and graphs). Figure 9.35b shows an example of a summary report displaying total daily credits enrolled by division.

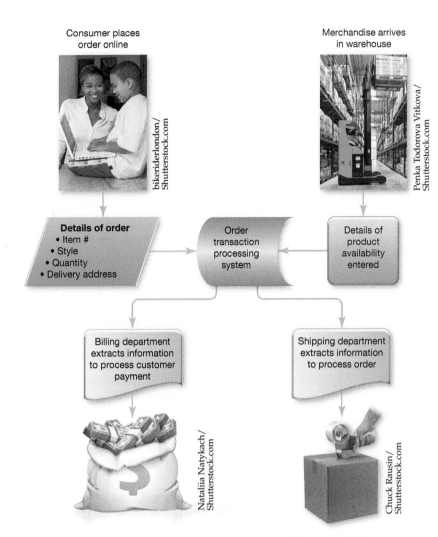

**Figure 9.34**

TPSs help capture and track critical business information needed for successful completion of business transactions such as selling merchandise over the Internet.

An **exception report** shows conditions that are unusual or that need attention by users of the system. The registrar at your college may get an exception report when all sections of a course are full, indicating that it may be time to schedule additional sections. Figure 9.35c shows an example of such an exception report.

## Decision Support Systems

**What is a decision support system?** A **decision support system (DSS)** is another type of business intelligence system designed to help managers develop solutions for specific problems. A DSS for a marketing department might provide statistical information on customer attributes (such as income levels, buying patterns, and so on) that would assist managers in making decisions regarding advertising strategy. A DSS not only uses data from databases and data warehouses, but also enables users to add

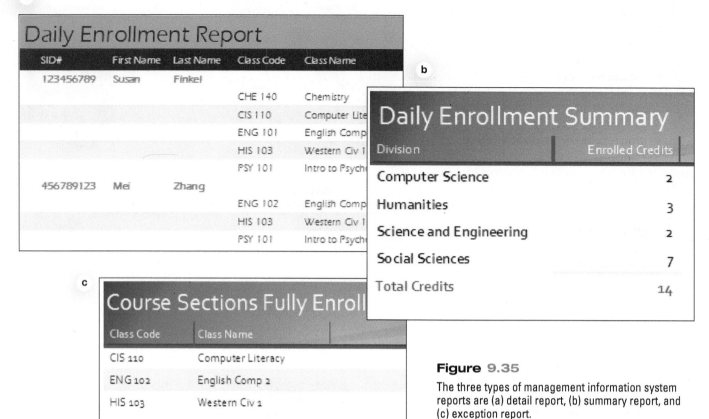

**a**

## Daily Enrollment Report

| SID# | First Name | Last Name | Class Code | Class Name |
|------|-----------|-----------|-----------|-----------|
| 123456789 | Susan | Finkel | | |
| | | | CHE 140 | Chemistry |
| | | | CIS 110 | Computer Lite |
| | | | ENG 101 | English Comp |
| | | | HIS 103 | Western Civ 1 |
| | | | PSY 101 | Intro to Psych |
| 456789123 | Mei | Zhang | | |
| | | | ENG 102 | English Comp |
| | | | HIS 103 | Western Civ 1 |
| | | | PSY 101 | Intro to Psych |

**b**

## Daily Enrollment Summary

| Division | Enrolled Credits |
|----------|-----------------|
| Computer Science | 2 |
| Humanities | 3 |
| Science and Engineering | 2 |
| Social Sciences | 7 |
| Total Credits | 14 |

**c**

## Course Sections Fully Enroll

| Class Code | Class Name | |
|-----------|-----------|---|
| CIS 110 | Computer Literacy | |
| ENG 102 | English Comp 2 | |
| HIS 103 | Western Civ 1 | |

**Figure 9.35**

The three types of management information system reports are (a) detail report, (b) summary report, and (c) exception report.

their own insights and experiences and apply them to the solution.

**What does a decision support system look like?** Database management systems, while playing an integral part of a DSS, are supplemented by additional software systems in a DSS. In a DSS, the user interface provides the means of interaction between the user and the system. An effective user interface must be easy to learn. The other major components of a DSS are internal and external data sources, model management systems, and knowledge-based systems. As shown in Figure 9.36, all of these systems work together to provide the user of the DSS with a broad base of information on which to base decisions.

### Internal and External Data Sources

**What are internal and external data sources for decision support systems?** Data can be fed into the DSS from a variety of sources. **Internal data sources** are maintained by the same company that operates the DSS. For example, internal TPSs can provide a wealth of statistical data about customers, ordering patterns, inventory

levels, and so on. An **external data source** is any source not owned by the company that owns the DSS, such as customer demographic data purchased from third parties, mailing lists, or statistics compiled by the federal government. Internal and external data sources provide a stream of data that is integrated into the DSS for analysis.

### Model Management Systems

**What function does a model management system perform?** A **model management system** is software that assists in building management models in DSSs. A management model is an analysis tool that, through the use of internal and external data, provides a view of a particular business situation for the purposes of decision making. Models can be built to describe any business situation, such as the classroom space requirements for next semester or a listing of alternative sales outlet locations.

Internal models (such as a spreadsheet that shows current classroom use on a college campus) are developed inside an organization. External models (such as statistics about populations of students at two-year

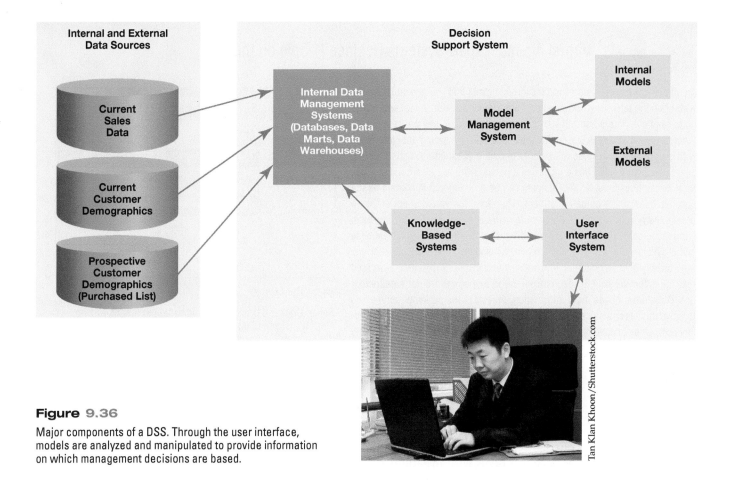

**Internal and External Data Sources**

**Decision Support System**

**Figure 9.36**

Major components of a DSS. Through the user interface, models are analyzed and manipulated to provide information on which management decisions are based.

Tan Klan Khoon/Shutterstock.com

colleges in the United States) are obtained from third parties. Model management systems typically contain financial and statistical analysis tools used to analyze the data provided by models or to create additional models.

### Knowledge-Based Systems

**What is a knowledge-based system, and how is it used in decision support systems?** A **knowledge-based system** provides additional intelligence that supplements the user's own intellect and makes the DSS more effective. It can be an **expert system** that tries to replicate the decision-making processes of human experts to solve specific problems. For example, an expert system might be designed to take the place of a physician in a remote location such as a scientific base in Antarctica. A physician expert system would ask the patient about symptoms just as a live physician would, and the system would make a diagnosis based on the algorithms programmed into it.

Another type of knowledge-based system is a **natural language processing (NLP) system**. NLP systems enable users to communicate with computer systems using a natural spoken or written language instead of using a computer programming language. Individuals with disabilities who cannot use a keyboard benefit greatly from NLP systems because they can just speak to the computer and have it understand what they are saying without using specific computer commands. Using an NLP system can simplify the user interface, making it much more efficient and user friendly. The speech-recognition feature of Microsoft Windows is a type of NLP system. Great strides are being made in developing computers with NLP systems, such as the IBM computer Watson that competed on the game show *Jeopardy* in 2011 against two human opponents. Watson was able to correctly decipher the questions and provide correct responses to them the majority of the time. In fact, the computer easily beat the two human champions it was competing against.

## Virtual Agents: Expert Systems Replace People on the Web

An offshoot of expert systems are the virtual agents that you encounter on the Web or on the telephone. Virtual agents are frequently used to deal with questions from customers and often try to appear as though they are real people themselves. However, virtual agents are a type of expert system that interfaces with a database to provide answers to people's questions. A typical virtual agent (see Figure 9.37) has a picture of a person (who has a name) and a box for entering questions. No virtual agent can be programmed to contain all the possible questions a human might ask. Therefore, the virtual agent software breaks the question down into key words and phrases, which it compares to a database containing question responses. It picks the most likely response and provides the answer, usually both in text and verbally. The customer can then usually give feedback as to whether the response adequately answered their question. Usually, if results from the virtual agent are not satisfactory or the customer needs more information, they have the option of connecting to a live customer service agent. Virtual agents, while not always perfect, allow companies to save money by answering common questions without using expensive human labor.

Courtesy of Gonzaga University

**Figure 9.37**

Spike, Gonzaga University's sports team mascot, has now been transformed into a virtual agent to direct people to the appropriate pages of the school's Web site.

All knowledge-based systems fall under the science of artificial intelligence. **Artificial intelligence (AI)** is the branch of computer science that deals with the attempt to create computers that think like humans. To date, no computers have been constructed that can replicate the thinking patterns of a human brain, because scientists still do not fully understand how humans store and integrate knowledge and experiences to form human intelligence.

**How does a knowledge-based system help in the decision-making process?** Databases and the models provided by model management systems tend to be extremely analytical and mathematical in nature. If we relied solely on databases and models to make decisions, then the answers would be derived with a "yes or no" mentality, allowing no room for human thought. Fortunately, human users are involved in these types of systems, providing an opportunity to inject human judgment and experience into the decision-making process.

The knowledge-based system also provides an opportunity to introduce experience into the mix. Knowledge-based systems support the concept of fuzzy logic. Normal logic is highly rigid: If "x" happens, then "y" will happen. **Fuzzy logic** enables the interjection of experiential learning into the equation by considering probabilities. Whereas

an algorithm in a database has to be specific, an algorithm in a knowledge-based system could state that if "x" happens, 70 percent of the time "y" will happen.

For instance, managers at Best Buy would find it extremely helpful if their DSSs informed them that 45 percent of customers who bought an iPad also bought a Smart Cover for it. This could suggest that designing a discount program for Smart Covers bought with iPads might spur sales. Fuzzy logic enables a system to be more flexible and to consider a wider range of possibilities than would conventional algorithmic thinking.

### Enterprise Resource Planning Systems

**What is an enterprise?** An enterprise is any business entity, large or small. It could be the pizza shop on the corner or a Fortune 500 manufacturer of sports apparel. All businesses have data and information to manage, and large, complex organizations can benefit from managing that information with a central piece of software.

**What does an enterprise resource planning system do?** An **enterprise resource planning (ERP) system** is a broad-based software system that integrates multiple data sources and ties together the various processes of an enterprise to enable information to flow more smoothly. ERP systems use a common database to store and integrate information. This enables the information to be used across multiple areas of an enterprise.

For instance, human resource functions (such as the management of hiring, firing, promotions, and benefits) and accounting functions (such as payroll) are often the first processes integrated into an ERP system. Historically, human resource records and accounting records were kept in separate databases, but having the information reside in one database makes the management and paying of employees more streamlined. If manufacturing operations were then integrated into the ERP system, the data that was already in place regarding the employees and payroll could be easily used for determining the cost of running an assembly line (because the workers on the assembly line get paid) or for scheduling workers to run the assembly line. The objective of ERP systems is to accumulate all information relevant to running a business in a central location and make it readily available to whoever needs that information to make decisions.

Almost all Fortune 500 companies have implemented ERP systems, and many medium-sized companies are implementing them also. Although the corner pizza shop probably does not need an ERP system, it would be difficult to coordinate the activities of a multinational corporation without one.

## Data Mining

Just because you have captured data in an organized fashion and have stored it in a format that seems to make sense doesn't mean that an analysis of the data will automatically reveal everything you need to know. Trends can sometimes be hard to spot if the data is not organized or analyzed in a particular way. To make data work harder, companies employ data-mining techniques.

**Data mining** is the process by which great amounts of data are analyzed and

**ACTIVE HELP-DESK**

Data Warehouses, Data Marts, and Information Systems

In this Active Helpdesk call, you'll play the role of a helpdesk staffer, fielding calls about data warehouses, data marts, and information systems.

investigated. The objective is to spot significant patterns or trends within the data that would otherwise not be obvious. For instance, by mining student enrollment data, a school may discover that 35 percent of new engineering degree students are Latino.

**Why do businesses mine their data?** The main reason businesses mine data is to understand their customers better. If a company can better understand the types of customers who buy its products and can learn what motivates its customers to do so, it can market effectively by concentrating its efforts on the populations that are most likely to buy.

**How do businesses mine their data?** Data mining enables managers to sift through data in several ways. Each method produces different information that managers can then base their decisions on. Managers make their data meaningful through the following activities:

- **Classification:** To analyze data, managers need to classify it. Therefore, before mining, managers define data classes that they think will be helpful in spotting trends. They then apply these class definitions to all unclassified data to prepare it for analysis. For example, "good credit risk" and "bad credit risk" are two data classes that managers could establish to determine whether to grant car loans to applicants. Managers would then identify factors (such as credit history and yearly income) that they could use to classify applicants as good or bad risks.

- **Estimation:** When managers classify data, the record either fits the classification criteria or it doesn't. Estimation enables managers to assign a value to data based on some criterion. For example, assume a bank wants to send out credit card offers to people who are likely to be granted a credit card. The bank may run the customers' data through a program that assigns them a score based on where they live, their household income, and their average bank balance. This provides managers with an estimate of the most likely credit card prospects so that they can include them in the mailing.

- **Affinity grouping (or association rules):** When mining data, managers also can determine which data goes together. In other words, they can apply affinity

# Data, Data Everywhere—But Is It Protected?

As databases have become commonplace, an ever-increasing amount of information about you and your habits has gone into various databases. Every time you purchase something with a credit card, there is a record of that transaction, and both the merchant from whom you purchased the item and the credit card company have information about your buying habits (see Figure 9.38).

Have you used a toll service that allows you to pay your tolls electronically by just driving through a lane without stopping? Toll records are routinely subpoenaed in court cases. Toll records were used in an Illinois court by a husband in a divorce case to prove his wife was rarely home and therefore unfit for custody of their son. All banking transactions are handled by computers (and hence databases) in the United States, and there is a high probability that your employer is electronically transferring your pay to your bank by direct deposit. If you engage in online banking and bill paying, yet another electronic trail of your financial life is being generated in databases.

Do you think you can avoid scrutiny by paying cash? Not if you are a member of a frequent shopper "club" (a popular promotion used by supermarkets and drug stores) and provide the checkout clerk with your personal information in exchange for coupons or a few dollars off your purchases. Remember, you never can be sure of how this data

might be used. In October 2004, a firefighter was arrested after his supermarket purchase records revealed he had purchased the same type of fire starters used in an arson case. After three months, the charges were dropped when another person pleaded guilty to committing the arson.

Because of the vast amount of electronic information processing that goes on today, you can't avoid having your personal information contained in databases. But do you actually know who has your data? You may have joined the frequent shopper club at CVS to get discounts and gave them your e-mail address and other contact information. But who did CVS give your e-mail address to?

Many consumers received a rude shock in March 2011 when they began receiving apologetic correspondence from companies alerting them that their e-mail addresses had potentially been exposed to misuse. Many companies (such as CVS) collect e-mail addresses so they can correspond with customers, but the e-mails don't come directly from those companies. Large marketing companies such as Epsilon are hired to manage customer e-mail programs for both large and small businesses. Unfortunately, Epsilon's database servers suffered an attack in March 2011 that exposed millions of individuals' e-mail

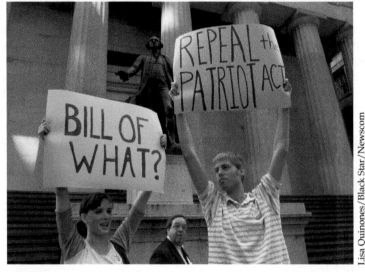

**Figure 9.38**

Demonstrators are protesting the perceived erosion of individual privacy rights for United States citizens. Do you feel your privacy rights are threatened?

grouping or association rules to the data. For example, suppose analysis of a sales database indicates that two items are bought together 60 percent of the time. Based on this data, managers might decide that these items should be pictured on the same page of their Web site.

- **Clustering:** Clustering involves organizing data into similar subgroups, or clusters. It is different from classification in that there are no predefined classes. The data-mining software makes the decision about what to group, and it is up to managers to determine whether the clusters are meaningful. For example,

the data-mining software may identify clusters of customers with similar buying patterns. Further analysis of the clusters may reveal that certain socioeconomic groups have similar buying patterns.

- **Description and visualization:** Often, the purpose of data mining is merely to describe data so that managers can visualize it. Sometimes having a clear picture of what is going on with the data helps people to interpret it in new and different ways. For example, if large amounts of data revealed that right-handed women who live in rural environments addresses. Inadvertently exposing information to inappropriate or unauthorized individuals is known as a *data breach*. Companies needed to warn their customers of potential spear phishing attacks that were likely to be launched against them.

Many phishing attacks are random. If a cyber-crook sends out 10,000 phishing e-mails claiming to be from Citibank, most of the people that receive them won't have a Citibank account and will ignore them. However, **spear phishing** attacks are more serious because they use e-mail addresses of customers that are known to have a relationship with a certain company. When you know you have e-mail addresses of customers that definitely have a relationship with a company, your phishing attacks are more likely to succeed . . . not unlike using a spear gun instead of a fish hook to hunt fish.

Although you might never be compromised as a result of this data breach, it does underscore the potential danger of having your information stolen by nefarious parties. What responsibility do companies to which you provide information have in safeguarding their data? Should they inform you that your data might be shared with other corporations and obtain your permission before sharing it? How should consumers be compensated (and by whom) if their data is misused?

### What Can You Do?

Providing information and having it recorded in databases are part of our way of life now. Because refusing to give information out at all is bound to be impractical, you should ask the following questions related to data you are providing:

- **For what purpose is the data being gathered?** When the clerk at the electronics superstore asks for your zip code, ask why she wants it. (It is probably for some marketing purpose.)
- **Are the reasons for gathering the data legitimate or important to you?** When you purchase a movie on Blu-ray, is asking for your zip code really a legitimate request? However, to validate the warranty on a large-screen TV, you may need to give a clerk your address and zip code. Similarly, disclosing medical information to key people (such as your pharmacist) may be important to receiving good care and therefore is extremely important to you. If you don't see the advantage, then ask more questions or don't reveal the information.

- **How will the information gathered be protected once it has been obtained?** Ask about data protection policies before you give information. Most Web sites provide access to their data protection policies—readily available through clickable links or pop-up boxes—when they ask for information. If an organization doesn't have a data protection policy, then be wary of giving them sensitive information unless there is a compelling advantage to doing so (such as receiving good medical care). Data protection doesn't just refer to keeping data secure. It also means restricting access to the data to employees of the organization that need to use that data. A shipping clerk might need to see your address, for example, but doesn't need to see your credit card information.
- **Will the information collected be used for purposes other than the purpose for which it was originally collected?** This might be covered in a data protection policy. If it isn't, then ask about it. Will your information be sold to or shared with other companies? Will it be used for marketing other products to you?
- **Could the information asked for be used for identity theft?** Identity thieves usually need your Social Security number and your birth date to open credit card accounts in your name. Be especially wary when asked for this information, and make sure there is a legitimate need for this information. Most organizations and businesses are shying away from using Social Security numbers to track customers, because of the risk of identity theft. And do you really need an e-mail from someone on your birthday advertising a product? It really isn't worth exposing your birth date to potential misuse.
- **Are organizations that already have your data safeguarding it?** Don't just consider new requests for information. Think about organizations, such as banks, that already have your information and monitor their performance. Have they been in the news lately because of a major data breach? (Is your bank a customer of Epsilon, for instance?) You might want to consider switching institutions if yours has a poor record of data security.

Think carefully before providing information and be vigilant about monitoring your data when you can. It may make the difference between invasion of privacy and peace of mind.

never take philosophy courses, it would most likely spark a heated discussion about the reasons why. It would certainly provide plenty of opportunities for additional study on the part of psychologists, sociologists, and college administrators!

You may have noticed that products are frequently moved around in supermarkets. This is usually the result of data mining. With electronic scanning of bar codes, each customer's purchase is recorded in a database. By classifying the data and using cluster analysis, supermarket managers can determine which products people usually purchase with other products. The store then places these products close to each other so that shoppers can find them easily. For instance, if analysis shows that people often buy potato chips with soft drinks, it makes sense to place these items in the same aisle.

As the human race continues to accumulate data, the development of faster and bigger databases will be a necessity. You can expect to interact with more and more databases every year, even if you don't realize you are doing so. While you may never have to create a database, understanding how databases work will enable you to interact with them more effectively.

**1. What is a database, and why is it beneficial to use databases?**

Databases are electronic collections of related data that can be organized so that it is more easily accessed and manipulated. Properly designed databases cut down on data redundancy and duplicate data by ensuring relevant data is recorded in only one place. This also helps eliminate data inconsistency, which comes from having different data about the same transaction recorded in two different places. When databases are used, multiple users can share and access information at the same time. Databases are used any time complex information needs to be organized or more than one person needs to access it. In these cases, lists (which are used to keep track of simple information) are no longer efficient.

**2. What components make up a database?**

The three main components of a database are fields, records, and tables. A category of information in a database is stored in a field. Each field is identified by a field name, which is a way of describing the field. Fields are assigned a data type that indicates what type of data can be stored in the field. Common data types include text, numeric, computational, date, memo, object, and hyperlink. A group of related fields is a record. A group of related records is a table or file. To keep records distinct, each record must have one field that has a value unique to that record. This unique field is a primary key (or a key field).

**3. What types of databases are there?**

The three major types of databases currently in use are relational, object-oriented, and multidimensional. Relational databases are characterized by two-dimensional tables of data in which a common field is maintained in each of two tables and the information in the tables is linked by this field. Object-oriented databases store data in objects, not in tables. The objects also contain instructions about how the data is to be manipulated or processed. Multidimensional databases represent data in three-dimensional cubes to enable faster retrieval of information from the database.

**4. What do database management systems do?**

Database management systems (DBMSs) are specially designed applications (such as Oracle or Microsoft Access) that interact with the user, other applications, and the database itself to capture and analyze data. The main operations of a DBMS are creating databases, entering data, viewing (or browsing) data, sorting (or indexing) data, extracting (or querying) data, and outputting data. A query language is used to extract records from a database. Almost all relational databases today use structured query language, or SQL. However, most DBMSs include wizards that enable you to query the database without learning a query language. The most common form of output for any database is a printed report.

**5. How do relational databases organize and manipulate data?**

Relational databases operate by organizing data into various tables based on logical groupings. Because not all of the data in a relational database is stored in the same table, a methodology must be implemented to link data between tables. In relational databases, the links between tables that define how the data is related are referred to as relationships. To establish a relationship between two tables, both tables must have a common field (or column). Once linked, information can be drawn from multiple tables through the use of queries (for on-screen viewing of data) or report generators (used to produce printed reports).

**6. What are data warehouses and data marts, and how are they used?**

A data warehouse is a large-scale electronic repository of data that contains and organizes in one place all the relevant data related to an organization. Data warehouses often contain information from multiple databases. Because it can be difficult to find information in a large data warehouse, small slices of the data warehouse called *data marts* are often created. The information in data marts pertains to a single department within the organization, for example. Data warehouses and data marts consolidate information from a wide variety of sources to provide comprehensive pictures of operations or transactions within a business.

7. **What is a business intelligence system, and what types of business intelligence systems are used by decision makers?**

Business intelligence systems are used to analyze and interpret data to enable managers to make informed decisions about how best to run a business. An office support system (OSS) is designed to assist employees in accomplishing their day-to-day tasks and improve communications. A transaction-processing system (TPS) is used to keep track of everyday business activities. A management information system (MIS) provides timely and accurate

information that enables managers to make critical business decisions. A decision support system (DSS) is designed to help managers develop solutions for specific problems. An enterprise resource planning (ERP) system is a large software system that gathers information from all parts of a business and integrates it to make it readily available for decision making. MIS, DSS, and ERP systems are all classified as business intelligence systems.

8. **What is data mining, and how does it work?**

Data mining is the process by which large amounts of data are analyzed to spot otherwise hidden trends. Through processes such as classification, estimation, affinity grouping, clustering, and description (visualization), data is organized so that it provides meaningful information that can be used by managers to identify business trends.

 ## Companion Website

The Companion Website includes a variety of additional materials to help you review and learn more about the topics in this chapter. Go to: *www.pearsonhighered.com/techinaction*

**key terms**

## Word Bank

- business intelligence system
- computational field
- data dictionary
- data mining
- data warehouse
- decision support system
- expert system
- join query
- memo field
- metadata
- object field
- primary key
- record
- relational algebra
- select query
- table
- text field
- transaction-processing system (TPS)

**Instructions:** Fill in the blanks using the words from the Word Bank above.

Relational databases store data in two-dimensional (1) _____s. Properly constructed relational databases use a field called a(n) (2) _____ that contains values that uniquely identify each (3) _____. In a database, data such as "Julia" or "red" are normally stored in a(n) (4) _____. The result of a formula such as (credit hours × cost per credit) should be stored in a(n) (5) _____, whereas an MP3 file would appropriately be stored in a(n) (6) _____. Extremely lengthy textual data is best stored in a(n) (7) _____. Data used to describe other data (such as data type) is referred to as (8) _____ and is contained in the (9) _____ of a database.

Queries are used to extract data from a database. In relational databases, information is drawn from multiple tables using a(n) (10) _____. If you were performing a simple operation such as extracting data from a single table, you could use a(n) (11) _____.

Systems that record routine business activities (such as sales) are classified as (12) _____s. (13) _____s are used to analyze and interpret data to enable managers to make informed decisions about how best to run a business. When a company needs a data storage facility that contains and organizes all the data related to an organization, (14) _____s are used instead of individual databases. To spot significant patterns or trends within data that would otherwise not be obvious, managers often use a technique known as (15) _____.

Your best friend, Julio, has decided to launch a t-shirt business (along the lines of **Threadless.com**) to feature the artwork of students from a local art college. He has engaged a Web designer to design his Web site, but has asked you to advise him on the types of information he needs to record to enable him to make sound decisions about running the business. He knows t-shirts, but he realizes you are much more computer savvy.

Write a proposal that outlines what you intend to do for Julio. What kinds of databases should be created for this business? What kind of data must be captured to run the business efficiently? How should that information be organized? Julio will probably be away from his manufacturing facility quite frequently. Can the databases for the business be accessed online (say with a smartphone)? Julio has limited funding. Are there open source database alternatives that would work for the types of databases he will need?

self-test

**Instructions:** Answer the multiple-choice and true–false questions below for more practice with key terms and concepts from this chapter.

## Multiple Choice

**1.** Two lists showing the same data about the same person is an example of
 a. data redundancy.
 b. data inconsistency.
 c. data disparity.
 d. data duplication errors.

**2.** Which of the following is NOT an advantage of using databases instead of lists?
 a. Data can be easily shared among users.
 b. Data entry errors can be minimized with databases.
 c. Data integrity can be ensured with a database.
 d. Databases are easier to build and maintain than lists.

**3.** In databases, tables are related using
 a. primary keys and foreign keys.
 b. boolean logic.
 c. data marts.
 d. database logic.

**4.** A field that has a unique entry for each record in a database table is called the
 a. logical key.
 b. master field.
 c. crucial field.
 d. primary key.

**5.** A primary key of one table that is also found in a related table is a
 a. linked key.
 b. foreign key.
 c. secondary key.
 d. subordinate key.

**6.** A(n) _____ database organizes data in two-dimensional tables.
 a. relational
 b. object-oriented
 c. rectangular
 d. multidimensional

**7.** Which of the following is one of the four main operations of a DBMS?
 a. querying data
 b. dissecting data
 c. structuring data
 d. consolidating data

**8.** Ensuring that a field must contain a number that is between two values is an example of a(n)
 a. alphabetic check.
 b. completeness check.
 c. range check.
 d. consistency check.

**9.** A system that is designed to help perform routine daily tasks is known as (a)n
 a. data mart.
 b. office support system.
 c. data warehouse.
 d. decision support system.

**10.** A system that tries to mimic human responses is an example of a(n)
 a. transaction-processing system.
 b. decision support system.
 c. expert system.
 d. knowledge-based system.

## True-False

_____ 1. A query is used to extract information from a database.

_____ 2. Validation checks ensure that required fields in a database are filled in completely.

_____ 3. Normalization of data involves reducing data redundancy by recording data only once.

_____ 4. A transaction-processing system (TPS) is an example of a business intelligence system.

_____ 5. Data mining is often used to spot customer trends.

## 1. Understanding Database Design

Go to Bestbuy.com and look at the iPads (and other tablet computers) that are for sale. Best Buy uses a very sophisticated database to process transactions. But every good database starts with good design by creating a field for each unique piece of data. List as many fields as you can identify used to record information for a tablet computer for sale at Best Buy. Assign each field you identify a data type and suggest a reasonable field length.

## 2. Privacy Settings on Facebook

Facebook is a large database. It is important to protect personal information that is contained in a database, and with Facebook you are responsible for making decisions about sharing your information. The owners of Facebook are constantly tweaking the privacy settings on the site. If you have not checked your privacy settings lately, you may not be aware of the personal information that you are sharing with anyone who can access Facebook.

a. Log in to your Facebook account and access your privacy settings. Which information about you is accessible to everyone? Is any of your information only visible to your friends? What types of information is viewable by friends of your friends?

b. Did any of the privacy settings surprise you? Which privacy settings do you think you need to change? Why? If you don't think any changes to your settings are necessary, explain why you feel secure with your current privacy settings.

## 3. Designing Your Own Database

A group of students at your school wants to collect and refurbish used computer equipment and donate it to underprivileged individuals. To help this group, you want to create a database to facilitate the tracking of the donated equipment. Determine the following:

a. What fields do you need to capture information about the clients who are donating the computing equipment? What would be the primary key of the "client" table? Why would it be a good primary key?

b. What fields do you need in your database for identifying and categorizing the computer equipment? What would be a good primary key to use for the "computer inventory" table? Why would it be a good primary key?

c. Design a table that tracks the donation transactions. What fields from the other two tables would need to be included in the "donation transaction" table? Justify your answer.

## 4. Comparing Databases

Amazon.com and eCampus.com are two sites students frequently use to buy textbooks. On both sites you interact with a database to search for and purchase your textbooks. Visit both sites and search for several textbooks such as the ones you are using this semester. Compare your experiences on both sites. Consider the following (and make sure you fully explain each answer):

a. Which site is easier to use?

b. Which site offers better options for refining the results of your search (query) for a textbook?

c. What fields did you search on to find your textbooks? Would searching on another field have produced more accurate results?

d. What enhancements would you suggest to the owners of both sites to improve your shopping experience?

## 1. Data Marts

You are a summer intern in the information technology group of a regional chain of sporting goods stores. The company has been in business for 20 years and operates 40 locations in seven states. The 40 locations are organized into four regions (north, south, east, and west) of 10 stores each. Regional managers are responsible for inventory management, procurement of inventory, sales, and marketing for their particular region. The company has been processing all transactions electronically (with customers and suppliers), and it has captured all the data in a large data warehouse. Unfortunately, the regional managers are complaining that there is now so much information in the data warehouse that it has become somewhat difficult to sort through it and extract meaningful data. You have just been placed on the team that will be designing a new data strategy for the company.

a. Setting up data marts would probably help with the accessibility of information. What type of data marts would you suggest setting up for this company? Make sure you explain who will benefit from the data marts you suggest.

b. For the data marts you identified in the previous question, list the data that should be stored in each data mart and explain how the regional managers could make use of that information to manage their group of stores.

## 2. Recovering from a Data Breach

You have an internship in the marketing department of XYZ Drugs (a large retail pharmacy chain) that has an established buyer loyalty program. The buyer loyalty program provides customers with discounts when they present their loyalty card when making purchases. XYZ collects e-mail addresses when customers enroll in the program and have engaged a third-party marketing company (ABC Marketing) to routinely send out e-mails to customers advertising special deals.

Unfortunately, ABC has just informed XYZ that their servers suffered a major data breach and all of the names and e-mail addresses of XYZ's customers in ABC's database were illegally copied by unknown hackers. The head of XYZ's marketing department has put you on the team to determine how best to inform and reassure XYZ's customers of the possible consequences of the data breach. You are currently working on the draft e-mail to be sent to XYZ's customers. Consider the following:

a. What are the risks that XYZ's customers face from the data breach?

b. What steps should the customers take to mitigate the risks you just identified? You need to be tactful and careful in your suggestions to the customers because you want them to continue to trust XYZ with their personal information.

c. Your friends and family have been asking you about this data breach. Prepare a list of precautions that they can take with their personal data to avoid being victims of these types of data breaches (which may include not providing as much personal information to retailers). Try searching on the Internet for ideas using search terms such as "data breach protection" or "e-mail breach safeguards."

**Instructions:** Some ideas are best understood by experimenting with them in our own minds. The following critical thinking questions are designed to demand your full attention but require only a comfortable chair—no technology.

## 1. Database Privacy Policies

Most likely you have provided quite a bit of personal information to various companies when you became their customer. Companies have an ethical responsibility to protect sensitive data obtained from customers. Consider the following:

a. Think about a retailer (such as Costco or Sears) that you have done business with recently. What personal information did you provide to that retailer? What personal information should a company be precluded from disclosing to others? What information does the company have of yours that you don't care if they share with (or sell to) other companies?

b. Most retailers have privacy policies that describe how your information will be used and safeguarded. Have you ever read a privacy policy from a retailer that you have done business with? If so, summarize the provisions of the policy. If not, review a privacy policy from a major online retailer and summarize its provisions. In your opinion, is the privacy policy you reviewed sufficient to protect your sensitive data?

## 2. Social Security Database

The U.S. Social Security Administration (SSA) maintains a large database containing a great deal of information on the personal income of individuals. The information in this database could be easily sorted and categorized by attributes such as geographic location and age. This information would be of great value to marketing professionals for targeting marketing programs to consumers. Currently, the SSA is prohibited from selling this information to third parties. However, the SSA and other government agencies face increasing pressure to find ways to generate revenue or decrease expenses.

a. Do you favor a change in the laws that would permit the SSA to sell names and addresses with household income information to third parties? Why or why not?

b. Would it be acceptable for the SSA to sell income information to marketing firms if it did not include personal information, but only included income statistics for certain geographic areas? How is this better (or worse) than selling personal information?

c. How would you feel about the SSA marketing financial products (such as investment opportunities and retirement plans) directly to consumers? Would this be a conflict of interest with the SSA's main mission, which is the collection of retirement taxes and the provision of old-age pensions?

## 3. Information About You on Facebook

Most likely you have a Facebook page or some other social networking page (MySpace, LinkedIn, etc.). Facebook is a database, and information from your page is often shared with other databases when you permit it by participating in various games and other applications that require access to your personal data as a condition of participation. Think about the information that you have on your Facebook page (including photos and videos).

a. What information is on your page that you wouldn't want your parents to know about? What information on your page might be of concern to a prospective employer? If you were considering transferring to another college or university, what things on your page might not impress the staff of the admissions office? What information might you consider removing from your Facebook page tonight?

b. How many games and other applications do you estimate have access to your information? Check your privacy settings for your Facebook page and look in the Apps, Games and Web sites section to see how many apps you actually are using. Were you surprised at the difference in the actual number of apps and your estimate? What apps do you think you should disable to prevent them from accessing your information? Give reasons for the ones you will disable (don't trust them, don't use them, etc.).

# Redesigning Facebook

### Problem

Facebook is the most popular social media site and is also a database. But as with any product, there is always room for improvement. Facebook management has made decisions about what data they require from users who create Facebook accounts. They also have set up specific areas to display what management considers to be pertinent information on a user's main Facebook page. But perhaps you as a user would have designed Facebook differently.

### Task

Your class has volunteered to work as a focus group for Facebook as part of a nationwide project to assess the usefulness of the information gathered by Facebook. Users often provide unique perspectives, and they should be consulted whenever possible during the design, implementation, and updates of Web sites. As heavy users of Facebook, management feels that student input is invaluable to ensuring currency and usability of its features.

### Process

Divide the class into small groups.

1. Your group members should examine their individual Facebook accounts. If anyone in your group does not have a Facebook account, they should set one up. If you all have Facebook accounts, you might want to consider going through the process of setting up an account to reacquaint yourselves with the information that is required (or can be entered) when a Facebook account is first set up. Pay particular attention to the profile area of your account. What fields in the profile do you consider to be most useful? Which fields do you think are totally unnecessary and could be eliminated? What fields are missing from the profile that you think would be useful to you and your friends?

2. Investigate your account settings and application settings, paying particular attention to items that are displayed on the main page of your account. What changes would you make to these settings? Are options missing that you would find helpful to configuring your Facebook page?

3. Present your group's findings to the class. Compare your suggestions to those of other groups. Be sure to think about the needs of other groups of users (such as your parents or your grandparents), because they probably use Facebook in ways that you might not.

4. Prepare a list of recommendations for improvements to the current Facebook home page and settings pages. Clearly indicate how the proposed changes will benefit both users and the management of Facebook (retaining users, being able to better target advertising to users, and so on).

### Conclusion

Facebook will most likely experience competition in the future from other social networking sites that will want to poach its huge base of users. To remain competitive, Facebook needs to consider the input of users like you to ensure that it delivers a cutting-edge product with features its customers want and need. Facebook's best chance of remaining on top of the social media heap is to be sensitive to the needs of its current users.

# Private Information on Public Databases

In this exercise, you will research and then role-play a complicated ethical situation. The role you play might or might not match your own personal beliefs; in either case, your research and use of logic will enable you to represent the view assigned. An arbitrator will watch and comment on both sides of the arguments, and together the team will agree on an ethical solution.

## Problem

As more tasks in our lives are conducted online, there is a tremendous amount of data that is accumulated about us in online databases. Unfortunately, much of this material is accessible in databases that are searchable by anyone with Internet access or to anyone willing to pay a small fee. Web sites such as **Spokeo.com** and **411.com** comb through publicly accessible databases such as social networking sites (Facebook or MySpace), online phone books, business sites where you have accounts (Yahoo! or MSN), and government (federal, state, and local) Web sites to compile information on individuals. There is probably a lot of information about you available on sites such as these that could expose you to risks such as identify theft.

## Research Areas to Consider

- Electronic information privacy
- Electronic Privacy Information Center (**epic.org**)
- Protecting your online privacy
- Protecting yourself on Facebook
- Protecting yourself from data breaches

## Process

1. Divide the class into teams.

2. Research the areas cited above and devise a scenario in which someone has complained about a Web site (such as **spokeo.com**) providing information that led to their identity being stolen.

3. Team members should write a summary that provides background information for their character—for example: victim of identity theft, Web site owner, or arbitrator—and details their character's behaviors to set the stage for the role-playing event. Then, team members should create an outline to use during the role-playing event.

4. Team members should arrange a mutually convenient time to meet for the exchange, either using the collaboration features of MyITLab, the discussion board feature of Blackboard, or meeting in person.

5. Team members should present their case to the class, or submit a PowerPoint presentation for review by the rest of the class, along with the summary and resolution they developed.

## Conclusion

As technology becomes ever more prevalent and integrated into our lives, more and more ethical dilemmas will present themselves. Being able to understand and evaluate both sides of the argument, while responding in a personally or socially ethical manner, will be an important skill.

# chapter 10
# using the internet:
## making the most of the Web's resources

cybrain/Shutterstock.com

### The Internet and How It Works

**OBJECTIVES:**

What is the origin of the Internet? *(p. 342)*

How does data travel on the Internet? *(p. 343)*

ra2 studio/Shutterstock.com

### Communicating and Collaborating Through the Internet

**OBJECTIVES:**

How can I communicate and collaborate using Web 2.0 technologies? *(p. 344)*

How can I communicate with e-mail? *(p. 346)*

 Sound Byte: Creating a Web-Based E-mail Account

 Sound Byte: Blogging

Angela Waye/Shutterstock.com

### Web Entertainment

**OBJECTIVE:**

What multimedia files are found on the Web, and what software is needed? *(p. 352)*

Maxx-Studio/Shutterstock.com

### Conducting Business over the Internet: E-Commerce

**OBJECTIVE:**

What is e-commerce, and what online safeguards are there? *(p. 356)*

 Active Helpdesk: Doing Business Online

marema/Shutterstock.com

### Using the Web Effectively

**OBJECTIVES:**

What is a Web browser, and what is a URL and its parts? *(p. 358)*

How can I use hyperlinks and other tools to get around the Web? *(p. 359)*

How do I search the Internet effectively, and how can I evaluate Web sites? *(p. 363)*

 Sound Byte: Welcome to the Web

 Active Helpdesk: Getting Around the Web

 Sound Byte: Finding Information on the Web

 Active Helpdesk: Using Subject Directories and Search Engines

*Scan here for more info on How Cool Is This?*

# how cool is *this?* Looking for answers on the Web? Check out WolframAlpha, a **new way to search** for information on the Web!

Where do you go when you need to find something online? Google? Dogpile? Although these and other common Internet tools **help** you find information, they generally lead you to where you can find an answer, but don't always provide the answer—or an answer that you trust. Enter WolframAlpha (**www.wolframalpha.com**), a "**computational knowledge engine**" that computes the answers to a wide range of questions that have factual answers.

For example, if you ask, "What is the monthly payment for a $20,000, five-year loan at 5% interest?" you'll get not only the payment, but also the total interest paid and the effective interest rate. A search for "pear" results in average nutrition facts, taxonomy information, and the digital representation of the color "pear." WolframAlpha **understands questions** and computes answers, unlike traditional Internet search tools that simply retrieve Web files that might contain an answer.

The foundation of this unique tool is a set of models from a variety of fields of knowledge, combined with **massive** amounts of data and algorithms that represent **real-world knowledge**.

It knows about technology, geography, cooking, business, travel, music, and more. The information it delivers uses more than 5,000 different **visual representations** such as tables and graphs. There are also several topic-specific mobile apps that relate to specific educational and professional areas such as statistics, calculus, and music theory.

Ask WolframAlpha a question today to see how cool it really is.

Lukiyanova Natalia / frenta/Shutterstock.com

# The Origin of the Internet

It's hard to imagine life without the **Internet**, the largest computer network in the world. The Internet is actually a network of networks that connects billions of computer users globally. We use it to shop, to communicate, to research, to find places and get directions, and to entertain ourselves (see Figure 10.1). It's accessible from our computers, smartphones, portable music players (PMPs), and gaming systems, and we can get to it while at home, at work, at school—even at Starbucks or in the car. But what exactly is the Internet, and how did it begin?

**Why was the Internet created?** The concept of the Internet was developed while the United States was in the midst of the Cold War with the Soviet Union. At that time, the U.S. armed forces needed a computer system that would operate efficiently

computers had been networked since the early 1960s, there was no reliable way to connect computers from different manufacturers because they used different proprietary designs and methods of communication. What was lacking was a common communications method that all computers could use. The Internet was created to respond to these two concerns: establishing a secure form of military communications and creating a means by which all computers could communicate.

**Who invented the Internet?** The modern Internet evolved from an early U.S. government-funded "internetworking" project called the Advanced Research Projects Agency Network (ARPANET). ARPANET began as a four-node network involving UCLA, Stanford Research Institute, the University of California at Santa Barbara, and the University of Utah in Salt Lake City. The first real communication occurred in late 1969 between the computer at Stanford and the computer at UCLA. Although the system crashed after the third letter was transmitted, it was the beginning of a revolution. Many people participated in the creation of the ARPANET, but two men

**Figure 10.1**

From buying shoes on eBay to getting directions on your cell phone to checking messages, the Internet makes it all possible.

© NetPhotos / Alamy

Oleksiy Mark / Shutterstock.com

and that was located in various parts of the country so that it could not be disrupted easily in the event of an attack.

At the same time, researchers hoped the Internet would address the problems involved with getting different computers to communicate with each other. Although

who worked on the project, Vinton Cerf and Robert Kahn, are generally acknowledged as the "fathers" of the Internet. They earned this honor because in the 1970s they were primarily responsible for developing the communications protocols (standards) that are still in use on the Internet today.

**So are the Web and the Internet the same thing?** Because the **World Wide Web** (**WWW** or the **Web**) is what we use the most, we sometimes think of the Internet and the Web as being interchangeable. However, the Web is a subset of the Internet, dedicated to broadcasting HTML pages and the means by which we access information over the Internet. The Web is based on the Hypertext Transfer Protocol (HTTP), hence the *http://* at the beginning of Web addresses. Other components of the Internet include FTP and BitTorrent, which will be discussed later in this chapter. What distinguishes the Web from the rest of the Internet is its use of:

- Common communications protocols that enable different computers to talk to each other and display information in compatible formats
- Special links that enable users to navigate from one place to another on the Web

**Did the same people who created the Internet create the Web?** The Web was created many years after the original Internet. In 1989, Tim Berners-Lee, a physicist at the European Organization for Nuclear Research (CERN), wanted a method for linking his research documents so that other researchers could access them. In conjunction with Robert Cailliau, Berners-Lee developed the basic architecture of the Web and created the first **Web browser** (or **browser**), software that enables a user to display and interact with text and other media on the Web. The original browser could handle only text and was usable only on computers running the NeXT operating system, a commercially unsuccessful operating system, which limited its usage. So Berners-Lee put out a call to the Internet community to assist with development of browsers for other platforms.

In 1993, the National Center for Supercomputing Applications released its Mosaic browser for use on the Macintosh and Windows operating systems. Mosaic could display graphics as well as text. The once-popular Netscape Navigator browser evolved from Mosaic and heralded the beginning of the Web's monumental growth.

## The Internet and How It Works

The Internet is an integral part of our lives, and our ability to use and interact with the Internet and the World Wide Web will only converge even more with our daily lives. Therefore, it's important to understand how the Internet works and the choices available for connecting to it.

### The Internet2 program

The Internet2 is a research and development consortium of more than 350 universities (supported by government and industry partners) that seeks to expand the possibilities of the Internet by developing new Internet technologies and disseminating them as rapidly as possible to the rest of the Internet community. Many of the current technologies of the commercial Internet are possible because of the research done by the Internet2 consortium. The Internet2 backbone supports extremely high-speed communications—up to 8.8 terabits per second (TBps)—and provides an excellent testing area for new data transmission technologies.

**How does the Internet work?** Computers connected to the Internet communicate with (or "talk" to) each other in turns, just as we do when we ask a question and get an answer. Thus, a computer connected to the Internet acts in one of two ways: it is either a **client**, a computer that asks for data, or it is a **server**, a computer that receives the request and returns the data to the client. Because the Internet uses clients and servers, it is referred to as a **client/server network**. We'll discuss such networks in more detail in Chapter 12.

**How do computers talk to each other?** Suppose you want to order something from **Amazon.com**. As Figure 10.2 illustrates, the following events take place:

1. When you type the address of a collection of Web pages, called a Web site, such as **www.Amazon.com** in your Web browser, your computer acts as a client computer because you are asking for data from Amazon's Web site.

2. Your browser's request for this data travels along several pathways that

**Figure** 10.2

How the Internet's client/server network works.

can be likened to interstate highways. The largest and fastest pathways are the main arteries of the Internet, called **Internet backbones**. All intermediary pathways connect to these backbones.

3. Your data flows along the backbone and then on to smaller pathways until it reaches its destination, which is the server computer for Amazon's Web site.

4. The server computer returns the requested data to your computer using the most expedient pathway system (which may be different from the pathway the request took).

5. Your Web browser interprets the data and displays it on your monitor.

**How does the data get sent to the correct computer?** Each time you connect to the Internet, your computer is assigned a unique identification number. This number, called an **Internet Protocol address** (or **IP address**), is a set of four numbers separated by periods and commonly referred to as a *dotted quad* or *dotted decimal*

such as 123.45.245.91. IP addresses are the means by which all computers connected to the Internet identify each other. Similarly, each Web site is assigned an IP address that uniquely identifies it. However, because the long strings of numbers that make up IP addresses are difficult for people to remember, Web sites are given text versions of their IP addresses. So Amazon's Web site has an IP address of 72.21.211.176 and a text name of www.amazon.com. When you type "www.amazon.com" into your browser window, your computer (with its own unique IP address) looks for Amazon's IP address (72.21.211.176). Data is exchanged between Amazon's server computer and your computer using these unique IP addresses.

# Communicating and Collaborating Through the Internet

Think of all the different ways you communicate with your friends, family, professors, and business associates over the Internet. You can use instant messaging, group communications, social networking, Web logs and video logs, wikis, podcasts, and Webcasts to communicate via the Internet. You can even talk over the phone through the Internet, which was discussed in Chapter 5. Over time, our use of the Internet has evolved from passively using Web content created for us to actively creating, sharing, and collaborating on our own Web content. **Web 2.0** describes an evolved type of Web interaction between people, software, and data. It can be classified as the *social Web*, in which the user is also a participant. Additionally, Web 2.0 describes a trend of new applications to combine the functionality of multiple applications. Hundreds of companies now exist to help us share, recommend, collaborate, create, and socialize (see Figure 10.3). The following discussions focus more on the social, collaborative, and communicative nature of Web 2.0 applications. Other Web-based productivity applications were discussed in Chapter 7. Like any other means of communication and collaboration, you need to know how to use these tools efficiently to get the most out of them.

## Social Networking

**What is social networking?** **Social networking** is a means by which people use the Internet to communicate and share

---

## BITS AND BYTES — Citing Web Site Sources

After you've evaluated a Web site and determined it to be a credible source of information that you will use in a research paper, you will need to list the source in the Works Cited section of your paper. There are formal guidelines as to how to cite Web content. Unlike those for citing books and periodicals, however, these standards are still being developed. At a minimum, the following components should be included in the citation: author, title of document or publication, date of publication or last revision, date accessed, and complete URL. Note that URL citations are no longer required by the MLA, but if a citation is still desired, it should appear in angle brackets. The following are examples of Web citations in both Modern Language Association (MLA) and American Psychological Association (APA) style for an article found in *Reuters* online:

**Example of MLA style**
Aspan, Maria. "ADP says investigating data breach." 15 June 2011. Reuters. 24 June 2011 <http://www.reuters.com/article/2011/06/15/us-adp-breach-idUSTRE75E5BB20110615>.

**Example of APA style**
Aspan, M. (2011, June 15). ADP says investigating data breach. Retrieved from http://www.reuters.com/article/2011/06/15/us-adp-breach-idUSTRE75E5BB20110615

The current version of Microsoft Word includes citation and bibliography formatting for most of the standard formats. If Word is not available, you can go to Son of Citation Machine (**www.citationmachine.net**), which is an interactive tool designed to output citations in proper MLA or APA format, using information you provide in an online form, as well as information from Purdue Online Writing Lab (**owl.english.purdue.edu**).

---

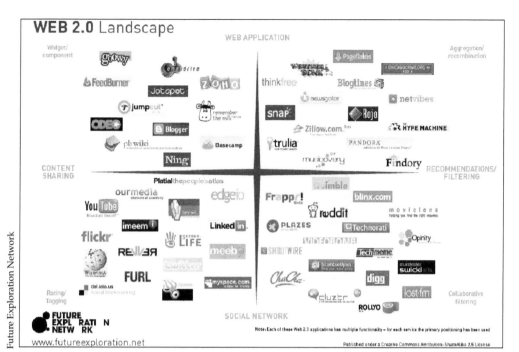

**Figure** 10.3

Hundreds of companies and Web sites make up the Web 2.0 landscape, which helps us share, recommend, collaborate, create, and socialize.

information among their immediate friends, and meet and connect with others through common interests, experiences, and friends. Social networking services such as Facebook (**www.facebook.com**) and Twitter (**www .twitter.com**) have become widely popular because they provide ways for members to communicate with their friends through a variety of means such as by voice, chat, instant message, and videoconference so that members don't need separate communication accounts. These services were first accepted broadly among the younger, nonprofessional population, but now many adults create their own social networking profiles. Most Facebook and Twitter users, for example, are over the age of 25. Ning (**www.ning.com**) is a social networking site that allows you to create your own network around a common topic or join a social networking group that has already been formed. Ning is not free, so if creating your own social network is of interest to you, you might also want to check out SocialGO (**www.socialgo.com**) and Mixxt (**www.mixxt .net**)—both are good free alternatives.

**How is social networking used in business?** Networking has long been a means of creating links between you and your friends—and their friends and acquaintances. Traditionally, networking has been helpful in the business community for the purposes of finding and filling open job positions as well as finding clients. The Internet, with its speedy connections and instantaneous means of communicating, facilitates such business networking as well as promoting more socially based networks. Professional, business-oriented online networks such as LinkedIn (**www.linkedin.com**) are helpful for members seeking potential clients, business opportunities, jobs, or job candidates. Like a true business network, LinkedIn helps you meet other professionals through the people you know. But, social networking has taken on an entirely different role in business in recent years. Now businesses use social networking for marketing and communicating directly with their customers. Often companies post special deals and offers on their Facebook page, or solicit responses from followers that may help with product development or future marketing campaigns (see Figure 10.4).

**Are there precautions I should take with my social networking content?** When social networking sites first became popular, there was huge concern over privacy issues, especially for young teenagers who put personal information on their pages without considering the possibility of that information being misused by a stalker or identity thief. Although those concerns still exist, many of the most popular social networking sites have improved their privacy policies, thereby reducing, but not eliminating, such concerns. Still, users must be cautious about the type of content they post on these sites. For example, think before you add information like "your

**Figure** 10.4

Social networking sites are becoming useful marketing and network-ing tools for businesses.

mother's maiden name" or "your first pet's name" because these are often security questions that are used to verify your identity.

Social networking sites are a great way to exchange photos, but again, use caution when posting images. Although privacy settings may offer some comfort, some images may be available for view through search engines and may not require site registration to be viewed. Online images may become public property and subject to reproduction, and there might be some images that you don't want distributed. Additionally, many employers and colleges use social networks as another means of gaining information about a potential applicant before granting an interview or extending a job offer. The responsibility for your content rests with you. Make sure your profile, images, and site content project an image that accurately represents you.

### E-Mail

**Why do I need e-mail?** Despite the popularity of social networking as a means of communication, e-mail is still the primary means of communication over the Internet. Approximately 89 percent of adult Americans who access the Internet send and receive e-mail. **E-mail** (short for **electronic mail**) is a written message that is sent and received over the Internet. The messages can be formatted and enhanced with graphics and may also include other files as attachments. E-mail is the primary method of electronic communication worldwide because it's fast and convenient. E-mail can be a means of exchanging and collaborating on documents via attachments, as well as creating documentation of

conversations. For social exchanges, e-mail often offers a more "private" conversation away from some of the very public exchanges on social networks.

**Is e-mail private?** Although e-mail is a more private exchange of information as compared to the very public social networking sites, e-mails really are not private. In fact, the information in e-mail is no more private than a postcard. E-mails can be easily viewed by others, by being either printed out or forwarded, so you never know who eventually could read your e-mail. Also, most e-mail is not encrypted, so you should never use e-mail to send personal or sensitive information such as bank account numbers or Social Security numbers. Doing so could lead to identity theft. Employers have access to e-mail sent from the workplace, so use caution when putting negative or controversial content in an e-mail. It could come back to haunt you. Finally, remember that even after you've deleted a message, it doesn't really vanish. Many Internet service providers and companies archive e-mail, which can then be accessed or subpoenaed in the event of a lawsuit or investigation.

**How do I write a good e-mail?** E-mail between friends does not have to follow any specific guidelines and can be as casual as your IM or texting exchanges. But when you send e-mail for professional reasons, like at your job, then you should be aware of proper e-mail etiquette. Following good e-mail etiquette maintains professionalism, increases efficiency, and might even help protect a company from costly lawsuits.

Common guidelines include being concise and to the point, using spell check, and avoiding texting abbreviations such as *u*, *r*, *LOL*, *BRB*, and others. Also, make sure you include a meaningful subject line. This helps recipients prioritize, organize, and categorize e-mails, and identify contents later on after the e-mail has been read. One problem with e-mail is that the meaning within the message often can be misinterpreted. Therefore, some means of conveying emotion (when necessary) can be helpful. Often emoticons—simple strings of characters that reflect facial expressions—can help reflect the writer's emotions. Use them sparingly to retain their effectiveness. Finally, include a signature line with your basic contact or corporate information.

**Are there different types of e-mail accounts?** Many people have more than one e-mail account. You may have a personal account, a work account, and an account you use when filling out forms on the Internet. To read, send, and organize your e-mail, you can use an **e-mail client**. E-mail clients such as Microsoft Outlook are software programs running on your computer that access your Internet service provider (ISP), which acts like an electronic post office. However, with these e-mail clients, you are able to view your e-mail only from the computer on which the e-mail client program has been installed, which can be less than convenient if you travel or want to view your e-mail when you're away from that computer.

Today, most high-speed providers and ISPs offer the services of a Web-based e-mail client so that users can look at their e-mail directly from the Web. Web-based e-mail uses the Internet as the e-mail client. Free e-mail accounts such as Yahoo! Mail, Hotmail, or Gmail are Web-based e-mail clients.

**What are the advantages of a Web-based e-mail account?** Unlike client-based e-mail, which is accessible only from a computer on which the e-mail client

is installed, Web-based e-mail accounts make your e-mail accessible from any device that can access the Internet. No special e-mail client software is necessary to install. Even if you use a client-based account, having a secondary Web-based e-mail account, such as Yahoo! or Gmail, also provides you with a more consistent e-mail address. Your other e-mail accounts and addresses may change when you switch ISPs or change employers, so having a consistent e-mail address is important.

**Why would I need a client-based e-mail program?** At one point, the biggest advantage of using a client-based e-mail program was that they were more full-featured programs than Web-based e-mail systems, enabling users to easily sort and organize their e-mail, and coordinate with corresponding calendars. Current Web-based e-mail systems are becoming more full-featured every year, so the advantages of having a client-based e-mail program are not as significant. However, although many free Web-based e-mail systems such as Yahoo! feature similar organizational tools as client-based e-mail programs, they are riddled with advertisements that can be annoying and distracting (see Figure 10.5). Additionally, a benefit of using a client-based e-mail program such as Microsoft Outlook is that it makes it easy to coordinate with others who are on the same corporate network (or virtual private network [VPN]), simplifying scheduling meetings and coordinating events.

### Instant Messaging

**What is instant messaging?** **Instant messaging (IM)** services are programs that enable you to communicate in real time with others who are online (see Figure 10.6). Although IM is most often used for casual conversations between friends, many businesses use IM as a means of quick and instant communication between coworkers. Students also use IM to communicate with their instructors as well as their classmates. Most instant messaging services provide integration with social networks, enabling you to get updates from your Facebook, Twitter, and other social network accounts without logging into each individual site. If you want to chat with more than one person, you can hold simultaneous individual conversations, or if you all want to chat together, you can create custom IM chat groups. Many IM services offer an audio chat feature so you can speak with your buddies

**SOUND BYTE**

### Creating a Web-Based E-mail Account

In this Sound Byte, you'll see a step-by-step demonstration that explains how to create a free Yahoo! Web-based e-mail account. You'll also learn the options available with such accounts.

E-mail folders

Client-based e-mail coordinates with tasks and calendar

Advertisements found in Web-based programs

Alan R. Evans

**Figure** 10.5

Both (a) client-based email programs and (b) Web-based e-mail have features to organize your inbox items into specific folders.

**Figure** 10.6

Instant messaging services such as Facebook Chat enable you to have real-time online conversations.

if you have a microphone and speakers. A Webcam allows you to conduct video chats.

AIM, Google Chat, Windows Live Messenger, and Yahoo! Messenger have become very popular instant-messaging services. Most of these services are proprietary, meaning you can chat only with those who share the same IM service. But there are universal chat services such as Trillian and Digsby that allow users of all the popular IMs to chat with each other regardless of the service they use. Meebo is a Web-based universal chat service that lets you communicate with users

on a variety of IM services from any computer anywhere.

**How do I keep track of my IM contacts?** When you use IM, you set up a list of contacts, often called a *buddy list*. To communicate (or chat) with someone from your buddy list, that person must be online at the same time as you are. When someone wants to chat with you, a window pops open with his or her message. If it's not convenient to chat at that time, you can close or ignore the message. Some programs such as Yahoo! and AOL's AIM offer stealth settings so that you can appear offline to certain buddies.

### Weblogs (Blogs) and Video Logs (Vlogs)

**What is a blog?** A blog or Weblog, is a personal log or journal posted on the Web. The beauty of blogs is that they are simple to create, manage, and read. Anyone can create a blog, and there are millions of blogs available to read, follow, and comment on.

Several key characteristics define a blog. Blogs are generally written by a single author and are arranged as a listing of entries on a single page, with the most recent blog (entry) appearing at the top of the list. In addition, blogs are public. Blogs have searchable and organized content, making them user friendly. They are accessible from anywhere using a Web browser.

The traditional form of a blog is primarily text-based but may also include images and audio. A **video log** (**vlog** or **video blog**) is a personal journal that uses video as the primary content. It can also contain text, images, and audio. Vlogs quickly are becoming a highly popular means of personal expression, and many can be found by searching the most popular video-sharing site, YouTube (**www.youtube.com**). Software such as Vlog It! makes adding video content to your blog easy, although you can also easily upload unedited video straight from your computer, video camera, or cell phone.

**Why would I want to create a blog?** Many people use blogs as a sort of personal scrapbook. Whenever the urge strikes, they just write a stream-of-consciousness flow of thoughts or a report of their daily activities. Many blogs, however, focus on a particular topic. For example, **www.themovieblog.com** contains reviews and opinions about movies, and **www.engadget.com** (see Figure 10.7) is a blog that devotes itself to discussing techno-gadgets. Many corporations, such as WalMart and Best Buy, have blogs written by employees. Technorati (**www.technorati.com**) and Blogcatalog (**www.blogcatalog.com**) are two of many blog directories that can help you find blogs that best fit your interests.

**How do I create a blog?** It is easy to write and maintain a blog, and many Web sites provide the necessary tools for you to create your own. Two sites that offer free blog hosting are Blogger (**www.blogger.com**) and WordPress (**www.wordpress.com**). You can add other features to your blog such as pictures or subpages. Another alternative is to host your blog yourself. Hosting your own blog requires that you have your own Web site and a URL so that people can access it.

**Are there problems with blogs?** The popularity of blogs has brought about a new problem: spam blogs (splogs), which are artificially created blog sites filled with fake articles or stolen text (a tactic known as *blog scraping*). Splogs, which contain links to other sites associated with the splog's creator, have the intention of either increasing traffic to, or increasing search engine rankings for, these usually disreputable or useless Web sites. Although not terribly bad, splogs are another unwanted form of content that continues to grow like weeds on the Web.

### Wikis

**What are wikis?** The viewer of a traditional Web site cannot change the content. In contrast, a **wiki** is a type of Web site that allows users to add, remove, or edit the content. Wikis add the extra benefit of tracking revisions so that past versions can be easily accessed at any time by any eligible reader. Like blogs, wikis can be used to express thoughts and opinions about certain topics. However, because wikis can be edited, they can present an emergent "common" opinion rather than the individual opinion of the initial writer.

**What are wikis used for?** Wikis provide an excellent source for collaborative writing, both in and out of the classroom. The popular collaborative online encyclopedia Wikipedia (**www.wikipedia.org**) uses wiki technology so that the content can be updated continually. Some Web-based document products, such as Google Docs (**docs.google.com**), have wiki-like features to promote online collaboration. Wikipedia is hosted by the Wikimedia Foundation, which

**Figure 10.7**

(a) Some blogs, like this one from Engadget, are set up as online reviews organized by category. (b) Alternatively, they can appear as personal journals that record a blogger's thoughts, viewpoints, and feelings in reverse chronological order.

**SOUND BYTE**

Blogging

In this Sound Byte, you'll see why blogs are one of today's most popular publishing mediums. You'll also learn how to create and publish your own blog.

also hosts other useful collaborative projects such as Wikibooks (textbooks), Wikiversity (learning tools), and Wikisource (document library), among others. Wiki technology is currently incorporated in course management systems such as Blackboard, to encourage collaborative learning in online courses. Wikis are also becoming popular tools for business collaboration. Rather than passing documents back and forth via e-mail and losing track of which updated version is the most recent, wikis allow all who have access to the wiki page to post their ideas and modify the content of just one document (see Figure 10.8). A history of all changes is kept so users can revert to earlier versions if desired.

These same collaborative efforts apply to a variety of other useful applications. For example, wikiHow (**www.wikihow.org**) is an online project that uses both wikis and the collaborative process to build a large, online how-to manual. Blender (**www.blender.org**), an open source software application for 3D modeling, uses MediaWiki, a more feature-rich wiki implementation product, to provide users with documentation, help with game development and 3D modeling, and tutorials for Blender software.

**How accurate is Web content that anyone can change?** The idea behind content that is managed and edited by many users, such as that found in Wikipedia and other large public wikis, is that the group will keep the content valid. Those challenging the validity of publicly editable wikis argue that the content cannot be trusted because wikis are easily tampered with, whereas supporters argue that the community of users can quickly catch erroneous content and correct it.

Wikipedia content has been continually measured for accuracy and has been found to be nearly as accurate as the *Encyclopedia Britannica,* but not as accurate as other reference sources. Free and easy access to edit pages can lead to improper manipulation and temporary inaccuracies, thus prompting caution when using a wiki as a source reference. Tighter access controls have been implemented to thwart malicious editing of the wiki content; users who want editing privileges are required to register. Citizendium (**www.citizendium.org**), another open wiki encyclopedia, requires contributors to provide real names and sign an ethics pledge, and all postings are monitored.

## Podcasts and Webcasts

**What is a podcast?** A **podcast** is a clip of audio or video content that is broadcast over the Internet using compressed audio and video files such as MP3s and MP4s. This content might include radio shows, audiobooks, magazines, and even educational programs. The word *podcast* is a combination of *broadcasting* and *iPod*—not because you have to use an iPod but because iPods are the most popular form of portable media player (PMP) and because people download audio files to listen to on their iPods. However, you don't have to listen to podcasts on a portable media player. You can listen to podcasts on your computer or even on a smartphone as long as the device can play the content. To listen to a podcast on your computer, you'll need a media player such as iTunes or Windows Media Player. If you want to enjoy a video podcast on your PMP, you need to make sure your mobile device can play video as well as audio files.

**So what makes podcasting different from just listening to an audio file on the computer or a PMP?** The difference is that podcasts are files that come to you through syndication so you do not have to search for the current episode once you have subscribed to the series. Perhaps you are used to getting your news from a certain Web site, but the only way you can determine that new content has been added is to go to the site and look for the newly added information.

**Figure** 10.8

Rather than collaborating by exchanging e-mails and attachments—and potentially losing track of the most recent version of a document—different users can collaborate on a wiki page.

Elijah provides initial text (in black)

**Project Home**
**Week 7: *Publicity Law***
*9/17/12 – 9/23/12*

***9/18/12***
Mackenzie-Jordan Law Associates has a significant number of celebrity clients. One of the most important aspects of our legal counsel to these individuals is to help protect the use of their images and likenesses.
Sometimes this is referred to as the right of publicity. This right is a valuable asset because there are endless licensing opportunities that can be quite lucrative.
Some states have a publicity law that protects a celebrity's image and likeness for 100 years, but as yet that law has not been enacted in the state of Texas.

***9/19/12***
The merchandising of celebrity images has become a huge source of income for many celebrities as well as others. In recent years, legal disputes have resulted from artists and illustrators manipulating celebrity images.
In the past, courts have typically protected the First Amendment rights of artists in these cases. But recently there have been a few cases where celebrities have been allowed to sue creators of fictional works for the violation of the right of publicity.
~~The right of publicity is intended to prevent others from capitalizing on a celebrity's fame.~~ Many people in the entertainment industry are fearful that unauthorized biographies, docudramas, and celebrity spoofs and satires will no longer be protected. Many entertainment lawyers say a celebrity's right to publicity is intended solely for ads and merchandise, not for literary works.

Jordan includes additional text (shaded yellow)

Stephanie removes text (shaded with green and shown with strikethrough)

In contrast, if you subscribe to podcasts, when the content changes, it is brought to you. Some podcasts provide opportunities for listeners to submit questions or even take listeners' calls live. What's more, if you have several favorite Web sites, rather than individually checking the content, you can collect all the site updates in one place. Podcasts are possible because of RSS technology, which makes it more efficient for you to gather updates to your favorite content.

**What is RSS?** **Really Simple Syndication (RSS)** is an XML-based format that facilitates the delivery of frequent content updates on Web pages. Using RSS, Web content can be formatted in such a way that aggregators can find it and download only the new content to your computer. **Aggregators** are software programs that go out and grab the latest updates of Web material according to your specifications. They are available for all major operating systems as well as some mobile devices such as smartphones.

**Where can I find podcasts?** Podcasts can be found all over the Web. Most newspapers, TV news organizations, and radio sites offer podcasts of their programs. Although many podcasts are news related, many podcasts offer more entertaining and informative content. The iTunes Store (**www.itunes.com**) puts thousands of free podcasts on its site. Subscribe to broadcasts from ABC or Bloomberg News, ESPN, TED Talks, or comedy from the Adam Carolla show. You can access lessons on yoga, a foreign language, or DIY tips. Many schools are beginning to recognize this format as a way to supply students with course content updates, and instructors create podcasts of their lectures.

iTunes, Podcast Alley (**www.podcastalley.com**), and Podcast Pickle (**www.podcastpickle.com**) are aggregators as well as great directories of podcasts, organized by genre, to help you easily locate podcasts of most interest to you (see Figure 10.9). If there is a particular topic for which you'd like to hear a podcast, Podscope (**www.podscope.com**) is a podcast-specific search engine that searches podcasts for specific words or phrases and then displays the results with audio clips. YouTube is also becoming a popular source of RSS feeds for video content.

**Can I create my own podcast?** It is simple to create audio content that can be delivered to the Web and then listened to by people all over the world. In fact, you could become a radio broadcaster overnight.

Although high-end equipment always will produce a more sophisticated output, you really need only the most basic equipment to make your own podcast.

To record the content, at the minimum you need a computer with a microphone. If you want to make a video podcast, you also need a Web camera (webcam) or video camera. Additional software may be needed to edit the digital audio and video content. After the podcast content has been recorded and edited, it needs to be exported to MP3 format. Sound-editing software, such as the freeware program Audacity (**audacity.sourceforge.net**), can be used to record and edit audio files and then export them to MP3 format. The last steps involve creating an RSS feed and then uploading the content to the Web.

**Figure 10.9**

Podcasts are available in a wide variety of topics and content. Web sites such as Podcast Pickle allow you to add your own podcast to their directories.

## The Internet Makes Business Startups Affordable

You, as well as many of your classmates, wear flip-flops year round—even in winter—and you think that flip-flops in school colors would be an extremely popular product. Your school's bookstore carries everything else with the school's colors and logo, just not flip-flops. You have asked your friends and several classmates, and most of them indicated they would buy flip-flops in the school's colors. So what do you do next? How do you move from product concept to actually selling your physical product?

Before the advent of the Internet and e-commerce, it would have been much more difficult and expensive to get your product produced and distributed. First, you would have needed to find someone with industrial design experience to design your flip-flops. Then, to make the flip-flops, you would have had to find a manufacturer, which likely required a high minimum order (maybe tens of thousands of pairs of flip-flops). You also would have needed a package design, marketing brochures, company logo (and other branding devices), a storage facility, and more. Finally, the largest hurdle would have been convincing a brick-and-mortar retailer, such as your campus bookstore, to carry your product.

Fortunately, the Internet brings the power of the global economy right to your door. For product design and manufacturing, you can visit a site like **www.Alibaba.com** (see Figure 10.10), which helps entrepreneurs locate manufacturers of all sorts of products located

in many different countries. And many manufacturers are happy to work with you to custom design your product. So if you find a flip-flop style you like, you probably can get it customized with your school colors.

But what happens if the bookstore doesn't want to sell your flip-flops? You can always set up a Web site to sell them yourself. But you'll probably need help with Web site design, company logo design, and Web programming to construct the site if you don't already have these skills.

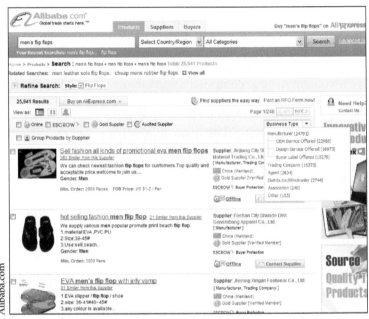

**Figure** 10.10

A search for men's flip-flops on Alibaba.com reveals nearly 26,000 suppliers with minimum order quantities as low as 1,000 units.

**What's a Webcast?** A **Webcast** is the broadcast of audio or video content over the Internet. Unlike podcasts that are prerecorded and made available for download, most Webcasts are live or one-time events. Webcasts are not updated automatically, but some, such as Microsoft's On-Demand Webcasts, are RSS feeds. Webcasts use a special kind of media technology that continuously feeds the audio and video content, which facilitates the viewing and downloading process of large audio and video files. Webcasts can include noninteractive content such as simulcasts of radio or TV broadcasts. More recent Webcasts invite interactive responses from the viewing or listening audience. For example, ORLive (**www.orlive.com**) provides surgical Webcasts that demonstrate the latest surgical innovations and techniques (see Figure 10.12). Webcasts also are used in the corporate world to broadcast annual meetings and in the educational arena to transmit seminars.

# Web Entertainment

Internet radio, music files such as MP3 and advanced audio coding (AAC), streaming video, and interactive gaming are all part of the entertainment world available over the Internet. What makes the Web appealing to many people is its rich **multimedia** content. Multimedia is anything that involves one or more forms of media in addition to text.

Many types of multimedia are used on the Web. Graphics (drawings, charts, and photos) are the most basic form of multimedia. Audio files are what give sound to the Web—the clips of music you hear when you visit certain Web sites, MP3 files that you download, or live broadcasts you can listen to through Internet radio. Video files on the Web range from the simple (such as short video clips) to the complex (such as hour-long live concerts). In addition to movies,

Fortunately, you can tap the global marketplace for skilled professionals by using sites such as Guru (**www.guru.com**) or Elance (**www.elance.com**) (see Figure 10.11). These sites help you locate freelance professionals to work on projects for you. You can create a description of the job you need done (say, logo design for a flip-flop company), post it on the site, and invite freelancers to bid on your job. You can contact freelancers that look promising, review samples of their work, and decide on someone who can help you—and at a competitive price. After your Web site is designed and up and running, you can place your business on social networking sites, such as Facebook, to help potential customers discover your product and spread the word about your great flip-flops. You probably already have lots of friends on Facebook who attend your school and would be good potential customers.

**Figure 10.11**

Need to design a package? Many freelancers at Elance are ready to help!

If you aren't selling your flip-flops in a physical store, where will you store them, and who will package and ship them when customers buy them? If your parents' basement isn't large enough, you can outsource warehousing and order fulfillment to Amazon.com. Fulfillment by Amazon is a service in which Amazon (for a fee) will warehouse your inventory and then package and ship it when customer orders are received. Orders do not have to come through Amazon's site (although that is an option); you can just provide ordering information to Amazon that is collected on your site, and Amazon will take care of all the tedious work.

Although there is always a cost to starting up a business, up-front costs are much lower when you take advantage of the global marketplace and Internet tools. So take that brilliant idea you have and turn it into a business today!

**Figure 10.12**

ORLive provides Webcasts that demonstrate the latest surgical techniques.

you can watch live or prerecorded television broadcasts, movie trailers, and sporting events. Hulu (**www.hulu.com**) is a great Web site where you can find popular TV shows and movies.

**What are streaming audio and video?** Because of the large file sizes of media content, watching video files such as movies or TV shows, listening to live audio broadcasting, and playing online games is possible because of streaming media. **Streaming audio** continuously feeds an audio file to your browser so you avoid having to wait for the entire file to download completely before listening to it. Likewise, **streaming video** continuously feeds a video file to your browser so that you can watch large files as they download instead of first

## What's Everyone Twittering About?

Twitter (**www.twitter.com**) is a social networking and microblogging service that enables you to exchange short text messages in real time with your friends or "followers" (see Figure 10.13). It lets you specify which Twitter users you want to follow so you can read their messages in one place. All you need is a device (such as your computer or mobile device) connected to the Internet.

Twitter messages, called tweets, are limited to 140 characters, so comments exchanged in Twitter are short and simple. While Twitter works well among close-knit groups for messages such as "Joe and I are going to Murphy's Café. See you there," it can also be used to gain a sense of the "pulse" of what the general public is talking about within a broader community. Businesses are using Twitter to respond to customer queries or to broadcast new services or products. Your Twitter account tracks the number of "followers," or people who are paying attention to your tweets, and the number of "friends," or people you are following. So, "tweet" away to stay connected.

AP Photo/Charlotte Observer, Robert Lahser

**Figure 10.13**

Twitter is a social networking and microblogging service for staying connected to "followers" in real time.

interactivity and online gaming. Many game Web sites, such as Addicting Games (**www .addictinggames.com**), offer thousands of free online games in arcade, puzzle, sports, shooting, word, and strategy categories. Simple multiplayer games such as backgammon, chess, and checkers became popular and offered users the chance to play the game with others from around the world.

In addition, there are many **multiplayer online games** in which play occurs among hundreds or thousands of other players over the Internet in a persistent (or always-on) game environment. In these games, you can interact with other players around the world in a meaningful context by trading, chatting, or playing cooperative or combative minigames. There are several types of **massively multiplayer online role-playing games (MMORPGs)** in which participants assume the role of a fictitious character in a virtual game world. World of Warcraft (**www.worldofwarcraft.com**), shown in Figure 10.14, and Guild Wars (**www .guildwars.com**) are among the most popular MMORPGs. Other types of multiplayer online game sites include first-person shooter games such as Battleground Europe (**www.battlegroundeurope.com**), sports games such as Football Superstars (**www .footballsuperstars.com**), and racing games such as Need for Speed (**www.needforspeed .com**). Second Life (**www.secondlife.com**) can also be considered an MMORPG, but with its own well-established, in-world virtual economy, it has transcended into a much bigger concept and function.

**Do I need anything besides a browser to view or hear multimedia on the Web?** Without any additional software, most graphics on the Web will appear in your browser. However, to view and hear some multimedia files—for example, podcasts, videos on YouTube, and audio files—you might need a special software program called a **plug-in** (or **player**). Figure 10.15 lists the most popular plug-ins.

If you purchased your computer within the past several years, many plug-ins probably came preinstalled on your computer. If a Web site requires a plug-in you don't have, then it usually displays a message on the screen that includes links to a site where you can download the plug-in free of charge. For example, to use streaming video, your browser might send you to the Adobe Web site, where you can download Flash Player.

having to download the files completely. Streaming videos make possible services such as Netflix or video on demand from your cable provider.

**What kinds of games are played on the Web?** Streaming audio and video helped to bring popularity to online user

**Figure 10.14**

World of Warcraft is a popular massive multiplayer online role-playing game.

Scripps Howard Photo Service/Newscom

**Figure 10.15** | POPULAR PLUG-INS AND PLAYERS AND THEIR USES

| Plug-In or Player Name | Where You Can Get It | What It Does |
| --- | --- | --- |
| Adobe Reader | **www.adobe.com** | Views and prints portable document format (PDF) files. |
| Flash Player | **www.adobe.com** | Plays animation and movies through Web browsers. |
| QuickTime Player | **www.apple.com** | Plays MP3 animation, music, musical instrument digital interface (MIDI), audio, and video files. |
| Shockwave Player | **www.adobe.com** | Plays interactive games, multimedia, graphics, and streaming audio and video on the Web. |
| Silverlight | **www.microsoft.com** | Similar to Flash. Plays Web-based animations and videos. |
| Windows Media Player | **www.microsoft.com** | Plays MP3 and WAV files, music files, and live audio, and movies and live video broadcasts on the Web. |

**Do I need to update players and plug-ins?** As with most technological resources, improvements and upgrades are available for players and plug-ins, and most will alert you to check for and download upgrades when they are available. It is best to keep the players and plug-ins as current as possible so that you get the full effects of the multimedia running with these players.

**Are there any risks with using plug-ins?** When a browser requires a plug-in to display particular Web content, it usually automatically accesses the plug-in. Depending on your settings, this access happens without asking you for consent to start the plug-in. Such automatic access can present security risks. To minimize such risks, update your plug-ins and browser software frequently so that you will have the most up-to-date remedies against identified security flaws.

**Is there any way to get multimedia Web content to load faster?** When you're on the Internet, your browser keeps track of the Web sites you've visited so that it can load them faster the next time you visit them. This *cache* (temporary storage place) of the text pages, images, and video files from recently visited Web sites can make your Internet surfing more efficient, but it also can congest your hard drive. Additionally, if you don't have your cache settings configured to check for updates to the Web page, your browser may not load the most recent content. To keep your system running efficiently, delete your temporary Internet cache periodically. To ensure the most recent Web site content is displayed, click Refresh or press the F5 key if you revisit a site in the same browsing session. All popular Web browsers have an option to clear the Internet cache manually, and most have a setting to allow you to clear the cache automatically every time you exit the browser.

### BITS AND BYTES

## Why Can't I Run Flash-Based Multimedia on My iPad or iPhone?

Your friend showed you a great video clip on their new Blackberry PlayBook. You try to load the same movie into your iPad, but it won't run. Why not? It's not because your iPad is broken, but because Apple devices don't run Flash files. Apple's Web site gives a complete explanation of Apple's "Thoughts on Flash" (**www.apple.com/ hotnews/thoughts-on-flash/**) but succinctly, Apple's main problem with Flash is that it is not "open" but rather 100% proprietary and therefore not easily controlled by Apple. Apple would rather use other open standard products such as HTML5, CSS, and JavaScript. Flash is also tough on battery consumption, has been tagged as having reliability and security issues, and doesn't work well on devices using touch commands rather than mice commands. But, what to do if you have an iPad, iPod Touch, or iPhone and want to view a Flash file? One work-around is to use the Skyfire Web browser, which turns Flash content into HTML on Skyfire's servers. The You-Tube app installed on all Apple devices shows YouTube content in a different format. Unfortunately, there are no good solutions if you want to play a Flash game on an Apple device, but as Apple suggests . . . there are lots of other games to choose from.

# Conducting Business over the Internet: E-Commerce

**E-commerce**, or **electronic commerce**, is the process of conducting business online, such as through advertising and selling products. A good example of an e-commerce business (also called an *e-business*) is Amazon.com. The company has no physical retail store presence, and its online presence offers customers a convenient way to shop for almost anything. Its success is the result of creative marketing, an expanding product line, and reliable customer service and product delivery—all hallmarks of traditional businesses as well.

**Are there different types of e-commerce businesses?** Traditional stores, those stores with a physical building to shop in, which also have an online presence, are referred to as *click-and-brick* businesses. These stores, such as Best Buy (**www.bestbuy.com**) and Target (**www.target.com**), provide a variety of services on their Web sites. Customers can visit their sites to check the availability of items or to get store locations and directions. Some click-and-bricks allow online purchases and in-store pickup and returns.

A significant portion of e-commerce consists of **business-to-consumer (B2C)** transactions—exchanges that take place between businesses and consumers—such as the purchases that consumers make at online stores. There is also a **business-to-business (B2B)** portion of e-commerce; this consists of businesses buying and selling goods and services to other businesses. An example is Omaha Paper Company (**www.omahapaper.com**), which distributes paper products to other companies. Finally, the **consumer-to-consumer (C2C)** portion of e-commerce consists of consumers selling to each other through online auction sites such as eBay (**www.ebay.com**) and exchange sites such as Freecycle (**www.freecycle.com**) and Craigslist (**www.craigslist.org**).

**What are the most popular e-commerce activities?** Approximately $200 billion each year is spent in the U.S. on goods purchased over the Internet, accounting for approximately 25 percent of all retail sales. So what is everyone buying online? Consumers buy books, music and videos, movie and event tickets, and toys and games more often online than in retail stores. Travel items such as plane tickets, hotel reservations, rental car reservations, and even automobile purchases are also frequently made online. With the advent of more lenient return policies, online retail sales of clothing and shoes also have increased. Sites such as eBay and Craigslist, together with payment exchange services such as PayPal and Google Checkout, are becoming the online equivalent of the weekend yard sale and have dramatically increased in popularity.

But e-commerce encompasses more than just shopping opportunities. Today, anything you can do inside your bank you can do online, and more than 50 percent of U.S. households do some form of online banking. Many people use online services to check their account balances, pay bills online, as well as check stock and mutual fund performance. Credit card companies allow you to view, schedule, and pay your credit card bill; brokerage houses allow you to conduct investment activities online.

## E-Commerce Safeguards

**Just how safe are online transactions?** When you buy something online, you most likely use a credit or debit card; therefore, the exchange of money is done directly between you and a bank. Because online shopping eliminates a salesclerk or other human intermediary from the transaction, it can actually be safer than traditional retail shopping. Still, because users are told to be wary of online transactions and because the integrity of online transactions is the backbone of e-commerce, businesses must have some form of security certification to give their customers a level of comfort.

Some sites have created secure logins that you can change to before signing in, which is safer than sending your login credentials unsecured. To certify that their online transactions are secure, businesses hire security companies such as VeriSign. But just seeing the VeriSign seal is not always a guarantee that the site is secure, because the seal can be copied and pasted onto virtually any site. Therefore, be sure to check that the beginning of the URL changes from "http://" to "https://"—with the "s" standing for **secure socket layer**. Another indication that a Web site is secure is the appearance of a small icon of a closed padlock in the toolbar (in both Microsoft Internet Explorer and Mozilla Firefox). The last visual clue to help identify a safe site is a

## Using PayPal for Safe Online Payments

Many people were not initially comfortable buying online from sites such as eBay because the sites required them to exchange personal financial information such as credit card numbers or banking information with complete strangers. PayPal (**www.paypal.com**) resolved that issue and is now a standard means of online payment exchanges for many online merchants. PayPal also offers buyer protection and dispute resolution services.

Here's how PayPal works (see Figure 10.16):

1. You provide your financial information to PayPal, which stores it on PayPal servers.
2. You provide only your PayPal e-mail address to the merchant.
3. The merchant receives payment from PayPal without seeing your financial information.

PayPal acts as a payment intermediary and allows anyone to pay with credit cards, bank accounts, or buyer credit without sharing financial information. PayPal is owned by eBay, the online auction site.

Google Checkout (**checkout.google.com**) offers similar services to PayPal, although there are some subtle differences. For example, you cannot pay directly from your bank account with Google Checkout, and only purchases within the U.S. can be made with Google Checkout. Google Checkout only provides customer support through forums and e-mail, whereas PayPal has increased its customer service considerably, and now you can chat live with PayPal representatives.

Provide your information to PayPal

PayPal securely stores your information

Merchant receives payment from PayPal

**Figure 10.16**

PayPal is an online payment intermediary, allowing anyone to shop without sharing financial information with the seller.

---

green-colored address bar as shown in Figure 10.17. Still, despite these indications, you also need to consider the validity of the site and place everything in context.

**How else can I shop safely online?** To ensure that your online shopping experience is a safe one, follow these guidelines:

- **Shop at well-known, reputable sites.** If you aren't familiar with a site, then investigate it with the Better Business Bureau (**www.bbb.org**) or at bizrate (**www.bizrate .com**). When you place an order, print a copy of the order and make sure you receive a confirmation number. Make sure the company has a phone number and street address in addition to a Web site.

- **Avoid making online transactions when using public computers.** Public computers might have programs that track and log your keystrokes, so you do not want to use public computers when typing sensitive information such as credit card numbers or bank account numbers. Public computers might also have other types of spyware installed to retrieve private information. Similarly, unless you have specific protection on your own notebook computer, avoid making wireless transactions in public hotspots.

- **Pay by credit card, not debit card.** Federal consumer credit laws protect credit card users, but debit card users do not have the same level of protection. If possible, reserve one credit card for Internet purchases only; even better, use a prepaid credit card that has a small credit limit. For an extra layer of security, find out if your credit card company has a service that confirms your identity with an extra password or code that only you know to use when making an online transaction or offers a one-time-use credit card number. Also, consider using a third-party payment processor such as PayPal or Google Checkout. PayPal also offers a security key that provides additional security to your PayPal account.

Harleysville Savings Bank

**Figure** 10.17

A closed padlock icon, "https" in the URL, and a green-shaded address bar are indications that the site is secure.

• **Check the return policy.** Print a copy and save it. If the site disappears overnight, this information may help you in filing a dispute or reporting a problem to a site such as the Better Business Bureau.

Whether you're doing business, playing games, or communicating with friends or colleagues, the Internet makes all of these activities more accessible. The Internet can potentially make these experiences and activities more enriched as well, although you must take precautions for the safest of experiences.

## Accessing the Web: Web Browsers

None of the activities for which we use the Web could happen without an important software application: a Web browser. Recall

### BITS AND BYTES

## It's Important to Keep Your Browser Software Up to Date

When new file formats are developed for the Web, browsers need new plug-ins to display content properly. Constantly downloading and installing plug-ins can be a tedious process. Although many Web sites provide links to sites that enable you to download plug-ins, not all do, resulting in frustration when you can't display the content you want. When new versions of browsers are released, they normally include the latest versions of popular plug-ins. Corrections of security breaches are typically included in these versions of browser software as well. Therefore, upgrading to the latest version of your browser software provides for safer, more convenient Web surfing. Fortunately, updates are free, and you can set most of the popular Web browsers to notify you when updates are available or to download the updates automatically.

that a Web browser, or browser, is software installed on your computer system that allows you to locate, view, and navigate the Web. Most browsers in use today are *graphical* browsers, meaning they can display pictures (graphics) in addition to text and other forms of multimedia such as sound and video.

**What are some common Web browsers?** Microsoft Internet Explorer (IE) is included in the Windows operating system. It has been the most widely used browser since 1999, and still enjoys predominant market share, although its popularity has slipped over the years. Other browsers, discussed below, have become popular alternatives to Internet Explorer.

• **Firefox** is a popular open source browser from Mozilla (**www.mozilla .org**). Firefox's popularity continues to increase, capturing approximately 28 percent of the U.S. browser market. Add-ons are available to customize and increase the functionality of Firefox. Examples include Video Download Helper that converts Web videos, like those found on YouTube, to files you can save, as well as a Facebook toolbar that integrates Facebook functionality into your browser. Other handy features found in Firefox are spell checking for e-mail, blogs, and other Web postings, as well as Session Restore, which brings back all your active Web pages if the browser or system shuts down unexpectedly.

• **Safari** is a browser developed by Apple (**www.apple.com/safari**). Although it was created as the default browser for Macintosh computers and is included with the Mac OS, a Windows-based version is also available. Safari has quickly gained public acceptance.

• **Google Chrome** is the newest browser on the market, distributed by Google (**www.google.com/chrome**) (see Figure 10.18), and has enjoyed growing market share since its inception. The unique features offered by Chrome include thumbnail access to your most recently visited sites from Chrome's main page and shortcuts to Google applications.

**What features do browsers offer?** Most of the popular Web browsers provide tabbed browsing for convenient navigation. With tabbed browsing, Web pages are loaded in "tabs" within the same browser window. Rather than having to switch among Web pages in several open windows, you can flip between the tabs in one window. You can even open several of your favorite Web sites from one folder and choose to display them as tabs. You may also save a group of tabs as a Favorites group, if there are several tabs you often open at the same time. Internet Explorer 9 offers other tab features such as "tear-off tabs" that facilitate rearranging open tabs, and "pinned tabs" that enable you to dock your most frequently accessed tabs in the task bar (see Figure 10.19). Another convenient navigation tool that most browsers share is providing thumbnail previews of all open Web pages in open tabs.

Other features shared by most of the favorite browsers include a built-in search box in which you can designate your preferred default search engine and tools for printing, page formatting, and security settings. For extra browsing privacy, most browsers also offer a privacy mode feature, such as InPrivate Browsing in Microsoft Internet Explorer, that allows users to surf without leaving a trace. Use the privacy mode when surfing the Web on public computers at college or at the public library, for example.

## Getting Around the Web: URLs, Hyperlinks, and Other Tools

You gain initial access to a particular **Web site** by typing its unique address, or **Uniform Resource Locator** (**URL**, pronounced "you-are-ell"), in your browser. For example, the URL of the Web site for *Popular Science* magazine is **www.popsci .com**. By typing this URL for *Popular Science* magazine, you connect to the **home page**, or main page, of the Web site. Once you are at the home page, you can move all around the site by clicking specially formatted pieces of

text called *hyperlinks*. Let's look at these and other navigation tools in more detail.

### URLs

**What do all the parts of the URL mean?** As noted earlier, a URL is a Web site's address. A Web site is composed of many different Web pages, each of which is a separate document with its own unique URL. Like a regular street address, a URL is composed of several parts that help identify the Web document it stands for (see Figure 10.20).

**Figure 10.18**
Google Chrome includes thumbnails of the most recently visited Web sites for easy access.

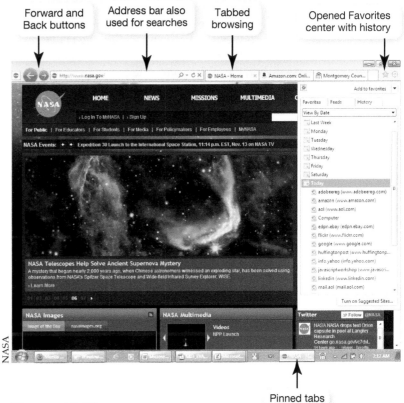

Forward and Back buttons

Address bar also used for searches

Tabbed browsing

Opened Favorites center with history

Pinned tabs

**Figure 10.19**
Internet Explorer (IE) includes tabbed browsing. Pinned tabs on the task bar make accessing your favorite sites even easier.

The first part of the URL indicates the *protocol* (set of rules) used to retrieve the specified document. The protocol is generally followed by a colon, two forward slashes, *www* (indicating *World Wide Web*), and the **domain name.** (Sometimes the domain name is also thought to include the *www.*) The domain name is also referred to as the *host name*. Individual pages within a Web site are further identified after the domain name, following another forward slash. These are referred to as the *path*. It should be noted that most current browsers no longer require you to enter the protocol and the www. Some, like Firefox, don't even require the domain if it's a .com. But even though these parts of the URL are not physically entered, they are still part of each Web site's URL.

**What's the protocol?** Most URLs begin with *http*, which is short for **Hypertext Transfer Protocol (HTTP)**. HTTP is the protocol that allows files to be transferred from a **Web server**—a computer that hosts the Web site you are requesting—so that you can see the Web site on your computer by using a browser. As discussed earlier, the HTTP protocol is what the Web is based on. Remember, the Web is only one component of the Internet. Other components, such as FTP and

**Figure 10.20**

The parts of a URL.

BitTorrent, are based on different protocols.

A common protocol used to transfer files over the Internet is **File Transfer Protocol (FTP)**. It is used to upload and download files from your computer to a Web server. FTP files use an FTP file server, whereas HTTP files use a Web server. To connect to most FTP servers, you need a user ID and a password. FTP addresses, like e-mail addresses or URLs, identify one location on the Internet. To upload and download files from FTP sites, you can use a Web browser or file transfer software such as WS_FTP, Fetch, Filezilla, or WinSCP.

BitTorrent, like FTP, is a protocol used to transfer large files. To use BitTorrent, you must install a software client program. It uses a peer-to-peer networking system, so that sharing occurs between connected computers that also have the BitTorrent client installed. BitTorrent was developed in 2001 and has been gaining popularity, especially among users who want to share music, movies, and games. Use caution, however, when accessing BitTorrent content. Since it is a peer-to-peer system, there are no restrictions. It is possible for copyrighted material to be shared illegally.

**What's in a domain name?** The domain name identifies the site's **host**, the location that maintains the computers that store the Web site files. For example, **www.berkeley.edu** is the domain name for the University of California at Berkeley.

The suffix in the domain name after the dot (such as .com or .edu) is called the **top-level domain**. This suffix indicates the kind of organization to which the host belongs. Figure 10.21 lists the most frequently used top-level domains.

Each country has its own top-level domain. These are two-letter designations such as .za for South Africa and .us for the United States. A sampling of country codes is shown in Figure 10.22. Within a country-specific domain, further subdivisions can be made for regions or states. For instance, the .us domain contains subdomains for each state, using the two-letter abbreviation of the state. For example, the URL for Pennsylvania's Web site is **www.state.pa.us**.

| Figure 10.21 | COMMON TOP-LEVEL DOMAINS AND THEIR AUTHORIZED USERS |
|---|---|
| **Domain Name** | **Who Can Use It** |
| .biz | Businesses |
| .com | Originally for commercial sites, but now can be used by anyone |
| .edu | Degree-granting institutions |
| .gov | Local, state, and federal U.S. government |
| .info | Information service providers |
| .mil | U.S. military |
| .name | Individuals |
| .net | Originally for networking organizations but no longer restricted |
| .org | Organizations (often not-for-profits) |

**Figure** 10.22

## EXAMPLES OF COUNTRY CODES

| Country Code | Country |
|---|---|
| .au | Australia |
| .ca | Canada |
| .jp | Japan |
| .uk | United Kingdom |

*Note:* For a full listing of country codes, refer to **www.iana.org/domains/root/db/**.

### What's the information after the domain name that I sometimes see?

When the URL is only the domain name (such as **www.nytimes.com**), you are requesting a site's home page. However, sometimes a forward slash and additional text follow the domain name, such as in **www.nytimes.com/pages/cartoons**. The information after the slash indicates a particular file or **path** (or **subdirectory**) within the Web site. The path or subdirectory is what identifies each different page within a particular Web site; it follows the top-level domain and is preceded by a slash. In Figure 10.20, you would connect to the cartoon pages on the *New York Times* site.

## Hyperlinks and Beyond

### What's the best way to get around in a Web site?

Unlike text in a book or a Microsoft Word document, which is linear (meaning you read it from top to bottom, left to right, one page after another), the Web is anything but linear. As its name implies, the Web is a series of connected paths, or links, that connect you to different Web sites. You can jump from one Web page (the document indicated by the path in the URL) to another Web page within the same Web site or navigate to another Web site altogether by clicking on a specially coded element called a **hyperlink**, as shown in Figure 10.23. Generally, text that operates as a hyperlink appears in a different color (often blue) and is underlined. When you pass your cursor over a hyperlinked image the cursor may change to a hand with a finger pointing upward. Sometimes images also act as hyperlinks. To access a hyperlink from an image, you simply click the image.

### How do I return to a Web page I've already visited?

To retrace your steps, some sites provide a **breadcrumb trail**—a list of pages within a Web site you've visited. It usually appears at the top of a page. Figure 10.23 shows an example of a breadcrumb trail. "Breadcrumbs" get their name from the fairy tale "Hansel and Gretel," in which the characters drop breadcrumbs on the trail to find their way out of a forest. By clicking on earlier links in a breadcrumb trail, you can retrace your steps back to the page on which you started.

To get back to your original location or visit a Web page you viewed previously, you use the browser's Back and Forward buttons. To back up more than one page, click the down arrow next to the Forward button to access a list of most recently visited Web sites. By selecting any one of these sites in the list, you can return directly

**Figure** 10.23

When you click on a hyperlink, you jump from one location on the Web to another. When you click on the links in a breadcrumb trail, you can navigate your way back through a Web site.

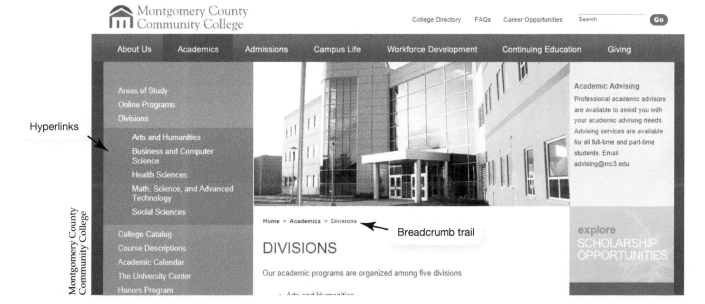

to that page without having to navigate through other Web sites and Web pages you've visited.

The History list on your browser's toolbar is also a handy feature. The History list shows all the Web sites and pages that you've visited over a certain period of time. These Web sites are organized according to date and can go back as far as three weeks. To access the history list in Internet Explorer, click the down arrow next to the navigation arrows.

### Favorites, Live Bookmarks, and Tagging

**What's the best way to mark a site so I can return to it later?** If you want an easy way to return to a specific Web page without having to remember to type in the address, you can use your browser's Favorites or Bookmarks feature. Internet Explorer and Safari call this feature **Favorites**; Firefox and Google Chrome call the same feature a **Bookmark**. This feature places a marker of the site's URL in an easily retrievable list in your browser's toolbar. To organize the sites into categories, most browsers offer tools to create folders. Most browsers also provide features to export the list of bookmarks to a file from which you can import to another computer or another browser.

Favorites and Bookmarks are great for quickly locating those sites you use the most, but they are accessible to you only when you are on your own computer. One way to access your Bookmarks and Favorites from any computer is to use MyBookmarks (**www.mybookmarks.com**), a free Internet service that stores your Bookmarks and Favorites online.

**What are live bookmarks?** The **live bookmark** feature of the Firefox browser adds the technology of RSS feeds to bookmarking. Because the Web is constantly changing, the site you bookmarked last week may subsequently change and add new content. Traditionally, you would notice the change only the next time you visited the site. With live bookmarks, the content comes to you. Instead of constantly checking your favorite Web pages for new content, a live bookmark delivers updates to you as soon as they become available. Live bookmarks are useful if you are interested in the most up-to-date news stories, sports scores, or stock prices.

**What is social bookmarking?** Social **bookmarking**, also known as **tagging**, lets you store, organize, and manage bookmarks (or tags) of Web pages. A social bookmark or tag is a **keyword** or term that is assigned to a piece of information such as a Web page, digital image, or video. A tag describes the item so that it can be found again by browsing or searching. Tags were popularized by Web 2.0 Web sites such as YouTube and Flickr.

The social bookmarking Web site Delicious (**www.delicious.com**) gives you the ability to add tags as bookmarks to your favorite Web sites (see Figure 10.24). The tag can be something meaningful to you, or you can select one from a list of suggested tags. Later, you can go back to Delicious, conduct a search using your tag, and find bookmarks tagged with the same word

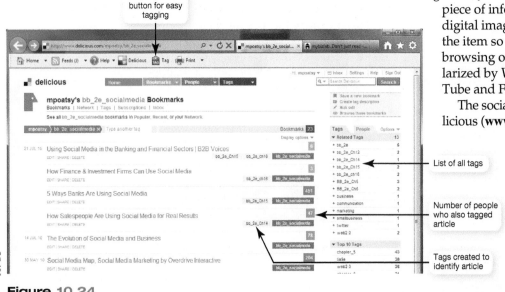

Installed toolbar button for easy tagging

List of all tags

Number of people who also tagged article

Tags created to identify article

**Figure 10.24**

Delicious is a social bookmarking Web site that allows you to organize and share your favorite Web sites.

AVOS

from everyone in your network. You can also see how many other Web users tagged the same site. Delicious offers convenient toolbars for your browsers, and many Web sites incorporate bookmarking icons for ease of use.

Figure 10.25 lists several popular social bookmarking tag tools. Diigo (**www.diigo.com**) allows you not only to tag and bookmark Web sites, but also to annotate the pages with highlights and sticky notes. Through Diigo, the Web pages can be archived, so they are always available. Digg (**www.digg.com**) and Newsvine (**www.newsvine.com**) offer similar systems for organizing news content. StumbleUpon (**www.stumbleupon.com**) is like a personalized search engine and recommends Web sites based on your personal interests and preferences, as well as the recommendations of people you know or the general surfing public.

## Searching the Web Effectively

With its billions of Web pages, the Web offers visitors access to masses of information on virtually any topic. To narrow down the quantity of Web information to something more useful, use a search engine and a keyword query. A **search engine** is a set of programs that searches the Web for keywords—specific words you wish to look for (*query*)—and then returns a list of the Web sites on which those keywords are found. Popular search engines include Google, Yahoo!, Bing, and Ask.com.

For some searches, you also can search the Web using a **subject directory**, which is a structured outline of Web sites organized by topics and subtopics. Librarians' Internet Index (**www.ipl.org**) is a subject directory, and some popular search engines such as Yahoo! also feature directories. If you can't decide which search engine is best, then you may want to try a metasearch engine. **Metasearch engines**, such as Dogpile (**www.dogpile.com**), search other search engines rather than individual Web sites. Figure 10.26 lists search engines and subject directories that are alternatives to Google, Yahoo!, Bing, and Ask.com.

### Search Engines

**How do search engines work?** Search engines have three components. The first component is a program called a spider. The **spider** constantly collects data on the Web,

© M4OS Photos / Alamy

The Canadian Press/Steve White
(Canadian Press via AP Images)

**Figure** 10.25

Icons of some popular social bookmarking Web sites.

following links in Web sites and reading Web pages. Spiders get their name because they crawl over the Web using multiple "legs" to visit many sites simultaneously. As the spider collects data, the second component of the search engine, an indexer program, organizes the data into a large database. When you use a search engine, you interact with the third component: the search engine software. This software searches the indexed data, pulling out relevant information according to your search. The resulting list appears in your Web browser as a list of hits (sites that match your search).

**Why don't I get the same results from all search engines?** Each search engine uses a unique formula, or *algorithm*, to formulate the search and create the resulting index of related sites. In addition, search engines differ in how they rank the search results. Most search engines rank their results based on the frequency of the appearance of your queried keywords in Web sites as well as the location of those words in the sites. Thus, sites that include the keywords in their URL or site name most likely appear at the top of the hit list. Thus, structuring Web pages to ensure their Web site appears at the top of a Google search has become an important part of a company's marketing strategy.

In addition, search engines differ as to which sites they search. For instance, Google and Ask.com search nearly the entire Web, whereas specialty search engines search only sites that are relevant to a particular subject. Specialty search engines exist for almost every industry or interest. For example, DailyStocks (**www.dailystocks.com**) is a search engine used primarily by investors that searches for corporate information to help them make educated decisions. Search Engine Watch (**www.searchenginewatch.com**) has a list of many specialty search engines organized by industry.

**Figure 10.26** | POPULAR SEARCH ENGINES AND SUBJECT DIRECTORIES

| Search Tools on the Internet | | |
|---|---|---|
| AltaVista | **www.altavista.com** | Keyword search engine. |
| ChaCha | **www.chacha.com** | This site lets you chat with a real live professional guide who helps you search, and it's free of charge. Also available by texting your questions to 242242. |
| CompletePlanet | **www.completeplanet.com** | Deep Web directory that searches databases not normally searched by typical search engines. |
| Dogpile | **www.dogpile.com** | Metasearch engine that searches Google, Yahoo!, and Bing. |
| Excite | **www.excite.com** | Portal with keyword search capabilities. |
| InfoMine | **www.infomine.com** | Subject directory of academic resources with keyword search engine capabilities. |
| Rollyo | **www.rollyo.com** | Short for "Roll Your Own Search Engine." This site lets you create your own search engine (searchroll) that searches just the sites you want it to search. |
| Open Directory Project | **www.dmoz.org** | Subject directory with keyword search capabilities. |
| Stumbleupon | **www.stumbleupon.com** | Lets you rate pages "thumbs up" or "thumbs down." As it learns your preferences, your search results improve. |
| Technorati | **www.technorati.com** | A great search engine for blog content. |
| Yippy | **www.yippy.com** | Keyword search engine that groups similar results into clouds (clusters). |

*Note:* For a complete list of search engines, go to **www.searchengineguide.com**.

## Searching to Do Good

There are many volunteer and charitable organizations to participate in, but for most of us it's hard to incorporate such activities into our daily lives, and it's equally difficult to contribute financially to them all. Now there is an easy way to "do good" while doing something we all do daily—use a search engine. GoodSearch (**www.goodsearch.com**) is a Yahoo!-powered search engine that donates half of its revenues to approved U.S. charities and schools that users designate. The money GoodSearch donates comes from the site's advertisers and amounts to approximately a penny per search.

If you're a big fan of the SPCA, a local hospital, or the neighborhood public elementary school, check to see if that particular organization has been approved. If so, you can add it as your designated charity and start searching. You can easily track how much GoodSearch has raised for your organization. Almost 100,000 charitable organizations are being helped by GoodSearch, but if the organization you are interested in is not on the list, as long as it is a registered U.S. not-for-profit organization, you can apply to have it added.

You can also contribute to your favorite charity by shopping online through GoodShop. Instead of going directly to your favorite Web shop, go to **www.Goodshop.com** first, find and click through to the store of your choice, and start shopping. Participating stores donate up to 30 percent of the purchased amount. So, search and shop away—and do some good!

**Can I use a search engine to search just for images and videos?** With the increasing popularity of multimedia, search engines such as Google, Ask.com, and Yahoo! have capabilities to search the Web for digital images and audio and video files. Use the Advanced Video Search in Google, for example, to find videos in a certain language or with subtitles, or of a specific duration or quality. Blinkx (**www.blinkx.com**) is a video search engine that helps you sift through all the video posted on the Web (see Figure 10.27).

**How can I refine my searches for better results?** When you conduct a Web search, you may receive a list of hits that includes thousands—even millions—of Web pages that have no relevance to the topic you're trying to search. Initially, Boolean operators were needed to help refine a search. **Boolean operators** are words such as *AND*, *NOT*, and *OR* that describe the relationships between keywords in a search.

Today, most search engines offer an advanced search page that provides the same types of strategies in a well-organized form (see Figure 10.28). Using the advanced search form can make your Internet research a lot more efficient. With the simple addition of a few words or constraints, you can narrow your search results to a more manageable and more meaningful list.

**Are there other helpful search strategies?** Instead of using the advanced search form, you can use other strategies to help refine your searches when entering your search phrases:

- **Search for a phrase.** To search for an exact phrase, place quotation marks around your keywords. The search engine will look for only those Web sites that contain the words in that exact order. For example, if you want information on the movie *The Green Hornet* and you type these words without quotation marks, your search results will contain pages that include either of the words *Green* and *Hornet*, although not necessarily in that order. Typing "The Green Hornet" in quotes guarantees that search results will include this exact phrase.

- **Search within a specific Web site.** To search just a specific Web site, you can use the search keyword, then *site:* followed by the Web site's URL. For example, searching with *processor site: www.wired.com* returns results about processors from the Wired.com Web site. The same method works for entire classes of sites in a given top-level domain or country code.

- **Use a wild card.** The asterisk "*" is a wild card, or placeholder, feature that is helpful when you need to search with unknown terms. Another way to think about the wild card search feature is as a "fill in the blank." For example, searching with *Congress voted * on the * bill* might bring up an article about the members of Congress who voted *no* on the *healthcare* bill or a different article about the members of Congress who voted *yes* on the *energy* bill.

**How else can I customize my searches?** A lot of other specialty search strategies and services are available. After

Blinkx

**Figure 10.27**

Video logs use video in addition to text, images, and audio. Blinkx is a video search engine that helps you sift through the increasing number of vlogs.

**Figure 10.28**

Most search engines have an advanced search form to help you refine your searches.

**ACTIVE HELP-DESK**

Getting Around the Web

In this Active Helpdesk call, you'll play the role of a helpdesk staffer, fielding calls about Web browsers, URLs, and how to use hyperlinks and other tools to get around the Web.

Google — Advanced Search

Advanced Search Tips

Use the form below and your advanced search will appear here

Find web pages that have...

| all these words: | |
| this exact wording or phrase: | |
| one or more of these words: | OR OR |

But don't show pages that have...

| any of these unwanted words: | |

Need more tools?

| Reading level: | no reading level displayed |
| Results per page: | 10 results | This option does not apply in Google Instant. |
| Language: | any language |
| File type: | any format |
| Search within a site or domain: | |
| | (e.g. youtube.com, .edu) |

Date, usage rights, region, and more

Advanced Search

Google

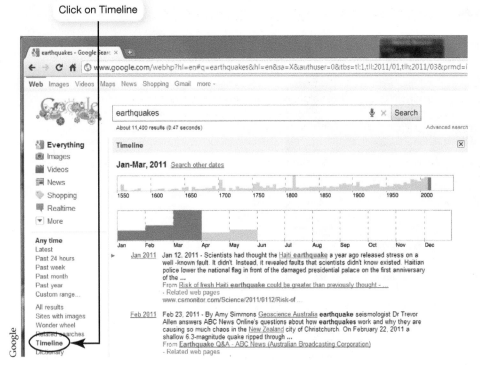

Click on Timeline

**Figure 10.29**

The Google Timeline enables you to zero in on search results from a specific period.

shows selected results from relevant time periods (see Figure 10.29).

## Evaluating Web Sites

**How can I make sure a Web site is appropriate to use for research?** When you're using the Internet for research, you shouldn't assume that everything you find is accurate and appropriate to use. Before you use an Internet resource, consider the following:

1. **Authority:** Who is the author of the article or the sponsor of the site? If the author is well known or the site is published by a reputable news source (such as the *New York Times*), then you can feel more confident using it as a source than if you are unable to locate such information. *Note:* Some sites include a page with information about the author or the site's sponsor.

2. **Bias:** Is the site biased? The purpose of many Web sites is to sell products or services or to persuade rather than inform. These sites, though useful in some situations, present a biased point of view. Look for sites that offer several sets of facts, or consider opinions from several sources.

3. **Relevance:** Is the information in the site current? Material can last a long time on the Web. Some research projects (such as historical accounts) depend on older records. However, if you're writing about cutting-edge technologies, you need to look for the most recent sources. Therefore, look for a date on information to make sure it is current.

you've entered your key search words, try clicking on the Timeline feature in the search options section of the left navigation pane. The Timeline helps narrow down articles to a particular time period (see Figure 10.29). In addition to the Timeline, you can narrow your search down by reading level, related searches, or pages you have or have not visited in the past.

Try clicking on the "more" hyperlink in the Google search engine for a listing of all the various search products Google offers. Google Scholar searches scholarly literature such as peer-reviewed papers, theses, and publications from academic organizations. Each search result contains bibliographic information as well. Google Custom Search enables you to create a customized search engine to search only a selected set of sites tailored to your specific needs. This specialized search engine can be added to a Web site or blog, or designed for a specific organization. Google Book Search enables you to search through the full-text content of millions of books. Google News searches through thousands of news stories from around the world. Google News can be further customized to search stories within specific categories such as Business or Entertainment, and a News Archives Timeline

  **Finding Information on the Web**

In this Sound Byte, you'll learn how and when to use search engines and subject directories. Through guided tours, you'll learn effective search techniques, including how to use Boolean operators and meta-search engines.

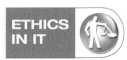

# ETHICS IN IT

## Plagiarism and Copyright Violation: What Can You Borrow from the Internet?

You've no doubt heard of plagiarism—claiming another person's words as your own. And you've probably heard the term *copyright violation*, especially if you've been following the music industry's battle to keep "free" music off the Web. But what constitutes plagiarism, and what constitutes copyright violation? And what can you borrow from the Web? Consider these scenarios:

1. You find a political cartoon that would be terrific in a PowerPoint presentation you're creating for your civics class. You copy it into your presentation.

2. Your hobby is writing children's books, which you later sell online. Most of what you create is your content, but sometimes you borrow story ideas from other children's books, and just change a few characters or situations. You do not obtain permission from the originators of the story ideas you borrow.

3. You're pressed for time and need to do research for a paper due tomorrow. You find information on an obscure Web site and copy it into your paper without documenting the source.

4. You download a song from the Internet and incorporate it into a PowerPoint presentation for a school project. Because you assume everyone knows the song, you don't credit it in your sources.

Which of the preceding scenarios represent copyright violations? Which represent plagiarism? The distinctions between these scenarios are narrow in some cases, but it's important to understand the differences.

As noted earlier, plagiarism occurs when you use someone else's ideas or words and represent them as your own. In today's computer society, it's easy to copy information from the Internet and paste it into a Word document, change a few words, and call it your own. To avoid plagiarism, use quotation marks around all words you borrow directly, and credit your sources for any ideas you paraphrase or borrow. Avoiding plagiarism means properly crediting all information you obtain from the Internet, including words, ideas, graphics, data, and audio and video clips.

Web sites such as Turnitin (**www.turnitin.com**) (for teachers and institutions) and WriteCheck (**www.writecheck.com**) (specifically for students), as shown in Figure 10.30, help check for plagiarism violations. WriteCheck compares your document to a database of magazines, newspapers, journals, and books, as well as Web content and previously submitted student papers. Although some common phrasing may be truly coincidental, real and purposeful plagiarism is reasonably easy to identify. Students can use WriteCheck before submitting an assignment to ensure their papers will not be confused with plagiarized work. In most schools, plagiarism is a serious offense, often resulting in a 0 for an assignment, or an F for the class. It's

best to ensure your paper doesn't even have unintended instances of plagiarized work.

Copyright violation is more serious because it, unlike plagiarism, is punishable by law. Copyright law assumes that all original work—including text, graphics, software, multimedia, audio and video clips, and other intellectual property—is copyrighted even if the work does not display the copyright symbol (©). Copyright violation occurs when you use another person's material for your own personal economic benefit, or when you take away from the economic benefit of the originator. Don't assume that by citing a source you're abiding by copyright laws. In most cases, you need to seek and receive written permission from the copyright holder.

There are exceptions to this rule. For example, there is no copyright on government documents, so you can download and reproduce material from NASA, for example, without violating copyright laws. The British Broadcasting Corporation (BBC) is also beginning to digitize and make available its archives of material to the public without copyright restrictions.

Teachers and students receive special consideration regarding copyright violations. This special consideration falls under a provision called academic fair use. As long as the material is being used for educational purposes only, limited copying and distribution is allowed. One standard applied to academic fair use is the effect the use has on the potential market. For example, an instructor could make copies of a book chapter and distribute it to her class one time but could not do it on a regular basis or over different semesters because that might affect the potential market or sales of the book. Similarly, a student can include a cartoon in a PowerPoint presentation without seeking permission from the artist. However, to avoid plagiarism in these situations, you still must credit your sources of information.

So, do you now know which of the four scenarios above are plagiarism or copyright violations? Let's review them.

1. You are not in violation because the use of the cartoon is for educational purposes and falls under the academic fair use provision. You must still credit the source, however.

2. You are in violation of copyright laws because you are presenting others' ideas for children's stories as your own.

3. You are guilty of plagiarism because you copied content from another source and implied it was your own work.

4. Again, because your copying is for a school project, you are not in violation because of the academic fair use provision. However, it's always important to document your sources.

**Figure 10.30**

By using WriteCheck, students can compare their work to a database of publications to check for unintended plagiarism.

4. **Audience:** For what audience is the site intended? Ensure that the content, tone, and style of the site match your needs. You probably wouldn't want to use information from a site geared toward teens if you were writing for adults, nor would you use a site that has a casual style and tone for serious research.

5. **Links:** Are the links available and appropriate? Check out the links provided on the site to determine whether they are still working and appropriate for your needs. Don't assume that the links provided are the only additional sources of information. Investigate other sites on your topic as well. You should also be able to find the same

---

## DIG DEEPER — Discovering the Semantic Web

How do we find information on the Web? Generally, we access Google or another search engine, type in the keyword or search phrase, and click the search button. As a result, millions of links to Web pages display. At best, we click on the first several links that seem reasonably relevant to our search. Rarely, if ever, do we explore all of the links that are found in the search results.

Similarly, think about all the other types of data on the Web that we access manually, such as contact information, appointment times, transportation schedules, entertainment schedules, medical treatments, and store types, locations, and hours. It would seem that computers would be helpful in plugging through all of this Web data, but oddly, that is not the case. Web pages are designed for people to read, not for computers to manipulate. Although computers can determine the parts and functionality of Web pages (headers, hyperlinks, etc.), as yet no reliable way exists for computers to process the meaning of the data so that they can use the information to see relationships or make decisions.

The **Semantic Web** (or **Web 3.0**) is an evolving extension of the World Wide Web in which information is defined in such a way to make it more easily readable by computers. Tim Berners-Lee, the inventor of the World Wide Web and the implementation of HTTP and HTML, thought up the Semantic Web.

Right now, search engines function by recognizing keywords such as appointment, dentist, and root canal, but they cannot determine in which office and on what days Dr. Smith works and what his available appointment times are. The Semantic Web would enable computers to find and manage that type of information and coordinate it with your other schedules and preferences.

Similarly, think about the convenience and efficiency that online shopping has brought to our lives. Then think about all the time we actually spend researching and comparing products, brands, stores, prices, and shipping options. Ultimately, after all that effort, we make the final buying decision and place the order. With the Semantic Web in place, you could enter your preferences into a computerized software agent, which would then search the Web for you, find the best option based on

your criteria, and place the order. Additionally, the agent would be able to record the financial transaction into your personal bookkeeping software and arrange for a technician to help install your purchase, if needed.

The Semantic Web would use software agents that roam from page to page, completing sophisticated tasks. These agents would not read words, look at pictures, and process information as humans do, but rather would search through metadata. Metadata is machine-readable data that describes other data in such a way that the agents can identify and define what they need to know. Like Web page coding, which is now done in HTML, XML, and other formats, metadata would be invisible to humans reading pages on the Web but would be clearly visible to computers, in essence turning the Web into a giant database.

The introduction of eXtensible Markup Language (XML) has helped make the user of the Web more of a participant. Web 2.0 technologies such as blogs, wikis, and social networking sites, as well as Web-based applications, are in part possible because of XML's tagging functionalities. RSS feeds also use technologies that are an underlying component of the Semantic Web.

The Semantic Web would build on this type of capability so that each Web site would have text and pictures (for people to read) and metadata (for computers to read) describing the information on the Web (see Figure 10.31). The metadata would contain all the attributes of the information, such as condition, price, or schedule availability, in a machine-readable format. Businesses, services, and software would all use the same categorization structures so that similar information would share the same attributes, ensuring consistency of metadata throughout the Web. Then, with Web data properly identified and categorized, computerized agents could read the metadata found on different sites, compare the information, and process the information based on user-defined criteria.

Although some of the Semantic Web functionalities are beginning to emerge in Web 2.0 technologies, such as Siri in the new iPhone 4S, the majority of the functionality and implementation of the Semantic Web is still in development. The World Wide Web Consortium (W3C), led by information on at least three different Web sites to help verify the information is accurate.

The answers to these questions will help you decide whether you should consider a Web site to be a good source of information.

I need a dentist appointment for a root canal.

SEARCH:
Dentist
Root canal
Seattle area
As soon as possible

STEP 6: Agent returns list of acceptable results and waits for action.

RESULTS:
Dr. Amid, 3/23 2 p.m.
Dr. Brett, 3/23 4 p.m.
Dr. Slade, 3/24 8 a.m.

STEP 1: User enters search criteria.

Schema and Ontology Tools

STEP 2: Agent takes search criteria and adds what is necessary to refine search.

STEP 5: Agent compares and ranks the information.

STEP 3: Agent transfers task to a specific Web service agent to check and compare services.

STEP 4: Web service agent collects the information, along with your availability.

Compare services

**Figure 10.31**

Web 2.0 technologies enable us to become creators and users of Internet content. The Semantic Web enables the computer to add context to Web content, providing meaning to information from different sources.

Tim Berners-Lee, is the primary organization leading the charge. The greatest challenge is recoding all the information currently available on the Web into the type of metadata that computers could recognize. The very grandeur of that task means that we will not see a fully functional Semantic Web until sometime in the distant future. In the meantime, we can continue to benefit from each small step toward that goal.

ten summary

**1. What is the origin of the Internet?**

The Internet is the largest computer network in the world, connecting millions of computers. Government and military officials developed the early Internet as a reliable way to communicate in the event of war. Eventually, scientists and educators used the Internet to exchange research. Today, we use the Internet and the Web (which is a part of the Internet) to shop, research, communicate, and entertain ourselves.

**2. How does data travel on the Internet?**

A computer connected to the Internet acts as either a client (a computer that asks for information) or a server (a computer that receives the request and returns the information to the client). Data travels between clients and servers along a system of communication lines or pathways. The largest and fastest of these pathways is the Internet backbone. To ensure that data is sent to the correct computer along the pathways, IP addresses (unique ID numbers) are assigned to all computers connected to the Internet.

**3. How can I communicate and collaborate using Web 2.0 technologies?**

Web 2.0 is a trend of Web interactions among people, software, and data. Examples of these technologies include blogs, wikis, and more. Blogs are journal entries posted to the Web that are generally organized by a topic or area of interest and are publicly available. Generally, one person writes the blog, and others can comment on the journal entries. Video logs are personal journals that use video as the primary content in addition to text, images, and audio. Wikis are a type of Web site that allows users to change content by adding, removing, or editing it. A wiki is designed to allow many users to collaborate on the content. Podcasts are audio or video content that is broadcast over the Internet. Users subscribe to receive updates to podcasts. Social networking sites enable users to communicate and share information with existing friends as well as to meet and connect with others through common interests, experiences, or friends.

**4. How can I communicate with e-mail?**

Communication was one of the reasons the Internet was developed and is one of the primary uses of the Internet today. E-mail allows users to communicate electronically without the parties involved being available at the same time, whereas instant-messaging services are programs that enable you to communicate in real time with others who are online at the same time.

**5. What multimedia files are found on the Web, and what software is needed?**

The Web is appealing because of its enriched multimedia content. Multimedia is anything that involves one or more forms of media in addition to text, such as graphics, audio, and video clips. Sometimes you need a special software program called a *plug-in* (or *player*) to view and hear multimedia files. Plug-ins are often installed in new computers or are offered free of charge at manufacturers' Web sites.

**6. What is e-commerce, and what online safeguards are there?**

E-commerce is the business of conducting business online. E-commerce includes transactions between businesses (B2B), between consumers (C2C), and between businesses and consumers (B2C). Because more business than ever before is conducted online, numerous safeguards have been put in place to ensure that transactions are protected.

**7. What is a Web browser, and what is a URL and its parts?**

Once you're connected to the Internet, in order to locate, navigate to, and view Web pages, you need to install special software called a Web browser on your system. The most common Web browsers are Internet Explorer, Firefox, Google Chrome, and Safari. You gain access to a Web site by typing in its address, called a Uniform Resource Locator (URL). A URL is composed of several parts, including the protocol, the domain, the top-level domain, and paths (or subdirectories).

8. **How can I use hyperlinks and other tools to get around the Web?**

One unique aspect of the Web is that you can jump from place to place by clicking on specially formatted pieces of text or images called *hyperlinks*. You can also use the Back and Forward buttons, History lists, breadcrumb trails, and Favorites or Bookmarks to navigate the Web. Favorites, live bookmarks, and social bookmarking help you return to specific Web pages without having to type in the URL and help you organize the Web content that is most important to you.

9. **How do I search the Internet effectively, and how can I evaluate Web sites?**

A search engine is a set of programs that searches the Web using specific keywords you wish to query and then returns a list of

the Web sites on which those keywords are found. Search engines can be used to search for images, podcasts, and videos in addition to traditional text-based Web content. A subject directory is a structured outline of Web sites organized by topic and subtopic. Metasearch engines search other search engines.

Not all Web sites are equal, and some are better sources for research than others. To evaluate whether it is appropriate to use a Web site as a resource, determine whether the author of the site is reputable and whether the site is intended for your particular needs. In addition, make sure that the site content is not biased, the information in the site is current, and all the links on the site are available and appropriate. If multiple sites offer the same content, then it is another indication that the information is accurate.

## Companion Website

The Companion Website includes a variety of additional materials to help you review and learn more about the topics in this chapter. Go to: *www.pearsonhighered.com/techinaction*

**key terms**

## Word Bank

- aggregator
- blogs (Weblogs)
- Bookmarks
- e-mail
- hyperlink
- instant messaging (IM)
- keyword
- metasearch engine
- podcast
- search engine
- social bookmarking
- social networking
- RSS feed
- tag
- Uniform Resource Locators (URLs)
- Web 2.0
- Web browser
- wiki

**Instructions:** Fill in the blanks using the words from the Word Bank above.

Knowing he has only a few minutes before class, Juan launches Internet Explorer, the (1) _____ software from Microsoft that allows him to connect to the Internet. He quickly goes to Facebook, the (2) _____ site, to catch up on the activities of his friends, and then checks his (3) _____ for any electronic mail communication he may have received from his professors. He also reads a few of the updates to the online journal **Engadget.com**, one of his favorite (4) _____.

At home, Juan types a(n) (5) _____ into Google, the (6) _____, to find Web sites he needs for a research paper. One of the first sites listed is Wikipedia, the online encyclopedia that takes advantage of the collaborative nature of (7) _____ technology. Because anyone can add, change, or edit content on Wikipedia, Juan knows that he can't rely completely on this information, but finds that it is usually a pretty good starting point for his research. Juan then checks out Dogpile.com, a(n) (8) _____ that searches the search engines Yahoo! and Bing in addition to Google. Juan clicks on a(n) (9) _____, the specially coded text in the resulting list in Dogpile, which links him to a Web site that will be useful in his research. He adds a(n) (10) _____ with a meaningful keyword in the (11) _____ site Delicious so he can see how many others find this Web page interesting, and what similar Web pages others have found that might also be helpful for Juan's research. Juan also notes the (12) _____ of the Web site so that he can add it to his bibliography. Finally, before going to bed, Juan opens up iTunes, a(n) (13) _____ that collects the latest updates of broadcasted media using a(n) (14) _____, which ensures that the latest content is available. Juan listens to the (15) _____ of one of his favorite radio shows that he subscribes to and then goes to sleep.

Using key terms from the chapter, create a presentation about all the various ways students and teachers can use social media and other communication tools to foster better communication and collaboration in the classroom, and to enrich the learning process.

**Instructions:** Answer the multiple-choice and true–false questions below for more practice with key terms and concepts from this chapter.

## Multiple Choice

**1.** Which is NOT true about the Internet?
   a. It is the largest computer network in the world.
   b. It was created to establish a secure form of military communications.
   c. It was developed as an additional means of commerce.
   d. It was invented as a way for all computers to communicate.

**2.** What do you need to read, send, and organize e-mail from *any* computer connected to the Internet?
   a. an e-mail client program
   b. an e-mail server
   c. a social networking account
   d. a Web-based e-mail account

**3.** Which is NOT an example of social networking?
   a. e-mail
   b. instant messaging
   c. blogging
   d. wiki

**4.** Which of the following is NOT a characteristic of a blog?
   a. Blogs are used to express opinions.
   b. Blogs are generally written by a single author.
   c. Blogs are private and require password access.
   d. Blogs are arranged as a listing of entries.

**5.** Which of the following is true about plug-ins?
   a. Plugs-ins rarely require updating.
   b. Plug-ins track the Web sites you've visited.

   c. Plug-ins are necessary for viewing most Web graphics.
   d. Plug-ins cannot present security risks.

**6.** What feature is a list of links you've visited within a Web site?
   a. Favorites
   b. breadcrumb trail
   c. Bookmarks
   d. history

**7.** Which is NOT a component of a search engine?
   a. spider
   b. indexer program
   c. subject directory
   d. search engine software

**8.** When using the Internet for research, you
   a. can assume that everything you find is accurate and appropriate.
   b. should evaluate sites for bias and relevance.
   c. should always use the most current sources.
   d. can assume that the links provided on the site are the only additional sources of information.

**9.** Which of the following is not an Internet protocol?
   a. ARPANET  b. HTTP
   c. FTP      d. BitTorrent

**10.** eBay and Craigslist are examples of what kind of electronic commerce?
   a. C2C      b. B2B
   c. B2C      d. C2B

## True–False

_____ 1. The information in e-mail is no more private than a postcard.

_____ 2. A search engine that searches other search engines is called a SuperSearch engine.

_____ 3. A green shaded address bar on a Web site indicates that the Web site is secure.

_____ 4. Each time you connect to the Internet, your computer is assigned the same IP address.

_____ 5. In the Web address www.facebook.com, facebook is the top-level domain.

1. **Online Support Facilities**

   Your school most likely has many online support facilities. Do you know what they are? Go to your school's Web site and search for online support.

   a. What kinds of online tutoring services are available?
   b. How do you reserve a book from the library online?
   c. How do you register for classes online?
   d. How do you take classes online?
   e. How do you buy books online?

2. **Plagiarism Policies**

   Does your school have a plagiarism policy?

   a. Search your school's Web site to find the school's plagiarism policy. What does it say?
   b. How well do you paraphrase? Find some Web sites that help test or evaluate your paraphrasing skills.
   c. Create an account at Turnitin. This Web site checks your written work against content on the Web and produces an originality report. Submit at least three different drafts of your work to Turnitin to check for any intended or unintended cases of plagiarism before submitting your final work for a grade. What were the results?

3. **Searching Beyond Google**

   While Google is probably your first choice among search engines, there are many other very good search engines that are good to know about. Conduct searches for inexpensive travel deals for spring break by using the following search engines. Record your results and a summary of the differences among search engines. Would you choose to use any of these search engines again? Why or why not?

   a. www.Yippy.com
   b. www.Dogpile.com
   c. www.Rollyo.com

4. **Free Speech Online**

   Leila was suspended from school for several days because her posts on Facebook about her teacher and a few of her classmates were "vulgar" and "derogatory." Daniel was expelled from his school because the picture he posted of himself was in violation of his school's code of conduct. Similarly, Bill, a local employer, changed his mind about a job offer to a recent graduate after seeing questionable content on the candidate's Facebook page.

   a. Should a person be penalized for his or her content on any Web site?
   b. Is the issue denial of free speech or prudent reactions to improper behavior?
   c. The Federal Bureau of Investigation (FBI) is working undercover in social networking sites to gather information. What are the benefits and drawbacks of this?

5. **Using Web 2.0 in Education**

   Social networking sites, blogs, and wikis are commonly referred to as Web 2.0 technologies. Sites that use Web 2.0 offer opportunities for collaboration, creativity, and enterprise. Describe how Web 2.0 sites such as Wikipedia, YouTube, Delicious, and Digg might change how you learn and manage information.

making the
transition to...
the workplace

making the transition to... the workplace

1. **Online Résumé Resources**

   Using a search engine, locate several Web resources that offer assistance in writing a résumé. For example, the University of Minnesota (**www1.umn.edu/ohr/careerdev/resources/resume**) has a résumé tutor that guides you as you write your résumé.

   a. What other Web sites can you find that help you write a résumé?

   b. Do these sites all offer the same services and have the same features?

2. **Online Job Search**

   After you've created a résumé, you need to know how to get it to the right people and manage the job search process. A wealth of online job search resources is available to help you with these details. Research the following Web sites and write a brief description of each that outlines the benefits and role in a job search:

   a. LinkedIn (**www.linkedin.com**)

   b. JibberJobber (**www.jibberjobber.com**)

   c. VisualCV (**www.visualcv.com**)

   d. Monster (**www.monster.com**)

3. **Evaluating Web 2.0 Content**

   You are aware of the guidelines you should use to evaluate the quality of content on a Web site, but you find yourself using other kinds of Web content such as blogs, wikis, social networking sites, and social bookmarks. Visit **library.albany.edu/usered/eval/evalweb** and review the new guidelines for evaluating Web content in the 2.0 environment. After reviewing the guidelines, describe the guidelines for evaluating Web content in the following:

   a. Blogs and wikis

   b. Google Scholar (**scholar.google.com**)

   c. California Digital Library (**www.cdlib.org**)

   d. Twitter (**www.twitter.com**)

   e. Delicious (**www.delicious.com**)

   f. Connotea (**www.connotea.org**)

4. **Using Social Media for Business**

   You work for a local bookstore that has so far been successful at attracting a good customer base, despite the lure of the big chain stores. At their last strategic planning meeting, the owners of the bookstore decided that they wanted to have a social media presence to better interact with their loyal customer base, but also to attract new customers. Research the various ways social media is being used for businesses.

   a. What are the pros and cons of using blogs, wikis, and social networking in the business community?

   b. Describe the social media strategy you would recommend to the owners.

5. **Facebook Privacy and Security**

   Your aunt contacted you last night. Your cousin, who is 14, wants a Facebook account. Your aunt has heard lots of stories of how difficult it is to protect your privacy on Facebook, and she wants your advice. Research the privacy and security settings on Facebook and create a "User's Guide" for your aunt to work through with your cousin. Make sure you include information on how to remove your cousin from Facebook search results, make contact information private, keep friendships private, adjust Wall posting visibility, set up photo album privacy, customize photo tagging, and explain what personal information should and should not be included on your cousin's profile.

**Instructions:** The following critical thinking questions are designed to demand your full attention but require only a comfortable chair—no technology.

1. **Social Networking and Society**

   Social networking seems to have taken over our lives! Almost everyone is on Facebook and Twitter. But is this a good thing?

   a. What advantages and disadvantages does social networking bring to your life?
   b. What positive and negative effects has social networking had on society as a whole?
   c. How are businesses using social networking?
   d. How might you see social networking evolving in the next two or three years?

2. **File Swapping Ethics**

   Downloading free music, movies, and other electronic media from the Internet, although illegal, still occurs on sites such as BitTorrent.

   a. Do you think you should have the ability to download free music files of your choice? Do you think the musicians who oppose online music sharing have made valid points?
   b. Discuss the differences you see between sharing music files online and sharing CDs with your friends.
   c. The current price to buy a song online is about $1. Is this a fair price? If not, what price would you consider to be fair?

3. **The Power of Google**

   Google is the largest and most popular search engine on the Internet today. Because of its size and popularity, some people claim that Google has enormous power to influence a Web user's search experience solely by its Web site ranking processes. What do you think about this potential power? How could it be used in negative or harmful ways?

   a. Some Web sites pay search engines to list them near the top of the results pages. These sponsors therefore get priority placement. What do you think of this policy?
   b. What effect (if any) do you think that Google has on Web site development? For example, do you think Web site developers intentionally include frequently searched words in their pages so that they will appear in more hits lists?
   c. When you google someone, you type their name in the Google search box to see what comes up. What privacy concerns do you think such googling could present? Have you ever googled yourself or your friends?

4. **Apple and Adobe Flash**

   Apple has made a corporate decision not to support Flash-based files on its devices. There are no good work-arounds if you want to play a Flash-based game on an Apple device, and some limited alternatives to help run other Flash-based content on an Apple device. Apple contends that working with other content written in open standard products is better for it as a company, and as a consumer, there are reasonable "alternatives" to Flash. What do you think of Apple's position? What would you recommend it to do?

team time

# Comparing Internet Search Methods

### Problem

With millions of sites on the Internet, finding useful information can be a daunting—and, at times, impossible—task. However, there are methods to make searching easier, some of which have been discussed in this chapter. In this Team Time, each team will search for specific items or pieces of information on the Internet and compare search methodologies.

### Process

Split your group into three or more teams, depending on class size. Each group will create a team wiki using free wiki software such as that found at **www.pbworks.com.** To appreciate the benefits of wiki collaboration fully, each team should have at least five or six members.

1. Each team should come up with a theme for its wiki. Suggestions include the following:
   - Best computer technology Web sites
   - Coolest new technology gadgets
   - All-time greatest musicians
   - All-time greatest athletes
   - Best places to visit in the United States
   - Best beaches in the United States
   - Best skiing areas around the world

2. Each student should pick one example to research and then must design a wiki page highlighting that subject. For example, if the team chose all-time greatest musicians, one student could select Bruce Springsteen and create a wiki page on Bruce Springsteen. The wiki page should contain links to other Web sites and, if possible, images and videos.

3. After the team wikis are created, teams should make their wikis available to the other teams for comments.

### Conclusion

After all the team wikis have been completed and shared, discuss the following with your class. What is the benefit of using wiki technology to create team pages? How did wikis help or hinder the team process? What other conclusions can the class draw about using wiki technology?

# Plagiarism

In this exercise, you will research and then role-play a complicated ethical situation. The role you play may or may not match your own personal beliefs, but your research and use of logic will enable you to represent whichever view is assigned. An arbitrator will watch and comment on both sides of the arguments, and together the team will agree on an ethical solution.

## Problem

Plagiarism, or portraying another's work as your own, has been around for a long while and extends well beyond the classroom. For example, Nick Simmons, the son of Gene Simmons (KISS) and a member of A&E's *Family Jewels* reality series, created a comic book series "Incarnate." Radical Publishing picked up the series but quickly stopped publication when Internet messages accused the author of copying from other similar series. Similarly, the Australian band Men at Work was cited for copying a melody from "Kookaburra Sits in the Old Gum Tree" for its 1980s hit "Down Under" and owes the owner years of royalties.

## Research Areas to Consider

- Plagiarism violations
- Comic book series "Incarnate"
- Australian band Men at Work
- Plagiarism consequences

## Process

Divide the class into teams.

1. Research the areas cited above and devise a scenario in which someone has violated plagiarism rules.

2. Team members should write a summary that provides background information for their character—for example: author, publisher, or arbitrator—and details their character's behaviors to set the stage for the role-playing event. Then team members should create an outline to use during the role-playing event.

3. Team members should arrange a mutually convenient time to meet for the exchange, using the chat room feature of MyITLab, the discussion board feature of Blackboard, or meeting in person.

4. Team members should present their case to the class, or submit a PowerPoint presentation for review by the rest of the class, along with the summary and resolution they developed.

## Conclusion

As technology becomes ever more prevalent and integrated into our lives, more and more ethical dilemmas will present themselves. Being able to understand and evaluate both sides of an argument, while responding in a personally or socially ethical manner, will be an important skill.

# chapter 11 information literacy

Taken from "Information Literacy Progression Standards: For use in New Jersey Colleges and Universities," by The Shared Information Literacy Committee of VALE, the User Education Committee of ACRL/NJLA, and the Academic Reference Librarians of CJRLC, October 2009

| STANDARDS | | Introductory/Novice Skills (to be met on completion of 30-32 credits) |
|---|---|---|
| **1. Identifies and addresses information need** | | a) Identifies research topic or information need.<br>b) Drafts research question(s) relevant to thesis or information need using unambiguous language.<br>c) Uses general information sources to identify relevant concepts/vocabulary and inform basic understanding of the research topic or information need. |
| **2. Accesses information effectively and efficiently** | **1. Selects search tools** | a) Identifies similarities and differences among types of information sources—books, journals, newspapers, Internet, reference materials.<br>b) Recognizes similarities and differences among different formats of information—print, electronic, human.<br>c) Identifies and selects appropriate tool for information need. |
| | **2. Constructs search strategies** | a) Identifies search terms relevant to research topic. |
| | **3. Retrieves information** | a) Uses library catalog and classification system to find books on shelves.<br>b) Uses multi-disciplinary databases.<br>c) Identifies issues related to on-and off-campus access of fee-based online sources.<br>d) Uses URLs to locate Web sites.<br>e) Identifies citation elements for information sources in different formats (e.g., book, article, chapter). |
| | **4. Refines search strategies** | a) Evaluates search results to determine relevance to topic.<br>b) Modifies search strategies to broaden or narrow topic. |
| | **5. Extracts, records & manages information sources** | a) Uses a variety of technologies to select and access resources.<br>b) Organizes gathered information.<br>c) Determines availability of item.<br>d) Demonstrates the ability to view/download/email references and articles.<br>e) Distinguishes between abstract and full text. |
| **3. Evaluates and thinks critically about information** | | a) Evaluates information sources for their relevance to need, appropriateness/audience, authority, reliability, currency, and point-of-view/bias.<br>b) Identifies a source's main idea and major points.<br>c) Distinguishes between scholarly vs. popular sources; articles vs. editorials vs. reviews.<br>d) Distinguishes between free Internet sources and library databases. |
| **4. Uses information effectively for a specific purpose** | | a) Completes a research product (e.g., project, paper, report, essay) that incorporates newly acquired and prior information.<br>b) Presents the research product effectively using the most appropriate medium for the intended audience (e.g., text, images, audiovisual). |
| **5. Uses information ethically and legally** | | a) Cites sources and compiles a bibliography or reference list, according to a standard format.<br>b) Demonstrates an understanding of copyright, plagiarism, intellectual property and academic integrity by completing a research product that meets institutional criteria. |

For more information, please visit http://www.valenj.org/sites/default/files/Information%20Literacy%20Progression%20Standards%202010.pdf

| STANDARDS | | Gateway/Developing Skills<br>(to be met on completion of 60-64 credits) |
|---|---|---|
| **1. Identifies and addresses information need** | | a) Uses subject or discipline-specific information sources to better inform an understanding of the research topic or information need and to determine the extent of available information sources before proceeding.<br>b) Establishes realistic timeline to accomplish research. |
| **2. Accesses information effectively and efficiently** | 1. Selects search tools | a) Recognizes differences between general and discipline-specific sources.<br>b) Utilizes appropriate specialized information sources, such as government documents and professional organizations. |
| | 2. Constructs search strategies | a) Conducts subject searches using appropriate controlled vocabulary.<br>b) Applies advanced search strategies, such as Boolean logic (and/or/not) and truncation. |
| | 3. Retrieves information | a) Requests/ accesses information beyond local resources (e.g., Interlibrary Loan, other libraries).<br>b) Uses subject or discipline-specific databases.<br>c) Uses bibliographies or citations to find materials. |
| | 4. Refines search strategies | a) Identifies gaps in information gathered.<br>b) Identifies alternative search tools. |
| | 5. Extracts, records & manages information sources | a) Uses advanced technologies (e.g., folders, RSS, preferences) to exploit functionality of information resources.<br>b) Uses electronic links to access information sources online. |
| **3. Evaluates and thinks critically about information** | | a) Analyzes the logic of arguments in the information gathered.<br>b) Recognizes and describes various aspects of a source that may impact its value for a *specific* research project (e.g., bias and currency may impact the value of the information).<br>c) Distinguishes between primary vs. secondary sources in a subject or discipline-specific context.<br>d) Distinguishes between trade publications and general sources.<br>e) Determines whether additional information, source types, and/or viewpoints are necessary. |
| **4. Uses information effectively for a specific purpose** | | a) Evaluates past and alternative strategies for integrating new and prior information into the completion of a research product.<br>b) Uses a range of formats and technologies, incorporating principles of design and communication, to present a research product. |
| **5. Uses information ethically and legally** | | a) Makes consistent and correct use of a citation style appropriate to the discipline.<br>b) Demonstrates knowledge of what constitutes plagiarism by properly representing content and ownership of original source materials. |

# IST101
# Information Literacy Project Process

Created by Andrea Lynch, Associate Professor at Mercer County Community College

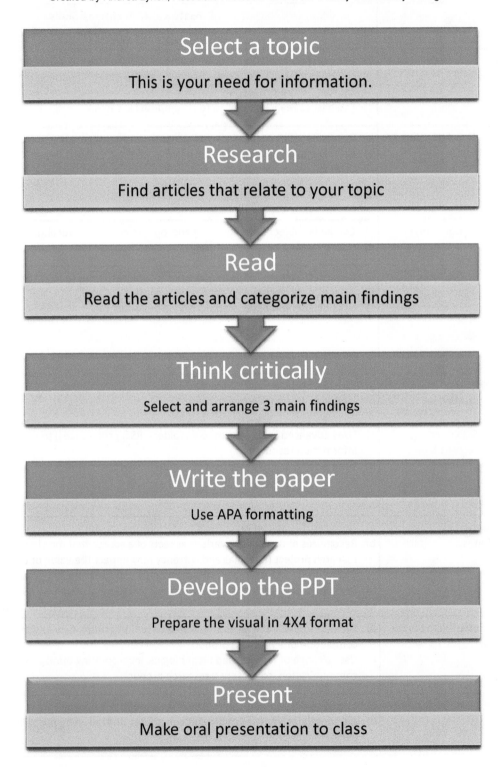

**Select a topic**

This is your need for information.

**Research**

Find articles that relate to your topic

**Read**

Read the articles and categorize main findings

**Think critically**

Select and arrange 3 main findings

**Write the paper**

Use APA formatting

**Develop the PPT**

Prepare the visual in 4X4 format

**Present**

Make oral presentation to class

Taken from *Computer Literacy for IC3 Unit 3: Living Online*, First Edition by John Preston, Sally Preston, Robert L. Ferrett. Adapted for Mercer County Community College by Andrea Lynch, Associate Professor.

# LESSON TWO
# Searching for Information

There are many sites on the Internet that offer free services, such as those sites that help us search for Web pages that contain information, pictures, services, or activities.

One problem in searching the Web is finding so many related Web pages that you cannot examine even a small fraction of them. If you search for a common term, you can often find a million or more Web pages that use the term—far too many to explore. To narrow the list of Web pages that might contain the information you want, you will study how Web pages are indexed and ranked.

## Automated Indexing and Ranking

In 1992, Tim Berners-Lee provided a list of all the Web servers on the Internet—all thirty of them. At that time, it was possible to make a directory of the Web pages that were available from the servers, which could be searched with relatively simple tools. In less than two decades, the number of Web pages has grown to more than 1 trillion and it is impossible to review, index, and rank these pages by having humans look at each one. Computer programs called **Web crawlers** or **spiders** search for Web pages, examine the content of pages, and then report their findings back to a central computer that performs the indexing, classifying, and ranking. The combination of these programs is

called a **search engine**. The companies that own these programs put up a Web page on which users can make a request for a list of Web pages that contain information related to their request. Examples of popular search engines are Google, Yahoo!, Live Search, Baidu (China), and Guruji (India), as shown in Figure 11.1.

The method used by the Web crawler and the main program that analyzes the data from the Web crawler is different for each search engine. If you enter the same request on competing search engines, you will get a different list of Web pages. The companies compete on which one can deliver a list of Web pages that provides the information you want within the first few items on the list. This makes the issue of ranking the Web pages important.

An early ranking method relies on keywords. The HTML code of Web pages can include a list of keywords. The Web crawler program can record this list and associate it with a page's address. The main program creates an index like the one at the back of a textbook. If you ask for a particular keyword, the program can produce all of the Web pages that include that keyword. The competition between websites to have their address display in the first page of a search engine's results is fierce. Because of this desire to be listed first, the authors of the Web-page code often include hundreds of keywords in hopes that their Web page will come up more often in the search. As a result, the search engines that use this system

Popular search engine in India

**Figure** 11.1

Guruji home page.

often display many Web pages that are not closely related to the subject of the search.

### Page Ranking

Another method of categorizing Web pages was popularized by Google. Their Web crawler made note of the hyperlinks in a Web page and the addresses to which those hyperlinks referred. Google reasoned that the Web pages that were referred to most by other Web pages with regard to a particular request for information contained the most relevant answers for the most people. This strategy was very successful and made Google the leader in the search engine field. The name of the company has entered the vocabulary as a verb. To **google** something means to use the Google search engine to find information on that subject.

Some companies still try to influence the ranking of their Web page by tricking the Web crawler or indexing programs, while others simply pay to have their Web page displayed on the first or second page of results. The addresses for these sites are usually labeled as **sponsored links**, as shown in Figure 11.2. Selling this space is a significant source of income for the companies that provide the search engine service.

One search strategy does not fit all needs. Other methods of helping users find the information they want are:

- categorizing—providing categories of sites (dir.yahoo.com)
- definitions—dictionaries (Dictionary.com)
- history of words—etymologies (etymonline.com)
- WikiAnswers—posting questions and inviting readers to answer or view previous exchanges (wiki.answers.com)

### Search Methods

To find the information you want, you can begin by searching for sites that are related to a few individual words. This method is called a **keyword search**.

Computers use a formal logic system called **Boolean logic** for making decisions, developed by George Boole in the 1800s. It uses the operators **and**, **or**, and **not**. Search engines combine Boolean logic with their own proprietary logic to choose which Web pages to display and how to rank them. To demonstrate how a search engine uses a mixture of Boolean and proprietary logic, you will search for recent authoritative information on the energy output of large wind turbines.

## To Refine a Search Using Logic Operators

1. **Start Internet Explorer.** The Internet Explorer window opens to the default Web page.
2. **In the Address box, type Google.com and then press ENTER.** The Google home page displays. Most browsers

**Figure** 11.2

Sponsored links.

Too many matches to examine

Sponsored links

**Figure** 11.3

Google search results.

will assume that you want to use the hypertext transfer protocol, so you do not have to type it unless the shortened address does not work.

3. **Below the Google logo, in the empty search box, type wind turbine, and then press ENTER.** The first ten websites are listed on the first page, along with a separate section of links to Web pages whose sponsors paid a fee to have their sites come up on the first page of the search, as shown in Figure 11.3. Google uses a proprietary logic to determine which pages to include. Notice

that the logic used by the Google search engine selected millions of Web pages that are related to wind turbines. This is far too many to examine, so the search must be refined.

4. **To the right of the Search button, click** *Advanced Search.* The Advanced Search window displays, as shown in Figure 11.4. Notice that the words used earlier are in the *all these words* box. The Google search engine combines its logic with the Boolean *and* logic to find sites that contain both words—*wind* and *turbine.*

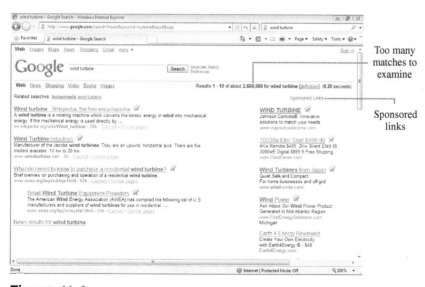

Too many matches to examine

Sponsored links

**Figure** 11.4

Google search results.

5. **In the *this exact wording or phrase* box, type *energy output*** Each of these words is commonly used in many ways. It is the exact combination of them that has meaning in this search.

6. **To the right of *one or more of these words*, in the first box, type *kwh* and, in the second box, type *mwh*** This is an example of the logical *or* operator. Energy output for large turbines can be measured in kilowatt hours (kwh) or megawatt hours (mwh). By searching for sites that contain either of these measurement terms, the results will be limited to sites that contain data with either of these energy labels.

7. **To the right of *any of these unwanted words*, in the box, type *small*** This criteria uses the logical not operator. This criterion will eliminate sites that describe small wind turbines that are more appropriate to home use.

8. **To the right of *Search within a site or domain*, in the box, type *.gov*** This will limit the search to government websites.

9. **To the left of *Date, usage rights, numeric range, and more*, click the plus sign. To the right of *Date: (how recent the page is)*, click the arrow on the box, and then click *past year*.** This criterion filters the websites by the date of posting to display only Web pages that have been posted in the last year, as shown in Figure 11.5. Be aware that the page might contain older information.

10. **Use the skills you practiced previously to start the Snipping Tool program and do a Window Snip of the Advanced Search window. Save a copy of this window to the folder where you store your files. Name the file *U3Ch-02SearchStudentName* substituting your name as indicated.**

11. **Scroll to the bottom of the browser window, if necessary, and click the Advanced Search button.** The combination of criteria applied with Boolean and proprietary logic reduces the number of Web pages from millions to a much smaller number. Notice the criteria in the Search box. If you know the codes, you can enter the advanced search criteria directly into the Search box.

12. **In the upper right corner of each open dialog box or window, click the Close button** 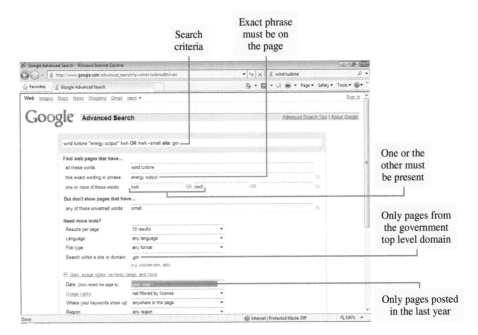.

13. **Submit your snip as directed by your instructor.**

**Figure 11.5**
Advanced search.

## To Extend Your Knowledge

### Search for Words within a Web Page

Some Web pages or the documents attached to them can be many screens or pages long. To find a particular word or phrase in the displayed page, the browser provides a Find feature that is similar to the one in a word processing program. The Find feature is found on the browser's menu bar in the Edit menu or may be started with CTRL + F.

Taken from *Computer Literacy for IC3 Unit 3: Living Online*, First Edition by John Preston, Sally Preston, Robert L. Ferrett. Adapted for Mercer County Community College by Andrea Lynch, Associate Professor.

## LESSON FIVE
## Security, Privacy, and Ethics

In this lesson, ethics, security and privacy are discussed as they pertain to using a Web browser and search engine on the Internet.

### Citing Sources

You can copy text and graphics from websites and use them for other purposes, such as reports or presentations. Before you copy anything from a website, you need to consider who owns the copyright to the material. A *copyright* is ownership of intelectual property and the exclusive right to use it or to choose who else uses it. Unauthorized copying is prohibited in most cases. There are copyright-free sites on the Web from which you can reproduce information and pictures; for example, the National Aeronautics and Space Administration (NASA), the National Oceanic and Atmospheric Administration (NOAA), and the U.S. Fish and Wildlife Service (FWS). Some pictures may have copyright notices indicating that the image is being used with permission from a copyright holder. You can also, under some circumstances, use copyrighted materials for education purposes. Regardless of whether the information is copyrighted, you must let the reader know what thoughts are yours and what has been copied from someone else.

When you see the term *copyright* or the copyright symbol (©), it means the author is reminding people that they should not use this material without permission. A copyright exists even if the author does not use the symbol. Copyrighted materials may be used without paying royalties for purposes of research, criticism, comment, news reporting, and teaching under the name of *fair use.* Specific information on U.S. copyright laws and rules is available from the Library of Congress at copyright. gov. Other protections of creative works include a *trademark*—a word or symbol that indicates ownership of a product or service and its use is reserved for the owner. A *patent* provides protection for the idea behind an invention.

In formal research papers, there are specific rules for *citing*—referencing—the source of someone else's text, pictures, or other work that is the result of a creative process. One of the important functions of a good citation is that it enables the reader to check the source material to see if it was taken out of context or misrepresented. When citing a Web page from which you have copied text or pictures, you need to provide enough information for someone else to find the same text or picture that you did.

The standards for citation that are commonly used in education in the U.S. are administered by the Modern Language Association (MLA) and the American Psychological Association (APA). Refer to Table 11.1 for a list of reference styles.

Citing Web pages poses problems that are different from citing traditionally published articles and books. The types of information in Web pages changes as new technologies are used, and some Web pages are assembled from pieces upon request and are not stored. Guidelines for citing references according to a particular standard are usually found at the organization's website where the standard is defined or in official organization publications.

There are electronic aids to help students create citations that meet most style requirements. Microsoft Word 2007 includes a feature that lets you fill in a form and, when you specify the reference style, provides a list of references and citations in that style. Third-party software like EndNote assists researchers to manage references. There are websites that perform similar services for free, such as Son of Citation Machine and Knight Cite.

**Table 11.1**

| Style | Where It Is Used |
|-------|------------------|
| APA | Research papers in the social sciences |
| Chicago | Publishing |
| GB7714 | China |
| GOST | Russia and former Societ-bloc countries |
| ISO-690 | International standard used in industry, manufacturing, and patent applications |
| MLA | English studies |
| SIST02 | Japan |
| Turabian | Academic research, particularly in musicology, history, and theology—based on Chicago style |

## Evaluating Quality Web Page Content

The ease with which anyone can publish a Web page means that there is little quality control. To determine the quality of the content of a website that appears as the result of a search, ask yourself the following questions:

- Is the content relevant to the topic I searched for?
- What does the Web address tell me? Look at the top-level domain to determine the type of domain (government, military, nonprofit) and if the domain name is hosted in a different country. Does the page come from a source that has an established reputation for accuracy and reliability or is it from an ISP like AOL that hosts sites posted by individuals?
- Is the source likely to be biased on this topic? For example, how does the issue affect the income of the site's sponsors or authors? Look for links such as *About Us, Philosophy,* or *Staff Biographies* that would provide an indication of bias on the topic. Is the author of the content qualified to provide an informed opinion?
- Is the information current? Old news stories can be recirculated in summaries where the summary has a recent date but the original article is old.
- Does the site contain references to authoritative sources? Look for hyperlinks to the sources the author uses as background for the article.

- Does the information go into enough detail and is it original? If the text is mostly someone else's ideas, follow the links back to the source and use that instead.
- Search for other articles by the same author or comments about the author, using a search engine like Google. Enclose the author's full name in quotation marks and include another word that describes the author's specialty to restrict the search.

If you have questions about a site, you can contact the site's creators if they provide a *Contact* link or an electronic mail address. It can be helpful to consider the ranking the search engine gave the site as an indication of how popular it is.

## Unethical Search Engine Practices

The ranking of websites on a search engine has considerable value. Commercial sites whose Web pages come up on the first page of a popular search engine are likely to have many more people visit their sites than if they appeared on the second page. This value can lead to unethical practices by the operators of search engines and by the authors of Web pages.

Because placement of a link on the first page of search results is valuable, some Web page sponsors simply pay the search engine company to place their link on the first page of results when someone searches for information on certain related topics. The search engine company keeps track of how many people actually click the link and charge the company an additional amount for each

Sponsored links
listed first but
less clearly marked

**Figure** 11.6

Sponsored links with lightly shaded background.

*click through* (clicking the link to connect to another website). An ethical search engine company will clearly label the sponsored links so the user can tell which ones are listed because they are appropriate matches for the search criteria and which links have been placed in a prominent location on the page for a fee. An unethical search engine company will not disclose that a sponsored link is at the top of the list because they paid for the location; they simply want to increase the number of click-throughs. Some search engines skirt the issue by shading

the sponsored links with a light grey background and labeling them using a small font that users might not notice, as shown in Figure 11.6.

Some Web sponsors use practices that are designed to raise their rankings at search engines without paying for special placement. For example, a group of sites might agree to place links on their pages to each of the other sites in the group. Some search engines, like Google, use the number of links on other pages as one of the ranking criteria, so the extra links increase the rankings of all the

Option to
turn on the
pop-up blocker

Displays
pop-up
blocker menu

Displays
menu

**Figure** 11.7

Pop-up blocker options.

pages in the group. Another practice is to create programs that repeatedly ask for the same Web page to increase the number of requests per day, which is another ranking criteria used by search engines. In general, practices that are designed to misrepresent a website's ranking in the list of search results are unethical because they are intended to deceive the user of the search engine.

### Searching Safely by Blocking Websites

The Internet has a wide variety of content, and because content crosses state and national boundaries easily, it is difficult to monitor and control. If there are categories of websites that you do not want to view, it is possible to block many of them by using the browser's content filter. Examples of these categories are adult and political content. Some countries block access to websites that contain political content that they deem to be subversive.

Another type of unwanted content is *pop-up* windows that contain unwanted messages, advertising, or surveys, as shown in Figure 11.7. A pop-up window appears as a result of clicking or even simply moving the pointer over a portion of the Web page. Some sites use pop-up windows for desirable purposes, but most pop-up windows display without the voluntary permission of the user. Display of pop-up windows can be disabled in most browser programs.

### Ethical Behavior on the Web

The basic concept behind ethical behavior is to treat others as you would have them treat you. When you use the Internet, consider the following and use them as guidelines:

- Respect the privacy of others.
- Treat the opinions of others with respect.
- Do not write something about another person or group that is not true.
- Do not use the Internet to harrass someone.
- Do not force offensive material on someone else.
- Respect the right of parents to limit their children's access to adult material.

Taken from *The Good, The Bad & The Ugly: or, Why It's a Good Idea to Evaluate Web Sources* by Susan E. Beck, April 27, 2009. *http://lib.nmsu.edu/instruction/evalcrit.html*

# Evaluation Criteria

### I. Authority

Is there an author? Is the page signed?

Is the author qualified? An expert?

Who is the sponsor?

Is the sponsor of the page reputable? How reputable?

Is there a link to information about the author or the sponsor?

If the page includes neither a signature nor indicates a sponsor, is there any other way to determine its origin?

Look for a header or footer showing affiliation.

Look at the URL. http://www.fbi.gov

Look at the domain. .edu, .com, .ac.uk, .org, .net

**Rationale**

1. Anyone can publish anything on the web.
2. It is often hard to determine a web page's authorship.
3. Even if a page is signed, qualifications are not usually provided.
4. Sponsorship is not always indicated.

### II. Accuracy

Is the information reliable and error-free?

Is there an editor or someone who verifies/checks the information?

**Rationale**

1. See number 1 above
2. Unlike traditional print resources, web resources rarely have editors or fact-checkers.
3. Currently, no web standards exist to ensure accuracy.

### III. Objectivity

Does the information show a minimum of bias?

Is the page designed to sway opinion?

Is there any advertising on the page?

**Rationale**

1. Frequently the goals of the sponsors/authors are not clearly stated.
2. Often the Web serves as a virtual "Hyde Park Corner", a soapbox.

### IV. Currency

Is the page dated?

If so, when was the last update?

How current are the links? Have some expired or moved?

**Rationale**

1. Publication or revision dates are not always provided.
2. If a date is provided, it may have various meanings. For example,

It may indicate when the material was first written

It may indicate when the material was first placed on the Web

It may indicate when the material was last revised

### V. Coverage

What topics are covered?

What does this page offer that is not found elsewhere?

What is its intrinsic value?

How in-depth is the material?

**Rationale**

1. Web coverage often differs from print coverage.
2. Frequently, it's difficult to determine the extent of coverage of a topic from a web page. The page may or may not include links to other web pages or print references.
3. Sometimes web information is "just for fun", a hoax, someone's personal expression that may be of interest to no one, or even outright silliness.

Taken from Purdue OWL, *http://owl.english.purdue.edu,* by Kristen Seas and Allen Brizee, April 21, 2010.
*http://owl.english.purdue.edu/owl/resource/664/01/*

# APA Style Workshop

**Summary:** This workshop provides an overview of APA (American Psychological Association) style and where to find help with different APA resources. It provides an annotated list of links to all of our APA materials and an APA overview. It is an excellent place to start to learn about APA format.

**Contributors:** Kristen Seas, Allen Brizee
**Last Edited:** 2010-04-21 07:52:46

Welcome to the OWL Workshop on APA Style! This workshop will introduce you to important aspects of using the American Psychological Association (APA) Style to write and format research papers. You should begin with the introductory material, which covers what APA Style is, why it is used, and who should apply it to their work. Then you are invited to work through the OWL's handouts on APA Formatting and Writing Style, as well as APA Citations and Reference Lists.

**NOTE:** This workshop should answer most of your basic questions about using APA Style. However, if you are writing a complex document such as a thesis or lengthy manuscript, or if you have detailed questions, you should consult The Publication Manual of the American Psychological Association (6th edition), which you can usually find at your local library or in many bookstores.

The APA also has a website that allows you to order the book online and read some of their frequently asked questions about APA style. Purdue's OWL also has a list of Additional Resources covering APA style that you can consult.

## What is APA Style?

APA Style establishes standards of written communication concerning:

- the organization of content
- writing style
- citing references
- and how to prepare a manuscript for publication in certain disciplines.

## Why Use APA?

Aside from simplifying the work of editors by having everyone use the same format for a given publication, using APA Style makes it easier for readers to understand a text by providing a familiar structure they can follow. Abiding by APA's standards as a writer will allow you to:

- Provide readers with cues they can use to follow your ideas more efficiently and to locate information of interest to them

- Allow readers to focus more on your ideas by not distracting them with unfamiliar formatting
- Establish your credibility or ethos in the field by demonstrating an awareness of your audience and their needs as fellow researchers

# Who Should Use APA?

APA Style describes rules for the preparation of manuscripts for writers and students in:

- Social Sciences, such as Psychology, Linguistics, Sociology, Economics, and Criminology
- Business
- Nursing

Before you adopt this style for your paper, you should check to see what citation style your discipline uses in its journals and for student research. If APA Style is appropriate for your writing project, then use this workshop to learn more about APA and how to follow its rules correctly in your own work.

# APA Formatting and Writing Style

You should start by becoming familiar with the general formatting requirements of APA Style, as well as the different standards for writing that are expected among APA writers. Because APA is different than other writing styles, you should pay attention to everything from general paper layout to word choice. The following pages will introduce you to some of these basic requirements of APA Style to get you started in the right direction.

## General APA Format

- Covers the basic page layout for a typical APA manuscript, including everything from margin widths to the use of headings and visuals
- Includes a general list of the basic components of an APA paper: title page, abstract, and reference page
- Also includes a PowerPoint slide presentation with detailed information about the APA citation style

## Types of APA Papers

- Describes the two most common types of APA papers: the literature review and the experimental report
- Outlines what sections must be included in each type of paper, from introductions to a methods section

## APA Stylistics: Basics

- Describes three basic areas of stylistic concerns when writing in an APA field: point of view, clarity/conciseness, and word choice
- Explains how poetic language and devices should be avoided in APA reviews and reports
- Suggestions and examples are given for each stylistic issue

## APA Stylistics: Things to Avoid

- Identifies the risk of bias in language concerning gender, race, disability, and sexuality when writing up research in APA fields
- Provides links to APA's official guidelines on avoiding bias
- Offers suggestions on finding alternatives to gendered pronouns and using different descriptors when identifying people in your research

# APA Citations and Reference List

Perhaps the trickiest part to mastering APA Style is understanding the requirements for citing and listing secondary sources accurately. The following pages walk you through the details of writing citations and developing a reference page at the end of your paper. Read these guidelines carefully! It is important that you refer to your sources according to APA Style so your readers can quickly follow the citations to the reference page and then, from there, locate any sources that might by of interest to them. They will expect this information to be presented in a particular style, and any deviations from that style could result in confusing your readers about where you obtained your information.

## In-Text Citations: The Basics

- Addresses the basic formatting requirements of using the APA Style for citing secondary sources within the text of your essay
- Provides guidance on how to incorporate different kinds of references to borrowed material, from short quotes to summaries or paraphrases

## In-Text Citations: Author/Authors

- Focuses on various details about referring to the authors of your sources within your essay, which can be difficult to do efficiently if the source has more than one author or has an unclear author (e.g. an organization)
- Describes how to cite indirect quotes, electronic sources, and/or sources without page numbers

# Footnotes and Endnotes

- Recommends using footnotes or endnotes to avoid long explanations in the text
- Covers two basic kinds of notes: bibliographic and digressive

# Reference List: Basic Rules

- Guides you through the general rules that apply to any reference list developed using APA Style
- Covers everything from where the reference list appears to the capitalization of words in the titles of sources
- Serves as a primer on formatting that will be followed in all of the following handouts on creating APA reference entries

# Reference List: Author/Authors

- Walks you through how to construct a reference entry for different text starting with a focus on author
- Notes how the references are different depending on the number of authors or if there are multiple works by the same author

# Reference List: Articles in Periodicals

- Builds from the previous handout by looking specifically at how to refer accurately to a periodical source
- Lists types of entries depending on the kind of journal (e.g. one paginated by volume), if the source is a magazine v. a newspaper, or the kind of article the source is (e.g. a letter to the editor)

# Reference List: Books

- Builds from the author handout by describing how to properly refer to book-length sources
- Addresses both the basic format as well as requirements for those unique book sources that require you to note specific details, such as whether it is a translation or part of a multivolume work

# Reference List: Other Print Sources

- Offers a short list of other less common print sources you might be citing in your manuscript and how to construct references for them
- Covers examples such as citing a source that is cited in another, or citing a government document

# Reference List: Electronic Sources

- Walks through the requirements and unique qualifications (see the Notes throughout the page) for constructing references for electronic sources
- Covers sources from online periodicals and scholarly databases, to emails.

# Reference List: Other Non-Print Sources

- Focuses primarily on how to reference video and audio texts that are used as sources, from movie clips to sound recordings
- Notes that personal communication (e.g. an interview or conversation) is not to be included in the reference list.

# In-Text Citations: The Basics

**Summary:** APA (American Psychological Association) is most commonly used to cite sources within the social sciences. This resource, revised according to the **6th edition,** second printing of the APA manual, offers examples for the general format of APA research papers, in-text citations, endnotes/footnotes, and the reference page. For more information, please consult the *Publication Manual of the American Psychological Association,* 6th edition, second printing.

**Contributors:** Joshua M. Paiz, Elizabeth Angeli, Jodi Wagner, Elena Lawrick, Kristen Moore, Michael Anderson, Lars Soderlund, Allen Brizee, Russell Keck
**Last Edited:** 2012-03-14 01:11:19

Reference citations in text are covered on pages 169-179 of the Publication Manual. What follows are some general guidelines for referring to the works of others in your essay.

**Note:** APA style requires authors to use the past tense or present perfect tense when using signal phrases to describe earlier research, for example, Jones (1998) **found** or Jones (1998) **has found**...

## APA Citation Basics

When using APA format, follow the author-date method of in-text citation. This means that the author's last name and the year of publication for the source should appear in the text, for example, (Jones, 1998), and a complete reference should appear in the reference list at the end of the paper.

If you are referring to an idea from another work but **NOT** directly quoting the material, or making reference to an entire book, article or other work, you only have to make reference to the author and year of publication and not the page number in your in-text reference. All sources that are cited in the text must appear in the reference list at the end of the paper.

## In-Text Citation Capitalization, Quotes, and Italics/Underlining

- Always capitalize proper nouns, including author names and initials: D. Jones.
- If you refer to the title of a source within your paper, capitalize all words that are four letters long or greater within the title of a source: *Permanence and Change*. Exceptions apply to short words that are verbs, nouns, pronouns, adjectives, and adverbs: *Writing New Media*, *There Is Nothing Left to Lose*.

  (**Note:** in your References list, only the first word of a title will be capitalized: Writing new media.)

- When capitalizing titles, capitalize both words in a hyphenated compound word: *Natural-Born Cyborgs*.
- Capitalize the first word after a dash or colon: "Defining Film Rhetoric: The Case of Hitchcock's *Vertigo*."
- Italicize or underline the titles of longer works such as books, edited collections, movies, television series, documentaries, or albums: *The Closing of the American Mind*; *The Wizard of Oz*; *Friends*.
- Put quotation marks around the titles of shorter works such as journal articles, articles from edited collections, television series episodes, and song titles: "Multimedia Narration: Constructing Possible Worlds"; "The One Where Chandler Can't Cry."

## Short Quotations

If you are directly quoting from a work, you will need to include the author, year of publication, and the page number for the reference (preceded by "p."). Introduce the quotation with a signal phrase that includes the author's last name followed by the date of publication in parentheses.

```
According to Jones (1998), "Students often had difficulty using

APA style, especially when it was their first time" (p. 199).
```

```
Jones (1998) found "students often had difficulty using APA

style" (p. 199); what implications does this have for teachers?
```

If the author is not named in a signal phrase, place the author's last name, the year of publication, and the page number in parentheses after the quotation.

```
She stated, "Students often had difficulty using APA style"

(Jones, 1998, p. 199), but she did not offer an explanation as to

why.
```

## Long Quotations

Place direct quotations longer than 40 words in a free-standing block of typewritten lines, and omit quotation marks. Start the quotation on a new line, indented 1/2 inch from the left margin, i.e., in the same place you would begin a new paragraph. Type the entire quotation on the new margin, and indent the first line of any subsequent paragraph within the quotation

1/2 inch from the new margin. Maintain double-spacing throughout. The parenthetical citation should come after the closing punctuation mark.

```
Jones's (1998) study found the following:

    Students often had difficulty using APA style,

    especially when it was their first time citing sources.

    This difficulty could be attributed to the fact that many

    students failed to  purchase a style manual or to ask

    their teacher for help. (p. 199)
```

## Summary or Paraphrase

If you are paraphrasing an idea from another work, you only have to make reference to the author and year of publication in your in-text reference, but APA guidelines encourage you to also provide the page number (although it is not required.)

```
According to Jones (1998), APA style is a difficult citation

format for first-time learners.

APA style is a difficult citation format for first-time learners

(Jones, 1998, p. 199).
```

# Reference List: Basic Rules

**Summary:** APA (American Psychological Association) is most commonly used to cite sources within the social sciences. This resource, revised according to the **6th edition,** second printing of the APA manual, offers examples for the general format of APA research papers, in-text citations, endnotes/footnotes, and the reference page. For more information, please consult the *Publication Manual of the American Psychological Association,* 6th edition, second printing.

**Contributors:** Joshua M. Paiz, Elizabeth Angeli, Jodi Wagner, Elena Lawrick, Kristen Moore, Michael Anderson, Lars Soderlund, Allen Brizee, Russell Keck
**Last Edited:** 2012-05-23 12:06:58

Your reference list should appear at the end of your paper. It provides the information necessary for a reader to locate and retrieve any source you cite in the body of the paper. Each source you cite in the paper must appear in your reference list; likewise, each entry in the reference list must be cited in your text.

Your references should begin on a new page separate from the text of the essay; label this page "References" centered at the top of the page (do NOT bold, underline, or use quotation marks for the title). All text should be double-spaced just like the rest of your essay.

## Basic Rules

- All lines after the first line of each entry in your reference list should be indented one-half inch from the left margin. This is called hanging indentation.
- Authors' names are inverted (last name first); give the last name and initials for all authors of a particular work for up to and including seven authors. If the work has more than seven authors, list the first six authors and then use ellipses after the sixth author's name. After the ellipses, list the last author's name of the work.
- Reference list entries should be alphabetized by the last name of the first author of each work.
- If you have more than one article by the same author, single-author references or multiple-author references with the exact same authors in the exact same order are listed in order by the year of publication, starting with the earliest.
- Present the journal title in full.
- Maintain the punctuation and capitalization that is used by the journal in its title.
  - For example: *ReCALL* not *RECALL* or *Knowledge Management Research & Practice* not *Knowledge Management Research and Practice.*
- Capitalize all major words in journal titles.

- When referring to books, chapters, articles, or Web pages, capitalize only the first letter of the first word of a title and subtitle, the first word after a colon or a dash in the title, and proper nouns. Do not capitalize the first letter of the second word in a hyphenated compound word.
- Italicize titles of longer works such as books and journals.
- Do not italicize, underline, or put quotes around the titles of shorter works such as journal articles or essays in edited collections.
- **Please note:** While the APA manual provides many examples of how to cite common types of sources, it does not provide rules on how to cite all types of sources. Therefore, if you have a source that APA does not include, APA suggests that you find the example that is most similar to your source and use that format. For more information, see page 193 of the *Publication Manual of the American Psychological Association*, sixth edition.

# Reference List: Electronic Sources (Web Publications)

**Summary:** APA (American Psychological Association) is most commonly used to cite sources within the social sciences. This resource, revised according to the **6th edition,** second printing of the APA manual, offers examples for the general format of APA research papers, in-text citations, endnotes/footnotes, and the reference page. For more information, please consult the *Publication Manual of the American Psychological Association,* 6th edition, second printing.

**Contributors:** Joshua M. Paiz, Elizabeth Angeli, Jodi Wagner, Elena Lawrick, Kristen Moore, Michael Anderson, Lars Soderlund, Allen Brizee, Russell Keck
**Last Edited:** 2012-06-06 10:56:48

**Please note:** There are no spaces used with brackets in APA. When possible, include the year, month, and date in references. If the month and date are not available, use the year of publication. Please note, too, that the OWL still includes information about print sources and databases for those still working with these sources.

## Article From an Online Periodical

Online articles follow the same guidelines for printed articles. Include all information the online host makes available, including an issue number in parentheses.

Author, A. A., & Author, B. B. (Date of publication). Title of

article.*Title of Online Periodical, volume number*(issue number if

available). Retrieved from

http://www.someaddress.com/full/url/

Bernstein, M. (2002). 10 tips on writing the living Web. *A list*

*apart: For people who make websites, 149.* Retrieved from

http://www.alistapart.com/articles/writeliving

## Online Scholarly Journal Article: Citing DOIs

Because online materials can potentially change URLs, APA recommends providing a Digital Object Identifier (DOI), when it is available, as opposed to the URL. DOIs are an attempt to provide stable, long-lasting links for online articles. They are unique to their documents and consist of a long alphanumeric code. Many-but not all-publishers will provide an article's DOI on the first page of the document.

Note that some online bibliographies provide an article's DOI but may "hide" the code under a button which may read "Article" or may be an abbreviation of a vendor's name like "CrossRef" or "PubMed." This button will usually lead the user to the full article which will include the DOI. Find DOI's from print publications or ones that go to dead links with CrossRef.org's "DOI Resolver," which is displayed in a central location on their home page.

# Article From an Online Periodical with DOI Assigned

Author, A. A., & Author, B. B. (Date of publication). Title of

article.*Title of Journal, volume number*, page range.

doi:0000000/000000000000

Brownlie, D. (2007). Toward effective poster presentations: An

annotated bibliography. *European Journal of Marketing, 41*, 1245-

1283. doi:10.1108/03090560710821161

# Article From an Online Periodical with no DOI Assigned

Online scholarly journal articles without a DOI require the URL of the journal home page. Remember that one goal of citations is to provide your readers with enough information to find the article; providing the journal home page aids readers in this process.

Author, A. A., & Author, B. B. (Date of publication). Title of

article.*Title of Journal, volume number*. Retrieved from

http://www.journalhomepage.com/full/url/

Kenneth, I. A. (2000). A Buddhist response to the nature of human

rights. *Journal of Buddhist Ethics, 8*. Retrieved from

http://www.cac.psu.edu/jbe/twocont.html

# Article From a Database

**Please note:** APA states that including database information in citations is not necessary because databases change over time (p. 192). However, the OWL still includes information about databases for those users who need database information.

When referencing a print article obtained from an online database (such as a database in the library), provide appropriate print citation information (formatted just like a "normal" print citation would be for that type of work). By providing this information, you allow people to retrieve the print version if they do not have access to the database from which you retrieved the article. You can also include the item number or accession number or database URL at the end, but the APA manual says that this is not required.

If you are citing an article from a database that is available in other places, such as a journal or magazine, include the homepage's URL. You may have to do a web search of the article's title, author, etc. to find the URL.

For articles that are easily located, do not provide database information. If the article is difficult to locate, then you can provide database information. Only use retrieval dates if the source could change, such as Wikis. For more about citing articles retrieved from electronic databases, see pages 187-192 of the Publication Manual.

Author, A. A., & Author, B. B. (Date of publication). Title of

article. *Title of Journal, volume number,* page range. Retrieved

from http://www.someaddress.com/full/url/

Smyth, A. M., Parker, A. L., & Pease, D. L. (2002). A study of

enjoyment of peas. *Journal of Abnormal Eating, 8*(3), 120-125.

Retrieved from

http://www.articlehomepage.com/full/url/

# Abstract

If you only cite an abstract but the full text of the article is also available, cite the online abstract as other online citations, adding "[Abstract]" after the article or source name.

Paterson, P. (2008). How well do young offenders with Asperger

    Syndrome cope in custody?: Two prison case studies

    [Abstract]. *British Journal of Learning Disabilities, 36*(1),

    54-58.

Bossong, G. Ergativity in Basque. *Linguistics, 22*(3), 341-392.

## Newspaper Article

Author, A. A. (Year, Month Day). Title of article. *Title of*

    *Newspaper*. Retrieved from

    http://www.someaddress.com/full/url/

Parker-Pope, T. (2008, May 6). Psychiatry handbook linked to drug

    industry. *The New York Times*. Retrieved from

    http://www.nytimes.com

## Electronic Books

Electronic books may include books found on personal websites, databases, or even in audio form. Use the following format if the book you are using is *only* provided in a digital format or is difficult to find in print. If the work is not directly available online or must be purchased, use "Available from," rather than "Retrieved from," and point readers to where they can find it. For books available in print form and electronic form, include the publish date in parentheses after the author's name.

De Huff, E. W. (n.d.). *Taytay's tales: Traditional Pueblo Indian*

    *tales*. Retrieved from

    http://digital.library.upenn.edu/women/dehuff/taytay/taytay.html

Davis, J. (n.d.). *Familiar birdsongs of the Northwest*. Available

    from http://www.powells.com/cgi-bin/biblio?inkey=1-

    9780931686108-0

# Chapter/Section of a Web Document or Online Book Chapter

Author, A. A., & Author, B. B. (Date of publication). Title of

article. In *Title of book or larger document* (chapter or section

number). Retrieved from http://www.someaddress.com/full/url/

Engelshcall, R. S. (1997). Module mod_rewrite: URL Rewriting Engine.

In *Apache HTTP Server Version 1.3 Documentation* (Apache modules).

Retrieved from

http://httpd.apache.org/docs/1.3/mod/mod_rewrite.html

Peckinpaugh, J. (2003). Change in the Nineties. In J. S. Bough and

G. B. DuBois (Eds.), *A century of growth in America*. Retrieved

from GoldStar database.

**NOTE**: Use a chapter or section identifier and provide a URL that links directly to the chapter section, not the home page of the Web site.

# Online Book Reviews

Cite the information as you normally would for the work you are quoting. (The first example below is from a newspaper article; the second is from a scholarly journal.) In brackets, write "Review of the book" and give the title of the reviewed work. Provide the web address after the words "Retrieved from," if the review is freely available to anyone. If the review comes from a subscription service or database, write "Available from" and provide the information where the review can be purchased.

Zacharek, S. (2008, April 27). Natural women [Review of the

book *Girls like us*]. *The New York Times*. Retrieved from

http://www.nytimes.com/2008/04/27/books/review/Zachareck

-t.html?pagewanted=2

Castle, G. (2007). New millennial Joyce [Review of the books *Twenty-

first Joyce, Joyce's critics: Transitions in reading and culture,* *and Joyce's messianism: Dante, negative existence, and the*

*messianic self]. Modern Fiction Studies, 50(1), 163-173.*

Available from Project MUSE Web site:

http://muse.jhu.edu/journals/modern_fiction_studies/toc/

mfs52.1.html

## Dissertation/Thesis from a Database

Biswas, S. (2008). *Dopamine D3 receptor: A neuroprotective treatment*

*target in Parkinson's disease.* Retrieved from ProQuest Digital

Dissertations. (AAT 3295214)

## Online Encyclopedias and Dictionaries

Often encyclopedias and dictionaries do not provide bylines (authors' names). When no byline is present, move the entry name to the front of the citation. Provide publication dates if present or specify (n.d.) if no date is present in the entry.

Feminism. (n.d.). In *Encyclopædia Britannica online.* Retrieved from

http://www.britannica.com/EBchecked/topic/724633/feminism

## Online Bibliographies and Annotated Bibliographies

Jürgens, R. (2005). *HIV/AIDS and HCV in Prisons: A Select Annotated*

*Bibliography.* Retrieved from http://www.hc-sc.gc.ca/ahc-

asc/alt_formats/hpb-dgps/pdf/intactiv/hiv-vih-aids-sida-prison-

carceral_e.pdf

## Data Sets

Point readers to raw data by providing a Web address (use "Retrieved from") or a general place that houses data sets on the site (use "Available from").

United States Department of Housing and Urban Development.

(2008). *Indiana income limits* [Data file]. Retrieved from

http://www.huduser.org/Datasets/IL/IL08/in_fy2008.pdf

## Graphic Data (e.g. Interactive Maps and Other Graphic Representations of Data)

Give the name of the researching organization followed by the date. In brackets, provide a brief explanation of what type of data is there and in what form it appears. Finally, provide the project name and retrieval information.

Solar Radiation and Climate Experiment. (2007). [Graph illustration

the SORCE Spectral Plot May 8, 2008]. *Solar Spectral Data Access*

*from the SIM, SOLSTICE, and XPS Instruments*. Retrieved from

http://lasp.colorado.edu/cgi-bin/ion-p?page=input_data_for_

spectra.ion

## Qualitative Data and Online Interviews

If an interview is not retrievable in audio or print form, cite the interview only in the text (not in the reference list) and provide the month, day, and year in the text. If an audio file or transcript is available online, use the following model, specifying the medium in brackets (e.g. [Interview transcript, Interview audio file]):

Butler, C. (Interviewer) & Stevenson, R. (Interviewee). (1999). *Oral*

*History 2* [Interview transcript]. Retrieved from Johnson Space

Center Oral Histories Project Web site: http://

www11.jsc.nasa.gov/history/oral_histories/oral_histories.htm

# Online Lecture Notes and Presentation Slides

When citing online lecture notes, be sure to provide the file format in brackets after the lecture title (e.g. PowerPoint slides, Word document).

Hallam, A. *Duality in consumer theory* [PDF document]. Retrieved from

    Lecture Notes Online Web site:

    http://www.econ.iastate.edu/classes/econ501/Hallam/

    index.html

Roberts, K. F. (1998). *Federal regulations of chemicals in the*

    *environment* [PowerPoint slides]. Retrieved from

    http://siri.uvm.edu/ppt/40hrenv/index.html

# Nonperiodical Web Document, Web Page, or Report

List as much of the following information as possible (you sometimes have to hunt around to find the information; don't be lazy. If there is a page like http://www.somesite.com/somepage.htm, and somepage.htm doesn't have the information you're looking for, move up the URL to http://www.somesite.com/):

Author, A. A., & Author, B. B. (Date of publication). Title of

    document. Retrieved from http://Web address

Angeli, E., Wagner, J., Lawrick, E., Moore, K., Anderson, M.,

    Soderland, L., & Brizee, A. (2010, May 5). General format.

    Retrieved from http://owl.english.purdue.edu/owl/resource/560/01/

**NOTE**: When an Internet document is more than one Web page, provide a URL that links to the home page or entry page for the document. Also, if there isn't a date available for the document use (n.d.) for no date.

# Computer Software/Downloaded Software

Do not cite standard office software (e.g. Word, Excel) or programming languages. Provide references only for specialized software.

Ludwig, T. (2002). PsychInquiry [computer software]. New York:

Worth.


Software that is downloaded from a Web site should provide the software's version and year when available.

Hayes, B., Tesar, B., & Zuraw, K. (2003). OTSoft: Optimality Theory

Software (Version 2.1) [Software]. Available from

http://www.linguistics.ucla.edu/people/hayes/otsoft/


# E-mail

E-mails are not included in the list of references, though you parenthetically cite them in your main text: (E. Robbins, personal communication, January 4, 2001).

# Online Forum or Discussion Board Posting

Include the title of the message, and the URL of the newsgroup or discussion board. Please note that titles for items in online communities (e.g. blogs, newsgroups, forums) are not italicized. If the author's name is not available, provide the screen name. Place identifiers like post or message numbers, if available, in brackets. If available, provide the URL where the message is archived (e.g. "Message posted to..., archived at...").

Frook, B. D. (1999, July 23). New inventions in the cyberworld of

toylandia [Msg 25]. Message posted to

http://groups.earthlink.com/forum/messages/00025.html


# Blog (Weblog) and Video Blog Post

Include the title of the message and the URL. Please note that titles for items in online communities (e.g. blogs, newsgroups, forums) are not italicized. If the author's name is not available, provide the screen name.

J Dean. (2008, May 7). When the self emerges: Is that me in the

mirror? [Web log comment]. Retrieved from

http://www.spring.org.uk/the1sttransport


Psychology Video Blog #3 [Video file]. Retrieved from

http://www.youtube.com/watch?v=1qM90eQi5-M


# Wikis

Please note that the *APA Style Guide to Electronic References* warns writers that wikis (like Wikipedia, for example) are collaborative projects that cannot guarantee the verifiability or expertise of their entries.

OLPC Peru/Arahuay. (n.d.). Retrieved April 29, 2011 from the OLPC

Wiki: http://wiki.laptop. org/go/OLPC_Peru/Arahuay


# Audio Podcast

For all podcasts, provide as much information as possible; not all of the following information will be available. Possible addition identifiers may include Producer, Director, etc.

Bell, T., & Phillips, T. (2008, May 6). A solar flare. *Science @*

*NASA Podcast*. Podcast retrieved from

http://science.nasa.gov/podcast.htm


# Video Podcasts

For all podcasts, provide as much information as possible; not all of the following information will be available. Possible addition identifiers may include Producer, Director, etc.

Scott, D. (Producer). (2007, January 5). The community college

classroom [Episode 7]. *Adventures in Education*. Podcast retrieved

from http://www.adveeducation.com

# chapter 12
# networking
## connecting computing devices

### Networking Fundamentals

*OBJECTIVE:*

What is a network, and what are the advantages/disadvantages of setting up one? *(p. 414)*

### Network Architecture and Components

*OBJECTIVES:*

What is the difference between a client/server network and a peer-to-peer network? *(p. 416)*

What are the main components of every network? *(p. 418)*

 Sound Byte: Installing a Home Computer Network

### Connecting to the Internet

*OBJECTIVE:*

What are my options for connecting to the Internet? *(p. 421)*

 Sound Byte: Connecting to the Internet

 Active Helpdesk: Connecting to the Internet

*Scan here for more info on How Cool Is This?*

### Home Networks

*OBJECTIVES:*

Which type of network is most commonly found in the home? *(p. 425)*

What equipment and software do I need to build a network in my home? *(p. 429)*

### Securing Wireless Networks

*OBJECTIVE:*

Why are wireless networks more vulnerable than wired networks, and what special precautions are required to ensure my wireless network is secure? *(p. 432)*

 Sound Byte: Securing Wireless Networks

 Active Helpdesk: Understanding Networking

### Configuring Software for Your Home Network

*OBJECTIVES:*

Besides computers, what other devices can I connect to a home network? *(p. 438)*

How do I configure the software on my computer and set up other devices to get my network up and running? *(p. 439)*

What problems might I encounter when setting up a wireless network? *(p. 441)*

# how cool is *this?* As you have probably

already experienced, wireless connectivity is not always free. Many businesses, such
as airports, **charge** customers for each device they want to connect, which
can become expensive for groups of friends trying to surf the Internet while waiting
to **catch a flight**. Connectify is free software that takes an existing Internet
connection and turns it into a wireless hotspot. So if you are connected to the Internet
on your Windows notebook or Android phone or tablet, the **Connectify** software
turns your computing device into a wireless hotspot
so that you and your friends can connect other
WiFi-enabled devices such as a phone
or **gaming** system through the
same Internet connection. The
hotspot you create features easy
connectivity and encryption of
data for solid **security**.

© Beboy / Fotolia

## Networking Fundamentals

Now that we are into the second decade of the 21st century, many homes have more than one computing device that is capable of connecting to the Internet. A typical family, like the Jones family (see Figure 12.1), might be engaged in the following: Robert (the father) is watching a movie, which he downloaded yesterday on the large-screen HDTV in the living room while checking his Gmail on his phone. Jennifer (the mother) is in the kitchen fixing lunch while checking

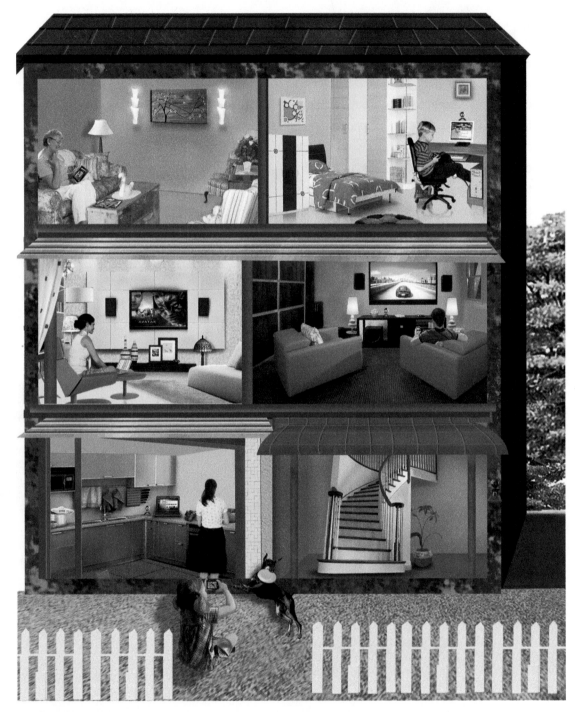

**Figure 12.1**

By setting up a home network, everyone in the family can connect their computing devices whenever and wherever they desire.

the weather forecast and watching YouTube videos. Andy, their nine-year-old son, is in his bedroom playing an online game with his friends (via his PlayStation) and is uploading a video he made for a class project to a Web site at school. Adriana, Andy's older sister, is in the den using her notebook computer to finish a report for school. She's also watching a Blu-ray Disc of *Avatar*, which is one of her all-time favorite movies. Grandma Rita is in the family room using her iPad to view pictures from the family's last vacation and is uploading to Facebook the pictures that she took of her grandchildren during their trip to the amusement park last week. And Andrea, the youngest daughter, is playing with Rojo in the backyard and uploading video that she took of him with her phone so that everyone can see it in the family room while they eat lunch. And because both Robert and Jennifer work outside the home, they use webcams to monitor activities in the house, like ensuring their kids arrive home safely from school while they are at work. What makes all this technology transfer and sharing possible? A home network!

**What is a computer network?** A computer **network** is simply two or more computers that are connected via software and hardware so that they can communicate with each other. You access networks all the time whether you realize it or not. When you use an ATM, get gasoline, or use the Internet (the world's largest network), you are interacting with a network. Each device connected to a network is referred to as a **node**. A node can be a computer, a peripheral (such as an all-in-one printer), a game console, a digital video recorder, or a communications device like a modem.

The main function for most home networks is to facilitate information sharing, but networks provide other benefits.

**What are the benefits of networks?** There are several benefits to having computers networked. Most home users want a network to facilitate resource sharing. For example, a network allows you to share the high-speed Internet connection coming into your home. Networks also allow you to share peripheral devices, such as printers. Figure 12.2a shows two computers that are not networked. The desktop computer is connected to the printer, but the notebook is not. To print files from the notebook, users have to transfer them using a flash drive or another storage medium to the desktop, or they have to disconnect the printer from the desktop and connect it to the notebook. Using a network, a notebook computer and an iPad, as shown in Figure 12.2b, can both print from the printer without transferring files or attaching the printer to

**Figure 12.2**

(a) Computers are not networked, and the notebook cannot access the printer. (b) Networking allows sharing of the printer.

**a**

Inkjet printer

Desktop

Printer cable

Notebook

**b**

iPad

Wireless connection

Inkjet printer

Notebook

a particular device. Using a wired or wireless network to share a printer saves the cost of buying one printer for each computing device.

**Besides peripheral and Internet connections, does networking facilitate any other types of resource sharing?** You can also easily share files between networked computers without having to use portable storage devices such as flash drives to transfer the files. In addition, you can set sharing options in Windows or OS X that allow the user of each computer on the network to access files (such as music or videos) stored on any other computer on the network, as shown in Figure 12.3.

This Windows network has five computers attached to it. ALAN-DESKTOP, ALAN-NOTEBOOK, and PAT-NOTEBOOK are running the Windows operating system. The two MACBOOKs are running OS X. The Public folders enable file sharing because the user of any computer on the network can access the Public folder's contents. And note the final advantage of networking: computers running different operating systems can communicate on the same network.

**Are there disadvantages to setting up a network?** Networks involve the purchase of additional equipment to set them up, so cost is one disadvantage. Also, networks need to be administered, at least to some degree. **Network administration** involves tasks such as: (1) installing new

computers and devices, (2) monitoring the network to ensure it is performing efficiently, (3) updating and installing new software on the network, and (4) configuring, or setting up, proper security for a network. Fortunately, most home networks do not require a great deal of administration after their initial configuration, and the benefits of using a network usually outweigh the disadvantages.

Now that you know the advantages of setting up a network, in the next two sections we'll explore the basic design and components of simple networks.

# Network Architectures

The term **network architecture** refers to the design of a network. Network architectures are classified according to the way in which they are controlled and the distance between their nodes.

## Describing Networks Based on Network Administration

**What different types of control do I have over my network?** A network can be administered, or managed, in either of two main ways: locally or centrally. Local administration means that the configuration and maintenance of the network must be performed on each individual computer attached to the network. A peer-to-peer network is the most common example of a locally administered network. Central administration means that tasks can be performed from one computer and affect the other computers on the network. The most common type of centrally administered network is a client/server network.

**What is a peer-to-peer network?** In a **peer-to-peer (P2P) network**, each node connected to the network can communicate directly with every other node on the network. Thus, all nodes on this type of network are peers (equals). When printing, for example, a computer on a P2P network doesn't have to go through the computer that's connected to the printer. Instead, it can communicate directly with the printer. Figure 12.2b, shown earlier, shows a very small peer-to-peer network. Because they are simple to set up, P2P networks are the most common type of

**Figure** 12.3

Windows Explorer showing five networked computers set up for sharing.

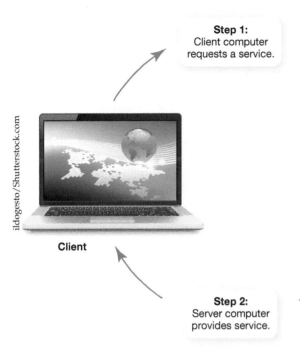

**Step 1:**
Client computer requests a service.

**Client**

**Step 2:**
Server computer provides service.

**Server**

## Figure 12.4

In a client/server network, a computer acts either as a client making requests for resources or as a server providing resources.

home network. Very small schools and offices may also use P2P networks. However, most networks that have 10 or more nodes are client/server networks.

### What are client/server networks?

A **client/server network** contains two different types of computers: clients and servers. A **client** is a computer on which users accomplish specific tasks (such as construct spreadsheets) and make specific requests (such as printing a file). The **server** is the computer that provides information or resources to the client computers on the network. The server on a client/server network also provides central administration for network functions such as printing. Figure 12.4 illustrates a client/server network in action.

As you learned in Chapter 10, the Internet is an example of a

## Figure 12.5

At only 8 inches high, the Acer Aspire easyStore server can perform a variety of tasks to simplify media management on a home network.

client/server network. When your computer is connected to the Internet, it is functioning as a client computer. When it accesses the Internet, your computer connects to a server computer maintained by your Internet service provider (the company that sells you Internet access). The server "serves up" resources to your computer so that you can interact with the Internet.

### Are client/server networks ever used as home networks?

Although client/server networks can be configured for home use, P2P networks are more often used in the home because they cost less than client/server networks and are easier to configure and maintain. However, specialized types of servers, such as servers for sharing files, are now appearing on P2P networks in the home.

Nowadays, people are accumulating vast numbers of media files from digital cameras, video downloads, and music downloads. Because users often want to share this media, specialized home network servers such as the Acer Aspire easyStore server featuring Windows Home Server are now available for home networks (see Figure 12.5). A **home network server** is designed to store media, share media across the network, and back up files on computers connected to the network. All computers connected to the network can access the server.

Even though a server may now be attached to a home network, that does not change the architecture of a home network from a P2P network to a client/server network. Except for the specialized functions of the home network server, all network administration tasks (such as installation of software and changing of configuration settings) must still be performed locally, and all the nodes on the network are still peers to each other.

### Describing Networks Based on Distance

**How does the distance between nodes define a network?** The distance between nodes on a network is another way to describe a network. A **home area network (HAN)** is a network located in a home. HANs are used to connect all of a home's digital devices, such as computers, peripherals, phones, gaming devices, digital video recorders (DVRs), and televisions. A **local area network (LAN)** is a network in which the nodes are located within a small geographic area. Examples include a network in a computer lab at school or at a fast-food restaurant.

**Is it possible to connect LANs?** A **wide area network (WAN)** is made up of LANs connected over long distances. Say a school has two campuses (east and west) located in different towns. Connecting the LAN at the east campus to the LAN at the west campus by telecommunications lines would allow the users on the two LANs to communicate. The two LANs would be described as a single WAN.

**Are wireless networks that cover large areas like cities considered WANs?** Technically, wireless networks like the one deployed in Minneapolis, which provides Internet access to city residents and visitors, are WANs. However, when a network is designed to provide access to a specific geographic area, such as an entire city, the network is usually called a **metropolitan area network (MAN)**. Many cities in the United States are now deploying MANs to provide Internet access to residents and provide convenience for tourists.

## Network Components

To function, all networks must include (1) a means of connecting the nodes on the network (cables or wireless technology), (2) special devices that allow the nodes to communicate with each other and to send data, and (3) software that allows the network to run. We discuss each of these components in this section (see Figure 12.6).

**Figure** 12.6

Network components.

Network adapter inside each node

Computer

Radio waves

Router

Printer

Network navigation device (used in some networks)

Transmission media (wireless or wired) connecting nodes

Networking software running on each computing device

iPad

## Transmission Media

**How are nodes on a network connected?** All network nodes are connected to each other and to the network by transmission media. **Transmission media** establish a communications channel between the nodes on a network and can be either wireless or wired.

Wireless networks use radio waves to connect nodes. With the proliferation of portable devices being connected to home networks, a network with wireless connectivity is required in most homes.

Wired networks use various types of cable (wire) to connect nodes. **Twisted-pair cable** is made up of copper wires that are twisted around each other and surrounded by a plastic jacket. Normal telephone cable is a type of twisted-pair cable, although phone cable won't work for connecting a home network; a slightly different type of twisted-pair cable is used. **Coaxial cable** (Figure 12.7a) consists of a single copper wire surrounded by layers of plastic. If you have cable TV, the cable running into your TV or cable box is most likely coaxial cable. **Fiber-optic cable** (Figure 12.7b) is made up of plastic or glass fibers that transmit data at extremely fast speeds.

**Does it matter what type of media you use to transfer data?** The media you choose depend on the requirements of a network's users. Using wireless media is critical when portable computing devices need to be connected to a network. However, higher speed connections than can be achieved by wireless connectivity are required for certain types of network activities, such as downloading large movie files. Different types of transmission media transmit data at different speeds.

**Data transfer rate** (also called **bandwidth**) is the maximum speed at which data can be transmitted between two nodes on a network. **Throughput** is the actual speed of data transfer that is achieved. Throughput is

### Figure 12.7

(a) Coaxial cable uses a copper core, whereas (b) fiber optic cable uses plastic or glass fibers.

always less than or equal to the data transfer rate. Data transfer rate and throughput are usually measured in megabits per second (Mbps). A megabit is 1 million bits. Twisted-pair cable, coaxial cable, and wireless media usually provide enough bandwidth for most home networks.

## Network Adapters

**How do the different nodes on the network communicate?** **Network adapters** are devices installed in network nodes that enable the nodes to communicate with each other and to access the network. All desktop and notebook computers (and many peripherals) sold today contain network adapters installed *inside* the device. This type of adapter is referred to as a **network interface card (NIC)**. Different NICs are designed to use different types of transmission media. Most NICs included in computing devices today are built to use wireless media, but many can use wired media as well. Your notebook computer most likely has a wireless NIC in it that allows you to connect to wireless networks at home, school, or the coffee shop. But most notebooks also have a port that accommodates cable for a wired connection to a network.

**Why would I ever consider using a wired connection with my notebook computer?** Wired connections can sometimes provide greater throughput than current high-speed wireless networks.

## Sharing Your Internet Connection with Your Neighbors: Legal? Ethical? Safe?

With the advances in wireless equipment, signals can travel well beyond the walls of your home. This makes it possible in an apartment or single family home (where homes are close together) for a group of neighbors to share a wireless signal and potentially save money by splitting the cost of one Internet connection among them. However, before jumping into this venture, you need to weigh a few issues carefully.

You probably aren't legally prohibited from sharing an Internet connection, but you should check on the state and local laws. Most laws are designed to prohibit piggybacking, which is using a network without the network owner's consent. However, if you are giving neighbors permission to share your connection, you probably don't violate any piggybacking laws.

Of course, your ISP might not permit you to share your Internet access with anyone. You probably have a personal account that is designed for one household. The terms of your agreement with the Internet service provider might prohibit you from sharing your connection with people outside your household. If you aren't allowed to share the type of account you have now, your ISP probably offers a type of account (such as a small business account) that will allow you to share a connection, but it will most likely be more expensive. The ISPs know that the more people that share an account, the more likely that account is to use bandwidth; so they price their accounts accordingly. You might be able to share a personal account without being detected by your ISP, but that certainly would be unethical because you should be paying for a higher level of access. Therefore, make sure to check with your ISP to determine that you have the right type of account.

The next thing you need to consider is whether the shared access should be open to all neighbors, or just to the neighbors that are contributing to the cost of the Internet connection. You could leave the connection open, like the connections at your local coffee shop, and let anyone who finds it log on and surf. You might consider this a very ethical action, because you are providing free Internet access for anyone who needs it. You could register your free hotspot with a service like JiWire (**www.jiwire .com**), and then people would be able to find it (see Figure 12.8). However, your neighbors who are helping pay the cost might have a different viewpoint and not want to fund free surfing for everyone. Make sure you work this out before proceeding.

If you are going to host a free and open hotspot, you still need to make sure that you set it up safely. You want to maintain a secure network for you and your neighbors while still allowing the occasional visiting surfer to use the connection. There are WiFi sharing services such as Fon (**www.fon.com**) or Chillifire (**www.chillifire.net**) that can provide you with special hardware or software that allows you to configure your hotspot so your network remains secure.

While offering free access to anyone will earn you lots of good karma, additional risks exist because you don't know what mischief or criminal activities someone might engage in while connected to the Internet through your account. Think very carefully before you proceed down the sharing path, and make sure you set your hotspot up to protect your internal network.

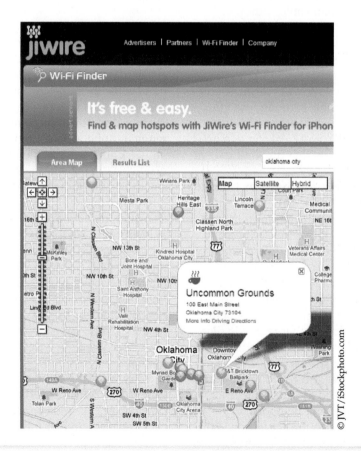

**Figure 12.8**

At JiWire, you can search and find free hotspots.

Some common reasons why wireless signals may have decreased throughput include:

- Wireless signals are more susceptible to interference from magnetic and electrical sources.
- Other wireless networks (such as your neighbor's network) can interfere with the signals on your network.
- Certain building materials (such as concrete and cinderblock) and metal (a refrigerator) can decrease throughput.
- Throughput varies depending on the distance from your networking equipment.

Wireless networks usually use specially coded signals to protect their data whereas wired connections don't protect their signals. This process of coding signals can slightly decrease throughput, although once coded, data travels at usual speeds.

Therefore, in situations where you want to achieve the highest possible throughput (transferring a large video), you may want to connect your notebook or other portable device to your home network using a wire temporarily. We'll discuss this type of connection in more depth when we talk about home Ethernet networks later in this chapter.

### Network Navigation Devices

**How is data sent through a network?** Network navigation devices facilitate and control the flow of data through a network. Data is sent over transmission media in bundles. Each bundle is called a **packet**. For computers to communicate, these packets of data must be able to flow between network nodes. Network navigation devices, which are themselves nodes on a network, enable the transmission of data between other nodes on the network that contain NICs.

**What network navigation devices will I use on my home network?** The two most common navigation devices are routers and switches. A **router** transfers packets of data between two or more networks. For example, if a home network is connected to the Internet, a router is required to send data between the two networks: the home network and the Internet. A **switch** is a "traffic cop" on a network. Switches receive data packets and send them to their intended nodes on the same network (not between different networks). All routers sold for home use have switches integrated into them.

**SOUND BYTE** Installing a Home Computer Network

Installing a network is relatively easy if you've seen someone else do it. In this Sound Byte, you'll learn how to install the hardware and configure Windows for a wired or wireless home network.

We discuss routers for home networks in more detail later in the chapter.

### Networking Software

**What software do home networks require?** Home networks need operating system (OS) software that supports P2P networking. The Windows, OS X, and Linux operating systems all support P2P networking. You can connect computers running any of these OSs to the same home network. We also cover configuring software for home networks later in the chapter.

**Is the same software used in client/server networks?** Client/server networks are controlled by centralized servers that have specialized **network operating system (NOS)** software installed on them. This software handles requests for information, Internet access, and the use of peripherals for the rest of the network nodes. As opposed to P2P networks, the nodes on a client/server network do not communicate directly with each other but communicate through a server. Communicating through a server is more efficient in a network with a large number of nodes, but requires more complex NOS software than is necessary for P2P networks. Examples of NOS software include Windows Server and SUSE Linux Enterprise Server.

Before considering the components you need to create a home network, you should consider your method of Internet access.

## Connecting to the Internet

One of the main reasons for setting up a home network is to share an Internet connection. You need to purchase Internet access from companies that specialize in providing this service known as **Internet service providers (or ISPs)**. ISPs may be specialized providers, like Juno, or companies that provide other services, such as phone and cable television, in addition to Internet access. You have two main choices for connections to the Internet: broadband or dial-up. Broadband uses high-speed data access whereas dial-up uses conventional phone lines and technology. Because of the higher speeds offered by broadband, over two-thirds of U.S. Internet users have broadband connections in their home. Although not completely obsolete, dial-up is fast becoming a legacy technology.

### Broadband Connections

**What is broadband?** Broadband, often referred to as "high-speed Internet," refers to a type of connection that offers a faster means to connect to the Internet. Broadband usually has a data transmission rate of 5 Mbps (megabits per second) or greater. This high rate of access is in contrast to dial-up Internet access, which has a maximum transmission speed of 56 Kbps (kilobits per second).

**What types of broadband are available?** The standard broadband technologies in most areas are **digital subscriber line (DSL)**, which uses the same types of wiring used in standard phone lines to connect your computer to the Internet, and cable, which uses cable from your television's cable service provider to connect to the Internet. **Fiber-optic service**, which uses plastic or glass cables to transfer data at the speed of light, has in the past few years become widely available as a broadband service to the home. Satellite broadband is mostly used in rural or mountain areas that cannot get DSL, cable, or fiber-optic service.

**How does cable Internet access work?** A cable Internet connection uses the same coaxial cable used by cable TV; however, cable TV and cable Internet are separate services. Cable TV is a one-way service in which the cable company feeds programming signals to your television. To bring two-way Internet connections to homes, cable companies had to upgrade

**SOUND BYTE** — Connecting to the Internet

In this Sound Byte, you'll learn the basics of connecting to the Internet from home, including useful information on the various types of Internet connections and selecting the right ISP.

**ACTIVE HELP-DESK** — Connecting to the Internet

In this Active Helpdesk call, you'll play the role of a helpdesk staffer. You will field calls about various options for connecting to the Internet and how to choose an Internet service provider.

their networks with two-way data transmission capabilities.

**How does DSL work?** Similar to a dial-up connection, DSL uses telephone lines to connect to the Internet. However, unlike dial-up, DSL allows phone and data transmission to share the same line, thus eliminating the need for an additional phone line. Phone lines are made of pairs of twisted copper wires known as twisted-pair wiring. The bandwidth of the copper wires is split into three sections, similar to a three-lane highway on which only one lane is used to carry voice data. DSL uses the remaining two lanes to send and receive data separately at much higher frequencies. Thus, although it uses a standard phone line, a DSL connection is much faster than a dial-up connection.

**Can anyone with a phone line have DSL?** Having a traditional phone line in your house doesn't mean that you have access to DSL service. Your local phone company must have special DSL technology to offer you the service. Although many phone companies offer DSL technology, many rural areas in the United States still do not have DSL service available.

**What are the limitations of DSL and cable?** Although cable and DSL speeds are about the same, each has its own particular limitations. DSL signals are sensitive to distance. There is a maximum distance of about 3 miles between where the signal originates, called the central office, and the customer's location. The further the connection is from the central office, the weaker the signal is. Although cable is not limited by distance like DSL, cable services are shared between users, so in peak usage times, cable connection speeds can slow down.

**How does fiber-optic service work?** Fiber-optic service uses fiber-optic lines, which are strands of optically pure glass or plastic that are as thin as a human hair. They are arranged in bundles called optical cables and transmit data via light signals over long distances. Because light travels so quickly, this technology can bring an enormous amount of data to your home at superfast speeds. When the data reaches your house, it's converted to electrical pulses that transmit digital signals your computer can "read." Fiber-optic service uses fiber-optic cable to run very fast data connections directly to your home, although fiber-optic cable is not usually run inside the home. On a fiber-optic network, twisted-pair or coaxial cable is still used inside the home to transport the network signals.

**What special equipment do I need to hook up to broadband?** A broadband Internet connection requires a modem. Depending on the type of broadband service you have, you will have either a cable modem or DSL modem. The modem works to translate the broadband signal into digital data and back again. With both cable and DSL services, the modem allows the data to travel on the unused capacity of the transmission medium. Often the ISP will rent the appropriate modem to the customer or specify what type of modem the customer must buy to work properly with the ISP's technology.

For example, a DSL modem separates voice signals from data signals so that they can travel in the right "lane" on the twisted-pair wiring. Voice data travels at a slower speed than digital data, which can travel at rates ranging from 500 Kbps to 6,000 Kbps [6 megabits per second (Mbps)].

As mentioned earlier, sharing your Internet connection with more than one computer requires a router. Your modem is usually located very near the router because the router must be plugged into the modem. Some ISPs provide combination modems and routers so you may only have one device in your home that serves both functions.

**What options exist when cable and DSL are not available?** Satellite Internet is another way to connect to the Internet. Most people choose satellite Internet when other high-speed options are unavailable. To take advantage of satellite Internet, you need a satellite dish (see Figure 12.9), which is placed outside your home and connected to your computer with coaxial cable, the same type of cable used for cable TV. Data from your computer is transmitted between your

personal satellite dish and the satellite company's receiving satellite dish by a satellite that sits in a geosynchronous orbit thousands of miles above the Earth.

**How does one access the Internet wirelessly?** To access the Internet wirelessly, you need to be in a **wireless fidelity (WiFi)** hotspot and have the right equipment on your mobile device. WiFi is a standard for wireless transmissions using radio waves that is used to connect computing devices to wireless networks and the Internet. Virtually all notebooks, smartphones, game systems, and personal media players sold today come with wireless capability built in. For your own personal WiFi, it's simple to set up wireless capability on your home network by using a router that features wireless capabilities. When you are away from home, you have two main choices for connecting to the Internet: use a WiFi hotspot or sign up for 3G or 4G Internet access with a cell phone provider.

**How can I access the Internet via a WiFi hotspot?** Many businesses and schools, as well as public places such as airports, libraries, bookstores, and restaurants, offer WiFi connections known as hotspots. Some public places offer free WiFi access, but others require you to buy wireless access through a wireless access service plan.

Ilene MacDonald / Alamy

**Figure** 12.9

ISPs that offer satellite Internet provide service even in remote areas.

To access pay WiFi services, you can pay for a single session or a monthly membership, or you can sign up for a longer-term subscription in which you receive monthly bills. Wi-Fi-FreeSpot (**www.wififreespot.com**) and WiFi HotSpot List (**www.wifihotspotlist.com**) will help you locate a free hotspot wherever you are planning to go.

In some cities and towns, local governments are installing municipal WiFi networks. The newest wireless access technology to be deployed for mobile and stationary broadband access is WiMAX. WiMAX is designed to extend local WiFi networks across greater distances, such as across a large college campus. Mobile WiMAX is an alternative to cellular transmission of voice and high-speed data. Even wireless in-flight Internet service is available! Gogo (**www.gogoinflight.com**) is a wireless broadband network that provides coverage on participating airlines across the continental United States, so when you are cleared to use your portable electronic devices, you can comfortably access wireless Internet from 35,000 feet.

**What is 3G and 4G access and how does it work?** 3G and 4G refer to the third and fourth generations, respectively, of cellular telephone networks. 4G is the latest service standard and offers the fastest data access speeds over cellular telephone networks. However, 3G and 4G data access is not just for phones any longer. Many devices such as iPads, Chromebooks, and notebook computers now are available with 3G or 4G capabilities built in. To utilize the 3G or 4G capabilities of a mobile device, you need to sign up for an access plan with a mobile data provider such as Verizon or AT&T.

If your computer does not have built-in 3G or 4G equipment, you can purchase a wireless data card, such as the ones shown in Figure 12.10. Wireless data cards, sometimes referred to as cellular modems, are devices that fit into either a USB port or a special slot on the side of a notebook called an Express card slot (also known as a PC card slot). The wireless data card enables users to access 3G or 4G networks. They also require a service plan.

### Dial-Up Connections

**Why would I ever want to consider a dial-up connection to the Internet?** About seventy percent of Internet users in the United States use high-speed Internet connections such as DSL, cable, or fiber-optic. But many people still use dial-up connections through conventional phone lines. The two main reasons people choose dial-up are the unavailability of high-speed service in their area (usually rural areas) or to save money. A dial-up connection is the least costly way to connect to the Internet.

**How does a dial-up connection work?** A dial-up connection needs only a standard phone line and a modem. The word modem is short for modulator/demodulator. A dial-up modem is a device that converts (modulates) the digital signals the computer understands into analog signals that can travel over phone lines. The computer on the other end also must have a modem to translate (demodulate) the received analog signal back to a digital signal that the receiving computer can understand. Many computers still come with internal modems built into the system unit, although some manufacturers have ceased including them as standard equipment.

**What are the disadvantages of dial-up?** The major downside to dial-up is speed. Dial-up modems transfer data at a much slower rate than that of a basic broadband connection. Also, when you're on the Internet using a dial-up connection, you

Sierra Wireless for the AirCard images.

**Figure 12.10**

Wireless data cards add 3G or 4G functionality to computing devices that don't have the capability built in.

**Figure 12.11** COMPARING DSL, CABLE, AND FIBER-OPTIC INTERNET CONNECTION OPTIONS.

| Network | DSL | Cable | Fiber-Optic |
|---|---|---|---|
| Maximum download speeds | Average speeds of 3.5 Mbps, with a maximum of 12 Mbps | Average speeds of 10 Mbps, with a maximum of 30 Mbps | Average speeds of 20 Mbps, with a maximum of 50 Mbps. |
| Pros | Lets you surf the Net and talk on the same phone line simultaneously. | Speeds are not dependent on distance from central office. | Increased speeds. Service is not shared or dependent on distance from central office. |
| Cons | Speed drops as you get farther from phone company's central office. Not every phone line will work. | Line is shared with others in neighborhood; speeds may vary due to peak and nonpeak usage. May require professional installation if cable not already present. | Cost. Although this is a diminishing concern as the technology continues to be deployed and accepted. Not available in all areas. |

*Note:* The data transfer rates listed in this table are approximations. As technologies improve, so do data transfer rates.

tie up your phone line if you don't have a separate line.

### Choosing the Right Internet Connection Option

**How do I choose which Internet connection option is best for me?** According to Internet World Stats, more than 77 percent of U.S. residents use the Internet. However, in 2011, the Federal Communications Commission reported that almost 100 million Americans either lack Internet access or only have access to dial-up services. Depending on the area in which you live, you might not have a choice as to the type of broadband connection that is available. Check with your local cable TV provider, phone company, and satellite TV provider(s) to determine what broadband options are available where you live and what the transfer rates are in your area.

Often the most difficult decision in choosing Internet service is choosing between high-speed plans offered by the same company. For instance, at the time of printing, Verizon offered three different fiber-optic plans that featured download speeds of either 15, 25, or 50 Mbps. While 15 Mbps is fine for streaming video, it may not be quite fast enough for streaming HD movies, especially if there are two people in the household streaming movies at the same time. Families with multiple users, especially serious gamers and children who are downloading streaming media at the same time, might very well need the 50 Mbps service. Consulting with friends and neighbors about the plan they have and whether it is meeting their needs can help you decide on the right plan for your household.

Finally, you may also need to consider which other services you want bundled into your payment, such as phone or TV. The table in Figure 12.11 compares several features of DSL, cable, and fiber-optic service to help you with your decision.

# Home Networks

Now that you understand the basic components of a home network and have selected an Internet service provider, you are probably wondering where to start on installing your home network. In the following sections, we'll discuss the most common types of networks found in the home and how to get the fastest data transfer rates from your home network. We'll also explore the various types of cabling used in wired networks.

### Ethernet Home Networks

**What type of peer-to-peer network should I install in my home?** The vast majority of home networks are Ethernet networks. An **Ethernet network** is so named because it uses the Ethernet protocol as the means (or standard) by which the nodes on the network communicate. The Ethernet protocol was developed by the Institute of Electrical and Electronics Engineers (IEEE). This nonprofit group develops many standard specifications for electronic data transmission that are adopted throughout the world. Each standard the IEEE develops is numbered, with 802.11 (wireless) and 802.3 (wired) being the standards for Ethernet networks. The Ethernet protocol makes Ethernet networks extremely efficient at moving data.

### What is the current wireless standard for Ethernet networks?

The current standard that governs wireless networking for Ethernet networks is the 802.11n standard, which was ratified in 2009. Establishing standards for networking is important so that devices from different manufacturers will work well together. The 802.11 standard is also known as WiFi. Four standards are currently defined under the 802.11 WiFi standard: 802.11a, 802.11b, 802.11g, and 802.11n. Since 802.11n features the fastest data transfer rates, it is now the most desirable choice for home networks. Devices using older standards, such as 802.11g, will still work with 802.11n networks, but they will operate with slower data transfer rates. This accommodation of current devices being able to use previously issued standards in addition to the current standards is known as **backward compatibility**.

### How do 802.11n wireless devices work?

Wireless routers and network adapters contain transceivers. A **transceiver** is a device that translates the electronic data that needs to be sent along the network into radio waves and then broadcasts these radio waves to other network nodes. Transceivers serve a dual function because they also receive the signals from other network nodes. Devices that use the 802.11n standard achieve higher throughput by using a technology known as Multiple Input Multiple Output (MIMO).

Devices using wireless standards developed prior to the 802.11n standard only utilized one antenna for transmitting and receiving data. Devices that use **Multiple Input Multiple Output (MIMO)** technology are designed to use multiple antennas for transmitting and receiving data. The multiple antennas break the data into multiple data streams and allow for faster transmission of the data. Thus, 802.11n devices can achieve throughput of 300 Mbps or higher under ideal conditions. But as mentioned previously, many factors can reduce the throughput of a wireless connection.

### How can I tell how fast the wireless connection to my network is on my computer?

You can install various utilities, such as Net Meter (available at **www.download.com**), on your computer that will measure your throughput. Net Meter (see Figure 12.13) shows you the throughput you are achieving on your computer's wireless connection to your network over a period of time. Hopefully, you'll achieve throughput in the range of 50 to 200 Mbps on your wireless network, which should be sufficient for most applications (even watching video). However, if you don't achieve acceptable throughput, you might want to consider a wired Ethernet connection.

### Is there any advantage to a wired connection?

Up to one gigabit per second (1,000 Mbps) of throughput is possible using the **gigabit Ethernet** standard, which is the most commonly used wired Ethernet standard deployed in devices designed for home networks. Computers generally ship with gigabit Ethernet cards installed in them. For even faster data transfer speeds, 10 gigabit

## Wake Up Your Computer Remotely

Having your computer on a home network with a shared Internet connection makes it possible to access your computer and its files even when you aren't at home. But if your computer is asleep, you need some way to "wake it up." Otherwise, you can't access it through the Internet. Fortunately for Mac users, there is an application called iNet WOL (Wake on LAN) designed to do this (see Figure 12.12). iNet WOL is compatible with the iPhone, iPod Touch, and iPad. The application allows you to use your portable device to wake up your computer via the Internet. Once your computer is awake, you can then use your remote access software to access it. Think of iNet WOL as an alarm clock for your computer.

**Figure 12.12**

The application iNet WOL (Wake on LAN) lets you use your iPhone, iPod Touch, or iPad to wake up your computer from a remote location.

**Figure 12.13**

Net Meter shows this computer is achieving a rather slow maximum connection of 1.65 Mbps on a shared wireless network at a hotel.

Ethernet is available, which provides a maximum throughput of 10 gigabits per second (Gbps). But 10 gigabit networks are primarily used in businesses with large data throughput needs. For gaming and streaming HD movies, gigabit Ethernet meets the needs of most home network users.

### Home Network Cabling

**What type of cable do I need to connect to a wired Ethernet network?** The most popular transmission media option for wired Ethernet networks is **unshielded twisted-pair (UTP) cable**. UTP cable is composed of four pairs of wires that are twisted around each other to reduce electrical interference. You can buy UTP cable in varying lengths with RJ-45 connectors (Ethernet connectors) already attached. RJ-45 connectors resemble standard phone connectors (called RJ-11 connectors) but are slightly larger and have contacts for eight wires (four pairs) instead of four wires (see Figure 12.14). You must use UTP cable with RJ-45 connectors on an Ethernet network because a phone cable will not work.

**Do all wired Ethernet networks use the same kind of UTP cable?** Figure 12.15 lists the three main types of UTP cable you would consider using in home-wired Ethernet networks—Cat 5E, Cat 6, and Cat 6a—and their data transfer rates. Although Cat 5E cable is the cheapest and is sufficient for many home networking tasks, it was designed for 100 Mbps wired Ethernet networks that were popular before gigabit Ethernet networks became the standard for home networking. Therefore,

you should probably not install Cat 5E cable even though it is still available in stores. Since **Cat 6 cable** is designed to achieve data transfer rates that support a gigabit Ethernet network, it is probably the best choice for home networking cable. Cat 6a cable is designed for Ultra-Fast Ethernet networks that run at speeds as fast as 10 Gbps. Installing a 10 gigabit Ethernet network in the home is probably unnecessary because today's home applications (even gaming and streaming media) don't require this rate of data transfer.

---

**BITS AND BYTES**

### Blazingly Fast Wireless Connections on the Horizon

Although most people want wireless connectivity throughout their home, wired connections still provide the best throughput. But the next generation of wireless standards, called WiGig and WirelessHD, are currently under development. These standards will be designed to provide between 7 and 25 Gbps of throughput. This speed will blow away current WiFi standards (which have a current theoretical maximum transfer rate of 600 Mbps) and wired gigabit connectivity. Whereas WiFi currently operates in the 5 GHz and 2.4 GHz bands, WiGig and WirelessHD will operate in the 60 GHz band, which is currently unlicensed by the FCC. This should prevent many of the interference issues that WiFi users currently experience. But don't start looking in the stores for this equipment just yet; we are still a few years away from devices using these standards.

**Figure 12.14**

(a) An RJ-45 (Ethernet) connector, which is used on UTP cables; and (b) a typical RJ-11 connector, which is used on standard phone cords.

**Figure** 12.15

Data transfer rates for popular home network cable types.

**Figure** 12.16

Wired and wireless connections using the same router.

Fortunately, you don't have to choose between a wired or a wireless network. Ethernet networks can handle your wired and wireless needs on the same network. This gives you the best of both worlds: portability and high throughput.

### Wired and Wireless on One Network

**Can I have wired and wireless nodes on one Ethernet network?** Yes, one Ethernet network can support nodes with

both wireless and wired connections. Most people will want to connect portable devices that are constantly being moved around the home wirelessly to their network. However, many of the devices that are connected to a network, such as televisions, DVRs, and game consoles, usually stay in one location. Although these devices probably feature wireless connectivity also, it may be desirable to hook them up to wired connections to take advantage of faster throughput achieved by wired connectivity. Routers sold for home networks facilitate wired and wireless connections. Figure 12.16 shows a router network listing with wired (desktop computer) and wireless devices (TiVo DVR and notebook) connected in a home network.

**Are there other types of P2P networks that can be installed in the home?** Non-Ethernet networks in the home are extremely rare. Because Ethernet networks (1) are based on a well-established standard, (2) feature easy setup, (3) provide good throughput for home networking needs, and (4) are cost effective, manufacturers of home networking equipment have overwhelmingly embraced Ethernet networks.

---

**My Network**                                                                                    **Connected Devices**

 **Alan-Notebook:**

| | | | Ethernet: 1 device(s) |
| Connection Type: | (((•))) | Wireless |
| IP Address: | 192.168.1.2 | | Coax: 0 device(s) |
| IP Address Allocation: | DHCP | |
| MAC Address: | 00:19:d2:28:21:ad | | (((•))) Wireless: 2 device(s) |

- Access Shared Files
- Website Blocking
- Block Internet Services
- Port Forwarding
- View Device Details
- Rename this Device

 **Alan-Desktop:**

| Connection Type: | ⊞ Ethernet |
| IP Address: | 192.168.1.3 |
| IP Address Allocation: | DHCP |
| MAC Address: | 00:25:11:09:99:cd |

- Access Shared Files
- Website Blocking
- Block Internet Services
- Port Forwarding
- View Device Details
- Rename this Device

**TIVO-6520201806A6969:**

| Connection Type: | (((•))) Wireless |
| IP Address: | 192.168.1.7 |
| IP Address Allocation: | DHCP |
| MAC Address: | 00:11:d9:00:f6:dd |

- Access Shared Files
- Website Blocking
- Block Internet Services
- Port Forwarding
- View Device Details

**Does the type of operating system I'm using affect my choice of a home networking standard?** Windows, OS X, and Linux all have built-in P2P networking software that will support connection to an Ethernet network. Therefore, an Ethernet network is appropriate for all computers using these three operating systems.

## Configuring Home Network Equipment

By now you should have enough information to decide what nodes on your network need to be connected wirelessly and which devices would benefit from wired connections. In this section, we'll explore the various types of equipment that you need to obtain to configure your home network. And we'll explore what devices your nodes need to contain to enable them to connect to your network.

### Routers and Switches: Moving Data Around Your Network

**What equipment do I need for a home Ethernet network?** Ethernet networks need network navigation devices to make them work; therefore, the first piece of equipment to consider is a router. Recall that routers are designed to transfer packets of data between two (or more) networks—in this case, your home network and the Internet. A router is essential on a home network to allow sharing of an Internet connection. For an Ethernet network to function properly, data must also be transmitted efficiently around the network. As you know, a switch is the device that is used on

Ethernet networks to route the data between nodes on the same network.

Because both a router and a switch are needed on home Ethernet networks, the manufacturers of home networking equipment make devices that are a combination of routers and switches. In most instances, these devices are called routers or broadband routers. But despite the name, these devices do include integrated switches. Although manufacturers do make routers with only wired capabilities, for the vast majority of home networks, people buy routers with wireless capabilities. When you examine a Windows 7 network with a router that includes an integrated switch, it can appear as two different devices (see Figure 12.17) even though there is only one device. On this home network, named GMVO5, the desktop computer is connected to the router with a cable. The two notebook computers are attached wirelessly to the router. The switch is contained within the router, even though the Windows network map shows them as two separate devices.

**What do switches do on an Ethernet network?** Data is transmitted through the transmission medium of an Ethernet network in packets. Imagine the data packets on an Ethernet network as cars on a road. If there were no traffic signals or rules of the road (such as stopping at a red light and proceeding on a green light), we'd see a lot more collisions between vehicles, and people wouldn't get where they were going as readily. Data packets can also suffer collisions. If data packets collide, the data in them is damaged or lost. In either case, the network doesn't function efficiently.

ALAN-DESKTOP

Pat-Notebook

Alan-Notebook

Switch

GMVO5

Wired/wireless router (on network named GMVO5)

Gateway

**Figure** 12.17
Windows network map showing three computers connected to an integrated router/switch.

As shown in Figure 12.18, a switch in an Ethernet network acts like a traffic signal (or a traffic cop) by enforcing the rules of the data road on the transmission media. The switch keeps track of the data packets and, in conjunction with network interface cards, helps the data packets find their destinations without running into each other. The switch also keeps track of all the nodes on the network and sends the data packets directly to the node for which they are headed. This keeps the network running efficiently.

**Figure 12.18**

A simplified explanation is that switches (working in conjunction with NICs) act like traffic signals or traffic cops. They enforce the rules of the data road on an Ethernet network and help prevent data packets from crashing into each other.

**Does my wireless router support wired connections?** Most home wireless routers have three or four Ethernet ports on the back of the router to support wired connections via twisted-pair cable (see Figure 12.19). If you have a lot of devices (such as a game console, HDTV, and a notebook) in your home that may be used simultaneously, you might want to consider connecting some of them via a wired connection to increase allocated bandwidth to each wireless device. This will help increase the throughput to each wireless device.

If you find that you need additional ports for plugging in wired connections to your network, you can buy a standalone switch and plug that into one of the ports on your router. This will give you additional ports for making wired connections to your network. Do not mistakenly buy another router with an embedded switch and try adding that to your network, because the two routers will cause conflicts as they fight for control over network navigation.

**Where do I obtain a router for my home network?** You can purchase a router at any electronics store (such as Best Buy) or online stores (such as **www.tigerdirect.com** or **www.newegg.com**) that carry home networking equipment. Also, since networks are so common in homes now, many ISPs offer home subscribers a device that combines a broadband modem and a wireless router. ISPs typically charge either a one-time or a monthly fee for this combination device. If you already have broadband access in your home, you at least have a modem. Check with your ISP if you are not sure whether you also already have a device that contains a router.

**How do I know which type of wireless networking my router supports?** If you do have a router provided by your ISP, make sure to ask what

Switch

Data packet 2

Data packet 3

Data packet 1

Data packet 4

ETHERNET MEDIA

ETHERNET MEDIA

bedo/iStockphoto.com

**Figure 12.19**

Rear view of typical wireless/wired router.

wireless networking standard the router supports. If it supports a standard older than 802.11n, you should consider having your ISP provide you with a new router. You want to have a router that supports the fastest wireless networking standard (802.11n) so that you can achieve the highest possible throughput on your wireless nodes. If all of your wireless devices have 802.11n network adapters, but your router only supports 802.11g, you will not achieve the best throughput available to you because 802.11g devices feature much slower transfer rates than 802.11n devices (about four to six times slower).

### Connecting Devices to Routers

**How many computers and other devices can be connected to a router in a home network?** Most home wireless routers can support up to 253 wireless connections at the same time. This number is a theoretical maximum, however—most home networks probably have fewer than ten wireless devices connected to the network. But regardless of how few or how many devices your home network has, those wireless devices share bandwidth when they are connected to a router. Therefore, the more devices actively transmitting data that you connect to a single router, the smaller the portion of the router's bandwidth each device receives.

To look at this another way, consider you have a pizza that represents your router's bandwidth. You can cut the pizza into six or eight pieces (that is, you can connect either six or eight devices to the network). If you cut the pizza into eight pieces, each person who gets a slice receives a smaller portion of pizza than they would if you had cut the pizza into six pieces. Similarly, when you connect eight devices to the network, each device has less bandwidth than it would have if only six devices were connected to the network.

**Where do I place the router on my network?** Your router should be connected directly to your broadband modem (see Figure 12.20). The connection is an Ethernet cable (Cat 6 cable) running from an Ethernet port on your modem to the modem port on your router.

**Are wireless routers for Windows and OS X networks different?** All routers that support the 802.11n standard should work with computers running Windows or OS X. However, Apple has designed routers that are optimized for working with Apple computers. So if you are connecting Apple computers to your network, you may wish to consider using an Apple AirPort router. (Windows machines can also connect to the AirPort routers.) The Apple AirPort Extreme (Figure 12.21) is a good choice for a home network. It supports up to 50 simultaneous wireless connections and has three gigabit Ethernet ports for wired connections.

**Figure** 12.20

A small network with a wireless router attached.

USB port    Modem port    Ethernet ports for wired connections

**Figure** 12.21

The AirPort Extreme router is often used for home networks with Apple computers.

**How do I set up my router so that I can use it to connect to the Internet?** If your ISP provided the router, it should already be configured properly. If you bought your own router, contact your ISP and find out about any special settings that you may need to configure your router to work with your ISP. Next, access your router from Internet Explorer (or another Web browser) by entering the router's IP address or default URL. You'll also need a username and password to log on to the router. You can usually find this information in the documentation that came with the router.

Many routers feature their own wizard (different from the Windows Networking wizards) that takes you through special configuration screens. Sometimes the wizards will ask questions such as whether IP addresses are assigned dynamically (meaning you are assigned a new IP address each time you connect to the Internet). If you're unsure of any information that needs to be entered to configure the router, contact your ISP and ask for guidance.

After ensuring that your router is set up properly, you need to consider the security of your wireless network before you begin attaching devices to it. Protecting your sensitive information is a high priority task.

## Securing Wireless Networks

All computers that connect to the Internet (whether or not they are on a network) need to be secured from intruders. This is usually accomplished by using a firewall, which is a hardware or software solution that helps shield your network from prying eyes. Wireless networks present special vulnerabilities; therefore, you should take additional specific steps to keep your wireless network safe. It is important to configure your network security before setting up and connecting all the nodes on your network.

**Why is a wireless network more vulnerable than a wired network?** With a wired network, it is fairly easy to tell if a **hacker**, someone who breaks into computer systems to create mischief or steal valuable information, is using your network. However, wireless 802.11n networks have wide ranges that may extend outside of your house. This makes it possible for a

hacker to access your network without your knowledge.

**Why should I be worried about someone logging onto my wireless network without my permission?** Some use of other people's wireless networks is unintentional. Houses are built close together. Apartments are clustered even closer together. Wireless signals can easily reach a neighbor's residence. Most wireless network adapters are set up to access the strongest wireless network signal detected. If your router is on the east side of your house and you and your notebook are on the west side, then you may get a stronger signal from your neighbor's wireless network than from your own. **Piggybacking** is connecting to a wireless network (other than your own) without the permission of the owner. This practice is illegal in many jurisdictions, but often happens inadvertently between neighbors.

Your neighbor probably isn't a hacker, but he might be using a lot of bandwidth— your bandwidth! If he's downloading a massive movie file while you're trying to do research for a term paper, he's probably slowing you down. In addition, when some less-than-honest neighbors discover they can log onto your wireless network, they may cancel their own Internet service to save money by using yours. Some neighbors might even be computer savvy enough to penetrate your unprotected wireless network and steal personal information, just as any other hackers would.

In addition, because computer criminal activities are traceable, hackers love to work their mischief from public computers (such as those in a library or college) so they can't be identified. If a hacker is sitting in her car outside your house and logging on to your wireless network, any cyberattacks she launches might be traced back to your IP address, and you might find law enforcement officials knocking on your door. This happened to a man in Buffalo, New York, in 2011 when the FBI showed up to arrest him for downloading child pornography. It was subsequently determined that a hacker used his unprotected wireless network to commit the crime.

**How is my wireless network vulnerable?** Packets of information on a wireless network are broadcast through the airwaves. Savvy hackers can intercept and decode information from your transmissions that may allow them to bypass any standard protections, such as a firewall, that you have set up on your network. Therefore, to secure a wireless network, you should take the additional precautions described in the Sound Byte "Securing Wireless Networks" and as summarized below:

1. **Change your network name (SSID).** Each wireless network has its own name to identify it, which is known as the **service set identifier (SSID)**. Unless you change this name when you set up your router, the router uses a default network name that all routers from that manufacturer use (such as "Wireless" or "Netgear"). Hackers know the default names and access codes for routers. If you haven't changed the SSID, it's advertising the fact that you probably haven't changed any of the other default settings for your router, either.

2. **Disable SSID broadcast.** Most routers are set up to broadcast their SSIDs so that other wireless devices can find them. If your router supports disabling SSID broadcasting, turn it off. This makes it more difficult for a hacker to detect your network and nearly impossible for a neighbor to inadvertently connect to your network.

3. **Change the default password on your router.** Hackers know the default passwords of most routers, and if they can access your router, they can probably break into your network. Change the password on your router to something hard to guess. Use at least eight characters that are a combination of letters, symbols, and numbers.

4. **Turn on security protocols.** Most routers ship with security protocols such as Wired Equivalent Privacy (WEP) or WiFi Protected Access (WPA). Both use encryption (a method of translating your data into code) to protect data in your wireless transmissions. WPA is a much stronger protocol than WEP, so enable WPA if you have it; enable WEP if you don't. When you enable these protocols, you are forced to create a security encryption key (passphrase). When you attempt to connect a node to a security-enabled network for the first time, you'll be required to enter

the security key. The security key or passphrase (see Figure 12.22) is the code that computers on your network need to decrypt (decode) data transmissions. Without this key, it is extremely difficult, if not impossible, to decrypt the data transmissions from your network. This prevents unauthorized access to your network because hackers won't know the correct key to use. The Windows 7 Connect to a Network dialog box shows all wireless networks within range (see Figure 12.23a). Moving your cursor over the network name will reveal details about the network such as whether or not it is a secured network. Clicking on a network name allows you to connect to it, or prompts you for more information such as the SSID name and security key (see Figure 12.23b).

5. **Implement media access control.** Each network adapter on your network has a unique number (like a serial number) assigned to it by the manufacturer. This

**Figure 12.22**

By accessing your router, you can configure the security protocols available on your router and change the SSID.

**Figure 12.23**

(a) The Windows 7 Connect to a network dialog box. (b) Manually connecting to a wireless network allows you to establish a connection if you know the network security key, encryption type, and SSID name.

>You can access the Network and Sharing Center by right-clicking the Network Connection icon on the taskbar and selecting **Open Network and Sharing Center** from the shortcut menu. Choose the **Set up a new connection or network** option, and then clicking on **Manually connect to a wireless network**.

is called a media access control (MAC) address, and it is a number printed right on the network adapter. Many routers allow you to restrict access to the network to only certain MAC

addresses. This helps ensure that only authorized devices can connect to your network.

6. **Limit your signal range.** Many routers allow you to adjust the transmitting power to low, medium, or high. Cutting down the power to low or medium could prevent your signal from reaching too far away from your home, making it tougher for interlopers to poach your signal.

7. **Apply firmware upgrades.** Your router has read-only memory that has software written to it. This software is known as **firmware**. As bugs are found in the firmware (which hackers might exploit), manufacturers issue patches, just as the makers of operating system software do. Periodically check the manufacturer's Web site and apply any necessary upgrades to your firmware.

If you follow these steps, you will greatly improve the security of your wireless network.

After securing your router, you are ready to begin connecting your computing devices to your network. You now need to ensure that all your nodes have the proper equipment to enable them to connect to your network.

# Connecting Devices to Networks

Aside from connecting computers to your home network, you probably have many other devices that would benefit from being attached to your network. Many peripheral devices, such as printers and graphics tablets, now come with built-in Ethernet adapters. Also, many home entertainment devices, portable devices, and power monitoring devices to reduce energy consumption in the home are also designed to attach to home networks. Such devices are usually described as being "network-ready."

## Connecting Computers

### How can I tell what network adapters are installed in my computer?

A network adapter is necessary to connect your computing device to your network. To see which network adapter(s) are installed in your Windows computer and to check whether the adapter is working, you should use the Device Manager utility program (see Figure 12.24). The installed adapters will be shown and then you can search for information on the Internet to determine the adapter's capability if you aren't sure which wireless standard it supports.

### Network-Ready Devices

**What is a network-ready device?**
A **network-ready device** (or Internet-ready device) can be connected directly to a router instead of to a computer on the network. Network-ready devices include Blu-ray players, televisions, game consoles, and even refrigerators. These devices contain wireless and/or wired network adapters inside them. The eventual goal may be to have all electronic devices in your home be nodes on your network.

**Why should I connect my printer to my home network?** With a network-ready printer, only the printer needs to be powered on for any computer on the network to print to it. If a printer were connected directly to another computer (via a cable) on the network instead of being a node on the network, that computer would need to be switched on so other computers could access the printer.

**What can I attach to my network to facilitate file sharing and backup of data?** Network-attached storage (NAS) devices are specialized computing devices designed to store and manage your data. People are generating tremendous quantities of data today with digital cameras and video cameras, as well as buying music files, and these files need to be stored and shared. Although data can always be stored on individual hard drives in computers on a network, NAS devices provide for centralized data storage and access.

Popular for years on business networks, NAS devices are now being widely marketed for home networks. You can think of them as specialized external hard drives. NAS devices, like the LinkStation series from Buffalo Technology (see Figure 12.25a), connect directly to the network through a router or switch. Specialized software can then be installed on computers attached to the network to ensure that all data saved to an individual computer is also stored on the NAS as a backup.

For Apple computers, the Time Capsule is a wireless router combined with a hard

drive for facilitating backups of all computers connected to the network. The Time Capsule looks very similar to the AirPort router, and it works in conjunction with the Time Machine backup feature of OS X (see Figure 12.25b). If you buy a Time Capsule, you won't need to buy an AirPort router (or other router) because the Time Capsule also fulfills this function on your network. When the Time Capsule is installed on your network, Macs connected to the network will ask the user if they want to use the Time Capsule as their source for Time Machine backups. The Time Capsule is another type of NAS device.

**Besides external hard drives, are there other NAS devices I could use on my network?** A more sophisticated type of NAS device is a home network server. Home network servers are specialized devices that are designed to provide a specific set of services to computers on a home network. Home servers do not convert a home peer-to-peer network into a client/server network because these servers perform only a limited set of functions instead of all the functions performed on client/server networks.

Home network servers, like the Acer Aspire easyStore server (shown earlier in Figure 12.5), are often configured with Windows Home Server and connect directly as a node on your network. Home servers

**Figure 12.24**
This Windows Device Manager window shows a wireless and a wired network adapter installed in a notebook.

>To access Device Manager: Click the Start Button, select **Control Panel**, click on the **Hardware and Sound** group, then click on **Device Manager**.

Courtesy of Buffalo Technology

Screenshots © Apple Inc. Reprinted by permission from Apple Inc.

**Figure** 12.25

(a) The LinkStation series from Buffalo Technology features NAS devices that can store 2 TB of data. (b) Time Machine, in conjunction with an external hard drive, provides easy backups of Macs on a network.

have the functionality of NAS devices and often handle the following tasks:

- Automatically back up all computers connected to the network
- Act as a repository for files to be shared across the network (such as music and video files)
- Function as an access gateway to allow any computer on the network to be accessed from a remote location via the Internet (see Figure 12.26)

You can access the media stored on your Windows Home Server through your Xbox 360 as long as the Xbox is also connected to your home network.

### Digital Entertainment Devices on a Network

**Why should I connect my digital entertainment devices to my network?** The main reason for connecting entertainment devices to your network is to access and share digital content. When you attach devices to the Internet, you can access more content, such as movies, videos, or music files. You can also use gaming devices to play multiplayer games with players all over the world. The content you access is either downloaded or streamed to your entertainment devices. Viewing Netflix movies delivered over the Internet on your computer or HDTV is an example of streaming media.

When media is streamed, it is sent directly to a device (such as a computer or HDTV) without being saved to a hard drive. This requires a lot of bandwidth, so a broadband connection is required to effectively view streaming media. Media can also be downloaded (saved) to a hard drive for viewing at a later time. Although services like Amazon Instant Video now offer streaming movies, they still offer the ability to download content to your computer, Blu-ray player, HDTV, DVR, or Xbox 360 so you can view it later.

**What types of digital entertainment devices can I use to view streaming or downloaded media?** Network-ready televisions and home theater systems allow for direct connection to your home network (wireless or wired). These devices are configured to receive streaming media directly from the Internet. Video on demand services such as HBO GO and Netflix can stream media directly to your Internet-ready devices (including smartphones and tablets).

**Figure** 12.26

Windows Home Server remote access interface.

However, many people prefer to own media and buy it on permanent formats such as Blu-ray Discs. Blu-ray Disc players, such as the Sony 3D Blu-ray Disc players, offer not only high-definition resolution, but also the capability to display 3D video. These Blu-ray players feature integrated wireless connectivity for connection to your network as well as the ability to receive streaming media from various Internet service providers. You can even view videos from YouTube and listen to Pandora Internet Radio right through your Blu-ray player.

In terms of controlling your devices such as televisions and Blu-ray players, more companies are developing applications that enable your portable devices, such as PlayStation Portables or iPhones, to act as remote controls. The Media Remote app by Sony (see Figure 12.27a) for the iPhone, iPod Touch, or iPad allows you to control Sony Blu-ray players and TVs. And the Remote app from Apple lets you use your iPhone or iPad to control your iTunes or Apple TV from your handheld device over your WiFi network instead of having to directly access your computer (see Figure 12.27b).

Digital video recorders (DVRs), like the TiVo Premiere, are often used in the home to record high-definition television programs. Connecting your TiVo to your network makes it possible to receive downloads of movies directly to your TiVo from services such as Amazon Instant Video. And some home network servers, like the Hewlett Packard MediaSmart servers, now work in conjunction with TiVo devices to provide additional storage for your TiVo devices. The TiVo Desktop software (see Figure 12.28), which you download from **www.tivo. com**, allows you to transfer shows recorded on your TiVo to your computer or to portable devices such as an iPod, iPhone, iPad, BlackBerry, or PSP.

**Can I connect my gaming consoles to my home network?** Current gaming

**Figure 12.27**

New software apps make it easy to just use your phone or iPad to control (a) Blu-ray players or (b) Apple TV.

systems, like the PlayStation 3 (PS3), offer much more than just games—they can function as a total entertainment platform when connected to your network and the Internet. The PS3 has a built-in Blu-ray drive and can play Blu-ray Discs as well as DVDs and music files. You can download movies, games, and videos directly to the PlayStation. It can also be used to share media across your network and import photos or video from cameras and phones. And if you have a

**Figure 12.28**

The TiVo® Desktop and TiVo® Desktop Plus software facilitate transfer of recorded shows from your PC to portable devices so you can enjoy your content on the go.

PS Vita, you can use an application called Remote Play (see Figure 12.29) to access features of your PlayStation from your Vita. You can use the Vita to turn your PlayStation on and off, access music and video files, access photos stored on your PlayStation, play games, and browse the Internet. Media is transmitted from your PlayStation and displayed on the Vita screen.

### Specialized Home Networking Devices

**What if I don't need the full functionality of a PC, but I still want to access Internet content?** The launch of the Apple iPad signaled a resurgence of Internet appliances. The main function of an **Internet appliance** is easy access to the Internet, social networking sites, e-mail, video, news, and entertainment. These devices fall into a category somewhere between smartphones and full-blown computers. They are light on calculation, but high on easy content delivery. Devices such as the Sony Dash Personal Internet viewer (see Figure 12.30) are popular in kitchens and bedside tables where access to Internet radio stations, short videos, and quick information updates (like Facebook updates and current weather conditions) are needed. Originally, Internet appliances were marketed toward older computer users since these devices feature easy operation and a shallow learning curve. But the Apple iPad is propelling this category of devices into the hands of much younger users.

**Figure 12.29**

The Remote Play feature of the PS Vita and the PS3 allows users to access PS3 features, like the PlayStation Store, directly from their Vita.

*Kyodo via AP Images*

**How can I use my home network to enhance photo sharing?** Digital picture frames that display an array of changing digital photos have become quite popular with the rise in digital photography. Now digital picture frames such as the Kodak Pulse Digital Frame (see Figure 12.31) come with built-in wireless adapters for easy connection to home networks. Featuring a touch screen interface, this frame can access photos stored on your network or on an online photo-sharing site and display them. You can set up an e-mail address for the picture frame so that friends and family can e-mail pictures directly to the frame as soon as they are taken. Wouldn't it be nice to come home to new photos of your friend's trip to Cancun tonight?

**How can I use my home network to enhance my home security?** Monitoring cameras, both for indoor and outdoor use, are now available for the home and feature wireless connectivity. The cameras can connect to your network and be monitored by software like the Logitech Alert System. Security monitoring software allows you to view real-time images from the cameras at your home using portable devices such as an iPhone or Android phone (see Figure 12.32). The software can be configured to alert you via e-mail or text message when

**ACTIVE HELP-DESK**

**Understanding Networking**

In this Active Helpdesk call, you'll play the role of a helpdesk staffer, fielding calls about home networks—their advantages, their main components, and the most common types—as well as about wireless networks and how they are created.

*Sony Electronics Inc.*

**Figure 12.30**

Quick access to information and entertainment is the key feature of Internet appliances.

Eastman Kodak Company, KODAK PULSE Digital Frame / W1030S / 10 in.

**Figure 12.31**

Sending pictures directly to an electronic frame from your phone is possible when the frame is connected to your network.

the cameras detect movement, such as a vehicle entering your driveway. Some systems also allow you to receive alerts when there is a lack of movement. This can be useful for monitoring an aging relative or for monitoring the arrival of children coming home from school at a certain time.

As time goes on, many more types of entertainment devices and home gadgets will eventually be connected to your home network.

# Configuring Software for Your Home Network

Once you install all the hardware for your network, you need to configure your operating system software for networking on your computers. In this section, you'll learn how to do just that using special Windows tools. Although configuration is different with Mac OS X, the setup is quick and easy. Linux is the most complex operating system to configure for a home network, though the difficulties are not insurmountable.

### Windows Configuration

**Is configuring software difficult?** Windows makes configuring software relatively simple if you are using the same version of Windows on all of your computers. The Windows examples in this section assume you are using Windows 7 on all of your computers. In Windows 7, the process of setting up a network is fairly automated by various software wizards. As you learned in Chapter 7, a wizard is a utility program included

with software that you can use to help you accomplish a specific task. You can launch the Windows wizards from the Network and Sharing Center, which can be accessed via the Network and Internet group in the Control Panel. Before running any wizards, you should do the following:

1. Make sure there are network adapters on each node.

2. For any wired connections, plug all the cables into the router, nodes, and so on.

3. Make sure your broadband modem is connected to your router and that the modem is connected to the Internet.

4. Turn on your equipment in the following order (allowing the modem and the router about one minute each to power up and configure):
   a. Your broadband modem
   b. Your router
   c. All computers and peripherals (printers, scanners, and so on)

Other devices, such as televisions, Blu-ray players, and gaming consoles, can be added to the network after configuring the computers.

After you have completed these steps, open the Network and Sharing Center from the Control Panel (see Figure 12.33). If your computer has a wired connection to the network, you should automatically be connected to your home network. The network name should be the SSID name that you gave to your router. If you are connecting wirelessly, click on the Connect to a Network option. You will need

Courtesy of Logitech, Inc.

**Figure 12.32**

Logitech security products can help you monitor your home's security from your mobile devices.

View your basic network information and set up connections

ALAN-DESKTOP
(This computer)

GMVO5

Internet

See full map

View your active networks

GMVO5
Home network

Connect or disconnect

Access type: Internet
HomeGroup: Ready to create
Connections: Wireless Network Connection
(GMVO5)

Click to create
a HomeGroup

Change your networking settings

Set up a new connection or network
Set up a wireless, broadband, dial-up, ad hoc, or VPN connection; or set up a router or access point.

Connect to a network ← Click to connect to your wireless network
Connect or reconnect to a wireless, wired, dial-up, or VPN network connection.

Choose homegroup and sharing options
Access files and printers located on other network computers, or change sharing settings.

**Figure 12.33**

The Windows Network and Sharing Center helps you configure your home network.

to enter your security passphrase to connect to your wireless network.

**What if I don't have the same version of Windows on all my computers?** Computers with various versions of Windows can coexist on the same network. Always set up the computers running the newest version of Windows first (Windows 7). Then consult the Microsoft Web site for guidance on how to proceed for configuring computers with previous versions of Windows on a Windows 7 network.

**How do I differentiate the computers on my network?** When you set up your Windows computer, you gave it a name. Each computer on a network needs a name that is different from the names of all other computers on the network so that the network can identify it. This unique name ensures that the network knows which computer is requesting services and data and can deliver data to the correct computer.

For ease of file and peripheral sharing, Windows 7 created a feature known as Home-

Group. If you have all Windows 7 computers on your network, you simply all join the same HomeGroup. After connecting your first Windows 7 computer to your network, you need to create a HomeGroup by clicking on the Ready to create link in the Network and Sharing Center (see Figure 12.33). The HomeGroup is a software device that makes it easier to allow computers on a Windows 7 network to share peripherals and information.

The first step in setting up a Home-Group (see Figure 12.34a) involves choosing sharing options for computers that belong to the HomeGroup. You can choose to share pictures, music, videos, documents, and printers with other Windows 7 computers that belong to the HomeGroup. Although these are global settings for every computer in the HomeGroup, you can change these settings on individual computers if you wish. In the second step of the HomeGroup setup, Windows generates a password (see Figure 12.34b). All other computers that subsequently are added to the network will need this password to join the HomeGroup. Once you have created the HomeGroup on the first computer, it will belong to that HomeGroup. You can then begin connecting other Windows 7 computers to the network and join them to the HomeGroup you created.

**How do Macs connect wirelessly to networks?** Generally, connecting Macs to a wireless network is a much easier process than connecting with Windows computers. You set up the security for a router on a Mac network just as was illustrated in the section on securing your wireless network. Therefore, logging your Mac onto the network will require knowing the SSID and its passphrase. When you boot up your Mac, the wireless card should be on by default. The network

**Figure 12.34**

The Create a HomeGroup wizard (a) allows you to configure sharing options and (b) provides a password required for other computers to join the HomeGroup.

>The Create a HomeGroup settings can be accessed by clicking the Computer link on the Start menu, then clicking the **HomeGroup** icon, and then clicking the **View HomeGroup** settings link.

login screen (see Figure 12.35) should appear with a list of available networks (that is, the ones the NIC in your Mac can detect). The locks next to the network names indicate a secure network, which will require a password. Enter the password for the network in the password box and click the Join button to connect to the network. For unsecure networks, the Join button can be clicked without entering anything in the password box.

**Why don't some networks appear as available?** Networks with SSID broadcast turned off will not appear on the list of available networks. To join one of these secure networks, click the Other button on the available wireless networks dialog box. This will cause the Enter the name of the network dialog box to appear (see Figure 12.36). Then just enter the SSID name for your network in the Network Name box and the security passphrase in the Password box. Clicking the Join button will then connect you to the network. Checking the Remember this network check box will cause the computer to automatically connect to the network when it is available (that is, it becomes one of your preferred networks). You can have multiple preferred networks such as your home, school, and local coffee shop networks.

Assuming you installed and configured everything properly, your home network should now be up and running, allowing you to share files, Internet connections, and peripherals. You are now ready to configure other non-computer devices to connect them to your network.

### Wireless Node Configuration and Testing

**How do I hook up devices like a TiVo or gaming console to my network?** For a wired connection, you would simply plug a cable into the device and your router. For wireless connections, there is usually a set of steps to follow in the setup menu for the device you are configuring. Assuming you set up a secure wireless network as described

**Figure** 12.35

The OS X available wireless networks dialog box.

in the security section of this chapter, you'll need to know the SSID name of your network and the security passphrase. Although each device's configuration steps will be slightly different, eventually, you will get to a screen where you need to input the SSID name and the passphrase. The Xbox 360 configuration screens are shown in Figure 12.38.

Once all your devices are connected to your network, you might want to check your Internet connection speed to see what kind of throughput you are achieving. You can check your speed on any device on your network that can access the Internet with a browser.

**How can I test my Internet connection speed?** Your ISP may have promised you certain speeds of downloading and uploading data. How can you tell if you are getting what was promised? There are numerous sites on the Internet, such as **www.speedtest.net** (see Figure 12.39) and **www.broadband.gov**, where you can test the speed of downloading files to your computer and uploading files to other computers. You can then see how your results compare to those of other users in your state and across the United States. Many factors can influence your Internet speeds, so be sure to run the test at several different times during the day over the course of a week before complaining to your ISP about not getting your promised speed.

**Figure** 12.36

The OS X Enter the name of the network dialog box.

### Troubleshooting Network Problems

**What types of problems can I run into when installing wireless networks?** The maximum range of wireless devices under the 802.11n standard is about 350 feet. But as you go farther away from your router, the throughput you achieve

**TRENDS IN IT**

## Where Should You Store Your Files? The Cloud Is Calling!

You probably own a lot of electronic media such as songs, videos, e-books, and pictures. You also have other electronic files that you need to access periodically such as files you've created for school projects, your tax returns, and so on. You need to store your media where it is secure—backed up regularly and not accessible to unauthorized individuals. You also need to be able to access your media whenever you need it. So should you store your media on your home network? That might work if your network-attached storage is accessible via the Internet. The latest trend, however, is to store your files in the cloud (on the Internet). But there are a plethora of choices as to where to store your files. Deciding which option to use depends on how you want to access your files, if the files need to be shared, and how you use your files.

### Files That Need Amending/Updating

If you use different computing devices such as a notebook, smartphone, and tablet, you may need to ensure that you have certain files with you at all times. Perhaps you are working on a term paper and you aren't sure what device you'll have with you the next time you have a brilliant idea to add to the paper. Having the current version of the file accessible on any device you use is critical in this instance, and means the file should probably be stored on each device. This ensures that you can work on the file even if your Internet access is interrupted or unavailable.

The most popular application for these types of files is Dropbox. Dropbox currently supports computers running the three most popular operating systems (Windows, OS X, and Linux) as well as Blackberrys, Android phones, iPhones, and iPads. After installing the Dropbox software on your devices, any files you store on your device in the Dropbox folder are automatically replicated to all your other devices via their Internet connection. Folders in Dropbox can be shared with other Dropbox users, which makes this an ideal application for sharing documents in group projects. Dropbox is free, but storage capacity is limited to between 2 GB and 8 GB for free accounts. Therefore, Dropbox is usually best for limited amounts of smaller files as opposed to sharing large media collections.

### Media on the Go

You might like to view/listen to your media on the go. But storing it on every device takes up a lot of space on the individual devices. Therefore, storing it out in the cloud and streaming exactly what you want to your computing device probably makes more sense. But that requires an active Internet connection. Companies like Apple and Amazon with their iCloud and Cloud Drive offerings are trying to entice you to store all your media (and other files) on their servers. Both iCloud and Cloud Drive offer limited amounts of space for free, but you can pay a yearly fee for additional storage for your 100 GB collection of HD movies. However, both of these options are designed primarily for single users

as opposed to sharing of media. And with limited free storage, these might not be the best options for large media collections.

### Large Media Collections That Need to Be Shared

For large media collections that you want to share with friends and relatives, sites like MediaFire and ADrive are popular choices. Both offer free accounts so you can test out the services. ADrive offers 50 GB of storage for free, but there is no limit to the amount of files you can store on MediaFire (even with their free account). You can easily share files with other individuals on either site. You can also post links to the files directly to Facebook or Twitter from MediaFire (Figure 12.37). However, with the MediaFire free account you can't upload files larger than 200 MB. This limit won't impact music or photos, but if you are planning on uploading HD movies, you'll need to opt for a pay account to enable uploading of files up to 10 GB per file.

The advantage of these sites is the large amount of free storage and the sharing abilities. However, the drawback to these sites is that they aren't designed for playing of streaming media (like iCloud and Cloud Drive are), so you need to download files to your device and store them locally before playing them.

No one solution is perfect for every file sharing situation, but the trend is definitely moving towards cloud storage as opposed to local network storage. You need to carefully examine the options available on each site to decide which one offers the features you need for the type of files you are storing and accessing. And make sure to carefully investigate file backup policies for each site, especially with free accounts. Some free accounts don't feature guaranteed backups of your media or the site might actually delete files in free accounts that haven't been accessed for a certain period of time. The pay accounts generally guarantee that the files are backed up on a regular basis. So don't ignore backup policies, because you want your files to be there when you need them!

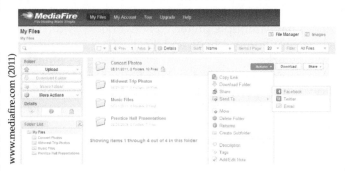

www.mediafire.com (2011)

**Figure 12.37**

MediaFire offers unlimited storage and file sharing for free.

---

will decrease. Obstacles between wireless nodes also decrease throughput. Walls, floors, and large metal objects are the most common sources of interference with wireless signals. For example, placing a computer with a wireless network adapter next to a refrigerator may prevent the signals from reaching the rest of the network. Similarly, a node that has four walls between it and the Internet connection will most likely have lower-than-maximum throughput.

**Figure** 12.38

Xbox 360 wireless configuration screens. (a) The Xbox will detect available networks. Select the Specify Unlisted Network option to enter the SSID name of your network. (b) Enter the security passphrase on the appropriate security screen.

## What if a node on the network can't get adequate throughput?

Repositioning the node within the same room (sometimes even just a few inches from the original position) can often affect communication between nodes. If this doesn't work, try moving the device closer to the router or to other rooms in your house. If these solutions don't work, you should consider adding a wireless range extender to your network.

A **wireless range extender** is a device that amplifies your wireless signal to get it out to parts of your home that are experiencing poor connectivity. As shown Figure 12.40, Notebook C on the back porch can't connect to the wireless network even though Computer B in the den can connect to the network. By placing a range extender in the den, where there is still good connectivity to the wireless network, the wireless signal is amplified and beamed farther out to the back porch. This improves the otherwise poor connectivity on the back porch and allows Notebook C to make a good connection to the network.

Courtesy of Speedtest.net

Hopefully, you'll now be able to connect all your computing devices to your home network and achieve the throughput you need to move your data efficiently around your home network.

**Figure** 12.39

Speed test showing a download speed of 23.02 Mbps and upload of 20.69 Mbps, which is extremely fast for a home Internet connection.

| Bedroom | Den | Back porch |
| --- | --- | --- |
| Computer A with wireless network adapter | Computer B with wireless range extender | Notebook C with wireless network adapter |

**Figure** 12.40

Because a wireless range extender is installed in the den, Notebook C on the back porch can now connect to the wireless network generated by the wireless router in the bedroom.

**summary**

1. **What is a network, and what are the advantages/disadvantages of setting up one?**

   A computer network is simply two or more computers that are connected using software and hardware so they can communicate. Advantages of networks include allowing users to (1) share an Internet connection, (2) share peripheral devices, and (3) share files. A disadvantage is that the network must be administered.

2. **What is the difference between a client/server network and a peer-to-peer network?**

   In peer-to-peer networks, each node connected to the network can communicate directly with every other node instead of having a separate device exercise central control over the network. P2P networks are the most common type of network installed in homes. Most networks that have 10 or more nodes are client/server networks. A client/server network contains two types of computers: a client computer on which users perform specific tasks and a server computer that provides resources to the clients and central control for the network.

3. **What are the main components of every network?**

   To function, any network must contain four components: (1) transmission media (cables or radio waves) to connect and establish communication between nodes, (2) network adapters that allow the nodes on the network to communicate, (3) network navigation devices (such as routers and switches) that move data around the network, and (4) software that allows the network to run.

4. **What are my options for connecting to the Internet?**

   Home users have many options for connecting to the Internet. A dial-up connection, in which you connect to the Internet using a standard phone line, was at one time the standard way to connect to the Internet. Today's broadband connections are faster and have made dial-up a legacy connection technology. Broadband connections include cable, DSL, and fiber-optic cable. Satellite is a connection option for those who do not have access to faster broadband technologies. WiFi allows users to connect to the Internet wirelessly, but is not as fast as a wired connection.

5. **Which type of network is most commonly found in the home?**

   Ethernet networks are the most common networks used in home networking. Most Ethernet networks use a combination of wired and wireless connections, depending upon the data throughput required. Wired connections usually achieve higher throughput than wireless connections.

6. **What equipment and software do I need to build a network in my home?**

   All computing equipment that will connect to a network has to contain a network adapter. Network adapters allow computers to communicate (either wired or wirelessly) with network navigation devices such as routers and switches. Wired connections are usually made with Cat 6 twisted-pair cable. A router is needed to share an Internet connection as it transmits data between two networks (the home network and the Internet).

7. **Why are wireless networks more vulnerable than wired networks, and what special precautions are required to ensure my wireless network is secure?**

   Wireless networks are even more susceptible to hacking than wired networks because the signals of most wireless networks extend beyond the walls of your home. Neighbors may unintentionally (or intentionally) connect to the Internet through your wireless connection, and hackers may try to access it. To prevent unwanted intrusions into your network, you should change the default password on your router to make it tougher for hackers to gain access, use a hard-to-guess SSID (network name), disable SSID broadcasting to make it harder for outsiders to detect your network, and enable security protocols such as WPA or WEP.

8. **Besides computers, what other devices can I connect to a home network?**

   Connecting peripherals such as printers directly to a network allows them to be easily shared by all users on the network. Network-attached storage (NAS) devices allow for the storage and sharing of data files such as movies and music as well as providing a central place for file backups. Connecting digital entertainment devices (such as gaming consoles) provides the ability to stream movies and other entertainment directly from the Internet.

9. **How do I configure the software on my computer and set up other devices to get my network up and running?**

   Windows 7 makes it easy to set up wired and wireless networks. Plug in the modem, router, and all cables, and then switch on the modem, router, and computers (in that order). Launch the Network and Sharing Center and select the appropriate links for setup. Make sure each computer has a distinct name and ensure that all computers are in the same HomeGroup. Devices such as gaming consoles each have their own setup procedures for connecting to wireless networks, but usually require the same information as needed for connecting a computer to a secured wireless network.

10. **What problems might I encounter when setting up a wireless network?**

    You may not get the throughput you need through a wireless connection, and therefore you may need to consider a wired connection for certain devices. Distance from the router as well as walls, floors, and large metal objects between a device and the router can interfere with wireless connectivity. Wireless range extenders can amplify signals to improve connectivity in areas of poor signal strength.

 ## Companion Website

The Companion Website includes a variety of additional materials to help you review and learn more about the topics in this chapter. Go to: **www.pearsonhighered.com/techinaction**

## Word Bank

- Cat 6 cable
- client/server
- data transfer rate
- hacker(s)
- home network server
- LAN

- network adapter(s)
- network-ready
- peer-to-peer (P2P)
- piggybacking
- router
- switch

- throughput
- twisted-pair cable
- WAN
- wired
- wireless
- wireless range extender

**Instructions:** Fill in the blanks using the words from the Word Bank above.

Cindy needed to network three computers for herself and her roommates, Liu and Rosita. She decided that a(n) (1) _____ network was the right type to install in their dorm suite because a(n) (2) _____ network was too complex. Because they all liked to stream digital movies from the Internet, they needed a high (3) _____, but doubted they would achieve the promised (4) _____ in any network they installed. Although they knew using (5) _____ media would provide the fastest Ethernet networks, they decided to use (6) _____ media so that they could use their notebooks wherever they were in their suite. Therefore they needed to buy a(n) (7) _____ with wireless capability that would allow them to share the broadband Internet connection that Sharon already had through a local ISP. This device would also double as a(n) (8) _____, preventing the need to purchase a separate device. Fortunately, all their computers already had wireless (9) _____ installed, making it easy to connect the computers to the network. Cindy knew they would need to purchase some (10) _____, since the Xbox 360 they wanted to share only had a wired Ethernet adapter in it.

Cindy's roommate Rosita wanted to know if they could hook into the (11) _____, or small network, that was already deployed for the students in the dorm. This student network was already hooked into the college's (12) _____, or large network, which spanned all three of the college's campuses. She knew they would need to be careful when connecting to the network, because some students from the dorm had accidentally been illegally (13) _____ on a network from the cafe across the street. The connectivity for notebooks in the lounge at the end of the hall was very poor, so they needed to consider purchasing a(n) (14) _____ to extend the range of the wireless signal. As a final detail, Rosita suggested they get a(n) (15) _____ printer that would plug right into the router and allow them all to print whenever they needed to do so.

Your grandmother has moved into a new retirement community. She is sharing a large living space with three other residents. All four retirees have their own notebook computers. Your grandmother has asked you to advise her and her roommates on an appropriate network to install so that they can share an Internet connection, a laser printer, and movies that they want to stream from Netflix via the Internet. And your grandmother is an avid photographer and has thousands of digital photographs on her computer. She is very concerned about forgetting to back up the photographs after she takes new ones and wants her family to be able to access her photos via the Internet.

**Instructions:** Using the preceding scenario, draft a networking plan for your grandmother and her roommates using as many of the keywords from the chapter as you can. Be sure that your grandmother, who is unfamiliar with many networking terms, can understand your suggestions.

**Instructions:** Answer the multiple-choice and true–false questions below for more practice with key terms and concepts from this chapter.

## Multiple Choice

**1.** Each device connected to a network is known as a
  a. peripheral.  b. network spoke.
  c. node.      d. computing unit.

**2.** Which of the following is a disadvantage of setting up a network?
  a. Peripherals are difficult to share.
  b. It is difficult to install Mac and Windows computers on the same network.
  c. Networks are too difficult for the average person to configure.
  d. Even peer-to-peer networks require some degree of network administration.

**3.** The most common type of network installed in the home is a
  a. peer-to-peer.
  b. client/server.
  c. peer/server.
  d. client-to-client.

**4.** A small network deployed in a home is referred to as a
  a. LAN.
  b. WAN.
  c. HAN.
  d. MAN.

**5.** The part of the network that establishes a communications channel between the nodes of the network is known as
  a. network operating software.
  b. transmission media.
  c. a network navigation device.
  d. a switch.

**6.** Throughput speed is always
  a. greater than bandwidth.
  b. the same as bandwidth.
  c. constant throughout a given transmission media.
  d. less than or equal to bandwidth.

**7.** The network navigation device that sends data packets to their intended node on a network is called a
  a. router.
  b. network interface card.
  c. switch.
  d. node facilitator.

**8.** The fastest broadband Internet service is usually
  a. fiber-optic.
  b. DSL.
  c. cable.
  d. satellite.

**9.** All of the following are methods to secure your wireless network except
  a. disable SSID broadcast.
  b. enable WPA.
  c. change your network name (SSID).
  d. disable WEP.

**10.** The device used to move data between two networks is called a
  a. gateway.
  b. switch.
  c. router.
  d. wireless range extender.

## True–False

_____ 1. Actual data throughput is usually higher on wired networks than on wireless networks.

_____ 2. Network-ready devices contain Ethernet switches.

_____ 3. Home network servers are a specialized type of NAS device.

_____ 4. LANs cover a larger geographic area than WANs.

_____ 5. Gaming consoles are often connected to home wireless networks.

**1. Dormitory Networking**

Mikel, Dylan, Sanjay, and Harrison were sitting in the common room of their campus suite and complaining about their wireless network. They inherited the equipment from the last residents of the suite, and unfortunately their router uses the outdated 802.11g standard. They all have notebooks that have 802.11n network adapters, but their throughput is poor. Since they are often all surfing the Internet at the same time and trying to download movies, their network's performance has become unacceptable.

Since they all just sold last semester's books back to the bookstore for a total of $600, they decided this would be a good time to upgrade their network and peripherals. Dylan has an inkjet printer that gobbles up expensive cartridges, and Phil has a laser printer that just broke. The guys figure one good networked all-in-one printer should meet their needs since it would also provide them with photocopying capabilities. Mikel is concerned about backups for his computer. His external hard drive fell on the floor and no longer works reliably. He has a tremendous amount of schoolwork and photos on his computer that he is concerned about losing if his hard drive fails. Since the guys don't know much about networking, the four roommates have asked for your guidance. Consider the following, keeping in mind their $600 budget:

a. Research network-ready laser printers on sites such as **www.hp.com**, **www.epson.com**, and **www.brother.com**. What network-ready all-in-one printer would you recommend? Why?

b. Research 802.11n wireless routers at sites such as **www.netgear.com**, **www.linksys.com**, and **www.dlink.com**. What router do you think will meet the roommates' needs? Why?

c. How would you recommend addressing Mikel's backup concerns? Would you recommend an NAS device for the network, or do they have enough money left in their budget for a home network server? Research these devices and make an affordable recommendation. Check sites such as **www.tigerdirect.com** and **www.newegg.com** for competitive pricing.

**2. Connecting Your Computer to Public Networks**

You are working for a local coffee shop that offers free wireless access to customers. Your supervisor has asked you to create a flyer for patrons that warns them of the potential dangers of surfing the Internet in public places. Conduct research on the Internet about using public hotspots to access the Internet. Prepare a flyer that lists specific steps that customers can take to protect their data when surfing on publicly accessible networks.

**3. Adding a Home Network Server for Backups to Your Network**

You know that adding a home network server to your network would facilitate sharing of your digital media and would make backing up your computers easier. You need to consider the following questions when selecting an appropriate home network server:

a. What is the volume of shared media that you need to store? (In other words, how many music files, movies, and other media files do you have?)

b. What are the sizes of the hard drives of the computers on your network (for backup purposes)? What size hard drive would you need on a home network server to ensure you could back up all your computers as well as store your shared media?

c. Would you need to access files on the home network server when you are away from home or allow others (such as your cousins) to access them?

Research home network servers using sites such as **www.hp.com**, **www.acer.com**, and **www.lenovo.com**, or use the term "home server" in a search engine. Select a server that is appropriate for your home network. Prepare a summary of your findings and include the reasons for your selection.

1. **Internet Access for a Small Business in a Remote Area**

   Your uncle owns a combination gas station/coffee shop/general store in a very small town in the Midwest. He currently is using dial-up Internet access to send e-mail and surf the Web. Some of his customers have indicated that they would love it if the store had broadband access. There is no local company that supplies broadband Internet service in the town where the business is located. Your uncle has asked you for ideas.

   Investigate three satellite Internet service providers and prepare a summary of features and prices for your uncle. Make sure to find out what the download and upload speeds are for each provider. Also, ensure that the service agreement provides for your uncle using the Internet connection to provide access to his customers. Which service would you recommend to your uncle? Why?

2. **Putting Computers to Work on Research Projects**

   Most computer CPUs use only a fraction of their computing power most of the time. Many medical research companies (such as those seeking cures for cancer and AIDS) could benefit from "borrowing" computer CPU time when computers are not being used or are being underutilized. Virtual supercomputers (which are really networks of computers) can be created using software installed on tens of thousands of computers. This type of computing is also known as *grid* or *distributed computing*. These virtual computing nets can be harnessed to solve complex problems when their owners are not using their computers. Assume that you are working for a business that has 100 computers and you would like to participate in a grid computing project. Investigate IBM's Worldwide Community Grid (**www.worldcommunitygrid.org**). Prepare a report for your boss that:

   a. Describes the Worldwide Community Grid (WCG) and its objectives.
   b. Lists current projects that the WCG is working on.
   c. Describes the process for installing the WCG software on the company's computers.
   d. Suggests a strategy for publicizing the company's participation in the WCG project that will encourage your employer's customers to participate.

3. **Testing Your Internet Connection Speed**

   Visit **www.speedtest.net** and **www.broadband.gov** and test the speed of your Internet connection at your home and in the computer lab at your school. Try to repeat the test at two different times during the day.

   a. What did you find out about download speeds at your home? Are you getting as much speed as was promised by your ISP? Would this speed be sufficient for a home-based business? What type of business packages does your ISP offer, and what speeds could you expect when paying for a business package?
   b. How does the connection speed at your school compare to the speed at your home? Where do you think you should have a faster connection—at your school or at your home? Why might the connection speed at your school be slower than you think it should be?

**Instructions:** Some ideas are best understood by experimenting with them in our own minds. The following critical thinking questions are designed to demand your full attention but require only a comfortable chair—no technology.

1. **Protecting Yourself on Public Wireless Networks**

   Many people use free public wireless networks to access the Internet. But many public networks don't have adequate security or may be under surveillance by hackers. To protect your sensitive data, there are certain activities you should not engage in on public networks. What types of activities should you avoid on a public network? What types of information should you only process on your secure home network?

2. **Adding Devices to Your Network**

   We discussed adding devices other than computers and computer peripherals to your network in this chapter. Consider the following for your home network:

   a. Do you currently stream or download movies from Netflix, Amazon Instant Video, or another service? If so, is your storage device sufficient, or do you need more capacity? If you don't currently download this type of entertainment, would your family do so if you had a device that was attached to your network? What type of device (DVR, home server, etc.) do you think would be most appropriate for the type of media that you enjoy? How much media would you need to download and view in a month to make purchasing equipment worthwhile?

   b. Do you have a need for a home security system? Would internal and external cameras be appropriate for monitoring your home? Are there people in your house (babysitters, housekeepers, contractors, etc.) on a regular basis that might need monitoring? Would you monitor these people in real time or make recordings for later review?

3. **Evaluating Your Network Storage Needs**

   You probably have media, such as videos, pictures, and music, that you access on a regular basis that you may already be sharing (or want to share) with family members. You could install an NAS device on your network to share the media, and perhaps you might even already have one. But this is usually only a good solution if the people you share media with are living in your household. For sharing media outside of the home, you could consider an NAS device that is accessible through the Internet or you could use an Internet-based media sharing solution. Consider the following:

   a. What types of media do you need to share? With whom do you need to share them? Where are these people located? Do they all use your home network? If not, do they all have access to the Internet? How much space will the media you need to store occupy? Consider what you already have on hand plus what you might be acquiring in the future.

   b. Investigate at least three different NAS devices (including home network servers) that feature the capacity you need. What is the cost of these devices? Can the devices be accessed over the Internet or do they require access to your network? What are the storage capacities of the devices?

   c. Research at least three Internet-based media storing/sharing solutions such as Dropbox, MediaFire, Amazon Cloud Drive, MiMedia, Mediashare, and Wixi. What is the cost associated with each service? Are there individual file size limitations for storage? What is the total volume of media you can store? Is the media you store on the site easily sharable with others? Does the service allow storage of all the types of media you need to store?

   d. Which solution would you implement? Be sure to justify your choice.

4. **Preparing for a Career in Computer Networking**

You've been told that preparing for a career as a network administrator, a person who installs and maintains networking equipment and software, might provide you with solid employment prospects after graduation. Research network administration careers on Web sites such as **www.bls.gov**, **www.careerbuilder.com**, and **www.salary.com**. Prepare a report that addresses the following:

a. What are the employment prospects for network administrators in the future? (The *Occupational Outlook Handbook* (**www.bls.gov/oco**) can provide you with projections.)

b. What types of salaries do entry-level positions command?

c. How much education do you need to prepare for this field?

d. What types of professional certifications are helpful in obtaining employment?

e. What are the typical duties of a network administrator?

f. Do you think you would pursue this type of job? What appeals to you about the position? What aspects of the job do you think you would not enjoy?

# Providing Wireless Internet Access to the Needy

## Problem

Wireless Internet access in the home is very desirable. However, not everyone is able to afford it, and this can put families, especially ones with school-aged children, at a severe disadvantage. Providing Internet access to the underprivileged is a way of closing the "digital divide" that exists between those who can afford Internet access and those who cannot.

## Task

You are volunteering for a charity that wants to begin installing wireless networks in homes for needy families. The project is funded by charitable grants with the objective of providing basic broadband Internet access and simple networking capabilities in the home at no cost to the recipients. The assumption is that the families already have two notebook computers per family (provided through another charity) that have 802.11n wireless capabilities. You have volunteered to research potential network and Internet solutions.

## Process

Break the class into three teams. Each team will be responsible for investigating one of the following issues:

1. **Internet service providers:** Research ISPs that serve the town where your school is located (don't forget to include satellite providers). Compare and contrast their lowest cost broadband access. Compare maximum upload and download speeds as well as costs. Be sure to consider the cost of the modems—whether they are purchased up front or rented on a monthly basis. Make sure to select what your group considers to be the best deal.
2. **Networking equipment and network-ready peripherals:** Each home needs to be provided with an 802.11n capable wireless router (to share the Internet access), a network-ready all-in-one printer, and a Blu-ray player capable of streaming digital video (for educational programs and movies). Research at least three different options for each of these devices. Since this is a grant and money is limited, be sure to consider price as well as functionality.
3. **Security:** The wireless networks need to be secured to keep hackers and piggybackers out. Work in conjunction with the group that is researching routers to determine the best type of router to purchase since it needs to support a strong wireless security protocol such as WPA. Make sure to consider what other types of protection are needed on the network, such as antivirus, anti-malware, and firewalls.

Present your findings to your class and come to a consensus about the solution you would propose for the charity. Provide your instructor with a report on your area suitable for presentation to the CEO of the charity.

## Conclusion

Providing technology to underserved populations on a cost-effective basis will go a long way towards closing the digital divide and ensuring that disadvantaged youth have the Internet access they need to pursue their education and compete effectively in today's society.

# Firing Employees for Expressing Views on Social Media Sites

In this exercise, you will research and then role-play a complicated ethical situation. The role you play may or may not match your own personal beliefs, but your research and use of logic will enable you to represent whichever view is assigned. An arbitrator will watch and comment on both sides of the arguments, and together the team will agree on an ethical solution.

## Problem

The largest network, the Internet, provides the capability for vast social interaction. Social media sites such as Facebook, YouTube, and Twitter, as well as blogs and wikis, give everyone convenient ways to express their opinions. However, employers often are intolerant of employees who freely express negative opinions or expose inside information about their employers on social media sites. Given that most jurisdictions in the United States use the doctrine of employment at-will (that is, employees can be fired at any time for any reason, or even no reason), many employers are quick to discipline or terminate employees who express opinions with which the company disagrees. When such cases come to court, the courts often find in favor of the employers. It is clear that individuals must exercise extreme care when posting work-related content.

## Research Areas to Consider

- Ellen Simonetti and Delta Airlines
- Fired for blogging about work
- Free speech
- Joyce Park or Michael Tunison

## Process

1. Divide the class into teams.
2. Research the areas cited above and devise a scenario in which someone has complained about an employee blogging about a sensitive workplace issue such as cleanliness at a food manufacturing facility or employee romances.
3. Team members should write a summary that provides background information for their character—for example: employee, human resources manager, or arbitrator—and details their character's behaviors to set the stage for the role-playing event. Then, team members should create an outline to use during the role-playing event.
4. Team members should arrange a mutually convenient time to meet for the exchange, either using the collaboration feature of MyITLab, the discussion board feature of Blackboard, or meeting in person.
5. Team members should present their case to the class, or submit a PowerPoint presentation for review by the rest of the class, along with the summary and resolution they developed.

## Conclusion

As technology becomes ever more prevalent and integrated into our lives, more and more ethical dilemmas will present themselves. Being able to understand and evaluate both sides of the argument, while responding in a personally or socially ethical manner, will be an important skill.

# TECHNOLOGY

# Careers
# in IT

t's hard to imagine an occupation in which computers are not used in some fashion. Even such previously low-tech industries as waste disposal and fast food use computers to manage inventories and order commodities. In this Technology in Focus feature, we explore various information technology (IT) career paths open to you.

# Rewards of Working in Information Technology

There are many great reasons to work in the exciting, ever-changing field of information technology. In this section, we'll explore some reasons why IT fields are so attractive to graduates looking for entry-level positions.

### IT Workers Are in Demand

If you want to investigate a career with computers, the first question you probably have is, "Will I be able to get a job?" After the dot-com bust in the early 2000s, many people thought the boom in computer-related jobs was over. However, current projections by the U.S. Department of Labor's Bureau of Labor Statistics report that computer-related jobs are among the

fastest-growing occupations through 2018 (see Figure 13.1). Recently, *Money* magazine and PayScale.com developed a list of the top 50 jobs in America based on job growth prospects, job satisfaction, and compensation for experienced workers. Software architects were number 1, and 14 of the top 50 jobs were IT careers. According to FINS Technology (**www.fins.com**), the average starting salary for IT jobs was increasing by 4.3 percent in 2011 from 2010 levels.

The number of students pursuing computer science degrees has been increasing over the past several years. The celebrity of IT icons such as Steve Jobs of Apple and Mark Zuckerberg of Facebook and the success of movies such as *The Social Network* are shining a positive spotlight on IT careers. The *New York Times* estimated that 11,000 computer science degrees would be awarded in the United States in 2011. This marks a reversal of a downward trend that had developed mainly because of the intense media discussion about the demise of Internet start-up companies in the early 2000s. Because of low enrollment since the "dot-com bust," shortages of computing professionals in the United States are projected over the next 5 to 10 years. In terms of job outlook, this is a perfect time to consider an IT career.

### IT Jobs Pay Well

As you can see from Figure 1, median salaries in IT careers are robust. But what exactly affects your salary in an IT position? Your skill set and your experience level are obvious answers, but the size of an employer and its geographic location are also factors. Large companies tend to pay more, so if you're pursuing a high salary, set your sights on a large corporation. But remember that making a lot of money isn't everything—be sure to consider other quality-of-life issues such as job satisfaction. Of course, choosing a computer career isn't a guarantee you'll get a high-paying job. Just as in any other profession, you will need appropriate training and on-the-job experience to earn a high salary.

**Figure 13.1** | HIGH-GROWTH IT TECHNOLOGY JOBS*

| Occupation | Median Pay | Top Pay | 10-Year Growth Rate | Total New Jobs |
|---|---|---|---|---|
| Computer software engineers | $94,180 | $143,330 | 32% | 295,000 |
| Computer systems analyst | 77,740 | 119,070 | 20 | 108,100 |
| Computer support specialists | 46,260 | 76,970 | 14 | 78,000 |
| Network and computer systems administrators | 69,160 | 108,090 | 23 | 78,900 |
| Database administrators | 73,490 | 115,660 | 20 | 24,400 |
| Computer and information research scientists | 100,660 | 153,120 | 24 | 7,000 |
| Computer and information systems managers | 115,780 | 166,400 | 17 | 49,500 |

*Excerpted from *Occupational Outlook Handbook*, 2010–2011 Edition, Bureau of Labor Statistics

So how much can you expect to start out earning? Although starting salaries for some IT positions (computer desktop support and helpdesk analysts) are in the modest range ($40,000 to $44,000), starting salaries for students with bachelor's degrees in information technology are fairly robust. But IT salaries vary widely, depending on experience level, the geographic location of the job, and the size of the employer.

To obtain the most accurate information, you should research salaries yourself in the geographic area where you expect to work. Job posting sites such as Monster .com can provide guidance, but Salary.com provides a free salary wizard to help you determine what IT professionals in your geographic area are making compared with national averages. You can add information such as your degree and the size of the company you are seeking to further fine-tune the figures. Figure 13.2 shows that for an entry-level programming position in Phoenix, Arizona, you could expect to earn a salary of between $43,285 and $70,048 at a company of 500 to 1,000 employees. Hundreds of IT job titles are listed, so you can tailor your search to the specific job in which you're interested.

## IT Jobs Are Not Going "Offshore"

In the global economy in which we now operate, job outlook includes the risk of jobs being outsourced, possibly to other countries. **Outsourcing** is a process whereby a business hires a third-party firm to provide business services (such as customer-support call centers) that were previously handled by in-house employees. **Offshoring** occurs when the outsourcing firm is located (or uses employees) outside the United States. India was the first country to offer its workforce and infrastructure for offshoring, and countries such as China, Romania, and other former Eastern Bloc countries now vie for a piece of the action. The big lure of outsourcing and offshoring is cost savings: The outsourcing firm can do the work more cheaply than in-house employees can. Considering that the standard of living and salaries are much lower in many countries than they are in the United States, offshoring is an attractive option for many U.S. employers. It may also be faster to hire outside assistance if a business does not already employ workers with the required skill set.

However, outsourcing and offshoring do not always deliver the vast cost savings that chief executive officers

**Figure 13.2**

The salary wizard at Salary.com is easy to tailor to your location.

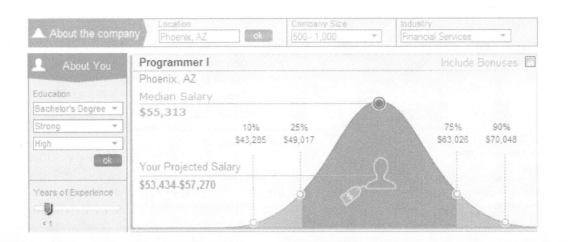

envision. TPI, a global sourcing advisory firm, conducted a survey that showed that the average cost savings from outsourcing was only 15 percent. Furthermore, other less-tangible factors can outweigh the cost savings from outsourcing. Some helpdesk jobs are being brought back to the United States because companies have experienced a backlash from consumers who have had difficulty understanding the employees with foreign accents who staff the support lines. Communications problems can arise between internal and external employees, for example, and cultural differences between the home country and the country doing the offshoring can result in software code that needs extensive rework by in-house employees to make it usable. Data also can be less secure in an external environment, or during the transfer between the company and an external vendor. A study by Deloitte Consulting found that 70 percent of survey participants had "negative experiences" with overseas outsourcing. And a survey in *CFO* magazine indicated that 22 percent of CFOs were planning to increase their outsourcing within the United States. Although outsourcing and offshoring won't be going away, companies are approaching these staffing alternatives with more caution and looking more to U.S. companies to provide resources.

So, many IT jobs are staying in the United States. According to *InformationWeek* magazine, most of the jobs in these three categories (see Figure 13.3) will stay put:

1. **Customer interaction:** Jobs that require direct input from customers or that involve systems with which customers interface daily.

2. **Enablers:** Jobs that involve getting key business projects accomplished, often requiring technical skills beyond the realm of IT, and good people skills.

3. **Infrastructure jobs:** Jobs that are fundamental to moving and storing the information that U.S.-based employees need to do their jobs.

Also, jobs that require specific knowledge of the U.S. marketplace and culture, such as social media managers, are also very likely to not be offshored.

## Women Are in High Demand in IT Departments

Currently, women make up about 25 percent of the IT workforce (per the National Center for Women and Information Technology). This presents a huge opportunity for women who have IT skills, because many IT departments are actively seeking to diversify their workforces. In addition, although a salary gender gap (the difference between what men and women earn for performing the same job) exists in IT careers, it's smaller than in most other professions.

## Choice of Working Location

In this case, location refers to the setting in which you work. IT jobs can be office-based, field-based, project-based, or home-based. Since not every situation is perfect for every individual, you can look for a job that suits your tastes and requirements. Figure 13.4 summarizes the major job types and their locations.

## Constant Changes Avoid Boredom

In IT, the playing field is always changing. New software and hardware are constantly being developed. You will need to work hard to keep your skills up to date. You will spend a lot of time in training and self-study trying to learn new systems and techniques. Many individuals thrive in this type of environment because it keeps their jobs from becoming dull or routine.

## You Work in Teams

When college and high school students are asked to describe their ideal jobs, the majority usually describe jobs that involve working in teams. Despite what many people think, IT professionals are not locked in lightless cubicles, basking in the glow of their monitors, and working on projects alone. Most IT jobs require constant interaction with other workers, usually in team settings. People skills are highly prized by IT departments. If you have good leadership and team-building skills, you will have the opportunity to exercise them in an IT job.

**Figure 13.3** | JOBS THAT SHOULD REMAIN ONSHORE

| Customer Interaction | Enablers | Infrastructure Jobs |
|---|---|---|
| Web application developers | Business process analysts | Network security |
| Web interface designers | Application developers (when customer interaction is critical) | Network installation technicians |
| Database and data warehouse designers/developers | Project managers (for systems with customers and business users who are located predominantly in the United States) | Network administrators (engineers) |
| Customer relationship management (CRM) analysts | | Wireless infrastructure managers and technicians |
| Enterprise resource planning (ERP) implementation specialists | | Disaster recovery planners and responders |

**Figure** 13.4 | WHERE DO YOU WANT TO WORK?

| Type of Job | Location and Hours | Special Considerations |
|---|---|---|
| Office-based | Report for work to the same location each day and interact with the same people on a regular basis. Requires regular hours of attendance (such as 9 A.M. to 5 P.M.). | May require working beyond "normal" working hours. May also require workers to be on call 24/7. |
| Field-based | Travel from place to place as needed and perform short-term jobs at each location. | Involve a great deal of travel and the ability to work independently. |
| Project-based | Work at client sites on specific projects for extended periods of time (weeks or months). | Can be especially attractive to individuals who like workplace situations that vary on a regular basis. |
| Home-based (telecommuting) | Work from home. | Involve very little day-to-day supervision and require an individual who is self-disciplined. |

## You Don't Need to Be a Mathematical Genius

Certain IT careers such as programming involve a fair bit of math. But even if you're not mathematically inclined, you can explore many other IT careers. IT employers also value such attributes as creativity, marketing, and artistic style, especially in jobs that involve working on the Internet or with social media.

## IT Skills Are Portable

Most computing skills are portable from industry to industry. A networking job in the clothing manufacturing industry uses the same primary skill set as a networking job for a supermarket chain. Therefore, if something disastrous happens to the industry you're in, you should be able to switch to another industry without having to learn an entire new skill set. Combining business courses with IT courses will also make you more marketable when changing jobs. For example, as an accounting major, if you minor in IT, employers may be more willing to hire you because working in accounting today means constantly interfacing with management information systems and manipulating data.

# Challenges of IT Careers

Although there are many positive aspects of IT careers, there can be some challenges as well. The discussions that follow are not meant to discourage you from pursuing an IT career, but merely to make you aware of exactly what challenges you may face in an IT department.

## Stress

Most IT jobs are hectic (see Figure 13.5). Whereas the average American works 42 hours a week, a survey by *InformationWeek* shows that the average IT staff person works 45 hours a week and is on call for another 24 hours. On-call time (hours an employee must be available to work in the event of a problem) has been increasing in recent years because more IT systems (such as e-commerce systems) require 24/7 availability. There are plenty of other high-stress jobs, such as air-traffic controller or physician, but IT jobs do tend to spawn more stressful situations and development

**Figure** 13.5

Stress comes from multiple directions in IT jobs.

timelines since availability of information is so critical to businesses today.

### I'm Just One of the "Guys"

A majority of IT jobs are filled by men, so some women view IT departments as *Dilbert*-like microcosms of antisocial geeks and don't feel they would fit in. Unfortunately, some mostly male IT departments do suffer from varying degrees of gender bias. Although some women may thrive on the challenge of enlightening these male enclaves and bringing them into the 21st century, others might find it difficult to work in such environments.

### Not Another Training Course!

Although the constantly changing nature of IT can alleviate boredom, keeping up with the changes can also cause some stress. You will need to take training courses, do self-study, and perhaps take additional college courses such as graduate degrees to keep up with the vast shifts of technology. You need to accept that the concept of lifelong learning is much more important in IT careers than in some other fields.

## What Realm of IT Should I Work In?

Figure 13.6 provides an organizational chart for a modern IT department that should help you understand the careers currently available and how they interrelate. The chief information officer (CIO) has overall responsibility for the development, implementation, and maintenance of information systems and infrastructure. Usually the CIO reports to the chief operating officer (COO).

The responsibilities below the CIO are generally grouped into two units: development and integration (responsible for the development of systems and Web sites) and technical services (responsible for the day-to-day operations of the company's information infrastructure and network, including all hardware and software deployed).

In large organizations, responsibilities are distinct and jobs are defined more narrowly. In medium-sized organizations, there can be overlap between position responsibilities. At a small shop, you might be the network administrator, database administrator, computer support technician, and social media manager all at the same time. Let's look at the typical jobs found in each department.

### Working in Development and Integration

Two distinct paths exist in this division: Web development and systems development. Because everything involves the Web today, there is often a great deal of overlap between these paths.

#### Web Development

When most people think of Web development careers, they usually equate them with being a **webmaster**. However, today's webmasters usually are supervisors with responsibility for certain aspects of Web development. At smaller companies, they may also be responsible for tasks that the other individuals in a Web development group usually do:

- **Web content creators** generate the words and images that appear on the Web. Journalists, other writers, editors, and marketing personnel prepare an enormous amount of Web content, whereas **video producers**, **graphic designers**, and **animators** create Web-based multimedia. **Interface designers** work with graphic designers and animators to create a look and feel for the site and make it easy to navigate. Content creators have a thorough understanding of their own fields as well as HTML/XHTML, PHP, and JavaScript. They also need to be familiar with the capabilities and limitations of modern Web development tools so that they know what the Web publishers can accomplish.

- **Web programmers** build Web pages to deploy the materials that the content creators develop. They wield the software tools (such as Adobe Dreamweaver and Microsoft Expression) that develop the Web pages and create links to databases (using products such as Oracle and SQL Server) to keep information flowing between users and Web pages. They must possess a solid understanding of client- and server-side Web languages (HTML/XHTML, XML, Java, JavaScript, ASP, PHP, Silverlight, and PERL) and development environments such as the Microsoft .NET Framework.

**Figure 13.6**

A typical structure for an IT department at a large corporation.

- **Customer interaction technicians** provide feedback to a Web site's customers. Major job responsibilities include answering e-mail, sending requested information, funneling questions to appropriate personnel (technical support, sales, and so on), and providing suggestions to Web publishers for site improvements. Extensive customer service training is essential to work effectively in this area.

- **Social media directors** are responsible for directing the strategy of the company on all social media sites where the company maintains a presence. Often supervising customer interaction technicians, these people make sure that customers have a quality experience while interacting with company employees and customers on sites such as Facebook, Twitter, and Yelp. Responding to comments left on

sites, developing promotional strategies, and designing functionality of the company's social media sites are common job responsibilities. In smaller companies, these duties might be done by customer interaction technicians.

As you can see in Figure 13.7, many different people can work on the same Web site. The education required varies widely for these jobs. Web programming jobs often require a four-year college degree in computer science, whereas graphic designers often are hired with two-year art degrees.

### Systems Development

Ask most people what systems developers do and they will answer, "programming." However, programming is only one aspect of systems development. Because large projects involve many people, there are many job opportunities in systems development. An explanation of each key area follows.

- **Systems analysts** spend most of their time in the beginning stages of the system development life cycle (SDLC). They talk with end users to gather information about problems and existing information systems. They document systems and propose solutions to problems. Having good people skills is essential to success as a systems analyst. In ad-

**Figure 13.7**
It takes a team to create and maintain a Web site.

Interface designers create navigation schemes

Content creators generate text

Social media directors monitor customer feedback

Graphic designers create art

dition, systems analysts work with programmers during the development phase to design appropriate programs to solve the problem at hand. Therefore, many organizations insist on hiring systems analysts who have both solid business backgrounds and previous programming experience (at least at a basic level). For entry-level jobs, a four-year degree is usually required. Many colleges and universities offer degrees in management information systems (MIS) that include a mixture of systems development, programming, and business courses.

- **Programmers** participate in the program development life cycle, attending meetings to document user needs and working closely with systems analysts during the design phase. Programmers need excellent written communication skills because they often generate detailed systems documentation for end-user training purposes. Because programming languages are mathematically based, it is essential for programmers to have strong math skills and an ability to think logically. Programmers should also be proficient at more than one programming language. A four-year degree is usually required for entry-level programming positions.

- **Project managers** usually have years of experience as programmers or systems analysts. This job is part of a career path upward from entry-level programming and systems analyst jobs. Project managers manage the overall systems development process: assigning staff, budgeting, reporting to management, coaching team members, and ensuring deadlines are met. Project managers need excellent time management skills because they are pulled in several directions at once. Many project managers obtain master's degrees to supplement their undergraduate degrees in computer science or MIS.

In addition to these key players, the following people are also involved in the systems development process:

- **Technical writers** generate systems documentation for end users and for programmers who may make modifications to the system in the future.

- **Network engineers** help the programmers and analysts design compatible systems, because many systems are required to run in certain environments (UNIX or Windows, for instance) and must work well in conjunction with other programs.

- **Database developers** design and build databases to support the software systems being developed.

Large development projects may have all of these team members on the project. Smaller projects may require an overlap of positions (such as a programmer also acting as a systems analyst). The majority of these jobs require four-year college degrees in computer science or management information systems. As shown in Figure 13.8, team members work together to build a system.

It is important to emphasize that all systems development careers are stressful. Deadlines are tight for development projects, especially if they involve getting a new product to market ahead of the competition. Nevertheless, if you enjoy challenges and can endure a fast-paced, dynamic environment, there should be plenty of opportunities for good systems developers in the decade ahead.

## Working in Technical Services

Technical services jobs are vital to keeping IT systems running. The people in these jobs install and maintain the infrastructure behind the IT systems and work with end users to make sure they can interact with the systems effectively. These also are the *least likely* IT jobs to be outsourced because hands-on work with equipment and users is required on a regular basis. The two major categories of technical services careers are information systems and support services.

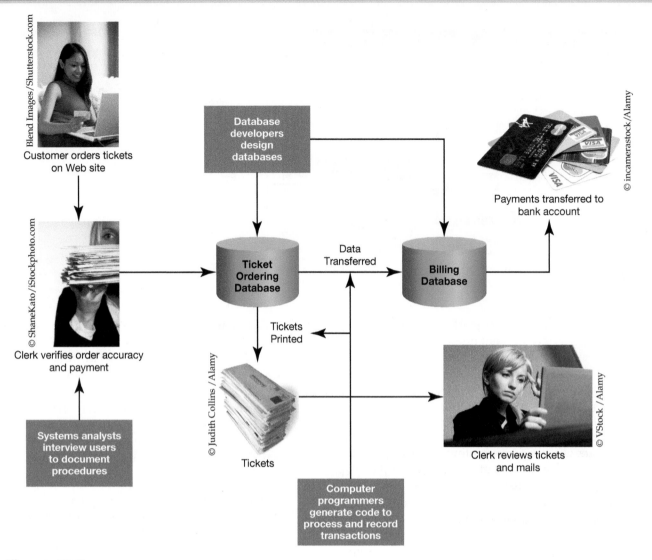

**Figure** 13.8

This is a flowchart of a ticket ordering system. Each member of the systems development team performs functions critical to the development process (as shown in the red boxes).

## Information Systems

The information systems department keeps the networks and telecommunications up and running at all times. Within the department, you'll find a variety of positions.

- **Network administrators** (sometimes called *network engineers*) install and configure servers, design and plan networks, and test new networking equipment (see Figure 13.9). Network administrators are involved in every stage of network planning and deployment. They decide what equipment to buy and what type of media to use, and they determine the correct topology for the network. They also often develop policies regarding network usage, security measures, and hardware and software standards.

  After the planning is complete, network administrators help install the network (either by supervising third-party contractors or by doing the work themselves). Typical installation tasks include configur-

ing and installing client computers and peripherals, running cable, and installing wireless media devices. Installing and configuring security devices and software are also critical jobs.

When equipment and cables break, network administrators must locate the source of the trouble and fix the problem. They also obtain and install updates to network software, and evaluate new equipment to determine whether the network should be upgraded. In addition, they monitor the network's performance to ensure that users' needs are met.

Because of the importance of the Internet to most organizations, network administrators ensure that the Internet connection is maintained at all times, which usually is a high priority on their to-do list. Finally, network administrators plan disaster recovery strategies (such as what to do if a fire destroys the server room).

**Figure 13.9**

At smaller companies, you may be fixing a user's computer in the morning, installing and configuring a new network operating system in the afternoon, and troubleshooting a wiring problem (shown here) in the evening.

- **Database administrators (DBAs)** install and configure database servers and ensure that the servers provide an adequate level of access to all users.
- **Web server administrators** install, configure, and maintain Web servers and ensure that the company maintains Internet connectivity at all times.
- **Telecommunications technicians** oversee the communications infrastructure, including training employees to use telecommunications equipment. They are often on call 24 hours a day.

### Support Services

As a member of the support services team, you interface with users (external customers or employees) and troubleshoot their computer problems. These positions include the following:

- **Helpdesk analysts** staff the phones, respond to Internet live chat, or respond to e-mail and solve problems for customers or employees, either remotely or in person. Often helpdesk personnel are called upon to train users on the latest software and hardware.
- **Computer support technicians** go to a user's physical location and fix software and hardware problems. They also often have to chase down and repair faults in the network infrastructure.

As important as these people are, they often receive a great deal of abuse by angry users whose computers are not working. When working in support services, you need to be patient and not be overly sensitive to insults! Technical services jobs often require two-year college degrees or training at trade schools or technical institutes. At smaller companies, job duties tend to overlap between the helpdesk and technician jobs. These jobs are in demand and require staffing in local markets, so they are

staying onshore. You can't repair a computer's power supply if you are located in another country!

## How Should I Prepare for a Job in IT?

A job in IT requires a robust skill set and formal training and preparation. Most employers today have an entry-level requirement of a college degree, a technical institute diploma, appropriate professional certifications, experience in the field, or a combination of these. How can you prepare for a job in IT?

1. **Get educated.** Two- and four-year colleges and universities normally offer three degrees to prepare students for IT careers: computer science, MIS, and information technology (although titles vary). Alternatives to colleges and universities are privately licensed technical (or trade) schools. Generally, these programs focus on building skill sets rapidly and qualifying for a job in a specific field. The main advantage of technical schools is that their programs usually take less time to complete than college degrees. However, to have a realistic chance of employment in IT fields other than networking or Web development, you should attend a degree-granting college or university.

2. **Investigate professional certifications.** Certifications attempt to provide a consistent method of measuring skill levels in specific areas of IT. Hundreds of IT certifications are available, most of which you get by passing a written exam. Software and hardware vendors (such as Microsoft and Cisco) and professional organizations (such as the Computing Technology Industry Association) often establish certification standards. Visit **www.microsoft.com**, **www.cisco.com**, **www.comptia.org**, and **www.sun.com** for more information on certifications.

   Employees with certifications generally earn more than employees who aren't certified. However, most employers don't view a certification as a substitute for a college degree or a trade school program. You should think of certifications as an extra edge beyond your formal education that will make you more attractive to employers. To ensure you're pursuing the right certifications, ask employers which certifications they respect, or explore online job sites to see which certifications are listed as desirable or required.

3. **Get experience.** In addition to education, employers want you to have experience, even for entry-level jobs. While you're still completing your education, consider getting an internship or part-time job in your field of study. Many colleges will help you find internships and allow you to earn credit toward your degree through internship programs.

4. **Do research.** Find out as much as you can about the company and the industry it is in before going on an interview. Start with the company's Web site and then expand your search to business and trade publications such as *Business Week* and *CIO* magazines.

## How Do I Get Started on My IT Career?

Training for a career is not useful unless you can find a job at the end of your training. Here are some tips on getting a job.

1. **Find an internship.** Many employers recruit at schools, and most schools maintain a placement office to help students find jobs. Employees in the placement office can help you with résumé preparation and interviewing skills, and provide you with leads for internships and jobs.

   You should also develop a relationship with your instructors. Many college instructors still work in or previously worked in the IT industry. They can often provide you with valuable advice and industry contacts.

2. **Start networking.** Many jobs are never advertised but instead are filled by word of mouth. Seek out contacts in your field and discuss job prospects with them. Find out what skills you need, and ask them to recommend others in the industry with whom you can speak. Professional organizations such as the Association for Computing Machinery (ACM) offer one way to network. These organizations often have chapters on college campuses and offer reduced membership rates for students.

   The contacts you make there could lead to your next job. Local user groups that are made up of working professionals with similar interests (such

as Microsoft programmers or Linux administrators) also are good sources of contacts. Figure 13.10 lists major professional organizations you should consider investigating.

If you are a woman and are thinking about pursuing an IT career, there are many resources and groups that cater to female IT professionals and students. The oldest and best-known organization is the Association for Women in Computing, founded in 1978. Figure 13.11 provides a list of resources to investigate.

3. **Check corporate Web sites for jobs.** Many corporate Web sites list current job opportunities. For example, Google provides searchable job listings by geographic location. Check the sites of companies in which you are interested and then do a search on the sites for job openings or, if provided, click their Employment links.

4. **Visit online employment sites.** Most IT jobs are advertised online at sites such as Monster.com and Dice.com. Most of these sites allow you to store your résumé online, and Dice (see Figure 13.12) allows employers to browse résumés to find qualified employees.

   Other sites also offer career resources, including **www.computerjobs.com, www.techcareers.com, www.justtechjobs.com, www.linkedin.com, www .computerwork.com, www.careerbuilder.com,** and **www.gamasutra.com.** Begin looking at job postings on these sites early in your education, because these job postings detail the skill sets employers require. Focusing on coursework that will provide you with desirable skill sets will make you more marketable.

The outlook for IT jobs should continue to be positive in the future. We wish you luck with your education and job search.

**Figure 13.10** | PROFESSIONAL ORGANIZATIONS

| Organization Name | Purpose | Web Site |
|---|---|---|
| Association for Computing Machinery (ACM) | Oldest scientific computing society. Maintains a strong focus on programming and systems development. | www.acm.org |
| Association for Information Systems (AIS) | Organization of professionals who work in academia and specialize in information systems. | www.aisnet.org |
| Association of Information Technology Professionals (AITP) | Heavy focus on IT education and development of seminars and learning materials. | www.aitp.org |
| Institute of Electrical and Electronics Engineers (IEEE) | Provides leadership and sets engineering standards for all types of network computing devices and protocols. | www.ieee.org |
| Information Systems Security Association (ISSA) | Not-for-profit, international organization of information security professionals and practitioners. | www.issa.org |

**Figure** 13.11 | RESOURCES FOR WOMEN IN IT

| Organization Name | Purpose | Web Site |
|---|---|---|
| Anita Borg Institute for Women and Technology | Organization whose aim is to "increase the impact of women on all aspects of technology." | **www.anitaborg.org** |
| Association for Women in Computing (AWC) | A not-for-profit organization dedicated to promoting the advancement of women in computing professions. | **www.awc-hq.org** |
| The Center for Women & Information Technology (CWIT) | Established at the University of Maryland, Baltimore County (UMBC), the organization is dedicated to providing global leadership in achieving women's full participation in all aspects of IT. | **www.umbc.edu/cwit** |
| Diversity/Careers in Engineering & Information Technology | An online magazine whose articles cover career issues focused on technical professionals who are members of minority groups, women, or people with disabilities. | **www.diversitycareers.com** |
| Women in Technology International (WITI) | A global trade association for tech-savvy, professional women. | **www.witi.com** |

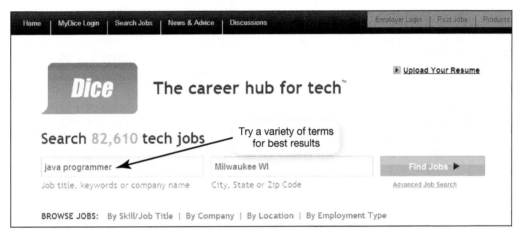

**Figure** 13.12

Employment sites such as Dice.com enable you to search for specific jobs within a defined geographic area.

The video gaming industry in the United States has surpassed the earning power of the Hollywood movie industry. In 2010, U.S. consumers bought over $18.5 billion worth of video games and accessories, whereas Hollywood took in just under $10.6 billion. Although some aspects of game development, such as scenery design and certain aspects of programming, are being sent offshore, the majority of game development requires a creative team whose members need to work in close proximity to each other. Therefore, it is anticipated that most game development jobs will stay in the United States. Consoles such as the Xbox 360 and the PlayStation 3 generate demand for large-scale games, but Xbox Live and PlayStation Network have also fueled demand for casual games. Also, the popularity of mobile devices such as smartphones and tablets is driving demand for lower-end, casual game applications. Casual games are games that can be played relatively quickly, often puzzle games. Demand for family-friendly games without violence, sex, and profanity is on the rise (see Figure 13.13). With all this demand, there are many opportunities for careers in game development.

Game development jobs usually are split along two paths: designers and programmers. Game designers tend to be artistic and are responsible for creating 2D and 3D art, game interfaces, video sequences, special effects, game levels, and scenarios. Game designers must master software packages such as Autodesk 3ds Max, Autodesk Maya, NewTek LightWave 3D, Adobe Photoshop, and Adobe Flash. Programmers are then responsible for coding the scenarios developed by these designers. Using languages and toolsets such as Objective-C, Unity, Apple Xcode, C, C++, Assembly, and Java, programmers build the game and ensure that it plays accurately.

Aside from programmers and designers, play testers and quality assurance professionals play the games with the intent of breaking them or discovering bugs within the game interfaces or worlds. **Play testing** is an essential part of the game development process because it assists designers in determining which aspects of the game are most intriguing to players and which parts of the game need to be repaired or enhanced.

No matter what job you may pursue in the realm of gaming, you will need to have a two- or four-year college degree. If you're interested in gaming, then look for a school with a solid animation or 3D art program or a computer game programming curriculum. Programming requires a strong background in mathematics and physics to enable you to realistically program environments that mimic the real world. Proficiency with mathematics (especially geometry) also helps with design careers. For more information on gaming careers, check out the International Game Developers Association site (**www.igda.org**) and Game Career Guide (**www.gamecareerguide.com**).

© Vinod Kurien / Alamy

**Figure 13.13**
Plants vs. Zombies, which has you grow plants to fend off encroaching zombie hordes, is an example of a popular casual game available for many different platforms.

# Multiple Choice

**Instructions:** Answer the multiple-choice questions below for more practice with key terms and concepts from this Technology in Focus feature.

1. The individuals responsible for making a Web site easy to navigate are referred to as
   a. network engineers.
   b. graphic designers.
   c. Web programmers.
   d. interface designers.

2. What type of job involves a great deal of travel and the ability to work independently?
   a. field-based
   b. project-based
   c. office-based
   d. home-based

3. Which position is *not* typically a part of the information systems department?
   a. helpdesk analysts
   b. telecommunications technicians
   c. network administrators
   d. W eb server administrators

4. Outsourcing is thought to be an attractive option for many companies because of
   a. the emphasis on employee training.
   b. the cost savings that can be realized.
   c. increased data security.
   d. the opportunity to experience new cultures and ideas.

5. Which role best describes those employees who design solutions to problems?
   a. project managers
   b. network engineers
   c. systems analysts
   d. database developers

6. Which of the following statements about IT careers is *true*?
   a. IT employers typically prefer certification to experience.
   b. Women who have IT skills have limited opportunities.
   c. Most IT jobs are being moved offshore.
   d. IT jobs require frequent interaction with others.

7. Which task is *not* typically performed by a network administrator?
   a. developing network usage policies
   b. installing networks
   c. planning for disaster recovery
   d. Web site programming

8. Social media directors are the people who are responsible for
   a. orchestrating the company strategy in online venues.
   b. providing feedback to Web site customers.
   c. creating the look and feel of a Web site.
   d. deploying the materials prepared by content creators.

9. The oldest scientific computing organization is the
   a. Institute of Electrical and Electronics Engineers.
   b. Association for Computing Machinery.
   c. Information Systems Security Association.
   d. Association for Women in Computing.

10. Which position is part of the Web development department?
    a. systems analyst
    b. Web content creator
    c. programmer
    d. technical writer

# Glossary

**3D sound card** An expansion card that enables a computer to produce sounds that are omnidirectional or three dimensional.

**802.11 standard** A wireless standard established in 1997 by the Institute of Electrical and Electronics Engineers; also known as WiFi (short for Wireless Fidelity), it enables wireless network devices to work seamlessly with other networks and devices.

## A

**access card reader** A device that reads information from a magnetic strip on the back of a credit card–like access card (such as a student ID card); card readers are easily programmed by adding authorized ID card numbers, Social Security numbers, and so on.

**access method** A program or hardware mechanism that controls which computer is allowed to use the transmission media in a network at a certain time.

**access time** The time it takes a storage device to locate its stored data.

**accounting software** An application program that helps business owners manage their finances more efficiently by providing tools for tracking accounting transactions such as sales, accounts receivable, inventory purchases, and accounts payable.

**ActionScript** A programming language included in Flash; similar to JavaScript in its keywords, operators, and classes.

**Active Server Pages (ASP)** A scripting environment in which users combine HyperText Markup Language (HTML), scripts, and reusable Microsoft ActiveX server components to create dynamically generated Web pages.

**active topology** A network topology in which each node on the network is responsible for retransmitting the token, or the data, to other nodes.

**Adobe Flash** A software product for developing Web-based multimedia.

**adware** A program that downloads on your computer when you install a freeware program, game, or utility. Generally, adware enables sponsored advertisements to appear in a section of your browser window or as a pop-up ad box.

**affective computing** A type of computing that relates to emotion or deliberately tries to influence emotion.

**aggregator** A software program that goes out and grabs the latest update of Web material (usually podcasts) according to your specifications.

**AJAX** A collection of technologies that allows the creation of Web applications that can update information on a page without requiring the user to do a page refresh or leave the page.

**algorithm** A set of specific, sequential steps that describe in natural language exactly what a computer program must do to complete its task.

**all-in-one computer** A desktop system unit that houses the computer's processor, memory, and monitor in a single unit.

**all-in-one printer** See *multifunction printer*.

**alphabetic check** Confirms that only textual characters are entered in a database field.

**analog** Waves that illustrate the loudness of a sound or the brightness of the colors in an image at a given moment in time.

**analog-to-digital converter chip** Converts analog signals into digital signals.

**antivirus software** Software that is specifically designed to detect viruses and protect a computer and files from harm.

**applet** A small program designed to be run from within another application. Java applets are often run on your computer by your browser through the Java Virtual Machine (an application built into current browsers).

**application programming interface (API)** A block of code in the operating system that software applications need to interact with.

**application server** A server that acts as a repository for application software.

**application software** The set of programs on a computer that helps a user carry out tasks such as word processing, sending e-mail, balancing a budget, creating presentations, editing photos, taking an online course, and playing games.

**artificial intelligence (AI)** The science that attempts to produce computers that display the same type of reasoning and intelligence that humans do.

**aspect ratio** The width-to-height proportion of a monitor.

**assembly language** A language that enables programmers to write their programs using a set of short, English-like commands that speak directly to the central processing unit (CPU) and give the programmer very direct control of hardware resources.

**audio editing software** Programs that perform basic editing tasks on audio files such as cutting dead air space from the beginning or end of a song or cutting a portion from the middle.

**augmented reality** A combination of our normal sense of the objects around us with an overlay of information displayed.

**authentication** The process of identifying a computer user, based on a login or username and password. The computer system determines whether the computer user is authorized and what level of access is to be granted on the network.

**authentication server** A server that keeps track of who is logging on to the network and which services on the network are available to each user.

**autonomy** The freedom to work without constant direction and control.

## B

**backdoor program** A program that enables a hacker to take complete control of a computer without the legitimate user's knowledge or permission.

**backup** A backup is a copy of computer files that you can use to replace the originals if they are lost or damaged.

**Backup and Restore** A Windows utility (found in the Control Panel) that allows the user to create a duplicate copy of all the data on a hard drive (or just the folders and files the user specifies) and copy it to another storage device, such as a DVD or external hard drive.

**backward compatibility** The accommodation of current devices being able to use previously issued software standards in addition to the current standards.

**bandwidth (data transfer rate)** The maximum speed at which data can be transmitted between two nodes on a network; usually measured in megabits per second (Mbps). See also *data transfer rate*.

**base class** The original object class from which other classes derive.

**base transceiver station** A large communications tower with antennas, amplifiers, and receivers/transmitters.

**basic input/output system (BIOS)** A program that manages the data between a computer's operating system and all the input and output devices attached to the computer; also responsible for loading the operating system (OS) from its permanent location on the hard drive to random access memory (RAM).

**bastion host** A heavily secured server located on a special perimeter network between a company's secure internal network and its firewall.

**batch processing** The process of accumulating transaction data until a certain point is reached, then processing those transactions all at once.

**beta version** A version of the software that is still under development. Many beta versions are available for a limited trial period, and are used to help the developers correct any errors before they launch the software on the market.

**binary decision** A decision point that can be answered in one of only two ways: *yes* (true) or *no* (false).

**binary digit (bit)** A digit that corresponds to the on and off states of a computer's switches. A bit contains a value of either 0 or 1.

**binary language** The language computers use to process data into information, consisting of only the values 0 and 1.

**binary large object (BLOB)** In databases, a type of object that holds extremely large chunks of data in binary form; this data is usually video clips, pictures, or audio clips.

**biometric authentication device** A device that uses some unique characteristic of human biology to identify authorized users.

**bit depth** The number of bits a video card uses to store data about each pixel on the monitor.

**black-hat hacker** A hacker who uses his knowledge to destroy information or for illegal gain.

**bloatware** The pre-installed software (often trial versions) on a new computer.

**BLOB** See *binary large object*.

**blog** See *Web log*.

**Blu-ray disc** A method of optical storage for digital data, developed for storing high-definition media. It has the largest storage capacity of all optical storage options.

**Bluetooth** A type of wireless technology that uses radio waves to transmit data over short distances (approximately 30 feet for Bluetooth 1 and 60 feet for Bluetooth 2). Often used to connect peripherals such as printers and keyboards to computers or headsets to cell phones.

**bookmark** A feature in some browsers that places a marker of a Web site's Uniform Resource Locator (URL) in an easily retrievable list. (Bookmarks are called Favorites in Microsoft Internet Explorer.)

**Boolean operator** A word used to refine logical searches. For Internet searches, the words AND, NOT, and OR describe the relationships between keywords in the search.

**boot process** The process for loading the operating system (OS) into random access memory (RAM) when the computer is turned on.

**boot-sector virus** A virus that replicates itself into the master boot record of a flash drive or hard drive.

**botnet** A large group of software applications (called *robots* or *bots*) that runs without user intervention on a large number of computers.

**breadcrumb list** A list that shows the hierarchy of previously viewed Web pages within the Web site that you are currently visiting. Shown at the top of some Web pages, it aids Web site navigation.

**bridge** A network device that is used to send data between two different local area networks (LANs) or two segments of the same LAN.

**brightness** A measure of the greatest amount of light showing when a monitor is displaying pure white; measured as candelas per square meter (cd/m2) or *nits*.

**broadband** A high-speed Internet connection such as cable, satellite, or digital subscriber line (DSL).

**browser** See *Web browser*.

**browsing** (1) The process of viewing database records. (2) The process of "surfing" the Web.

**brute force attack** An attack delivered by specialized hacking software that tries many combinations of letters, numbers, and pieces of a user ID in an attempt to discover a user password.

**bus (linear bus) topology** A system of networking connections in which all devices are connected to a central cable called the *bus* (or backbone).

**business intelligence systems** Used to analyze and interpret data to enable managers to make informed decisions about how best to run a business.

**business-to-business (B2B)** E-commerce transactions between businesses.

**business-to-consumer (B2C)** E-commerce transactions between businesses and consumers.

**byte** Eight binary digits (bits).

## C

**C** The predecessor language of C++; developed originally for system programmers by Brian Kernighan and Dennis Ritchie of AT&T Bell Laboratories in 1978. It provides higher-level programming language features (such as if statements and for loops) but still allows programmers to manipulate the system memory and central processing unit (CPU) registers directly.

**C#** A programming language released by Microsoft to compete with Java. Pronounced *see sharp*.

**C++** The successor language to C. Developed by Bjarne Stroustrup, C++ uses all of the same symbols and keywords as C but extends the language with additional keywords, better security, and more support for the reuse of existing code through object-oriented design.

**cache memory** Small blocks of memory, located directly on and next to the central processing unit (CPU) chip, that act as holding places for recently or frequently used instructions or data that the CPU accesses the most. When these instructions or data are stored in cache memory, the CPU can more quickly retrieve them than if it had to access the instructions or data from random access memory (RAM).

**cascading style sheets (CSS)** A list of statements (also known as rules) that define in one single location how HTML/XHTML elements are to be displayed.

**Cat 6 cable** A UTP cable type that provides more than 1 GB of throughput.

**cellular phone (cell phone)** A telephone that operates over a wireless network. Cell phones can also offer Internet access, text messaging, personal information management (PIM) features, and more.

**central processing unit (CPU or processor)** The part of the system unit of a computer that is responsible for data processing (the "brains" of the computer); it is the largest and most important chip in the computer. The CPU controls all the functions performed by the computer's other components and processes all the commands issued to it by software instructions.

**centralized** A type of network design in which users are not responsible for creating their own data backups or providing security for their computers; instead, those tasks are handled by a centralized server, software, and a system administrator.

**CGI script** A computer program that conforms to the Common Gateway Interface (CGI) specification, which provides a method for sending data between end users (browser users) and Web servers.

**cgi-bin** A directory where Common Gateway Interface (CGI) scripts are normally placed.

**circuit switching** A method of communication in which a dedicated connection is formed between two points (such as two people on telephones) and the connection remains active for the duration of the transmission.

**class** A collection of descriptive variables and active functions that together define a set of common properties. Actual examples of the class are known as *objects*.

**classless interdomain routing (CIDR)** Pronounced "cider," this is an addressing scheme that allows a single IP address to represent several unique IP addresses by adding a network prefix (a slash and a number) to the end of the last octet; also known as *supernetting*.

**clickstream data** Information captured about each click that users make as they navigate a Web site.

**client** A computer that requests information from a server in a client/server network (such as your computer when you are connected to the Internet).

**client/server model** A way of describing typical network functions. Client computers (such as your desktop PC) request services, and servers provide ("serve up") those services to the clients.

**client/server network (server-based network)** A type of network that uses servers to deliver services to computers that are requesting them (clients).

**client-side program** A computer program that runs on the client computer and requires no interaction with a Web server.

**clock speed** The steady and constant pace at which a computer goes through machine cycles, measured in hertz (Hz).

**cloud server** Servers that are maintained by hosting companies, such as Rackspace Hosting, and that are connected to networks via the Internet.

**coaxial cable** A single copper wire surrounded by layers of plastic insulation and sheathing; used mainly in cable television and cable Internet service.

**code editing** The step in which a programmer physically types the code into the computer.

**codec** A rule, implemented in either software or hardware, which squeezes a given amount of audio and video information into less space.

**coding** The process of translating an algorithm into a programming language.

**cold boot** The process of starting a computer from a powered-down or off state.

**collaborative consumption** Joining together as a group to use a specific product more efficiently.

**command-driven interface** Interface between user and computer in which the user enters commands to communicate with the computer system.

**comment (remark)** A plain English notation inserted into program code for documentation. The comment is not ever seen by the compiler.

**commerce server** A computer that hosts software that enables consumers to purchase goods and services over the Web. These servers generally use special security protocols to protect sensitive information (such as credit card numbers) from being intercepted.

**Common Gateway Interface (CGI)** Provides a methodology by which a browser can request that a program file be executed (or run) instead of just being delivered to the browser.

**communications server** A server that handles all communications between the network and other networks, including managing Internet connectivity.

**compact disc (CD)** A method of optical storage for digital data; originally developed for storing digital audio.

**compilation** The process by which code is converted into machine language, or the language the central processing unit (CPU) can understand.

**compiler** The program that understands both the syntax of the programming language and the exact structure of the central processing unit (CPU) and its machine language. It can "read" the source code and translate the source code directly into machine language.

**completeness check** A process that ensures that all database fields defined as "required" have data entered into them.

**computational field (computed field)** A numeric field in a database that is filled as the result of a computation.

**computer** A data-processing device that gathers, processes, outputs, and stores data and information.

**computer forensics** The application of computer systems and techniques to gather potential legal evidence; a law enforcement specialty used to fight high-tech crime.

**computer literate** Being familiar enough with computers that you understand their capabilities and limitations and know how to use them.

**computer protocol** A set of rules for accomplishing electronic information exchange. If the Internet is the information superhighway, then protocols are the driving rules.

**computer-aided design (CAD)** A 3D modeling program used to create automated designs, technical drawings, and model visualizations.

**connectionless protocol** A protocol that a host computer can use to send data over the network without establishing a direct connection with any specific recipient computer.

**connection-oriented protocol** A protocol that requires two computers to exchange control packets, which set up the parameters of the data exchange session, before sending packets that contain data.

**connectivity port** A port that enables the computer (or other device) to be connected to other devices or systems such as networks, modems, and the Internet.

**consistency check** The process of comparing the value of data in a database field against established parameters to determine whether the value is reasonable.

**consumer-to-consumer (C2C)** E-commerce transactions between consumers through online sites such as eBay.com.

**contrast ratio** A measure of the difference in light intensity between the brightest white and the darkest black colors that a monitor can produce. If the contrast ratio is too low, colors tend to fade when the brightness is adjusted to a high or low setting.

**control structure** The general term used for keywords in a programming language that allow the programmer to control, or redirect, the flow of the program based on a decision.

**cookie** A small text file that some Web sites automatically store on a client computer's hard drive when a user visits the site.

**copyleft** A simplified licensing scheme that enables copyright holders to grant certain rights to a work while retaining other rights.

**core** A complete processing section from a CPU, embedded into one physical chip.

**course management software** A program that provides traditional classroom tools,

such as calendars and grade books, over the Internet, as well as areas for students to exchange ideas and information in chat rooms, discussion forums, and e-mail.

**CPU benchmarks** Measurements used to compare performance between processors.

**CPU usage graph** Records your CPU usage for the past several seconds.

**creative surplus** A term used to describe the ability of the world's populace to volunteer and collaborate on large projects.

**crisis mapping tool** A tool that collects information from e-mails, text messages, blog posts, and Twitter tweets and maps them, making the information instantly publicly available.

**crowdsourcing** The process of taking a task that an employee or a contractor usually performs (such as product design) and instead outsourcing that task to a large group of people, usually via the Internet.

**CSMA/CD** A method of data collision detection in which a node connected to the network listens (that is, has carrier sense) to determine that no other nodes are currently transmitting data signals; short for Carrier Sense Multiple Access with Collision Detection.

**custom installation** The process of installing only those features of a software program that a user wants on the hard drive.

**customer relationship management (CRM) software** A business program used for storing sales and client contact information in one central database.

**cybercrime** Any criminal action perpetrated primarily through the use of a computer.

**cybercriminal** An individual who uses computers, networks, and the Internet to perpetrate crime.

**cyberloafing** Doing anything with a computer that is unrelated to a job (such as playing video games), while one is supposed to be working. Also called *cyberslacking*.

**data** Numbers, words, pictures, or sounds that represent facts, figures, or ideas.

**data breach** When sensitive or confidential information is copied, transmitted, or viewed by an individual who was never authorized to handle the data.

**data centralization** Having all data in one central location (usually a database). Data centralization helps ensure data integrity by requiring data to be updated only in one place if the data changes.

**data collision** When two computers send data at the same time and the sets of data collide somewhere in the media.

**data dictionary (database schema)** A file that defines the name, data type, and length of each field in the database.

**data file** File that contains stored data.

**data inconsistency** Any difference in data in lists caused when data exists in multiple lists and not all lists are updated when a piece of data changes.

**data integrity** The process of ensuring that data contained in a database is accurate and reliable.

**data mart** Small slices of a data warehouse.

**data mining** The process by which great amounts of data are analyzed and investigated. The objective is to spot significant patterns or trends within the data that would otherwise not be obvious.

**data plan** A connectivity plan or text messaging plan in which data charges are separate from cell phone calling charges and are provided at rates different from those for voice calls.

**data redundancy** When the same data exists in more than one place in a database.

**data staging** A three-step process: extracting data from source databases, transforming (reformatting) the data, and storing the data in a data warehouse.

**data transfer rate (bandwidth)** The maximum speed at which data can be transmitted between two nodes on a network; usually measured in megabits per second (Mbps).

**data type (field type)** An attribute of a data field that determines what type of data can be stored in the database field or memory location.

**data warehouse** A large-scale electronic repository of data that contains and organizes in one place all the data related to an organization.

**database** A collection of related data that can be easily stored, sorted, organized, and queried.

**database administrator (database designer)** An individual trained in the design, construction, and maintenance of databases.

**database designer** See *database administrator.*

**database management system (DBMS)** A type of specially designed application software (such as Oracle or Microsoft Access) that interacts with the user, other applications, and the database to capture and analyze data.

**database query** An inquiry the user poses to a database to extract a meaningful subset of data.

**database server** A server that provides client computers with access to information stored in a database.

**database software** An electronic filing system best used for larger and more complicated groups of data that require more than one table and the ability to group, sort, and retrieve data and generate reports.

**data-flow diagram** Diagram that traces all data in an information system from the point at which data enters the system to its final resting place (storage or output).

**date field** A field in a database that holds date data such as birthdays, due dates, and so on.

**debugger** A tool that helps programmers step through a program as it runs to locate errors.

**debugging** The process of repeatedly running a program to find errors and to make sure the program behaves in the way it should.

**decentralized** A type of network in which users are responsible for creating their own data backups and for providing security for their computers.

**decision point** A point at which a computer program must choose from a set of different actions based on the value of its current inputs.

**decision support system (DSS)** A system designed to help managers develop solutions for specific problems.

**dedicated server** A server used to fulfill one specific function (such as handling e-mail).

**default value** The value a database will use for a field unless the user enters another value.

**denial-of-service (DoS) attack** An attack that occurs when legitimate users are denied access to a computer system because a hacker is repeatedly making requests of that computer system that tie up its resources and deny legitimate users access.

**derivative work** Intellectual property that is based on an original work but is modified in some way.

**derived class** A class created based on a previously existing class (i.e., a base class). Derived classes inherit all of the member variables and methods of the base class from which they are derived.

**desktop** As its name implies, the computer's desktop puts at your fingertips all of the elements necessary for a productive work session and that are typically found on or near the top of a traditional desk, such as files and folders.

**desktop computer** A computer that is intended for use at a single location. A desktop computer consists of a case that houses the main components of the computer, plus peripheral devices.

**desktop publishing (DTP) software** Programs for incorporating and arranging graphics and text to produce creative documents.

**detail report** A report generated with data from a database that shows the individual transactions that occurred during a certain time period.

**device driver** Software that facilitates the communication between a device and the operating system.

**Device Manager** A feature in the Windows operating system that lets individuals view and change the properties of all hardware devices attached to the computer.

**digital convergence** The use of a single unifying device to handle media, Internet, entertainment, and telephony needs; is expressed in the range of devices now on the market.

**digital divide** The discrepancy between those who have access to the opportunities and knowledge computers and the Internet offer and those who do not.

**digital rights management (DRM)** A system of access control that allows only limited use of material that has been legally purchased.

**digital signal processor** A specialized chip that processes digital information and transmits signals very quickly.

**digital subscriber line (DSL)** A type of connection that uses telephone lines to connect to the Internet and that allows both phone and data transmissions to share the same line.

**digital video (or versatile) disc (DVD)** A method of optical storage for digital data that has greater storage capacity than compact discs.

**digital video editing software** A program for editing digital video.

**digital video interface (DVI)** Video interface technology that newer LCD monitors, as well as other multimedia devices such as televisions, DVD players, and projectors, use to connect to a PC.

**directory** A hierarchical structure that include files, folders, and drives used to create a more organized and efficient computer.

**Disk Cleanup** A Windows utility that removes unnecessary files from the hard drive.

**disk defragmenter** A utility that regroups related pieces of files on the hard drive, enabling faster retrieval of the data.

**distributed denial of service (DDoS) attack** An automated attack that is launched from more than one zombie computer at the same time.

**Document Object Model (DOM)** A means to organize objects and page elements in a Web page. DOM defines every item on a Web page, such as graphics, tables, and headers, as an object.

**documentation** A description of the development and technical details of a computer program, including how the code works and how the user interacts with the program.

**domain name** A part of a Uniform Resource Locator (URL). Domain names consist of two parts: the site's host and a suffix that indicates the type of organization. (Example: popsci.com)

**Domain Name System (DNS) server** A server that contains location information for domains on the Internet and functions like a phone book for the Internet.

**dotted decimal number (dotted quad)** One of the numbers in an Internet Protocol (IP) address.

**drawing software (illustration software)** Programs for creating or editing two-dimensional line-based drawings.

**drive bay** A special shelf inside a computer that is designed to hold storage devices.

**drive-by download** The use of malicious software to attack your computer by downloading harmful programs onto your computer, without your knowledge, while you are surfing a Web site.

**dynamic addressing** The process of assigning Internet Protocol (IP) addresses when users log on using their Internet service provider (ISP). The computer is assigned an address from an available pool of IP addresses.

**dynamic decision making** A mechanism that allows a Web page to decide how to display itself, based on the choices the reader makes as he or she looks at the page.

**Dynamic Host Configuration Protocol (DHCP)** The protocol that handles dynamic addressing. Part of the Transmission Control Protocol/Internet Protocol (TCP/IP) protocol suite, DHCP takes a pool of IP addresses and shares them with hosts on the network on an as-needed basis.

**Dynamic HyperText Markup Language (DHTML or dynamic HTML)** A combination of Web development technologies including HTML, cascading style sheets, and a scripting language that are used to add interactivity to a Web site after the Web site has been loaded onto the client computer.

# E

**e-commerce (electric commerce)** The process of conducting business online for purposes ranging from fund-raising to advertising to selling products.

**e-mail (electronic mail)** Internet-based communication in which senders and recipients correspond.

**e-mail client** A software program that runs on a computer and is used to send and receive e-mail through the ISP's server.

**e-mail server** A server that processes and delivers incoming and outgoing e-mail.

**e-mail virus** A virus transmitted by e-mail that often uses the address book in the victim's e-mail system to distribute itself.

**editor** A tool that helps programmers as they enter code, highlighting keywords and alerting the programmers to typos.

**electronic text (etext)** Textual information stored as digital information so it can be stored, manipulated, and transmitted by electronic devices.

**element** The tags and the text between the tags in HyperText Markup Language (HTML).

**embedded computer** A specially designed computer chip that resides inside another device, such as a car. These self-contained computer devices have their own programming and typically neither receive input from users nor interact with other systems.

**encryption** The process of encoding data (ciphering) so that only the person with a corresponding decryption key (the intended recipient) can decode (or decipher) and read the message.

**encryption virus** A malicious program that searches for common data files and compresses them into a file using a complex encryption key, thereby rendering the files unusable.

**enterprise resource planning (ERP) system** Used to control many "back office" operations and processing functions such as billing, production, inventory management, and human resources management.

**entertainment software** Programs designed to provide users with entertainment. Computer games make up the vast majority of entertainment software.

**ereader** A device that can display etext and has supporting tools, like note taking, bookmarks, and integrated dictionaries.

**ergonomics** How a user sets up his or her computer and other equipment to minimize risk of injury or discomfort.

**error handling** In programming, the instructions that a program runs if the input data is incorrect or another error is encountered.

**Error-Checking** A Windows utility that checks for lost files and fragments as well as physical errors on a hard drive.

**Ethernet network** A network that uses the Ethernet protocol as the means (or standard) by which the nodes on the network communicate.

**Ethernet port** A port that is slightly larger than a standard phone jack and transfers data at speeds of up to 10,000 Mbps; used to connect a computer to a DSL or cable modem or a network.

**event** The result of an action, such as a keystroke, mouse click, or signal to the printer, in the respective device (keyboard, mouse, or printer) to which the operating system responds.

**exception report** A report that shows conditions that are unusual or that need attention by users of a system.

**executable program** The binary sequence (code) that instructs the central processing unit (CPU) to perform certain calculations.

**expansion card (adapter card)** A circuit board with specific functions that augment the computer's basic functions and provide connections to other devices; examples include the sound card and the video card.

**expert system** A system designed to replicate the decision-making processes of human experts to solve specific problems.

**export** The process of putting data into an electronic file in a format that another application can understand.

**ExpressCard** Notebooks are often equipped with an ExpressCard slot. The ExpressCard can add a solid state drive (SSD), eSATA and FireWire ports, and other capabilities to your system.

**Extensible HyperText Markup Language (XHTML)** A standard established by the World Wide Web Consortium (W3C) that combines elements from both Extensible Markup Language (XML) and HyperText Markup Language (HTML). XHTML has much more stringent rules than HTML does regarding tagging.

**Extensible Markup Language (XML)** A language that enables designers to define their own tags, making it much easier to transfer data between Web sites and Web servers.

**extension (file type)** In a file name, the three letters that follow the user-supplied file name after the dot (.); the extension identifies what kind of family of files the file belongs to, or which application should be used to read the file.

**external data source** Any source not owned by the company that owns a decision support system, such as customer demographic data purchased from third parties.

**external hard drive** An internal hard drive that is enclosed in a protective case to make it portable; the drive is connected to the computer with a data transfer cable and is often used to back up data.

**external SATA (eSATA)** A port that will connect to some external hard drive models.

**extranet** The portion of a company's intranet that is used to share business information with business partners such as vendors, suppliers, and customers.

# F

**Favorites** A feature in Microsoft Internet Explorer that places a marker of a Web site's Uniform Resource Locator (URL) in an easily retrievable list in the browser's toolbar. (Called Bookmarks in some browsers.)

**fiber-optic cable** A cable that transmits data at close to the speed of light along glass or plastic fibers.

**fiber-optic service (FiOS)** Internet access that is enabled by transmitting data at the speed of light through glass or plastic fibers.

**field** A field where a category of information in a database is stored. Fields are displayed in columns.

**field constraint** Any property that must be satisfied for an entry to be accepted into the database field.

**field name** An identifying name assigned to each field in a database.

**field size** The maximum number of characters (or numbers) that a field in a database can contain.

**fifth-generation language (5GL)** A computer language that uses natural

language processing or expert systems to make the programming experience better matched to human thinking processes.

**file** A collection of related pieces of information stored together for easy reference; in database terminology, a file or *table* is a group of related records.

**file allocation table (FAT)** An index of all sector numbers that the hard drive stores in a table to keep track of which sectors hold which files.

**file compression utility** A program that takes out redundancies in a file to reduce the file size.

**file management** The process by which humans or computer software provide organizational structure to a computer's contents.

**file name** The first part of the label applied to a file; it is generally the name a user assigns to the file when saving it.

**file path** The exact location of a file, starting with the drive in which the file is located, and including all folders, subfolders (if any), the file name, and the extension. (Example: C:\Users\username\Documents\Illustrations\EBronte.jpg)

**file server** A computer deployed to provide remote storage space or to act as a repository for files that users can access.

**File Transfer Protocol (FTP)** A protocol used to upload and download files from one computer to another over the Internet.

**financial planning software** Programs for managing finances, such as Intuit's Quicken and Microsoft Money, which include electronic checkbook registers and automatic bill payment tools.

**firewall** A software program or hardware device designed to prevent unauthorized access to computers or networks.

**FireWire 400 (IEEE 1394)** An interface port that transfers data at 400 Mbps.

**FireWire 800** One of the fastest ports available, moving data at 800 Mbps.

**firmware** System software that controls hardware devices.

**first-generation language (1GL)** The actual machine language of a central processing unit (CPU); the sequence of bits—1s and 0s—that the CPU understands.

**flash drive** A drive that plugs into a universal serial bus (USB) port on a computer and stores data digitally. Also called *USB drive, jump drive,* or *thumb drive.*

**flash memory** Portable, nonvolatile memory.

**flash memory card** A form of portable storage; this removable memory card is often used in digital cameras, portable media players, and personal digital assistants (PDAs).

**flowchart** A visual representation of the patterns an algorithm comprises.

**folder** A collection of files stored on a computer.

**for** Keyword in Visual Basic used with the Next keyword to implement a loop.

**foreign key** The primary key of another database table that is included for purposes of establishing relationships with another table.

**fourth-generation language (4GL)** A sophisticated level of programming language such as a report generator or database query language.

**frame** A container designed to hold multiple data packets.

**freeware** Any copyrighted software that can be used for free.

**front side bus (FSB)** See *local bus.*

**full installation** The process of installing all the files and programs from the distribution CD to the computer's hard drive.

**fuzzy logic** A type of logic that allows the interjection of experiential learning into an equation by considering probabilities.

# G

**gadget** A mini-application that runs on the desktop, offering easy access to a frequently used tool such as weather or a calendar item.

**gateway** See *wireless router.*

**general availability (GA)** After the RTM is issued, the product is ready to be purchased by the public.

**geotag** Data attached to a photograph that indicate the latitude and longitude where you were standing when you took the photo.

**gigabit Ethernet** The most commonly used wired Ethernet standard deployed in devices designed for home networks which provides bandwidth of up to 1 Gbps.

**gigabyte (GB)** About a billion bytes.

**gigahertz (GHz)** One billion hertz.

**Global Positioning System (GPS)** A system of 21 satellites (plus 3 working spares), built and operated by the U.S. military, that constantly orbit the earth. They provide information to GPS-capable devices to pinpoint locations on the earth.

**graphical user interface (GUI)** Unlike the command- and menu-driven interfaces used in earlier software, GUIs display graphics and use the point-and-click technology of the mouse and cursor, making them much more user-friendly.

**graphics double data rate 5 (GDDR5)** A standard of video memory.

**graphics processing unit (GPU)** A specialized logic chip that is dedicated to quickly displaying and calculating visual data such as shadows, textures, and luminosity.

**grey hat hackers** A cross between black and white—they will often illegally break into systems merely to flaunt their expertise to the administrator of the system they penetrated or to attempt to sell their services in repairing security breaches.

**guest server** Virtual servers running on a host machine.

# H

**hacker** Anyone who unlawfully breaks into a computer system (whether an individual computer or a network).

**handshaking** The process of two computers exchanging control packets that set up the parameters of a data exchange.

**hard drive** A device that holds all permanently stored programs and data; can be located inside the system unit or attached to the system unit via a USB port.

**hardware** Any part of the computer you can physically touch.

**head crash** Impact of read/write head against magnetic platter of the hard drive; often results in data loss.

**hexadecimal notation** A number system that uses 16 digits to represent numbers; also called a *base 16 number system*.

**hibernate** A power-management mode that saves the current state of the current system to the computer's hard drive.

**high definition (HD)** A standard of digital television signal that guarantees a specific level of resolution and a specific *aspect ratio*, which is the rectangular shape of the image.

**high-definition multimedia interface (HDMI)** A compact audio–video interface standard that carries both high-definition video and uncompressed digital audio.

**hoax** An e-mail message or Web site that contains information that is untrue, and is published with the purpose of deceiving others.

**home area network (HAN)** A network located in a home that is used to connect all of its digital devices.

**home network server** A device designed to store media, share media across the network, and back up files on computers connected to a home network.

**home page** The main or opening page of a Web site.

**honey pot** A computer system that is set up to attract unauthorized users by appearing to be a key part of a network or a system that contains something of great value.

**host** The portion of a domain name that identifies who maintains a given Web site. For example, *berkeley.edu* is the domain name for the University of California at Berkeley, which maintains that site.

**HTML tag** The bracketed information that surrounds elements of a Web page in order to convey information about them and define how their content is to be displayed.

**HTML/XHTML embedded scripting language** A client-side method of embedding programming language code directly within the HTML/XHTML code of a Web page.

**hybrid topology** A topology comprised of several topologies and combined into one network.

**hyperlink** A type of specially coded text that, when clicked, enables a user to jump from one location, or Web page, to another

within a Web site or to another Web site altogether.

**hyperlink field** A field in a database that stores hyperlinks to Web pages.

**hypertext** Text that is linked to other documents or media (such as video clips or pictures).

**HyperText Markup Language (HTML)** A set of rules for marking up blocks of text so that a Web browser knows how to display them. It uses a series of tags that defines the display of text on a Web page.

**HyperText Transfer Protocol (HTTP)** The protocol that allows files to be transferred from a Web server so that you can see them on your computer by using a browser.

**HyperText Transfer Protocol Secure (or Over SSL)** A protocol that will encrypt the information sent between your browser and the server.

**hyperthreading** A technology that permits quicker processing of information by enabling a new set of instructions to start executing before the previous set has finished.

# I

**icon** A picture on a computer display that represents an object such as a software application or a file or folder.

**identity theft** The process by which someone uses personal information about someone else (such as the victim's name, address, and Social Security number) to assume the victim's identity for the purpose of defrauding others.

**if else** In the programming language C++, keywords for a binary decision within an algorithm.

**image backup** A copy of an entire computer system, created for restoration purposes.

**image editing software (photo editing software)** Programs for editing photographs and other images.

**impact printer** A printer that has tiny hammer-like keys that strike the paper through an inked ribbon, thus making a mark on the paper. The most common impact printer is the dot-matrix printer.

**incremental backup** A type of backup that only backs up files that have changed since the last time files were backed up.

**information** Data that has been organized or presented in a meaningful fashion.

**information assurance** The set of measures intended to protect and defend information and information systems by ensuring their availability, integrity, authentication, confidentiality, and nonrepudiation.

**information system** A system that includes data, people, procedures, hardware, and software and that is used to gather and analyze information.

**information technology (IT)** The set of techniques used in processing and retrieving information.

**inheritance** The ability of a new class of objects to pick up all of the data and methods of an existing class automatically and then extend and customize those to fit its own specific needs.

**initial value** A beginning point in a loop.

**inkjet printer** A nonimpact printer that sprays tiny drops of ink onto paper.

**inoculation** A process used by antivirus software; compares old and current qualities of files to detect viral activity.

**input device** A hardware device used to enter, or input, data (text, images, and sounds) and instructions (user responses and commands) into a computer. Some input devices are keyboards and mice.

**input form** A form that provides a view of the data fields to be filled in a database, with appropriate labels to assist database users in populating the database.

**instant messaging (IM)** A program that enables users to communicate online in real time with others who are also online.

**integrated development environment (IDE)** A development tool that helps programmers write, compile, and test their programs.

**integrated help** Documentation for a software product that is built directly into the software.

**Internet** A network of networks that is the largest network in the world, connecting millions of computers from more than one hundred countries.

**Internet appliance** A device used for easy access to the Internet, social networking sites, e-mail, video, news, and entertainment. These devices fall into a category somewhere between smartphones and full-blown computers.

**Internet backbone** The main pathway of high-speed communications lines over which all Internet traffic flows.

**Internet cache** A section of your hard drive that stores information that you may need again for surfing (such as IP addresses and frequently accessed Web pages).

**Internet Corporation for Assigned Names and Numbers (ICANN)** The organization responsible for allocating IP addresses to organizations to ensure they are unique and have not been assigned to other users.

**Internet exchange point** A device that allows different Internet service providers to exchange information between networks.

**Internet Protocol (IP)** A protocol for sending data between computers on the Internet.

**Internet Protocol address (IP address)** The means by which all computers connected to the Internet identify each other. It consists of a unique set of four numbers separated by dots such as 123.45.178.91.

**Internet Protocol version 4 (IPv4)** The original IP addressing scheme.

**Internet Protocol version 6 (IPv6)** A proposed IP addressing scheme that makes IP addresses longer, thereby providing more available IP addresses. It uses eight groups of 16-bit numbers.

**Internet service provider (ISP)** Companies that specialize in providing Internet access. ISPs may be specialized providers, like Juno, or companies that provide other services in addition to Internet access (such as phone and cable television).

**Internet tablet** A very light, portable computing device without a keyboard.

**interpreter** A software program that translates source code into an intermediate form line by line. Each line is then executed as it is translated.

**interrupt** A signal that tells the operating system that it is in need of immediate attention.

**interrupt handler** A special numerical code that prioritizes requests from various devices. These requests then are placed in the interrupt table in the computer's primary memory.

**intranet** A private corporate network that is used exclusively by company employees to facilitate information sharing, database access, group scheduling, videoconferencing, and other employee and customer collaborations.

**IP address** See *Internet Protocol address.*

## J

**jam signal** A special signal sent to all network nodes, alerting them that a data collision has occurred.

**Java** A platform-independent programming language that Sun Microsystems introduced in the early 1990s. It quickly became popular because its object-oriented model enables Java programmers to benefit from its set of existing classes.

**Java applet** A small Java-based program.

**Java Server Pages (JSP)** An extension of the Java servlet technology with dynamic scripting capability.

**JavaScript** A scripting language often used to add interactivity to Web pages. JavaScript is not as fully featured as Java, but its syntax, keywords, data types, and operators are a subset of Java's.

**join query** A database query that links (or joins) two database tables using a common field in both tables and extracts the relevant data from each.

## K

**kernel (supervisor program)** The essential component of the operating system that is responsible for managing the processor and all other components of the computer system. Because it stays in random access memory (RAM) the entire time the computer is powered on, the kernel is called *memory resident.*

**kernel memory** The memory that the computer's operating system uses.

**key pair** A public and a private key used for coding and decoding encrypted data.

**keyboard** A hardware device used to enter typed data and commands into a computer.

**keystroke logger** A type of spyware program that monitors keystrokes with the intent of stealing passwords, login IDs, or credit card information.

**keyword** (1) A specific word a user wishes to query (or look for) in an Internet search. (2) A specific word that has a predefined meaning in a particular programming language.

**kilobyte (KB)** A unit of computer storage equal to approximately one thousand bytes.

**knowledge-based system** A support system that provides additional intelligence that supplements the user's own intellect and makes a decision support system (DSS) more effective.

# L

**laser printer** A nonimpact printer known for quick and quiet production and high-quality printouts.

**Last Known Good Configuration** A Windows feature that starts the computer by using the registry information that was saved during the last shutdown.

**latency** The process that occurs after the read/write head of the hard drive locates the correct track, and then waits for the correct sector to spin to the read/write head.

**legacy technology** Comprises computing devices, software, or peripherals that use techniques, parts, and methods from an earlier time that are no longer popular.

**library** In Windows 7, a folder that is used to display files from different locations as if they were all saved in a single folder, regardless of where they are actually stored in the file hierarchy.

**light-emitting diode (LED) display** A newer, more energy efficient type of monitor. It may have better color accuracy and thinner panels than traditional LCD monitors.

**Linux** An open source operating system based on UNIX. Because of the stable nature of this operating system, it is often used on Web servers.

**liquid crystal display (LCD)** The technology used in flat-panel computer monitors.

**live bookmark** A bookmark that delivers updates to you as soon as they become

available, using Really Simple Syndication (RSS).

**local area network (LAN)** A network in which the nodes are located within a small geographic area.

**logic bomb** A computer virus that runs when a certain set of conditions is met, such as when specific dates are reached on the computer's internal clock.

**logical error** A mistake in the design and planning of the algorithm itself rather than in the use of syntax in the coding.

**logical port** A virtual communications gateway or path that enables a computer to organize requests for information (such as Web page downloads and e-mail routing) from other networks or computers.

**logical port blocking** A condition in which a firewall is configured to ignore all incoming packets that request access to a certain port so that no unwanted requests will get through to the computer.

**loop** An algorithm that performs a repeating set of actions. A logical yes/no expression is evaluated. As long as the expression evaluates to TRUE (yes), the algorithm will perform the same set of actions and continue to loop around. When the answer to the question is FALSE (no), the algorithm breaks free of the looping structure and moves on to the next step.

# M

**Mac OS** The first commercially available operating system to incorporate a graphical user interface (GUI) with user-friendly point-and-click technology.

**machine language** A set of instructions executed directly by the central processing unit (CPU).

**macro** A small program that groups a series of commands to run as a single command.

**macro virus** A virus that is distributed by hiding it inside a macro.

**mainframe** A large, expensive computer that supports hundreds or thousands of users simultaneously and executes many different programs at the same time.

**malware** Software that is intended to render a system temporarily or

permanently useless or to penetrate a computer system completely for purposes of information gathering. Examples include spyware, viruses, worms, and Trojan horses.

**management information system (MIS)** A system that provides timely and accurate information that enables managers to make critical business decisions.

**many-to-many relationship** A database relationship in which one record in a database table (A) can have many related records in another table (B), and any record in table B can have many related records in table A.

**mapping program** Software that provides street maps and written directions to locations.

**massively multiplayer online role-playing games (MMORPG)** A gaming environment in which thousands of participants interact in a virtual game world by assuming roles of fictitious characters.

**master boot record (MBR)** A small program that runs whenever a computer boots up.

**mastery** The feeling of confidence and excitement from seeing your own skills progress.

**media access control (MAC) address** A physical address, similar to a serial number on an appliance, that is assigned to each network adapter; it is made up of six 2-digit characters such as 01:40:87:44:79:A5.

**megabyte (MB)** A unit of computer storage equal to approximately 1 million bytes.

**memo field** A text field in a database that is used to hold long pieces of text.

**memory module (memory card)** A small circuit board that holds a series of random access memory (RAM) chips.

**menu** A list of commands that displays on the screen.

**menu-driven interface** A user interface in which the user chooses a command from menus displayed on the screen.

**metadata** Data that describes other data.

**metasearch engine** A metasearch engine, such as Dogpile, searches other search engines rather than individual Web sites.

**metropolitan area network (MAN)** A wide area network (WAN) that links users in a specific geographic area (such as within a city or county).

**microbrowser** Software that makes it possible to access the Internet from a smartphone.

**microphone (mic)** A device that allows you to capture sound waves, such as those created by your voice, and transfer them to digital format on your computer.

**Microsoft Disk Operating System (MS-DOS)** A single-user, single-task operating system created by Microsoft. MS-DOS was the first widely installed operating system in personal computers.

**mobile switching center** A central location that receives cell phone requests for service from a base station.

**model management system** A type of software that assists in building management models in decision support systems (DSSs).

**modem** A communication device that works to translate digital data into an analog signal and back again.

**modem card** An expansion card that provides the computer with a connection to the Internet via conventional phone lines.

**modem port** A port that uses a traditional telephone signal to connect a computer to the Internet.

**monitor (display screen)** A common output device that displays text, graphics, and video as soft copies (copies that can be seen only on screen).

**Moore's Law** A prediction, named after Gordon Moore, the cofounder of Intel; states that the number of transistors on a CPU chip will double every two years.

**motherboard** A special circuit board in the system unit that contains the central processing unit (CPU), the memory (RAM) chips, and the slots available for expansion cards; all of the other boards (video cards, sound cards, and so on) connect to it to receive power and to communicate.

**mouse** A hardware device used to enter user responses and commands into a computer.

**multidimensional database** A database that stores data in multiple dimensions and is organized in a cube format.

**multimedia** Anything that involves one or more forms of media plus text.

**multimedia message service (MMS)** An extension of short message service (SMS) that enables messages that include text, sound, images, and video clips to be sent from a cell phone to other phones or e-mail addresses.

**multimedia software** Programs that include image, video, and audio editing software, animation software, and other specialty software required to produce computer games, animations, and movies.

**multipartite virus** Literally meaning "multipart" virus; a type of computer virus that attempts to infect both the boot sector and executable files at the same time.

**multiplayer online game** An online game in which play occurs among hundreds or thousands of other players over the Internet in a persistent or ever-on game environment. In some games, players can interact with other players through trading, chatting, or playing cooperative or combative mini-games.

**Multiple Input Multiple Output (MIMO)** A design in routers that provides for faster wireless data transmission by utilizing more than one antenna to transmit and receive data.

**Multipurpose Internet Mail Extensions (MIME)** A specification that was introduced in 1991 to simplify attachments to e-mail messages. All e-mail client software now uses this protocol for attaching files.

**multitask** The ability of an operating system to perform more than one process at a time.

**multiuser operating system (network operating system)** An operating system (OS) that enables more than one user to access the computer system at one time by efficiently juggling all the requests from multiple users.

# N

**natural language processing (NLP) system** A system that enables users to communicate with computer systems using a natural spoken or written language as opposed to using computer programming languages.

**negative acknowledgment (NAK)** What computer Y sends to computer X if a packet is unreadable, indicating the packet was not received in understandable form.

**netbook** A computing device that runs a full-featured operating system but weighs two pounds or less.

**network** A group of two or more computers (or nodes) that are configured to share information and resources such as printers, files, and databases.

**network adapter** A device that enables the computer (or peripheral) to communicate with the network using a common data communication language, or protocol.

**network address translation (NAT)** A process that firewalls use to assign internal Internet Protocol (IP) addresses on a network.

**network administration** Involves tasks such as: (1) installing new computers and devices, (2) monitoring the network to ensure it is performing efficiently, (3) updating and installing new software on the network, and (4) configuring, or setting up, proper security for a network.

**network administrator** Someone who has training in computer and peripheral maintenance and repair, network design, and the installation of network software; installs new equipment, configures computers for users, repairs equipment, and assigns network access to users.

**network architecture** The design of a computer network; includes both physical and logical design.

**network-attached storage (NAS) device** A specialized computing device designed to store and manage network data.

**network interface card (NIC)** An expansion card that enables a computer to connect other computers or to a cable modem to facilitate a high-speed Internet connection.

**network navigation device** A device on a network such as a router, hub, and switch that moves data signals around the network.

**network operating system (NOS)** Software that handles requests for information, Internet access, and the use of peripherals for the rest of the network nodes.

**network prefix** The part of a network address under the CIDR IP addressing scheme. It consists of a slash and a number added to the end of the last octet in an IP address.

**network topology** The layout and structure of the network.

**network-ready device** A device (such as a printer or external hard drive) that can be attached directly to a network instead of needing to attach to a computer on the network.

**Next** In the Visual Basic programming language, the keyword used to implement a loop.

**node** A device connected to a network such as a computer, a peripheral (such as a printer), or a communications device (such as a modem).

**nonimpact printer** A printer that sprays ink or uses laser beams to make marks on the paper. The most common nonimpact printers are inkjet and laser printers.

**nonvolatile storage** Permanent storage, as in read-only memory (ROM).

**normalization** The process of recording data only once in a database to reduce data redundancy.

**notebook computer** A small, compact portable computer.

**numeric check** A data validation routine that confirms that only numbers are entered in a database field.

**numeric field** A field in a database that stores numbers.

**object** A variable in a program that is an example of a class. Each object in a specific class is constructed from similar data and methods.

**object field** A field in a database that holds objects such as pictures, video clips, or entire documents.

**Object Query Language (OQL)** A query language that is used to extract information from an object-oriented database.

**Objective C** The language most often used to program applications to run under Mac OS X.

**object-oriented analysis** An approach to software design that differs from the traditional "top-down" design. In object-oriented (OO) analysis, programmers first identify all of the classes (collections of data and methods) that are required to describe completely the problem the program is trying to solve.

**object-oriented database** A database that stores data in objects, not in tables.

**octet** Eight bits. For example, each of the four numbers in the dotted decimal notation of an Internet Protocol (IP) address is represented by an octet.

**office support system (OSS)** A system (such as Microsoft Office) designed to assist employees in accomplishing their day-to-day tasks and to improve communications.

**offshore** The process of sending jobs formerly performed in the U.S. to other countries.

**one-to-many relationship** A database relationship in which one record in a data table can have many related records in another data table.

**one-to-one relationship** A database relationship in which one record in a data table has only one related record in another data table.

**online mapping service** An alternative to more traditional mapping software programs; easily accessible with any Internet connection and updated more frequently than offline services. Examples include MapQuest, Yahoo! Maps, and Google Maps.

**online transaction processing (OLTP)** The immediate processing of user requests or transactions.

**open source software** Program code made publicly available for free; it can be copied, distributed, or changed without the stringent copyright protections of proprietary software products.

**open system** A system whose designs are public, enabling access by any interested party.

**Open Systems Interconnection (OSI)** Established by the Institute of Electrical and Electronics Engineers (IEE), a standard of communications adopted throughout the computing world that provides the protocol guidelines for all modern networks.

**operating system (OS)** The system software that controls the way in which a computer system functions, including the management of hardware, peripherals, and software.

**operator** Any of the coding symbols that represent the fundamental actions of a computer language.

**optical drive** A hardware device that uses lasers or light to read from, and maybe even write to, CDs, DVDs, or Blu-ray discs.

**optical media** Portable storage devices, such as CDs, DVDs, and Blu-ray discs, that use a laser to read and write data.

**optical mouse** A mouse that uses an internal sensor or laser to control the mouse's movement. The sensor sends signals to the computer, telling it where to move the pointer on the screen.

**organic light-emitting diode (OLED) display** A display that uses organic compounds to produce light when exposed to an electric current. Unlike LCDs, OLEDs do not require a backlight to function and therefore draw less power and have a much thinner display, sometimes as thin as 3 mm.

**output device** A device that sends processed data and information out of a computer in the form of text, pictures (graphics), sounds (audio), or video.

**packet (data packet)** A small segment of data that is bundled for sending over transmission media. Each packet contains the address of the computer or peripheral device to which it is being sent.

**packet analyzer (sniffer)** A computer hardware device or software program designed to detect and record digital information being transmitted over a network.

**packet filtering** A feature found in firewalls that filters out unwanted data packets sent to specific logical ports.

**packet screening** A process that involves examining incoming data packets to ensure they originated from, or are authorized by, valid users on the internal network.

**packet switching** A communications methodology in which data is broken into small chunks (called packets) and sent over various routes at the same time. When the packets reach their destination, they are reassembled by the receiving computer.

**paging** The process of swapping data or instructions that have been placed in the swap file for later use back into active random access memory (RAM). The contents of the hard drive's swap file then become less active data or instructions.

**Pascal** The only modern computer language that was specifically designed as a teaching language; it is seldom taught now at the college level.

**passive topology** When data merely travels the entire length of the communications medium and is received by all network devices.

**path (subdirectory)** The information after the slash indicates a particular file or path (or subdirectory) within the Web site.

**path separator** The backslash mark (\) used by Microsoft Windows and DOS in file names. Mac files use a colon (:), and UNIX and Linux use the forward slash (/) as the path separator.

**peer-to-peer (P2P) network** A network in which each node connected to the network can communicate directly with every other node on the network.

**peer-to-peer (P2P) sharing** The process of users transferring files between computers.

**peripheral device** A device such as a monitor, printer, or keyboard that connects to the system unit through a data port.

**personal area network (PAN)** A network used to connect wireless devices (such as Bluetooth-enabled devices) in close proximity to each other.

**personal firewall** A firewall specifically designed for home networks.

**personal information manager (PIM) software** Programs such as Microsoft Outlook or Lotus Organizer that strive to replace the various management tools found on a traditional desk such as a calendar, address book, notepad, and to-do lists.

**pharming** Planting malicious code on a computer that alters the browser's ability to find Web addresses and directs users to bogus Web sites.

**phishing** The process of sending e-mail messages to lure Internet users into revealing personal information such as credit card or Social Security numbers or other sensitive information that could lead to identity theft.

**PHP (Hypertext Preprocessor)** A scripting language used to produce dynamic Web pages.

**physical memory** The amount of random access memory (RAM) that is installed in a computer.

**piggybacking** The process of connecting to a wireless network without the permission of the owner of the network.

**pixel** A single point that creates the images on a computer monitor. Pixels are illuminated by an electron beam that passes rapidly back and forth across the back of the screen so that the pixels appear to glow continuously.

**platform** The combination of a computer's operating system and processor. The two most common platform types are the PC and the Apple Macintosh.

**platter** A thin, round, metallic storage plate stacked onto the hard drive spindle.

**plotter** A large printer that uses a computer-controlled pen to produce oversize pictures that require precise continuous lines to be drawn, such as maps and architectural plans.

**Plug and Play (PnP)** The technology that enables the operating system, once it is booted up, to recognize automatically any new peripherals and configure them to work with the system.

**plug-in (player)** A small software program that "plugs in" to a Web browser to enable a specific function—for example, to view and hear certain multimedia files on the Web.

**podcast** A clip of audio or video content that is broadcast over the Internet using compressed audio or video files in formats such as MP3.

**point of presence (POP)** A bank of modems through which many users can connect to an Internet service provider (ISP) simultaneously.

**polymorphic virus** A virus that changes its virus signature (the binary pattern that makes the virus identifiable) every time it infects a new file. This makes it more difficult for antivirus programs to detect the virus.

**port** An interface through which external devices are connected to the computer.

**portability** The capability to move a completed solution easily from one type of computer to another.

**portable media player (PMP)** A small portable device (such as an iPod) that enables you to carry your MP3s or other media files around with you.

**positive acknowledgment (ACK)** What computer Y sends when it receives a data packet that it can read from computer X.

**possessed object** Any object that a user carries to identify him- or herself and that grants the user access to a computer system or computer facility.

**power supply** A power supply regulates the wall voltage to the voltages required by computer chips; it is housed inside the system unit.

**power-on self-test (POST)** The first job the basic input/output system (BIOS) performs, ensuring that essential peripheral devices are attached and operational. This process consists of a test on the video card and video memory, a BIOS identification process (during which the BIOS version, manufacturer, and data are displayed on the monitor), and a memory test to ensure memory chips are working properly.

**preemptive multitasking** When the operating system processes the task assigned a higher priority before processing a task that has been assigned a lower priority.

**presentation software** An application program for creating dynamic slide shows such as Microsoft PowerPoint or Apple Keynote.

**pretexting** The act of creating an invented scenario (the pretext) to convince someone to divulge information.

**Pretty Good Privacy (PGP)** A popular public-key encryption package.

**primary key (key field)** The unique field that each database record in a table must have.

**print queue** A software holding area for printing jobs.

**print server** A server that manages all client-requested printing jobs for all printers on the network.

**printer** A common output device that creates tangible or hard copies of text and graphics.

**private key** One-half of a pair of binary files that is needed to decrypt an encrypted message. The private key is kept only by the individual who created the key pair and is never distributed to anyone else. The private key is used to decrypt messages created with the corresponding public key.

**private-key encryption** A procedure in which only the two parties involved in sending a message have the code. This could be a simple shift code where letters of the alphabet are shifted to a new position.

**problem statement** A clear description of which tasks the computer program must accomplish and how the program will execute these tasks and respond to unusual situations. It is the starting point of programming work.

**processing** Manipulating or organizing data into information.

**productivity software** Programs that enable a user to perform various tasks generally required in home, school, and business. Examples include word processing, spreadsheet, presentation, personal information management (PIM), and database programs.

**program** A series of instructions to be followed by a computer to accomplish a task.

**program development life cycle (PDLC)** A number of stages, from conception to final deployment, which a programming project follows.

**program file** A file that is used in the running of software programs and does not store data.

**program specification** A clear statement of the goals and objectives of the project.

**programming** The process of translating a task into a series of commands a computer will use to perform that task.

**programming language** A kind of "code" for the set of instructions the central processing unit (CPU) knows how to perform.

**project management software** An application program, such as Microsoft Project, that helps project managers generate charts and tables used to manage aspects of a project.

**projector** A device that can project images from your computer onto a wall or viewing screen.

**proprietary software** Custom software application that is owned and controlled by the company that created it.

**proprietary system** A software product whose code is not generally available (is kept private) and that is generally developed and marketed by a single company.

**protocol** (1) A set of rules for exchanging data and communication. (2) The first part of the Uniform Resource Locator (URL) indicating the set of rules used to retrieve the specified document.

**prototype** A small model of a computer program, often built at the beginning of a large project.

**proxy server** Acts as a go-between for computers on the internal network and the external network (often the Internet).

**pseudocode** A text-based approach to documenting an algorithm.

**public key** One-half of a pair of binary files that is needed to decrypt an encrypted message. After creating the keys, the user distributes the public key to anyone he wishes to send him encrypted messages. A message encrypted with a public key can be unencrypted only using the corresponding private key.

**public-key encryption** A procedure in which the key for coding is generally distributed as a public key that may be placed on a Web site. Anyone wishing to send a message codes it using the public key. The recipient decodes the message with a private key.

**purpose** The understanding that you are working for something larger than yourself.

 **Q**

**QR (quick response) code** A technology that lets any piece of print in the real world host a live link to online information and video content.

**quarantining** The placement (by antivirus software) of a computer virus in a secure area on the hard drive so that it won't spread infection to other files.

**query** The process of requesting information from a database.

**query language** A language used to retrieve and display records from a database. A query language consists of its own vocabulary and sentence structure, used to frame the requests.

**QWERTY keyboard** A keyboard that gets its name from the first six letters on the top-left row of alphabetic keys on the keyboard.

 **R**

**random access memory (RAM)** The computer's temporary storage space or short-term memory. It is located in a set of chips on the system unit's motherboard, and its capacity is measured in megabytes or gigabytes.

**range check** A type of data validation used in databases to ensure that a value entered falls within a specified range (such as requiring a person's age to fall in a range of between 1 and 120).

**rapid application development (RAD)** A method of system development in which developers create a prototype first, generating system documents as they use and remodel the product.

**read/write head** The mechanism that retrieves (reads) and records (writes) the magnetic data to and from a data disk.

**read-only memory (ROM)** A set of memory chips, located on the motherboard, which stores data and instructions that cannot be changed or erased; it holds all the instructions the computer needs to start up.

**real-time operating system (RTOS)** A program with a specific purpose that must guarantee certain response times for particular computing tasks, or else the machine's application is useless. Real-time operating systems are found in many types of robotic equipment.

**real-time processing** The process of updating a database (or information system) immediately as changes are made.

**Really Simple Syndication (RSS) technology** An XML-based format that allows frequent updates of content on the World Wide Web.

**record** A collection of related fields in a database.

**Recycle Bin** A folder on a Windows desktop in which deleted files from the hard drive are held until permanently purged from the system.

**redundant array of independent disks (RAID)** A set of strategies for using more than one drive in a system.

**referential integrity** For each value in the foreign key of one table, there is a corresponding value in the primary key of the related table.

**registry** A portion of the hard drive containing all the different configurations (settings) used by the Windows operating system (OS) as well as by other applications.

**relation** A database table that contains related data.

**relational algebra** The use of English-like expressions that have variables and operations, much like algebraic equations.

**relational database** A database that logically groups similar data into relations (or tables).

**relationship** In relational databases, the link between tables that defines how the data are related.

**release to manufacturers (RTM)** The point in the software release cycle when changes are made after beta testing and the product re releases to other manufacturers.

**resolution** The clearness or sharpness of an image, which is controlled by the number of pixels displayed on the screen.

**response time** The measurement (in milliseconds) of the time it takes for a pixel to change color; the lower the response time, the smoother moving images will appear on the monitor.

**reusability** The ability to reuse existing classes of objects from other projects, enabling programmers to produce new code quickly.

**ribbon** An interface in the Microsoft Office suite that groups related commands into tabs for easy access.

**ring (loop) topology** A network configuration in which the computers and peripherals are laid out in a configuration resembling a circle. Data flows around the circle from device to device in one direction only.

**root directory** The top level of the filing structure in a computer system. In Windows computers, the root directory of the hard drive is represented as C:\.

**root DNS server** A group of servers maintained throughout the Internet to which ISP Web servers connect to locate the master listings for an entire top-level domain.

**rootkit** Programs that allow hackers to gain access to your computer and take almost complete control of it without your knowledge. These programs are designed to subvert normal logon procedures to a computer and to hide their operations from normal detection methods.

**router** A device that routes packets of data between two or more networks.

**runtime error** An error in the problem logic that is only caught when the program executes.

# S

**Safe mode** A special diagnostic mode designed for troubleshooting errors that occur during the boot process.

**sampling rate** The number of times per second a signal is measured and converted to a digital value. Sampling rates are measured in kilobits per second.

**satellite Internet** A way to connect to the Internet using a small satellite dish, which is placed outside the home and is connected to a computer with coaxial cable. The satellite company then sends the data to a satellite orbiting the Earth. The satellite, in turn, sends the data back to the satellite dish and to the computer.

**scalability** The ability to easily add more users to a network without affecting the performance of the other network nodes (computers or peripherals).

**scareware** A type of malware that is downloaded onto your computer and tries to convince you that your computer is infected with a virus or other type of malware.

**scope creep** In project management, an ever-changing set of requests from the clients for additional features as they wait longer and longer to see a working prototype.

**script** A list of commands (mini-programs or macros) that can be executed on a computer without user interaction.

**scripting language** A simple programming language that is limited to performing a specific set of specialized tasks.

**scrollbar** On the desktop, the bar that appears at the side or bottom of the window and controls which part of the information is displayed on the screen.

**search engine** A set of programs that searches the Web for specific words (or keywords) you wish to query (or look for) and then returns a list of the Web sites on which those keywords are found.

**second-generation language (2GL)** Also known as an assembly language. Second-generation languages deal directly with system hardware but provide acronyms that are easier for human programmers to work with.

**second-level domain** A domain that falls within top-level domains of the Internet. Each second-level domain needs to be unique within that particular domain but not necessarily unique to all top-level domains.

**sector** A section of a hard drive platter, wedge-shaped from the center of the platter to the edge.

**Secure Sockets Layer (SSL)** A protocol that provides for the encryption of data transmitted using the Internet. The current versions of all major Web browsers support SSL.

**seek time** The time it takes for the hard drive's read/write heads to move over the surface of the disk to the correct track.

**select query** A query that displays a subset of data from a table based on the criteria the user specifies.

**Semantic Web (Web 3.0)** An evolving extension of the World Wide Web in which information is defined in such a way to make it more easily readable by computers.

**Serial Advanced Technology Attachment (Serial ATA)** A type of hard drive that uses much thinner cables, and can transfer data more quickly than IDE drives.

**server** A computer that provides resources to other computers on a network.

**server-side program** A program that is run on a Web server as opposed to inside a Web browser.

**service pack** Software updates to problems in a program after its commercial release to the public. Users can download these software modules to repair errors identified in the program code.

**service set identifier (SSID)** A network name that wireless routers use to identify themselves.

**shareware** Software that enables users to "test" the software by running it for a limited time free of charge.

**shielded twisted pair (STP) cable** Twisted pair cable that contains a layer of foil shielding to reduce interference.

**short message service (SMS)** Technology that enables short text messages (up to 160 characters) to be sent over mobile networks.

**Simple Mail Transfer Protocol (SMTP)** A protocol for sending e-mail along the Internet to its destination.

**simulation program** Software, often used for training purposes, which allows the user to experience or control an event as if it is reality.

**sleep mode** A low-power mode for electronic devices such as computers that saves electric power consumption and saves the last-used settings. When the device is "woken up," work is resumed more quickly than when cold booting the computer.

**smartphone** A device that combines the functionality of a cell phone, a PMP, and a PDA into one unit. Smartphones have sophisticated operating systems, Web browsers, and the capability to run software applications.

**social bookmark (tag)** A keyword or term that Internet users assign to a Web resource such as a Web page, digital image, or video.

**social engineering** Any technique that uses social skills to generate human interaction for the purpose of enticing individuals to reveal sensitive information.

**social networking** A means by which people use the Internet to communicate and share information among their immediate friends, and meet and connect with others through common interests, experiences, and friends.

**software** The set of computer programs or instructions that tells the computer what to do and enables it to perform different tasks.

**Software as a Service (SaaS)** Software that is delivered on demand over the Internet.

**software license** An agreement between the user and the software developer that must be accepted before installing the software on a computer.

**software piracy** Violating a software license agreement by copying an application onto more computers than the license agreement permits.

**software suite** A collection of software programs that have been bundled together as a package.

**solid state drive (SSD)** A storage device that uses the same kind of memory that flash drives use, but can reach data in only a tenth of the time a flash drive requires.

**sort (index)** The process of organizing data in a database into a particular order.

**sound card** An expansion card that attaches to the motherboard inside the system unit and that enables the computer to produce sounds by providing a connection for the speakers and microphone.

**source code** The instructions programmers write in a higher-level language.

**spam** Unwanted or junk e-mail.

**spam filter** An option you can select in your e-mail account that places known or suspected spam messages into a folder other than your inbox.

**speaker** An output device for sound.

**spear phishing** Spear phishing is a targeted phishing attack that sends e-mails to people known to be customers of a company. Such attacks have a much greater chance of successfully getting individuals to reveal sensitive data.

**spider** A program used by search engines that constantly collects information on the Web, following links in Web sites and reading Web pages. Spiders get their name because they crawl over the Web using multiple "legs" to visit many sites simultaneously.

**spooler** A program that helps coordinate all print jobs being sent to the printer at the same time.

**spreadsheet software** An application program such as Microsoft Excel or Lotus 1-2-3 that enables a user to do calculations and numerical analyses easily.

**spyware** An unwanted piggyback program that downloads with the software you want to install from the Internet and then runs in the background of your system.

**star topology** An active topology (meaning that data is retransmitted) in which the nodes connect to a central communications device called a *switch*. The switch receives a signal from the sending node and retransmits it to the node that should receive it.

**statement** A sentence in programming code.

**static addressing** A means of assigning an Internet Protocol (IP) address that never changes and is most likely assigned manually by a network administrator.

**stealth virus** A virus that temporarily erases its code from the files where it resides and hides in the active memory of the computer.

**streaming audio** Technology that enables audio files to be fed to a browser continuously. This lets users avoid having to download an entire file before listening.

**streaming video** Technology that enables video files to be fed to a browser continuously. This lets users avoid having to download the entire file before viewing.

**structured (analytical) data** Data that can be identified and classified as discrete bits of information (such as a name or phone number). Unstructured data includes nontraditional data such as audio clips (including MP3 files), video clips, and pictures that must be viewed in their entirety rather than in discrete segments.

**Structured Query Language (SQL)** The most popular database query language today.

**stylus** A pen-shaped device used to tap or write on touch-sensitive screens.

**subject directory** A structured outline of Web sites organized by topics and subtopics.

**summary report** A report that summarizes data in some fashion (such as a total of the day's concession sales at an amusement park). Also known as a *summary data report*.

**supercomputer** A specially designed computer that can perform complex calculations extremely rapidly; used in situations in which complex models requiring intensive mathematical calculations are needed (such as weather forecasting or atomic energy research).

**SuperFetch** A memory-management technique used by Windows 7. Monitors the applications you use the most and preloads them into your system memory so that they'll be ready to go.

**surge protector** A device that protects computers and other electronic devices from power surges.

**surround sound** A type of audio processing that makes the listener experience sound as if it were coming from all directions.

**surround-sound speakers** Speaker systems set up in such a way that they surround an entire area (and the people in it) with sound.

**S-video (super video)** A type of technology used to transmit video signals; used on newer LCD monitors, as well as other multimedia devices such as televisions, DVD players, and projectors.

**swap file (page file)** A temporary storage area on the hard drive where the operating system "swaps out" or moves the data or instructions from random access memory (RAM) that have not recently been used. This process takes place when more RAM space is needed.

**switch** A device for transmitting data on a network. A switch makes decisions, based on the media access control (MAC) address of the data, as to where the data is to be sent.

**syncing (or synchronizing)** The process of updating data on portable devices (such as a cell phone or iPod) and computer so that they contain the same data.

**syntax** An agreed-upon set of rules defining how a programming language must be structured.

**syntax error** An error that violates the strict, precise set of rules that defines a programming language.

**system development life cycle (SDLC)** An organized process (or set of steps) for developing an information processing system.

**system evaluation** The process of looking at a computer's subsystems, what they do, and how they perform to determine whether the computer system has the right hardware components to do what the user ultimately wants it to do.

**system file** Any of the main files of an operating system.

**system requirements** The set of minimum storage, memory capacity, and processing standards recommended by the software manufacturer to ensure proper operation of a software application.

**System Restore** A utility in Windows that restores system settings to a specific previous date when everything was working properly.

**system restore point** In Windows, a snapshot of your entire system's settings used for restoring your system to a prior point in time.

**system software** The set of programs that enables a computer's hardware devices and application software to work together; it includes the operating system and utility programs.

**system unit** The metal or plastic case that holds all the physical parts of the computer together, including the computer's processor (its brains), its memory, and the many circuit boards that help the computer function.

# T

**T line** A high-speed fiber-optic communications line that is designed to provide much higher throughput than conventional voice (telephone) and data (DSL or cable) lines.

**table** In database terminology, a group of related records. Also called a *file*.

**tablet computer** A mobile computer, such as the Apple iPad or Motorola XOOM,

integrated into a flat multitouch-sensitive screen. It uses an onscreen virtual keyboard, but separate keyboards can be connected via Bluetooth or wires.

**tablet PC** A notebook computer designed specifically to work with handwriting recognition technology.

**Task Manager** A Windows utility that shows programs currently running and permits you to exit nonresponsive programs when you click End Task.

**Task Scheduler** A Windows utility that enables you to schedule tasks to run automatically at predetermined times with no interaction necessary on your part.

**taskbar** In later versions of Windows operating systems, a feature that displays open and favorite applications for easy access.

**tax preparation software** An application program, such as Intuit's TurboTax or H&R Block's TaxCut, for preparing state and federal taxes. Each program offers a complete set of tax forms and instructions as well as expert advice on how to complete each form.

**TCP/IP** The main suite of protocols used on the Internet.

**telephony** The use of equipment to provide voice communications over a distance.

**template** A form included in many productivity applications that provides the basic structure for a particular kind of document, spreadsheet, or presentation.

**terabyte** 1,099,511,627,776 bytes or $2^{40}$ bytes.

**terminator** A device that absorbs a signal so that it is not reflected back onto parts of the network that have already received it.

**test condition** A check in software programming to see whether a loop is completed.

**testing plan** In the problem statement, a plan that lists specific input numbers that a software program would typically expect the user to enter. It then lists the precise output values that a perfect program would return for those input values.

**tethering** Approach which makes sure that as long as you have a 3G signal, your computer can access the Internet even when it tells you there are no available wireless networks. Several smartphones offer this capability.

**text field** A database field that can hold any combination of alphanumeric data (letters or numbers) and is most often used to hold text.

**thermal printer** A printer that works either by melting wax-based ink onto ordinary paper (in a process called *thermal wax transfer printing*) or by burning dots onto specially coated paper (in a process called *direct thermal printing*).

**third-generation language (3GL, or high-level language)** A computer language that uses symbols and commands to help programmers tell the computer what to do.

**thrashing** A condition of excessive paging in which the operating system becomes sluggish.

**three-way handshake** A process used by the Transmission Control Protocol (TCP) to establish a connection.

**throughput** The actual speed of data transfer that is achieved. It is usually less than the data transfer rate and is measured in megabits per second (Mbps).

**time bomb** A virus that is triggered by the passage of time or on a certain date.

**time-variant data** Data that doesn't all pertain to one period in time—for example, data in a data warehouse.

**token** A special packet containing data.

**token method** The access method that ring networks use to avoid data collisions.

**toolbar** A group of icons collected for easy access.

**top-down design** A systematic approach in which a programming problem is broken down into a series of high-level tasks.

**top-level domain (TLD)** The suffix, often of three letters, in the domain name (such as .com or .edu) that indicates the kind of organization the host is.

**touch pad (track pad)** A small, touch-sensitive screen at the base of a notebook keyboard that is used to direct the cursor.

**touch screen** A type of monitor (or display in a notebook or PDA) that accepts input from a user touching the screen.

**track** A concentric circle that serves as a storage area on a hard drive platter.

**trackpoint device** A small, joystick-like nub that enables you to move the cursor with the tip of your finger.

**transaction processing system (TPS)** A system used to keep track of everyday business activities (such as sales of products).

**transceiver** In a wireless network, a device that translates the electronic data that needs to be sent along the network into radio waves and then broadcasts these radio waves to other network nodes.

**Transmission Control Protocol (TCP)** A protocol that prepares data for transmission and provides for error checking and resending lost data.

**transmission media** The radio waves or cable that transport data on a network.

**Transport Layer Security (TLS)** A protocol that provides data integrity and security for transmissions over the Internet.

**Trojan horse** A computer program that appears to be something useful or desirable (such as a game or a screen saver), but at the same time does something malicious in the background without the user's knowledge.

**tunneling**  The main technology for achieving a VPN (virtual private network). In tunneling, data packets are placed inside other data packets. The format of these external data packets is encrypted and is understood only by the sending and receiving hardware, which is known as a *tunnel interface*. The hardware is optimized to seek efficient routes of transmission through the Internet, making information much more difficult to intercept and decrypt.

**twisted pair cable** Cables made of copper wires that are twisted around each other and are surrounded by a plastic jacket (such as traditional home phone wire).

# U

**Uniform Resource Locator (URL)** A Web site's unique address; an example is microsoft.com.

**uninterruptible power supply (UPS)** A device designed to power a computer from large batteries for a brief period during a loss of electrical power.

**universal serial bus (USB) port** A port that can connect a wide variety of peripheral devices to the computer, including keyboards, printers, mice, smartphones, PDAs, flash drives, and digital cameras.

**UNIX** An operating system originally conceived in 1969 by Ken Thompson and Dennis Ritchie of AT&T's Bell Labs. In 1974, the UNIX code was rewritten in the standard programming language C. Today there are various commercial versions of UNIX.

**unshielded twisted pair (UTP) cable** The most popular transmission media option for Ethernet networks. UTP cable is composed of four pairs of wires that are twisted around each other to reduce electrical interference.

**unstructured data** Nontraditional database data such as audio clips (including MP3 files), video clips, pictures, and extremely large documents. Data of this type is known as a *binary large object* (BLOB) because it is actually encoded in binary form.

**urban legend** A hoax that becomes so well known that it is accepted by society as true even though it is false. Also known as an *urban myth*.

**User Datagram Protocol (UDP)** A protocol that prepares data for transmission but that has no resending capabilities.

**user interface** Part of the operating system that enables individuals to interact with the computer.

**utility program** A small program that performs many of the general housekeeping tasks for the computer, such as system maintenance and file compression.

# V

**validation** The process of ensuring that data entered into a database is correct (or at least reasonable) and complete.

**validation rule** A rule that is set up in a database to alert the user to possible wrong entries.

**variable** A name or symbol that stands for a value.

**variable declaration** A line of programming code that alerts the operating system that the program needs to allocate storage space in random access memory (RAM) for the variable.

**VBScript** A subset of Visual Basic; also used to introduce interactivity to Web pages.

**vertical market software** Software that is developed for and customized to a specific industry's needs (such as a wood inventory system for a sawmill) as opposed to software that is useful across a range of industries (such as word processing software).

**video card (video adapter)** An expansion card that is installed inside a system unit to translate binary data (the 1s and 0s the computer uses) into the images viewed on the monitor.

**video graphics array (VGA) port** A port to which a CRT monitor connects.

**video log (vlog or video blog)** A personal online journal that uses video as the primary content in addition to text, images, and audio.

**video memory** RAM that is included as part of a video card.

**viewing angle** Measured in degrees, this is the maximum angle at which a monitor can be viewed before the image quality degrades to unacceptable levels.

**virtual memory** The space on the hard drive where the operating system stores data if there isn't enough random access memory (RAM) to hold all of the programs you're currently trying to run.

**virtual private network (VPN)** A network that uses public communication pathways (usually the Internet) to provide branch offices or employees who are not at the office with secure access to the company network. VPNs maintain privacy by using secure data communication protocols.

**virtualization** Involves using specialized software to make individual physical servers behave as though they are more than one physical device. Each virtual server can operate as its own separate device and can even run its own operating system.

**virus** A computer program that attaches itself to another computer program (known as the host program) and attempts to spread itself to other computers when files are exchanged.

**virus signature** A portion of the virus code that is unique to a particular computer virus and makes it identifiable by antivirus software.

**Visual Basic (VB)** A programming language used to build a wide range of Windows applications quickly.

**visual programming** A technique for automatically writing code when the programmer says the layout is complete. It helps programmers produce a final application much more quickly.

**VoIP (Voice over Internet Protocol)** A technology that facilitates making telephone calls across the Internet instead of using conventional telephone lines.

**volatile storage** Temporary storage, such as in random access memory (RAM). When the power is off, the data in volatile storage is cleared out.

# W

**warm boot** The process of restarting the system while it's powered on.

**Web 2.0** Tools and Web-based services that emphasize online collaboration and sharing among users.

**Web browser (browser)** Software installed on a computer system that allows individuals to locate, view, and navigate the Web.

**Web page authoring software** Programs you can use to design interactive Web pages without knowing any HyperText Markup Language (HTML) code.

**Web server** A computer running a specialized operating system that enables it to host Web pages (and other information) and provide requested Web pages to clients.

**Web service** A program used by a Web site to make information available to other Web sites.

**Web site** A location on the Web.

**Web-based application** A program that is hosted on a Web site and does not require installation on the computer.

**webcam** A small camera that sits on top of a computer monitor (connected to the computer by a cable) or is built into a

notebook computer and is usually used to transfer live video.

**webcast** The broadcast of audio or video content over the Internet. Unlike a podcast, a webcast is not updated automatically.

**white-hat hacker** A hacker who breaks into systems just for the challenge of it (and who doesn't wish to steal or wreak havoc on the systems). Such hackers tout themselves as experts who are performing a needed service for society by helping companies realize the vulnerabilities that exist in their systems.

**whole-house surge protector** A surge protector that is installed on (or near) the breaker panel of a home and protects all electronic devices in the home from power surges.

**wide area network (WAN)** A network made up of local area networks (LANs) connected over long distances.

**widget** A mini-application developed for the Macintosh platform.

**wiki** A type of Web site that allows anyone visiting the site to change its content by adding, removing, or editing the content.

**window** In a graphical user interface, a rectangular box that contains programs displayed on the screen.

**Windows** An operating system by Microsoft that incorporates a user-friendly, graphical interface.

**Windows 7** Microsoft operating system that builds upon the security and user interface upgrades that the Windows Vista release provided, and gives users with touch-screen monitors the ability to use touch commands to scroll, resize windows, pan, and zoom.

**Windows Explorer** The main tool for finding, viewing, and managing the contents of your computer by showing the location and contents of every drive, folder, and file.

**wireless access point (WAP)** A device similar to a switch in an Ethernet network. It takes the place of a wireless network adapter and helps relay data between network nodes.

**Wireless Application Protocol (WAP)** The standard that dictates how handheld devices will access information on the Internet.

**wireless fidelity (WiFi)** The 802.11 standard for wireless data transmissions established by the Institute of Electrical and Electronics Engineers (IEEE).

**wireless Internet service provider (wireless ISP)** An ISP that provides service to wireless devices such as PDA/smartphones.

**Wireless Markup Language (WML)** A format for writing content viewed on a cellular phone or personal digital assistant (PDA) that is text-based and contains no graphics.

**wireless media** Communications media that do not use cables but instead rely on radio waves to communicate.

**wireless network interface card (wireless NIC)** A card installed in a system that connects with wireless access points on the network.

**wireless range extender** A device that amplifies your wireless signal to get it out to parts of your home that are experiencing poor connectivity.

**wizard** A step-by-step guide that walks a user through the necessary steps to complete a complicated task.

**word processing software** Programs used to create and edit written documents such as papers, letters, and résumés.

**World Wide Web (WWW or Web)** The part of the Internet used the most. What distinguishes the Web from the rest of the Internet are (1) its use of common communication protocols (such as Transmission Control Protocol/ Internet Protocol, or TCP/IP) and special languages (such as the HyperText Markup Language, or HTML) that enable different computers to talk to each other and display information in compatible formats; and (2) its use of special links (called hyperlinks) that enable users to jump from one place to another in the Web.

**worm** A program that attempts to travel between systems through network connections to spread infections. Worms can run independently of host file execution and are active in spreading themselves.

## z

**zombie** A computer that is controlled by a hacker who uses it to launch attacks on other computer systems.

# Index